MW01065849

The New Zealand
Bed *&* Breakfast
Guide

2006

Published in New Zealand and Australia by The B&B Book
Published by arrangement in the rest of the world by
    Pelican Publishing Company, Inc.

Pelican editions
        First edition, January 2005
        Second edition, January 2006

ISBN-13: 9781589803992
Prices in this guide are quoted in New Zealand dollars.

Published by Pelican Publishing Company, Inc.
1000 Burmaster Street, Gretna, Louisiana 70053

Cover illustration *Ascot Street, Thorndon, Wellington* from an etching by Mary Taylor,
courtesy of Millwood Gallery, Wellington.

Welcome to this edition of The Bed & Breakfast Book. Bed & Breakfast in New Zealand means a warm welcome and a unique holiday experience. Most B&B accommodation is in private homes with a sprinkling of guesthouses and small hotels. Each listing in the guide has been written by the host themselves and you will discover their warmth and personality through their writing. The New Zealand Bed & Breakfast Book is not just an accommodation guide – it is an introduction to a uniquely New Zealand holiday experience. The best holidays are often remembered by the friends one makes. How many of us have loved a country because of one or two memorable individuals we encountered? For the traveller who wants to experience the real New Zealand and get to know its people, bed and breakfast offers an opportunity to do just that. We recommend you don't try to travel too far in one day. Take time to enjoy the company of your hosts and other local people. You will find New Zealand hosts friendly and generous, and eager to share their local knowledge with you.

We have carefully inspected every property;

B&B Approved; All B&Bs in The Bed & Breakfast Book have been inspected on joining. They conform to the Schedule of Standards on page 508. As important as the requirement of meeting a physical standard, we expect that all of our properties will offer excellent hospitality. Some hosts who are members of associations or marketing groups, which also undertake inspections, have chosen to display the logos below.

The **@home NEW ZEALAND** logo represents the largest organisation of hosted accommodation providers in New Zealand. It assures you of a warm welcome from friendly, helpful hosts. Accommodations displaying this logo are regularly assessed every two years and have met the quality standards set by the Association.

Qualmark™ is New Zealand tourism's official mark of quality. All Qualmark™ licenced accommodation listed in this directory means they have been independently assessed as professional and trustworthy, so you can book and buy with confidence. They will meet your essential requirements of cleanliness, safety, security and comfort; and offer a range and quality of services appropriate to their star grade.

Heritage Inns; A collection of luxury historic hosted character bed and breakfast lodges across NZ, are superior and often recommended by tourists. Our B&Bs have knowledgeable and friendly hosts. Our luxury accommodation ranges from the quiet honeymoon lodge in boutique romantic locations to central city accommodation - rivaling superior apartments, hotels or motels. Alternatively, enjoy the genuine NZ experience of an idyllic farmstay, lodge or luxury country B&B.

Superior Inns; Superior Inns of New Zealand properties are specially selected. All offer a true bed and breakfast experience, highlights of your visit to New Zealand. The specially selected bed and breakfast properties offer spacious bedrooms with bathrooms, luxury fittings, private guest lounges, fabulous delectable breakfasts and a chance to meet other visitors or be on your own. Our hosts can organise airport pickups, rental cars, restaurant bookings, honeymoon packages and short stay options.

Finding your way around

We travel from north to south listing the towns as we come to them. In addition, we've divided New Zealand into geographical regions, a map of which is included at the start of each chapter. In some regions, such as Southland, our listings take a detour off the north to south route, and follow their nose - it will soon become obvious.

Happy Travelling
The B&B Book Team

Our Guarantee

Hosts in The New Zealand Bed & Breakfast Book are committed to offering quality hospitality. If you receive hospitality which is less than you expected please discuss your concerns with your hosts at the time. If you are not satisfied you should contact the publishers who will take up the matter with the hosts. If you are still not satisfied the publishers will refund their assessment of a fair proportion of the tariff you paid.

Your comments

We welcome your views on The Bed & Breakfast Book and the hosts you meet. Please visit our website **www.bnb.co.nz** or write to us at, PO Box 6843, Wellington, New Zealand.

Comment Forms

Please help us to maintain our high standards by sending us comments about where you stayed. Guest Comments forms are available from your hosts.

- You may submit your comment on our website **www.bnb.co.nz**

- Or your hosts will give you a comment form.

- Or simply cut one from the back of the book.

- Each comment returned will be in our ongoing monthly draw for a free night's B&B.

- Each person staying can submit a comment for an increased chance of success.

- Guest comments are displayed on the hosts' pages at **www.bnb.co.nz**

About Bed & Breakfast

Our B&Bs range from homely to luxurious, but you can always be assured of generous hospitality.

Types of accommodation
Traditional B&B
Generally small owner-occupied home accommodation usually with private guest living and dining areas.
Homestay
A homestay is a B&B where you share the family's living area.
Farmstay
Country accommodation, usually on a working farm.
Self-contained
Separate self-contained accommodation, with kitchen and living/dining room. Breakfast provisions usually provided at least for the first night.
Separate/suite
Similar to self-contained but without kitchen facilities. Living/dining facilities may be limited.

Bathrooms
Ensuite and private bathrooms are for your use exclusively.
Guests share bathroom means you will be sharing with other guests.
Family share means you will be sharing with the family.

Tariff
The prices listed are in New Zealand dollars and include GST. Prices listed are subject to change, and any change to listed prices will be stated at time of booking. Some hosts offer a discount for children - this applies to age 12 or under unless otherwise stated. Most of our B&Bs will accept credit cards.

Reservations
We recommend you contact your hosts well in advance to be sure of confirming your accommodation. Most hosts require a deposit so make sure you understand their cancellation policy. Please let your hosts know if you have to cancel, they will have spent time preparing for you. You may also book accommodation through some travel agents or via specialised B&B reservation services.

Breakfast & Dinner
Breakfast is included in the tariff, with each host offering their own menu. You'll be surprised at the range of delicious breakfasts available, many using local produce. If you would like dinner most hosts require 24 hours notice.

Smoking
Most of our B&Bs are non-smoking, but smoking is permitted outside. Listings displaying the no smoking logo do not permit smoking anywhere on the property. B&Bs which have a smoking area inside mention this in their text.

Accessibility
♿ Certified as being wheelchair accessible.

Schedule of Standards

General
Friendly, warm greeting at door by host
Local tourism and transport information available to guests
Property appearance neat and tidy, internally and externally
Absolute cleanliness of the home in all areas used by the guests
Absolute cleanliness of kitchen, refrigerator and food storage areas
Gate or roadside identification of property
Protective clothing and footwear available for farmstay guests
Hosts accept responsibility to comply with local body bylaws
Host will be present to welcome and farewell guests
Hosts' pets and young children mentioned in listing
Smoke alarms in each guest bedroom and above each landing
Evacuation advice card displayed in each bedroom (recommended)
Working torch beside every bed
Suitable fire extinguisher in kitchen and on landing of each upper floor (recommended)
Fire blanket in kitchen (recommended)

Hosts accept responsibility to comply with applicable laws and regulations
Fire safety laws and requirements
Insurances
Swimming and spa pool regulations
Other laws impacting on operation of a B&B

Bedrooms
Each bedroom solely dedicated to guests with...
Bed heating
Heating
Light controlled from the bed
Wardrobe space with variety of hangers
Drawers
Good quality floor covering
Mirror
Power point near a mirror
Waste paper basket
Drinking glasses
Clean pillows with additional available
No Host family items stored in the room
Night light for guidance to w.c. if not adjacent to bedroom
Blinds or curtains on all windows where appropriate
Good quality mattresses in sound condition on a sound base
Clean bedding appropriate to the climate, with extra available

Bathroom & toilet facilities
At least one bathroom adequately ventilated and equipped with...
Bath or shower
Wash handbasin and mirror
Covered wastebasket in bathroom
Extra toilet roll
Lock on bathroom and toilet doors
Electric razor point if bedrooms are without a suitable power point
Soap, towels, bathmat, facecloths, fresh for each new guest
Towels changed or dried daily for guests staying more than one night
Sufficient bathroom and toilet facilities to serve family and guests

New Zealand and Regions

Northland

Whangarei

Auckland

Coromandel

Bay of Plenty

Tauranga

Waikato, King Country

Hamilton

Rotorua

Gisborne

Gisborne

Taranaki, Wanganui,
Ruapehu, Rangitikei

New Plymouth

Napier

Manawatu, Horowhenua

Hawkes Bay

Nelson, Golden Bay

Palmerston North

Wairarapa

Masterton

Nelson

Blenheim

Wellington

West Coast

Marlborough

Greymouth

Canterbury

Christchurch

Timaru

South Canterbury,
North Otago

Queenstown

Dunedin

Otago, North Catlins

Invercargill

Southland,
South Catlins

Stewart Island

Contents

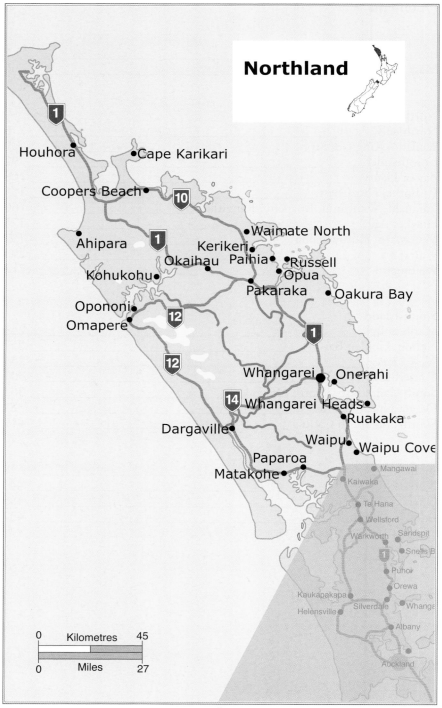

Northland

Houhora
Cape Karikari
Coopers Beach
10
Waimate North
Ahipara
1
Kerikeri
Okaihau
Paihia
Russell
Kohukohu
Opua
Pakaraka
Oakura Bay
Opononi
12
Omapere
12
1
Whangarei
Onerahi
14
Whangarei Heads
Ruakaka
Dargaville
Waipu
Waipu Cove
Paparoa
Mangawai
Matakohe
Kaiwaka
Te Hana
Wellsford
Warkworth
Sandspit
Snells B
1
Puhoi
Orewa
Kaukapakapa
Helensville
Silverdale
Whanga
Albany
Auckland

0   Kilometres   45

0   Miles   27

Houhora *44 km N of Kaitaia*

Houhora Lodge & Homestay *Homestay*
Jacqui & Bruce Malcolm
3994 Far North Road, Houhora, RD 4, Kaitaia

Tel (09) 409 7884 or 021 926 992
Fax (09) 409 7884
houhora.homestay@xtra.co.nz
www.topstay.co.nz

Double $125-$160 Single $90-$100 (Full breakfast)
Dinner $40 by arrangement
Visa MC accepted Children welcome
3 King/Twin 3 Single (3 bdrm)
Bathrooms: 2 Ensuite 1 Private

We have fled our largest city to live on the shores of Houhora Harbour, and look forward to sharing this special part of New Zealand with you. Come and enjoy remote coastal walks, shell-collecting, Cape Reinga, 90 Mile Beach and other attractions. We can arrange 4x4 trips, sport or game fishing and provide relaxed and quality accommodation on your return. Home-made bread, home-grown fruit, home-pressed olive oil, vegetables and eggs. Fresh or smoked fish a speciality. Email, internet, fax and laundry facilities available.

Cape Karikari - Whatuwhiwhi *30min SE of Kaitaia*

Riviera Lodge *Luxury B&B Cottage with Kitchen*
Janine & Rex Honeyfield
69 Whatuwhiwhi Road, RD 3, Cape Karikari, Kaitaia

Tel (09) 406 7596 or 021 277 2510
Fax (09) 406 7581
riviera.lodge@xtra.co.nz   www.rivieralodge.co.nz

Double $120-$200 Single $100-$160 (Continental)
Child over 12 $40 High rate 20 December-31 January
including public holidays
Visa MC accepted Children welcome
1 Queen 1 Double 1 Single (5 in Cottage bdrm)
Bathrooms: 1 Ensuite 1 Guest share Shower

Opened in October 2004. Riviera Lodge a new B&B nestled on the edge of Doubtless Bay set alongside native bush, 15 minutes off Highway 10 Whatuwhiwhi, Cape Karikari. Recreational activities: rock fishing, diving, swimming, also fishing trips by arrangement. Walk to Perihipi Bay, handy to Matai Bay, Rangiputa and Tokerau beach, where you can take a stroll. Just minutes from Carrington Resort which has a 18 hole golf course, winery and restaurant. Whatuwhiwhi has a service station and dairy. Janine, Rex, our dog Duke, cat Brandy welcome you to the winterless north.

Coopers Beach *3 km N of Mangonui*

Mac'n'Mo's *B&B*
Maureen & Malcolm MacMillan
PO Box 177, 104 State Highway 10,
Coopers Beach, Mangonui

Tel (09) 406 0538 Fax (09) 406 0538
MacNMo@xtra.co.nz

Double $80-$90 Single $50-$60 (Continental)
Dinner $25 by arrangement
1 Queen 1 Double 1 Twin (3 bdrm)
Bathrooms: 2 Ensuite 1 Private

Enjoy a million dollar view of Doubtless Bay while you enjoy Mac's smoked fish on your toast. The bus to Cape Reinga stops at our gate, you may go on a craft or wine trail, swim with dolphins, go fishing, diving or just relax on our unpolluted uncrowded beaches, there's one across the road. There are several fine restaurants and the world famous fish and chip shop nearby. Have a memorable stay with Mac'n'Mo, they will take good care of you.

Coopers Beach *4 km N of Mangonui*

Doubtless Bay Lodge *B&B*

Barbara & Ian

33 Cable Bay Block Road, Coopers Beach, Mangonui

Tel (09) 406 1661 or 021 824 571
Fax (09) 406 1662
enquiries@doubtlessbaylodge.co.nz

Double $75-$110 Single $55-$80 (Full breakfast)
Child $20
Visa MC Eftpos accepted Children welcome
3 Queen 1 Twin (4 bdrm)
Bathrooms: 4 Ensuite

Experience the outstanding views over Doubtless Bay and surrounding countryside. Top of the range B&B an hour north of Paihia. Short walk to the golden sands of Coopers Beach and local shops. Each room has an ensuite bathroom, Sky TV, fridge, tea and coffee making facilities. Guest laundry and barbeque available. Scenic bus tours to Cape Reinga, fishing trips and golf games can be arranged. Visit the many historic places, isolated beaches, local wineries in the area. Let us help you make this the perfect holiday destination.

Kerikeri *3 km E of Kerikeri*

Matariki Orchard *B&B Homestay*

Alison & David Bridgman

14 Pa Road, Kerikeri, Bay of Islands

Tel (09) 407 7577 or 027 408 0621
Fax (09) 407 7593 matarikihomestay@xtra.co.nz
www.kerikeri.co.nz/matariki

Double $140-$160 Single $100 (Full breakfast)
Child negotiable Dinner $50pp
Visa MC accepted Pet free home Children welcome
1 King 1 Queen 2 Single (3 bdrm)
Bathrooms: 1 Ensuite 1 Guest share 1 Private

We welcome guests to our home, large garden, swimming pool and subtropical orchard, within walking distance to historic area. 4 minutes by car to township. David has a vintage car that is used for personalised tours. A short complimentary tour is offered of historic area to guests. We are retired farmers and David a local tour operator for 9 years loves to help with where to go and what to do. Can arrange tour bookings. We enjoy providing dinner with NZ wine. No pets or children. Phone for directions.

Kerikeri - Okaihau *12 km W of Kerikeri*

Clotworthy Farmstay *B&B Farmstay*

Shennett & Neville Clotworthy

914 Wiroa Road, RD 1, Okaihau, Bay of Islands

Tel (09) 401 9371 or 025 941 759
Fax (09) 401 9371

Double $90 Single $50 (Full breakfast)
Dinner $25 by arrangement
Visa MC accepted
1 Queen 2 Single (2 bdrm)
Bathrooms: 1 Guest share

We farm cattle, sheep and horses on our 310 acres. There are panoramic views of the Bay of Islands area from our home 1000 feet above sea level. Of 1840s pioneering descent, our interests are travel, farming, genealogy and equestrian activities. We have an extensive library on Northland history and families. Directions: SH10 take Wiroa/Airport Road at the Kerikeri intersection. 9km on the right. Or SH1, take Kerikeri Road just south of Okaihau. We are fourth house on the left, past the golf course (8km).

Kerikeri *8 km S of Kerikeri*
Puriri Park *B&B Cottage No Kitchen*
Charmian & Paul Treadwell
Puriri Park Orchard, State Highway 10,
Box 572, Kerikeri

Tel (09) 407 9818 Fax (09) 407 9498
puriri@xtra.co.nz

Double $95 Single $75 (Full breakfast)
Child $10 Dinner $35
Visa MC accepted
Children welcome
1 Queen 2 Double 2 Twin 1 Single (4 bdrm)
Bathrooms: 2 Guest share 2 Private

Puriri Park has long been known for its hospitality in the Far North. Guests are welcome to wander around our large garden, explore the kiwifruit and avocado orchards, sit by the lilypond or feed our flock of fantail pigeons. We have 5 acres of bird-filled native bush, mostly totara and puriri. We are in an excellent situation for trips to Cape Reinga and sailing or cruising on the beautiful Bay of Islands. We can arrange tours for you or pick you up from the airport.

Kerikeri *10 km N of Kerikeri Central*
Kerikeri Inlet View *B&B Homestay Farmstay*
Trish & Ryan Daniells
99C Furness Road, RD 3, Kerikeri

Tel (09) 407 7477 Fax (09) 407 7478
kerikeri_inlet_view@hotmail.com

Double $75 Single $45 (Full breakfast)
Child $15 Dinner $18 by arrangement
Backpackers $15 (no breakfast or water view)
Children and pets welcome
1 Queen 2 Double 2 Single (3 bdrm)
Bathrooms: 1 Ensuite 1 Guest share 1 Private

We welcome you to our spacious home on top of our 1100 acre beef and sheep farm. Enjoy the superb views of the Kerikeri Inlet and the Bay of Islands while you relax in our spa pool. Join us for breakfast consisting of seasonal fruit, homemade bread and butter, free-range chook eggs, our own sausages and or bacon, before exploring the many attractions around Kerikeri. Backpackers has private lockable bedrooms, lounge, kitchen/laundry. Note: please phone first for bookings, detailed directions or pick-up. We can speak Japanese.

Kerikeri *12 km E of Kerikeri*
Oversley *Homestay*
Maire & Tone Coyte
Doves Bay Road, RD 1, Kerikeri

Tel (09) 407 8744 or 0274 959 207
Fax (09) 407 4487
oversley@xtra.co.nz
www.bnb.co.nz/hosts/oversley.html

Double $150-$180 Single $130-$160 (Full breakfast)
Dinner by arrangement
Visa MC accepted
1 King/Twin 1 Queen 2 Single (3 bdrm)
Bathrooms: 2 Ensuite 1 Private

Oversley Homestay offers magnificent panoramic water views, sweeping lawns and private native bush walks to the water. Our spacious, comfortable home, set in 18 acres, has a friendly relaxed atmosphere with high quality accommodation. Laundry facilities available. We are an easy going, well travelled, retired couple,who enjoy all sports, which includes golfing on the many surrounding first class courses. Kerikeri course 15 minutes away (Kauri Cliffs course only 40 minutes). Holly, our little bichon, enjoys good company as much as we do.

Kerikeri *2 km S of Kerikeri*

Gannaway House *B&B Homestay*
Jill & Roger Gardner
Kerikeri Road, RD 3, Kerikeri

Tel (09) 407 1432 or 027 479 8115
Fax (09) 407 1431
gannaway@xtra.co.nz
www.bnb.co.nz/hosts/gannawayhouse.html

Double $95-$125 **Single** $65-$95 (Full breakfast)
Child $30
Visa MC accepted
2 Queen 1 Twin (3 bdrm)
Bathrooms: 1 Ensuite 1 Guest share

Jill and Roger welcome you to Gannaway House. Our comfortable home, set in 2 acres of garden and orchard is situated down a tree-lined driveway, close to town but in the quiet of the country. We offer 1 large ground floor room with ensuite and private entrance. Upstairs, 2 rooms (1 Queen and 1 twin) with shared facilities. Relax in our garden, visit the many arts & crafts shops and wineries in the area, or we can arrange trips for you. We are also breeders of very sociable Burmese cats.

Kerikeri *20 km S of Paihia*

Glenfalloch *B&B Homestay*
Bojka & Keith
48 Landing Road, Kerikeri

Tel (09) 407 5471 Fax (09) 407 5473
glenfalloch@ihug.co.nz
www.kerikeri-accommodation.co.nz

Double $90-$110 **Single** $80-$90 (Full breakfast)
Child $25 Dinner $30pp by arrangement
Visa MC Diners accepted
Children welcome
1 Queen 1 Double 1 Single (3 bdrm)
Bathrooms: 2 Ensuite

Venture down Glenfalloch's driveway to our secluded bed and breakfast, nestled in a garden paradise. Enjoy the hospitality of Keith and Bojka, who comes from Slovenia. Relax in the spa and swimming pool and on teh decks, or for the energetic there is lawn tennis. Glenfalloch is just 500 metres from Kerikeri's Stone Store and Kemp Mission House, and adjacent to the lovely Rainbow Falls walking track. Kerikeri is unique and offers some good golf courses within short distances, lovely shops and excellent restaurants.

Pakaraka - Paihia *10 km N of Kawakawa*

Bay of Islands Farmstay - B&B Highland Farm *B&B Farmstay*
Glenis & Ken Mackintosh
Pakaraka, 6627 State Highway 1, RD 2, Kaikohe 0400

Tel (09) 404 0430 or 027 249 8296
Fax (09) 404 0430 Ken@infobiz.co.nz
www.bnb.co.nz/bayofislandfarmstaybb.html

Double $95 **Single** $65 (Full breakfast)
Child $10 Dinner $20-$30 (byo & comp)
Twin room $90
Visa MC accepted Pet free home Children welcome
1 Double 1 Twin 3 Single (2 bdrm)
Bathrooms: 2 Ensuite

Beautiful 51 acres, stone walls, barberry hedges. Sheep, cattle. Ken, a sheep-dog trialist, trains dogs and pups daily! Enjoy watching, help shift animals. Meet and photograph with animals on your farm walk. Enjoy your visit. Swimming pool or cosy warm home in winter. Access to internet. Good central base! 5 golf courses, beaches, hot pools, shopping! Situated 15 minutes from Paihia, Kerikeri, Kaikohe. Welcome to Bay of Islands. Book early or take pot luck! (10 minutes north Kawakawa, 2 south of Pakaraka Junction). "Highland Farm" on entrance.

Pakaraka *20 km N of Pahia/ Kerikeri/Kaikohe*

Jarvis Family Farmstay & Equestrian Centre *B&B Farmstay*

Frederika & Douglas Jarvis
State Highway 1, Pakaraka, RD 2
Ohaeawai, Bay of Islands

Tel (09) 405 9606 or 021 259 1120 Fax (09) 405 9607
baystay@igrin.co.nz www.nzbaystay.com

Double $100-$120 Single $60 (Special breakfast)
Child half price
Dinner $30 by arrangement
Visa MC accepted
Children and pets welcome
1 Queen 1 Double 1 Twin (2 bdrm)
Bathrooms: 3 Private spa bathroom

For a charming and relaxing break, look no further!
Beautiful subtropical gardens with water features
surround our spacious family home where you can
choose between indoor and outdoor living.

Our 4 poster suite includes its own lounge with two
single beds, TV/video plus a private deck in the wishing
well garden. Fredi and Douglas emigrated from the UK
in 1990, where they ran one of England's top country
inns: so they are no strangers to hospitality. We have 30
acres for you to enjoy with extensive equestrian facilities
and walks. Just bring a smile with you.

Here are some quotes from our visitors book: "Wow!
What a fabulous time. Fredi's musical talent, a
sing-a-long on the porch. The food, the dogs &
horses, wanted to take everyone home." USA. "Lovely
stay, perfect surroundings for our honeymoon." UK.
"Thankyou for sharing your little bit of heaven." USA

Pakaraka is centrally based for touring the Bay, West
and North Coasts with all the popular tourist, dolphin
and marine discoveries. We are a pet friendly country
stay.

Northland

Paihia *4 km N of Paihia*

Lakeview Homestay *Homestay*
Heather and Maurice Pickup
12 The Anchorage, Watea RD 1, Paihia

Tel (09) 402 8152 Fax (09) 402 8152
lakeviewwatea@slingshot.co.nz

Double $120 **Single** $90 (Full breakfast)
Dinner $35
Visa MC accepted
Not suitable for children
1 Queen (1 bdrm)
Bathrooms: 1 Private

Our modern wooden home is set in quiet countryside.
A small lake at the bottom of the garden which is home to many native birds and black swans. We are of
English/NZ origins, but have American connections too. The guest bedroom has a view of the lake. We
are close to Haruru Falls, Waitangi, beaches, walks, golf and historic places. Breakfasts feature home-
made breads and preserves and more. We can book tours and cruises. Complimentary refreshments on
arrival. We have 1 old dog.

Paihia *7 km N of Paihia*

Lily Pond Estate B&B (Est 1989) *B&B*
Allwyn & Graeme Sutherland
725 Puketona Road, RD 1, Paihia,
Lily Pond Estate sign at gate

Tel (09) 402 7041

Double $85-$100 **Single** $50 (Full breakfast)
1 Double 1 Twin 1 Single (3 bdrm)
Bathrooms: 1 Guest share 1 Private

Drive in through an avenue of mature Liquid Amber
trees to our comfortable timber home on our 5 acre
country estate growing citrus and pip fruit. The guest
wing has views of the fountain, bird aviary, small lake
and black swan with the double and twin rooms having private verandah access. Fresh orange juice, fruit
and home-made jams are served at breakfast. We are born New Zealanders, sailed thousands of miles
living aboard our 50 foot yacht in the Pacific and will gladly share our Bay of Island knowledge to make
your visit most memorable.

Paihia *1.5 km S of Paihia*

Te Haumi House *B&B Homestay*
Enid & Ernie Walker
12 Seaview Road, Paihia

Tel (09) 402 8046 Fax (09) 402 8046
enidanderniewalker@xtra.co.nz

Double $80-$90 **Single** $60 (Continental)
Visa MC accepted
2 Queen 1 Single (2 bdrm)
Bathrooms: 1 Family share 1 Guest share

Millennium Sunrise. Welcome to our modern
waterfront home, set amongst subtropical gardens with
expansive harbour views, just minutes from tourist
activities and town centre. Guests enjoy privacy through a clever split-level design. Buffet breakfast with
a choice of dining room, garden deck or courtyard. Laundry facilities, ample off-street parking and
courtesy pick up from bus available. Descendants of early settlers, we have a good knowledge of local
history. Ernie is a Masonic Lodge member.

Paihia *In Central Paihia*
Craicor Accommodation *Apartment with Kitchen*
Garth Craig & Anne Corbett
PO Box 15, 49 Kings Road, Paihia, Bay of Islands

Tel (09) 402 7882 Fax (09) 402 7883
craicor@actrix.gen.nz
www.craicor-accom.co.nz

Double $130 Single $95 (Breakfast by arrangement)
Continental breakfast optional $7.50pp
Visa MC Amex accepted
Not suitable for children
2 King 2 Single (2 bdrm)
Bathrooms: 2 Ensuite

The perfect spot for those seeking a quiet, sunny and central location. Discover the Garden Suite and Tree House. Self-contained modern units nestled in a garden setting with trees that almost hug you, native birds and sea views. Each unit has ensuite bathroom, fully equipped kitchen for self-catering, super king bed, TV, insect screens and is tastefully decorated to reflect the natural colours of the surroundings. Safe off-street parking, all within a 5 minute stroll to the waterfront, restaurants and town centre.

Paihia *1 km N of Paihia*
Bay of Islands Bed & Breakfast *B&B Homestay*
Laraine & Sid Dyer
48 Tahuna Road, Paihia, Bay of Islands

Tel (09) 402 8551 Fax (09) 402 8551
bayofislandsbnb@slingshot.co.nz

Double $90 Single $45 (Continental)
1 Queen 1 Double 1 Single (3 bdrm)
Bathrooms: 1 Family share

We invite you to stay and relax in our home, only minutes from the beach, with bush walks and golf course nearby. On arrival a warm welcome awaits you, with tea or coffee and a chance to unwind. Assistance with your itinerary is offered should you need help. We look forward to the pleasure of your company and ensuring your stay is as comfortable and memorable as possible. Our courtesy car will meet you if travelling by bus. We have a dog named Lucy.

Paihia *In Paihia Central*
Marlin House *Luxury B&B Cottage with Kitchen*
Christopher & Angela Houry
15 Bayview Road, Paihia, Bay of Islands New Zealand

Tel (09) 402 8550 Fax (09) 402 6770
marlinhouse@xtra.co.nz

Double $170 Single $120 (Special breakfast)
Laundry $10
Visa MC accepted
Not suitable for children
1 King 1 Queen 1 Twin (3 bdrm)
Bathrooms: 3 Ensuite

Marlin House is a large comfortable colonial-style house with spacious luxury accommodation in 3 self-contained ensuites with fridge microwave and TV, all with seperate entrances onto decks with seating overlooking the bay. Ample off-road parking is available. Situated in a quiet tree-clad spot above Paihia with beautiful sea views and only 4 minutes easy walk to the beach shops and restaurants. Special breakfasts with home-baking. Benny the cat is outside (minimum 2 night stay).

Northland

Paihia *0.5 km NW of Paihia*

Windermere *B&B Apartment with Kitchen*
Richard & Jill Burrows
168 Marsden Road, Paihia, Bay of Islands

Tel (09) 402 8696 or 021 115 7436
Fax (09) 402 5095 windermere@igrin.co.nz
www.windermere.co.nz

Double $100-$175 Single $80-$15 (Continental)
Child $25 Extra adult $50
Visa MC accepted
2 Queen 2 Single (2 bdrm)
Bathrooms: 2 Ensuite

Windermere is a large modern family home set
in a bush setting and yet located right on one of the best beaches in the Bay of Islands. Superior
accommodation is provided with suites having their own ensuite and kitchen facilities. For longer stays
1 suite has its own laundry, dryer and fully equipped kitchen. The other suite has microwave and fridge
only. Each suite has its own decks where you can sit and enjoy the view enhanced by spectacular sunsets.
Sky TV. Outdoor Spa.

Paihia *6 km W of Paihia*

Appledore Lodge *Luxury B&B Separate Suite Cottage with Kitchen*
Janet & Jim Pugh
Puketona Road, Paihia, Bay of Islands

Tel (09) 402 8007 Fax (09) 402 8007
appledorelodge@xtra.co.nz
www.appledorelodge.co.nz

Double $100-$230 Single $100-$180 (Continental)
Minimum 4 nights over Christmas & New Year
Visa MC Amex accepted Not suitable for children
2 King/Twin 1 Queen 1 Double (4 bdrm)
Bathrooms: 4 Ensuite

Miniature waterfalls and rapids await your discovery
as the Waitangi River gently tumbles by your bedroom window just 25 meters away. House guests in the
Victoria Room with romantic 4 poster are served a special home made breakfast on our antique Kauri
table or grand deck. Luxury Riverside Suite & Self-contained superior Riverside Cottage & Studio take
delight in an all home-made breakfast basket. We enjoy classic cars, golf, travel and meeting new guests.
Janet, Jim & our golden retriever look forward to making your stay truly memorable.

Paihia

Fallsview B&B *B&B Homestay*
Clive & Shirley Welch
4 Fallsview Road, Haruru, Paihia RD 1

Tel (09) 402 7871 or 025 627 1652
Fax (09) 402 7861
fallsviewbb@slingshot.co.nz
www.fallsview.co.nz

Double $100-$110 Single $60-$60 (Full breakfast)
Child negotiable
Visa MC accepted
Children welcome
1 Queen 1 Twin 1 Single (3 bdrm)
Bathrooms: 1 Guest share 1 Bath seperate shower

A modern apartment with all the comforts of home, as in very comfortable beds, a beautiful sunny
lounge with fridge, microwave, stereo, TV, tea/coffee and laundry facilities. Be as private or as sociable
as you wish. Extra twin beds available upstairs. Breakfast also upstairs with glorious views of the
surrounding countryside. Our other team members are Mac our miniature poodle, whose job it is to
make sure you feel most welcome, and 2 cats. Situated 3km from all main tourist attractions.

Paihia *In Paihia-Central*

Allegra House *B&B Apartment with Kitchen*
Heinz & Brita Marti
39 Bayview Road, Paihia, Bay of Islands

Tel (09) 402 7932 or 027 470 1137
Fax (09) 402 7930 allegrahouse@xtra.co.nz
www.allegra.co.nz

Double $125-$190 Single $120-$190 (Continental)
Child negotiable
Apartment $145-$220
Visa MC accepted Children welcome
1 King/Twin 2 Queen (3 bdrm)
Bathrooms: 3 Ensuite

Allegra House, our spacious, modern home is centrally located, just up the hill from Paihia's wharf, shops and restaurants. Spectacular views from all rooms. B&B rooms have ensuite bathroom,tea/coffee making facilities, fridge, TV and balcony. Or self-catering apartment with separate bedroom, large bathroom, fully equipped kitchen and spacious lounge opening onto a large balcony. Each room has its own air conditioning and the whole house is smoke-free. BBQ,laundry facilities and internet access. Plenty of good local information.

Paihia *.5 km SW of Post Office*

Decks of Paihia *B&B Country B&B*
Philip & Wendy Hopkinson
69 School Road, Paihia, Bay of Islands

Tel (09) 402 6146 or 021 278 7558
Fax (09) 402 6147
info@decksofpaihia.com
www.decksofpaihia.com

Double $145-$190
(Special breakfast)
Visa MC accepted Not suitable for children
3 King/Twin (3 bdrm)
Bathrooms: 3 Ensuite

Newly constructed purpose built home incorporating 3 guest suites all with private ensuite bathrooms. Quiet peaceful central Paihia location, stylishly furnished and very comfortable interior with ample living space. Beautiful sun drenched decks allow a choice of breakfast spots to enjoy the lovely views over Paihia and the Bay of Islands. Philip and Wendy have enjoyed many years in the hospitality industry and are happy to share their extensive knowledge of the Bay of Islands and Northland with you. Philip has strong links to the area - his great grandfather Patrick McGovern was the police constable in Russell in the 1880s.

Paihia - Opua *5 km S of Paihia*

Rose Cottage *B&B Separate Suite*
Pat & Don Jansen
37A Oromahoe Road, Opua 0290, Bay of Islands

Tel (09) 402 8099 Fax (09) 402 8096
rosecottageopua@paradise.net.nz
www.bnb.co.nz/rosecottageopua.html

Double $80-$120 (Continental)
Not suitable for children
1 Queen 1 Double (2 bdrm)
Bathrooms: 1 Private

Our home overlooks a native bush garden and picturesque upper harbour and rural views. The guest wing is separate from host accommodation with private entrance, fridge, microwave, tea/coffee facilities and TV. Private bathroom and separate toilet for exclusive guest use with the option of one party or shared facilities. Comfortable rooms enjoy sea views. We are both retired and have been hosting guests since 1987. Our interests include local history, gardening fishing, sailing and walking. We look forward to helping you enjoy your stay. Inspections welcome.

Paihia - Opua *300m km E of Opua*
Sinclair B&B *B&B Homestay Separate Suite*
Margaret Sinclair
7 Franklin Street, Opua

Tel (09) 402 8285 Fax (09) 402 8285
bbopua@xtra.co.nz

Double $80-$100 Single $50 (Continental)
Self-contained flat $80-$100 double $10 single
Children welcome
1 Double 2 Single (2 bdrm)
Bathrooms: 1 Family share

Welcome to my lovely home above Opua Harbour.
Enjoy panoramic views of water and boat activities
- always something happening. Tourist activities are nearby. Relax in the spa after your day's outing. You
may like to wander in my garden - my big interest. Downstairs is a 2 roomed unit with separate shower,
toilet and private deck with stunning views. Take the Whangarei - Paihia road. Turn right for Opua
- Russel Ferry. This is Franklin Street. My house is clearly visible on the seaward side.

≈

Paihia - Opua *5 km S of Paihia*
Seascape *B&B Homestay Self-contained Flat*
Vanessa & Frank Leadley
17 English Bay Road, Opua, Bay of Islands

Tel (09) 402 7650 or 027 475 6793
Fax (09) 402 7650
frankleadley@xtra.co.nz

Double $110-$140 Single $80 (Continental)
Self-contained flat $110-$140
Visa MC accepted
1 Queen 2 Single (2 bdrm)
Bathrooms: 1 Ensuite 1 Family share

Seascape is on a tranquil bush-clad ridge. Enjoy
spectacular views, stroll through bush to the coastal walk-way, enjoy our beautifully landscaped garden,
experience the many activities in the bay, or relax on your deck. We are keen NZ and international
travellers. Other interests include music, gardening, fishing, boating, and Rotary. Our fully self-
contained flat has queen-size bed, TV, laundry, kitchen, BBQ, own entrance and deck. Join us for
breakfast, or look after yourselves. Guest Room with shared facilities also available.

≈

Paihia - Opua *5 km S of Paihia*
Pt Veronica Lodge *B&B Homestay*
Audrey & John McKiernan
39 Point Veronica Drive, Opua 290, Bay of Islands

Tel (09) 402 5579 Fax (09) 402 5579
stay@ptveronicalodge.co.nz
www.ptveronicalodge.co.nz

Double $130-$180 Single $100-$160
(Special breakfast)
Visa MC Diners accepted
2 Queen (2 bdrm)
Bathrooms: 2 Ensuite

Qualmark 4 Star guest & hosted property at Veronica
Point between Paihia and Opua. Access to the coastal track and views of the bay towards Paihia and
Russell; this is our special place. Peaceful, romantic and restful with wonderful bush and coastal walks
from the house. Soak in our spa or rest on the decks. TV in your room and Sky channels in the lounge.
Golf, sailing, fishing & historic buildings within 10 minutes drive. Audrey, John and Bonnie & Clyde,
our friendly dogs welcome you.

Paihia - Opua *5 km S of Paihia*
Waterview Lodge *B&B Cottage No Kitchen*
Antionette & Jess Cherrington
14 Franklin Street, Opua, Bay of Islands 0290

Tel (09) 402 7595 Fax (09) 402 7596
info@waterviewlodge.co.nz www.waterviewlodge.com

Double $140-$230 Single $90-$140 (Continental)
Child $20 Dinner $40-$50
Studio apartment $120-$180
Cottage $150-$250
Visa MC Amex Eftpos accepted Children welcome
2 King 5 Queen 1 Twin 5 Single (8 bdrm)
Bathrooms: 3 Ensuite 2 Private bath in cottage

Overlooking the picturesque Port of Opua, Waterview Lodge is a quality accommodation establishment. The Harbour and River Suites, with private balconies, have expansive sea views of Opua and the upper harbour. Our 3 bedroom cottage also has beautiful sea views. Our 2 bedroom Garden Unit is located downstairs next to the Garden Suite, with access to a private garden and native bush backdrop. Both my husband and I are originally from the Bay of Islands. We enjoy living at Waterview Lodge with our 2 sons, Ben 17 and Oliver 10, and our little dog Amy.

Paihia - Opua *5 km S of Paihia*
Mako Lodge *B&B Self-contained*
June & John Pearce
18 Point Veronica Drive, Opua 0290, Bay of Islands

Tel (09) 402 7957 Fax (09) 402 5957
info@makolodge.co.nz
www.makolodge.co.nz

Double $140-$175 Single $130-$140 (Full breakfast)
Visa MC accepted
Pet free home Children welcome
1 King/Twin 2 Queen (3 bdrm)
Bathrooms: 3 Ensuite One ensuite has additional bath and seperate shower

Our Lodge completed at Point Veronica in 2003 is in an outstanding peaceful coastal location with breathtaking views from our decks of sea and bush. Walkers have easy access to the bush/coastal path in the area. Yet we are only 5km from Paihia and Waitangi and its popular activities for tourists. All bedrooms have sea views with fridge, complimentary tea and coffee making facilities, TV with Sky, VCR, access to video library and clock radio alarms. Enjoy our spa pool, location and spectacular sunsets. Charter fishing also available by arrangement

Paihia - Opua *5 km S of Piahia*
Edge Water Opua *Apartment with Kitchen*
Edge Water Opua
12 Beechy Street, Opua 0290, Bay of Islands

Tel (09) 402 5631 or 025 209 8482
theedgewater@xtra.co.nz

Double $250 (Full breakfast provisions)
Pet free home Not suitable for children
1 King (1 bdrm)
Bathrooms: 1 Private

Step out of your door onto a safe sheltered beach and swim before breakfast. Edgewater Opua apartments is new, ultra-modern, all day sun with large balconies overlooking the harbour marina with many tourist, charter and pleasure boats, kayaking and coastal walking tracks. Restaurants and yacht club 5 minutes walk or go fishing and cook a fish on the BBQ. Watch Sky TV.

Northland

Russell *In Russell Central*

Te Manaaki *B&B Apartment with Kitchen*
Sharyn & Dudley Smith
2 Robertson Road, Russell

Tel (09) 403 7200 or 027 424 4391
Fax (09) 403 7537
triple.b@xtra.co.nz
www.bay-of-islands.co.nz/accomm/tmanaaki.html

Double $150-$280 Single $150-$280 (Full breakfast)
Child $20
Visa MC accepted   Children welcome
2 SuperKing/Twin (2 bdrm)
Bathrooms: 2 Ensuite

Te Manaaki overlooks the picturesque harbour and village of historic Russell with its delightful seaside restaurants, shops and wharf a gentle stroll away. Magnificent harbour, bush and village views are a feature of guests private accommodation. The Villa is an attractively appointed sunny spacious deluxe unit set in its own grounds (with garden spa) adjacent to the main house. The Studio is a self-contained suite-styled apartment on the ground floor of our new modern home. Both units have mini-kitchen facilities, Sky TV & off-street parking.

Russell - Okiato *9 km S of Russell*

Aimeo Cottage *B&B Cottage with Kitchen*
Annie & Helmuth Hormann
Russell 26 Okiato Point Road,

Tel (09) 403 7494 Fax (09) 403 7494
aimeo@xtra.co.nz

Double $120-$145 Single $110-$135
(Special breakfast) Child $25
3 bedroom holiday home by request
Visa MC accepted
Children welcome
4 King/Twin 1 Single (2 bdrm)
Bathrooms: 1 Ensuite 1 Private

A quiet place to relax. We have sailed half way around the world to find this beautiful quiet place in the heart of the Bay of Islands and would be happy to share this with you for a while. Aimeo Cottage is built on the hill of Okiato Point, a secluded peninsula overlooking the bay. In 10 minutes you are in New Zealand's first capital, Russell, the site of many historic buildings, an interesting museum and art galleries. Children are welcome. For golfers, a complimentary complete set of clubs available (men's and women's).

Russell *1 km E of Russell*

Lesley's *B&B*
Lesley Coleman
1 Pomare Road, Russell, Northland

Tel (09) 403 7099 or 021 108 0369
three.gs@xtra.co.nz
www.bay-of-islands.co.nz/accomm/lesley.html

Double $130-$150 Single $95-$110 (Special breakfast)
Child $30 Dinner $25
Visa MC accepted Children welcome
1 Double 1 Single (1 bdrm)
Bathrooms: 1 Private

Walk beside a palm cluster to our secluded home inspired by living in Greece. See Matauwhi Bay and overseas yachts from the deck. Enjoy breakfast (with organic emphasis) and eggs from our hens in the cosy guest conservatory. Our guest room has its own entrance and tea/coffee making facilities. Lesley's original artwork is on the walls and the private bathroom features a clawfoot bath. Guestbook comments: "We came exhausted and left refreshed!" "Awesome waffles." Billy the terrior lives here too. Welcome.

Russell - Te Wahapu *7 km S of Russell*

Brisa Cottages *B&B Cottage with Kitchen*
Jenny & Peter Sharpe
92B Te Wahapu Road, RD 1, Russell

Tel (09) 403 7757 or 0800 274 727 Fax (09) 403 7758
brisa@xtra.co.nz   www.bay-of-islands.net.nz/

Double $160-$220 Single $160 (Special breakfast)
Dinner $40pp by arrangement
Visa MC accepted
Not suitable for children
1 King/Twin 3 Queen 1 Single (4 bdrm)
Bathrooms: 4 Ensuite

Our cottages and garden are hidden among the trees at the water's edge. In the morning wake to the sound of the birds and the sunrise over Orongo Bay. We offer warm hospitality and quiet, clean, high quality accommodation with safe off-street parking. Our guests can enjoy total privacy within a self-contained cottage which has a kitchenette, a spacious bedroom/lounge area and ensuite bathroom.

Each cottage has its own area of flowers shrubs and trees, a separate entrance and large deck that overlooks the bay. The emphasis is on tasteful, comfortable surroundings with all the essential extras such as fresh flowers, home-baking, toiletries and bathrobes. Top quality beds and bedding, cotton sheets and soft absorbent towels ensure a feeling of luxury. In each suite a television, books and magazines are provided for your enjoyment.

Our breakfast table is set with white linen, silver and fine china and features fresh baking, home-grown fruit, our own preserves and eggs from our free range hens. The menu changes daily. Picnic hampers and dinners are also available by arrangement.

A dinghy is at hand for a leisurely paddle from our beach and historic Russell's museum, restaurants and galleries are just 7 minutes away by car. Come and enjoy this private and tranquil place with us.

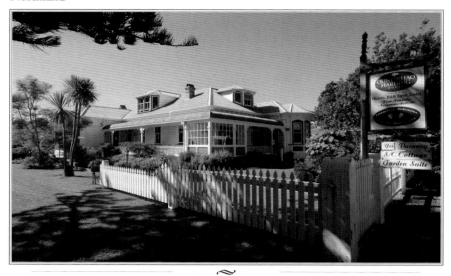

Russell - Matauwhi Bay *1 km E of Russell*

Ounuwhao B&B *B&B Cottage with Kitchen Seperate Suite*

Marilyn & Allan Nicklin

Matauwhi Bay, Russell, The Heart of the Bay of Islands

Tel (09) 403 7310 Fax (09) 403 8310
thenicklins@xtra.co.nz
www.bay-of-islands.co.nz/ounuwhao

Double $185-$225 Single $135-$170 (Full breakfast)
Child under 12 $45
Self-contained garden suite double $200-$250
Visa MC accepted
1 King/Twin 4 Queen 2 Twin 2 Single (7 bdrm)
Bathrooms: 5 Ensuite 2 Private

Welcome to historic Russell, the Heart of the Bay of Islands and the first settled area of NZ. Take a step back into a bygone era and spend some time with us in our delightful, nostalgic, immaculately restored Victorian villa (Circa 1894).

Enjoy your own large guest lounge; tea/coffee and biscuits always available, with open fire in the cooler months, and wrap-around verandahs for you to relax and take in the warm sea breezes. Each of our 4 queen rooms have traditional wallpapers and paintwork, with hand-made patchwork quilts and fresh flowers to create a lovingly detailed, traditional romantic interior.

Breakfast is served in our farmhouse kitchen around the large kauri dining table or alfresco on the verandah if you wish. It is an all home-made affair; from the freshly baked fruit and nut bread, to the yummy daily special and the jam conserves.

Our self-contained cottage is set in park-like grounds for your privacy and enjoyment: with 2 double bedrooms, it is ideal for a family or 2 couples travelling together. It has a large lounge overlooking the reserve and out into the bay, a sunroom and fully self-contained kitchen. Wonderful for people looking for that special place for peace and time-out. Maximum 4 persons. Breakfast is available if required. Complimentary afternoon tea on arrival. Laundry service available.

We look forward to meeting you soon. Our homes are SMOKE-FREE. We are closed June and July. EXPERIENCE OUR HISTORIC B&B. ENJOY A WORLD OF DIFFERENCE.

Russell *0.5 km N of Russell*

La Veduta *Homestay*
Danielle & Dino Fossi
11 Gould Street, Russell, Bay of Islands

Tel (09) 403 8299 Fax (09) 403 8299
laveduta@xtra.co.nz
www.laveduta.co.nz

Double $180-$200 **Single** $130-$150 (Full breakfast)
King-size room $220
Visa MC accepted
1 King 1 Queen 2 Double 1 Single (4 bdrm)
Bathrooms: 3 Ensuite 2 Private

La Veduta. Enjoy our mix of traditional European
culture in the midst of the beautiful Bay of Islands. Historic heartland of New Zealand. La Veduta is the
perfect pied a terre for your Northland holiday. We offer our guests a warm welcome and personalised
service. A delicious cooked breakfast is served on the balcony. Enjoy refreshments watching the sunset
over the bay. We can arrange tours and activities. Restaurants, beach, ferries handy. French and Italian
spoken. Complimentary afternoon tea. A friendly family dog.

Russell *0.4 km N of Russell Central*

A Place in the Sun *B&B Separate Suite Apartment with Kitchen*
Pip & Oliver Campbell
57 Upper Wellington Street, Russell, Bay of Islands

Tel (09) 403 7615 Fax (09) 403 7610
sailing@paradise.net.nz
www.aplaceinthesun.co.nz

Double $120-$170 **Single** $100-$140 (Continental)
Group of 4 $270
Visa MC accepted
Pet free home
2 Queen 1 Double (3 bdrm)
Bathrooms: 2 Ensuite

Welcome to our special place. Explore historic 'Romantic Russell'. Share this retired Kiwi sailing
couple's perfect anchorage. Choose from two private en-suite apartments offering comfortable queen
bedrooms, TV, barbecue, plus great views overlooking Russell village and across the Bay, ideal for relaxing
holidays or honeymoons. Your ranch-sliders open to patio and garden, (no stairs). Enjoy a sunny,
peaceful setting, bordering bush reserve (kiwi habitat). Stroll around Russell Wharf, discover uncrowded
beaches, heritage trails, try rock- or gamefishing. Cruise, sail or simply unwind. It's Paradise.

Russell *In Russell Central*

Villa Russell *B&B Guest House*
Sue & Steve Western
2 Little Queen Street, Russell, Bay of Islands

Tel (09) 403 8845 or 027 492 8912
Fax (09) 403 8845
info@kingfishercharters.co.nz
www.kingfishercharters.co.nz

Double $155 (Full breakfast)
Visa MC accepted
1 King/Twin 2 Queen (3 bdrm)
Bathrooms: 1 Ensuite 2 Private

Enjoy a welcoming visit to Villa Russell, 2 minutes
from the beach and Russell's restaurants. Relax with magnificent views of the bay and wharf from the
deck of our beautifully restored 1910 Villa or from your spacious guest room, with own ensuite. A short
walk takes you to Long Bay surf beach or up to historic Flagstaff Hill and native bush. Off-street parking
provided. Charters on our 11.6 metre yacht Kingfisher may also be arranged to sail the Bay of Islands.
Friendly family dog.

Northland

Kohukohu *80 km S of Kaitaia*
Harbour Views Guest House *B&B Homestay*
Jacky Kelly & Bill Thomson
32B Rakautapu Road, Kohukohu, Northland

Tel (09) 405 5815 Fax (09) 405 5865

Double $90 **Single** $45 (Full breakfast)
Dinner $20
Not suitable for children
1 Queen 2 Single (2 bdrm)
Bathrooms: 1 Private

Historic Kohukohu, now a friendly and charming
village, is situated on the north side of the Hokianga
Harbour. Our beautifully restored kauri home is set in
2 acres of gardens and trees and commands a spectacular view of the harbour. The guest rooms, opening
on to a sunny verandah, are in a private wing of the house. Meals are prepared using home-grown
produce in season. We are interested in, and knowledgeable about, the history and geography of the area.
We have 2 cats.

≈

Opononi *50 km W of Kaikohe*
Koutu Lodge *B&B Homestay*
Tony and Sylvia Stockman
Koutu Loop Road, Opononi, RD 3, Kaikohe

Tel (09) 405 8882 Fax (09) 405 8893
koutulodgebnb@xtra.co.nz
www.waireboulders.co.nz/koutulodge

Double $80-$100 **Single** $65 (Full breakfast)
Dinner $35 by arrangement
Visa MC accepted
1 King 1 Queen 1 Double (3 bdrm)
Bathrooms: 2 Ensuite 1 Private

Situated on Koutu Point overlooking the beautiful
Hokianga Harbour, our home has views both rural and sea. Two rooms have private entrances, decks,
and ensuites, and are very comfortable. We are a friendly, relaxed Kiwi couple, and our aim is to provide
a memorable stay in the true B&B tradition. Stay a while and enjoy everything the historic Hokianga
has to offer.Koutu Loop Rd is 4.3 kms north of Opononi then left 2.3 kms on tar seal to Lodge on right.

≈

Opononi *57 km W of Kaikohe*
Opononi Dolphin Lodge *B&B Separate Suite*
Sue & John Reynard
Corner of SH12 & Fairlie Crescent, Opononi

Tel (09) 405 8451
Fax (09) 405 8451
opononidolphinlodge@xtra.co.nz

Double $75-$95 **Single** $65-$75 (Continental)
Visa MC accepted
1 Queen 1 Double 1 Twin 1 Single (3 bdrm)
Bathrooms: 2 Ensuite 1 Private

Situated on the corner of Fairlie Crescent and SH12,
opposite a beach reserve on the edge of the pristine
Hokianga Harbour. Our sunsets are breathtaking. 20 minutes from "Tane Mahuta" the largest kauri tree
in the world. Step outside for picture postcard views of beautiful blue beconing waters and huge sand
dunes. Visit the boulders, sand board, walking tracks, boating, great fishing, local crafts. Come, enjoy the
friendly hospitality. The West Coast Diamond in the North awaits you.

Omapere *55 km W of Kaikohe*
Harbourside Bed & Breakfast *B&B*
Joy & Garth Coulter
State Highway 12, 1 Pioneer Walk, Omapere

Tel (09) 405 8246
harboursidebnb@xtra.co.nz

Double $90 Single $60 (Continental)
Visa MC accepted
1 Queen 2 Single (2 bdrm)
Bathrooms: 2 Ensuite

Our beachfront home on corner State Highway 12
and Pioneer Walk overlooking the Hokianga Harbour
is within walking distance of restaurants and bars. Both
rooms have ensuites, tea making facilities, refrigerators and TV with separate entrances onto private
decks to relax and enjoy superb views. We're close to the Waipoua Forest, West Coast beaches, sand hills
and historic Rawene. We have an interest in farming, forestry and education. Stay and share our home
and cat.Also available self catering flat.

Omapere *60 km W of Kaikohe*
Hokianga Haven Omapere Beachfront *B&B*
Heather Randerson
226 State Highway 12, Omapere, Hokianga

Tel (09) 405 8285 or 021 393 973
Fax (09) 405 8215 tikanga2000@xtra.co.nz
www.hokiangahaven.co.nz

Double $130-$180 (Continental)
2 night minimum stay October to March
1 Queen (1 bdrm)
Bathrooms: 1 Private

Snuggled into this peaceful private, beachfront location,
our comfortable home embraces the continuously
inspiring seascape of the dramatic harbour entrance and magnificent dune. Simply relaxing in this
harbourside haven is revitalizing. Bush and forest walks, horse riding, harbour cruising, fishing, river and
coastal swimming are some of the natural delights to be enjoyed in this historic area. Our dog will be a
willing walking companion. Star gazing in the warmth of the hot tub is a wonderful way to finish the day.
Range of healing therapies available.

Omapere *55 km W of Kaikohe*
McKenzie's Accommodation *B&B*
Leonie & Doug McKenzie
4 Pioneer Walk, Omapere, South Hokianga

Tel (09) 405 8068 Fax (09) 405 8068
dlmk@xtra.co.nz
www.mckenziesaccommodation.co.nz

Double $90 Single $70 (Continental)
Child $15
Visa MC accepted
Children welcome
1 Queen 1 Single (1 bdrm in B&B, 2 in cottage)
Bathrooms: 1 Private

Our home is right on the beach of the scenic Hokianga Harbour. This photo is taken from just outside
the house. The B&B room has separate outside entrance at ground level, TV, fridge, jug, heater. Separate
bathroom and toilet exclusively for guests. We also have a separate 2 bedroom self-contained unit which
can be self-catering or B&B. Close to the Waipoua Kauri Forest. Less than 5 mins walk to restaurant.
Relax and enjoy this unique environment. Your friendly hosts have extensive local knowledge.

Dargaville *1.5 km S of Dargaville*
Kauri House Lodge *Farmstay*

Doug Blaxall
PO Box 382, Bowen Street, Dargaville

Tel (09) 439 8082 or 025 547769
Fax (09) 439 8082 kaurihouse@xtra.co.nz

Double $200-$275 Single $200
(Full breakfast)
Visa MC accepted
1 King/Twin 2 King (3 bdrm)
Bathrooms: 3 Ensuite

Kauri House Lodge sits high above Dargaville amongst mature trees. The 1880s villa retains all it's charm, style and grace with original kauri panelling and period antiques in all rooms.

Start your day woken by native birds, walk through extensive landscaped grounds or read in our library. In summer enjoy a dip in the large swimming pool. In winter our billiard room log fire is a cosy spot to relax for the evening.

Join us to explore beautiful mature native bush on our nearby farm overlooking the Wairoa River and Kaipara Harbour. The area offers many activities including deserted beaches, lakes, river tours, horse treks, walks and restaurants.

THE MOST COMMON COMMENT IN OUR VISITOR BOOK: "SAVE THE BEST TO LAST".

We have been hosting bed & breakfast for 30 years.

Dargaville *2 km N of Dargaville*
Awakino Point Boutique Motel *Separate Suite*
June & Mick
State Highway 14, Dargaville, PO Box 168 Dargaville

Tel (09) 439 7870 or 027 451 9474
027 479 2126 Fax (09) 439 7580
awakinopoint@xtra.co.nz www.awakinopoint.co.nz

Double $85-$100 (Continental)
Dinner by arrangement
2 bedroom unit 4 persons $145-$160 Rates seasonal
Visa MC Amex accepted
3 Queen 4 Twin (5 bdrm)
Bathrooms: 3 Ensuite

Unique property set on its own acreage surrounded by attractive gardens, just 2km drive from Dargaville on SH14 (The Whangarei Road). The best features of a NZ motel and bed & breakfast have been amalgamated to produce something a little different. You will enjoy your own self-contained suite with private bathroom, friendly service and a good breakfast. 3 well appointed 1 and 2 bedroom self-contained ground floor units. 1 has a seperate lounge kitchenette, bath and log fire. Guest laundry & BBQ available. Smoke-free Indoors.

Bayly's Beach - Dargaville *12 km W of Dargaville*
Ocean View *Cottage No Kitchen*
Paula & John Powell
7 Ocean View Terrace, Baylys Beach, RD 7, Dargaville

Tel (09) 439 6256 or 021 0400 511
baylys@win.co.nz
www.bnb.co.nz/oceanview.html

Double $90 Single $60 (Continental provisions)
Child under 12 $10 Extra adult $10
Visa MC accepted
Children welcome
1 Double 1 Single (1 bdrm)
Bathrooms: 1 Ensuite

Just off the trail, this expansive west coast beach is a wonderful place to relax. With a glimpse of the sea, your cottage is 2 minutes walk to the beach and clifftop walkways. Locally we have 2 great cafes and 18 hole golf course. Kai Iwi Lakes and Waipoua Forests are an easy day trip. Enjoy your sunny, comfortable cottage and breakfast at your leisure - provided in cottage for you. With our 2 children, sleepy cat and delightful Jack Russell, we look forward to welcoming you.

Dargaville *2 km S of Dargaville*
Turiwiri B&B *B&B*
Bruce & Jennifer Crawford
Turiwiri RAPID 6775, State Highway 12, Dargaville

Tel (09) 439 6003 Fax (09) 439 6003
crawford@igrin.co.nz

Double $80 Single $40 (Continental)
2 Queen (2 bdrm)
Bathrooms: 1 Guest share

We enjoy sharing our local knowledge with guests in our modern, 1 level home. Excellent parking for vehicles and an expansive garden in the midst of our 37 acre working farmlet. Our family of 3 grown children all live away from home. Interests include family, farming, Rotary International, gardening and big game fishing. We have 2 friendly cats and a Jack Russell house dog, that loves everyone.

Dargaville
Birch's B&B *B&B Cottage with Kitchen*
Anson & Pat Clapcott
18 Kauri Street, Dargaville,

Tel (09) 439 7565 Fax (09) 439 7520
p.clapcott@quicksilver.net.nz
birch@kauricoast.co.nz

Double $75-$90 Single $45-$60 (Continental)
Child negotiable Dinner by arrangement
Self-contained 2 bedroom cottage $85-$125
Visa MC accepted
3 Queen 3 Twin (6 bdrm)
Bathrooms: 1 Private

You will need several days in the Dargaville area to fully appreciate the beauty of the Kauri Coast. We have 2 queen and 2 twin rooms. There is a large family lounge with fireplace and a modern kitchen with dining area. Enjoy a complimentary beverage from the balcony overlooking beautiful gardens and native trees or stay in our cute self-contained cottage with its own kauri trees. We're a walkable distance to the town, with excellent dining or dinner by arrangement. 1 dog, 1 Kiwi and 1 American to greet you.

~

Matakohe *9 km S of Matakohe*
Petite Provence *B&B Homestay*
Linda & Guy Bucchi
703C Tinopai Road, RD 1, Matakohe

Tel (09) 431 7552 Fax (09) 431 7552
petite-provence@clear.net.nz
petiteprovence.co.nz

Double $130 Single $90 (Continental)
Dinner $35 by arrangement
2 Queen 1 Twin (3 bdrm)
Bathrooms: 2 Ensuite 1 Private

Bienvenue to Petite Provence set on rolling farmland (distant Kaipara harbour views). 9km south of Matakohe Kauri Museum. Guy is French, Linda a New Zealander, our family home in the south of France was also a homestay. Mediterranean/vegetarian/local cuisine (home-grown produce, local seafood) Smoking outdoors. Pets: Loopy our outside dog. Bookings preferred. Directions: from Matakohe Museum travel 2km south, take Tinopai Road, drive approximately 7km. We are at end (500 metres) of private road on left. Sign on street frontage.

~

Paparoa *1 km S of Paparoa Township*
Pioneer B&B *B&B*
Rowie & Pete Panhuis
The Pines Road, Paparoa

Tel (09) 431 6033 Fax (09) 431 6677
officeworkshop@xtra.co.nz

Double $115 Single $85 (Full breakfast)
Child $25 Dinner $30 by arrangement
Children welcome
1 Queen 1 Twin (2 bdrm)
Bathrooms: 1 Ensuite

Pete and Rowie welcome you to their historic homestead. Step back in time and relax in our charmingly restored cottage with ensuite and open fireplace. Enhanced by surrounding native bush and cottage gardens, this is a delightful place to enjoy some country hospitality. Evening meals are cooked on our coal range using fresh local produce if you care to join us, or local restaurants are nearby. We have a passion for local history and memorabilia with the famous Kauri Museum close by. Pets on property.

Paparoa *7 km W of Paparoa*
Palm House *B&B Cottage with Kitchen*
Jenny & Hector MacKinnon
Pahi, RD 1, Paparoa

Tel (09) 431 6689 palmhouse@paradise.net.nz

Double $100-$105 Single $70 (Full breakfast)
Child $55 Dinner $35
Garden cottage $100
Visa MC accepted
Children welcome
2 King/Twin 2 Queen (3 bdrm)
Bathrooms: 1 Ensuite 1 Guest share

Hector & Jenny are reknowned for their relaxed, friendly hospitality, candlelit meals of fine local produce and NZ wines. Enjoy staying at peaceful Pahi. Stroll along the tideline or stand on the wharf and watch the fish jump. Visit the largest Morton Bay Fig Tree in the Southern Hemisphere. Just 13km from Matakohe Museum and en route to the spectacular Kauri Forest. Signposted on the main State Highway 12, travel 7km down Pahi Road and reach Palm House.

Paparoa *1/2 km E of Paparoa*
The Old Post Office Guesthouse *B&B Guest House*
Janice Booth
Corner of State Highway 12 & Oakleigh Road
PO Box 79, Paparoa

Tel (09) 431 6444 Fax (09) 431 6444
paparoa.jan@xtra.co.nz

Double $85-$100 Single $50 (Continental)
Dinner $25 2 bedroom suite from $150
Visa MC accepted
Children welcome
2 Queen 2 Double 7 Twin 1 Single (6 bdrm)
Bathrooms: 5 Private

From the moment you step inside you will succumb to the character and charm of this lovely old historic building (circa 1903), with delightful cottage garden and rural backdrop. Enjoy our true Kiwi hospitality, cuisine and homely atmosphere with separate guests lounges and free tea/coffee. Local restaurants nearby. Spend a day at the world famous Matakohe Kauri Museum only 8km away or if, like us, you enjoy the outdoors, our kayaks are available to explore the nearby Kaipara Harbour. 2 cats on property.

Oakura Bay *45 km NE of Whangarei*
Robin's Nest *Luxury B&B*
Robin & Peter Cusdin
32 Ohawini Road, Oakura Bay, Northland

Tel (09) 433 6035 or 021 188 9000
Fax (09) 433 6039 robin@robinsnest.co.nz
www.robinsnest.co.nz

Double $90-$130 (Full breakfast)
Studio $130-$190 Breakfast & dinner by arrangement
Visa MC accepted
Not suitable for children
1 King/Twin 1 Queen (2 bdrm)
Bathrooms: 2 Ensuite

Our luxury studio is self-contained with superb sea views, TV, CD player, underfloor heating, private decks and gas barbecue. Breakfast available if required at extra cost. The queen room in our home has tea making facilities, ensuite, heated towel-rail, TV, with breakfast included, plus glorious sea views. Enjoy scenic coastal and native forest drives on the Old Russell Road to the Bay of Islands, fishing trips, boat & kayak hire, horse trekking, rock/beach walks and rock casting. Guests are greeted by our old dog Cagney who is a delightful golden retriever.

Whangarei *17 km E of Whangarei*

Parua House *Homestay Farmstay*
Pat & Peter Heaslip
Parua Bay, RD 4, Whangarei

Tel (09) 436 5855 or 021 186 5002
paruahomestay@clear.net.nz
www.paruahomestay.homestead.com

Double $150 Single $90 (Full breakfast)
Child half price Dinner $35
Visa MC accepted
Children welcome
2 Queen 2 Twin 1 Single (4 bdrm)
Bathrooms: 2 Ensuite 1 Private

Parua House is a classical colonial house, built in 1883, comfortably restored and occupying an elevated site with panoramic views of Parua Bay and the Whangarei Harbour.

The property covers 29 hectares of farmland including 2 protected reserves, which are rich in native trees (including kauri) and birds. Guests are welcome to explore the farm and bush, milk the jersey cow, explore the olive grove and sub-tropical orchard, or just relax in the spa pool or on the veranda. A safe swimming beach adjoins the farm, with a short walk to the fishing jetty; 2 marinas and an excellent golf course are are 2 minutes away.

Our wide interests include photography, patchwork quilting and horticulture. The house is attractively appointed with antique furniture and a rare collection of spinning wheels.

Awake to home-baked bread and freshly squeezed orange juice. Dine in elegant surroundings with generous helpings of home produce with our own eggs, home grown vegetables, olives and sub-tropical fruit (home-made ice cream a speciality). Pre-meal drinks and wine are provided to add to the bonhomie of an evening around a large French oak refectory table. As featured on TV's "Ansett NZ Time of Your Life" and "Corban's Taste NZ".

Whangarei *16 km W of Whangarei*
Taraire Grove *B&B Homestay*
Jan & Brian Newman
Tatton Road, RD 9, Whangarei

Tel (09) 434 7279 Fax (09) 434 7279
briannewman@xtra.co.nz

Double $90 **Single** $55 (Full breakfast)
Child half price
Dinner $15-$25pp
Visa MC accepted Children welcome
1 Queen 2 Single (2 bdrm)
Bathrooms: 1 Guest share

We welcome you to our charming country residence at
Maungatapere, within easy driving distances to east and west coast beaches. We are a semi-retired couple, and welcome the opportunity to return hospitality experienced overseas. Our home overlooks a stream and we are gradually developing the 3 and a half acres into lawns, gardens and ponds. 2 resident pets. The guest wing is private with TV room and tea/coffee making facilities. Whangarei, 15 minutes away, has excellent restaurants or you can choose to dine with us and enjoy hospitality.

Whangarei *10 km NE of Whangarei CBD*
Country Garden Tearooms *Cottage with Kitchen*
Margaret & John Pool
526 Ngunguru Road, RD 3, Whangarei

Tel (09) 437 5127 or 025 519 476
www.countrygarden.co.nz

Double $95-$110 **Single** $65-$70 (Full breakfast)
Dinner $30 by arrangement
2 Queen (2 bdrm)
Bathrooms: 2 Ensuite

Enjoy a warm friendly welcome. We have over 3
acres of beautiful trees, shrubs, bulbs, perennials,
succulents and a large variety of bird life. Feel at home
in a spacious self-contained unit with fridge, microwave and tea making facilities. Enjoy cooked or continental breakfast in our dining room overlooking the garden. We are 10km from central Whangarei on Ngunguru-Tutukaka highway. 5km from Whangarei Falls. Beautiful beaches, restaurants, diving, fishing and golfing within 10km.

Whangarei *12 km SW of Whangarei*
Owaitokamotu *B&B Homestay*
Minnie & George Whitehead
727 Otaika Valley Road, Otaika, Whangarei

Tel (09) 434 7554 Fax (09) 434 7554
minniegeorge@xtra.co.nz

Double $85-$100 **Single** $65 (Full breakfast)
Dinner $25 by arrangement
Children and pets welcome
2 King/Twin 2 Queen (3 bdrm)
Bathrooms: 2 Guest share

Come, enjoy the tranquility of Owaitokamotu, place
of water. Magnificent rocks of all shapes and sizes,
pristine bush, rambling walks, set in 10 acres, easy contour. Created gardens, featuring ponds, bridges, archways, windmill, 1850s style shanty and more. Home wheelchair friendly. All bedrooms private access from exterior. TV, tea/coffee facilities. Join us for 3 course evening meal, $25 by arrangement. Restaurants nearby. Interests: travel, wood carving, our garden. Smoke-free indoors. Laundry facilities available. Warm welcome awaits you.

Northland

Whangarei *25 km SE of Whangarei*

Vealbrook B&B *B&B Homestay Cottage No Kitchen*
Bob & Pre Sturge
2013 McLeod Bay, Whangarei Heads, RD 4,
Whangarei Heads Road, Whangarei

Tel (09) 434 0098 Fax (09) 434 0098
pretoria@clear.net.nz

Double $100 **Single** $95 (Special breakfast)
Child $15 Dinner $25
Self-contained unit $120
Children welcome
1 Queen 1 Double 1 Twin 3 Single (3 bdrm)
Bathrooms: 1 Guest share

Stunning harbour views. Coastal scenic walks. Mountains to climb. 20 metres to the beach. Safe swimming, snorkelling, kayaking, good fishing at jetty. Local dairy nearby. Pine Golf Course 15 minutes away. Surfing ocean beach. Pleasant drive round beautiful ocean bays. The house is arranged with antique furniture. Antique lace garments on display. For breakfast enjoy Bob's home-made marmalades jellies. Freshly picked fruit and fruit juice. Vegetables, subtropical fruits. Dinner supplied on request. Pre-meal drinks. Enjoy warmth and friendliness of your hosts

Whangarei - Onerahi *9 km SE of Whangarei*

Channel Vista *B&B Cottage with Kitchen*
Braia & Paul Larsen
254 Beach Road, Onerahi, Whangarei

Tel (09) 436 5529 or 027 448 8507
Fax (09) 436 5529
channelvista@igrin.co.nz
www.homestays.net.nz/channelvista.htm

Double $170 **Single** $100 (Full breakfast)
Visa MC accepted
Children welcome
2 Queen (2 bdrm)
Bathrooms: 2 Ensuite

Channel Vista is situated on the shores of Whangarei Harbour. We have 2 self-contained units each with their own private decks where you can relax and watch boats go by. Laundry, fax and email facilities available. Local shopping centre only 3 minutes away, 5 minute walk along waterfront to top restaurant. Sports facilities eg, golf, diving, game fishing, bowls etc nearby. We are 1 hour from the Bay of Islands, so it is a good place to base yourself for your Northland holiday.

Whangarei *20 km E of Whangarei*

Juniper House *B&B Homestay*
Diane & Mike James
49 Proctor Road, RD 9, Whangarei

Tel (09) 434 6399 or 027 422 4498
Fax (09) 434 6399
diane.james@xtra.co.nz

Double $120-$135 **Single** $60-$70 (Full breakfast)
1 Queen 1 Double 2 Single (3 bdrm)
Bathrooms: 1 Ensuite 1 Guest share

Juniper House is a comfortable welcoming home set in a young avocado orchard. Relax in our extensive gardens, enjoy a game of tennis or swim in our saltwater pool. For the snooker enthusiast we have a ful-size billiard table. We are an easy 15 minute drive from the Museum & Kiwi House, golf courses, cafes, galleries and Whangarei yacht basin. We offer full breakfast, dinner and drinks by arrangement. Our interests include sailing, fishing and decorative art. Orchard cat.

Whangarei - Onerahi *25 km E of Whangarei*

Tidesong *B&B Homestay Apartment with Kitchen*
Ros & Hugh Cole-Baker
Beasley Road, RD 1, Onerahi, Whangarei

Tel (09) 436 1959 or 027 636 5888
stay@tidesong.co.nz
www.stay@tidesong.co.nz

Double $95-$110 Single $70-$80 (Full breakfast)
Dinner $25-$30
Children welcome
3 Queen 1 Single (3 bdrm)
Bathrooms: 2 Ensuite 1 Guest share

From Whangarei drive east for 25 minutes to Taiharuru Estuary. Comfortable secluded accommodation in a separate upstairs flat. Full breakfast with extra home-cooked meals available. Safe kayaking and other boating from our jetty. Large garden with bush tracks and outdoor games. Close to fishing, shellfish, varied birdlife,and great walks on surf beaches and spectacular ridges. Relax afterwards in the gas-fired outdoor garden bath. We look forward to showing you warm and friendly Northland hospitality.

Whangarei *4.5 km NE of Whangarei*

Luxury At The Lake, *B&B Private Lake Setting, Luxury Self-contained Retreat*
Diane & Jim Watson
18 Takahe Street, Tikipunga, Whangarei

Tel (09) 437 1989 or 027 444 1174
Fax (09) 437 1989
relax@lakeluxuryretreat.co.nz
www.lakeluxuryretreat.co.nz

Double $100-$250 (Full provisions)
Dinner options available
Visa MC Eftpos accepted Pet free home
1 King/Twin 1 Queen (2 bdrm)
Bathrooms: 1 Ensuite 1 Private

Situated just 10 minutes from town, we provide a quiet and unique ideal base for the discerning traveller who likes comfort, beautiful surroundings, privacy and security. We welcome you to our romantic retreat which is fully self-contained with tasteful, comfortable furnishings and all the amenities of home. Private patio and barbeque. Included is full self-catering breakfast with 12 noon checkout. Our bed & breakfast has it's own bathroom and toilet, with private entrance and balcony overlooking the lake. A continental breakfast supplied with 10am checkout.

Whangarei *7 km N of Whangarei City*

Lotus Lodge *B&B Farmstay*
Keith & Jill Clarke
58 Great North Road, Springs Flat, Kamo, Whangarei

Tel (09) 435 2294 Fax (09) 435 2294
lotuslodge@clear.net.nz

Double $100-$140 Single $65-$80 (Continental)
Dinner by arrangement
2 Double 1 Twin (3 bdrm)
Bathrooms: 1 Guest share

We invite you to share in our 200 acres of paradise. Sheba the Bermese will welcome you to the peace and tranquility that Lotus Lodge has to offer. 2 minutes from Kamo, 5 minutes to golf course. Experience ñ moving cattle/sheep with farm dog Del, view native bush, find amazing limestone rocks,laze in the quietness of the garden, or read in the lounge. Make this your stop for seeing the north ñ beaches, fishing, diving, kauri forests, shopping, all in a days outing. Our interests: gardening, classic cars, travel, art and people.

Northland

Whangarei Heads *31 km SE of Whangarei*

Manaia Gardens *Cottage with Kitchen*
Audrey & Colin Arnold
2487 Whangarei Heads Road, Taurikura, Whangarei

Tel (09) 434 0797 arnoldac@igrin.co.nz

Double $70 **Single** $60 (Accomodation only)
Child under 5 free
Extra person $10
Visa MC accepted
Pet free home Children welcome
2 Queen 1 Double (3 bdrm)
Bathrooms: 2 Private

We have a small farm with two quaint old self-contained cabins in the garden. They have comfortable beds and basic cooking facilities ,(2-burner gas cooker or electric frypan), microwave,toaster frig. etc.There are nearby shops and galleries.Freezer space, laundry, barbecue and rowboat available. This is a beautiful area with rocky bush clad hills, harbour and ocean beaches, lots of Conservation land for walks. Or just relax in private. We are the only buildings in the bay. Mailbox 2487 on the Whangarei Heads Road.

Whangarei Heads *28 km SE of Whangarei*

Bantry *Homestay*
Karel & Robin Lieffering
Little Munro Bay, RD 4, Whangarei Heads

Tel (09) 434 0751 Fax (09) 434 0754
robinl@igrin.co.nz

Double $110 **Single** $55 (Full breakfast)
Child under 12 half price Dinner $35
Children and pets welcome
1 Queen 2 Single (2 bdrm)
Bathrooms: 1 Guest share 1 Private

We are a semi-retired couple with dog. We speak Dutch, French, German, Japanese and we like to laugh. Our unusual home with some natural rock interior walls is on the edge of a safe swimming beach, and bush reserve with walking tracks and several good fishing spots. A photographically fascinating area with wonderful views of coastal mountains. Guests have own entrance and sitting room all with sea views. Enjoyable food and NZ wine. Phone, fax or email us for reservations and directions. One party bookings only.

Whangarei Heads *30 km SE of Whangarei*

The Retreat *B&B Separate Suite*
Heather Logue & Trevor Harris
9 Taurikura Street, Taurikura, Whangarei Heads

Tel (09) 434 0204 or 029 927 5064
Fax (09) 434 0204
nantrev2@xtra.co.nz

Double $120 **Single** $90 (Full breakfast)
Dinner $35
Visa MC accepted
Pet free home Not suitable for children
1 Queen (1 bdrm)
Bathrooms: 1 Ensuite

Come and enjoy a waterfront paradise with Heather & Trevor. Rest in a comfortable self-contained unit in peaceful surroundings, or let us spoil you and enjoy scruptious home-cooked meals. Amble through the garden onto a sandy shore. Swim, snorkel, fish or canoe. Dive trips arranged. Golf course, art galleries and cafes nearby. We have no children or pets. We have had a lifetime in agriculture and enjoy sharing our knowledge. The retreat is half an hour south east of Whangarei.

Ruakaka *30 km S of Whangarei*

Bream Bay Farmstay *B&B Farmstay Separate Suite*
Joyce & Vince Roberts
34/27 Doctors Hill Road, Waipu, Ruakaka

Tel (09) 432 7842 or 027 441 9585
021 419 515 Fax (09) 432 7842
robertsb.b@xtra.co.nz www.breambay.orcon.net.nz

Double $80-$110 Single $50 (Full breakfast)
Child $20 Dinner $25
Visa MC accepted
Children and pets welcome
2 Queen 2 Single (3 bdrm)
Bathrooms: 3 Ensuite

Spectacular is the only words to describe the sea views from this brand new home built especially for the discerning travelers. Your own kitchen & laundry. Free tour by arrangement over our 100 acre dry stock farm and bush. Beautiful beaches, golf course, racetrack where Vince trains our racehorses and good restaurants are a short drive from our home. Meals include our home-grown lamb. As ex-dairy farmers with grown up family of 4, we have enjoyed hosting B&B for 14 years, other interests include travel, golf and gardening.

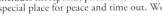

Ruakaka *30 km S of Whangarei*

Waterview Bream Bay *B&B Farmstay Cottage with Kitchen*
Gayle Tilly & Rodney McPhee
34 Doctors Hill Road, Waipu, Ruakaka

Tel (09) 433 0050 Fax (09) 433 0050
rodneyandgaylesb.b@xtra.co.nz

Double $80 Single $50 (Full provisions)
Child $20 Dinner $25
Children and pets welcome
2 Queen 2 Single (3 bdrm)
Bathrooms: 1 Family share 1 Private

Waterview Bream Bay offers a self-contained unit with panoramic sea and rural views. Beautiful beaches, golf course, race track, fishing, horse treks and restaurants are all within a few minutes drive away. Our property has large gardens and children are welcome. Cot available. Wildlife appearing at our home includes moreporks, pheasants, ducks and the rare brown bitton. Wonderful for people looking for that special place for peace and time out. We look forward to meeting you soon.

Waipu *10 km S of Waipu*

labonte@xtra.co.nz *Homestay Farmstay Apartment with Kitchen*
Andre & Robin La Bonte
PO Box 60, Waipu, Northland

Tel (09) 432 0645 Fax (09) 432 0645
labonte@xtra.co.nz

Double $80 Single $50 (Continental)
Dinner $20 by arrangement
Visa MC accepted
1 King 1 Queen 2 Double 2 Single (3 bdrm)
Bathrooms: 2 Private

Sleep to the sound of the ocean in a separate studio apartment or in guest bedrooms on our 36 acre seaside farm. Explore our limestone rock formations or just sit and relax under the mature trees that grace our shoreline. The beach at Waipu Cove is a 10 minute walk along the sea. We are a licensed fish farm, graze cattle and have flea-free cats. Glowworm caves, deep-sea fishing, scuba diving and golf available locally. No smoking please. American spoken. Bookings recommended.

Waipu *6.5 km SE of Waipu*

The Stone House *B&B Farmstay Separate Suite Cottage with Kitchen*
Gillian & John Devine
Cove Road, Waipu

Tel (09) 432 0432 Fax (09) 432 0432
stonehousewaipu@xtra.co.nz

Double $80-$120 Single $60-$70 (Full breakfast)
Child $20 Dinner $25
Visa MC accepted
Children and pets welcome
1 King/Twin 2 Queen 3 Single (4 bdrm)
Bathrooms: 2 Ensuite 1 Private

Relax in a charming seaside cottage or with your
hosts Gillian & John in their unique solid Stonehouse. Either way you will enjoy the green pastures of
our farm, fringed with mature pohutakawa trees and the sound of surf on our magnificent ocean beach.
Picturesque rock gardens, croquet lawn and sheltered patios complete the setting. Canoes and dinghys
are available for exploring the adjacent lagoon and bird sanctuary. A touch of Cornwall with warm
company around a log fire. German spoken.

Waipu Cove *8 km SE of Waipu*

Flower Haven *B&B Self-contained Downstairs Flat*
Shirley & Brian Flower
53 St Anne Road, Waipu Cove, RD 2, Waipu 0254

Tel (09) 432 0421
bnb@flowerhaven.com
www.flowerhaven.com

Double $95-$110(Continental)
Visa MC accepted
Pet free home Not suitable for children
2 Double (2 bdrm)
Bathrooms: 1 Private

Flower Haven is elevated with panoramic coastal views,
being developed as a garden retreat. The accommodation is a self-contained downstairs flat with separate
access; kitchen includes stove, microwave, fridge/freezer. Washing machine, radio, TV, linen, duvets,
blankets and bath towels provided. Reduced tariff if continental breakfast not required. Our interests
are gardening, genealogy and meeting people. Near to restaurants, museums, golf, horse treks, fishing,
walking tracks, oil refinery. 5 minutes to shop, sandy surf beach, rocks. Whangarei 35 minutes, Auckland
1 and a half hours.

Waipu Cove *9 km SE of Waipu*

Melody Lodge *B&B Homestay*
Melody Gard
996 Cove Road, Waipu, Northland

Tel (09) 432 0939 Fax (09) 432 0939
melody@melodylodge.co.nz
www.melodylodge.co.nz

Double $85-$110 Single $65-$90 (Continental)
Not suitable for children
1 Queen 1 Double 2 Single (3 bdrm)
Bathrooms: 1 Ensuite 1 Guest share

Situated between the popular beaches of Waipu Cove
and Langs Beach, Melody Lodge overlooks the whole of Bream Bay. Stunning sea views from all rooms.
New cedar house with garden and spectacular stand of native bush adjacent. Resident artist and cat.
Attached Art Gallery features local artworks, exclusive screenprinted souvenirs and cards. Swim at Waipu,
stroll Langs Beach, study birdlife, experience the bush, a round of golf, horseriding, kayaking, fishing.
Bush, sea, music, art and good conversation... relax and enjoy it all from Melody Lodge.

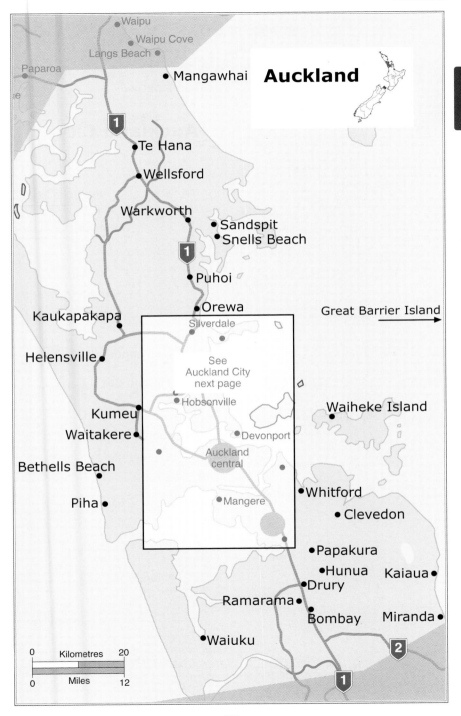

Auckland

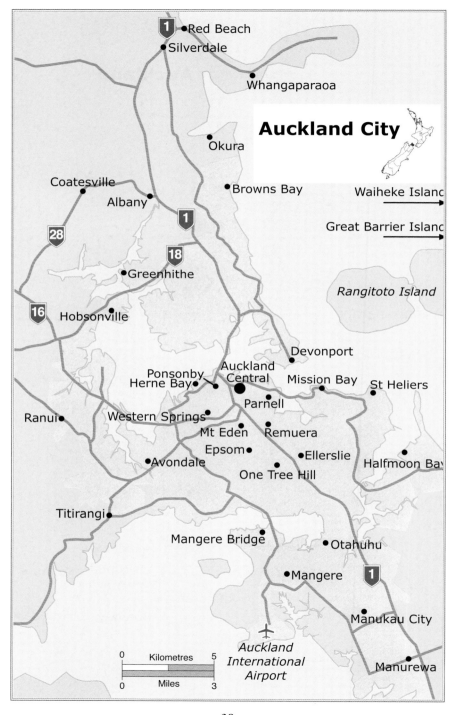

Auckland City

Red Beach
Silverdale
Whangaparaoa
Okura
Coatesville
Albany
Browns Bay
Waiheke Island
Great Barrier Island
Greenhithe
Rangitoto Island
Hobsonville
Devonport
Ponsonby
Herne Bay
Auckland Central
Mission Bay
St Heliers
Parnell
Ranui
Western Springs
Mt Eden
Remuera
Epsom
Ellerslie
Avondale
Halfmoon Bay
One Tree Hill
Titirangi
Mangere Bridge
Otahuhu
Mangere
Manukau City
Auckland International Airport
Manurewa

0 Kilometres 5
0 Miles 3

Wellsford - Te Hana *6 km N of Wellsford*
The Retreat Historic Farmhouse *Farmstay*
Colleen & Tony Moore
Te Hana, RD 5, Wellsford

Tel (09) 423 8547 enquiry@sheepfarmstay.com
www.sheepfarmstay.com

Double $95-$120 (Full breakfast)
Dinner $25pp by arrangement
Self-contained cottage $95
Visa MC Diners accepted
2 Queen 1 Double 1 Single (3 bdrm)
Bathrooms: 1 Ensuite 1 Private

Tony and Colleen welcome you to The Retreat,
a spacious 1860s farmhouse built for a family
with 12 children. Set well back from the road, the
house is surrounded by an extensive landscaped
garden, including a productive vegetable garden
and orchard. Fresh produce from the garden is a
feature in our home cooking.

Colleen is a spinner and weaver and our flock of sheep provides the raw material for the woollen goods
that are hand-made and for sale from the studio. If you haven't got close up to a sheep this is your
chance, as we always have friendly sheep to hand feed. We have hosted guests at The Retreat since 1988
and appreciate what you require.

We know New Zealand well, our families have lived in NZ for several generations and we have visited
most places in our beautiful country, so if you have any questions on what to see or do, we are well
equipped to provide the answers.

Also available is a self-contained cottage, close to the house, with the option of having meals with us, or
self-catering.

The Retreat is very easy to find. Travelling North on SH1, we are 6km north of Wellsford, look for
the Weaving Studio sign on your left. You will pass through Te Hana before arriving at The Retreat.
Kaiwaka is 13km north of The Retreat.

Auckland

Wellsford

Rosandra Homestay *B&B Farmstay*
Ross & Sandra Williams
557 SH1, RD 5, Wellsford

Tel (09) 423 9343 Fax (09) 423 9343
rosandra@xtra.co.nz

Double $100 Single $60 (Full breakfast)
3 Queen 1 Twin (4 bdrm)
Bathrooms: 1 Ensuite

Welcome to our 90 acre lifestyle farm. Beautifully
covered with mature trees, where our sheep and beef
cattle graze. Privately set in landscaped gardens our
modern home offers you warm spacious guest rooms
with ensuite, private lounge with big screen TV, opening on to a sunny outdoor deck area. Swim all year
round in the indoor 15 metre heated pool or relax in the spa pool. Situated close to golf courses and East
Coast beaches, find us easily on SH1, 7km north of Wellsford and opposite Mangawhai turn off. 2 cats.

Warkworth *0.5 km N of Warkworth*

Homewood Cottage *B&B Separate Suite*
Ina & Trevor Shaw
17 View Road, Warkworth

Tel (09) 425 8667 or 0211176457
Fax (09) 425 9610   ina.homewoodcottage@xtra.co.nz

Double $90 (Special breakfast)
Visa MC accepted
1 Queen 1 Twin (2 bdrm)
Bathrooms: 2 Ensuite

Welcome to our home in a peaceful garden with views
of Warkworth and the hills. The spacious rooms ensure
privacy and quiet. The new beds are comfortable with
electric blankets and quilts. Each room has TV, teamaking, own entrance, and car park. No cooking.
Afternoon tea and substantial continental breakfast served. Ina is an artist who also enjoys walking, music
and her guests. Restaurants are two minutes away, beaches vineyards and crafts close by. A smoke free
home. View Road is off Hill Street.

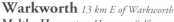

Warkworth *13 km E of Warkworth*

Maltby Homestay *Homestay Self-contained*
Barbara & John Maltby
Omaha Orchards, 282 Point Wells Road, RD 6,
Warkworth

Tel (09) 422 7415 Fax (09) 422 7419
jandbmaltby@value.net.nz

Double $60-$85 Single $60-$75 (Continental)
Dinner $15-$25 by arrangement Extra guests $12
In-house accommodation available if required
1 Queen 1 Double (1 bdrm)
Bathrooms: 1 Ensuite

Our home and self-contained unit (built 1999) is set
on 11 acres nestled beside the Whangateau Harbour. Relax in the extensive gardens and swim in the
beautifully appointed pool. Nearby is Omaha Beach, golf course, tennis courts, restaurants, art and craft
studios, pottery works, museum, Sheep World, Honey Centre and Kawau Island. This is some of the
prettiest coastline in New Zealand. John and Barbara look forward to sharing their little slice of paradise
with you.

Warkworth - Sandspit *7 km E of Warkworth*

Belvedere Homestay *Homestay*

M & R Everett
38 Kanuka Road, RD 2, Warkworth

Tel (09) 425 7201 or Mobil 027 284 4771
Fax (09) 425 7201
belvederehomestay@xtra.co.nz
www.belvederehomestay.co.nz

Double $130-$145 Single $95 (Special breakfast)
Dinner $45pp
Visa MC accepted
2 Queen 1 Twin (3 bdrm)
Bathrooms: 1 Ensuite 2 Private

Sandspit the perfect stop to and from The Bay
of Islands. Belvedere has 360 degree views, sea to
countryside; it's awesome.

Relaxing decks, barbecue, garden, orchards, native birds
and bush, peace and tranquillity with good parking.
Air-conditioned, spa, games room, comfortable beds are
all here for your comfort.

Many attractions are within 7km and Margaret's
flair with cooking is a great way to relax after an
adventurous day with pre-drinks, 2 course meal and
wine. Have a warm and relaxing stay with Margaret &
Ron.

**Sandspit - the perfect stop to and from the
Bay of Islands.**

Warkworth - Sandspit *10 km E of Warkworth*
Sea Breeze *Apartment with Kitchen*
Di & Robin Grant
14 Puriri Place, RD 2, Sandspit Heights, Warkworth

Tel (09) 425 7220 or 021 65 7220
Fax (09) 425 7220 robindi.grant@xtra.co.nz
www.bnb.co.nz/hosts/seabreeze.html

Double $120 Single $100 (Continental)
Visa MC accepted
1 Queen (1 bdrm)
Bathrooms: 1 Ensuite

Sea Breeze is a self-contained luxury apartment with magnificent sea views and surrounding bush. Breakfast is provided in the kitchenette to be enjoyed at your leisure and a bed-settee in the lounge doubles for extra guests. There are easy bush walks to the beaches immediately below the property. Take a cruise to Kawau Island or visit the many vineyards, galleries and cafes. Your hosts have travelled extensively and now enjoy gardening and boating in their spare time. Phone/fax for directions.

Warkworth *2.5 km S of Warkworth*
Warkworth Country House *B&B*
Alan & Pauline Waddington
18 Wilson Road, RD 1, Warkworth

Tel (09) 422 2485 Fax (09) 422 2485
paulalan@xtra.co.nz

Double $115-$135 Single $80-$100 (Full breakfast)
Child by arrangement Visa MC accepted
Children welcome
1 Queen 1 Twin (2 bdrm)
Bathrooms: 2 Ensuite

Situated in 2 peaceful acres with country and estuary views, just 45 minutes north of Auckland. Each tasteful room has ensuite, private entrance and patio,TV, tea/coffee making facilities, heater, electric blankets, radio alarm and toiletries. Enjoy a delicious full breakfast in our country-style dining room then visit one of many local places of interest in this lovely part of New Zealand. Warkworth township with its variety of shops and restaurants is just 3 minutes drive away. A warm welcome awaits you.

Warkworth - Sandspit *6 km E of Warkworth*
Jacaranda House B&B *B&B Apartment with Kitchen*
Gillian Irons & Richard Bray
1186 Sandspit Road, RD 2, Warkworth

Tel (09) 422 2394 or 027 283 7772
Fax (09) 422 2395 jacarandahouse@xtra.co.nz

Double $125 Single $90 (Continental)
Not suitable for children
1 Queen (1 bdrm)
Bathrooms: 1 Ensuite 1 Private

We are on the Matakana Estuary and a short walk to the Sandspit Wharf, gateway to Kawau Island. A few minutes drive to restaurants, cafes, vineyards and pottery in the Matakana region. Enjoy your continental breakfast on our north facing deck with 180 degree view of the estuary, or enjoy the privacy of your self-contained unit. You will have your own ground level entrance, Sky TV and parking. Oscar, our house cat, is no bother.

Warkworth - Rural *8 km SE of Warkworth*

The Cedar House *B&B Homestay*
Shona & Julian Huxtable
60 Cowan Bay Road, RD 3, Warkworth 1241,

Tel (09) 422 2579 or 021 238 3850
thecedarhouse@xtra.co.nz

Double $130-$150 (Full breakfast)
Dinner $40 by prior arrangement
2 Queen (2 bdrm)
Bathrooms: 2 Ensuite

Set in 7 acres, The Cedar House commands magnificent views over rolling pasture and native bush to Kawau, Little and Great Barrier Islands. You are invited to share our home and perhaps swim in the pool or stroll around the gardens with our pet collies, Frank & Bonnie. Enjoy a relaxing breakfast, often served outside. We also offer a 3 course dinner, enhanced by the use of fresh produce from the garden and a glass of wine.

Warkworth *4.5 km W of Warkworth*

Willow Lodge *B&B Self Contained Suite with Kitchenette*
Colin Hilditch & Vicki Webster
541 Woodcocks Road, RD 1, Warkworth 1241

Tel (09) 425 7676 or 021 104 1807
021 064 5567 Fax (09) 425 7676
willow_lodge@xtra.co.nz

Double $100-$120 **Single** $60-$80 (Full breakfast)
Child $20 Dinner $30 by arrangement
1 Queen 2 Double 4 Single (4 bdrm)
Bathrooms: 2 Ensuite 1 Private

You've just found what you were looking for - peace and old world charm, 5 minutes drive from picturesque Warkworth (45 minutes from Auckland). Willow Lodge is nestled amid 2 acres of landscaped gardens. We offer in-house or self-contained semi-detached accommodation. Enjoy guest TV lounge, tea/coffee, BBQ all of which opens onto a private courtyard. Colin & Vicki, with their dog and 2 cats look forward to warmly welcoming you to their home. Much to explore, plenty to enjoy and treasured memories to be created.

Puhoi *9 km N of Orewa*

Westwell Ho *B&B*
Fae & David England
34 Saleyards Road, Puhoi 1240,

Tel (09) 422 0064 or 027 280 5795
Fax (09) 422 0064   dhengland@xtra.co.nz

Double $115 **Single** $80 (Full breakfast)
Child $35
Visa MC Amex accepted
Children welcome
1 Queen 1 Double 1 Single (2 bdrm)
Bathrooms: 1 Ensuite 1 Private

We welcome you to our sunny colonial-style home in the lovely Puhoi Valley. We are only 2 minutes by car west of Main North Highway up a small road behind the old pub in this historic Puhoi Village. The homestead has wide verandahs around 3 sides where you can relax as you view the gardens and beautiful trees. Nearby are the fantastic Waiwera Thermal Pools, or you could hire a canoe and paddle down the Puhoi River to Wenderholm Beach and Park. Sky TV available.

Orewa *20 mins N of Auckland Central*
Villa Orewa *B&B Homestay*
Sandra & Ian Burrow
264 Hibiscus Coast Highway, Orewa, Auckland

Tel (09) 426 3073 Fax (09) 426 3053
rooms@villaorewa.co.nz
www.villaorewa.co.nz

Double $150-$225 (Special breakfast)
Dinner by arrangement
Visa MC accepted
1 King/Twin 2 Queen (3 bdrm)
Bathrooms: 3 Ensuite

Welcome to our beautifully appointed Mediterranean style home, with white-washed walls and blue vaulted roofs. A taste of the Greek Isles on beautiful Orewa Beach. Stay in 1 of our self-contained rooms, each with private balcony, and enjoy the panoramic beach and sea views, or socialise with us in our spacious living areas. Orewa offers a great range of activities and amenities; with cafes, restaurants, and shopping all within a short level walk. We are sure your stay will be enjoyable and memorable.

Orewa - Red Beach *5 km S of Orewa*
Hibiscus House *B&B*
Judy & Brian Marsden
13A Marellen Drive, Red Beach,
Whangaparaoa - Hibiscus Coast

Tel (09) 427 6303 or 025 492 025
025 472 056 Fax (09) 427 6303
jb.marsden@xtra.co.nz

Double $95 Single $75 (Full breakfast)
Dinner $25
2 Queen 2 Twin (3 bdrm)
Bathrooms: 2 Ensuite 1 Private

We offer quality bed & breakfast, opposite a beach for the relaxing break you deserve, on route to Northland. Judy and Brian give friendly, personal hospitality in a very convenient location. Handy to shops, markets, cinema, beaches, golf courses and a leisure centre complex with heated swimming pool. Easy walks to surf, tennis and squash clubs. RSA 5 minutes away. Gulf Harbour Marina for ferries, fishing and sailing. Restaurants/bars/cafes for all tastes and occasions 5-15 minutes away. Sorry no pets. Children over 12 welcome.

Orewa - Puawai Bay *40 km N of Auckland*

Puawai Bay *B&B Apartment with Kitchen*
Audrey & Robert
31 Glenelg Road, Red Beach, Hibiscus Coast

Tel (09) 426 1165 Fax (09) 426 1165
bookings@puawaibay.co.nz
www.puawaibay.co.nz

Double $100 (Continental)
Apartment $150 per night
Visa MC Diners Eftpos accepted
Not suitable for children
2 Queen (4 bdrm)
Bathrooms: 2 Ensuite

Set on a picturesque cliff-edge site with steps down to the beach and its own vineyard. This 4 bedroom Pacific style home has 2 bedrooms allocated to B&B and a self-contained apartment. Puawai Bay has a gym, sauna, billiard room and library. Handy to all local attractions and perfect for swimmers, sunbathers, surfers, kayakers and fishermen.

Please let us know
how you enjoyed your B&B experience.
Ask your host for a comment form
or leave a comment on www.bnb.co.nz

Silverdale *1 km S of Silverdale*

The Ambers Luxury B&B *Luxury B&B*
Diane & Gerard Zwier
146 Pine Valley Road, Silverdale, Auckland

Tel (09) 426 0015 Fax (09) 426 0015
diane@the-ambers.co.nz
www.the-ambers.co.nz

Double $160 Single $115 (Full breakfast)
Child $75 Family attic suite
Visa MC Diners Amex accepted Children welcome
2 King/Twin 2 Double (4 bdrm)
Bathrooms: 3 Ensuite

The Ambers is a charming old-style Georgian country house set on 14 acres with formal rose gardens, fountains and mature trees. There are beautiful beaches, golf courses and restaurants nearby. The Ambers offers elegant country accommodation inclusive of full cooked breakfast. We have 4 double bedrooms, 3 with ensuites. Choose from our elegant Regency Room or French style Blue Room, both on the first floor, or our romantic attic suite with antique claw-footed bath. The 2 attic rooms make an ideal family suite.

Silverdale - Wainui *8 km SW of Silverdale*

Whitehills Country Stay *B&B Self-contained with kitchen, deck and own entrance*
Maureen & Dennis Evans
224 Whitehills Road, Wainui, RD 1 Kaukapakapa

Tel (09) 420 5666 or 027 448 9503
Fax (09) 420 5666 d-mevans@xtra.co.nz
www.bnbauckland.co.nz

Double $120 **Single** $75 (Continental)
Child negotiable Dinner $30 by arrangement
Self-contained $115-$130 double
Visa MC accepted Children welcome
1 Queen 5 Single (3 bdrm)
Bathrooms: 2 Private

Relax and unwind at Whitehills situated 25 minutes from Auckland Harbour Bridge and 7 minutes from the Silverdale Motorway exit. Convenient for shops, beaches and golf courses. B&B is available in the main house or enjoy a comfortable, self-contained studio with its own kitchen, entrance and deck. Breakfast provisions can be provided. You are most welcome to wander around our garden, walk in the 6 acres of native bush or simply relax on the covered verandah. We, and our friendly border collie, look forward to meeting you.

Whangaparaoa *4 km E of Orewa*

Duncansby by the Sea *B&B*
Kathy & Ken Grieve
72 Duncansby Road, Whale Cove,
Stanmore Bay, Whangaparaoa

Tel (09) 424 0025 or 027 200 9688,
027 442 2278 Fax (09) 424 3607
duncansby@xtra.co.nz
www.duncansby-bnb.co.nz

Double $110 **Single** $80 (Full breakfast)
Visa MC accepted
2 Queen (2 bdrm)
Bathrooms: 1 Ensuite 1 Private

Duncansby, our brand new home, offers relaxing panoramic sea views of the Hibiscus Coast. Located at Whale Cove between Red Beach and Stanmore Bay, our modern sunny well appointed rooms have own entrances, TV, decks, white linen, tea/coffee facilities. Paradise for golfers with 3 local golf courses including International Gulf Harbour Course with its boating and fishing marina. Visit Tiritiri Bird Sanctuary, walk Shakespeare Park. Enjoy 9 superb beaches, excellent local restaurants and cafes. Only 35 minutes north of Auckland City, we welcome you.

Helensville *4 km SW of Helensville*

Rose Cottage *B&B Cottage with Kitchen*
Dianne & Richard Kidd
2191 State Highway 16, RD 2, Helensville

Tel (09) 420 8007 or 027 459 9135
Fax (09) 420 7966 kidds@xtra.co.nz
www.babs.co.nz/whenuanui

Double $110 **Single** $80 (Full breakfast)
Visa MC accepted
1 Queen (1 bdrm)
Bathrooms: 1 Ensuite

Rose Cottage offers comfort and privacy set within peaceful gardens. Whenuanui is a 350 hectare Helensville sheep and beef farm providing magnificent farm walks. The family homestead and gardens have panoramic views over Helensville and the Kaipara Valley. Tasteful accommodation includes ensuite, TV and kitchenette. All-weather tennis court available for guests to use. Just 35 minutes from downtown Auckland on State Highway 16. A base to explore the Kaipara region or a great start or end to your Northland tour. Smoking outdoors appreciated.

Kumeu *26 km NW of Auckland*

Calico Lodge *B&B Homestay Countrystay B & B*
Kay & Kerry Hamilton
250 Matua Road, RD 1, Kumeu

Tel (09) 412 8167 or 0800 501 850
025 286 6064
bed@calicolodge.co.nz
www.calicolodge.co.nz

Double $120-$175 Single $95-$150 (Full breakfast)
Visa MC accepted Children welcome
1 King/Twin 2 Queen (3 bdrm)
Bathrooms: 2 Ensuite 1 Private

Kerry and Kay, Zippy our little dog, 3 cats and tame sheep welcome you to Calico Lodge. Amidst the wineries, wedding venues, and cafes, near west coast beaches, 25 minutes NW of Auckland our modern home on 4 acres has beautiful trees and gardens. Hand made teddy bears and patchwork quilting (for sale) adorn the bedrooms and lounge in separate guest wing. 2 minutes SH16, peace and beautiful bush views complete the picture. We love to share our little piece of paradise.

The difference between a B&B and a hotel
is that you don't hug the hotel staff when you leave.

Hobsonville *15mins NW of Auckland*

Eastview *B&B Homestay Separate Suite*
Joane & Don Clarke
2 Parkside Road, Hobsonville, Auckland

Tel (09) 416 9254 Fax (09) 416 9254
enquiries@eastview.co.nz
www.eastview.co.nz

Double $100-$120 Single $85-$100 (Full breakfast)
Child $30 Dinner by arrangement
Extra adult discount
Visa MC accepted Children welcome
2 Queen 2 Single (3 bdrm)
Bathrooms: 2 Private

Situated at the western end of Auckland's beautiful harbour. Eastview is easy to find from the airport or travel routes north and south. Well located for exploring Auckland. Panoramic water/city views. Near to Kumeu wine country (popular for weddings), superb beaches, rainforest clad hills, gannet colony. We offer many personal homely touches. 2 sunny accommodation areas. A 2 bedroomed suite, and a queen bedroom with private bathroom. A great place to relax after your trip or a day's sightseeing. Be welcomed by cat Rosie and small dog Pebbles.

Auckland

Bethells Beach *15 km W of Swanson*

Bethell's Beach Cottages *Cottage with Kitchen*
Self-contained cottages & 100 seater Summer Pavilion
Trude & John Bethell-Paice
PO Box 95057, Swanson, Auckland

Tel (09) 810 9581 Fax (09) 810 8677
info@bethellsbeach.com
www.bethellsbeach.com

Double $250-$350 (Special breakfast)
Child under 12 half price
Dinner 2 course $35pp 3 course $45pp
Breakfast $25pp + GST
Visa MC accepted Children welcome
2 Queen 2 Double 3 Single (3 bdrm)
Bathrooms: 2 Private

"To Give is to Love & To Love is to Live"
Trude Bethell-Paice

D rive 30 minutes from Auckland City to one of the most unique parts of the West Coast. The Bethell's settled this area 6 generations ago and Trude and John continue the long family tradition of hospitality.

They have created magic cottages and venue in this spectacular place where the best sunsets and seaviews are to be experienced - as seen in: Next (NZ), Cuisine (NZ), Elle (UK), Fodors (USA), Turquiose Holiday (UK) 2003. The cottages have a sunny north facing aspect and are surrounded by 200 year old pohutukawa's (NZ Christmas tree). Each one is totally separate, private and has a large brick barbecue. The vast front lawn is ideal for games and the gardens are thoughtfully designed for relaxation.

The cottages are made up with your holiday in mind - not only are beds made and towels/linen put out, but Trude and John have attended to too many details to mention and laundry facilities are available. Even the cats will welcome you. As seen in Vogue Australia 1998. Life/The Observer (Great Britain 1998) - 'one of twenty great world wide destinations'. British TV Travel Show 1998. She magazine (February 1999) - 'one of the 10 most romantic places to stay in NZ'. North and South magazine (January 1999) - 'one of the 14 best Bed and Breakfasts in NZ' Oct 2002 - USA Fodors travel guide.

'Turehu' Cottage has a studio atmosphere with double bi-folding doors from the conservatory. For outdoor dining sit under a pohutukawa tree at your own bench and table on the hillside with views over the beach and Bethell's valley. Cork floor in the kitchen, TV and bedroom area, gentle cream walls and white trim. Warm slate floors in the conservatory with lounge, dining table and bathroom (shower and toilet). Kitchen has microwave, large fridge/freezer, stove and coffee plunger, with all kitchen and dining amenities. Suitable for a couple and 1 child or 2 friends.

'Te Koinga' Cottage, this superb home away from home is 80 square metre and has two bi-folding doors onto a 35 square metre wooden deck for outdoor dining and relaxation in this sun trap. Set under the shade of a magnificent spralling pohutukawa tree and surrounded by garden. A fireplace for winter warmth and 16 seater dining table. The 2 bedrooms have carpet and terracotta tiles expand to the dining, kitchen, bathroom and toilet. Wood panelled and cream/tan rag rolled walls for a relaxing atmosphere. The bathroom offers a bath and shower. Open planned kitchen has microwave, large fridge/freezer, stove, dishwasher and coffee maker. Suitable for a family, 2 couples or a small function. Trude is a marriage celebrant and Civil Union Celebrant and Trude and John specialise in weddings, private functions and company workshops. A local professional chef is available for these occasions.

Local Adventures - Bethell's beach is a short drive or walk. Pack a picnic lunch and discover Lake Wainamu for fresh water swimming and expansive sand dunes or go on a bush walk with excellent examples of New Zealand native flora. If you head in the direction of the beach you may enjoy exploring the caves (at night the magic of glowworms and phosphorescence in the shallows), or go surfing or fishing. You are close to many world class vineyards and restaurants/cafes. You may fancy a game of golf - 2 courses within 10-20 minutes drive from your cottage. Many more activities in a short driving distance. No pets please. Children under 12 half price.

Bethells Valley - West Auckland *15 km W of Henderson*
Greenmead Farm *Self-contained Cottage with Kitchen*

Averil & Jon Bateman
115 Bethells Road, RD 1, Henderson

Tel (09) 810 9363 Fax (09) 810 8363
jabat@greenmead.co.nz
www.greenmead.co.nz

Double $110
Extra guests $20pp
Children welcome
4 Single (2 bdrm)
Bathrooms: 1 Private

Guests have sole use of comfortable holiday home - 2 bedrooms, bathroom, lounge (TV) and large kitchen/dining room with excellent cooking facilities. Additional guests $20 each. Breakfast extra. The main house and guest cottage are surrounded by a large country garden - swings for children. Cattle, 2 border collie working dogs. Peaceful location in rural valley in the Waitakere Ranges. Good walking tracks in the area - rainforest, beach and lake. 30 minutes drive west of central Auckland. Beach 6 minutes.

Waitakere Ranges - Swanson *4 km W of Swanson*
Panorama Heights *B&B Cottage No Kitchen*

Allison & Paul Ingram
42 Kitewaho Road, Swanson,
Waitakere City, Auckland

Tel (09) 832 4777 or 0800 692624 Outside Auckland
Fax (09) 833 7773 nzbnb4u@clear.net.nz
www.panoramaheights.co.nz

Double $140 Single $100 (Full breakfast)
Dinner by request Visa MC accepted
2 Queen 1 Twin 1 Single (4 bdrm)
Bathrooms: 3 Ensuite 1 Private

Private and peaceful breathtaking panoramic views located high in the Waitakere Ranges on the Twin Coast Discovery Route. Watch the sun rise across native kauri trees, bush and Auckland City beyond. Within easy access to over 250km of walking tracks through 17,000 hectares of native rainforest. 10-15 minutes from West Coast beaches (Piha, Bethells, Karekare, Muriwai), West Auckland wineries, 2 scenic golf courses, art trails, shopping centers. We offer you excellent quality accommodation at a very affordable price. Please phone/email for bookings/directions.

Waitakere - Swanson *02 km N of Waitakere township*
Waitakere Alpacas *B&B Farmstay*
Hans Roecoert & Christine Walton
97 Arrowsmith Road, RD 2, Waitakere (Auckland)

Tel (09) 810 7136 Fax (09) 810 7138
info@waitakerealpacas.co.nz
www.waitakerealpacas.co.nz

Double $95-$120 Single $95-$120 (Continental)
Child $50
Dinner (3 course menu) $35pp
Transfers from railway station by arrangement
Visa MC Eftpos accepted Children welcome
1 Queen 2 Twin (2 bdrm)
Bathrooms: 1 Guest share

Waitakere Alpacas is situated in the Waitakere foothills, west of Auckland. Walk amongst and feed the beautiful alpacas. Craft shop, spinning demo, game room, spa pool. Close to west coast beaches and the Kumeu wine trail, we offer you more then 35 years of hospitality experience. 100 alpacas, 4 cats, 1 dog, 8 chickens, ducks and Billy the goat will give you the best time of your life.

Auckland

Ranui *15mins km W of Auckland*

The Garrett *B&B Homestay*
Alma & Rod Mackay
295 Swanson Road, Waitakere City, Auckland 8

Tel (09) 833 6018
Fax (09) 833 6018

Double $85 Single $50 (Continental)
Child $22-$30
2 King/Twin1 King 2 Single (2 bdrm)
Bathrooms: 1 Ensuite

Just 15 minutes from Auckland City and 5 minutes from Henderson, The Garrett offers villa style accommodation with ensuite and terrace. Twin beds or king-size available. We can accommodate extra guests with folding beds on request; suitable for business people. High ceilings, period furniture and decor create an atmosphere of old in this delightful homestay, just minutes away from Waitakere City. Leading attractions include wine trails, Art Out West - including Lopdell House Gallery, Waitakere Ranges, bush walks, Aratiki Environment Centre, and golf courses. West City Shopping Centre, Lynn Mall and St Lukes.

Ranui *15mins km W of Auckland*

The Brushmakers Cottage *B&B Apartment with Kitchen*
Jeanette & Roger Brown
20 Clearview Heights, Ranui,
Waitakere City, Auckland

Tel (09) 833 8476 mobile 0274 596 334
r.g.brown@xtra.co.nz

Double $85-$150 Single $70-$100 (Full breakfast)
Dinner by arrangement
Extra guests $20
Not suitable for children
2 Queen 1 Double 1 Twin (4 bdrm)
Bathrooms: 1 Ensuite 1 Family share 2 Private

Choose between luxury self-contained apartment, featuring full kitchen, dishwasher, dining/lounge, TV/DVD, laundry, or traditional B&B. Backing onto a vineyard this peaceful location has views of both the Waitakere ranges and central Auckland. 10 minutes walk from train and bus stations and only 15 minutes drive from downtown Auckland. Close to both east and west coast beaches, gannet colony, golf courses, winery, cafes, restaurants and shopping malls. A great base for exploring Auckland. Ask about discounts. Some gluten-free food available.

Piha *20 km NW of Titirangi*

Piha Cottage *Cottage with Kitchen*
Tracey & Steve Skidmore
PO Box 48, Piha, Waitakere City, Auckland

Tel (09) 812 8514 Fax (09) 812 8514
info@pihacottage.co.nz
www.pihacottage.co.nz

Double $110-$130 Single $95-$120 (Full provisions)
Child $20 Pet free home
Children welcome
1 Double 1 Single (1 bdrm)
Bathrooms: 1 Private

Leave the city behind. Beautiful Piha Cottage is hidden on a sunny, quiet bush setting, within easy walking distance of the surf beach and walking tracks. This spacious open plan home includes a well-equipped kitchen, dining, living and sleeping areas. After a delicious self-serve breakfast (including waffles and maple syrup) go surfing, swimming or choose from one of Piha's outstanding walking tracks, through lush rainforest or along spectacular coastline. We, and our two young daughters, welcome you warmly and then leave you in peace to enjoy the tranquility.

Piha *40mins W of Auckland*
Piha Lodge *Apartment with Kitchen Units with kitchenette*
Shirley Bond
117 Piha Road, Piha Beach, Auckland

Tel (09) 812 8595 or 021 639 529
Fax (09) 812 8583 pihalodge@xtra.co.nz
www.pihalodge.co.nz

home

Double $140 (Continental)
Child $20 Dinner $35 by prior arrangement
Extra adult $30 Visa MC accepted Pets welcome
3 Queen 3 Double 1 Single (6 bdrm)
Bathrooms: 1 Ensuite 2 Private 1 bath in ensuite

Awarded Best Accommodation. Our 2 quality self-
contained units plus enquire about apartment, have satellite TV, own BBQ's, stunning panoramic sea
and bush views, all the comforts of home plus privacy and security. Situated in the subtropical rainforest
of the Waitakere Ranges and on the wild West Coast, Piha is a world famous surfing beach with
legendary sunsets. Enjoy the bush walks, climb Lion Rock, visit the fairytale Kitekite Falls or relax in the
swimming pool, hot spa or games room. Internet access, laundry. Our 2 friendly little bichon dogs are
kept separately.

Piha *25 km W of Henderson*
Westwood Cottage *Cottage with Kitchen*
Dianne & Don Sparrow
95 Glenesk Road, Piha, Auckland

Tel (09) 812 8203 Fax (09) 812 8203
westwoodcottage.piha@xtra.co.nz

Double $120-$140 (Continental provisions)
Child $20
Visa MC accepted
Children welcome
1 Queen 1 Double (2 bdrm)
Bathrooms: 1 Private

Westwood Cottage offers a unique experience. Nestled
in a secluded corner of our property, amongst beautiful bush overlooking Piha Valley. The Cottage is
self-contained, open plan design, flowing on to a private deck. Full kitchen facilities with continental
breakfast supplied. A cozy log fire for your enjoyment on cooler evenings. Off-road parking provided.
Children 5 and over welcome. A short walk leads to Piha Surf Beach and bush walks include Kitekite
Waterfall and Black Rock Dam. Forward book to avoid dissapointment.

Okura *20 km N of Auckland Central*
Okura B&B *B&B Separate Suite*
Judie & Ian Greig
20 Valerie Crescent, Okura,
North Shore City, Auckland

Tel (09) 473 0792 Fax (09) 473 1072
ibgreig@paradise.net.nz

Double $95 Single $75 (Full breakfast)
Visa MC accepted
1 Queen 1 Single (2 bdrm)
Bathrooms: 1 Private

Situated on Auckland's North Shore, Okura is a small
settlement bounded by farmland and the Okura River,
an estuary edged with native forest. If you like peace, quiet, with only bird song nearby, estuary and
forest views, then this is for you. Accommodation includes your own, not shared, TV lounge, tea-making
facilities, fridge, shower and toilet. Nearby is a wide variety of cafes, shops, beaches, walks, North Shore
Stadium, Massey University and golf courses. Okura - one of Auckland's best kept secrets.

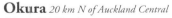

Auckland

Albany - Coatesville *7 km N of Albany*

Camperdown *Farmstay*
Chris & David Hempleman
455 Coatesville/Riverhead Highway,
RD 3, Albany, Auckland

Tel (09) 415 9009 Fax (09) 415 9023
chris@camperdown.co.nz
www.camperdown.co.nz

Double $135 Single $95 (Full breakfast)
Child $45 Dinner $40
Children welcome
1 King/Twin 2 Queen 2 Single (4 bdrm)
Bathrooms: 1 Guest share 2 Private

We are only 20 minutes from Auckland City, relax in secluded tranquillity. Our home opens into beautiful gardens, native bush and stream offering the best of hospitality in a friendly relaxed atmosphere. On the farm we have sheep, cattle and pet lambs Our spacious guest areas consist of the entire upstairs. Guests may use our games room, play tennis on our new court, row a boat on the lake, or just stroll by the stream. Camperdown is easy travelling to the main tourist route north.

Albany - Coatesville *3 km N of Albany*

Te Harinui Country Homestay *B&B*
Mike & Sue Blanchard
102 Coatesville/Riverhead Highway, RD 3,
Albany, Auckland

Tel (09) 415 9295 sue@teharinui.co.nz
www.teharinui.co.nz

Double $95 Single $75 (Full breakfast)
Child by arrangement
Dinner $30 by arrangement
Children welcome
1 Queen 2 Single (2 bdrm)
Bathrooms: 1 Guest share

Country hospitality as it used to be. A home from home in the country only 20 minutes from the city. Relax in the large garden, feed our pet coloured sheep and old horse, our dog and cat are friendly. Learn to spin and browse our craft shop. We can arrange outings to local attractions including gardens, orchards and beaches. Close to stadium and Massey University, buses to the city. Generous breakfasts; coffee and teas are always available. Sue speaks French and is learning Mandarin.

Our B&Bs range from homely to luxurious,
but you can always be assured of superior hospitality.

52

Greenhithe *15 km N of Auckland*

B&B
Approved

Waiata Tui Lodge (The Song of the Tui) *B&B Homestay*
Therese & Ned Jujnovich
177 Upper Harbour Drive, Greenhithe, Auckland

Tel (09) 413 9270 Fax (09) 413 9217
theresewa@xtra.co.nz   www.bnb.co.nz/waiata

Double $100-$115 Single $70 (Special breakfast)
Child negotiable, cot available
Dinner $25 Visa MC Amex accepted
2 Queen 1 Twin 2 Single (3 bdrm)
Bathrooms: 2 Private 1 Guest share

A warm welcome to our haven. 8 acres of native forest and pasture only 15 minutes from NZ's largest city, yet so peaceful you could be in the heart of the countryside. A handy relaxing stay before your journey north. Spectacular views from over the kauri trees to the tranquil water below, with the distant Waitakere Ranges beyond.

Waken to tui song and the smell of freshly baked bread. A delicious healthy breakfast will be served: home-grown or local in season fruit, various cereals, home-made yoghurt and spreads as well as a cooked breakfast, fruit juice, tea or coffee. From our large kauri breakfast table you can look out to the west and see the changing patterns of trees, water and tide. Perhaps a tui or a kereru (NZ's largest colourful pigeon) will stop for a drink at the birdbath on the adjoining deck.

You may like to walk in our lush rain forest with tree ferns and massive trees down to the waters edge or you can relax in the bush hammock with a book. Do some bird watching or wander around our large garden usually bright with seasonal flowers. Swim in the pool in summer. Meet Harry, our friendly goat.

We have both travelled extensively overseas and within NZ and will be pleased to help you with your travel plans.

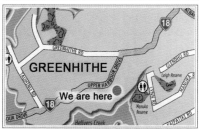

GREENHITHE

We are here

A Lockwood (solid-timber) home built for our family 30 years ago has been a homestay since 1987. Only 5km to Albany and Glenfield. 5 minutes to Greenhithe Village & restaurants.

Waken to tui song and the smell of freshly baked bread.

53

Browns Bay *1.5 km W of Browns Bay*

Amoritz House *B&B*
Carol & Gary Moffatt
730 East Coast Road, Browns Bay, Auckland

Tel (09) 479 6338 or 025 806 958
Fax (09) 479 6338 amoritz@ihug.co.nz
www.aucklandaccommodation.co.nz

Double $90-$120 Single $70-$90 (Full breakfast)
Dinner $10-$30pp Visa MC accepted
2 King/Twin 1 Double 1 Single (3 bdrm)
Bathrooms: 2 Ensuite 1 Private

Spend some peaceful nights in our quiet guest
bedrooms with Sky TV, garden and rural outlooks.
Separate guest entrance leads into kitchenette with fridge, microwave, washing machine, dryer etc.
Adjoining dining room. Internet, email, fax etc available. Minutes from North Harbour Stadium,
Millennium Stadium, Massey University, a variety of cafes, restaurants, beaches, shopping and Auckland
City centre with all its attractions. Bus stop at door. Barbeque. Off-street parking, 2 minutes to
Motorway. Non-smoking. Dinners $10, $20, $30 per person with prior notice.

~

Browns Bay *1.7 km W of Browns Bay*

St Clair B&B *B&B*
Raeburn Van Lierop
30 St Clair Place, Browns Bay, Auckland

Tel (09) 475 5230 or 027 620 7704
Fax (09) 475 5303
st_clair@xtra.co.nz

Double $130 Single $80 (Full breakfast)
Dinner $35
1 King 1 Queen (2 bdrm)
Bathrooms: 1 Ensuite 1 Private

Welcome to my modern New-England style purpose
built B&B. Enjoy the antiques, bric-a-brac and
memorabilia or maybe relax on the spacious deck with magic views of Coromandel, Rakino Island and
the Noises. Minutes drive to Browns Bay shops and beach, North Harbour Stadium, Albany Mega
Centre and Motorway. Queen bed, ensuite, kitchenette or king bed, private spa/bathroom. Private
balcony. Off-street parking. Well behaved family dog.

~

Devonport *1 km N of Devonport*

Rainbow Villa *B&B*
Judy McGrath
17 Rattray Street, Devonport, Auckland

Tel (09) 445 3597 Fax (09) 445 4597
rainbowvilla@xtra.co.nz

Double $130-$160 Single $100-$130 (Full breakfast)
Visa MC Amex accepted
1 King 1 Queen 2 Twin 2 Single (3 bdrm)
Bathrooms: 3 Ensuite

Welcome to our Victorian villa (1885) nestled in a
quiet cul-de-sac on the lower slopes of Mt Victoria. 3
elegant spacious rooms with ensuites, Sky TV. Spa pool
in the garden. We serve a delicious full breakfast, coffee and tea available at all times. Situated just 100
metres from historic Devonport Village, 5 minute walk to ferry, only 10 minute 'cruise' to downtown
Auckland. Directions: Rattray Street is first on left past Picture theatre. Shuttles available at airport. Not
suitable for children or pets. www.rainbowvilla.co.nz, e-mail rainbowvilla@xtra.co.nz.

Devonport *4 km N of Auckland Central*
Karin's Garden Villa *B&B Cottage with Kitchen*
Karin Loesch & Family
14 Sinclair Street, Devonport, Auckland 1309

Tel (09) 445 8689 Fax (09) 445 8689
stay@karinsvilla.com
www.karinsvilla.com

Double $145-$175 Single $90-$130
(Continental Breakfast)
Child $25 Dinner by arrangement
Self-contained cottage $185 Visa MC accepted
1 King/Twin 2 Double 3 Single (4 bdrm)
Bathrooms: 1 Ensuite 1 Private 1 Guest share

Tucked away at the end of a quiet cul-de-sac, Karin's Garden Villa - a **Devonport Dream** - offers real home comfort with its light cosy rooms, easy relaxed atmosphere and the warmest of welcome from Karin and her family.

A beautifully restored spacious Victorian villa surrounded by large lawns and old fruit trees. Karin's Garden Villa has also been featured on NZ and Australian television advertising for its relaxed, peaceful setting. Just 5 minutes stroll from tree-lined Cheltenham Beach, sailing, golf, tennis, shops and restaurants and only a short drive or pleasant 10 minute walk past extinct volcanoes to the picturesque Devonport centre with its many attractions.

Your comfortable room offers separate private access through french doors, opening onto wide verandahs and cottage garden. And for those visitors wanting ultimate comfort and privacy, there is even a self-contained studio cottage with balcony and full kitchen facilities to rent (minimum 3 days). Sit down to a nutritious breakfast in the sunny dining room with its large bay windows overlooking everflowering purple lavender and native gardens. Guests are welcome to join the family barbecue and relax on our large lawn. We welcome longer stays and can arrange favourable discounts accordingly.

Help yourself to tea and German-style coffee and biscuits anytime, check your email and feel free to use the kitchen and laundry. Karin comes from Germany and she and her family have lived in Indonesia for a number of years. We have seen a lot of the world and enjoy meeting other travellers. Always happy to help you arrange island cruises, rental cars, bikes and tours.

From the airport take a shuttle bus to our doorstep or to downtown ferry terminal. Courtesy pick up from Devonport Wharf. By car: after crossing Harbour Bridge, take Takapuna-Devonport turnoff. Right at T-junction, follow Lake Road to end, left into Albert, Vauxhall Road and then first left into Sinclair Street.

Devonport *1.5 km N of Devonport*
Ducks Crossing Cottage *B&B Homestay*
Gwenda & Peter Mark-Woods
58 Seabreeze Road, Devonport, Auckland

Tel (09) 445 8102 Fax (09) 445 8102
duckxing@splurge.net.nz

Double $90-$130 Single $65-$85 (Full breakfast)
Child $30 Pet free home Children welcome
1 King/Twin 1 Queen 1 Single (3 bdrm)
Bathrooms: 1 Ensuite 2 Private

Welcome to our charming modern home in a garden setting. Peaceful, spacious, sunny bedrooms with television and clock radios. Tea, coffee and home-cooking available. We overlook Waitemata Golf Course and are 5 minutes from Narrow Neck Beach. Devonport Village, with cafes, restaurants and antique shops is 2 minutes by car or 15 minutes walk. Hosts are well travelled,informative and enjoy hospitality. Directions:airport door to door shuttle, or drive Route 26, Seabreeze Road, first house on left. Good off-street parking, courtesy ferry pick up on request.

Devonport *75m km N of Ferry Terminal*
The Jasmine Cottage *B&B Cottage No Kitchen*
Joan & John Lewis
20 Buchanan Street, Devonport, Auckland

Tel (09) 445 8825 Fax (09) 445 8605
joanjohnlewis@xtra.co.nz
www.photoalbum.co.nz/jasmine/

Double $100 (Full breakfast)
1 night only $110
1 Queen (1 bdrm)
Bathrooms: 1 Ensuite

Welcome to our cosy smoke-free quiet and private guest cottage. We are right in the heart of historic Devonport Village with all its attractions, cafes, beaches, golf course, scenic walks. The ferry to Auckland City and the Hauraki Gulf is 3 minutes walk away. A breakfast basket is delivered to your door and provides fruit juice, cereals, home made muesli and yoghurt, a platter of seasonal fruits, breads, English muffins, jams, spreads, cheeses, free-range eggs, breakfast teas and freshly brewed coffee. TV, fax.

Waiheke Island
Blue Horizon *B&B*
David & Marion Aim
41 Coromandel Road, Sandy Bay, Waiheke Island

Tel (09) 372 5632

Double $80-$95 Single $55-$70 (Continental)
2 Queen (2 bdrm)
Bathrooms: 1 Ensuite 1 Family share

We live above Sandy Bay, which is 2-3 minutes walk away with spectacular sea views. All the rooms of our modest home face due north, catching the sun all day. Waiheke caters for adventuring, dining out, sandy beaches, rock pools, which we enjoy after farming and owning a garden centre which our 4 children helped with. We really enjoy our B&B and look forward to sharing our beautiful island with you. Directions: ferry from Auckland. Car ferry Howick. Complimentary ferry transfers.

Great Barrier Island *1 km S of Mulberry Grove*

Pigeons Lodge *B&B Apartment with Kitchen Guest House*
Jim & Anne Robertson
179 Shoal Bay Road, Tryphena, Great Barrier Island

Tel (09) 429 0437
PIGEONS.LODGE@xtra.co.nz
www.pigeonslodge.co.nz

Double $120-$150 Single $110-$140 (Full breakfast)
Visa MC accepted
Pet free home
Not suitable for children
5 Queen 1 Twin (3 bdrms in B&B, 2 in apartments)
Bathrooms: 5 Ensuite

Pigeons Lodge is the perfect accommodation to experience the magic that is Great Barrier Island - a world of its own. The lodge is situated on the water's edge in mature native bush and you will delight in the pigeons, kakas and tuis that entertain you over a leisurely breakfast on the deck. Jim & Anne provide hospitality which is legendary, and they will advise you the best ways to explore the walks, enjoy the beaches, and immerse yourself in this world of natural wonders and simple pleasures.

Auckland - Herne Bay *2.5 km W of Auckland central*

Moana Vista *B&B Homestay*
Tim Kennedy & Matthew Moran
60 Hamilton Road, Herne Bay, Auckland

Tel (09) 376 5028 or 0800 213 761
Fax (09) 376 5025
info@moanavista.co.nz
www.moanavista.co.nz

Double $180-$240 Single $160-$180 (Continental)
Visa MC accepted Children welcome
2 Queen 1 Twin (3 bdrm)
Bathrooms: 2 Ensuite 1 Private

Close to Ponsonby and Auckland city Moanavista is nestled in the exclusive enclave of Herne Bay. This charming, renovated 2 storey villa is owned and operated by your friendly hosts, Tim and Matthew. 2 of the upper rooms have lovely harbour views. they also offer complimentary use of TV, internet/email services, tea, coffee and a glass of wine. You will be treated to a continental breakfast of fresh seasonal fruits, cereals and bakery. You can wander up the road to visit any one of the award winning local restaurants.

Auckland - Ponsonby *3 km W of Auckland Central*

The Big Blue House *B&B Homestay*
Kate Prebble & Lynne Giddings
103 Garnet Road, Westmere, Auckland

Tel (09) 360 6384
kate-lynne@xtra.co.nz
www.thebigbluehouse.co.nz

Double $110-$140 Single $60-$120 (Continental)
Child $10 Dinner $35 by arrangment
Visa MC Eftpos accepted
Children welcome
2 King 3 Single (3 bdrm)
Bathrooms: 1 Ensuite 2 Family share

Kate and Lynne warmly invite you to enjoy our unique homestay environment close to Auckland's central city and harbour. Be greeted by our friendly cat and dog. Enjoy the luxury of spacious rooms with sea/hill views, TV, tea/coffee facilities, writing desk, electric blankets,heated towels and bathrobes. Generous continental breakfast. Luxuriate in our spa, splash in the pool. Take an easy stroll to the Auckland Zoo, Western Springs Stadium, cafes or seashore. Children welcome. Make yourself at home!

Auckland - Ponsonby *In Auckland Central*

The Great Ponsonby *Small Hotel*
Sally James & Gerard Hill
30 Ponsonby Terrace, Ponsonby, Auckland

Tel (09) 376 5989 or 0800 766 792
Fax (09) 376 5527
info@greatpons.co.nz
www.greatpons.co.nz

Double $210-$350 **Single** $180-$275 (Special breakfast)
Visa MC Diners Amex accepted
6 King/Twin 5 Queen (11 bdrm)
Bathrooms: 11 Ensuite

Delightful small hotel bed & breakfast. Stay in a heritage 1890's villa restored with charm and flair providing you with quiet and peace.

Your hotel is just 2 minutes stroll to Ponsonby's vibrant cafes , bistros, restaurants, art and craft galleries and just 5 minutes by taxi to the waterfront and central Auckland.

11 individually designed guestrooms with Pacific and New Zealand artworks. Accommodation choices include courtyard and palm garden studios, villa rooms and upstairs penthouse suite.

Leisurely breakfast in the dining room or alfresco on the balcony. Freshly prepared cooked selection plus juices, fresh fruits and plunger coffee or tea choices, Delicious!

Free wireless internet. Socialise or read in the large comfortable lounge, balconies and courtyards. Friendly dog and cat - part of the family.

Auckland - Ponsonby *In Auckland Central*

Colonial Cottage *B&B Homestay*
Grae Glieu
35 Clarence Street, Ponsonby, Auckland 1034

Tel (09) 360 2820 Fax (09) 360 3436
bnb@colonial-cottage.com

Double $100-$120 Single $80-$100 (Special breakfast)
Dinner $25 by arrangement
1 King 1 Queen 1 Single (3 bdrm)
Bathrooms: 1 Guest share

Delightful olde-world charm with modern amenities
to assure your comfort - accent on quality. Hospitable
and relaxing. Quiet with green outlook. Close to Herne
Bay and Ponsonby Road cafes and quality restaurants. Airport shuttle service door-to-door. Handy to
public transport, city attractions and motorways. Smoke-free indoors. Alternative health therapies and
massage available. Special dietary requirements catered for. Organic emphasis. Single party bookings
available.

Auckland - Ponsonby *1 km W of Inner City*

Amitee's on Ponsonby *Luxury B&B Hotel*
Ian Stewart & Jill Slee
237 Ponsonby Road, Ponsonby, Auckland

Tel (09) 378 6325 Fax (09) 378 6329
info@amitees.co.nz
www.amitees.com

Double $180-$275 (Continental)
Penthouse Suite $400 Visa MC Amex Eftpos accepted
Not suitable for children
2 King 3 Queen 1 Double 1 Twin (7 bdrm)
Bathrooms: 7 Ensuite High pressure shower,
Toilet & Vanity with luxury toiletries

Welcome to the only boutique hotel on vibrant Ponsonby Road. Relax in your choice of 6 spacious,
comfortable and beautifully appointed bedrooms; or the luxury penthouse suite with stunning city views.
You will love the sumptuous bedding, luxurious robes and extras such as ensuites, Sky TV, DD phones
and free internet access. Experience Auckland's finest restaurants, cafes and boutique shopping right
outside the door, or the city centre only minutes away. Top choice for Auckland by New York Times, 31
Oct 2004. For business or leisure, Amitee's is your perfect choice.

Auckland - Ponsonby *2 km W of Information centre*

Ponsonbynb *B&B Separate Suite with Kitchen*
Chrissy and Reg Price
9 Picton Street, Ponsonby, Auckland

Tel (09) 376 0250 or 021 336 640
prices@xtra.co.nz
www.ponsonbynb.co.nz

Double $210 Single $180 (Continental)
Child $30
Special off season rates
Visa MC Amex accepted
Pet free home Children welcome
1 King 1 Double (1 bdrm)
Bathrooms: 1 Ensuite Separate shower

We are close to cafes and shops of Ponsonby, yet nestled in a tree lined street of early 1900s wooden
villas. The modern studio is completely separate and self-contained with kitchen. There's a great outlook,
but still a cozy, warm and private feeling inside a stone walled compound with subtropical gardens.
Featured in Travel & Leisure magazine. Our cream persian cat, Safari, rules the roost.

Auckland - Parnell *1.5 km E of Auckland Central*

Ascot Parnell 'a small b&b hotel' *Luxury B&B Homestay Hotel Guest House*

Therese & Bart Blommaert

St Stephens Avenue, Parnell, Auckland 1

Tel (09) 309 9012 Fax (09) 309 3729
info@ascotparnell.com
www.ascotparnell.com

Double $185-$365 Single $135-$295 (Full breakfast)
Child 8 years plus welcome
50 restaurants in walking distance
Ask us about our winter packages
Visa MC Diners Amex accepted
1 King/Twin 2 Queen 3 Twin 2 Single (3 bdrm)
Bathrooms: 3 Ensuite in all rooms

Ascot Parnell: Your bed & breakfast for the 21st century. Superbly equipped **centrally located B&B** hidden from the main street in tranquil garden surroundings. All is super-modern, with the large, open living space drawing your eye - and your entire body - out to the balcony for the city and harbour view.

Uniquely located at a moment's stroll from Parnell Village. Walk to numerous cafes, restaurants, art galleries and boutiques and only 1.5km to downtown Auckland city. The Rose Gardens and Auckland Museum is an easy 5 minute walk. **The Airport Shuttle-Bus brings you to the door** and if you come by car, there is secure underground parking.

Bedrooms are bright and spacious, with large windows that open, some with balconies and have either garden or harbour views. Rooms are all non-smoking with air-conditioning, phone and internet connection. Every practical detail has been minutely considered from your point of view... and only the highest quality has been sought in all things. There is much solid wood, pebbles in pot plants, marble in bathrooms, thick glass showers, mirrors, modern art, warm simple colours, perfect white linen on new beds. Mod cons include an open-plan kitchen with a coffee-maker, free juice & cookies. There is a Mac for guest use, a heated swimming pool, security-swiper for the lift, a piano, CD player, laundry, the list goes on...

Breakfast is a five-course feast with freshly squeezed juice, seasonal or tropical fruits, yoghurt, cereals and homemade muesli, gourmet omelettes, bacon and eggs, Belgian pancakes, French toast etc.

Your hosts, Bart and Therese could not care more enthusiastically about their guests. (French, German, Flemish/Dutch spoken). They will help you book tours, rental cars and accommodations for your onward journey. Reservations are essential.

Auckland - Parnell *1.5 km N of Auckland City*

St Georges Bay Lodge *B&B*
Carol & Steven Quilliam
43 St Georges Bay Road, Parnell, Auckland

Tel (09) 303 1050 or 021-214 1473
Fax (09) 360 7392 carol@stgeorge.co.nz
www.stgeorge.co.nz

Double $215-$265 Single $195-$215 (Full breakfast)
Without ensuite $135-$165 Visa MC accepted
Pet free home Children welcome
4 King/Twin 1 Double (5 bdrm)
Bathrooms: 4 Ensuite 1 Family share

St Georges Bay Lodge is an elegant Victorian villa which has the charm of a by-gone era, with the comfort of modern amenities. There is no better location for your stay in Auckland City. We are minutes from: picturesque Parnell Village, designer boutiques and speciality stores, great cafes, restaurants, and night club life, health centres, swimming pools, gardens, parks, and the Museum in Auckland Domain and Holy Trinity Cathedral. Also within walking distance: Newmarket, casino, more restaurants and city

∼

Auckland CBD *In Auckland CBD*

Braemar on Parliament Street *B&B*
Susan Sweetman
7 Parliament Street, Auckland City Central

Tel (09) 377 5463 or 021 640 688
Fax (09) 377 3056
braemar@aucklandbedandbreakfast.com
www.aucklandbedandbreakfast.com

Double $150-$295 (Full breakfast)
Visa MC Diners Amex Eftpos accepted
Children and pets welcome by arangement
2 Queen 2 Double (4 bdrm)
Bathrooms: 1 Ensuite 1 Guest share 1 Private

A lovingly restored Edwardian townhouse in the Auckland CBD, Braemar provides luxurious and elegant accommodation to the discerning traveller. The Batten Suite has 3 rooms including private bathroom and lounge with open fireplace. Our other 2 guestrooms share the original and large bathroom. All bathrooms with showers and claw foot baths. All upstairs bedrooms with posturepedic beds. Complimentary toiletries, tea & coffee.

**All our B&Bs are non-smoking
unless stated otherwise in the text.**

∼

Auckland CBD *In Auckland CBD*
Redwood Vista Bed & Breakfast *B&B*
Dawn Feickert

4D Kingsbridge apartments,
72 Wellesley Street, Auckland

Tel (09) 373 4903 or 0800 349 742
027 475 8996 Fax (09) 373 4903
kotuku@wave.co.nz
www.redwood-bed-breakfast.ws

Double $135-$165 Single $100-$135 (Special breakfast)
Visa MC accepted
Pet free home
2 Queen 2 Twin (2 bdrm)
Bathrooms: 1 Ensuite 1 Family share

The Redwood Vista is a convenient central location in the heart of Auckland City with stunning views day and night. Walk to all the city attractions including art galleries, museums, theatres, cinemas, restaurants, shopping arcades, try your luck at Sky City Casino. Go sailing, stroll around the Viaduct yacht basin, along the waterfront, and through the renowned parks and reserves. Run down to the heated baths and gym.

Ideal for the business traveller where everything is close by in the CBD plus walk to the Auckland University and Hospital. The Auckland Airport shuttles are available door to door on request 24 hours a day. The ferry terminal is 15 minutes walk away. The link bus and city buses are close by to take you to places like the Parnell Village the Rose Gardens, Ponsonby, Kelly Tarlton's Underwater world. We are also close to motorways-North and South. You have several golf courses available, close to beaches.

From our fourth floor spacious and private apartment with views of the Harbour Bridge, Sky Tower and Waitemata Harbour enjoy a gourmet breakfast with choices of fresh fruit, yoghurt, cereals daily baked muffins, scones, breads and pastries as well as special dishes. This is served in the dining room or you can wander onto the verandah.

Our rooms are non-smoking, comfortable and have queen and single beds with all the conveniences you would expect, including colour TV plus tea & coffee making facilities.

We are well travelled with a great interest in wine and every effort has been made to ensure your stay - be it business or pleasure is an enjoyable one. Email and office facilities available. Please phone for directions to the apartment.

Auckland - Epsom *5 km S of Auckland City Centre*

Millars Epsom Homestay *Homestay*

Janet & Jim Millar

10 Ngaroma Road, Epsom, Auckland 1003

Tel (09) 625 7336
jmillar@xtra.co.nz
www.jasons.co.nz/brochure_rack/millars

B&B
Approved

Double $100-$110 Single $60-$70 (Full breakfast)
Child $10-$20 Dinner $50
Visa MC accepted
Children welcome
1 King 1 Queen 2 Twin 1 Single (3 bdrm)
Bathrooms: 1 Ensuite 2 Private

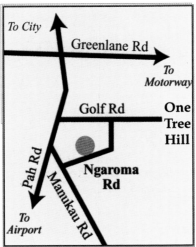

Our home, a spacious 1919 wooden bungalow, is surprisingly quiet and restful, set in a garden suburb in a tree-lined street, 200 metres from Greenwoods Corner Village with its bank, post office, reasonably priced non-tourist restaurants, and bus stop on direct route (15 minutes to the CBD).

There is a short walk to One Tree Hill, one of Auckland's loveliest parks with a playground, farm animals, groves of trees, the observatory, and a magnificent panorama of Auckland from the summit. A 15 minute walk through the park leads to the Expo Centre and Greenlane Hospital.

There are 2 accommodation areas - either the Garden Suite with its queen-sized double bedroom, large lounge with 3 single beds, patio, desk and TV, own bathroom, and which is the area we find really suitable for families; or the upstairs bedroom (king-size, can be converted to twin beds) with own ensuite, desk and TV.

We have travelled widely both in NZ and overseas (our son lives in Finland) and very much like conversing with guests and assisting in making their stay as pleasant as possible in our country and especially in this attractive suburb of Auckland. We are a smoke-free family. Jim and I were both born in NZ, and we belong to @Home NZ.

Auckland - Epsom *5 km S of Auckland Central*

Auckland Homestay Bed & Breakfast *B&B Homestay*

Isobel & Ian Thompson
37 Torrance Street, Epsom, Auckland

Tel (09) 624 3714
aucklandhomestay@xtra.co.nz
www.aucklandhomestay.co.nz

Double $125-$145 Single $85-$110 (Full breakfast)
Child negotiable
Dinner by arrangement
Visa MC accepted
Children welcome
2 Queen 1 Single (3 bdrm)
Bathrooms: 1 Ensuite 1 Guest share

Experience warm, friendly hospitality in our large modern home in a quiet tree lined street. Just 5 minutes from motorway and 15 minutes from airport and city CBD. Our central location is ideally positioned to explore the many attractions, whether by car or one of the nearby bus routes. Use of full laundry facilities. Telephone, email by request. Evening meals by prior arrangement. Off-street parking. We look forward to sharing our non-smoking home with you.

Auckland - Mt Eden *Auckland Central*

811 Bed & Breakfast *B&B*

Bryan Condon & David Fitchew
811 Dominion Road, Mt Eden, Auckland 1003

Tel (09) 620 4284 Fax (09) 620 4286
811bnb@quicksilver.net.nz

Double $85 Single $55 (Full breakfast)
2 Double 1 Twin (3 bdrm)
Bathrooms: 2 Guest share

All are welcome at 811 Bed & Breakfast. Your hosts and their irish water spaniels welcome you to their turn of the century home. Our home reflects years of collecting and living overseas. Located on Dominion Road (which is an extension of Queen Street city centre). The bus stop at the door, only 10 minutes to city and 20 minutes to airport, shuttle bus from airport. Easy walking to Balmoral shopping area (excellent restaurants). Our breakfast gives you a beaut start to your day.

Auckland - Mt Eden *2 km S of Auckland Central*

Bavaria B&B Hotel *B&B*

Ulrike & Rudolf
83 Valley Road, Mt Eden, Auckland 3

Tel (09) 638 9641 Fax (09) 638 9665
bavaria@xtra.co.nz
www.bavariabandbhotel.co.nz

Double $110-$139 Single $74-$95 (Full breakfast)
Child over 2 $12
Reduced rates May-September
Visa MC Amex accepted Children welcome
1 King/Twin 4 Queen 2 Double
2 Twin 2 Single (11 bdrm)
Bathrooms: 11 Ensuite

Charming small hotel in quiet residential location, close to city with excellent connections to town, Mt. Eden summit with panoramic views easily accessible, immaculate quality rooms with ensuites, phones and internet access for your laptop, healthy breakfast buffet-style, complimentary tea/coffee/biscuits, sunny lounge and peaceful garden, good shopping, cafes, restaurants and internet cafes nearby, off-street parking, friendly and welcoming atmosphere. Ask us for advice on rental cars, tours etc.

Auckland - Western Springs *6mins W of Town*

Hastings Hall *B&B Hotel*
Malcolm Martel
99 Western Springs Road, Western Springs

Tel (09) 845 8550 or 021 300 006
Fax (09) 845 8554 unique@hastingshall.co.nz
www.hastingshall.co.nz

Double $165-$375 Single $145-$295 (Full breakfast)
Visa MC Amex Eftpos accepted
Children and pets welcome
1 King 8 Queen (9 bdrm)
Bathrooms: 7 Ensuite 2 Private

Magnificently restored 1878 mansion, extensive
grounds 5 minutes to city centre. Ideal for tourists, businesspersons or a retreat away to unwind. Enjoy gourmet breakfasts. There are 9 themed guest rooms all with marble ensuites. The Grand Williams suite with private lounge to the Moulin Rouge loft suite in the Stables. Tropically landscaped grounds, formal lounge and large pool lounge with library, home theatre & computer, email & fax facilities. Furnished with antiques from the period, fine linen and warm fluffy towels. Ideal for small conferences, functions, meetings or seminars.

Auckland - Remuera *7 km N of Auckland Central*

Woodlands *B&B Homestay*
Jude & Roger Harwood
18 Waiatarua Road, Remuera, Auckland 1005

Tel (09) 524 6990 Fax (09) 524 6993
jude.harwood@xtra.co.nz
www.babs.co.nz/woodlands

Double $125-$145 Single $100 (Special breakfast)
Child not suitable Dinner $65pp Visa MC accepted
Pet free home Not suitable for children
1 King 1 Double 1 Twin 1 Single (3 bdrm)
Bathrooms: 1 Ensuite 1 Private

Guest book comments: "Absolutely purr-fect." "Very
comfortable with stunning food." "A lovely oasis of calm with wonderful breakfasts." "Peaceful retreat with excellent breakfasts." Our breakfasts ARE special using seasonal fruit and produce. Join us for a Cordon Bleu candlelit evening dinner - booking essential. Woodlands is very quiet, surrounded by native trees and palms and central to many places of interest. The 3 guest bedrooms have tea/coffee facilities, heated towel rails, swimming towels and colour TVs. Fridge. Safe off-street carparking. Arrive a guest - leave a friend.

Auckland - Remuera

Lillington Villa *B&B Homestay Apartment with Kitchen*
Carol & Peter Dossor
24 Lillington Road, Remuera, Auckland

Tel (09) 523 2035 Fax (09) 523 2036
caropet@xtra.co.nz
babs.co.nz/lillington

Double $150 Single $140 (Full breakfast)
Child $20 Dinner $40
Full week $550-$650
Children welcome
1 Queen 3 Single (2 bdrm)
Bathrooms: 1 Ensuite

Home away from home. 2 large, sunny, luxurious flats in well-restored villa 10 minutes from central
Auckland. Own entrances and courtyards. Lock-up garages. Security and fire alarm systems. Gas heating. Telephone, video, Sky TV. Full modern open-plan kitchens and well-equipped bathrooms. Dishwasher, microwave, fridge/freezer, stove, washing machine, dryer. Quality fittings and equipment. 1 bedroom flat has queen and single beds. 2 bedroom family flat has queen and 3 single beds.

Auckland - Remuera *1.5 km E of Newmarket*

Green Oasis *B&B Homestay Apartment with Kitchen*
James & Joy Foote
25A Portland Road, Remuera, Auckland 5

Tel (09) 520 1921 Fax (09) 522 9004
footes1@xtra.co.nz
www.babs.co.nz/greenoasis

Double $120-$130 Single $75-$90 (Full breakfast)
Child $65 Visa MC accepted Children welcome
1 Queen 1 Single (2 bdrm)
Bathrooms: 1 Private

Green Oasis, a secluded, tranquil location in a much
loved garden of native trees and ferns, 10 minutes
to city centre. Close to the museum, antique & specialty shops, restaurants & cafes of Remuera,
Newmarket or Parnell. An informal home of natural timbers, sunny decks where you will find us
relaxed and welcoming, sensitive to your needs, be it to withdraw and rest, or to engage with us. Your
accommodation, entered from a private garden, is self-contained with fully equipped kitchen, tea/coffee
making facilities, washing machine, TV. Special breakfast of seasonal and home-made taste sensations!

Auckland - Remuera *3 km E of Auckland Central*

Omahu Lodge *Luxury B&B*
Robyn & Ken Booth
33 Omahu Road, Remuera, Auckland

Tel (09) 524 5648 or 021 954 333
Fax (09) 524 5108 omahulodge@xtra.co.nz
www.omahulodge.co.nz

Double $175-$225 Single $160-$200 (Full breakfast)
Dinner by arrangement Visa MC accepted
Pet free home Not suitable for children
2 Queen 2 Double (4 bdrm)
Bathrooms: 4 Ensuite

Omahu Lodge is a spacious home with total privacy
in a peaceful, residential setting. Choose from four spacious and beautifully appointed bedrooms all
with ensuites, heated towels, bath robes and tea/coffee facilities. Rooms having views of One Tree
Hill, Mt Hobson and Auckland's eastern and southern suburbs. Enjoy a sauna, spa or swim in the solar
heated pool. Restaurants, parks, antique shops and public transport are within easy walking distance.
The city centre and Auckland's renowned harbour just ten minutes away by car. Dinner is available by
arrangement.

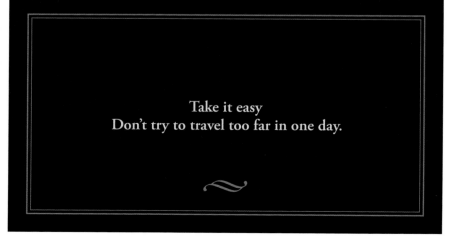

Take it easy
Don't try to travel too far in one day.

Auckland - One Tree Hill *3 km S of Newmarket*

Greenlane Bed and Breakfast *Homestay*
Clare & Don Boyd & Winston
21 Atarangi Road, Greenlane

Tel (09) 523 3419 or 0800 254 419,
027 281 3222
Fax (09) 524 8506
Stay@Paradise.net.nz
www.CityStay.net.nz

Double $100 **Single** $60
(Full breakfast)
Visa MC accepted
2 Queen 1 Twin 4 Single (4 bdrm)
Bathrooms: 1 Ensuite, 2 Guest Share

For tourists and business people alike, our
100 year old home has modern facilities
with a huge 400 acre treed park at the end
of our short street. We are close to Great
South Road & The NZ Expo Centre
(Auckland Showgrounds). Rooms have
TV, phone, DSL, and desk. Available: laundry, fax, computer, off street parking. Frequent buses to city
centre.

Directions: Exit Route 1 at Green Lane East, head west 300 metres, free left turn at lights, then second
street on right.

Auckland - Ellerslie *5 km SE of Auckland*
Ellerslie Bed & Breakfast Inn *Hosted B&B*
AnnaBella & Brian Gillies
6 Walpole Street, Ellerslie, Auckland

Tel (09) 589 1997 or 021 258 2632, 0800 5891997
Fax (09) 589 1994
info@ellersliebbi.co.nz   www.ellersliebbi.co.nz

Double $130-$160 Single $100-$130 (Full breakfast)
Dinner $65pp and only by prior arrangement
Visa MC accepted   Not suitable for children
2 Queen 1 Twin 2 Single (3 bdrm)
Bathrooms: 3 Ensuite

Greetings, We invite you to share in our wonderful new purpose built brick home, situated in the centrally located suburb of Ellerslie, close to Motorway ON and OFF ramps and on a bus route - and yet only 15 minutes, north or south to downtown Auckland or airport. Pubs, restaurants, specialty shops, Ellerslie Race Course & Convention Centre, Parnell, Newmarket, all within easy reach.

Our cosy Guest-only lounge boasts an area set up with Sky digital TV. The Guest PC on DSL wireless offers free internet. A Bridge table and chairs offers the chance to gamble a penny or two amongst friends! Or if its privacy your looking for then curl up in your comfy queen bed in your cosy ensuite bedroom, tucked under pure cotton sheets and your down duvet, and catch a movie or a sport (whoever wins the toss!) on your private in room LCD TV.

Special cooked breakfasts, changing daily, offering pancakes, french toast with Canadian maple syrup, Omelettes to die for, or a scramble in filo with bacon and tomatoes. These served after the usual starters of juice, fruits, cereals, yoghurts; you will not need lunch!

Ideally suited for the tourist or the corporate traveller, we will do our best to accommodate your schedule. Plenty of off street parking.

Your hosts, AnnaBella (a Canadian) & Brian (a Kiwi and a chef) both well travelled, offer as one guest wrote a "Warm Welcome", "Excellent Hospitality" and a "can't do enough for you" attitude.

Unsuitable for children. Smoke-free. We have a gorgeous burmese called Purrkins. And we do look forward to meeting you.

Auckland - Orakei - Okahu Bay *4.8 km E of Auckland Central*

Nautical Nook/Free Sailing *B&B Homestay*
Trish & Keith Janes & Irish Setter
23B Watene Crescent, Orakei, Auckland

Tel (09) 521 2544 or 0800 360 544
027 439 7116 nauticalnook@bigfoot.com
www.nauticalnook.com

Double $120-$140 Single $90-$100 (Full breakfast)
Visa MC accepted Children welcome
2 Queen 1 Single (3 bdrm)
Bathrooms: 1 Ensuite 2 Private

Friendly, relaxed beachside hospitality overlooking
park/harbour, 4.8km from downtown. 100 metres
from Okahu Bay, fringed by pohutukawa trees. Gourmet breakfast. Stroll along picturesque promenade
to Kelly Tarlton's Underwater World, Mission Bay beach and cafes, Te Pa Cultural Visitors Centre. Bus
at door to downtown, ferry terminal, museums. Unwind for 2-3 day stopover. Complimentary sailing
on the sparkling harbour on our 34' yacht. We have a wealth of local knowledge and international travel
experience and can assist with sightseeing, travel planning. Welcome! Pay cash and deduct 10% off listed
rates. Excellent website!

Auckland - Mission Bay *6 km E of Auckland Central*

Cockell Homestay *Homestay*
Jean & Bryan Cockell
41 Nihill Cresent, Mission Bay, Auckland

Tel (09) 528 3809
cockells@xtra.co.nz

Double $95 Single $75 (Full breakfast)
Dinner $25 by arrangement
Visa MC accepted
Not suitable for children
1 Double (1 bdrm)
Bathrooms: 1 Private

We warmly welcome you to our comfortable split level
home. The upper level is for your exclusive use including a private lounge. 5 minutes walk to Mission
Bay beach, cafes and restaurants and 10 minutes scenic car or bus ride to down town Auckland and ferry
terminal for harbour and islands in the Gulf. We are retired and look forward to sharing our special part
of Auckland with you. Please phone for directions or airport shuttle bus to our door. Please no smoking.

Auckland - St Heliers *10 km E of Auckland*

McPherson B&B *B&B*
Jill & Ron McPherson
102 Maskell Street, St Heliers, Auckland

Tel (09) 575 9738 Fax (09) 575 0051
ron&jill_mcpherson@xtra.co.nz

Double $120 Single $85 (Continental)
1 Queen 1 Twin (2 bdrm)
Bathrooms: 1 Private

Welcome to our modern home with off-street parking
in a smoke-free environment. 1 group of guests is
accommodated at a time. Having travelled extensively
ourselves we are fully aware of tourists' needs. 8

minutes walk to St Heliers Bay beach, shops, restaurants, cafes, banks and post office. Picturesque
12 minutes drive along the Auckland waterfront past Kelly Tarlton's Antarctic and Underwater
Encounter to downtown Auckland. Interests including all sports, gardening and Jill is a keen cross-stitch
embroiderer. Not suitable for children/pets.

Auckland - St Heliers *10 km E of Auckland Central*

Pippi's Bed and Breakfast *B&B Homestay*
Pippi & Philip Wells
15 Tuhimata Street, St Heliers, Auckland

Tel (09) 575 6057 or 021 989 643
Fax (09) 575 6055 pswells@xtra.co.nz
http://go.to/pippis

Double $150-$175 Single $100-$140 (Full breakfast)
Visa MC accepted
1 Queen 1 Double (3 bdrm)
Bathrooms: 1 Ensuite 1 Private

Our character home with pretty cottage garden offers
guests a sunny retreat only a short walk to lovely
beach, village and restaurants. Spacious bedroom with easy access, ensuite bathroom, electric blankets,
feather duvets, Sky TV, tea/coffee etc. Delicious breakfast of fruit, home-made bread/muesli, and/or full
breakfast, espresso coffee/tea. Telephone, fax, email, hairdryer, laundry, off-street parking available. With
Bertie (toy poodle) and Rags (cat) we look forward to offering you a warm welcome to our smoke-free
home.

Auckland - St Heliers *12 km E of Auckland Central*

The Munro's *B&B Homestay*
Margaret and Don Munro
12 Emerson Street, St Heliers, Auckland 1005

Tel (09) 528 0459 Fax (09) 528 0459
dmlmunro@xtra.co.nz

Double $98-$120 Single $80-$90 (Full breakfast)
Dinner by arrangement
Visa MC accepted
Pet free home
1 King/Twin1 King (1 bdrm)
Bathrooms: 1 Ensuite

Our spacious guestroom has a king or twin
comfortable bed(s), ensuite, private entry and patio area. There are tea/coffee facilities. Off-street parking.
Located only 2km from St Heliers Bay with a 10 kilometre scenic waterfront drive to central Auckland.
The airport is a 45 minute drive, or a taxi/shuttle bus will bring you to our door. Dinner is available
by prior arrangement. We are a retired Scottish couple who have lived in the tropics, enjoy travel and
conversation. No smoking please.

Auckland - Titirangi *20min km W of Auckland City*

Kaurigrove *B&B*
Gaby & Peter Wunderlich
120 Konini Road, Titirangi, Auckland 7

Tel (09) 817 5608 or 025 275 0574
Fax (09) 817 5608
kaurigrove@yahoo.co.nz

Double $95-$100 Single $60
Visa MC Diners Amex accepted
1 Queen 1 Single (2 bdrm)
Bathrooms: 1 Guest share

Welcome to our home! Kaurigrove offers a tranquil
location amidst kauri trees in a park-like setting yet
close to shops, cafes and restaurants. Situated at Titirangi, we are near Auckland's historic west coast with
its magnificent beaches and vast native bush with a wonder-world of walking tracks. Gaby and Peter,
your hosts of German background, are keen trampers themselves and are happy to introduce you to
the highlights of Auckland and its surrounding areas. PS: We have a shy cat called Coco. Non-smoking
inside residence.

Auckland - Avondale *10 km W of Auckland Central*

Kodesh Community *Homestay Cottage No Kitchen*
Kodesh Trust
31B Cradock Street, Avondale, Auckland

Tel (09) 828 5672 Fax (09) 828 5684
Kodeshtrust@xtra.co.nz

Double $60 Single $40 (Continental)
Child $20 Dinner $8
Flat-2 people $70-$90
Eftpos accepted
2 Queen 1 Double 3 Twin 2 Single (8 bdrm)
Bathrooms: 1 Family share 2 Private

Kodesh is an ecumenical, cross-cultural Christian
community of around 25 residents, 8 minutes by car from downtown Auckland. Guest rooms are in a
large modern home. 1 self-contained flat sleeps 4, the other 7. Group rates available. An evening meal is
available in the community dining room Monday-Friday. Bookings essential. The atmosphere is relaxed
and guests can amalgamate into the life of the community as much or little as desired. No smoking, no
pets, children under 12 welcome in self-contained unit.

Auckland Airport - Mangere Bridge *14 km S of Auckland Central*

Mangere Bridge Homestay *Homestay*
Carol & Brian
1 Boyd Ave, Mangere Bridge, Auckland

Tel (09) 636 6346 Fax (09) 636 6345

Double $80-$95 Single $60-$75 (Full breakfast)
Child 12 & under $20
Dinner $25 by prior arrangement
2 King/Twin 1 Double (3 bdrm)
Bathrooms: 3 Ensuite

We invite you to share our home, which is within ten
minutes of Auckland Airport, an ideal location for your
arrival or departure of New Zealand. We enjoy meeting
people and look forward to making your stay an enjoyable one. We welcome you to join us for dinner
by prior arrangement. Courtesy car to or from airport, bus and rail. Off street parking available. Handy
to public transport. Short stroll to the waterfront. Please no smoking indoors. Our cat requests no pets.
Inspection welcome.

Auckland - Mangere *4 km N of Airport*

Airport Bed & Breakfast *B&B*
Laurel Blakey
1 Westney Road, Corner of Kirkbride Road, Mangere

Tel (09) 275 0533 Fax (09) 275 0968
airportbnb@xtra.co.nz
www.airportbnb.co.nz

Double $90-$120 Single $75-$10 (Continental)
Visa MC Diners Amex Eftpos accepted
1 King 3 Queen 5 Double 1 Twin 7 Single (10 bdrm)
Bathrooms: 4 Ensuite 3 Guest share

Just 5 minutes drive from Auckland Airport a friendly
welcome and great value accommodation awaits. 10

quality rooms, 4 ensuites, central heating, large TV/Sky/dining room. Internet access. 2 minutes walk
to city bus stop - see Auckland by bus and ferry on the $9 day pass. Restaurants/takeaways nearby. Car,
cycle and luggage storage. Rental cars and NZ wide sightseeing tours booked. Courtesy airport transfer
(not 24 hour), free phone at airport, dial 28. Buffet breakfast, complimentary tea/coffee.

Auckland Airport - Mangere *2 km N of Mangere*
Airport Homestay/B&B *B&B Homestay*
May Pepperell
288 Kirkbride Road, Mangere, Auckland

Tel (09) 275 6777 or 025 289 8200
Fax (09) 275 6728

Double $70 **Single** $45 (Continental)
Child $20
3 Single (2 bdrm)
Bathrooms: 1 Guest share

Clean comfortable home 5 minutes from airport but not on flight path. Easy walk to shops and restaurants. 10 minutes from shopping centres and Telstra Events Centre at Manukau. Aviation Golf Course near airport, also Villa Maria Winery. My interests are people, travel, Ladies' Probus and voluntary work. Beds have woollen underlays and electric blankets. There is a sunny terrace and fenced swimming pool. Courtesy car to/from airport at reasonable hour. Vehicles minded while you're away from $1 day. Bus stop very close.

Auckland Airport - Mangere Bridge *7.5 km N of Auckland Airport*
Mountain View B&B *B&B Homestay*
Ian & Jenny (and cat Oscar) Davis
85A Wallace Road, Mangere Bridge, Auckland

Tel (09) 636 6535 Fax (09) 636 6126
mtviewbb@xtra.co.nz
www.bnb.co.nz/mountainviewbb.html

Double $95-$150 **Single** $75-$95 (Full breakfast)
Child $20 Dinner by arrangement
Visa MC accepted Children welcome
1 King/Twin 4 Queen 2 Twin 3 Single (6 bdrm)
Bathrooms: 4 Ensuite 1 Guest share

8 Minutes from Auckland Airport. Exit via George Bolt Drive, left into Kirkbride Road, follow through to Wallace Road, we're 1.2km on right from roundabout, up long driveway with curved brick entrance. Spacious home on half an acre, quiet locality not on flight-path, convenient off-street parking, public transport at gate. Enjoy spectacular harbour views whilst eating divine breakfasts. Typed navigational assistance to north, south or city. Central to many attractions and sport venues. Guests state: "nice, quiet, friendly, comfortable, good info. First Class." T's, UK.

Auckland - Otahuhu *17 km S of Auckland*
Oasis in Otahuhu *B&B*
Jerrine & Gerard Fecteau
70 Mangere Road, Otahuhu, Auckland

Tel (09) 276 9335 Fax (09) 276 9235
oasisbb@xtra.co.nz

Double $70 **Single** $50 (Continental)
Child negotiable Dinner $20
Visa MC accepted
Children and pets welcome
1 Queen 1 Double 1 Twin (3 bdrm)
Bathrooms: 2 Guest share

We welcome you to the Oasis in Otahuhu with the best Canuck-Kiwi hospitality. We are 15 minutes from the airport and 5 minutes from the train and motorway. We are collectors of many things: coins of the world, brass, Canadian Indian art. Cactus garden. We can help you plan your holiday and get a rental car. In addition to breakfast you can join us for dinner by arrangement or dine at one of the many restaurants in Otahuhu. Please phone, fax or email and our courtesy van will pick you up.

Auckland - Manukau *6.5 km NE of Manukau City*

Tanglewood *Homestay*
Roseanne & Ian Devereux
5 Inchinnam Road, Flat Bush, Auckland

Tel (09) 274 8280 Fax (09) 634 6896
tanglewood@clear.net.nz

Double $100 Single $70 (Full breakfast)
Visa MC accepted
Children welcome
1 Queen 1 Double (2 bdrm)
Bathrooms: 1 Ensuite 1 Private

Our homely cottage, set in 2 acres is close to the international airport. The garden loft is separate from the house with ensuite, TV, fridge, deck overlooking large peaceful gardens and ponds. Accommodation inside the house has its own bathroom. We are 30 minutes from downtown Auckland, close to Botany Shopping Centre and a stroll to local restaurants. Delicious home-cooked breakfast includes eggs from our free-range hens. We have a swimming pool and friendly dog, Daisy. We offer you warm and relaxed hospitality.

Auckland - Manukau *6.5 km NE of Manukau*

Calico Cottage *B&B*
Patty & Murray Glenie
7 Inchinnam Road, Flat Bush, Auckland

Tel (09) 274 8527 Fax (09) 274 8528
MG-PT@xtra.co.nz

Double $100 Single $70 (Full breakfast)
Child $15
Visa MC accepted
Children and pets welcome
1 Queen 1 Single (2 bdrm)
Bathrooms: 1 Ensuite

Welcome to Calico Cottage. We are on 2 acres with garden, paddocks, sheep, chickens - free range eggs, and 2 dogs who live outdoors. Peaceful and yet only 10 minutes from both Manukau City Centre and Botany Town Centre and 20 minutes from Auckland Airport. Transport to and from airport arranged if required. We have a double bedroom with new ensuite and a TV room adjoining for your own use. We look forward to your visit.

Auckland - Manurewa *2 km S of Manukau City*

Hillpark Homestay *B&B*
Katrine & Graham Paton
16 Collie Street, Manurewa, Auckland 1702

Tel (09) 267 6847 or 021 207 2559
Fax (09) 267 8718 hillpark.homestay@xtra.co.nz
www.hillpark.co.nz

Double $90-$100 Single $60-$60 (Full breakfast)
Child $20 Dinner $20 by arrangement
Visa MC accepted Children welcome
1 Double 4 Single (3 bdrm)
Bathrooms: 1 Ensuite 1 Guest share

Welcome to our sunny, spacious home and meet our friendly tonkinese cat. We are 15 minutes from Auckland Airport, 20 minutes from Auckland City centre, on the route south and the Pacific Coast Highway. Nearby are restaurants, Regional Botanic Gardens (Ellerslie Flower Show), TelstraClear Pacific Events Centre, Tipapa Events Centre, Manukau City Shopping Centre, Manukau Superclinic and Surgery Centre. Our interests include teaching, classical music, painting, gardening, photography, Christian activities, reading and travel. We are a smoke-free home. Directions: please phone or visit our website.

Auckland - Half Moon Bay *2 km W of Howick*

Parkland Lodge *Luxury B&B*
Janette & John Fielding
15 Elimar Drive, Farm Cove,
Half Moon Bay (near Howick)

Tel (09) 576 5683 or 021 260 0461
fielding@ihug.co.nz

Double $190-$435 (Special breakfast)
Dinner by arrangement
Visa MC accepted
2 King/Twin 1 King (3 bdrm)
Bathrooms: 2 Ensuite 1 Private Seperate powder room

Parkland Lodge is nestled in 1 acre of mature

landscaped private grounds with magical seaviews to Rangitoto and Browns Island. Ideal base to savour Auckland's attractions being a short enjoyable ferry ride from Half Moon Bay or 15 minutes by car. Exclusive guest entrance and lounge with open fire ensures comfort and privacy. Swimming pool, spa, billiard room, reading room, home theatre and Oscar (border collie). Airport collection available. Complement your NZ visit in our romantic Kauri Cottage in Russell Bay of Islands

Whitford *25 km SE of Auckland*

Springhill Country Homestay *Farmstay*
Judy & Derek Stubbs
Polo Lane, Whitford, RD, Manurewa, Auckland

Tel (09) 530 8674 Fax (09) 530 8274
djstubbs@ihug.co.nz

Double $120 Single $80 (Full breakfast)
Child $40 (1 room suitable for children)
Visa MC accepted
Children and pets welcome
1 Queen (1 bdrm)
Bathrooms: 1 Ensuite

Springhill is an 8 hectare farm in Whitford, an

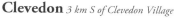

attractive rural area approximately 25km south-east of Auckland. We are close to a beautiful golf course, beaches and Auckland Airport. We farm angora goats, sheep and free-range hens, pets include a cat and a dog. Guest accommodation is 1 detached double room with ensuite, but children can be accommodated. TV, tea/coffee making facilities, and a private spa pool are available. Directions: left off Whitford Park Road. 1km past Golf Course.

Clevedon *3 km S of Clevedon Village*

The Gables *B&B Cottage with Kitchen*
Phil & Cathy Foulkes
122 Tourist Road, Clevedon, RD 2 Papakura

Tel (09) 292 8373 or 027 494 1249
Fax (09) 292 8372 foulkes@xtra.co.nz
www.the-gables.co.nz

Double $100-$120 Single $90 (Continental provisions)
Child $20 Dinner by arrangement Extra person $20
Visa MC accepted Children welcome
2 Queen 2 Double (2 bdrm)
Bathrooms: 2 Ensuite

In 1988 Phil & Cathy Foulkes set out to create a

dream country home and garden for themselves and their family. Tucked away in their garden are 2 self-contained spacious cottage units where they invite guests to share their hospitality. Set on 10 acres, handy to Clevedon Village each cottage unit offers a queen-size bedroom with ensuite, lounge/dining room with double bed settee, laundry and cooking facilities. Clevedon features green pastures, friendly people and old fashioned hospitality within 30 minutes drive from Auckland CBD and International Airport.

Clevedon *20 km SE of Clevedon*

Pemberley *Farmstay*
Mark & Vanya Bailey
660 Kawakawa-Orere Road, RD 5, Papakura

Tel (09) 292 2698 Fax (09) 292 2698
mvbailey@xtra.co.nz

Double $120 Single $70 (Full breakfast)
Child $40 (5 and over) Dinner $30pp by arrangement
Childcare available Visa MC accepted
Children welcome
1 Double 1 Twin (2 bdrm)
Bathrooms: 2 Ensuite

Haere mai. We're hunter-gatherers living the good
life on a bush farmlet with donkeys, coloured sheep, 2 fat cows, chooks and 2 cheeky in-house terriers!
We're into home-baking, hearty meals, good coffee and wine. Vanya is also trained in vego/Asian
cooking. Swim and relax at our riverside, walk or hunt in the native forest, gather fruit and eggs or tinker
in Mark's Kiwi bloke's shed. Close by are beaches, parks, Hunua Ranges, Miranda hot pools and bird
sanctuary, polo and Ardmore (Warbirds) Airport. Childcare available.

Kaiaua *85 km SE of Auckland*

Kaiaua Seaside Lodge *B&B*
Fran Joseph & Denis Martinovich
1336 Pacific Coast Highway, Kaiaua

Tel (09) 232 2696 or 027 274 0534
Fax (09) 232 2699 kaiaua_lodge@xtra.co.nz

Double $100-$120 Single $75 (Special breakfast)
Children welcome
3 Queen 2 Single (5 bdrm)
Bathrooms: 2 Ensuite 1 Guest share

Situated on the water's edge, 4km north of Kaiaua
township, the Lodge features attractive beach gardens
and panoramic views of the Coromandel. It is ideally
positioned for leisurely seashore strolls or more active tramps in the Hunua Ranges. Boating and fishing
facilities are available and breakfast includes flounder or snapper, in season. Ensuite rooms are spacious
and the separate guest lounge has a refrigerator and television. The Seabird Coast is renowned for its
birdlife, thermal hot pools, nearby Regional Parks and "fish 'n chips".

Kaiaua *82 km SE of Auckland*

Tikapa Moana Lodge *Luxury FarmstayCottage with Kitchen*
Bill Brownell & Marilyn Fisher
30 Pukekereru Lane, Kaiaua, RD 3, Pokeno

Tel (09) 232 2550 or (027) 296 4082
Fax (09) 232 2577 tikapalodge@seabirdcoast.co.nz
www.tikapamoanalodge.co.nz

Double $90 Single $75 (Breakfast extra $15)
1 Queen 1 Single in sitting room.(1bdrm)
Bathroom: 1 Private
Holiday house for larger families & groups ($210 for 8)
4 Double, 2 Single (3 bdrm + lounge)
Bathrooms: 1 Guest share (+ second toilet)

Seaside cottage and B&B in rammed earth house, both situated in 4 acre organic orchard and vegetable
gardens featuring 30 varieties of exotic fruits. Only 30 minutes from Coromandel Peninsula. Hosts:
Marilyn is a Watsu aquatic therapist offering treatments at nearby Miranda Hot Springs (also therapeutic
massage). Bill is a coastal/marine ecologist and keen tramper and kayaker. Kea is our placid old resident
german shepherd. 2 licensed restaurants in Kaiaua (7 minutes drive south) On parle Francais; se habla
Espanol.

Auckland

Miranda *30 km SE of Bombay Hills Freeway*

Miranda Views B&B *B&B Cottage with Kitchen*

Millie & Wayne Taylor

1213 Miranda Road, Miranda, 1872

Tel (09) 232 7800 or 025 942 780
Fax (09) 232 7811
mill@xtra.co.nz

Double $135 **Single** $100 (Full provisions)
Child $30
Visa MC Eftpos accepted
Children welcome
1 Queen 3 Single (2 bdrm)
Bathrooms: 2 Guest share

Our lifestyle farm is situated in the beautiful Miranda Valley; less than an hours drive south from Auckland Airport. Enjoy the panoramic views of our lush valley, the Firth of Thames and Coromandel Ranges in the background. Relax and unwind in your own private chalet, take in views on your own balcony, stroll around our farm, visit some of our local attractions, or just watch a bit of TV. We along with our daughter Ashley and our 2 spoilt cats and 2 friendly dogs welcome you.

~

Papakura *5 km E of Papakura*

Hunua Gorge Country House *B&B Farmstay*

Ben, Brandi and Joy Calway

482 Hunua Road, Papakura, South Auckland

Tel (09) 299 7926 Fax (09) 299 7926
hunuagorge@xtra.co.nz
www.friars.co.nz/hosts/hunua.html

Double $110-$150 **Single** $90 (Full breakfast)
Child depending on age Dinner $25-$35
Visa MC accepted Children welcome
1 King 1 Queen 1 Double 2 Twin 2 Single (5 bdrm)
Bathrooms: 1 Ensuite 1 Family share 1 Private

Welcome to our rural home close to the Auckland Airport and city. On route to Coromandel, a great place to start or end your NZ holiday. Great food, magic sunsets, wild scenery, leafy greenery, starry skies, and views from all rooms. Large comfortable newly decorated home, verandahs, lawns, garden, bush and rural setting on 50 acres with cattle and birdlife. Stay a few days and discover the wonders of Auckland. Fresh food, fresh air, comfortable beds guaranteed. Please phone. Dinner from $25 or $35, 3 courses by prior arrangement. Children welcome.

~

Papakura *1.5 km W of Papakura*

Campbell Clan House *B&B*

Colin & Anna Mieke Campbell

57 Rushgreen Avenue, Papakura

Tel (09) 298 8231 or 027 496 7754
Fax (09) 298 7792 colam@pl.net
www.campbellclan.co.nz

Double $110-$120 **Single** $70-$80 (Full breakfast)
Child negotiable
Dinner $25-$35 by arrangement
Visa MC accepted Children welcome
2 Queen 2 Single (3 bdrm)
Bathrooms: 2 Ensuite 1 Private

Our peaceful location is within walking distance of trains and buses, shopping centre and restaurants. We are 2 minutes from motorway north/south, 15 minutes from airport and enroute to Pacific Coast Scenic Highway. Our separate upstairs guest accomodation includes 3 double bedrooms, large comfortable lounge with tea/coffee, tourist information, TV and private balcony with lovely view. We are happy to assist with any holiday arrangements, car hire, transfers and offer internet and laundry facilities. Discount for 3 or more nights.

Hunua - Paparimu *18 km S of Papakura*
Erathcree Countrystay *B&B Cottage with Kitchen*
Rob & Gillian Wakelin
10 Wilson Road, Paparimu, RD 3, Papakura, Auckland

Tel (09) 292 5062 or 021 128 1547
Fax (09) 292 5064 gillrob@xtra.co.nz

Double $130 Single $100 (Full breakfast)
Child under 12 reduced rate, cot available
Dinner $40pp by arrangement
Additional person $30pp
Visa MC accepted Children and pets welcome
1 Queen 1 Double (1 bdrm & fold out in lounge)
Bathrooms: 1 Private

An easy drive to Auckland Airport/City (40 minutes), quick access to State Highway 2 for travel south ... but in its own tranquil world of green countryside, tree filled garden and Hunua Ranges backdrop. Well travelled hosts offer a warm, helpful welcome, the pets are friendly and the atmosphere relaxed. The cottage is a short garden stroll away from the house, with comfortable beds, fresh fruit and flowers, and small luxuries to make your stay special. Wheelchairs; ground floor access.

Drury *5 km S of Drury*

Tuhimata Park *B&B*
Susan & Pat Baker
697B Runciman Road, Runciman, RD 2, Drury

Tel (09) 294 8748 Fax (09) 294 8749
tuhimata@iprolink.co.nz

Double $90-$120 Single $60-$80 (Full breakfast)
Child negotiable
Visa MC accepted
Children welcome
2 Queen 2 Single (3 bdrm)
Bathrooms: 2 Ensuite 1 Guest share

Our spacious, comfortable, and relaxing home is an ideal place to start or finish a NZ holiday. Only 20 minutes from Auckland Airport and 30 minutes from the city centre. Set in expansive lawns and giant oak trees, with wide verandahs, overlooking rolling green farmland, indoor garden and BBQ in a large conservatory, tennis court, swimming pool, spa pool, and games room. Laundry facilities. Proud members of @home New Zealand - a guarantee of qualitiy accommodation.

Drury *3 km E of Drury*

The Drury Homestead *B&B*
Carolyn & Ron Booker
349 Drury Hills Road, Drury, South Auckland

Tel (09) 294 9030 Fax (09) 294 9035
druryhome@paradise.net.nz

Double $100-$130 Single $70 (Special breakfast)
Child negotiable
Dinner $30
3 Queen 1 Twin (4 bdrm)
Bathrooms: 3 Ensuite 1 Private

Hosts Carolyn and Ron, have undertaken a labour of love in restoring an early colonial home to its former glory. The Drury Homestead was originally built circa 1879 and is set in majestic rolling farmland, bordered by native bush and a glorious tumbling stream. Choose from 4 character filled rooms, all with their own special views. Refurbished with an emphasis on comfort and style. Your comfort our style! Dine with us, enjoying the best of fresh local produce or choose from nearby restaurants. Family cat and dog.

Auckland

Ramarama *1 km N of Bombay*

Thistledown Lodge *B&B Homestay*
Sue & Archie McPherson
1810 Great South Road, Ramarama, Drury RD 3

Tel (09) 236 0044
inquiries@thistledownlodge.co.nz
www.thistledownlodge.co.nz

Double $110-$130 Single $80 (Special breakfast)
Child negotiable Dinner by arrangement
Visa MC accepted Children welcome
1 King 2 Queen 3 Single (4 bdrm)
Bathrooms: 2 Ensuite 2 Private

Relax in a peaceful country setting - it will be the perfect start or end to your holiday. Find out why guests remember Archie's special breakfasts and keep returning for more. Spacious second floor bedrooms in the English colonial style home have TV and welcoming extras. Unwind in the heated swimming pool, spa (jacuzzi) or infrared sauna. You'll enjoy meeting Big Ears and her Suffolk sheep friends and Eric the friendly Highland steer. Easy to find from Ramarama or Bombay motorway exits, secure off-street parking and just 30 minutes from Auckland Airport.

Waiuku *5 km E of Waiuku*

Totara Downs *Homestay*
Janet & Christopher de Tracy-Gould
355 Baldhill Road, RD 1, Waiuku,
Franklin District, Auckland 1852

Tel (09) 235 8505 or 021 118 1616
Fax (09) 235 8504
totaradw@ihug.co.nz
www.totaradowns.co.nz

Double $150 Single $100 (Full breakfast)
Visa MC accepted
1 King/Twin 1 Queen (2 bdrm)
Bathrooms: 1 Ensuite 1 Private

Just 50 minutes drive south from Auckland International Airport and city, Totara Downs is found on a quiet country road. Set in large country house gardens with breath taking rural views. We offer feather and downs pillows and duvets, sitting room with open fire, swimming pool, lawn croquet. Historic Waiuku boasts wonderful peninsula beaches and country garden tours. With Flora our westie and 2 cats we look forward to meeting you. Not suitable for children under 12. Smoke-free home.

Bombay *12 km E of Pukekohe*

Pinnacle Farm Countrystay *B&B Guest House*
Robin & Alton Ross
438 Pinnacle Hill Road, RD Bombay 1850, Auckland

Tel (09) 236 0956 or 021 250 5651
021 060 5359 Fax (09) 236 0957
nzgolfing@clear.net.nz

Double $150 Single $140 (Continental provisions)
Child $30 Children welcome
2 King/Twin 1 Queen (2 bdrm)
Bathrooms: 1 Private

Self-catering, two bedroom guesthouse on 10 acres, 6km from Southern Motorway, 4km from SH2 to Coromandel and Bay of Plenty, & 15 minutes from Pukekohe Racetrack. Exclusive use, with private entrance, own balcony with views, sitting room, TV, kitchenette and electric blankets on each bed. Continental breakfast provisions delivered, other meals available in Bombay (6km), Pukekohe (12km) or self-catering. Chocolate ladrador dog on property under control. A quiet place for your first or last nights in New Zealand. We are 40 minutes south of Auckland Airport.

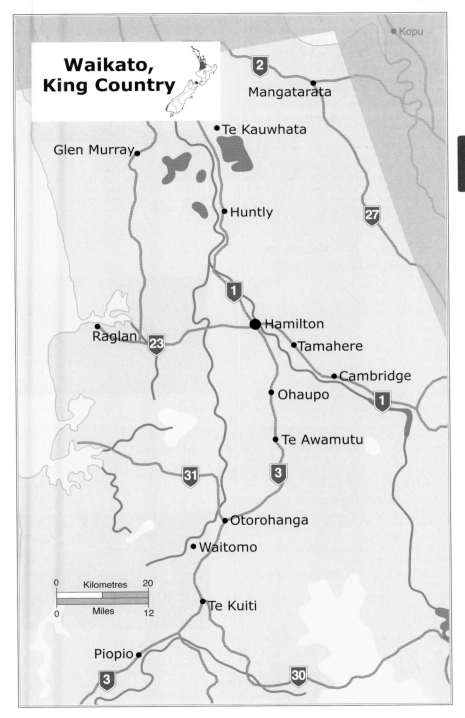

Waikato, King Country

Waikato

Te Kauwhata *7 km E of Te Kauwhata*
Herons Ridge *Farmstay Cottage No Kitchen*
David Sharland
1131 Lake Waikare Scenic Drive, RD 1, Te Kauwhata

Tel (07) 826 4646 Fax (07) 826 4646
herons.ridge@xtra.co.nz
www.huntly.net.nz/herons.html

Double $100-$140 Single $60-$80 (Full breakfast)
Child discounted Dinner by arrangement
Self-contained studio $140
Children and pets welcome
1 King 2 Queen 1 Double 1 Twin 1 Single (4 bdrm)
Bathrooms: 2 Ensuite 1 Private

Welcome to your home in the Waikato. Our quality inhouse family suite and superb garden studio overlooking the pool and garden are the perfect setting for your stay. The horse stud, set amongst ponds and pinewoods, enhance our rural location close to Lake Waikare. Meals are served inhouse. Horse riding, country walks, golf and hot springs - the choice is yours. From SH1 go through Te Kauwhata Village, 6km east along Waerenga Road, 1km on right - Welcome.

~

Glen Murray - Te Kauwhata *22 km W of Te Kauwhata*
Awaroa Vineyard Cottage *Luxury B&B Farmstay Cottage with Kitchen*
Jan and Brian White
121 Insoll Road, Glen Murray

Tel (09) 233 3289 or 021 773 327
Fax (09) 233 3290 jan_white@xtra.co.nz

Double $120 Single $80 (Full provisions)
Dinner $35
Visa MC accepted
Children welcome
1 King/Twin 1 Queen (2 bdrm)
Bathrooms: 1 Private

Awaroa Cottage offers attractive self-contained accommodation with panoramic rural views. Guests can relax in the lounge, barbecue in the private garden or stroll around our boutique vineyard. Dine under the stars and fall asleep to sound of the morepork calling. Our hamper breakfast ensures you wake and dine at your leisure. We share the historic homestead with our 2 cats. Just 1 hour from Auckland and Hamilton and within easy reach of Te Kauwhata cafes, wineries, excellent golf courses and other tourist attractions.

~

Huntly *4 km NW of Huntly*
Parnassus Farm & Garden *B&B Farmstay Cottage with Kitchen*
Sharon & David Payne
Te Ohaki Road, RD 1, Huntly

Tel (07) 828 8781 or 021 458 525
Fax (07) 828 8781 parnassus@xtra.co.nz
www.parnassus.co.nz

Double $120-$140 Single $70-$100 (Full breakfast)
Child according to age
Dinner by arrangement
Visa MC accepted
Children welcome
2 King/Twin 2 Double 2 Single (3 bdrm)
Bathrooms: 1 Guest share 3 Private

Experience farm life or simply relax on a working farm 1 hour south of Auckland & only 4km off SH1. All bedrooms beautifully appointed with private facilities. Our home gardens supply produce & preserves for the Farm to Fork dinning experience we are renowned for & showcase a diverse range of trees & shrubs, fruits & vegetables. Farm, bush & wetland walks all easily accessible. Leave SH1 at traffic lights by Huntly KFC. Cross river, right, Harris Street 2km, right, Te Ohaki Road, number 191.

Raglan *20 km S of Raglan*
Matawha *Farmstay*
Jenny & Peter Thomson
61 Matawha Road, RD 2, Raglan

Tel (07) 825 6709 Fax (07) 825 6715
jennyt@wave.co.nz

Double $100-$120 Single $50-$60 (Full breakfast)
Cash or cheque only please Dinner $20
1 King 1 Double 4 Single (3 bdrm)
Bathrooms: 1 Family share 1 Private

We live on the west coast and our family has farmed this land for 100 years. Come and enjoy our private beach, expansive garden, home-grown vegetables, spa, 2 cats and the peace of no other buildings or people for miles. Take bush or mountain walks, a scenic drive, go surfing or fishing, or maybe find the hot-water beach!
Directions: Take Hamilton/Raglan route 23, turn left at Bridal Veil Falls sign, right at Te Mata onto Ruapuke Rd, left onto Tuturimu Road and follow to T-junction, straight ahead across cattlestop – 61 Matawha Road. Auckland 2.5hrs, Hamilton 1hr, Raglan 30min.

Hamilton *3 km N of Hamilton*
Kantara *Homestay*
Mrs Esther Kelly
7 Delamare Road, Bryant Park, Hamilton

Tel (07) 849 2070
esther@slingshot.co.nz

Double $100-$125 Single $65 (Full breakfast)
Dinner $25
Pet free home Not suitable for children
1 Double 1 Twin (2 bdrm)
Bathrooms: 1 Ensuite 1 Private

I have travelled extensively throughout New Zealand and overseas and welcome tourists to my comfortable home. I live close to the Waikato River with its tranquil river walks and St Andrews Golf Course. My interests are travel, golf, tramping, Mah Jong and gardening. Tea/coffee making facilities are available. I look forward to offering you friendly hospitality. Directions: from Auckland - leave main Highway north of Hamilton at second round intersection into Bryant Road. Turn left into Sandwich Road and second street on right.

Hamilton *1.5 km E of Hamilton Central*
Matthews B&B *B&B Homestay*
Maureen & Graeme Matthews
24 Pearson Avenue, Claudelands, Hamilton

Tel (07) 855 4269 or 027 474 7758
Fax (07) 855 4269 mgm@xtra.co.nz
www.matthewsbnb.co.nz

Double $75-$90 Single $50-$60 (Full breakfast)
Child half price Dinner $20
Visa MC accepted
1 Double 1 Twin (2 bdrm)
Bathrooms: 1 Family share 1 Guest share

Welcome to our home 2 seconds off the city bypass on Routes 7 & 9 at Five Crossroads. We are adjacent to the Waikato Events Centre, Ruakura Research Station, handy to the university and only 3 minutes from central city. Our home is a lived-in comfortable home, warm in winter and cool in summer, with a pool available. We enjoy spending time with visitors from NZ and overseas. We have travelled extensively and enjoy helping to plan your holiday. Dinner by arrangement.

Waikato

Hamilton *In Hamilton Central*
Ebbett Homestay *B&B Homestay*
Glenys & John Ebbett
162 Beerescourt Road, Hamilton

Tel (07) 849 2005
johnebbett@xtra.co.nz

Double $95 **Single** $65 (Full breakfast)
Dinner $25 Pet free home
Not suitable for children
2 Single (1 bdrm)
Bathrooms: 1 Private

Only minutes from town centre, our 14 year old home
has a spectacular view of the Waikato River (New
Zealand's longest) and easy access to Hamilton's popular river walk. We enjoy sharing travel anecdotes,
but also respect our guests' wish for privacy. Your room has its own tea/coffee facility and private
bathroom. 85 minutes from Auckland International Airport, we appeal to tourists arriving or departing
New Zealand. Our interests include people, music, sport, travel, gardening and community. We have
had 12 years of happy hosting.

Hamilton *In Hamilton Central*
Dixon Homestay *Homestay*
Judy & Brian Dixon
50A Queenwood Avenue, Chartwell, Hamilton

Tel (07) 855 7324
ju.dixon@xtra.co.nz
www.opotiki2.co.nz/waiotahi

Double $80 **Single** $50 (Continental)
1 Queen 1 Single (1 bdrm)
Bathrooms: 1 Private

Haere mai - Welcome to our comfortable smoke-
free, homely Lockwood nestled within a quiet garden.
Guests have sole access to their bathroom and bedroom.
Our aim is to provide a warm environment where guests relax and enjoy themselves. Within walking
distance are popular Cafe en Q, The Platter Place, Chartwell Square and Waikato River walks. We also
have a beach home with magnificent sea views near Opotiki if requested. We share our home with a
friendly cat named Zapper. Directions: please phone.

Hamilton - Ohaupo *4 km SW of Hamilton*
Green Gables of Rukuhia *B&B Homestay*
Earl & Judi McWhirter
35 Rukuhia Road, RD 2, Ohaupo

Tel (07) 843 8511 Fax (07) 843 8514
judi.earl@clear.net.nz

Double $80-$90 **Single** $40-$50 (Continental)
Dinner by arrangement
Visa MC accepted
2 Double 3 Single (3 bdrm)
Bathrooms: 1 Guest share

Warm, comfortable smoke-free family home in a quiet rural setting,
close to Hamilton, airport and field days (Mystery Creek). Free pick up/delivery airport, bus, train
terminal all part of the friendly service. 5km to Vilagrad Winery; 2 minutes walk to Gostiona Restaurant.
2 storeyed house with guest rooms, lounge downstairs; dining, hosts upstairs. Fresh home-baked bread
and selection of coffees to suit. Judi lectures statistics, University of Waikato. Earl is a "retired" school
teacher. 1 teenage daughter still lives at home. Non-smokers preferred.

Hamilton *4 km S of Hamilton*
The Poplars *Home & Garden*
Lesley & Peter Ramsay
402 Matangi Road, RD 4, Hamilton

Tel (07) 829 5551 or 027 668 0985
pramsay@ihug.co.nz
www.geocities.com/thepoplarsnz/

Double $95 Single $70 (Full breakfast)
Dinner $30pp by arrangement
Visa MC accepted   Children and pets welcome
1 King 1 Twin (2 bdrm)
Bathrooms: 1 Private

Just minutes from Hamilton, Mystery Creek and Cambridge, The Poplars offers a haven of peace and quiet. Set in a majestic 3 acre garden with internationally acclaimed daffodils, 500 roses and many water features. Each guest room has tea and coffee making facilities, electric blankets and TV. Solar heated swimming pool and spa are adjacent to guest rooms. Hosts Peter and Lesley, themselves seasoned travellers, offer you the charms of country living. A warm welcome shared with family pets awaits you. A unique and special place to stay. Directions: Please phone.

Hamilton *28 km S of Hamilton*
Country Quarters Homestay *B&B Homestay*
Ngaere & Jack Waite
11 Corcoran Road, Te Pahu, Hamilton

Tel (07) 825 9727 graeme.waite@xtra.co.nz

Double $80 Single $40 (Full breakfast)
Child $10 Dinner $25 Caravan $15
Children and pets welcome
1 Queen 1 Twin 3 Single (5 bdrm)
Bathrooms: 1 Guest share

We welcome you to the peace and tranquillity of country life. Our place is central from Te Awamutu and Hamilton, located in the little farming community of Te Pahu, right under Mount Pirongia. We are in the middle of a block of chestnut trees and are quite secluded. We have our small dog and 2 fat cats. Our home is very large and roomy and we have special facilities for the elderly person. Comfort and nice meals is what we offer you.

Hamilton - Tamahere *10 km S of Hamilton*
Lenvor B&B *B&B Homestay*
Lenora & Trevor Shelley
540E Oaklea Lane, RD 3, Tamahere, Hamilton

Tel (07) 856 2027 Fax (07) 856 4173
lenvor@clear.net.nz

Double $110 Single $65 (Full breakfast)
Child $10-$25
Dinner by arrangement
Children welcome
3 Queen 3 Single (4 bdrm)
Bathrooms: 1 Ensuite 1 Family share 2 Guest share

Lenora and Trevor warmly invite you to relax and to share the comfort of our home Lenvor, which is set in a rural area, down a country lane. Our 2 storeyed home has guest rooms and small lounge upstairs; dining, lounge and hosts downstairs. 10 minutes to Hamilton or Cambridge, 5 minutes to Mystery Creek or airport. Lenora's interests are floral art and cake icing. Trevor enjoys vintage cars. Centrally situated for day trips to Coromandel, Tauranga, Rotorua, Taupo and Waitomo Caves.

Hamilton *10 km E of Hamilton*

A&A Country Stay *Farmstay Cottage with Kitchen*
Ann & Alan Marsh
275 Vaile Road, RD 4, Hamilton

Tel (07) 824 1908 or (07) 8241909
027 476 3014 Fax (07) 824 1908
aacountrystay@ callplus.net.nz

Double $100 Single $60 (Provisions first night)
Child $20 Weekly rates for long-term stays
Visa MC Diners accepted
Children and pets welcome
1 Queen 2 Single (2 bdrm)
Bathrooms: 1 Private

The Cottage is fully self-contained, 2 bedrooms, including laundry and Sky digital. Peaceful surroundings set in 2 acres of garden with a large pond. Sit, relax in privacy out on the veranda, have our ducks and doves visit you for that bit of bread while overlooking our 47 acres with sheep and cattle. Have a talk to our clydesdale (Sarah) and our miniature (Sha) who love people staying especially when they have apples in their hand. 2 Jack Russells who will also welcome you.

Ohaupo *15 km S of Hamilton*

Ridge House *B&B*
Margaret Birtles & Matthew Harris
15 Main Road, Ohaupo

Tel (07) 823 6555 Fax (07) 823 6550
m.a.birtles@xtra.co.nz

Double $80-$90 Single $65 (Continental)
Child $15 Dinner $20 by arrangement
Visa MC accepted
Children and pets welcome
1 Queen 2 Double 1 Single (3 bdrm)
Bathrooms: 1 Ensuite 1 Guest share

We welcome you to come and visit our home with its
wonderful lake and pastoral views. Our home is shared with our dog, Zoe, who loves to welcome visitors. We are just 6 minutes to Hamilton International Airport and can arrange pick up from there and car storage ($10). This is an ideal base for trips to Hamilton, Te Awamutu, Waitomo Caves, Cambridge, Rotorua and Tauranga. Mystery Creek (home of the Field Days) and popular golf courses are close by. Travel well.

Hamilton *12 km SW of Hamilton*

Uliveto Countrystay *Countrystay B&B*
Peter & Daphne Searle
164 Finlayson Road, RD 10, Ngahinapouri, Hamilton

Tel (07) 825 2116 or 027 200 5320
peedee@wave.co.nz www.uliveto.co.nz

Double up to $120 Single $90 (Full breakfast)
Dinner by arrangement
Pet free home
Children welcome
2 Queen (2 bdrm)
Bathrooms: 2 Ensuite Private ensuite

We offer peace and tranquility in a brand new purpose
built house, set in a newly planted olive grove located down a quiet no exit road, directly off SH39, in the Waikato countryside. Each bedroom has a comfortable, queen-size bed with own private ensuite. External access from your own deck allows you complete privacy and a place to relax in the tranquil surroundings. Shared guest lounge with tea/coffee making facilities, Sky TV, stereo. Relaxing therapeutic spa available. Only 20 minutes drive to central Hamilton.

Cambridge *In Cambridge Central*
Park House *B&B*
Pat & Bill Hargreaves
70 Queen Street, Cambridge

Tel (07) 827 6368 Fax (07) 827 4094
Park.House@xtra.co.nz www.parkhouse.co.nz

Double up to $160 Single $120 (Full breakfast)
Visa MC Amex accepted
Not suitable for children
1 King/Twin 1 Queen (2 bdrm)
Bathrooms: 1 Ensuite 1 Private

Park House, circa 1920, is for guests of discernment who appreciate quality and comfort. For 18 years we have offered this superb setting for guests. Throughout this large home are antiques, traditional furniture, patchworks and stained glass windows creating an elegant and restful ambience. The guest lounge features an elaborately carved fireplace, fine art, library, TV and complimentary sherry. Bedrooms in separate wing upstairs ensues privacy. Unbeatable quiet location overlooking village green, 2 minute walk to restaurants, antique and craft shops.

≈

Cambridge *5 km SW of Cambridge*
Birches *B&B Farmstay Cottage No Kitchen*
Sheri Mitchell & Hugh Jellie
263 Maungatautari Road, PO Box 194, Cambridge

Tel (07) 827 6556 or 021 882 216
Fax (07) 827 3552 birches@ihug.co.nz
www.birches.co.nz

Double $100 Single $65 (Full breakfast)
Child by arrangement Dinner by arrangement
Visa MC Amex accepted
Children and pets welcome
1 Queen 1 Double 1 Single (2 bdrm)
Bathrooms: 1 Ensuite 1 Private

Our 1930's character farmhouse offers open fires in guests' sitting room, tennis and swimming pool set in country garden amongst picturesque horse studs. Proximity to Cambridge and Lake Karapiro makes Birches an ideal base for lake users. Hugh, a veterinarian, and I are widely travelled. Olivia, 13, is happy to show her farm pets and cat. Little Cherry Tree Cottage (queen/ensuite) is ideal for couples wanting privacy. The twin room in farmhouse has private bathroom with spa bath. We serve delicious farmhouse breakfasts alfresco or in dining room.

≈

Cambridge *2 km S of Cambridge*
Glenelg *B&B Homestay*
Shirley & Ken Geary
6 Curnow Place, Cambridge

Tel (07) 823 0084 Fax (07) 823 4279
glenelgbnb@ihug.co.nz

Double $100 Single $65 (Full breakfast)
Child $20 Dinner $20 by arrangement
Visa MC accepted
Children and pets welcome
3 Queen 1 Twin (4 bdrm)
Bathrooms: 3 Ensuite 1 Private

Glenelg welcomes you to Cambridge to a new home with quality spacious accommodation - warm quiet and private overlooking Waikato farmland, with plenty of off-street parking. Beds have electric blankets and woolrests. 200 rose bushes in the garden. 5 minutes to Lake Karapiro. Mystery Creek, where NZ National Field Days and many other functions are held is only 15 minutes away. Laundry facilities available. No smoking indoors please. Home away from home. For a brochure and directions please phone. Evening dinner by arrangement. Pets and children are welcome.

Waikato

Cambridge *10 km N of Cambridge*
Dunfarmin *B&B Countrystay B & B*
Jackie & Bob Clarke
46 Oaklea Lane, RD 3, Hamilton

Tel (07) 856 6643 Fax (07) 856 6032
dunfarmin@wave.co.nz

Double $100 Single $60 (Full breakfast)
Child $25 Dinner $25 by arrangement
Visa MC accepted
Children welcome
2 Queen 2 Single (3 bdrm)
Bathrooms: 1 Ensuite 1 Guest share

Welcome to our new home built among chestnut trees
in a rural area, We are situated mid-way between Cambridge and Hamilton, 2 minutes off Highway
1. 5 minutes away are the Hamilton Airport and Mystery Creek. Close by is the Waikato River with its
lovely river walks and the paddle steamer and Hamilton Gardens. Cambridge has many cafes, restaurants,
antique and craft shops. We are ex-farmers with now only alpacas, Mary the cow and Possum the cat.

Cambridge *2 km S of Cambridge*
Pamade B&B *B&B Cottage with Kitchen*
Paul & Marion Derikx
229 Shakespeare Street, Cambridge - Leamington,
- opposite turn off to Karapiro Lake

Tel (07) 827 4916 Fax (07) 827 4988
pamades@slingshot.co.nz

Double $85-$95 Single $55-$65 (Special breakfast)
Dinner by arrangement
1 King 1 Queen 1 Twin 4 Single (3 bdrm)
Bathrooms: 2 Ensuite 1 Private

Pamade is a character home, very comfortable with
beautiful gardens. We are situated 2 minutes from
central Cambridge with its wonderful selection of fascinating art, craft, boutique and antique shops,
restaurants, stud farms and golf course. Just around the corner from Lake Karapiro (5 minutes drive),
with its water skiing, rowing and other aquatic sports. Mystery Creek (Fieldays) is only 10 minutes drive
away. Self-contained unit plus large double room (ensuite and coffee and tea arrangements) with private
exit. Ideal for longer stays. Great breakfast guaranteed. Dinner by prior arrangement.

Cambridge *1 km S of Cambridge*
Cambridge Handi Homestay *B&B Homestay*
Isobel & Harry Hopkins
7 Marlowe Drive, Cambridge

Tel (07) 823 2142 Fax (07) 823 2143
handi.homestay@xtra.co.nz
www.handi-homestay.co.nz

Double $85-$100 Single $55-$65 (Full breakfast)
Child $20 (under 5 free if sharing parents room)
Children welcome
1 Queen 1 Double 1 Twin (3 bdrm)
Bathrooms: 1 Ensuite

A warm welcome awaits you at our home close to
the Waikato River. Spacious guestrooms have TV, tea and coffee facilities. Superb breakfast. Easily
located with tranquil gardens, a pleasant stroll to town centre - close to childrens playgrounds. Drive to
South end of Victoria Street (Main Street), cross bridge and turn right at roundabout onto Pope Street
- Highway to Te Awamutu. Marlowe Drive is first on the right.

Cambridge *1 km NE of Cambridge*

Bacton House *B&B*

Mary & John Cubitt

46 Williams Street, Cambridge

Tel (07) 827 3353 or 027 696 7594
Fax (07) 827 3353
mjcubitt@wave.co.nz
www.bactonhouse.co.nz

Double $100-$110 Single $90 (Full breakfast)
Visa MC accepted
2 Queen (2 bdrm)
Bathrooms: 1 Ensuite 1 Private

Welcome to Bacton House. Centrally situated, Bacton House offers large rooms with complete quiet and privacy. Enjoy the large garden and swimming pool. Bedrooms have been completely refurbished using quality materials and with your comfort in mind. Queen-size beds, electric blankets, comfortable lounge chairs, television, tea/coffee making facilities, private bathroom/ensuite, power showers. A delicious cooked breakfast is offered in the guest's dining room. Lady Grey is our resident cat.

Te Awamutu *4.5 km N of Te Awamutu*

Bleskie Farmstay *Farmstay*

Mrs R Bleskie & C Bleskie

Storey Road, Te Awamutu

Tel (07) 871 3301
sophy@ihug.co.nz

Double $115 Single $60 (Full breakfast)
Child $25 Dinner $25
Children and pets welcome
1 Double 8 Single (5 bdrm)
Bathrooms: 1 Ensuite 1 Family share 1 Guest share

The 85 acre farm, situated in beautiful country side with cattle, horses, pigs, poultry, sheep, goats and pets.
A spacious home welcomes you with swimming pool and tennis court. Large guest rooms with doors to garden. Specials: horseback riding and gig rides for children and adults for $10 a ride. Raspberry picking in season and access to the milking of 500 dairy cows.

Te Awamutu *2 km S of Te Awamutu*

Leger Farm *B&B Farmstay*

Beverley & Peter Bryant

114 St Leger Road, Te Awamutu

Tel (07) 871 6676 Fax (07) 871 6679

Double $125-$140 Single $85-$10 (Full breakfast)
Dinner $35
1 Queen 1 Double 1 Twin 3 Single (4 bdrm)
Bathrooms: 1 Ensuite 1 Guest share 1 Private

Leger Farm is a private residence with country living at its finest. The discerning leisure traveller seeking quality accommodation, in peaceful, relaxing surroundings, will find warm hospitality and every comfort here. Spacious bedrooms share stunning panoramic views of surrounding countryside. Each bedroom has its own balcony with beautiful garden vistas. We farm cattle and sheep, and are centrally based for visiting Waitomo Caves and black water rafting, Rotorua with its thermal activity and NZ's dramatic West Coast and ironstone sands. Golf course nearby for relaxation. Smoke-free home.

Waikato

Te Awamutu *4 km S of Te Awamutu*
Morton Homestay *B&B Homestay*
Marg & Dick Morton
10 Brill Road, RD 5, Te Awamutu

Tel (07) 871 8814 Fax (07) 871 8865

Double $80 Single $50 (Full breakfast)
Dinner $25 by arrangement
Rates negotiable for 3 or more people
Visa MC accepted
1 Double 4 Single (3 bdrm)
Bathrooms: 1 Private

We welcome visitors to enjoy our hospitality and the peacefulness of our home 5 minutes from the centre of New Zealand's Rosetown. Waitomo, Rotorua and Lake Taupo are within easy driving distance from us. Hamilton Airport and Mystery Creek are 20 minutes away. Te Awamutu is an excellent base for bushwalking, golfing, fishing and garden visits. Gardening, philately and music are among our interests. We also have an interest in classic cars. Direction. Please phone or fax for reservations and directions.

Otorohanga - Waitomo District *8 km NW of Otorohanga*
Meadowland *B&B Farmstay Cottage with Kitchen*
Jill & Tony Webber
746 State Highway 31, RD 3, Otorohanga

Tel (07) 873 7729 Fax (07) 873 7719
meadowland@xtra.co.nz

Double $85 Single $60 (Full breakfast)
Child $20
Visa MC accepted
Children welcome
2 Queen 1 Double 1 Twin 2 Single (5 bdrm)
Bathrooms: 1 Guest share 1 Private

Welcome to Meadowland. Our accommodation is: a self-contained unit which can sleep up to 6 - extra adults $25. 1 twin and 2 double bedrooms in homestead with guest shared bathroom and separate toilet. All beds have woolrests and electric blankets. We have a tennis court, swimming pool and spa pool on site. We are 5 minutes from the Otorohanga Kiwi House & Aviary, 20 minutes from Waitomo Caves area, 20 minutes to 3 golf courses. Non-smokers preferred. Subsequent nights $20 less.

Waitomo Caves *9.7 km W of Waitomo Village*
Te Tiro *B&B Farmstay Cottage with Kitchen*
Rachel & Angus Stubbs
970 Caves Te Anga Road, RD 8 Te Kuiti

Tel (07) 878 6328 Fax (07) 878 6328
stubbs.a_r@xtra.co.nz www.waitomocavesnz.com

Double $90-$100 Single $70 (Continental provisions)
Child $15
Visa MC accepted
Children and pets welcome
2 Queen 4 Single (2 bdrm)
Bathrooms: 2 Private

Te Tiro (The View) welcomes you. Enjoy fantastic panoramic views of the central North Island and mountains. At night enjoy glowworms nestled in lush NZ bush only metres from your cottage. Situated on an established sheep farm with 350 acres of reserve bush. Our self-contained pioneer style cottages can accommodate up to 5 people in a cosy open plan room. Hosts Rachel and Angus have 30 years of tourism experience between them and would be happy to advise you on the wonders of Waitomo.

Waitomo Caves *16 km S of Otorohanga*
Waitomo Caves Guest Lodge *B&B Separate units*
Janet & Colin Beeston
PO Box 16, Waitomo Caves

Tel (07) 878 7641 Fax (07) 878 7466
jancolbeeston@xtra.co.nz
www.waitomocavesguestlodge.co.nz

Double $80-$90 Single $60 (Continental)
Child $10 Extra adult $20
Visa MC accepted
Children welcome
6 Queen 1 Twin 5 Single (7 bdrm)
Bathrooms: 7 Ensuite

We are located right in the centre of Waitomo Caves Village, next to the store and an easy walking distance to the Information Centre and Museum, the glowworm caves and various eating places. Our quality ensuite units are in a beautiful, peaceful garden setting, with lovely views over the Waitomo Domain and surrounding bush. You can expect a warm welcome from Janet, Colin & Gypsy, the family dog. We have travelled widely in New Zealand and can advise you knowledgeably on your itinerary.

Te Kuiti - Waitomo District *20 km NW of Te Kuiti*
Tapanui Country Home *Luxury B&B Homestay Farmstay Separate Suite*
Sue & Mark Perry
1714 Oparure Road, Te Kuiti

Tel (07) 877 8549 or 027 494 9873
Fax (07) 877 8541 tapanuibnb@ihug.co.nz
www.tapanui.co.nz

Double $180-$195 Single $170-$185 (Full breakfast)
Dinner by arrangement Visa MC Diners accepted
Not suitable for children
2 King/Twin 1 Single (2 bdrm)
Bathrooms: 1 Ensuite 1 Private

Elegant country retreat near the Waitomo attractions. Enjoy elegance, peace and uninterrupted views of hill country pasture. Relax and recharge with comfortable, quality super-king/twin beds, cotton waffle bathrobes & slippers, hair dryers, quality towels, heated towel rails, spacious ensuite and private bathroom. Experience New Zealand farming hospitality and delicious cooked meals with NZ wine while recharging from Waitomo adventures and activities. Meet the family of hand-reared sheep, pig, goat, donkey & resident cat on 770-hectare sheep and beef farm. Guests welcome after 4pm. Adults only.

Te Kuiti - Waitomo District *6 km E of Te Kuiti*
Panorama Farm *B&B Homestay Farmstay*
Raema & Michael Warriner
65 Carter Road, RD 2, Te Kuiti

Tel (07) 878 5104 Fax (07) 878 8104
panoramab.b@xtra.co.nz

Double $72 Single $36 (Full breakfast)
Child $18 Dinner $20
Visa MC accepted
Children and pets welcome
1 Double 3 Single (2 bdrm)
Bathrooms: 1 Guest share

Raema, Michael and the cat welcome you to our hill top home, overlooking bush clad hills, fertile valleys and distant peaks with golden dawns and spectacular sunsets. We offer comfortable beds and the quiet surroundings of a 30 hectare farm plus 40 years experience of the district and its attractions. Waitomo is 25 minutes away, Rotorua, Taupo 2 hours so come and enjoy the company, the scenery and a good night's rest. Arriving or departing from Auckland - we are 2 1/2 hours to the airport.

Waikato

Te Kuiti - Waitomo District *1 km S of Te Kuiti Post Office*

Sanaig House *B&B Homestay*
Sue & Mike Wagstaff
35 Awakino Road, Te Kuiti

Tel (07) 878 7128 Fax (07) 878 7128
sanaig@xtra.co.nz

Double $100 **Single** $70 (Continental)
2 Queen 1 Double (3 bdrm)
Bathrooms: 1 Ensuite 1 Private

Sanaig House built in 1903 is one of Te Kuiti's gracious homesteads. Our guest bedrooms are attractive, spacious and overlook a garden with lovely mature trees. The Waitomo area, famous for its glowworm caves, has a variety of other exciting outdoor adventures: blackwater rafting, abseiling, quad bike riding and horse riding. Relaxing bush walks, fishing, bird watching and garden visits can all be arranged. Sanaig House is only 500 metres from a good restaurant and there is a selection of cafes and other restaurants in Te Kuiti.

Te Kuiti - Waitomo District *2 km N of Te Kuiti*

Simply the Best B&B *B&B Farmstay Campervans welcome $20pp*
Margaret & Graeme Churstain
129 Gadsby Road, RD 5, Te Kuiti

Tel (07) 878 8191 Fax (07) 878 5949
enquiry@simplythebestbnb.co.nz
www.simplythebestbnb.co.nz

Double $80 **Single** $40 (Continental)
Dinner $20pp by arrangement
Children welcome
1 Queen 1 Double 1 Twin (3 bdrm)
Bathrooms: 1 Ensuite 1 Private

Welcome to our peaceful farmlet signposted off SH3, northern end of Te Kuiti (Shearing Capital of the World). Stay away from the commercial sector for a day or 2 and enjoy stunning rural views, comfortable living and good kiwi hospitality. The Waitomo Caves are 10 minutes away or enjoy a scenic west coast day trip. Sheepshearing, dairy milking shed viewings and trout fishing can be arranged. Within 2.5 hours of Auckland International Airport this is simply the best way to begin or end your New Zealand journey.

Te Kuiti - Waitomo District *2 km N of Te Kuiti*

Gadsby Heights *B&B Homestay Farmstay*
Janis & Ross MacDonald
137 Gadsby Road, RD 5, Te Kuiti

Tel (07) 878 3361 or 027 696 7122
Fax (07) 878 3361 info@gadsbyheights.co.nz
www.gadsbyheights.co.nz

Double $85-$100 **Single** $50-$60 (Full breakfast)
Child $15 Dinner $25pp by arrangement
Visa MC accepted
Children welcome   Pets welcome
1 Queen 1 Double 2 Single (2 bdrm)
Bathrooms: 1 Ensuite 1 Private

Fantastic views, farm animals, lovely gardens, just 2 minutes from Te Kuiti and 10 minutes to Waitomo. Ross, Janis, Sophie (6) and Sox the cat welcome you to Gadsby Heights. Warm and friendly accommodation, conveniently located for you to take advantage of all that the Waitomo area and the central North Island have to offer. We have sheep shearing, dog demonstration, farm visits by appointment and a tour service available to take you off the beaten track, to out of the way places and beyond. We look forward to meeting you.

Pio Pio - Waitomo District *19 km S of Te Kuiti*

Carmel Farm *B&B Homestay Farmstay*
Barbara & Leo Anselmi
Main Road, PO Box 93, Pio Pio

Tel (07) 877 8130 Fax (07) 877 8130
Carmelfarms@xtra.co.nz

Double $100 Single $50 (Continental)
Dinner $25pp
Children and pets welcome
2 King/Twin 4 Single (4 bdrm)
Bathrooms: 1 Ensuite 1 Family share

Barbara and Leo Anselmi own and operate a 2000 acre sheep, beef and dairy farm. You will be welcomed into a 3000 square feet modern home set in picturesque gardens, in a lovely limestone valley.

You will be treated to delicious home-cooked meals and the warmth of our friendship.

Whether enjoying the excitement of mustering mobs of cattle and sheep, viewing the milking of 550 cows, driving around the rolling hills on the 4 wheeled farm-bike, relaxing as you bask in the sun by the pool or wandering through the gardens, you will experience unforgettable memories of breathtaking scenery, a clean green environment.

We have farm pets who love the attention of our guests. The donkeys are waiting to be fed. We look over a beautiful 18 hole golf course which welcomes visitors.

The property is a short distance from black water rafting and canoeing activities, The Lost World Cavern, and the famous Waitomo Caves. Nearby are bush walks and the home of the rare kokako bird. We can help to arrange activities for people of all ages and interests including garden visits and horse riding. Please let us know your preference. We are 140km from Rotorua/Taupo.

Directions: Travel 19km south of Te Kuiti on SH3 towards Piopio. Carmel Farm is on the right. We can arrange to pick up from Otorohanga, Te Kuiti or Waitomo, if required.

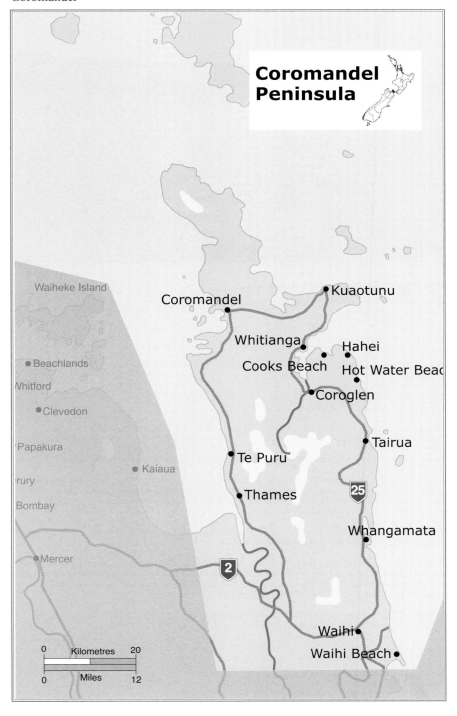

Coromandel
Peninsula

Waiheke Island

Kuaotunu

Coromandel

Whitianga

Hahei

Cooks Beach

Hot Water Beach

● Beachlands

Coroglen

Whitford

● Clevedon

Papakura

Tairua

● Kaiaua

rury

Te Puru

Bombay

25

Thames

Whangamata

● Mercer

2

Waihi

Waihi Beach

0   Kilometres   20

0   Miles   12

Thames *8 km SE of Thames*

Wharfedale Farmstay *Farmstay Cottage No Kitchen*
Rosemary Burks
RD 1, Kopu, Thames

Tel (07) 868 8929 Fax (07) 868 8926
wharfedale@xtra.co.nz

Double $100-$135 **Single** $95 (Full breakfast)
Not suitable children Visa MC accepted
1 Double 2 Single (2 bdrm)
Bathrooms: 2 Private

For 15 years our guests have enjoyed the beauty of
Wharfedale which has featured in Air NZ's "Airwaves"
and Japan's "My Country" magazines. We invite
you to share our idyllic lifestyle set in 9 acres of park-like paddocks and gardens, surrounded by native
bush. Delight in private river swimming, abundant bird life, our dairy goats. We enjoy wholefood and
organically grown produce. There are cooking facilities in the studio apartment. We have no children or
indoor animals. Cool shade in summer and cozy log fires and electric blankets in winter.

Thames *6.4 km E of Thames*

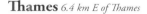

Mountain Top B&B *Homestay*

Elizabeth McCracken & Allan Berry
452 Kauaeranga Valley Road, RD 2, Thames

Tel (07) 868 9662 Fax (07) 868 9662
nzh_mountain.top@xtra.co.nz

Double $115-$120 **Single** $80 (Full breakfast)
Child half price Dinner $30-$35
Visa MC Diners Amex accepted
Children and pets welcome
1 Queen 2 Twin (2 bdrm)
Bathrooms: 1 Guest share

Allan and I grow mandarins, native trees and raise
coloured sheep on a small organic farm. Our private,
peaceful, guest wing with lounge, TV and extensive
library has bedrooms and decks with superb views overlooking river, forest swimming pools and
mountains. Nearby Coromandel Forest Park has wonderful walking tracks. We have a productive,
rambly garden, Jack Russell Roly, cat Priscilla. No cell phone coverage - best to phone mornings or
evenings. We love entertaining and cooking for people, mostly from farm produce. Let's look after you.

Thames *4 km E of Thames*

Acorn Lodge *B&B*
Dennis & Pat
161 Kauaeranga Valley, RD 2, Thames

Tel (07) 868 8723
Fax (07) 868 8713
AcornLodge@xtra.co.nz

Double $110 **Single** $70 (Full breakfast)
Child negotiable
Visa MC accepted
1 Queen 1 Double 1 Single (3 bdrm)
Bathrooms: 2 Private

Relax and enjoy the tranquil views from our spacious
home set in 2 acres of park-like grounds. Enjoy a pot of tea or coffee and home-baking on your sunny
patio or relax in your comfortable lounge featuring an atrium and waterfall. At night marvel at the
glowworms - only 2 minutes walk. Our interests include tramping in the nearby Forest Park, fishing and
gardening. Dennis and Pat, along with Penny, our cat and Coco, our friendly german shepherd, assure
you of a warm welcome.

Coromandel

Thames *3 km S of Thames*

Totara Valley Barns *B&B*
Shona & Bruz MacGregor
65 Totara Valley Road, RD 1, Thames

Tel (07) 868 9730 or 027 310 3644
Fax (07) 868 9730
info@totarabarns.co.nz
www.totarabarns.co.nz

Double $100-$120 Single $75 (Continental)
Child $25 Dinner $35
Visa MC accepted Children welcome
2 Queen (2 bdrm)
Bathrooms: 2 Ensuite

Unique, newly converted barn-style accommodation in a tranquil rural setting with large separate guest lounge. Easily accessible to Coromandel, Hot Water Beach and Cathedral Cove, Totara Valley Barns is perfect for a relaxing indulgent getaway. Enjoy a generous continental breakfast, enough for a packed lunch, and delicious home-cooked dinners are a specialty. Your hosts, Shona and Bruz, would love to share their knowledge of the area and with those extra touches, can assure you of Kiwi hospitality at its best.

~

Thames *8 km E of Thames*

Huia Lodge *B&B*
Celia & Murray Newby
589 Kauaeranga Valley Road, Thames

Tel (07) 868 6557 Fax (07) 868 6557
celian@wave.co.nz
www.thames-info.co.nz/HuiaLodge

Double $90 Single $60 (Full breakfast)
Child $20
Visa MC accepted
Children welcome
2 Queen 2 Single (2 bdrm)
Bathrooms: 2 Ensuite

Each unit has an ensuite and tea/coffee facilities. Relax and enjoy the tranquility of the valley, hike in the nearby Forest Park or circle the peninsula to view the famous Coromandel scenery. We enjoy meeting travellers, love the rural lifestyle, grow fruit/vegetables, and enjoy the peace with our pet dog and cat on our 3 acre paradise. Turn at BP corner (south end of township) into Banks Street then follow Parawai Road into the valley. We're 8km from BP. Just 1 1/2 hours from Auckland.

~

Thames Coast - Te Puru *12 km N of Thames*

Te Puru Coast Bed & Breakfast *B&B Homestay Cottage No Kitchen*
Bill & Paula Olsen
2A Tatahi Street, Te Puru, Thames Coast, Coromandel

Tel (07) 868 2866 Fax (07) 868 2866
tepurucoastbnb@xtra.co.nz
www.tepurucoastbnb.co.nz

Double $110 Single $70 (Full breakfast)
Child $25 Dinner $30pp
Self-contained unit $125 double Children welcome
1 Queen 2 Double 1 Twin 2 Single (4 bdrm)
Bathrooms: 1 Ensuite 2 Private

Welcome to the beautiful Thames Coast. Our modern comfortable home is 80 metres off the main coast road with off-street parking. Guest lounge has TV and tea & coffee facilities. You may choose a continental or cooked breakfast and evening meals are on request with complimentary New Zealand wine or beer. Our large deck is yours to enjoy or take a 2 minute walk to the beach. Fishermen welcome. The separate self-contained unit has own laundry, kitchen/dining, bathroom, BBQ.

Coromandel *11 km S of Coromandel*
Coromandel Homestay *Homestay*
Hilary & Vic Matthews
74 Kowhai Drive, Te Kouma Bay, Coromandel

Tel (07) 866 8046 Fax (07) 866 8046
vc.hm.matthews@xtra.co.nz

Double $95-$120 Single $75 (Continental)
Dinner $40 by arrangement Visa MC accepted
Pet free home Not suitable for children
2 Queen 1 Single (2 bdrm)
Bathrooms: 2 Ensuite

Our homestay is near an attractive safe beach. We have a bush setting and beautiful views of Coromandel Harbour. The area is very quiet and peaceful. Vic is a professional furniture/designer maker. Hilary enjoys gardening, spinning and woodturning. We have a cat. Take State Highway 25 for 50km travelling north from Thames. Turn sharp left into Te Kouma Road. After 3km turn left into Kowhai Drive. We are 15 minutes drive south of Coromandel town. Dinner by prior arrangement.

Coromandel *0.5 km E of Coromandel*
Country Touch *B&B Cottage No Kitchen*
Colleen & Geoff Innis
39 Whangapoua Road, Coromandel

Tel (07) 866 8310
Fax (07) 866 8310
countrytouch@xtra.co.nz
www.country-touch.com.nz

Double $95 Single $65 (Continental)
Child $10
Visa MC accepted
Children welcome
2 Queen 2 Twin (4 bdrm)
Bathrooms: 4 Ensuite

Geoff and I are a retired couple who enjoy meeting people, and invite you to a restful holiday in a country setting. With newly established trees and gardens, roses a speciality. You have the independence of 4 units situated apart from our home, all with fold out sofas, TV, fridge, tea and coffee making facilities. You have a country touch feeling with only a 10 minute stroll to Coromandel township, where you can enjoy our local arts, crafts and restaurants. Come and enjoy.

Coromandel *10 km S of Coromandel*
AJ's Homestay *Homestay*
Annette & Ray Hintz
24 Kowhai Drive, Te Kouma, RD, Coromandel

Tel (07) 866 7057 or 027 458 1624
Fax (07) 866 7057
rm.aj.hintz@actrix.gen.nz

Double $95-$120 Single $80 (Continental)
Dinner $30-$40
Visa MC accepted
Children welcome
3 Queen 1 Twin (3 bdrm)
Bathrooms: 1 Ensuite 1 Family share

AJ's Homestay with panoramic sea views overlooking the Coromandel Harbour, spectacular sunsets. 5 minute walk to a safe swimming beach. Most mornings breakfast is served on the terrace. Our games room has a billiard and table tennis table. Dinner can be arranged. Directions: Thames coast main road (SH25) approximately 50 minutes. At the bottom of the last hill overlooking the Coromandel Harbour. Turn sharp left, at the Te Kouma Road sign. Travel past the boat ramp, next turn left. Kowhai Drive, we are number 24.

Coromandel *0.5 km S of Coromandel*

The Green House *B&B*
Gwen Whitmore
505 Tiki Road, Coromandel

Tel (07) 866 7303 or 0800 473 364
whitmore@wave.co.nz
www.greenhousebandb.co.nz

Double $110-$150 **Single** $90-$110 (Special breakfast)
Child negotiable Visa MC accepted
1 King/Twin 2 Queen (3 bdrm)
Bathrooms: 3 Ensuite

This relaxed home with very comfortable facilities,
lovely views over hills and sea, is just minutes walk
from excellent restaurants etc. Upstairs dedicated guest lounge with quality furnishings, tea/coffee, fridge,
TV, videos, CDs etc. Also 2 ensuite bedrooms, 1 with private deck, the other sea views. A third ensuite
bedroom is downstairs. Generous hospitality is offered, and guest feedback to Qualmark is consistently
"Excellent and exceeds expectations". Advance bookings advised, freephone in NZ for this very clean,
friendly great place to stay. Small friendly dog on property.

~

Coromandel *3 km S of Coromandel*

Jacaranda Lodge *B&B*
Robin Münch
3195 Tiki Road, Coromandel, RD 1

Tel (07) 866 8002 or 021 252 6892
Fax (07) 866 8002
info@jacarandalodge.co.nz
www.jacarandalodge.co.nz

Double $100-$145 **Single** $55-$120 (Continental)
Visa MC accepted Children welcome
4 Queen 1 Twin 1 Single (6 bdrm)
Bathrooms: 2 Ensuite 1 Guest share 1 Private

Robin invites you to share her spacious home set on 6
acres of tranquil country paradise. Located 3km south of Coromandel Town, Jacaranda Lodge provides
the perfect escape: relax in one of the guest lounges; stroll around the delightful gardens; or experience
Coromandel's walks, galleries, unique attractions and spectacular coastline. Delicious continental
breakfasts include fresh organic produce from Jacaranda's orchard. Large, comfortable bedrooms. Ensuite,
private or shared bathrooms. Fully equipped guest kitchen. Special dietary needs catered for, including
kosher. Sleep, eat, enjoy.

~

Kuaotunu *17 km N of Whitianga*

Kaeppeli's *B&B Coastal Country*
Jill & Robert Kaeppeli
Grays Avenue, Kuaotunu, RD 2, Whitianga

Tel (07) 866 2445 or 025 656 3442
Fax (07) 866 2445
kaeppelis@paradise.net.nz
www.kaeppeli.co.nz

Double $120-$160 **Single** $85-$120 (Full breakfast)
Child negotiable Dinner $35 by arrangement
Visa MC accepted Children and pets welcome
2 King 4 Single (4 bdrm)
Bathrooms: 4 Ensuite

Country living in style and comfort with exquisite meals. Robert's an excellent Swiss Chef using top
quality produce and the wood fired oven. Meals served in our panoramic gazebo or guests dining room.
Relax and enjoy the peace and tranquility of Kuaotunu, it's choice of clean safe beaches, bush walks,
fishing, tennis, kayaking, swimming. Matarangi's Bob Charles designed golf course and horse trekking
nearby. Our daughter and pets make children welcome. Ideal for exploring the Coromandel Peninsula.
And our view? Just the best!!

Kuaotunu *16 km N of Whitianga*
@ The Peacheys *B&B Homestay*
Yvonne & Dale Peachey
15 Kawhero Drive, Kuaotunu RD 2, Whitianga

Tel (07) 866 5290 Fax (07) 866 4592
DYPeachey@xtra.co.nz
www.thepeacheys.co.nz

Double $100-$130 Single $90 (Special breakfast)
Dinner $30pp Visa MC accepted
Not suitable for children
1 King 1 Queen 3 Single (2 bdrm)
Bathrooms: 2 Ensuite

Welcome to our bed & breakfast. Take a few days to enjoy Kuaotunu's relaxed lifestyle. It really is too good to miss. Explore beaches (ours is only 50 metres from your room), forest & coastal walks, Coromandel & Whitianga and their attractions. Experience our incredible night sky, no light pollution & amazing sunsets. Massage therepist next door (by appointment). Resturaunts in Whitianga and Matarangi, or arrange dinner with us. Bathrobes, beach towels, refrigerator, tea & coffee in your spacious and comfortable room.

Kuaotunu *18 km N of Whitianga*
Kuaotunu Bay Lodge *B&B Separate Suite*
Lorraine & Bill Muir
State Highway 25, Kuaotunu, RD 2, Whitianga

Tel (07) 866 4396 or 027 601 3665
Fax (07) 866 4396
muir@kuaotunubay.co.nz
www.kuaotunubay.co.nz

Double $150-$200 Single $160-$180
(Special breakfast) Visa MC accepted
3 Queen 2 Single (4 bdrm)
Bathrooms: 3 Ensuite 1 Private

An elegant beach house overlooking Kuaotunu Bay on 4 hectares of bush and pasture 18km north of Whitianga with panoramic views of the peninsula and islands. purpose built for guest with ensuites, decks, private entrances. Watch the waves from your bed, enjoy a swim before a hearty breakfast. All activities within easy reach. Savour some of the fine restaurants in Whitianga. spending 2 or 3 days with us gives you time to explore the whole peninsula. We offer affordable luxury and a true Kiwi experience.

Kuaotunu *17 km N of Whitianga*
Blue Penguin *B&B*
Glenda Mawhinney & Barbara Meredith
11 Cuvier Crescent, Kuaotunu, RD 2, Whitianga, Coromandel Peninsula

Tel (07) 866 2222 Fax (07) 866 0228
holidayhomes@bluepenguin.co.nz
www.bluepenguin.co.nz

Double $110-$130 Single $75 (Continental)
Child $35 Full house available Dec-Feb, 3 brm, 2 bath
Visa MC accepted Children and pets welcome
1 King/Twin 2 Double 2 Single (2 bdrm)
Bathrooms: 1 Guest share

We welcome you to our architecturally designed home with spectacular views over the beach and pohutukawa trees to the Mercury Islands and Great Barrier. The master guestroom has king bed, window seats and small private balcony. Children love the family guestroom, 2 doubles, 2 singles, cot, TV/video, toys & games. We have a retriever, poodle and little foxy. We are two professional women who also manage 300 private beach houses which are available for holiday rental - see our website for full descriptions, colour photographs, seasonal rates and availability calendars.

Coromandel

Coromandel

Kuaotunu *17 km N of Whitianga*
Drift In B&B *B&B Homestay*
Yvonne & Peppe Thompson
16 Grays Avenue, Kuaotunu, RD 2, Whitianga

Tel (07) 866 4321 or 025 245 3632
Fax (07) 866 4321
driftin@paradise.net.nz
www.coromandelfun.co.nz/driftin

Double $110-$110 Single $65-$65 (Full breakfast)
Child 5-12 years $30 Dinner $28 by arrangement
Visa MC accepted Children welcome
1 Queen 2 Single (2 bdrm)
Bathrooms: 1 Guest share

Welcome is assured. This tranquil comfortable modern cedar home is designed to take full advantage of the sun and breathtaking island views by day and moonlit night. An unique beach theme pervades house and garden with small dog in residence. Just a minute stroll to white sand beaches for safe swimming and fossicking. Breakfast is a memorable occasion with sight and sounds of birds and sea complementing an excellent range of home cooking. Delicious evening meals available by prior arrangement. Drift in, relax and enjoy this unique and special part of New Zealand.

~

Whitianga *1 km S of Whitianga*
Cosy Cat Cottage *B&B Cottage with Kitchen*
Gordon Pearce
41 South Highway (town end), Whitianga

Tel (07) 866 4488 or 025 798 745
Fax (07) 866 4488
cosycat@xtra.co.nz
www.cosycat.co.nz

Double $85-$105 Single $55-$75 (Full breakfast)
Cottage $90-$160
Visa MC accepted Children welcome
2 Queen 1 Double 1 Single (3 bdrm)
Bathrooms: 2 Ensuite 1 Private

Welcome to our picturesque 2 storied cottage filled with feline memorabilia! Relax with complimentary tea or coffee served on the veranda or in the guest lounge. Enjoy a good nights rest in comfortable beds and choose a variety of treats from our breakfast blackboard menu. You will probably like to meet Sylvie the cat or perhaps visit the cat hotel in the garden. A separate cottage is available with queen beds, bathrooms and kitchen. Friendly helpful service is assured - hope to see you soon!

~

Whitianga *In Whitianga Central*
Anne's Haven *B&B Homestay*
Anne & Bob
119 Albert St, Whitianga

Tel (07) 866 5550
anneshaven@paradise.net.nz

Double $70 Single $50 (Full breakfast)
Child $20 Dinner $20
1 Double 2 Single (2 bdrm)
Bathrooms: 1 Family share

Welcome to our comfortable modern home and the tranquillity of the garden. Guests share the lounge/TV room. The shower, toilet and bathroom are each separate rooms for easy access. Breakfast includes homemade bread and jams. We are 400 metres from shops and restaurants and within walking distance to six lovely beaches. Bob enjoys building and flying radio controlled model planes. Anne makes pottery, dabbles with watercolours and gardens. Let us make your stay a memorable one. Our moggie 'Gordon Bennett' is also friendly.

Whitianga - Cooks Beach *17 km N of Tairua*
Mercury Orchard *B&B Cottage with Kitchen*
Heather and Barry Scott
141 Purangi Road, Cooks Beach, Whitianga

Tel (07) 866 3119 Fax (07) 866 3115
relax@mercuryorchard.co.nz
www.mercuryorchard.co.nz

Double $130-$160 Single $110 (Full breakfast)
Child $15 Dinner $25
Fig Tree Cottage $150 or Paua bach $160
Visa MC accepted Children welcome
1 King 3 Queen 1 Single (4 bdrm)
Bathrooms: 3 Ensuite

Paua Bach and Fig Tree Cottage are nestled amongst 5 acres of peaceful country gardens and orchard. Self- contained country style luxury with french doors opening onto your private deck with barbeque. Crisp cotton bed linen, bathrobes, fresh fruit, flowers and candles. Special to the Bach, an old fashioned outdoor bath. Quiet. Relaxing. Enjoy a Mercury Orchard full breakfast while listening to the birdsong. Hot Water Beach and Cathedral Cove are 7-8 minutes drive. We share our home with 2 small dogs and cat.

Whitianga *4 km N of Whitianga*
At Parkland Place *B&B*
Maria & Guy Clark
14 Parkland Place, Brophys Beach, Whitianga

Tel (07) 866 4987 or 021 404 923
Fax (07) 866 4946
parklandplace@wave.co.nz
www.atparklandplace.co.nz

Double $135-$200 Single $100-$150 (Special b'fast)
Child negotiable Dinner by arrangement
Visa MC Diners Amex accepted Children welcome
1 King/Twin3 King 2 Queen 3 Single (5 bdrm)
Bathrooms: 5 Ensuite 1 Guest share

Enjoy European hospitality in Whitianga's most luxurious boutique accommodation. Maria, a ship's chef from Poland and New Zealand husband Guy, a master mariner, will make your stay a memorable experience. Large luxuriously appointed rooms. Magnificent breakfasts. Superb candle-lit dinners or BBQ by arrangement. Sunny picturesque outdoor area with spa pool. Large guest lounge with TV, library, music and refreshments. Situated near the beach and next to reserves and farmland ensures absolute peace and quiet. Privacy and discretion assured. You will not regret coming.

Whitianga - Coroglen *14 km S of Whitianga*
Coroglen Lodge *B&B Farmstay Separate Suite*
Wendy & Nigel Davidson
2221 State Highway 25, RD 1, Whitianga 2856

Tel (07) 866 3225 Fax (07) 866 3235
clover@wave.co.nz
www.mercurybay.co.nz/coroglen.html

Double $85-$100 Single $60-$80 (Continental)
Visa MC accepted
Children welcome
2 Queen 2 Single (3 bdrm)
Bathrooms: 2 Guest share

Coroglen Lodge is situated on 17 acres of farmland with cattle, sheep and alpacas. Nestled in the hills with views of the Coromandel Ranges, this is rural tranquillity. Halfway between Whitianga township and Hot Water Beach there is easy access to both areas and all attractions. Guest area is separate, relaxed, and spacious with a large sunny lounge area for your comfort. Wendy spins and knits with wool from her sheep and alpacas, and Nigel has a collection of vintage tractors.

Coromandel

Whitianga *22 km N of Coroglen*

Coppers Creek Farmstay *B&B Farmstay Cottage with Kitchen*
Graham & Pamela Caddy
1587 State Highway 25, Coroglen,
RD 1, Whitianga 2856

Tel (07) 866 3960 Fax (07) 866 3960
caddy.copperscreek@xtra.co.nz
www.copperscreekfarmstay.co.nz

Double $90-$75 Single $65 (Full breakfast)
Child $20-$15 Visa MC accepted
Children welcome
1 Queen 3 Single (2 bdrm)
Bathrooms: 1 Ensuite 1 Private

Coppers Creek is a small working beef breeding farm comprising of 120 acres of pasture, bush and streams. We have the usual assortment of farm animals including the odd teenager. Enjoy the freedom of our self-contained studio apartment and adjacent childrens bedroom, with private entrance and BBQ area, with fresh produce available from the farm garden in season. We are only 15 minutes drive from Hot Water Beach, Hahei, Cooks Beach and Whitianga. We enjoy boating, kayaking, fishing, diving and bush walks.

Whitianga *4 km N of Whitianga*

Centennial Heights B&B *B&B*
Paul & Johanna Blackman
141 Centennial Drive, Whitianga

Tel (07) 866 0279 Fax (07) 866 0276
Blackmanmathis@xtra.co.nz
www.centennialheights.unitrental.com/

Double $130 Single $75 (Special breakfast)
Child $20
2 Queen 1 Single (3 bdrm)
Bathrooms: 2 Ensuite 1 Private

Centennial Heights overlooks the sparkling waters
of Whitianga Harbour. Paul & Johanna (who speaks
fluent German and French) and Mollie (our border collie) offer warm hospitality in elegant surroundings. Over complimentary pre-dinner drinks we can assist you with information on the areas attractions including fishing, kayaking, tramping, scuba diving, snorkelling, boat cruises and dining out etc. We offer a delicious cooked breakfast which can be enjoyed with spectacular sea views. We look forward to welcoming you and making your stay a pleasant and memorable one.

Hahei *38 km S of Whitianga*

The Church *B&B Cottages No Kitchen & Cottages with Kitchen*
Richard Agnew & Karen Blair
87 Beach Road, Hahei, RD 1, Whitianga

Tel (07) 866 3533 or 025 596 877
Fax (07) 866 3055
thechurchhahei@xtra.co.nz
www.thechurchhahei.co.nz

Double $95-$150 (Continental)
Child $10-$150 Dinner Menu Extra Adult $20-$25
Visa MC accepted Children welcome
11 Queen 1 Double 11 Twin 13 Single (11 bdrm)
Bathrooms: 11 Ensuite

The Church is Hahei's most unique accommodation
and dining experience. The Church building provides a character dining room/licensed restaurant for wholesome breakfasts and delicious evening meals. 11 cosy wooden cottages scattered through delightful bush and gardens offer a range of accommodation and tariffs, with ensuites, fridges, tea and coffee facilities. Some cottages fully self-contained with woodstoves for winter. Enjoy the wonders of Cathedral Cove, Hot Water Beach, and the Coromandel Peninsula. Seasonal rates. Smoking outside.

Hahei Beach *200m NE of Hahei shops and cafes*
Hawleys Bed and Breakfast Hahei *B&B*
Peter and Rhonda Hawley
19 Hahei Beach Road, RD 1, Whitianga

Tel (07) 866 3272 or 027 497 1090
Fax (07) 866 3273
hawleys@haheibeach.co.nz
www.haheibeach.co.nz

Double $150 Single $130 (Full breakfast)
Visa MC accepted
Children and pets welcome
1 Queen 2 Single (2 bdrm)
Bathrooms: 1 Guest share 1 Private

Situated on the flat, half-way (200m) between the beach and the shops and cafes. Ideal for those who enjoy extra space and comfort. The purpose built 2 double bedrooms (house completed mid 2000) and spacious bathroom and take up all of the second storey at the rear of the house. The larger room has a balcony and a queen size bed and the smaller room 2 single beds. A cot is available. There is secure garaging. No children at home and no pets.

Hahei *36 km SE of Whitianga*
Hahei Horizon *B&B Homestay*
Peter & Kay Harrison
20 Grierson Close, Hahei, RD 1, Whitianga

Tel (07) 866 3281 or 027 480 9273
021 160 7213
pkharrison@xtra.co.nz
www.haheihorizon.co.nz

Double $140-$220 (Full breakfast)
Child by arrangement Children welcome
1 King/Twin 1 Queen (2 bdrm)
Bathrooms: 2 Ensuite

Peter & Kay invite you to share our little piece of this special part of New Zealand. Hahei Horizon is our home on the hill which has also been specifically designed for bed & breakfast. Every room has stunning views of the coast and its surroundings. With down to earth Kiwi hospitality, relaxation is hard to avoid. All rooms are large with quality linen, tea/coffee, fridge, ensuites. Internet available. Easy walk to beach and cafes - Hahei has all the traveller desires!

Hahei *400m SW of Hahei*
Hahei B&B *B&B*
Mark Cederman
6 Jackson Place, Hahei, RD 1 Whitianga

Tel (07) 866 3730 or 027 499 8879
Fax (07) 866 3750
info@haheibandb.co.nz
www.haheibandb.co.nz

Double $140-$200 (Full breakfast)
Visa MC accepted
Children welcome
2 Queen 1 Double 1 Twin 4 Single (4 bdrm)
Bathrooms: 1 Ensuite 1 Guest share 1 Private

A warm welcome awaits you at Hahei Bed & Breakfast. This is a modern, purpose built home with a large swimming pool, beautiful gardens and sun drenched decks. Continental or cooked breakfast served in the privacy of your own rooms, or alfresco on the deck overlooking Hahei and the gardens. Local features and attractions include bush walks, diving and snorkelling in close proximity to digging your own hot pool at Hot Water Beach or walking to picturesque Cathedral Cove.

Coromandel

Hot Water Beach 28 km N of Tairua
Auntie Dawns Place *Apartment with Kitchen*
Dawn & Joe Nelmes
15 Radar Road, Hot Water Beach, Whitianga RD 1

Tel (07) 866 3707 Fax (07) 866 3701
enquiries@auntiedawn.co.nz
www.auntiedawn.co.nz

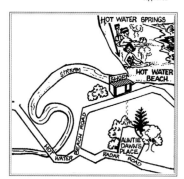

Double $90-$120 Single $50 (Continental)
Visa MC accepted
2 Queen 1 Double 1 Single (2 bdrm)
Bathrooms: 2 Private

Hot Water Beach is a surf beach. At low tide hot water
bubbles up in the sand and you dig yourself a 'hot pool'. Our
house is surrounded by huge Pohutukawa trees, 3 minutes
walk from the hot springs. We have a terrier and Joe makes
home-brew beer. Each apartment is comfortably furnished
with a queen bedroom, and a spare bed in the living room.
We provide tea, coffee, bread, butter, jam, milk and cereals. Guests prepare breakfast at preferred time.
Nearest restaurant at Hahei. Directions: turn right into Radar Road 200 metres before shop.

Hot Water Beach 32 km S of Whitianga
Hot Water Beach B&B *B&B Homestay*
Gail & Trevor Knight
48 Pye Place, Hot Water Beach, RD 1,
Coromandel Peninsula

Tel (07) 866 3991 or 0800 146 889
025 799620 Fax (07) 866 3291
TKnight@xtra.co.nz
www.hotwaterbedandbreakfast.co.nz

Double $160-$200 Single $140-$180 (Full breakfast)
Visa MC Diners Amex accepted
2 Queen (2 bdrm)
Bathrooms: 2 Ensuite

We have a spacious elevated home with extensive decks, on which you can have fresh coffee or juice,
while enjoying sweeping panoramic sea/beach views. Sit under the brilliant southern stars in our spa pool
or play on our full sized billiard table. You can swim, surf, dive, fish, kayak, play golf, bushwalk, horse
trek or visit spectacular Cathedral Cove or alternatively just dig a hole and soak in the natural hot springs
on our beach. We have a cat and a sociable boxer.

Tairua 45 km E of Thames
Harbour View Lodge *B&B*
Sheryl Allan & John Goldstone
179 Main Road, Tairua

Tel (07) 864 7040 or 021 303 982
Fax (07) 864 7042
info@harbourviewlodge.co.nz
www.harbourviewlodge.co.nz

Double $145-$185 Single $130-$150 (Full breakfast)
Visa MC accepted Not suitable for children
1 King/Twin 2 Queen (3 bdrm)
Bathrooms: 3 Ensuite

Situated on the foothills of Tairua. Our B&B has been
furnished with the finest of linens and interior design. All rooms have their own ensuite, hair dryers,
electric blankets, tea/coffee facilities. Guest Lounge, swimming pool, off street parking, internet facilities
available. Continental/full cooked breakfast is served in the dining room with its ever-changing views
of Tairua Harbour and Paku Mountain. Enjoy our beaches, bush walks,18 hole golf course. 5 minute
level walk to local restaurants. Close to Cathedral Cove & Hot Water Beach.

Tairua *40 km E of Thames*
Dell Cote Homestay *B&B Homestay*
Barry & Trish Oldham
37 Rewrewa Valley Road, Tairua 2853
PO Box 45, Tairua 2853

Tel (07) 864 8142 Fax (07) 864 8142
homestay@dellcote.com
www.dellcote.co.nz

Double $180 Single $160 (Special breakfast)
Visa MC accepted Not suitable for children
3 Queen 1 King Single (3 bdrm)
Bathrooms: 2 Ensuite 1 Private

A welcoming eco friendly home, set in an acre of garden and orchard in the bush clad Rewarewa Valley. Rooms have private access, quality cotton bed linen, electric blankets, toiletries, hair dryer, heated towel rails & fresh flowers. Generous breakfast choices, continental/cooked options, with home-grown seasonal produce and preserves. Guest lounge. Off-street parking. Peaceful location. Pleasant walking to Tairua Village, art galleries, cafes, restaurants. Enjoy the beach, bush walks, golf, fishing & diving. 20 minutes to Hot Water Beach, Catherdral Cove, Pauanui.

Whangamata *200m N of town centre*
Sandy Rose Bed & Breakfast *B&B*
Shirley & Murray Calman
Corner Hetherington & Rutherford Roads,
Whangamata

Tel (07) 865 6911 Fax (07) 865 6911
sandyrose@whangamata.co.nz
sandyrose.whangamata.co.nz

Double $120-$120 Single $90-$90 (Special breakfast)
Visa MC accepted Not suitable for children
2 King/Twin 1 Queen 1 Double (3 bdrm)
Bathrooms: 3 Ensuite

A charming B&B in the Coromandel Peninsula's popular holiday destination, we have 3 tastefully decorated guest bedrooms, all with ensuite bathrooms, comfortable beds and in-room TVs. Complimentary tea & coffee is available in the guest lounge. We are ideally located, close to Whangamata's shops, cafes and restaurants, and an easy stroll to the surf beach, harbour and wharf. Enjoy our extensive continental breakfast and use our home as a base to relax and enjoy the natural attractions that Whangamata and area has to offer.

Whangamata *2 km S of Town Centre*
Kotuku *B&B Self-contained Studio Unit*
Linda & Peter Bigge
422 Otahu Road, Whangamata,

Tel (07) 865 6128 or 021 149 1584
Fax (07) 865 6128
lindapeter@internet.co.nz
www.kotukuhomestay.co.nz

Double $108-$120 (Full breakfast)
 Studio Unit $80
Visa MC Diners accepted Children welcome
3 Queen (3 bdrm)
Bathrooms: 3 Ensuite

We offer comfortable accommodation in a purpose built home. Rosie, our friendly Labrador cross and Elizabeth the cat, will welcome you. Relax in the spacious lounge or private patio, enjoy the Coromandel sunset from our deluxe outdoor spa. Kotuku is situated at the quieter end of Whangamata, just a 2 minute stroll to the lovely Otahu Estuary and Reserve; ideal for walking, swimming, kayaking or just take a picnic lunch and watch the fascinating shorebirds. Bikes, kayaks and a surfboard are available for your use.

Coromandel

Whangamata *8 km N of Whangamata*
Copsefield *B&B*
Lynn & Wayne Cruickshank
1055 State highway 25, RD 1, Whangamata

Tel (07) 865 9555 Fax (09) 865 9510
copsefield@xtra.co.nz
www.copsefield.co.nz

Double $180 **Single** $130 (Full breakfast)
Dinner $25pp
Visa MC accepted
2 Queen 2 Single (3 bdrm)
Bathrooms: 3 Ensuite

Character country home situated on 3 acres at the
southern end of the stunning Coromandel Peninsula. Copsefield is purpose built for your comfort,with
3 ensuite rooms. 2 beaches close by. Canoes, bikes, walks, spa pool, 6 hole pitch & putt golf course. Peace
and tranquility beside native bush and river. Guest lounge with TV, tea & coffee. Evening meal by
arrangement. Enjoy our full breakfast including fresh-grown fruit and juices. Lynn and Wayne offer you
a warm and friendly welcome and personal attention.

Waihi *1 km S of Waihi*
West Wind Gardens *B&B Homestay*
Josie & Merv Scott
58 Adams Street, Waihi

Tel (07) 863 7208 westwindgarden@xtra.co.nz

Double $75 **Single** $40 (Continental)
Child $20 Dinner $20
Visa MC accepted
Children welcome
1 Double 2 Single (2 bdrm)
Bathrooms: 1 Guest share

We offer a friendly restful smoke-free stay in our
modern home and garden. Waihi is the gate way to
both the Coromandel with its beautiful beaches and the Bay of Plenty. Waihi is a historic town with
vintage railway running to Waikino, a working gold mine discovered 1878 closed 1952. Reopened in
1989 as a open-cast mine. Free mine tours available. Beach 10 minutes away, beautiful bush walks, golf
courses, trout fishing. Enjoy a home cooked meal or sample our restaurants. Our interests are gardening,
dancing and travel.

Waihi Beach *11 km E of Waihi*
Waterfront Homestay *Apartment with Kitchen*
Kay & John Morgan
17 The Esplanade (off Hinemoa Street),
Waihi Beach

Tel (07) 863 4342 or 021 170 5058
Fax (07) 863 4342
k.morgan@xtra.co.nz

Double $100 **Single** $75 (Continental)
Visa MC accepted
Children welcome
1 Queen 1 Double 1 Single (2 bdrm)
Bathrooms: 1 Private

Waterfront Homestay. Fully self-contained, 2 double bedrooms plus single bed. Suitable for 2 couples
or small family group. Unit is lower floor of family home on waterfront of beautiful uncrowded ocean
beach. Walk from front door directly onto sandy beach. Safe ocean swimming, surfcasting, surfing and
coastal walks. Restaurant within walking distance or use facilities provided with accommodation.

Waihi *5 km N of Waihi*
The French Provincial Country House *B&B*
Margaret van Duyvenbooden
Golden Valley - Trig Road North, RD 1, Waihi

Tel (07) 863 7339 Fax (07) 863 7330

Double $165-$195 Single $140 (Continental)
Visa MC accepted
1 King (1 bdrm)
Bathrooms: 1 Ensuite 1 Guest share

A warm welcome awaits you at The French Provincial Country House, with fine accommodation. Sited on farmland in a picturesque valley only 5km from an historic township, close to all attractions.

Upstairs is a private, large luxurious suite with lovely rural views, 2 private balconies, super king bed, ensuite bathroom, TV, fresh flowers, crisp white bed linen, electric blanket, hairdryer, toiletries and big soft bath towels. Serviced daily.

A generous continental breakfast is served at a time to suit. Fresh fruit salad, yogurt, assortment of cereals and home-made muesli. Croissants or muffins, fresh orange juice, tea and coffee. This home is not suitable for children and is smoke-free.

In summer there are colourful gardens with large shade trees and front door parking for guests. Close to beautiful beaches for swimming and fishing, gold mining tours, cafes and restaurants. A day trip to the beautiful Coromandel Peninsula is recommended. 1 night in this beautiful area is not long enough. Please make an early reservation to save disappointment.

"One night in this beautiful area is not long enough."

Waihi *1.5 km W of Waihi*

Trout & Chicken at Drift House *B&B Homestay Cottage with Kitchen*
Michael & Adrienne Muir
9137 State Highway 2, RD 2, Waihi

Tel (07) 863 6964 or 027 206 4080 Fax (07) 863 6966
troutandchicken@paradise.net.nz
www.troutandchicken.co.nz

Double $120-$180 Single $90-$110 (Special breakfast)
Child in cottage only Dinner by arrangement
Studio $50pp Visa MC accepted Children welcome
2 King/Twin 2 Queen 1 Twin (2 in B&B, 1 in Cottage)
Bathrooms: 2 Ensuite 1 Guest share
Cottage has 1 bathroom

Come and experience some affordable luxury in our purpose built home, hidden 350 metres from the highway, on an organic bluberry orchard beside Waitete Stream. Enjoy the peace and quiet, spacious ensuited bedrooms, large guest lounge with open fire, your own deck, special breakfast in the dining room or alfresco. Visit the spectacular gorge, gold mine, museum and art gallery, antique shops etc. Check out this historic area. Let us organise guided or self drive tours, trout fishing, art lessons, massage, dinner in town. We have pets at home.

Waihi *2 km W of Waihi*

Ashtree House *B&B*
Anne & Bill Ashdown
20 Riflerange Road, Waihi

Tel (07) 863 6448 or 021 2924 987
Fax (07) 863 6443

Double $80 Single $50 (Full breakfast)
Child under 10 $10 Dinner $20pp
Garden Unit $35pp
Children welcome
1 Queen 1 Double 2 Single (3 bdrm)
Bathrooms: 1 Guest share 2 Private

Modern brick home set on the side of a hill with extensive views and access to trout river. Private guest wing comprising 2 double bedrooms, large private bathroom with shower and bath. Guest lounge with TV, stereo and large selection of New Zealand books. Laundry and separate toilet. 8 acres, large attractive garden and pond area. 1 house dog. Situated 2 minutes to centre of Waihi, complete privacy and quiet guaranteed. Self-contained unit with wheelchair facilities. 5 minutes to beautiful Karangahake Gorge.

Waihi *0.5 km W of Waihi*

Chez Nous *B&B Homestay*
Sara Parish
41 Seddon Avenue, Waihi

Tel (07) 863 7538 Sara.P@xtra.co.nz

Double $65 Single $45 (Continental)
Child $20
Dinner $20pp by arrangement
Visa MC accepted
Children welcome
1 Queen 1 Twin (2 bdrm)
Bathrooms: 1 Guest share

Enjoy a relaxed and friendly atmosphere in a spacious, modern home in an attractive garden setting. Shops and restaurants are within easy walking distance. Discover past and present gold mining activities (tours available), sandy surf beaches, bush walks, 18 hole golf course, art, craft and wine trails. Waihi is an ideal stopover for the traveller who wants to explore the Coromandel Peninsula, Bay of Plenty and Waikato.

Waihi Beach *11 km E of Waihi*
Coq on Fyfe *B&B*
Robyn & Dave Smith
33 Fyfe Road, Waihi Beach

Tel (07) 863 4627
Fax (07) 863 4627
daverobynsmith@xtra.co.nz

Double $100 (Continental)
Visa MC accepted
Not suitable for children

1 Queen (1 bdrm)
Bathrooms: 1 Ensuite

At 33 on Fyfe we can offer you peace and quiet. Awake
to the sound of tuis and be lulled to sleep by the sound of the ocean. Enjoy bush and beach walks only
minutes away. Dine out at one of several nearby cafes. Your unit has its own heated bathroom, tea and
coffee making facilities and room to relax.Stroll around our lush tropical garden with panoramic sea and
bush views. Internet available.

Waihi Beach *11 km E of Waihi*
Seagulls Bed & Breakfast *B&B*
Marie & Steve Quinlan
8 West Street (off Pacific Road),
Waihi Beach

Tel (07) 863 4633 or 027 492 0033
Fax (07) 863 4634
seagullsquinlan@clear.net.nz

Double $100-$125 Single $85-$95 (Full breakfast)
2 Queen 1 Single (2 bdrm)
Bathrooms: 1 Guest share

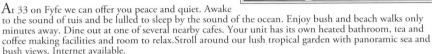

Relax and unwind at beautiful Waihi Beach - gateway
to Coromandel Peninsular and the sunny Bay of Plenty.
Enjoy the spectacular panoramic views of beach (3minutes walk) and Mayor Island. Listen to tuis sing in
bush on our boundary. See the sunrise. Modern spacious luxury home with your own double bedroom,
lounge and bathroom. Excellent outdoor areas. Cafes, restaurant, fishing, golf, tennis, beach and bush
walks nearby. Breakfast include fresh seasonal fruits and organic produce when available. Our foxy Jacky
will meet you.

Please let us know
how you enjoyed your B&B experience.
Ask your host for a comment form
or leave a comment on www.bnb.co.nz

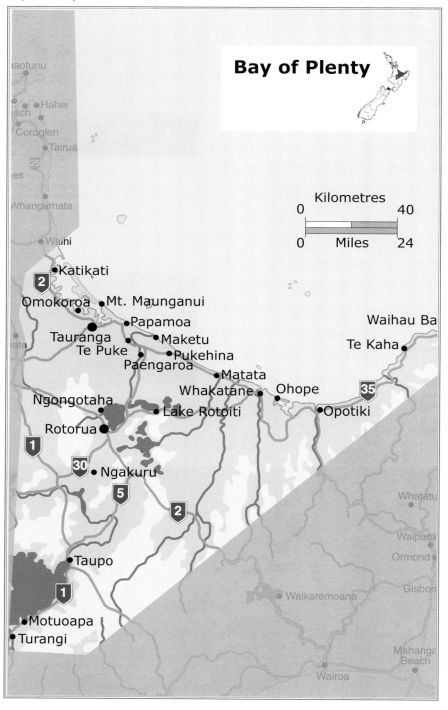

Bay of Plenty

Katikati *30 km N of Tauranga*

Fallowfield Chalet at Jacaranda Cottage *Self-catering Chalet*
Lynlie & Rick Watson
230 Thompson's Track, RD 2, Katikati

Tel (07) 549 0616 or 025 272 8710
Fax (07) 549 0616   relax@jacaranda-cottage.co.nz
www.jacaranda-cottage.co.nz

Double $95 (Accommodation only)
Minimum stay 2 nights   Child discounted by age
Extra adult $25   Whole week $565
Whole month $1425   Children welcome
1 Double 1 Single (1 bdrm)
Bathrooms: 1 Ensuite

Spectacular views from forests and farmlands to mountains and the sea - the backdrop for your stay on our 5 acre farmlet 8km south of Katikati Mural Town. Relax and unwind in Fallowfield, our clean and warm, fully equipped self-catering hillside Chalet. Enjoy your privacy, or opt for more contact with friendly Kiwi hosts. Children welcome to 'help' with quiet smallfarm animals. Glowworm expeditions offered. Near beaches, tramping, golf, horse treks, hot pools, bird gardens, winery, restaurants, arts/crafts, over 40 fascinating murals.

≈

Katikati *20 km S of Katikati*

Jones Lifestyle *Apartment with Kitchen*
Thora & Trevor Jones
Pahoia Road, RD 2, Tauranga

Tel (07) 548 0661 Fax (07) 548 0661
joneslifestyle@clear.net.nz

Double $90 Single $60 (Continental provisions)
Child $20
Visa MC Diners accepted
1 Queen (1 bdrm)
Bathrooms: 1 Private

Situated on Pahoia Peninsula and within easy reach of Tauranga and Katikati, our self-contained apartment is a very peaceful place to stay, with spectacular views of Tauranga Harbour and sunset over the Kaimai Ranges. It is a short walk to the beach. Our large garden is alive with birdsong. Amenities include fully eqipped kitchen, bathroom, laundry, lounge with convertible sofa, games rooms (billiards, table tennis etc.). Extra bedrooms and private bathroom are available in main house. Deluxe continental breakfast (optional) provided for self service.

≈

Katikati *3 km N of Katikati*

Aberfeldy *B&B Farmstay*
Mary Anne & Rod Calver
164 Lindemann Road, RD 1, Katikati

Tel (07) 549 0363 or 0800 309 064
027 590 9710 Fax (07) 549 0363
aberfeldy@xtra.co.nz
www.aberfeldy.co.nz

Double $110 Single $70 (Full breakfast)
Child $40   Dinner by arrangement
Visa MC accepted   Children and pets welcome
1 Queen 1 Twin 1 Single (2 bdrm)
Bathrooms: 1 Private

Large attractive home set in extensive gardens with private sunny guest accommodation. The private lounge opens onto a patio, and has TV and coffee making facilities. 1 party at a time in guest accommodation. We farm sheep and cattle. Rod's associated with Kiwifruit and is a Rotarian. Panoramic views of bush-clad hills, farmland and harbour. Activities include bush and farm walks, meeting tame animals especially Sue & Lucy the Kune Kune pigs. Golf course, horse riding, and beaches nearby. Jax, our Australian terrier will welcome you.

Bay of Plenty

Katikati *1 km N of Katikati*

Waterford House (katikati.8k.com) *B&B*
Alan & Helen Cook
15 Crossley Street, Katikati 3063

Tel (07) 549 0757 www.katikati.8k.com

Double $70 Single $45 (Full breakfast)
Child discounted Dinner $20 by arrangement
Visa MC accepted Children welcome
1 Queen 1 Double 2 Twin 1 Single (5 bdrm)
Bathrooms: 3 Guest share

Waterford House, situated in a quiet semi-rural area,
provides spacious accommodation with wheelchair
access throughout. A large comfortable lounge with
television, stereo-radio, fridge-freezer, microwave and tea/coffee making facilities. Cot and highchair are
available. Local attractions include Twickenham Homestead Cafe, Morton Estate Winery, bird gardens,
Ballantyne Golf Course, Sapphire Springs Hot Pools, Kaimai bush walks, Uretara River Walkway and
craft workshops. 32 murals and sculptures depict the history of Katikati "Mural Town", located on
Pacific Coast Highway. Our cat is called Matilda.

Katikati *8 km N of Katikati*

Cotswold Lodge Countrystay *B&B*
Alison & Des Belsham
183 Ongare Point Road, RD 1, Katikati

Tel (07) 549 2110 Fax (07) 549 2109
cotswold@ihug.co.nz
www.cotswold.co.nz

Double $125-$145 Single $95-$100 (Special breakfast)
Dinner by arrangement Visa MC accepted
2 Queen 1 Double 1 Single (3 bdrm)
Bathrooms: 3 Ensuite

We offer warm Kiwi hospitality, a little luxury and
a relaxed peaceful environment in our rural home,
Cotswold Lodge. Gourmet breakfasts. Evening meals by prior arrangement. Wander through the gardens,
Kiwifruit orchard or down to the Harbour. Sit on the deck and watch the sunset over the Kaimai
Ranges or relax in the hot spa and listen to the birds. All rooms have ensuite bathrooms, bathrobes,
toiletries, hairdryers etc. Guest refrigerator, tea and coffee making facilities. We have a friendly labrador.
Restaurants, golf etc nearby.

Katikati *9 km N of Katikati*

Panorama Country Lodge *Luxury B&B Private Suites*
Barbara & Phil McKernon
901 Pacific Coast Highway (SH2), RD 1, Katikati

Tel (07) 549 1882 or 0211 655875
Fax (07) 549 1882 mckernon@xtra.co.nz
www.panoramalodge.co.nz

Double $140-$180 Single $100-$120
(Special breakfast) Visa MC accepted
1 King 1 Queen 2 Single (3 bdrm)
Bathrooms: 1 Ensuite 1 Private

Perfectly situated between beautiful Waihi Beach and Katikati. Nestling
in the foothills of the Kaimai Ranges and commanding magnificent
Pacific and Island views from every room! Relax in spacious and peaceful private guest suites, with
ensuite and private facilities, quality furnishings, french doors to swimming pool and terrace, TV &
CD, DVD, slippers & robes, coffee & tea, delicious breakfasts, served: in-suite, terrace or dining room.
Explore the grounds, orchards, paddocks and meet 'our boys' the alpacas, not forgetting our very friendly
dog, Kaimai. Nearby: cafes, wineries, beaches, golf, bushwalks, etc. 'We love it here...so will you!'

Katikati *15 km S of Waihi*
Paradiso *B&B Cottage with Kitchen*
Theo & Gerda Blok
101 Athenree Road, RD 1, Katikati

Tel (07) 863 5350 Fax (07) 863 5678
paradijs@xtra.co.nz
www.paradisobb.co.nz

Double $100 Single $50 (Continental)
Child under 5 $10 Children welcome
1 Queen 2 Single (1 bdrm)
Bathrooms: 1 Private

Paradiso, 5 acres of park-like gardens, with children's playground, nestled on the edge of Tauranga Harbour. A double-seated kayak is available to explore the harbour, native bush walks nearby. 5km from Waihi Beach. We offer friendly B&B in clean, comfortable studio-style accommodation, or you can self-cater, be as private as you wish. We came from Holland 36 years ago and lived on a dairy farm for 30 years, and we have found paradise. For more information, look on our website.

Katikati *12 km N of Katikati*
The Candy's B&B *B&B*
Gloria & Neil Candy
43 Athenree Road, RD 1, Katikati

Tel (07) 863 1159 Fax (07) 863 1196
neilcandy@ihug.co.nz

Double $110 Single $80-$90 (Continental)
Dinner $32pp
1 King 2 Twin (2 bdrm)
Bathrooms: 1 Ensuite 1 Guest share

Take time out: relax. Our new home is on three acres, with beautiful harbour views: each room has a patio. Walk to Athenree Hotpools, drive 3 minutes to Waihi Surf Beach, 10 minutes south to Katikati, 2 Local Golf Courses, Morton Winery, Lavender Farm. 10 minutes north to Waihi Goldmine, walks and excellent restaurants. Neil loves fishing, and is an ex-chef, Gloria loves crafts. Meals on request. This is paradise and our city pets agree.

Katikati *2.5 km W of Katikati*
Busby Lodge *Luxury Homestay*
Elaine & Guy Robertson
251 Busby Road, RD 1, Katikati

Tel (07) 549 0189 or 027 490 8199
Fax (07) 549 0184 busbylodge@xtra.co.nz

Double $200 Single $120 (Full breakfast)
Visa MC accepted
1 King 1 Twin (2 bdrm)
Bathrooms: 2 Ensuite

Enjoy breathtaking, panoramic views from our new, friendly, warm homestay. Situated 2.5km from Katikati and close to many attractions, including golf courses, walking tracks, wineries and beaches. We will share our wonderful lifestyle with you. Our spaniel Bess, with tail wagging, will guide you through our home, which offers ensuite bedrooms, large comfortable lounge, laundry facilities and wheelchair access. we are relaxed retired couple, with interests in aviation, boating, fishing, world affairs and good conversation. Home away from home.

Omokoroa *15 km N of Tauranga*

Walnut Cottage *B&B Cottage with kitchenette*
Ken & Betty Curreen
309 Plummers Point Road, Omokoroa,
RD 2, Tauranga

Tel (07) 548 0692 Fax (07) 548 1764
walnuthomestay@actrix.co.nz
www.cybersurf.co.nz/curreen

Double $90-$110 Single $60-$90 (Continental)
Dinner $20
1 Queen 1 Double (2 bdrm)
Bathrooms: 1 Ensuite 1 Private

Situated on scenic Plummers Point Peninsula overlooking Tauranga Harbour we invite our guests to enjoy the tranquility our little corner of the world has to offer. Stroll along the Peninsula with its superb views, boat jetty and reserve. In the vicinity we have mineral hot pools, golf course, fountain & quarry gardens, tramping tracks, wineries and eating houses. Walnut Cottage is self-contained. Kowhai Suite has own entrance and conservatory with tea/coffee, T.V. Directions: Plummers Point Road is opposite Caltex Service Station on SH2.

Omokoroa *13 km N of Tauranga*

Serendipity *B&B Homestay*
Sarath and Linda Vidanage
77 Harbour View Road, Omokoroa, Tauranga

Tel (07) 548 2044
sarathv@yahoo.com
www.serendipitybnb.co.nz

Double $120 Single $85 (Full breakfast)
Child $30 Dinner $40 Children welcome
2 Queen 2 Double (2 bdrm)
Bathrooms: 2 Private

Welcome to our home and garden nestled above spectacular Omokoroa Beach. The beach is a short walk down the steps. Leisurely walking treks take you through the groves and gardens of the peninsula. A beautiful golf course and local hot pools are minutes away. We are a well-traveled couple who have found our paradise. We love to cook and offer a varied cuisine from traditional to exotic. In one stop you will experience the best of Tauranga and The Bay of Plenty.

Omokoroa *17 km N of Tauranga*

Seascape *B&B*
Sue & Geoff Gripton
5 Waterview Terrace, Omokoroa

Tel (07) 548 1027 or 021 1711936
grippos@xtra.co.nz
www.seascape.i8.com

Double $90-$100 Single $65 (Full breakfast)
1 Double 2 Single (2 bdrm)
Bathrooms: 1 Ensuite

Come share our stunning views of Tauranga Harbour and Kaimais. On our doorstep are beaches, walkways, golf, hot pools, boat ramps etc. Just halfway (15 minutes) between Tauranga and Katikati, we offer a double room with ensuite and TV, twin room with shared bathroom, both with tea/coffee. Enjoy a cooked or continental breakfast with homemade bread and jams while gazing at the ever-changing view. Only 3 1/2 kilometres from SH2, left at roundabout, 1st right, 1st left into Waterview Terrace. Geoff, Sue and our cat will welcome you.

Omokoroa *20 km N of Tauranga*

Bay Watch *B&B*
Allan & Jan Baldock
31 Harbour View Road, Omokoroa, Tauranga

Tel (07) 548 2725 Fax (07) 548 2725
janb@wave.co.nz

Double $110 Single $75 (Full breakfast)
Visa MC accepted
Children welcome
1 Queen 1 Double (1 bdrm)
Bathrooms: 1 Ensuite 1 Private

Welcome to our new Mediteranean Style House, with stunning views of Tauranga Harbour and foreshore.
We offer a self-contained unit, with private ensuite, kitchen/lounge and Sky TV. Across the road from Omokoroa Beach, park, boat ramp, jetty, shops and restaurant. Also walk the beachfront around the Peninsula. 5 minutes to the golf course and hot pools. Fishing charters arranged. Our interests include fishing, golf and rugby. We look forward to giving you a Kiwi experience.

Tauranga *2 km W of Tauranga*

Ross Homestay *B&B Homestay*
Christine Ross
8A Vale Street, Bureta, Tauranga

Tel (07) 576 8895
rossvale@xtra.co.nz

Double $80 Single $50 (Continental)
Visa MC accepted
1 Twin 1 Single (2 bdrm)
Bathrooms: 2 Private

Welcome. We are located close to town, with a golf course and licensed restaurants nearby and a park opposite. Twin room has every comfort and large private bathroom. The single guest room has own facilities and TV. You can enjoy our spacious lounge and sunny balcony, or take a short stroll to harbour edge. Your hostess Christine, is a miniaturist and doll maker and has travelled extensively and is enjoying retirement. Breakfast of your choice. Off-street parking plus a garage. Will meet public transport.

Tauranga - Oropi *9 km S of Tauranga*

Grenofen *B&B Homestay*
Jennie & Norm Reeve
85 Castles Road, Oropi, RD 3, Tauranga

Tel (07) 543 3953 Fax (07) 543 3951
n.reeve@wave.co.nz

Double $120-$140 Single $80-$90 (Full breakfast)
Child by age Dinner $35
Children welcome
1 King 2 Single (2 bdrm)
Bathrooms: 2 Ensuite

We invite you to stay with us in our spacious home overlooking the countryside, sea, Tauranga City and Mt Maunganui. Our property is a sheltered 3 1/2 acres with trees, gardens and lawns. You may relax in quiet and privacy, enjoy the spa, or swim in our pool. both rooms have ensuite, electric blankets, TV, and comfortable chairs. Tea facilities in guest area, laundry done overnight if required. We love to share our home and travel experiences with guests. Be sure of a warm welcome.

Tauranga - Bethlehem *6 km NW of Tauranga*
Hollies *B&B*
Shirley & Michael Creak
Westridge Drive, Bethlehem, Tauranga 3001

Tel (07) 577 9678 Fax (07) 579 1678
stay@hollies.co.nz
www.hollies.co.nz

Double $120-$250 Single $105-$200
(Special breakfast)
Dinner $40pp Visa MC accepted
2 King/Twin 1 Queen 2 Single (3 bdrm)
Bathrooms: 1 Ensuite 2 Private

Hollies offers peace and tranquility. Elegant modern
country house,large luxuriously appointed guest lounge and bedrooms. Acre of beautiful gardens,
swimming pool. The spacious suite has super king (or twin) bed, ensuite, lounge & TV, kitchenette,
private entrance and balcony. Perfect for longer stays. Hairdryers, bathrobes and toiletries, fresh flowers,
chocolates and crisp linen and every attention to detail combine to ensure your stay is truly memorable.
Complimentary tea/coffee. Breakfast: healthy or indulgent, fresh fruit, croissants tempting cooked dishes.
Winery and restaurants 5 minutes. Muffee our cat.

Tauranga *5 km N of Tauranga*
Matua Bed and Breakfast *B&B*
Anne & Peter Seaton
34 Tainui Street, Matua, Tauranga

Tel (07) 576 8083 or 027 491 5566
Fax (07) 576 8086
pa_seaton@clear.net.nz
www.matuabedandbreakfast.co.nz

Double $85-$100 Single $60-$70 (Continental)
Child $30 Pet free home Children welcome
1 Queen 1 Twin (2 bdrm)
Bathrooms: 1 Guest share

Welcome to our quality 1 level well appointed home
set in a peaceful garden, only 200 metres to the estuary beach. Enjoy a generous continental breakfast
overlooking our picturesque garden. Tea, coffee, home-baking & laundry facilities are available anytime.
We have travelled extensively. Let us help you plan your sightseeing visits to local and regional places of
interest . We look forward to offering you friendly Kiwi hospitality making your stay very special. Please
phone for directions or the free pick up service from public transport.

Tauranga *3 km N of Tauranga Central*
Harbinger House *B&B Homestay*
Helen & Doug Fisher
209 Fraser Street, Tauranga

Tel (07) 578 8801 or 027 458 3049
Fax (07) 579 4101
d-h.fisher@xtra.co.nz
www.harbinger.co.nz

Double $80-$95 Single $60-$75 (Special breakfast)
Child half price Dinner $25 Visa MC accepted
2 Queen 2 Single (3 bdrm)
Bathrooms: 1 Guest share

Harbinger House provides affordable luxury in the
heart of Tauranga, being close to hospital, conference facilities, downtown and a new shopping mall
100 metres away. Our upstairs has been renovated with your comfort in mind, using quality furnishings,
linen, bathrobes, fresh flowers, tea and coffee. A guest phone and laundry facilities are available. The
queen rooms have separate vanities and private balconies. Breakfast is a gourmet event. We offer
complimentary pick up from public transport depots and off-street parking is available.

Please let us know
how you enjoyed your B&B experience.
Ask your host for a comment form
or leave a comment on www.bnb.co.nz

Bay of Plenty

Tauranga *10 km W of Tauranga*

The Lavender Patch Countrystay B & B *B&B Apartment with Kitchen*
Mike & Pamela Mail
136 Kennedy Road, Pyes Pa, RD 3, Tauranga

Tel (07) 543 2113 or 027 252 4441
Fax (07) 543 2731   mikemail@xtra.co.nz
www.lavenderpatch.co.nz

Double $120-$145 **Single** $105-$120
(Special breakfast) Child $15, under 10 free
Dinner $30pp Extra adult $20, limit 1
Visa MC accepted Children welcome
1 Queen 1 Single (1 bdrm)
Bathrooms: 1 Ensuite

Idyllic country-style apartment overlooking peaceful lavender gardens - a hint of the Provence. Your own private patio to relax outdoors. Separate entrance, sole occupancy, quiet location. Queen bed with fresh cotton linen scented with lavender. Shower with our own lovely lavender-scented shower gel and use our home-made lavender soap. Friendly but unobtrusive hosting guaranteed. Generous healthy breakfast with home-made preserves. Phone, fax, email and laundry services available. Visa/Mastercard. Children welcome. Pets - Winnie cat.

Tauranga *3 km W of Tauranga City Centre*

Be Our Guest *B&B motel studio unit*
Aileen & Lang Pringle
160 Waihi Road, Tauranga City

Tel (07) 571 8862 or 021 030 9627
Fax (07) 571 8862   beourguest@xtra.co.nz
www.beourguest.co.nz

Double $90-$100 **Single** $60-$80 (Full breakfast)
Child under 12 $15 Dinner $25
Self-contained studio units $80-$100
Visa MC Eftpos accepted Children welcome
1 Queen bed plus twin beds, 1Queen bed plus single bed
(2 bdrm and separate motel studio units)
Bathrooms: 1 Guest share

Welcome to warm Kiwi hospitality, with itinerary help. Our rooms all have TV, electric blankets, internet & laundry facilities available. Just a few minutes away are shopping in the city, wonderful cafes, hot mineral pools, bush walks, water falls, surf beaches, fishing, golf, horse riding, boating and more. Lang is a therapeutic masseur, Aileen loves to cook. Complimentary pick-up within city. Fresh coffee/tea & home-made biscuits are always available. Aileen & Lang would love to share some time with you.

Bay of Plenty

Contact us today

Tauranga - Tauriko *10 km SW of Tauranga*

Redwood Heights *B&B Farmstay*
Chrissy & Errol Jefferson
50 Redwood Lane, Tauriko RD 1, Tauranga

Tel (07) 543 1116 or 027 417 2891
Fax (07) 543 1742 redwoodheights@value.net.nz

Double $95 Single $70 (Full breakfast)
Child according to age, cot available
Dinner $25 by arrangement
Visa MC accepted Children welcome
1 King 2 Single (2 bdrm)
Bathrooms: 1 Private

Welcome to our 30 acre farm overlooking the Wairoa River and home of our belted galloway cattle, various animals and outside pets. We have a swimming pool, spa pool, extensive gardens with ponds and waterfall, kayaking, fishing on the river and walks. Only 5 minutes to winery and restaurants, 12 minutes to downtown Tauranga. Guest lounge with tea/coffee, tv/video or join us and exchange travel experiences. Relax and unwind with nothing to disturb you but the sounds of nature.

Tauranga *10 km SW of Tauranga*

Redwood Villa *B&B*
Bridget & Rod Hill
17 Redwood Lane, Tauriko RD 1, Tauranga

Tel (07) 543 2880 or (021) 779 589
Fax (07) 543 4780
redwoodvilla@xtra.co.nz
www.redwoodvilla.co.nz

Double $105-$145 (Continental)
Rates for multiple nights on request
Visa MC accepted Children welcome
2 Queen (2 bdrm)
Bathrooms: 1 Ensuite

Relax, enjoy, recharge amongst the ambience of the giant Redwood and Oak trees in our 100 year old villa. As the original Tauriko Trading Post (10km from Tauranga) servicing the district at the turn of the last century, much of the yesteryear charm remains. If you are looking for a home away from home, want to be treated to something special, enjoy your own space, or simply looking for a place to stay for a night or 2, give us a call. Complimentary refreshments on arrival.

Tauranga *8 km NW of Tauranga*

Oakridge Views *B&B*
Diane & Trevor Hinton
557 Cambridge Road, Tauriko, Tauranga

Tel (07) 543 0292 or 027 285 2189
Fax (07) 543 0294
oakridge.views@xtra.co.nz
www.oakridgeviews.co.nz

Double $90-$120 Single $50-$70 (Full breakfast)
Child under 12 $20
1 Queen 1 Twin (2 bdrm)
Bathrooms: 1 Ensuite 1 Private

Welcome to Oakridge Views, where your comfort is our concern. Enjoy our panoramic views of gardens and rolling hills. Relax in our comfortable 1 level home away from home with an acre of gardens. Handy to some of the top restaurants in the bay. Only 10 minutes to downtown Tauranga and over the harbour bridge to Mt Maunganui. Attractions include garden walks, tramping, parks, wineries, beaches, golf courses. Spa pool available. We love our small pooch, Molly.

Tauranga - Matua

Aramoana *B&B*

Doreen Anderson

9 Seaway Terrace, Matua, Tauranga

Tel (07) 576 3058 or 027 320 0203
Fax (07) 576 3758
andersondem@xtra.co.nz

Double $90 Single $70 (Breakfast by arrangement)
Children welcome
1 Queen 1 Twin (2 bdrm)
Bathrooms: 1 Guest share

Relax in comfort by the sea with fabulous views of the harbour and Mt Maunganui. Watch the ships coming and going to the port. Enjoy the lights at night and the moonlight sparkling on the water. Walk along the beach to parks and playgrounds. Dine or shop in the nearby village of Cherrywood or drive to golf, the nearest course only 4 minutes away. Use Aramoana as your base to explore the bay. Your host has extensive knowledge of the area and will make you very welcome.

Tauranga

Frog Cottage *Luxury B&B Self Contained*

Sally Morrison

379 Devonport Road, Tauranga

Tel (07) 571 5474 or 025 963 916
sally.morrison@xtra.co.nz
www.frogcottage.co.nz

Double $385 (Full provisions)
Visa MC accepted Not suitable for children
1 Queen 2 Single (2 bdrm)
Bathrooms: 1 Guest share Clawfoot bath

A 'gingerbread style' cottage built in 1939. French country style interior design. Totally self-contained luxury accommodation featuring an antique claw foot bath, opening fire, finest Egyptian cotton bed linen, fresh flowers and continental breakfast. Off-street parking, short stroll to CBD, cafes and harbour. Complimentary home-made macadamia and white chocolate biscuits.

Mt Maunganui *4 km N of Mt Maunganui*

Homestay on the Beach *Luxury Homestay Apartment with Kitchen*

Bernie & Lolly Cotter

85C Oceanbeach Road, Mt Maunganui

Tel (07) 575 4879 Fax (07) 575 4828
bernie.cotter@xtra.co.nz

Double $130 Single $90 (Continental)
Child negotiable Suite Double $160
Extra guests $25pp Children welcome
2 Queen 1 Single (2 bdrm)
Bathrooms: 1 Ensuite 1 Private

Welcome to our magnificent home by the sea. Choose from our self-contained suite, sleeping 2 couples and 1 single (suitable for children) with private deck. 1 min to beach for those casual walks. Upstairs is our Queen ensuite with TV. Your continental breakfast includes eggs any style. International golf course 500 metres. The famous "Mount Walk" up or around with 360 degree views is breathtaking. 4kms to shops, hot salt water pools, and restaurants for your enjoyment. Sorry no pets. Off street parking. Look forward to having you stay.

Bay of Plenty

Mt Maunganui *8 km S of Mt Maunganui*

Bermuda Homestay *Homestay*
Barbara Marsh
19 Bermuda Drive, Papamoa, Mount Maunganui

Tel (07) 575 5592 Fax (07) 575 5592
b.marsh@clear.net.nz

Double $100 **Single** $70 (Continental)
Visa MC accepted
1 Queen 2 Single (2 bdrm)
Bathrooms: 1 Guest share

Welcome to our modern, quiet home, a short walk
from one of New Zealand's finest beaches. Excellent
shopping available at both Bayfair Mall or Palm Beach
Shopping Plaza, only minutes away. Local activities include golf courses, hot salt pools, great restaurants
and cafes, fishing, swimming, surfing and walks around and up the glorious Mount. Relax in our private
outdoor garden and make yourself at your home away from home. Your well travelled hostess looks
forward to having you stay and assures unique hospitality.

Mt Maunganui *3 km S of Mt Maunganui*

Fairways *B&B Apartment with Kitchen*
Philippa & John Davies
170 Ocean Beach Road, Mt Maunganui

Tel (07) 575 5325 Fax (07) 578 2362
pipjohn@clear.net.nz

Double $95 **Single** $75 (Full breakfast)
Dinner $35pp including wine by arrangement
1 Queen 1 Double (2 bdrm)
Bathrooms: 1 Ensuite 1 Family share

A Golfer's paradise. Our comfortable, timbered,
character home adjoins the eighth fairway of the
Mount golf course, and is across the road from the
wonderful ocean beach. Enjoy with us interesting food, wine, art, music, conversation, and a bonus golf
lesson. John is a retired solicitor, teacher and former scratch golfer, and Pippa a registered nurse involved
in natural health. Our leisurely dinners are fun occasions, and John's desserts legendary. We are well
travelled both in New Zealand and abroad, and look forward to meeting you.

Mt Maunganui *9 km S of Mt Maunganui*

Pembroke House *B&B*
Cathy & Graham Burgess
12 Santa Fe Key, Royal Palm Beach,
Papamoa/ Mt Maunganui

Tel (07) 572 1000
PembrokeHouse@xtra.co.nz
www.pembrokehouse.co.nz

Double $90-$120 **Single** $70-$95 (Full breakfast)
Child $35 Visa MC accepted
2 Queen 1 Twin (3 bdrm)
Bathrooms: 2 Ensuite 1 Private

A modern home. Cross the road to the Ocean Beach,
where you can enjoy swimming, surfing and beach walks. Enjoy stunning sea views while dining at
breakfast. Near Palm Beach Shopping Plaza, restaurants and golf courses. Close proximity to Mount
Maunganui, Tauranga, Rotorua and Whakatane. Separate guest lounge with TV and tea making
facilities. Cathy, a schoolteacher, and Graham, semi-retired - your hosts. We are widely travelled and
both enjoy meeting people. Our home is shared with our Persian cat, Crystal. Unsuitable for pre-
schoolers.

Mt Maunganui - Papamoa *9 km SE of Mt Maunganui*
Hesford House *B&B Homestay*
Sally & Derek Hesford
45 Gravatt Road, Royal Palm Beach,
Papamoa/Mt Maunganui

Tel (07) 572 2825
derek.sally@clear.net.nz
www.hesfordhouse.co.nz

Double $90-$130 **Single** $60-$70 (Full breakfast)
Child $25 Children welcome
2 Queen 1 Twin (3 bdrm)
Bathrooms: 1 Ensuite

We invite you to stay in our tastefully decorated
modern, architecturally designed character home. Enjoy panoramic views of the Papamoa Hills together with exquisite sunsets. A short stroll to the shopping plaza or through the lakes to the beach. Close to restaurants, cafes and popular tourist attractions. Relax in a beautiful outdoor garden setting. Complimentary tea/coffee facilities, fridge and TVs in each room. Our unique location offers you magnificent beaches and only 50 minutes drive to Rotorua and Whakatane. Courtesy pickup from public transport.

Mt Maunganui *3 km S of Mt. Maunganui*
Beachside *B&B Homestay*
Lorraine & Jim Robertson
21B Oceanbeach Road, Mt Maunganui

Tel (07) 574 0960 or 021 238 0598
Fax (07) 574 0960 beachside@ihug.co.nz
www.beachsidebnb.co.nz

Double $90-$120 **Single** $75 (Full breakfast)
Visa MC accepted
1 King/Twin 2 Queen (3 bdrm)
Bathrooms: 2 Ensuite 1 Private

We are close to the action and golf courses but far enough away to be quiet. And only 30 seconds to NZ's most popular beach. Off-street parking & laundry facilities available. Courtesy transport from local airport, buses & information centre. Relax or indulge with Jim's cappuccinos and enjoy great sea views from our third storey guest lounge. Our generous breakfast includes a seasonal fresh fruit salad and home-baked bread. We are widely travelled and enjoy meeting people. We would love to help you to have a memorable stay in our beautiful locality.

Mt Maunganui *4 km SE of Mt Maunganui*
Wedge 'n' Wood *B&B*
Peter & Alison Watson
10 Fairway Avenue, Mount Maunganui

Tel (07) 574 6641 or 021 030 9393
Fax (07) 574 6641
wedgenwood@clear.net.nz

Double $120-$150 **Single** $90-$110 (Full breakfast)
2 King/Twin (2 bdrm)
Bathrooms: 2 Ensuite

Our new home is ideally situated for golfers, or anyone coming to enjoy what Mt Maunganui and the bay and beaches has to offer. We have 2 ground floor luxury rooms with super king/twin beds, own ensuite, fridge, sky TV, complimentary tea/coffee facilites. 2 minutes walk to Mt Maunganui golf course, or an easy 10 minute drive to Mount and Tauranga shops. Courtesy pick up from public transport. Breakfast for a king in our sunroom, where our aquarium filled with tropical fish swim lazily about.

Maketu Beach - Te Puke *8 km E of Te Puke*
Blue Tides Beachfront B&B/Homestay plus Sea View Unit
B&B & Apartment with Kitchen
Patricia Haine
7 Te Awhe Road, Maketu Beach, Bay of Plenty

Tel (07) 533 2023 or 025 2613077.
0800 359 191 Fax (07) 533 2023
info@bluetides.co.nz
www.bluetides.co.nz

Double $130-$165 Single $110-$130 (Full breakfast)
Unit $130 double Visa MC accepted
2 King/Twin 2 Queen (4 bdrm)
Bathrooms: 4 Ensuite

Qualmarked 3+. Stay in an historic seaside village, white sand beach and cafe across the road. Regional Award Winner 02-03 quality accommodation with many thoughtful extras. delicious full breakfasts with home-made local produce. Awesome coastal views, romantic sunsets and stunning starry night skies. Easy drive to Rotorua, Tauranga, Whakatane & the Junction. Home of kiwifruit. Recommended at least a 2 night stay. Also a self-catering sea view unit, full kitchen, separate entrance and garage. A special place I'd love to share with you.

Paengaroa *5 km E of Te Puke*
A Restful Retreat *B&B Homestay Cottage with Kitchen*
Linda Ross
45 Conway Road, Paengaroa, Bay of Plenty

Tel 025 956 874 or (07) 533 1375
lindaross@xtra.co.nz

Double $85 (Continental)
Child $55 Children and pets welcome
1 Queen 1 Single (1 bdrm)
Bathrooms: 1 Private

Stylish, sunny and cosy, double, self-contained within lovely home nestled in woodlands paradise at The Junction, Paengaroa in sunny Bay of Plenty. Paengaroa is central and enroute to Tauranga, Whakatane and Rotorua and very handy to Comvita, the internationally famous honey manufacturer. You will relax and unwind in this very tranquil setting. Cook your own dinner, dine with the family or enjoy our local take out or cafe cuisine. Children welcome (maximum 2) , Pets will be considered.

Pukehina Beach *21 km E of Te Puke*
Homestay on the Beach *Homestay*
Alison & Paul Carter
217 Pukehina Parade, Pukehina Beach, RD 9, Te Puke

Tel (07) 533 3988 or 027 276 7305
Fax (07) 533 3988 p.a.carter@pukehina-beach.co.nz
www.homestays.net.nz/pukehina.htm

Double $110-$120 Single $70 (Full breakfast)
Child half price Dinner $30 Unit $140
Visa MC accepted Pet free home Children welcome
2 Double (2 bdrm)
Bathrooms: 1 Guest share

Welcome to our absolute beachfront home situated on the Pacific Ocean. Your accommodation situated downstairs, allowing complete privacy if you so wish, includes, TV lounge with coffee/tea, fridge, microwave and laundry facilities, also available at separate rate. Enjoy magnificent views from your own sundeck, including White Island volcano and occasional visits from friendly dolphins. A golf course 13km away. 30-40 minute drive from Tauranga, Mount Maunganui, Whakatane and Rotorua. A licensed restaurant 2km, surf casting, swimming, walks or relax and enjoy our unique paradise.

~

Matata - Pikowai *30 km NW of Whakatane*
Fothergills on Mimiha *S/C B&B   Cottage with kitchen, deck and own entrance*
Bev & Hilton Fothergill
84 Mimiha Road, Pikowai/Matata, Whakatane

Tel (07) 322 2224 or 021 131 5171
027 460 5958 Fax (07) 322 2224
beverlyf@xtra.co.nz www.fothergills.co.nz

Double $120-$140 Single $90-$120 (Continental)
Extra person $20 Dinner $40 by arrangement
Cottage $150-170 per night, $650-$750 per week
Visa MC accepted Children welcome
2 Queen 1 Twin 1 Single (4 bdrm)
Bathrooms: 2 Private very good shower pressure

Hilton & Bev offer you their modern upstairs B&B unit
or their self-service cottage situated on their beautiful rural
property on a quiet country road halfway between Te Puke
and Whakatane, and less than 1km from the main road and
beach.

Our lovely B&B unit has TV in each bedroom, plus a
kitchenette with fridge, microwave, frypan to cater for
yourself if desired. New comfortable beds, black-out
blinds, insect screens, coordinated colours, comfy chairs all
contribute to the high standard we aspire to. The bathroom,
downstairs, boasts a really great shower! Breakfast can be

provided in the unit to enjoy when you want, or you can come to the house. Fresh, home-grown, home-made!

Mimiha Cottage is built on its own site beside the Mimiha Stream. A 2-bedroomed cottage, this is fully
equipped, sunny & warm, wheelchair accessible and comfortably, tastefully furnished. New and comfortable
beds & bedding assure you of a good night's sleep in this peaceful place. Lots of good space for lounging and
living, with TV, excellent gas heating, large dining table, everything provided including your first breakfast.
Outside a paved courtyard, trellising and shade-covers protect & provide privacy for you as you dine in the
outdoor area, cook your BBQ, or just relax! Our very large country-style garden is waiting to delight you.

Wide flower borders with 220 roses, perennials, shrubs, trees provide beauty whatever the season. As well we
grow a wide variety of edibles, - vegetables, herbs, fruits, from which we make special preserves which we offer
as appetizers, at meals and for sale. Our friendly fox terrier, Mo, will show you the way when you walk up the
farm hill, follow the winding stream round the garden perimeter, or inspect the new pond in the fenced-off
area west of the house. Come & enjoy this special place!

121

Bay of Plenty

Matata *34 km W of Whakatane*

Pohutukawa Beach B&B & Cottage *B&B Farmstay Cottage with Kitchen*
Jorg & Charlotte Prinz
693 State Highway 2, RD 4, Whakatane

Tel (07) 322 2182 Fax (07) 322 2186
joe@prinztours.co.nz
www.prinztours.co.nz/bube.html

Double $110 **Single** $90 (Continental)
Dinner $35
Self-contained cottage (sleeps 4) $150-$180
Visa MC accepted Children welcome
1 King/Twin 2 Queen 1 Double (4 bdrm)
Bathrooms: 2 Ensuite 1 Private

Pohutukawa Beach B&B and Cottage are set in a picturesque location at the beach of the Pacific Ocean with views to active volcano White Island. Sometimes dolphins and whales pass by. We offer warm hospitality, sharing our home and cottage with travellers. The B&B is base for our tour company Prinz Tours, specialised in guided day tours and personalised itineraries New Zealand wide. Dinners with ingredients from the organic garden and cattle farm on request. We speak German.

Whakatane *18 km S of Whakatane*

Omataroa Deer Farm *Farmstay*
Jill & John Needham
Paul Road, RD 2, Whakatane

Tel (07) 322 8399 Fax (07) 322 8399
jill-needham@xtra.co.nz

Double $90 **Single** $60 (Full breakfast)
Child $40 Dinner $25
1 King 1 Queen (2 bdrm)
Bathrooms: 1 Ensuite 1 Private

We invite you to stay with us in our contemporary home which sits high on a hill commanding panoramic views. We farm deer organically and grow hydrangeas for export. You will be the only guest so you have sole use of a quiet private wing. Your evening meal will be venison, lamb or fresh seafood with home-grown vegetables. We dive, fish, tramp, ski, golf and love to travel. We have a friendly chocolate labrador and a burmese cat. Laundry available.

Whakatane *In Whakatane Central*

Travellers Rest *Homestay*
Karen & Jeff Winterson
28 Henderson Street, Whakatane 3080

Tel (07) 307 1015 travrest@wave.co.nz

Double $70-$80 **Single** up to $40 (Continental)
Modern undercover caravan available
Visa MC accepted
Children and pets welcome
1 King/Twin 1 Double (2 bdrm)
Bathrooms: 1 Guest share

Needing time out? Join Jeff & Karen in their quiet home and garden beside the Whakatane River. Enjoy scenic river walks, rest in their garden, or visit the vibrant local, art, craft, or garden trail.
Take a short drive to Ohope Beach, hot pools, river or sea activities. Our interests are: family, caravaning, gardening, photography, model cars, and stamp collecting. We look forward to sharing time with our guests, as do our friendly cat and dog. Internet facility available. Unavailable Sept 05 to Feb 06

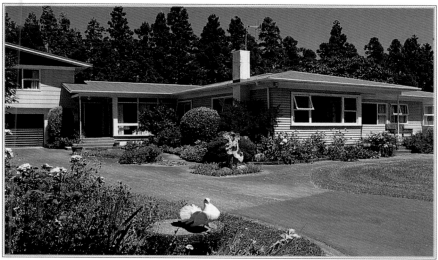

Whakatane *7 km W of Whakatane*

Whakatane Homestay- Leaburn Farm *Homestay*
Kathleen & Jim Law
237 Thornton Road, RD 4, Whakatane

Tel (07) 308 7487 or (07) 308 7955
Fax (07) 308 7487
kath.law@theredbarn.co.nz
www.whakatanehomestay.co.nz

Double $85-$95 Single $55-$65 (Full breakfast)
Dinner $25
Visa MC accepted
Pets welcome
1 Queen 2 Single (2 bdrm)
Bathrooms: 1 Guest share

Looking for peace and quiet, or do you want to explore this sunshine coast? If stimulating conversation or a browse in an extensive library is something you enjoy, you are welcome here.

Other guests comments over the 23 years we have been home-hosting, include: "thanks for your warm hospitality, sharing your lovely home. We especially enjoyed talking with you and creating a new friendship." Ron & Dorothy, USA "Yummy home-cooked meals and fantastic hosts." Steve, Australia "Wished we could have stayed longer." Dave & Margaret, UK As young oldies, we enjoy company, farming tales, travel, business interests, and your choice of topic.

We are handy to the golf course, 7km to thriving Whakatane Township. Special interests of genealogy, Lions Club, bowls and crafts. We have a craft shop and cafe/restaurant on the property.

Our queen-bedded guest room is adjacent to a spa bathroom, separate shower and toilet, and is shared only with other guests if the twin bedroom is occupied. Be as busy as you like or enjoy restful country atmosphere. Pamper yourselves at our place.

Whakatane *10 km S of Whakatane*

Baker's *B&B Homestay Cottage with Kitchen*
Lynne & Bruce Baker
40 Butler Road, RD 2, Whakatane

Tel (07) 307 0368 or 027 284 6996
Fax (07) 307 0368 bakers@world-net.co.nz
www.bakershomestay.co.nz

Double $120-$130 Single $90 (Continental)
Child $20 Dinner $30 by arrangement
Self-contained private cottage available
Visa MC accepted Children and pets welcome
1 King/Twin 2 Queen 2 Single (4 bdrm)
Bathrooms: 2 Ensuite 1 Private

You will be sure of a friendly welcome to our lovely country home nestled amongst mature gardens, croquet lawn, pentaque court swimming and spa pool to enjoy and relax in. Choose between our delightful fully self-contained 2 bedroom cottage or be pampered with bed & breakfast in our warm spacious home. Guest lounge has Sky TV, tea/coffee and treats. Lynne and Bruce are keen outdoor hosts enjoying fishing, surfing, gardening and travel. White Island tours, dolphin watching, deep-sea fishing and diving activities can be arranged for your memorable stay.

Whakatane *1.5 km S of Whakatane Central*

Crestwood Homestay *B&B Separate Suite*
Janet & Peter McKechnie
2 Crestwood Rise, Whakatane, Bay of Plenty

Tel (07) 308 7554 or 0800 111 449
025 624 6248 Fax (07) 308 7551
pandjmckechnie@xtra.co.nz
www.crestwood-homestay.co.nz

Double $90-$12 Single $70-$90 (Continental)
Dinner $30 by arrangement Visa MC accepted
1 Queen 1 Twin (2 bdrm)
Bathrooms: 1 Private Two or more guests travelling
together have the option of shared facilities

Close to town, wharf and coastal walkway, an ideal base to stay if visiting White Island, dolphin watching, or scenic coastal walkway. Quiet surroundings with extensive sea views from all rooms. Separate upstairs area for guests with all home comforts. Private access, spacious rooms, lounge, kitchenette, sunny deck and safe off-road parking. Breakfast and evening meals are served downstairs where we enjoy conversation, give helpful advice and arrange activities. Trout fishing rivers and lakes, golf, beaches and hot springs a short drive away. Option of single party booking or shared facilities

Whakatane *13 km W of Whakatane*

Kanuka Cottage *B&B Farmstay Kitchen/laundry share*
Carol & Ian Boyd
880A Thornton Road, RD 4, Whakatane

Tel (07) 304 6001 Fax (07) 304 6001
kanuka1@xtra.co.nz

Double $80-$100 (Full breakfast)
Child $15 Dinner $25 by arrangement
Visa MC accepted Children welcome
1 King/Twin 1 Queen 3 Single (2 bdrm)
Bathrooms: 2 Ensuite

Enjoy expansive sea and active volcano views from our B&B and self-contained units. Set in 23 secluded acres of coastal kanuka with private access to sandy surf beach. Good surfcasting and kontiki fishing. White Island tours, deep-sea fishing, and other recreational activities arranged. Handy to golf courses. Large and interesting succulent, cacti and bromeliad gardens with plants for sale. Feed our friendly alpaca, boer goats, ducks and chickens. Sample our fresh vegetables, fruit and eggs organically produced on our property. We are on the Pacific Coast Highway.

Whakatane

Lake View Bed & Breakfast *B&B*

Susan & Steven Barton
181 King Street, Whakatane

Tel (07) 306 0800 or 0800 161 820
Fax (07) 306 0081
susan@pascoebarton.co.nz

Double $110-$125 Single $100-$115 (Full breakfast)
Visa MC accepted
Not suitable for children
1 King (1 bdrm)
Bathrooms: 1 Ensuite

Relax and enjoy our tranquil setting on Sullivan
Lakefront with its wonderful birdlife. Your room has everything to ensure a comfortable and pampered stay, complete with a quality king-size bed and handcrafted rimu furniture. The large ensuite has a large spa bath for 2 and separate shower. Coffee/teamaking facilities, Sky television, and leather couch are included in the room. Your room opens onto a private courtyard where breakfast can be served or choose to have breakfast overlooking the lake from the dining room. 2 children.

Ohope Beach *6 km E of Whakatane*

Shiloah *B&B Homestay*

Pat & Brian Tolley
27 Westend, Ohope Beach

Tel (07) 312 4401 Fax (07) 312 4401

Double $66-$90 Single $35-$45 (Full breakfast)
Child half price Dinner $18-25 by arrangement
Self-contained unit available
1 Queen 1 Twin 4 Single (2 bdrm)
Bathrooms: 1 Guest share 2 Private

Homestay: paradise on the beach - view White Island
and enjoy our hospitality. Facilities available for
disabled guests. Classic car enthusiasts - well travelled.
Also available is a self-catered unit, separate from our B&B, with 1 twin bedroom, 1 single bed and 2 bed settees if required, complete with shower and kitchenette. Tariff; $30-50 own bedding, extra if supplied. Access to beach across road. Fishing, swimming, surfing, and bush walks.

Ohope Beach *8 km SE of Whakatane*

Oceanspray Homestay *Homestay Separate Cottage with Kitchen*

Frances & John Galbraith
283A Pohutukawa Avenue, Ohope, Bay of Plenty

Tel (07) 312 4112 or Mobile 027 286 6824
Fax (07) 312 4192 frances@oceanspray.co.nz
www.oceanspray.co.nz

Double $120-$150 Single $80-$100 (Full provisions)
Child negotiable Visa MC accepted
Children welcome
3 Queen 2 Twin (5 bdrm)
Bathrooms: 1 Ensuite 2 Private

Welcome to our beachfront home. Wonderful sea
views from our upstairs decks. Our modern downstairs 3 bedroom apartment is self-contained with own kitchen, lounge, two bathrooms (one en-suite). Adjacent to our house, a 2 bedroom, modern, self-contained cottage. Families welcome. Home comforts - Sky TV, books, videos/toys for children. Continental breakfast provisions are supplied into your unit. John's pursuits are kayaking and longline fishing. Frances enjoys entertaining and providing excellent cuisine. Our cat and labrador dog also make you welcome.

Ohope Beach *8 km N of Whakatane*

The Rafters *Apartment with Kitchen*
Pat Rafter
261A Pohutukawa Avenue, Ohope Beach

Tel (07) 312 4856 Fax (07) 312 4856
The_Rafters_Ohope@xtra.co.nz
www.wave.co.nz/pages/macaulay/The_Rafters.htm

Double $80 **Single** $75 (Accomodation only)
Child $10
Extra adult $20, limit 1
Children and pets welcome
1 King 1 Single (2 bdrm)
Bathrooms: 1 Ensuite

Breakfast is not supplied, Unit is self-contained.
Minimum 2 night stay. Maximum 3 guests.

Panoramic sea views: White, Whale islands, East Coast. Safe swimming. Many interesting walks. Golf, tennis, bowls, all within minutes.

Licensed Chartered Club Restaurant opposite. Trips to volcanic White Island, fishing, jet boating, diving, swimming with dolphins arranged.

Full cooking facilities; private entrance, sunken garden, BBQ. Complimentary: tea, coffee, biscuits, fruit, newspaper, personal laundry service.

Pat's interests are: philosophy, theology, history, English literature, the making of grape wines and all spirits, golf, bowls, music and tramping. I have a friendly weimaraner dog.

Courtesy car available. House trained animals welcomed. 4 restaurants and oyster farm within 5 minutes drive. I look forward to your company and assure you unique hospitality.

Directions: on reaching Ohope Beach turn right, proceed 2km to 261A (beach-side) name "Rafters" on a brick letterbox with illuminated B&B sign.

Ohope Beach *10 km NE of Whakatane*
Tawai House *B&B Cottage No Kitchen*
Audrey & Ray Butler
13 Tawai Street, Ohope Beach 3085

Tel (07) 312 4332

Double $85-$90 Single $60 (Continental)
1 Double 2 Single (2 bdrm)
Bathrooms: 1 Private

Our home is situated 100 metres from the ocean beach, swimming and surfing. Ray an experienced fisherman will enjoy taking you fishing. You may enjoy cooking on the barbeque in your own private secluded area. Only minutes from the Chartered Club, restaurants, golf, bowls and bush walks. Directions: Tawai Street left off Harbour Road.

Ohope *10 km SE of Whakatane*
Moanarua Beach Cottage *Cottage with Kitchen*
Miria & Taroi Black
2 Hoterini Street, Ohope

Tel (07) 312 5924 or 021 255 6192
info@moanarua.co.nz
www.moanarua.co.nz

Double $110-$140 Single $90-$130 (Continental)
Child 1 baby or small child
Dinner by arrangement
Children and pets welcome
1 King (1 bdrm cottage)
Bathrooms: 1 Ensuite

Naumai, haeremai - Ohope the place of fun, surf, sand and sunshine! Miria and Taroi of Moanarua Beach Cottage offer you a romantic hideaway nestled between the ocean and the harbour. Feel free to use our kayaks, BBQ, expansive decks with sea views of both sides and luxury spa. Chat with us about local history and the displays of contemporary Maori art works that adorn our home, cottage and garden. Kick back and relax in your private fully self-contained cottage or enjoy some of the many local activities.

Ohope Beach *6 km E of Whakatane*
Memorymakers *B&B Apartment with Kitchen*
Lionel Korach
186 Ocean Road, Ohope

Tel (07) 312 5404 or 027 454 5597
memorymakers@xtra.co.nz
www.memorymakers.co.nz

Double $100-$150 Single $100 (Special breakfast)
Child negotiable
Dinner by arrangement
Children welcome
1 King 2 Single (2 bdrm)
Bathrooms: 1 Ensuite

Hi from your hosts, Hilary & Lionel, we have a modern 2 bedroom self-contained apartment with sundeck especially for you. We are perfectly situated with the beach across the road, handy access to cafes, restaurants or try our cusine. We have stacks of off-road parking for car and boat. We have options available for fishing or scenic trips on our boat. Bush walks,trout fishing beach walks, or guided trips around the bay. Use us, or on your own, or a bit of both.

Bay of Plenty

Opotiki *18 km E of Opotiki*

Coral's B&B *B&B Farmstay Cottage with Kitchen*
Coral Parkinson
Morice's Bay, Highway 35, RD 1, Opotiki

Tel (07) 315 8052 Fax (07) 315 8052
coralsb.b@wxc.net.nz

Double $80-$120 Single up to $70
(Breakfast by arrangement) Child $10
Dinner $25 Breakfast $15pp by arrangement
Children and pets welcome
1 Queen 1 Double 2 Single (3 bdrm)
Bathrooms: 1 Private

We provide self-contained accommodation located
on our hobby farm. As well as pets and farm animals we collect varied memorabilia. Enjoy the beach
and bird life; swim at nearby sandy surf beach. Fish, ramble over the rocks, explore caves. Our 2 storied
cottage features lead-light windows, native timbers, large decks look out across the bay and native bush.
3 golf courses within an hours drive; covered parking, home-made bread and preserves. We have a clasic
English Daimler car and offer visits in it to our local Marae.

Opotiki - Tirohanga *7 km E of Opotiki*

Tirohanga Beach Holiday Home *Cottage with Kitchen*
Natalie & Jeff Jaffarian
787 State Highway 35E, Opotiki

Tel (07) 315 8899 Fax (07) 315 8896
jaffarian@xtra.co.nz
www.beachholidayhomenewzealand.com/

Double $90 Single $90 (Breakfast by arrangement)
Dinner by arrangement Weekly & monthly rates
Visa MC accepted
1 Queen 1 Double 1 Twin 3 Single (4 bdrm)
Bathrooms: 2 Private

Each Unit has a tub shower bath, full kitchen with
fridge, stove, microwave, kettle, and utensils. Barbecue, washing machine, internet access and telephone
may be available. Tirohanga Beach Holiday Home is an ideal get-away for all seasons. Beautiful beach
extends for miles in each direction. Swimming, surfing, fishing, beach walking at your doorstep. Enjoy
breathtaking sun-rises and sun-sets from the large deck overlooking White and Whale Islands.

Opotiki *11 km W of Opotiki*

Fantail Cottage *Homestay*
Meg & Mike Collins
336 Ohiwa Harbour Road, RD 2, Opotiki

Tel (07) 315 4981 Fax (07) 315 4981
wendylyn@wave.co.nz

Double $85 Single $50 (Full breakfast)
Dinner $25pp
1 Double (1 bdrm)
Bathrooms: 1 Ensuite

Set on a bush-clad spur, your cosy room and hot spa
have expansive views of the tidal Ohiwa Harbour. A
birdwatcher's paradise, on one of the best coastal
birding sites in the North Island. Meg and Mike have travelled widely overseas and offer a classic NZ
experience. Enjoy organic home grown produce, fishing, swimming or walking on the beach. 34 km
from Whakatane, 15 km from Opotiki. From SH2 turn at Waiotahi Bridge. Follow signs to Ohiwa
Holiday Park and Fantail Cottage.

Opotiki - Te Kaha *66 km E of Opotiki*

Tui Lodge *B&B*
Joyce, Rex & Peter Carpenter
200 Copenhagen Road, Te Kaha, BOP 3093

Tel (07) 325 2922 Fax (07) 325 2922
jorex@xtra.co.nz
www.tuilodge.co.nz

Double $115-$140 Single $95-$110 (Full breakfast)
Child POA Dinner $30pp
Visa MC accepted Pets welcome
3 Queen 2 Twin 1 Single (6 bdrm)
Bathrooms: 4 Ensuite 1 Private

Tui Lodge offers comfort and tranquility without
equal on the coast. Purpose built in 1998, the lodge is in complete harmony with our forest surrounds
and semi-tropical gardens. We think we do it well but what do our guests think? "This is paradise reborn
I could stay for life." - Marianne Vidon, France. "So gracious & so beautiful with absolute comfort."
- Jerry & Cobi, USA. The best B&B we have stayed in across the world - Helen & Paul Milmine, NZ

Opotiki - Waihau Bay *112 km N of Opotiki*

Waihau Bay Homestay *B&B Homestay Apartment with Kitchen*
Noelene & Merv Topia
RD 3, Opotiki

Tel (07) 325 3674 or 0800 240 170
Fax (07) 325 3679 n.topia@clear.net.nz
www.nzhomestay.co.nz/topia.html

Double $85-$10 Single $55-$75 (Full breakfast)
Child half price Dinner $25
Visa MC Eftpos accepted
Children and pets welcome
2 King/Twin 1 Queen 2 Twin 2 Single (4 bdrm)
Bathrooms: 2 Ensuite 1 Guest share 2 Private

Surrounded by unspoiled beauty we invite you to come and enjoy magnificent views, stunning sunsets,
swim, go diving, kayaking (we have kayaks) or just walk along the sandy beach. You are most welcome
to join Merv when he checks his craypots each morning and his catches are our cuisine specialty. Fishing
trips, horse treks and guided cultural walks are also available. We have 2 self-contained units with
disabled facilities, and a double room with ensuite. Our cats Whiskey & Tosca enjoy making new friends.

Rotorua - Lake Rotoiti *20 km NE of Rotorua*

Lakestay Rotoiti *B&B*
Graeme & Raewyn Natusch
173 Tumoana Road, Lake Rotoiti, RD 4 Rotorua

Tel (07) 345 4089 or 027 4188404
Fax (07) 345 4089
lakestayrotoiti@xtra.co.nz

Double $120-$150 Single $80-$100 (Full breakfast)
Dinner $30 Self-contained studio $120-$150
Off season rates May-October
2 Queen (2 bdrm)
Bathrooms: 2 Ensuite

Lakestay Rotoiti, a very special destination for the
discerning couple or individual travellers both summer and winter with friendly informative hosts and
siamese cat. One of just 3 lakefront properties in a beautiful secluded sandy bay surrounded by native
bush, forest and stunning lake views from all living and guest bedrooms. Excellent swimming, trout
fishing, walking tracks and natural rejuvinating hot baths nearby. Guests enjoy complimentary use
of kyaks, dingy, windsurfer and bicycles. Wonderful evening dinner by arrangement. Directions are
essential. A truely unique experience.

Rotorua *2 km N of Rotorua centre*

Rotorua's Legend on the Lake Homestay *Homestay Apartment with Kitchen*

Murray & Heather Watson

33 Haumoana Street, Koutu, Rotorua

Tel (07) 347 1123 or 027 492 7122
Fax (07) 347 1313 muzzandheb@kol.co.nz
www.troutnz.co.nz

Double $135 Single $100 (Full breakfast)
Child $20 Minimum stay 2 nights
Discount for 3 or more nights Visa MC accepted
1 Queen (1 bdrm)
Bathrooms: 1 Ensuite

On arrival you will be greeted with our magnificent, quiet and secluded lakes-edge view and a genuine Kiwi welcome. Please join us on the lawn beside the lake for refreshments as we would love to help you plan your stay by sharing our local knowledge of the area and its many attractions. Hearing the tranquil lapping of the lake you will find it hard to believe you are only 5 minutes drive from the city centre. You will find your self-contained apartment to have all the comforts of home (washing machine, TV, DVD, video, stereo, oven, microwave and dishwasher). Separate bedroom (queen) and living area/kitchen with ensuite access from both rooms.

Our smoke-free apartment ensures a freshness you will enjoy. Breakfast includes fruit, yoghurt, cereal, juice and tea/coffee followed by a cooked breakfast - all this you can choose the time you would like to have it served. Breakfast is a great time to get to know us and for us to help you make the most of your time in this volcanic thermal paradise. We are more than happy to assist with local bookings and recommend you sample some of the strong local Maori culture.

Murray operates a trout fishing charter business on Lake Rotorua and Heather runs a gourmet food business, we have both travelled extensively, internationally and throughout New Zealand and enjoy meeting people from all over the world. We have been running homestays for the last 10 years and really know how to make your time here enjoyable and comfortable. Feel free to sit on the lawn or in the conservatory and watch the spectacular sunsets we are lucky enough to enjoy almost every night. We hope you will arrive as our guests and leave as our friends.

Rotorua - Ngongotaha *17 km N of Rotorua*

Deer Pine Lodge *B&B Farmstay*
John Insch
255 Jackson Road, Ngongotaha, Rotorua

Tel (07) 332 3458 or 027 312 0338
Fax (07) 332 3458 deerpine@clear.net.nz

Double $60-$100 Single $70-$85 (Continental)
Child $20-$25 Dinner $30 by arrangement
Visa MC accepted
3 King 1 Queen 4 Single (5 bdrm)
Bathrooms: 5 Ensuite

Welcome to Deer Pine Lodge. We farm deer, our property surrounded with trees planted by the New Zealand Forest Research as experimental shelter belts on our accredited deer farm.

The nearby city of Rotorua is fast becoming New Zealand's most popular tourist destination offering all sorts of entertainment. We have a cat and a boxer (Jake), very gentle. Our 4 children have grown up and left the nest.

Our bed & breakfast units/rooms are private with ensuites, TV, radio, fridge, microwave, electric blankets on all beds, tea/coffee making facilities, heaters. Heaters and hair dryers also in bathrooms. Our 2 bedroom fully self-contained units, designed by prominent Rotorua architect Gerald Stock, each having private balcony, carport, sundeck, ensuite, spacious lounge, kitchen, TV, radio, heater etc. Cot and highchair available, also laundry facilities. Security arms fitted on all windows, smoke detectors installed in all bedrooms and lounges, fire extinguisher installed in all kitchens.

Holding NZ certificate in food hygiene ensuring high standards of food preparation and serving. Guests are free to do the conducted tour and observe the different species of deer and get first hand knowledge of all aspects of deer farming after breakfast. If interested please inform host on arrival. 3 course meal of beef, lamb, or venison by prior arrangement, pre-dinner drinks.

Hosts John and Betty, originally from Scotland have travelled extensively overseas and have many years experience in hosting look forward to your stay with us. Prefer guests to smoke outside.

Bay of Plenty

Rotorua *2 km N of Rotorua centre*

Rotorua Lakeside Homestay *Homestay*
Ursula & Lindsay Prince
3 Raukura Place, Rotorua

Tel (07) 347 0140 or 0800 223 624
Fax (07) 347 0107
the-princes@xtra.co.nz

Double $100-$110 Single $80-$90 (Special breakfast)
MINIMUM STAY OF TWO NIGHTS
Discount of $5 per night for 3 or more nights
1 King/Twin 1 Queen (2 bdrm)
Bathrooms: 1 Ensuite 1 Private

We invite you to share our spacious, modern home in
its tranquil lake setting. Hosts since 1988, our interests include world affairs and environmental issues.
We enjoy outdoor activities - feel free to use our Canadian canoe. Now retired, we have lived overseas
and still travel extensively. At breakfast (home-made goodies) we'll help you plan activities and arrange
bookings. Directions: From Lake Road turn into Bennetts Road, then first left into Koutu Road, then
first right into Karenga Street. Turn RIGHT into Haumona Street, a left turn at the end brings you
down Raukura Place to our door.

~

Rotorua *4 km SW of Rotorua*

Hunts Farm *Farmstay*
Maureen & John Hunt
363 Pukehangi Road, Rotorua

Tel (07) 348 1352

Double $100 Single $70 (Full breakfast)
Child $25
1 King/Twin 1 Queen 2 Single (2 bdrm)
Bathrooms: 2 Ensuite

Come rest in our new home as we help you plan your
itinerary and book your local tours. Explore by foot or
farm vehicle our 150 acre farm running beef and deer. Now children have flown, Tigger, our trusty farm
dog, who lives in the garden, is chief helper. Views are magical, 360 degrees of lake, island, forest, city
and farm. Guest area has private entrance, includes lounge tea coffee facilities, TV, fridge. 2 triple rooms,
each with ensuite lead out to sunny private terraces.

~

Rotorua - Ngakuru *32 km S of Rotorua*

Te Ana Farmstay *Farmstay*
The Oberer Residence: Heather Oberer
Poutakataka Road, Ngakuru, RD 1, Rotorua

Tel (07) 333 2720 or 021 828 151
Fax (07) 333 2720   teanafarmstay@xtra.co.nz
www.teanafarmstay.co.nz

Double $100-$150 Single $75 (Special breakfast)
Child $20-$35 Dinner by prior arrangement
Children welcome
2 Queen 4 Single (4 bdrm)
Bathrooms: 2 Ensuite 1 Family share

Te Ana, a 569 acre dairy beef and sheep property, offers peace and tranquility in a spacious rural garden
setting affording magnificent views of lake, volcanically-formed hills and lush farmland. Enjoy a leisurely
stroll before joining host for a very generous country breakfast. Ideal base from which to explore the
Rotorua and Taupo attractions, Waiotapu and Waimungu Thermal Reserves, Waikite Thermal mineral
swimming pool and Tamaki Tours Hangi. Families welcomed by Sam, our loyal Jack Russell. Farm tour,
canoe and fishing rod available.

Rotorua *4 km S of Rotorua*

Serendipity Homestay *B&B Homestay*
Kate & Brian Gore
3 Kerswell Terrace, Tihi-o-Tonga, Rotorua

Tel (07) 347 9385 or 025 609 3268
b.gore@clear.net.nz
www.serendipityhomestay.co.nz

Double $120-$130 Single $75 (Special breakfast)
Child under 12 $35 Dinner $35 by arrangement
Visa MC accepted
Pet free home Children welcome
1 Queen 2 Twin (2 bdrm)
Bathrooms: 1 Private spa bath plus shower

Marvel - at unsurpassed views of geysers, city, lakes and beyond. Relax - in all day sun, on the deck, in the conservatory or in the privacy of our garden. Indulge - in comfort, home-cooked cuisine and the friendly folk who have been enjoying hosting for many years. Our interests are, golf, tramping, travel, the environment, antiques and sharing our extensive local and national knowledge with you. Let us advise you on the 'must see' list while in Rotorua and other highlights of our beautiful country. Welcome!

Rotorua - Ngongotaha *8 km N of Rotorua*

Suncrest Ngongotaha B&B *B&B*
Amanda & Gary Gower
74 Hall Road, Ngongotaha, Rotorua

Tel (07) 357 4336 or 0800 357 4336
Fax (07) 357 4336 gandagower@xtra.co.nz

Double $130-$140   Single $100-$110 (Full breakfast)
Dinner by arrangement Visa MC accepted
1 Queen 1 Twin (2 bdrm)
Bathrooms: 1 Guest share 1 and a half bathrooms, Main bathroom has spa bath and walk-in shower, toilet also has a vanity.

We welcome you to our brand new home in Ngongotaha. A wonderful view of Lake Rotorua and Mt Tarawera from our lounge, especially at sunrise and dusk. Private courtyard to relax in and enjoy our developing garden. Close to many tourist attractions. We can assist you with bookings, information etc. for Rotorua's attractions and restaurants. A short distance to lake, fishing streams and beautiful walks. Free pick up from transport terminals, off-street parking. Laundry available. Complimentary tea/coffee. Our interests, travel, music, arts & crafts.

Rotorua *1.5 km S of Rotorua*

Heather's Homestay *B&B Homestay*
Heather Radford
5A Marguerita Street, Rotorua

Tel (07) 349 4303
heathermr@xtra.co.nz

Double $80 Single $50 (Full breakfast)
Visa MC Amex accepted
Children welcome
2 Queen 1 Twin (2 bdrm)
Bathrooms: 2 Private

Haeremai - Welcome to my comfortable home in the heart of the thermal area, minutes from the city centre yet quiet and private. Rotorua born and bred I am proud of my city and enjoy sharing what knowledge I have with guests. A keen tramper/walker, I also enjoy showing off the lovely walks in the area. For 10 years I have been a B&B host and look forward to many more visitors to my home and unique city. Directions: off Fenton Street.

Rotorua - Ngongotaha *10 km N of Rotorua*

Waiteti Lakeside Lodge *Homestay*
Val & Brian Blewett
2 Arnold Street, Ngongotaha, Rotorua

Tel (07) 357 2311 Fax (07) 357 2311
waitetilodge@xtra.co.nz
www.waitetilodge.co.nz

Double $170-$270 **Single** $150-$250 (Full breakfast)
Child over 10 $50 Multiple night rates available
Visa MC Amex accepted Pet free home
4 Queen 2 Single (5 bdrm)
Bathrooms: 3 Ensuite 2 Guest share 1 Private

Waiteti Lakeside Lodge is situated on the shores of Lake Rotorua at the mouth of the picturesque Waiteti Trout Stream, away from the sulphur fumes and traffic noise of Rotorua City but close to all of Rotorua's attractions, fine restaurants, and Maori culture.

The timber and natural stone lodge offers luxury private accommodation in traditional style and an extremely quiet and tranquil setting. There are 5 supremely comfortable bedrooms, 3 with ensuites, 1 private or 2 sharing a bathroom. The ensuite rooms have TVs and open on to balconies overlooking the lake, and in addition there is a private guests' lounge with satellite TV, video, library, pool table, and tea and coffee facilities. All rooms enjoy spectacular views of the lake and stream mouth, and the lodge's gardens extend to the water's edge, home to numerous native birds and waterfowl.

Enjoy trout fishing (with or without professional guide) from the lodge's grounds, on the lake in the lodge's own charter boat, or on one of the many productive local trout streams - your catch can be fresh smoked for a superb breakfast or lunch treat.

Alternatively you may prefer to take a guided boat trip to historic Mokoia Island, a sacred Maori site and wildlife sanctuary, where native flora and birdlife, including several rare and endangered species, abound. Your experienced hosts Brian and Val Blewett are available to advise and/or guide you at all times to ensure that your stay is highly enjoyable. Brian is a professional fishing guide with more than 30 years experience, so success is virtually guaranteed. Brian and Val will arrange bookings for all local attractions and activities including: Rotorua's best cafes and restaurants Maori culture and entertainment 6 golf courses back country/wilderness trout fishing white water rafting canoeing forest walks mountain biking float plane trips from the lodge.

Directions: Take Highway 5 from Rotorua to Ngongotaha, through town centre, over the railway line, turn second right into Waiteti Road. At the end turn right into Arnold Street and the lodge is at the end of the street next to the footbridge.

Rotorua *14 km NE of Rotorua*

Brunswick *Homestay*
Joy & Lin Cathcart
99 Brunswick Drive, RD 4, Rotorua 3221

Tel (07) 350 1472 or 021 256 5355 (mobile)
Fax (07) 350 1472
joylin@clear.net.nz

Double $110 Single $70 (Full breakfast)
Dinner by arrangement
Visa MC accepted
Pet free home Not suitable for children
1 King (1 bdrm)
Bathrooms: 1 Private adjacent to the bedroom

With peaceful surroundings and beautiful views over Lake Rotorua "Brunswick"is 15 mins from Rotorua City centre and 5mins from Rotorua Airport.Having retired from dairy farming Lin now enjoys his golf-Joy plays bridge and gardening is a shared hobby.Our guest room has TV, hot drink facilities-guest refrigerator available.We are smoke-free and have no pets.After 15years of hosting and many return guests, a cuppa, Joy's homebaking and a warm welcome awaits you!

Rotorua *5 km SE of Rotorua*

Walker Homestay & B&B *B&B Homestay Cottage with Kitchen*
Colleen & Isaac Walker
13 Glenfield Road, Owhata, Rotorua

Tel (07) 345 3882 or 021 050 9633
Fax (07) 345 3856 colleen.walker@clear.net.nz

Double $85-$90 Single $50-$55
(Continental provisions)
Child half price Dinner $25 by arrangement
Extra guest $15 Visa MC accepted Children welcome
1 Queen 1 Double 1 Twin 1 Single (3 bdrm)
Bathrooms: 1 Ensuite in house
1 Private in self-contained unit

2 Bedroom cottage in own garden area has lounge, kitchen, bathroom,and laundry. Room in house has ensuite; tea/coffee facilities; microwave; separate entrance and access to hosts living area. Have complete privacy or be one of the family. BBQ available. Colleen is a business administration tutor and Ike is a NZ Maori. He is a coach driver with a background of farming and paper industry, a keen fisherman and golfer. 2 friendly dachshund dogs will welcome you. 24 hours notice for evening meal. Off-road parking.

Rotorua *3 km W of Rotorua*

West Brook *B&B Homestay*
Judy & Brian Bain
378 Malfroy Road, Rotorua

Tel (07) 347 8073 Fax (07) 347 8073

Double $80 Single $50 (Continental)
Child under 12 half price Dinner $25
Children welcome
4 Single (2 bdrm)
Bathrooms: 1 Family share

Retired farmers with years of hospitality involvement, live 3km from city on western outskirts. Interests include meeting people, farming, international current affairs. Brian a Rotorua Host Lions member, Judy's interest extend to all aspects of homemaking and gardening. Both well appointed comfy guest rooms are equipped with electric blankets. The friendly front door welcome and chatter over the meal table add up to our motto: home away from home. Assistance with sightseeing planning and transport to and from tourist centre available.

Rotorua - Ngongotaha *17 km N of Rotorua*
Clover Downs Estate *B&B Homestay Farmstay*
Lyn & Lloyd Ferris
175 Jackson Road, RD 2, Ngongotaha, Rotorua

Tel (07) 332 2366 or 0800 3687 5323
021 712 866 Fax (07) 332 2367
Reservations@cloverdowns.co.nz
www.accommodationinrotorua.co.nz

Double $215-$305 Single $195-$290
(Special breakfast) Child negotiable
Visa MC Diners Amex accepted
Children welcome
3 King/Twin1 King (4 bdrm)
Bathrooms: 4 Ensuite

Welcome to our fine country Bed & Breaskfast accommodation on a deer and ostrich farm, nestled in a peaceful country setting just 15 minutes drive north of Rotorua city.

We can offer a choice of four individually decorated spacious king-size suites each comprising ensuite bathroom, tea/coffee making facilities, refrigerator, telephone, ironing facilities, hairdryer, TV, VCR, stereo & individual outdoor decks. We serve a leisurely breakfast each morning which, if you desire, is followed by our popular free deer and ostrich farm tour.

Visit our awesome cultural and scenic attractions.
Minutes drive from our property you will discover a myriad of things to do and see: stand on active volcanoes, peer into craters, see boiling mud or just soak in a mineral pool. We can advise you on trout fishing at one of the many lakes and rivers in the area, walk cool forest glades or maybe play a round of golf. With days as busy as this you'll be glad to come home to our gracious haven of relaxation. If you wish to go out, Rotorua has some wonderful restaurants and cafes. or you may like to enjoy a Maori hangi and concert. We strive to exceed our guests' expectations through an ineffable blend of warmth, generosity and detail.

Directions: Take State Highway 5 to roundabout. Travel thru Ngongotaha village on Hamurana Road - go over railway line then take third left into Central Road. Turn first right into Jackson Road - Clover Downs Estate is number 175 on left hand side.

Rotorua *3 km S of Rotorua*

Thermal Stay *B&B Homestay*

Wendy & Rod Davenhill
367 Old Taupo Road, Springfield, Rotorua 3201

Tel (07) 349 1605 or 025 377 122
Fax (07) 349 1641 davenhill@clear.net.nz
www.thermalstay.co.nz

Double $95-$120 Single $65-$80 (Full breakfast)
Dinner $30pp by arrangement
Visa MC accepted
Children (over 7 years) welcome
1 King 2 Queen 2 Single (3 bdrm)
Bathrooms: 2 Private 1 Guest share

An Oasis In the City. Quiet location, central, private. Thermally heated home and swimming pool, hot tub in winter. Secluded, tranquil gardens featuring waterfall, fish and native birdlife. Close to city centre, nearby thermal activities, forests, trout stream and 2 golf courses. Well travelled hosts who enjoy good food, wine and conversation. Our company, or time in the guest lounge with private patio, your choice. Dine with us or sample a local restaurant or Maori hangi/concert. Off road parking, laundry, email and fax available.

Rotorua *12 km NE of Rotorua*

Eucalyptus Tree Country Homestay *B&B Homestay Farmstay*

Manfred & Is Fischer
66 State Highway 33, RD 4, Rotorua

Tel (07) 345 5325 Fax (07) 345 5325
euc.countryhome@ihug.co.nz
homepages.ihug.co.nz/~euc.countryhome

Double $90 Single $60 (Full breakfast)
Dinner $30
1 King/Twin 2 Queen 1 Double (3 bdrm)
Bathrooms: 1 Family share 1 Guest share

Welcome to our quiet, smoke-free, high quality country home. On our small farm near Lake Rotorua, close to Lake Rotoiti and Okataina, we have a donkey, calves, sheep, chickens, rabbits, organic vegetables and fruit trees. Native bush drive to clear trophy trout fishing lakes and bush walks, thermal area, Maori culture, hot pools, horse riding, skydiving, whitewater rafting. Our hobbies are trout fishing from boat, and fly fishing in lakes and rivers, hunting and shooting. We lived in the USA, Canada, Indonesia, Mexico and Germany and speak their languages.

Rotorua *20 km E of Rotorua*

Lakeside B&B *B&B Homestay*

Laurice & Bill Unwin
155G Okere Road, RD 4, Rotorua

Tel (07) 362 4288 or 027 452 1483
Fax (07) 362 4288 laurice.bill@xtra.co.nz
www.lakesidebnb.co.nz

Double $150-$160 Single $120 (Full breakfast)
Child $10-22 Dinner $35pp Visa MC accepted
Pet free home Children welcome
1 King/Twin 2 Queen 1 Single (3 bdrm)
Bathrooms: 2 Ensuite 1 Private

From the house you will enjoy the views from your bedrooms overlooking Lake Rotoiti. Birdlife abounds on the lake. Each bedroom has very comfortable beds with pure cotton sheets, hairdryer, television, refrigerator and tea/coffee making facilities. Robes available. Nearby are bush walks to Okere Falls, river and lake fishing and an evening stroll to the glowworms. Meals at 24 hours notice. Laundry and email facilities. Maori concert and hangi closeby. Our place is 1 minute off Highway 33 at Okere Falls. Ring for directions.

Bay of Plenty

Rotorua *4 km E of Rotorua*
Aroden B&B Homestay *B&B Homestay*
Leonie & Paul Kibblewhite
2 Hilton Road, Lynmore, Rotorua

Tel (07) 345 6303 Fax (07) 345 6353
aroden@xtra.co.nz

Double $120 Single $90 (Full breakfast)
Child negotiable Visa MC Diners accepted
2 Queen (2 bdrm)
Bathrooms: 1 Ensuite 1 Private

A great central location: city 5 minutes,
Whakarewarewa Forest adjacent (glowworms at
night!), en route to lakes. Enjoy Aroden's comfort
and character: 2 lounge areas, well-appointed rooms, comfortable beds with quality linen, modern
tiled bathrooms (excellent showers), central heating/open fire, patio, luxuriant garden with native tree
collection. Leonie, background in teaching, and Paul, scientist, are fifth generation Kiwi with a real
knowledge of this remarkable area. And meet Taupo, Paul's engaging guide dog. Breakfast is special
- this couple enjoys food! Leonie parle francais.

Rotorua - Lake Tarawera *15 km SE of Rotorua*
Boatshed Bay Lodge *B&B Homestay Cottage with Kitchen*
Lorraine & Steve Jones
95 Spencer Road, Lake Tarawera, RD 5, Rotorua

Tel (07) 362 8441 Fax (07) 362 8441
boatshedbay@xtra.co.nz

Double $120 Single $90 (Full breakfast)
Child $25 Dinner $40pp
Self-contained $95
Visa MC accepted
2 Queen 1 Double 2 Single (2 bdrm)
Bathrooms: 2 Ensuite

Boatshed Bay is located on the shore of scenic Lake
Tarawera with its sparkling waters fringed by native bush at the foot of majestic Mount Tarawera. We
offer boat charter, world-renowned trout fishing, tramping (mountain trek), bushwalks or just relax in
peace and tranquillity only 15km from Rotorua. All facilities are available, including laundry, kitchen
and nearby licensed restaurant The Landing Cafe. We provide home-style breakfast and meals on request.
Your hosts Lorraine and Steve are well travelled and enjoy meeting people. Our place is your place.

Rotorua - Lake Tarawera *20 km SE of Rotorua*
Lake Tarawera Rheinland Lodge *B&B Homestay*
Gunter & Maria
484 Spencer Road, RD 5, Rotorua

Tel (07) 362 8838 Fax (07) 362 8838
tarawera@ihug.co.nz

Double $100-$130 Single $75-$95 (Special breakfast)
Child half price Dinner $30
1 King/Twin 1 Queen (2 bdrm)
Bathrooms: 1 Family share 1 Private

Located at the magic Lake Tarawera renowned for
its scenery and history we offer warm hospitality with
a personal touch. Expect total privacy, magnificent
lake views, luxurious and relaxing outdoor whirlpool, spacious bathroom with shower and bath, fitness
area, stereo, TV, internet connection, lake beach 5 minutes on foot, sea 45 minutes by car, bush walks,
fishing and hunting trips by arrangement, home-made bread, German cuisine on request, organic garden,
German/English spoken,

Rotorua *10 km W of Rotorua*
Rhodohill *B&B Apartment with Kitchen*
Ailsa & Dave Stewart
569 Paradise Valley Road, Rotorua

Tel (07) 348 9010 Fax (07) 348 9041
rhodohill@xtra.co.nz

Double $80-$90 Single $60-$70 (Continental)
Child $20
Visa MC accepted
Children welcome
1 Queen (1 bdrm)
Bathrooms: 1 Ensuite

Rhodohill is set in a mature 4 acre garden in
picturesque Paradise Valley, 10km west of Rotorua. Its hillside setting, large trees and hundreds of
rhododendrons, camellias etc. and many native birds offer a relaxing retreat within easy distance of major
tourist attractions, golf courses and cafes and restaurants. The renowned Ngongotaha trout stream flows
through the valley. Modern, self-contained accommodation with own entrance, ensuite bathroom, fully
equipped kitchen, dining room-lounge. Smoke-free indoors. We also operate a specialist plant nursery.

Rotorua - Central *In Rotorua Central*
Tresco *B&B*
Trinka & Trevor Brine
3 Toko Street, Rotorua

Tel (07) 348 9611 or Freephone 0800 873 726
021 355 777 Fax (07) 348 9611
trescorotorua@xtra.co.nz
www.trescorotorua.co.nz

Double $90 Single $50-$75 (Full breakfast)
Single ensuite $75 Triple $120
Visa MC accepted
1 King/Twin 3 Queen 2 Twin 2 Single (6 bdrm)
Bathrooms: 3 Ensuite 2 Guest share 1 Private

Central location - A warm welcome awaits you at our comfortable friendly home, situated on a tree-
lined street only 150 metres from Central Rotorua with its many attractions and excellent restaurants.
Established for over 35 years and recently renovated, Tresco offers all the comforts of home. We serve a
substantial breakfast and 24-hour complimentary refreshments. Genuine hot mineral pool. Free pick-up
from airport or bus terminal. Off-street parking. Laundry/drying facility. Guest survey gives us top marks
for friendliness, cleanliness and location.

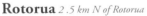

Rotorua *2.5 km N of Rotorua*
Ferntree Cottage *B&B Homestay Separate Suite*
Val & Geoff Brannan
1 Tatai Street, Rotorua

Tel 0800 398 633 or (07) 348 0000
021 049 1910, 021 104 7203
v.g.brannan@xtra.co.nz   www.ferntreecottage.co.nz

Double $100-$130 Single $80-$100 (Special breakfast)
Child negotiable Dinner by arrangement
Stay 3nights or more and receive a free bottle of 'NZ' wine
Families negotiable Visa MC accepted
1 Queen 1 Double (2 bdrm)
Bathrooms: 1 Ensuite 1 Family share

Experience the warm hospitality, comfortable beds, well appointed bathrooms and highly rated
breakfasts at Ferntree Cottage. You will wake up to pretty garden views and hear the bird's chorus.
Ideally situated close to Lake Rotorua, the city and world-famous attractions. Excite your senses with the
many adventures and sightseeing available within a short drive of your Bed & Breakfast accommodation.
Your hosts have a wide range of interests including theatre, music, gardening, vintage vehicles and boats,
travel and entertaining. Snappercat and little Josiedog enjoy company.

Rotorua - Okere Falls *20 km N of Rotorua*
At The Ferns Bed & Breakfast *B&B Homestay Cottage with Kitchen*
Carol & Bernie Mason
48 Taheke Road, RD 4, Okere Falls

Tel (07) 362 4087 or 027 251 7932
Fax (07) 362 4087 bcmason@xtra.co.nz
www.attheferns.co.nz

Double $120 (Full breakfast)
Dinner $45 each by arrangement
Extra person $15
Breakfast in self-contained $15
Visa MC accepted Children welcome
1 King 1 Double 1 Single (2 bdrm)
Bathrooms: 1 Ensuite 1 Private

Secluded Okere Falls Rotorua accommodation, surrounded by tree ferns, bird song and close to shady walks and great trout fishing. If you enjoy peace and quiet and relish the chance to relax and enjoy nature, At The Ferns is the ideal place. Walk to Okere Falls and fish for trout, kayak, white water raft or watch the fun. Choose from your own little self-contained cottage in the lower garden or have bed & breakfast where the guest room gives you privacy with all the comforts of home.

Rotorua - Ngongotaha *8 km N of Rotorua*
Bayadere Lodge *B&B Homestay*
Cynthia and Neil Clark
38 Hall Road, Ngongotaha, Rotorua

Tel (07) 357 5965 or 027 292 8520
027 292 8447 Fax (07) 357 5965
c.clark@clear.net.nz
www.bayaderlodge.com

Double $150-$180 Single $110-$140 (Full breakfast)
Child negotiable Dinner $45pp
Visa MC Diners accepted Pet free home
2 King/Twin1 King (3 bdrm)
Bathrooms: 3 Ensuite

Bayadere Lodge, a modern spacious home,with splendid views of Lake Rotorua. It is 8km from Rotorua and has no sulphur fumes. Walking distance to the world famous Ngongotaha and Waiteti trout streams. Tea and coffee making facilities, hairdryers, electric blankets. Our guest lounge that has an ajoining decking where you may sit in the peaceful garden. Within 3km of the tourist attractions. Rainbow Springs, Skyline Rides, Luge, Matai Cultural Show & the Agrodome Show. You wil be welcomed as a special guests in our home.

Rotorua *2 km N of Rotorua*
Moana Rose Lakeside Bed & Breakfast *B&B Homestay*
Pauline & Bruce Kingston
23 Haumoana Street, Koutu, Rotorua

Tel (07) 349 2980 Fax (07) 349 2997
moanarose@bktours.co.nz
www.bktours.co.nz

Double $120-$140 Single $80-$90 (Full breakfast)
Child $35 Visa MC accepted
Children welcome
1 Queen 1 Twin (2 bdrm)
Bathrooms: 1 Private

Situated on the lake edge, 2km from the city centre, we offer a quiet relaxed atmosphere, including separate entrance, comfortable spacious bedrooms, electric blankets, own bathroom and a delightful garden spa. Enjoy our company or the privacy of your own sitting room, including Sky TV, fridge, tea/coffee facilities. From our sun deck walk down to the lake and watch the bird life grazing on the reserve with Lizzie our cat in hot pursuit. Bruce is a licensed tour operator and will gladly assist with your tour options. Welcome, Kia Ora.

Lake Rotoiti - Rotorua *20 km NE of Rotorua*

Kamahi Cottage *Cottage No Kitchen*
Sheryl & Kevin Jensen
137 Okere Road, RD 4, Lake Rotoiti, Rotorua

Tel (07) 362 4244 or 027 457 0496
021 206 2724 Fax (07) 362 4244
S&KJensen@xtra.co.nz

Double $100-$110 Single $70 (Continental provisions)
Child $15
Visa MC accepted
Children welcome
1 Queen 1 Twin (2 bdrm)
Bathrooms: 1 Private

Kamahi (ka-ma-he) is a cottage, separate from our home, with beautiful views of Lake Rotoiti - a few steps to the water edge. Kayaks available. Handy to Okere Falls, white water rafting, bush walks, fishing, golf course. Breakfast provisions in cottage/kitchenette facilities. Fish smoker and BBQ available. Endless lake views, the colourful garden and surrounding area invite you to relax and enjoy your stay. We are friendly New Zealanders and love meeting with you on the shared deck. 2 friendly small dogs.

Rotorua *10 km E of Rotorua*

Peppertree Farm *B&B Farmstay*
Robyn Panther & Barry Morris
25 Cookson Road, RD 4, Rotorua

Tel (07) 345 3718 Fax (07) 345 3718
peppertree.farm@xtra.co.nz

Double $95-$105 Single $65 (Full breakfast)
Child half price
Visa MC accepted
Children welcome
1 Double 2 Twin (3 bdrm)
Bathrooms: 1 Ensuite 1 Guest share

Handy to the airport our quiet rural retreat overlooking Lake Rotorua provides a picturesque and homely welcome. Farm animals are horses, cows, sheep, a young donkey and chickens. Lucy, our cavalier King Charles spaniel, is a house pet, and Ben, our very friendly labrador lives outside. We are knowledgable locals who enjoy horse racing, rugby, most sports and meeting interesting people! If you wish to attend a Maori concert and hangi, we can arrange pick up and delivery back to the farm.

Rotorua Central *1 km S of Rotorua Central*

Innes Cottage *B&B Homestay*
Chris & Gill Innes
18A Wylie Street, Central Rotorua, Central Rotorua

Tel 0800 24 30 30 or (07) 349 1839
Fax (07) 349 1890 chris@clican.com
www.innescottage.co.nz

Double $100-$130 Single $85-$100 (Continental)
Child POA Dinner by arrangement
Visa MC Diners Amex accepted
Children and pets welcome
2 Queen 2 Single (3 bdrm)
Bathrooms: 1 Ensuite 1 Guest share 1 Private

Centrally situated in easy walking distance to the city, set in a treelined quiet neighborhood only 100 metres from the main road. Close to Whakarewarewa thermal area, Rotorua Golf Club, major tourist attractions are easily accessible. After 130 years heritage in the beverage industry we have travelled extensively, have collected a wealth of knowledge and many valuable contacts. Let us assist and advise you on the most popular and "must see" attractions and other highlights of our beautiful country. We have a cat.

Bay of Plenty

Rotorua *1.5 km SW of Rotorua*
Golf View Chalet *Cottage No Kitchen*
Fred and Caroline Windner
83 Springfield Road, Rotorua

Tel (07) 347 8168 Fax (07) 347 8134
golfchalet@xtra.co.nz

Double $135 Single $80 (Continental)
1 King/Twin 2 Single (1 bdrm)
Bathrooms: 1 Ensuite

Separate private chalet, 1km west of Whakarewarewa,
our famous Pohutu Geyser. Approximately 2km to
the city centre. We have off-street parking and your
continental breakfast provisions are supplied. Not
suitable for children or pets. Besides all the recreational facilities Rotorua offers, you can perfect your
chipping and putting on the Springfield Golf Course. Access through our property. We are Austrian
Kiwis.

Rotorua *10 km N of Rotorua*
Ngongotaha Lakeside Lodge *B&B Lake Stay*
Lyndsay & Graham Butcher
41 Operiana Street, Ngongotaha, Rotorua

Tel (07) 357 4020 or 0800 144 020
Fax (07) 357 4020 lake.edge@xtra.co.nz
www.rotorualakesidelodge.co.nz

Double $150-$210 Single $130-$150 (Full breakfast)
Child over 12 negotiable
Visa MC accepted
1 King 1 Queen 2 Twin 1 Single (3 bdrm)
Bathrooms: 3 Ensuite

Absolute lake edge, stunning panaramic views, fishing,
bird watching, great food and warm hospitality are what you will find at our spacious comfortable home.
The upper level is exclusively for guests with fully equipped lounge/conservatory overlooking the lake. All
bedrooms have ensuite facilities with everything provided. The famous Waiteti Stream is only metres
away, with Rainbow and Brown Trout waiting to be caught. Free use of fishing gear and canoe.... You
catch and we'll cook. Smoke free inside. Safe parking and sulphur free. Multiple night discounts.

Rotorua *10 km NE of Rotorua centre*
Lake Okareka B&B *Homestay Apartment with Kitchen*
Patricia & Ken Scott
10 Okareka Loop Road, RD 5, Rotorua

Tel (07) 362 8245 or 0800-652-735
patricia.scott@xtra.co.nz
www.lakeokarekabnb.co.nz

Double $100-$120 Single $65 (Full breakfast)
Dinner by arrangement
Children welcome
1 Queen 1 Double 1 Single (3 bdrm)
Bathrooms: 2 Ensuite

Welcome to our modern home set in beautiful
tranquil surroundings with stunning views by Lake Okareka. Stroll along the waters edge, enjoy the
native bush, ferns and birdlife or have free use of our kayaks. Our environment is relaxing, friendly
and peaceful. We have a double room with ensuite, a single room and a self-contained studio unit with
private entrance. Guests are welcome to 3 spacious living areas. We are 10 minutes drive from city
centre; conveniently situated for all tourist attractions and activities.

Rotorua

Robertson House *B&B*

Patrice Legrand & John Ballard
70 Pererika Street, Rotorua

Tel (07) 343 7559
Fax (07) 343 7559
info@robertsonhouse.co.nz

Double $110-$170 Single $80-$140 (Continental)
Extra person $50
1 King/Twin 2 Queen 2 Double 2 Single (5 bdrm)
Bathrooms: 3 Ensuite

Our historic home, only 2 minutes drive from city centre, was built by one of Rotoruas forefathers, in 1905. Under the auspices of the Historic Places Trust it has been carefully renovated, retaining its colonial charm. Relax in its warm comfortable atmosphere, or take time out on the verandah and enjoy our old English cottage garden resplendent with colour and fragrance, citrus trees and grape vines. Our friendly hosts are happy to assist with information and bookings for Rotorua's Maori cultural and sightseeing attractions.

Okere Falls - Rotorua *22 km E of Rotorua*

Bush Haven Cottage and B&B *B&B Cottage with Kitchen*

George & Sheryll Beveridge
146 Okere Road, Okere Falls, RD 4, Rotorua

Tel (07) 362 4497 or 021 396 709
Fax (07) 362 4417
georgesheryll@xtra.co.nz

Double $120 Single $80 (Continental)
Extra person with double $20
Visa MC accepted
Children and pets welcome
1 Queen 1 Double 2 Single (2 bdrm)
Bathrooms: 1 Private

As the name suggests, our property is a restful peaceful retreat surrounded by ferns, native bush and native birds. Waken to the call of the tuis and have breakfast delivered to the door of your cosy, private, fully self-contained 2 bedroom cottage including washing machine and spa pool. The lake and Okere Falls are within a short walking distance. Rotorua, the leading tourist destination in the North Island, is only 15 mintues drive away.

Taupo - Acacia Bay *6 km W of Taupo*

Leece's Homestay *Homestay*

Marlene & Bob Leece
98 Wakeman Road, Acacia Bay, Taupo 2736

Tel (07) 378 6099 Fax (07) 378 6092

Double $90 Single $60 (Continental)
1 King 1 Double 2 Single (2 bdrm)
Visa MC accepted
Bathrooms: 1 Guest share

Your hosts Bob, Marlene & Jaspa extend a warm welcome to our large wood interior home with woodfire for winter and north facing sunny deck from guest bedroom. Also magnificent view of Lake Taupo from lounge and front deck. There are bush walks and steps down to lake to swim in summer. We are awaiting your arrival with anticipation of making friends. Please phone for directions.

Taupo *2 km E of Taupo*

Yeoman's Lakeview Homestay *B&B Homestay*

Colleen & Bob Yeoman

23 Rokino Road, Taupo 2730

Tel (07) 377 0283 Fax (07) 377 4683

Double $110-$120 Single $60 (Full breakfast)
Child $25 Dinner $30 by arrangement
Children welcome
1 Queen 3 Single (3 bdrm)
Bathrooms: 1 Ensuite 1 Guest share

Bob and I have enjoyed hosting for many years,
our Lakeview Homestay with beautiful mountains
backdrop makes our guests' stay in Taupo very special.
Our home is spacious, comfortable and relaxing. All Taupo's attractions are nearby, golf courses, thermal
pools, Huka Falls and fishing. We are retired sheep and cattle farmers, Bob excels at golf and is in charge
of cooked breakfasts. Home-made jams and marmalade are my specialty. Turn into Huia Street from
lakefront, take fourth turn on the right into Rokino Road. Off-street parking.

~

Taupo *3 km S of Taupo*

Hawai Homestay *Homestay Cottage with Kitchen*

Jeanette Jones

18 Hawai Street, 2 Mile Bay, Taupo

Tel (07) 377 3242 or 021 069 6224
jeanettej@xtra.co.nz
www.beds-n-leisure.com/hawai.htm

Double $90 Single $60 (Full breakfast)
Child $20 Dinner $20
Marmite Cottage $65 double
Visa MC accepted
Children and pets welcome
1 Queen 1 Twin (2 bdrm)
Bathrooms: 1 Guest share

Come and relax and unwind in our comfortable modern warm home. Befriend our adorable Shitzu
who just loves visitors. Enjoy our hearty breakfasts, which include homemade muesli, muffins, bread and
preserves. We are close to hot pools, good walking paths, the lake and restaurants. The self-contained
cottage is ideal for families. A typical kiwi bach, sleeps 7 - linen, firewood, books and games provided.
Interests include church, travel, roses and crafts. Hawai St comes off SH1.

~

Taupo - Acacia Bay *5 km W of Taupo*

Pariroa Homestay *Homestay*

Joan & Eric Leersnijder

77A Wakeman Road, Acacia Bay, Taupo

Tel (07) 378 3861
pariroa@xtra.co.nz

Double $80 Single $65 (Full breakfast)
Visa MC accepted
Not suitable for children
1 Queen 2 Single (2 bdrm)
Bathrooms: 1 Guest share

Views views! Our home is Scandinavian style with
wooden interior. Situated in a very quiet area and
minutes from the beach, we have magnificent, uninterrupted views of Lake Taupo and The Ranges
from bedrooms and living room. We have travelled extensively and Eric was previously a tea planter in
Indonesia, having lived in The Netherlands, Spain and Italy. Directions: Turn down between 95 and 99
Wakeman Road. We are the last house on this short road (200 metres).

Taupo *1 km S of Taupo*
Pataka House *Homestay Separate Suite*
Raewyn & Neil Alexander
8 Pataka Road, Taupo

Tel (07) 378 5481 Fax (07) 378 5461
pataka-homestay@xtra.co.nz
www.patakahouse.co.nz

Double $110 Single $75 (Full breakfast)
Child $30
Seperate suite $130
Children welcome
2 Queen 4 Twin (4 bdrm)
Bathrooms: 1 Ensuite 1 Guest share 1 Private 1

Pataka House is highly recommended for its hospitality. We assure guests that their stay lives up to New Zealand's reputation as being a home away from home. We are easily located just 1 turn off the lake front and up a tree-lined driveway. Our garden room is privately situated, has an appealing decor and extremely popular to young and old alike. Stay for 1 night or stay for more as Lake Taupo will truly be the highlight of your holiday. Mika, a burmese, loves visitors.

Taupo *15 km W of Taupo*
Ben Lomond *Cottage with Kitchen*
Mary & Jack Weston
1434 Poihipi Road, RD 1, Taupo

Tel (07) 377 6033 or 025 774 080
Fax (07) 377 6033
benlomond@xtra.co.nz

Double call for prices (Continental provisions)
Cottage $100
Visa MC accepted
Children and pets welcome
1 Queen 2 Single (2 bdrm)
Bathrooms: 1 Guest share

Welcome to Ben Lomond. Jack and I have farmed here for 40 years and our comfortable family home is set in a mature garden. There is a self-contained cottage in the garden where you can do your own thing or pop to the house for breakfast. We have interests in fishing, golf and the equestrian world and are familiar with the attractions on the Central Plateau. Our pets include dogs and cats who wander in and out. Taupo restaurants are 15 minutes away.

Taupo *1 km N of Taupo Central*
Lakeland Homestay *Homestay*
Lesley, Chris & Pussycats
11 Williams Street, Taupo

Tel (07) 378 1952 or 025 877 971
Fax (07) 378 1912
lakeland.bb@xtra.co.nz

Double $120-$130 Single $65 (Continental)
Visa MC accepted
1 Queen 2 Twin (2 bdrm)
Bathrooms: 1 Ensuite 1 Family share

Nestled in a restful tree-lined street, a mere 5 minutes stroll from the lake's edge and shopping centre
Lakeland Homestay is a cheerful and cosy home that enjoys views of the lake and mountains. Keen gardeners, anglers and golfers Chris and Lesley work and play in an adventure oasis. For extra warmth on winter nights all beds have electric blankets, and laundry facilities are available. A courtesy car is available for coach travellers and there is off-street parking. Please phone for directions.

Bay of Plenty

Bay of Plenty

Taupo - Countryside *35 km NW of Taupo*
South Claragh & Bird Cottage *B&B Homestay Cottage with Kitchen*

Lesley & Paul Hill
South Claragh, 3245 Poihipi Road, RD 1 Mangakino

Tel (07) 372 8848 Fax (07) 372 8047
welcome@countryaccommodation.co.nz
www.countryaccommodation.co.nz

Double $100-$140 Single $80-$90 (Full breakfast)
Child $10 in cottage, $45 in B&B Dinner $45pp
Bird Cottage $100-$140 double Visa MC accepted
1 Queen 1 Double 1 Single (1 bdrm in cottage,
2 in B&B) Bathrooms: 2 Private

Turn into our leafy driveway and relax in tranquil,
rambling gardens with donkeys, sheep, outdoor dog and cat. Accommodation options: 1. Enjoy bed &
breakfast in our comfortable, centrally heated farmhouse with delicious farm breakfasts. The freshest
home-grown produce and excellent cooking make dining recommended. 2. Settle into Bird Cottage
- cosy, with delightful views. Perfect for 2, but will sleep 3-4. Firewood and linen provided, cot available.
As there is a kitchen, no meals included in tariff, but happily prepared for you, by arrangement. Children
welcome. Details and pictures on our web site.

Taupo *2 km S of Taupo*
Bramham *B&B Homestay*

Julia & John Bates
7 Waipahihi Avenue, Taupo

Tel (07) 378 0064 or 027 240 9643
021 240 9643 Fax (07) 378 0065
info@bramham.co.nz
www.bramham.co.nz

Double $100-$110 Single $60-$80 (Full breakfast)
1 Double 2 Twin 1 Single (3 bdrm)
Bathrooms: 3 Ensuite

Bramham is situated just 2 minutes walk form the hot
beach of Lake Taupo and offers tremendous views of
the lake and mountains to the south. John and Julia, having spent 24 years in the RNZAF, including
service with the USAF in Tucson Arizona, welcome you to our quiet, homely and peaceful atmosphere.
Hearty breakfasts are our specialty. Local knowledge is our business. Bus terminal and airport service
complimentary. Being a non-smoker our dog Koko, ask you not to smoke in our home.

Taupo *14 km NW of Taupo*
Minarapa *B&B Homestay*

Barbara & Dermot Grainger
620 Oruanui Road, RD 1, Taupo

Tel (07) 378 1931 info@minarapa.co.nz
www.minarapa.co.nz

Double $115-$140 Single $95-$110 (Full breakfast)
Child price on application
Dinner by arrangement
Visa MC accepted
1 King/Twin 2 Queen 2 Twin (4 bdrm)
Bathrooms: 2 Ensuite 1 Private

Wend your way along a wonderful tree-lined drive
into rural tranquillity. Minarapa, our 11 acre country retreat, 12 minutes from Taupo, 45 minutes from
Rotorua and central to the region's main tourist attractions, is a great place to unwind. Here you may
wander among colourful tree-sheltered gardens, play tennis, billiards, or ball with Toby the dog, or relax
in our guest lounge/billiard room. Retire to spacious guest rooms, two with balcony, appointed with
your comfort in mind. Barbara speaks fluent German.

146

Taupo *3 km S of Taupo*
Woodend Cottage *B&B Homestay Cottage No Kitchen*
Judi Thomson
15A Mere Road, Taupo

Tel (07) 378 4558 or 027 555 3123
Fax (07) 378 4071
jude.thomson@orcon.net.nz
www.abovethelake.co.nz

Double $110 Single $85 (Full breakfast)
Child by arrangement
Visa MC accepted
1 King (1 bdrm)
Bathrooms: 1 Private

Welcome to our completely private guest area which includes queen-size bed, television, ensuite and views over the lake to the mountains. Georgia, our social labrador, looks forward to your company. We are happy to suggest 'what's hot and what's not' for local activities and eateries.

Taupo *2 km S of Info Centre*
Gillies of Taupo - Gillies Lodge *B&B*
Margi Martin & Alan Malpas
77 Gillies Avenue, Taupo, Box 1924, Taupo

Tel (07) 377 2377 Fax (07) 377 2373
info@gilliesoftaupo.co.nz
www.gilliesoftaupo.co.nz

Double $115-$125 Single $75-$95 (Full breakfast)
Not suitable for children
4 Double 8 Single (9 bdrm)
Bathrooms: 9 Ensuite

Taupo's original licensed guest house. 9 rooms all ensuited. A perfect base to explore Taupo's many attractions and make day trips to Rotorua, Napier, Waitomo Caves and National Parks. Peaceful, sunny, central and quiet with off-street parking. Relax and enjoy the views or sunsets from the lounge with log fire and library. Breakfast with your hosts and share their intimate local knowledge and sense of history. A true B&B experience. Good old fashioned values, genteel decor and ambience. Ideal venue for small groups. Reservations essential.

Taupo *10 km NW of Taupo*
Whitiora Farm *Farmstay*
Judith & Jim McGrath
1281 Mapara Road, RD 1, West Taupo

Tel (07) 378 6491 Fax (07) 378 6491
mcg.whitiora@xtra.co.nz

Double $100 Single $60 (Continental)
Child $25 Dinner $30
Lunch $15 by arrangement
Children welcome
1 Queen 3 Single (3 bdrm)
Bathrooms: 1 Family share 1 Private

3 Course dinner, booking essential. Breakfast: your choice of cereal, home-grown fruit, home-made bread and conserves, coffee, English and herb tea. Our 461 acre 'one-man working-farm' grazes sheep, cattle, deer & thoroughbred horses, which we breed and Jim trains and races. Judith enjoys gardening, and serving home-grown produce. We enjoy sharing our large comfortable home, garden, farm, and welcome children (5-12 half price, under 5 negotiable). We appreciate you not smoking in our home. Please book to avoid disappointment.

Bay of Plenty

Taupo *13 km N of Taupo*

Bellbird Ridge Alpaca Farm *B&B Farmstay Cottage with Kitchen*

Mike & Lorraine Harrison
68 Tangye Road, RD 1, Taupo

Tel (07) 377 1996 or 025 668 7754
Fax (07) 377 1992 lharrison@xtra.co.nz
www.bellbirdridge.co.nz

Double $130-$140 Single $100-$120 (Full provisions)
Child $30 Dinner $40pp by arrangement
Visa MC accepted
Children and pets welcome
2 Queen 1 Twin 1 Single (4 bdrm)
Bathrooms: 1 Ensuite 1 Private

Our farm, only 15 minutes from Taupo and Kinloch, is the perfect place to base your holiday in the central north island. Take a break from your travels and unwind in our charming and secluded self-contained cottage, enjoy our beautiful garden and friendly alpacas. The cottage has a queen-sized bed with feather duvet; separate kitchen/dining/lounge area, gas heating and generous breakfast provisions are included. Also available in our house, where you would be our only guests, are double, twin and single bedrooms with your own bathroom.

Taupo *5 km S of Taupo centre*

Beside Lake Taupo *B&B Homestay*

Irene & Roger Foote
8 Chad Street, Taupo

Tel (07) 378 5847 Fax (07) 378 5847
besidelaketaupo@xtra.co.nz
www.besidelaketaupo.co.nz

Double $220-$250 (Full breakfast)
Visa MC Diners Eftpos accepted
1 King/Twin 2 Queen 1 Twin (3 bdrm)
Bathrooms: 1 Ensuite 2 Private

Our luxury, shoreline, eco-friendly home has garaging with internal access to house and elevator. Rooms have lake views, balcony or terrace, Sky TV, guest controlled air-conditioning/heating and tea/coffee. Organic ingredients for the breakfast of your choice. Laundry, email, fax, hairdryers and robes for guest use. Enjoy the lakeshore bird life. Kayaks and dinghy provided. Walks, boating, fishing and swimming from site. Explore the volcanic countryside and experience the numerous adventure and leisure activities available locally. Enjoy your break beside the lake.

Taupo *2.5 km S of Taupo*

Fairviews *Homestay*

Brenda Watson-Hughes & Mike Hughes
8 Fairview Terrace, Taupo

Tel (07) 377 0773 fairviews@reap.org.nz
www.reap.org.nz/~fairviews

Double $115-$145 Single $95-$110 (Full breakfast)
Visa MC accepted
1 Queen 1 Twin (2 bdrm)
Bathrooms: 1 Ensuite 1 Private

You are invited to stay at our modern smoke-free homestay situated in a tranquil neighbourhood within walking distance of hot pools and lake. Relax and enjoy Fairviews' gardens. Be as private as you wish or socialise with hosts. Rooms are tastefully decorated and comfortable. Double room is large with private entrance, TV, fridge, tea/coffee facilities, robe and hairdryer. Generous breakfasts provided. Email facilities and laundry are available at small charge. Our regional knowledge is extensive. Interests include theatre, travel, cycling, tramping, antiques/collectables.

Taupo *2 km SE of Taupo*
Finial House *B&B Homestay*
Jan & Neil Fleming
51 Ngauruhoe Street, Taupo

Tel (07) 377 4347 or 027 685 8255
Fax (07) 377 4348
n.j.fleming@xtra.co.nz
www.finial-homestay.co.nz

Double $120-$150 Single $90-$120 (Full breakfast)
Dinner $25-$35 by arrangement
Visa MC accepted
2 King/Twin 2 Queen (3 bdrm)
Bathrooms: 2 Ensuite 1 Family share one

Finial House is a spacious home in a peaceful setting. Enjoy the magnificent views of the lake and volcanic mountains from our extensive lounge, or deck with a relaxing spa pool. Close to town and lake with their many attractions. We are ex-dairy farmers who enjoy talking with you about your travels and interests. Our interests are: sports, travel, music, walking, running and gardening. Our 3 children have families of their own and we are left with our 2 timid cats.

Taupo - Acacia Bay *7 km W of Taupo*
Hazeldene Lodge *B&B Homestay*
Judy & Tony Pratt
119 Acacia Heights Drive, Acacia Bay, Taupo

Tel (07) 377 0560 or 021 066 5512
Fax (07) 377 0560 hazeldene@xtra.co.nz
www.hazeldenelodge.co.nz

Double $195-$275 Single $185-$265 (Full breakfast)
Child POA Dinner by arrangement
Visa MC accepted
Children welcome
1 Super King/Twin 3 Queen (4 bdrm)
Bathrooms: 4 Ensuite

We warmly invite you to come and stay with us, we are set in 2 acres of landscaped gardens planted with many native shrubs and bushes. From here you can easily access the nearby attractions of the town, Huka Falls, golf courses, geothermal activity, and excellent restaurants. All bedrooms have been fitted out with TV, electric blankets, hair dryers, iron and ironing board, coffee and tea making facilities. Your rooms have spectacular views during the day, and by night twinkling lights of Taupo township.

Taupo - Acacia Bay *5 km W of Taupo*
Bay View Homestay *Homestay*
Marion & Guy Whitehouse
50/1 Wakeman Road, Acacia Bay, Taupo

Tel (07) 378 7873 or 021 211 2904
Fax (07) 378 7893

Double $100 Single $60 (Continental)
Dinner by arrangement
1 Queen 1 Twin (2 bdrm)
Bathrooms: 1 Guest share

Enjoy the warm hospitality with your hosts Marion and Guy, retired deer farmers and friendly cat Kita. Our quiet, relaxing, modern, contemporary home of native timbers offers open-plan living, air conditioning, double glazing, off-road parking. Spectacular panoramic views of Lake Taupo and mountains. Taupo's shimmering lights by night. Minutes from lake, fishing, tennis, native walks, restaurant. 5km to Taupo township and local attracions, thermal pools, Huka Falls, Huka Jet, chartered fishing, bungy, golf. Bookings can be arranged. Please phone for directions.

Bay of Plenty

Taupo - Acacia Bay *5 km W of Taupo*
The Loft *B&B*

home

Grace Andrews & Peter Rosieur
3 Wakeman Road, Acacia Bay, Taupo

Tel (07) 377 1040 or 027 485 1347
Fax (07) 377 1049 book@theloftnz.com
www.theloftnz.com

Double $130-$175 Single $90-$120 (Full breakfast)
Child $50-$75 Dinner $30-$45 Washing/internet
Visa MC accepted   Children welcome
3 Queen 2 Single (3 bdrm)
Bathrooms: 3 Ensuite

Situated 5 minutes from Taupo township and a few
minutes walk to Lake Taupo, *The Loft* is set in a small
cottage garden adjacent to a native bush reserve.

Your hosts, Peter & Grace, are friendly people who
delight in the best things in life. Both have travelled
extensively throughout New Zealand and the rest of
the world. Their passions vary from food and fine wine
to tramping and gardening. Enjoy their scrumptious
breakfast of fresh fruit salad, freshly squeezed orange
juice, freshly baked muffins and croissants; wonderful
scrambled eggs with mushrooms, bacon and home
grown tomatoes, an experience not to be missed.
Arrange an evening meal at *The Loft* and be treated to
a pleasurable 3-course dinner that will leave you with
a lasting memory of New Zealand hospitality. After
dinner, join your hosts for a complimentary port before retiring for a good nights sleep.

The upstairs guest accommodation comprises 3 private bedrooms with queen size beds and ensuite
bathrooms. Their style is rustic, romantic and warm where attention to detail shows that your comfort
takes top priority. The guest lounge, with an open fire welcomes you to relax and chat about the Taupo
region and your sight seeing plans. Trout fishing trips and adventure treks can be arranged by your hosts
along with a myriad of other more relaxing activities.

Grace & Peter look forward to sharing their home and their company with you, assuring you of a warm
welcome and a luxurious stay. Turtle, the red-eared turtle, completes the family.
Directions: www.theloftnz.com

Taupo *16 km N of Taupo*
Brackenhurst *B&B Homestay Farmstay Cottage with Kitchen*
Barbara & Ray Graham
801 Oruanui Road, RD 1, Taupo

Tel (07) 377 6451 or 027 445 6217 (mobile)
Fax (07) 377 6451 rgbg@xtra.co.nz

Double $100-$110 Single $60 (Full breakfast)
Child $30 Dinner $40
Visa MC accepted
Pet free home Children and pets welcome
1 Queen 1 Double 4 Single (3 bdrm)
Bathrooms: 2 Ensuite 2 Private

Brackenhurst is a modern Lockwood home on 14 acres of peaceful countryside with fantails, tuis and bellbirds in the large garden. friendly highland cattle and lovely donkeys. A warm welcome with peace and tranquility. Practise your chipping and putting. We are half a kilometre from SH1 and close to Huka Falls, geothermal activities, golf courses and a days outing to Rotorua, Waitomo Caves or Napier. Private guests wing in the house or separate annex offer away from home comforts. Breakfast to suit, continental style or full English. Dinner is available by arrangement.

Taupo *3 km S of Taupo*
Moorhill *B&B Boutique Accommodation*
Liz & Peter Sharland
27 Korimako Road, Taupo

Tel (07) 377 1069 or 021 300 455
Fax (07) 377 1069 petenlizr@xtra.co.nz
www.moorhill.co.nz

Double $135-$175 (Special breakfast)
Dinner by arrangement
Visa MC accepted
Pet free home Not suitable for children
1 King/Twin1 King 1 Queen (2 bdrm)
Bathrooms: 2 Ensuite

A warm welcome awaits you at Moorhill, an elegant home set in a private, mature garden, close to Lake Taupo, botanical gardens, thermal pools and restaurants. Relax and enjoy our spacious rooms, comfortable beds and delicious cooked breakfasts. Both well appointed ensuite bedrooms have quality linen, duvets, electric blankets, hairdryer, fridge, tea/coffee making and ironing facilities. The tastefully furnished guest lounge, with TV, opens onto sunny decks and garden - a great place to enjoy a glass of wine and share travel experiences. Ample off-street parking.

Taupo *15 km N of Taupo*
Maimoa House *B&B Homestay Farmstay*
Margaret & Godfrey Ellis
41 Oak Drive, off Palmer Mill Road, Taupo

Tel (07) 376 9000
mewestview@xtra.co.nz
www.maimoahomestay.co.nz

Double $95-$110 Single $65 (Special breakfast)
Child $30 Dinner $30 by arrangement
10% discount for 3 nights or more
Visa MC accepted Children and pets welcome
1 Queen 1 Double 1 Twin (3 bdrm)
Bathrooms: 1 Guest share with large spa bath and seperate shower & toilet

Hello and welcome to our peaceful home with spectacular views over the mountains to the lake. Enjoy a special breakfast with home-made bread and excellent fruit platter. Join us for a 3 course dinner (allergies catered for) with wine. Dine in or out on our sunny patio. Borrow our tandem or single bikes. We have a friendly lab dog, a cat and a few cows. Our interests include church activities and travelling.

Taupo *1 km N of Town Centre*
Magnifique *B&B Homestay*
Gay & Rex Eden
52 Woodward Street, Taupo

Tel (07) 378 4915 Fax (07) 378 4915
info@magnifique.co.nz
www.magnifique.co.nz

Double $125-$135 Single $85-$100 (Special breakfast)
Dinner $35pp including wine by arrangement
Visa MC accepted
Pet free home
2 Queen 2 Single (3 bdrm)
Bathrooms: 2 Private

We welcome you with refreshments and home-baking while you take in the magnificent sweeping views of town, lake and mountains. You may leave your car and walk just 6 minutes to Taupo's lovely restaurants and shops. Our focus in life is people, so be assured of a warm welcome and the highest standards of comfort and hospitality. Each room has tea making facilities, fridge, TV. We will treat you with our special breakfasts which have not yet failed to delight our guests.

Turangi *1.5 km E of Turangi Central*
The Andersons *B&B Homestay Cottage with Kitchen*
Betty & Jack Anderson
3 Poto Street, Turangi

Tel (07) 386 8272 Fax (07) 386 8272
jbanderson@xtra.co.nz
www.taupo.com/accommodation/andersons/

Double $100 Single $80 (Full breakfast)
Child in cottage only
Self-contained cottage $80-$150
Visa MC accepted
2 Queen 1 Twin (3 bdrm)
Bathrooms: 3 Ensuite

Welcome to our smoke-free home, in a quiet street, beside Tongariro River walkway, handy to restaurants and town and fishing. Arranged transport to Tongariro National Park at your door. Lake Taupo and thermal baths 5 minutes drive. Upstairs rooms with balconies, queen beds, ensuites, fridge/tea/coffee, separated for privacy by landing. Downstairs twin suite, own entry, bathroom, fridge/tea/coffee, laundry and lounge to share interests in flying, skiing, fishing, tramping, and maps of our volcanic area. Guest-shy cat. Cottage suitable for families.

Turangi *53 km S of Taupo*
Akepiro Cottage *B&B Cottage with Kitchen*
Jenny & John Wilcox
169 Taupahi Road, Turangi

Tel (07) 386 7384
jennywilcox@xtra.co.nz

Double $100 Single $60 (Breakfast by arrangement)
Child $15 Twin $100
Continental breakfast $10
Visa MC accepted
Children welcome
2 Queen 2 Single (2 bdrm)
Bathrooms: 1 Private with shower over bath

Half-acre woodland garden, featuring rhododendrons and native plants, attracting many species of birds. Access through garden gate to Tongariro River, major fishing pools. Perfect retreat for restful break. Close to excellent 18 hole golf course, half hour to the mountains, the Tongariro Crossing. Many walking tracks and World Heritage Park. Our home and garden are adjacent, but utmost privacy maintained. Full kitchen, laundry, linen & power incl TV, BBQ. Breakfast must be requested if required. Come, share this corner of nature's paradise.

Turangi - Motuoapa *10 km N of Turangi*
Meredith House *B&B Cottage with Kitchen*
Frances & Ian Meredith
45 Kahotea Drive, Motuoapa, RD 2, Turangi

Tel (07) 386 5266 or 027 444 06135
Fax (07) 386 5270
meredith.house@xtra.co.nz

Double $90 Single $60 (Breakfast by arrangement)
Self-contained $100-$120
Visa MC accepted Children welcome
1 Queen 3 Single (2 bdrm)
Bathrooms: 2 Ensuite

Stop and enjoy this outdoor Paradise. Just off
SH1 (B&B Sign). Overlooking Lake Taupo, our 2 storey home offers ground-floor self-contained
accommodation with own entrance. Full breakfast on request. Fully equipped kitchen, dining room,
lounge. 2 cosy bedrooms (each with TV). Vehicle/boat off-street parking. Minutes to marina and world-
renowned lake/river fishing. Beautiful bush walks. 45 minutes to ski fields and Tongariro National Park.
Our association with Tongariro/Taupo area spans over 30 years, through work and outdoor pursuits.
Welcome to our retreat.

Turangi *54 km S of Taupo*
Founders at Turangi *B&B Homestay*
Peter & Chris Stewart
253 Taupahi Road, Turangi

Tel (07) 386 8539 Fax (07) 386 8534
founders@ihug.co.nz
www.founders.co.nz

Double $170 Single $120 (Special breakfast)
Whole lodge (sleeps 12-13) negotiable
Visa MC Eftpos accepted
Not suitable for children
1 King/Twin1 King 3 Queen (4 bdrm)
Bathrooms: 4 Ensuite

Welcome to Turangi and to our New Zealand colonial-style home. Relax and enjoy the unique beauty
of the trout fishing capital of the world. Many outdoor activities are available at this place for all seasons,
with the Tongariro River, mountains of Tongariro National Park and magnificent Lake Taupo on our
doorstep. 4 ensuite bedrooms open on to the veranda. Enjoy breakfast in our sunny dining room or
pre-dinner drinks by the fire apres ski in the winter! Our friendly dog lives outdoors.

Turangi *52 km S of Taupo*
The Birches *B&B Homestay*
Tineke & Peter Baldwin
13 Koura Street, Turangi

Tel (07) 386 5140 or 021 149 6594
Fax (07) 386 5149
tineke.peter@xtra.co.nz
www.bnb.co.nz/thebirches.html

Double $150 Single $120 (Special breakfast)
Dinner by arrangement
Visa MC accepted
Pet free home Not suitable for children
1 Queen (1 bdrm)
Bathrooms: 1 Ensuite

Close to the world renowned Tongariro River we offer a charming residence in a quiet street. This
unique setting is ideally situated for fly fishing,tramping, skiing, rafting and other outdoor pursuits.
Enjoy a superior and spacious bedsitting room with ensuite, TV and coffee/tea making facilities in a
separate part of the house. Your Dutch/Canadian hosts have considerable international experience and
can also speak Dutch and French. Dinner by arrangement.

Turangi *16 km NW of Turangi*
Wills' Place *B&B*

Jill & Brian Wills
145 Omori Road, Omori

Tel (07) 386 7339 or 027 228 8960
Fax (07) 386 7339 willsplace@wave.co.nz
www.willsplace.co.nz

Double $125 Single $90 (Full breakfast)
Child negotiable Dinner by arrangement
Visa MC accepted
Pet free home Children welcome
2 Queen 3 Single (2 bdrm)
Bathrooms: 1 Private

Our home is lakeside in the beautiful southwest corner of Lake Taupo with wonderful views, excellent fishing, boating, swimming, walks. Just off the beaten track, yet only 10-15 minutes to shops, restaurants, thermal pools, Tongariro River, rafting, kayaking, etc. 40 minutes to Tongariro National Park and ski fields. We offer you a superior comfortable and spacious 2 bedroom suite with separate living area, a fullsize bathroom with bath and shower. Tea-making facilities, fridge, microwave, television, laundry. Separate entry and complete privacy.

Turangi *2 km N of Turangi*
Dyden Cottage *B&B Cottage with Kitchen*

Sarah & Graeme Henshaw
Old Mill Lane, 134 Grace Road RD 2, Turangi

Tel (07) 386 6050 or 021 402 278
Fax (07) 386 6052
dydencottage@xtra.co.nz

Double $100 Single $70 (Full provisions)
Child $10
Dinner $35 by arrangement
Visa MC accepted Children welcome
1 Queen 1 Single (1 bdrm)
Bathrooms: 1 Ensuite

Dyden Cottage offers self-contained accommodation set in 5 acres of mature gardens and farmland. It has a separate entrance and private outdoor area. The cottage sleeps 3 and includes an ensuite bathroom and living area with television. The kitchen is stocked with everything you need for breakfast, including fresh eggs from the property. Enjoy the peace and tranquility of your surroundings or take advantage of the world class fly fishing, bush walks, golf, boating, river rafting and skiing all within easy reach of Turangi.

Turangi *1 km N of Turangi*
At the Tongariro Riverside B&B and Homestay *B&B Homestay*

Leslie Wilson
72 Herekiekie Street, Turangi

Tel (07) 386 7447 or 021 074 0749
thewilsonsathome@clear.net.nz
www.tongariroriversidebandb.com

Double $100 Single $85 (Continental)
Not suitable for children
1 King (1 bdrm)
Bathrooms: 1 Ensuite

Absolute riverside property - right on the banks of the Tongariro River. We are 35 minutes south of Taupo, and just 40 minutes from the Mt Ruapehu Skifields and the Tongariro World Heritage National Park and the Tongariro Crossing. We have a delightful home in a peaceful no exit street. The large bedroom has a king-size bed and window seat overlooking the river, Sky TV, tea and coffee making facilities and opens out into a glass covered conservatory. The ensuite has a large bath and shower, toilet and bidet. Sauna is available for guest use. Generous breakfast provided. Safe parking within property. Lunch and dinner available by arrangement.

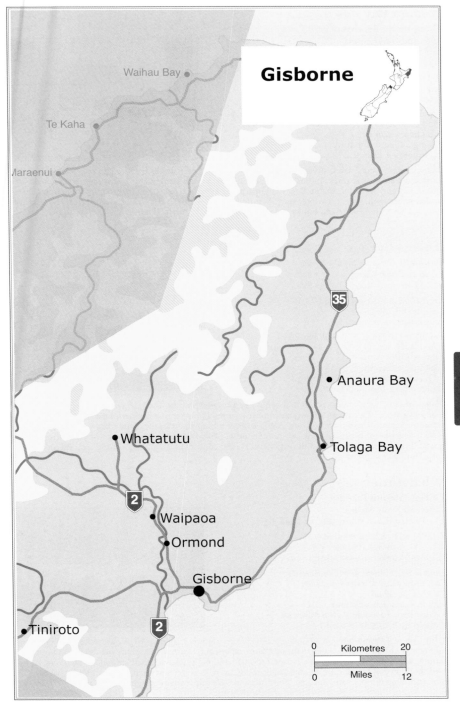

Gisborne

Anaura Bay *71 km N of Gisborne*

Rangimarie Beachstay *B&B Cottage with Kitchen*
Judy and David Newell
930 Anaura Road, Anaura Bay, East Coast
(Postal Address PO Box 53, Tolaga Bay, East Coast)

Tel 021 633372 Fax (06) 868 9340
anaurastay@xtra.co.nz
www.anaura-stay.co.nz

Double $90-$130 Single $75-$110 (Full breakfast)
Child $20 Dinner $30
Children welcome
1 King 2 Queen (3 bdrm)
Bathrooms: 1 Ensuite 2 Private

Rangimarie covers 2 acres, sweeps down to a white sandy beach and is bordered on one side by a native bush reserve. Second storey studios in Rangimarie Cottage and Rangimarie House have sensational views of sunrises and beautiful Anaura Bay. Rangimarie Cottage has a large tiled bathroom with double shower and clawfoot bath, great for winter stays. We are happy to prepare all meals by arrangement. Rangimarie Cottage has a kitchenette and bunks and is available for self-contained rental.

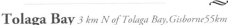

Tolaga Bay *3 km N of Tolaga Bay, Gisborne 55km*

Papatahi *Homestay Separate Suite*
Nicki & Bruce Jefferd
427 Main Road North, Tolaga Bay

Tel (06) 862 6623 or 021 283 7178
Fax (06) 862 6623
nickibrucej@xtra.co.nz

Double $110 Single $70 (Full breakfast)
Child half price
Dinner $30pp
Children welcome
1 Queen 1 Double 2 Single (3 bdrm)
Bathrooms: 1 Ensuite 1 Guest share

Papatahi Homestay is very easy to find being just 3km north of the Tolaga Bay township, on the Pacific Coast Highway. We have a comfortable, modern, sunny home set in a wonderful garden. Papatahi offers separate accommodation with ensuite. A golf course, fishing charters, the Tolaga Bay Cashmere Co. and several magnificent beaches are all just minutes away. Daily farm activities are often of interest to our guests. Friendly farm pets add to the experience! Great country meals and good wine are a speciality. Inspection will impress!

Whatatutu *50 km NE of Gisborne*

Te Hau Station *Farmstay*
Chris and Jenny Meban
332 Te Hau Road, Whatatutu, Eastland 3871

Tel (06) 862 1822 or 0800 686 218
, 021 251 4186 Fax (06) 862 1997
tehaustn@xtra.co.nz www.tehau.co.nz

Double $110 Single $70 (Continental)
Child half price Dinner from $20
Visa MC accepted
Children and pets welcome
1 King/Twin 2 Double 1 Twin (3 bdrm)
Bathrooms: 1 Ensuite 1 Family share

Our Colonial Farmhouse, on a 6000 acre hill country station, is an easy 40 minute drive from Gisborne, off State Highway 2 north. Enjoy hands-on farm experiences, learning about life on a sheep and cattle station; watch the shepherds riding horses, expertly handling stock with their sheepdogs. Walking, claybird shooting and hunting are all options, or choose to relax and enjoy the many facilities we have to offer including our pool and hot spa. Our 2 sons take pleasure in showing guests their many pets. Horse riding $20 per hour. All meals available, dine with hosts.

Waipaoa *20 km N of Gisborne*
The Willows *Farmstay*
Rosemary & Graham Johnson &
Montgomerie the Labrador
Waipaoa, RD 1, Gisborne

Tel (06) 862 5605 or 027 483 7365
Fax (06) 862 5601

Double $80 Single $50 (Full breakfast)
Child 10% discount
Dinner $30 by arrangement
2 Queen 2 Single (3 bdrm)
Bathrooms: 1 Guest share 1 Private

Our home is situated on a hill amid a park like garden
with some wonderful trees planted by our forefathers. We enjoy the amenities available in the city and
also the country life on our 440 acre property involving deer, cattle, sheep, grapes and cropping. We
now offer a double bedroom with a private bathroom. The bedroom has its own access so you can enjoy
privacy if you so desire. We are situated 20km north of Gisborne on SH2 through the scenic Waioeka
Gorge.

≈

Ormond *18 km N of Gisborne*
Goldspree Kiwifruit Orchard Stay *Self-contained Unit*
Marjorie & Mark Hayes
37 Bond Road, RD 1 Ormond, Gisborne

Tel (06) 862 5688 or 027 469 5916
Fax (06) 862 5688
goldspree@xtra.co.nz

Double $120 Single $95 (Continental)
Child $25 Extra guests $25
2 Queen 2 Single (2 bdrm)
Bathrooms: 1 Private

Set amongst the Chardonnay capital of NZ. Country
living with style and comfort. Stay in our self-contained
large modern villa nestled amongst the kiwifruit vines. Spend lazy afternoons wine tasting or walking
along the beautiful Gisborne beaches, or just relax with our family and pets in a peaceful setting. 5
minutes to restaurant bar/grill. Fax, email, internet and swimming pool available.

Gisborne

≈

Gisborne *5 km NE of Gisborne*
Beach Stay *B&B*
Peter & Dorothy Rouse
111 Wairere Road, Wainui Beach, Gisborne

Tel (06) 868 8111 Fax (06) 868 8162
pete.dot@xtra.co.nz

Double $85 Single $50 (Full breakfast)
Child $10 Dinner $25
Visa MC accepted
1 Queen 2 Double 2 Single (2 bdrm)
Bathrooms: 1 Ensuite 1 Private

We welcome you to our home which is situated right
on the beach front at Wainui. The steps from the lawn
lead down to the beach, which is renowned for its lovely clean sand, surf, pleasant walking and good
swimming. Gisborne can also offer a host of entertainment, including golf on 1 of the finest golf courses,
charter fishing trips, wine trails, Eastwood Hill Arboretum, horse trekking etc, or you may wish to relax
on the beach for the day with a light luncheon provided.

Gisborne *In Gisborne Central*

Sea View *B&B Homestay*
Kerry & Barry Crosby
68 Salisbury Road, Gisborne

Tel (06) 867 3879 or 025 899 253
kerry.barry@xtra.co.nz

Double $95 Single $70 (Continental)
Children welcome
2 Double 1 Twin 1 Single (3 bdrm)
Bathrooms: 2 Private

Absolute luxury and comfort. Beachfront bed & breakfast. Seaview is situated on the foreshore of Waikanae beach with unsurpassed panoramic views of Young Nicks Head and beautiful Poverty Bay. Just 50 metres from front door to golden sand, and warm blue waters of Poverty Bay. Only 2 minutes drive to the city (easy walking distance) and visitor information centre. Relax and enjoy safe swimming and great surfing. 5 minutes to international golf course and Olympic pool complex. We offer 2 double bedrooms and twin room. 2 private bathrooms. Internet facilities available.

Gisborne *8 km N of Gisborne*

Makorori Heights *Homestay*
Roger & Morag Shanks
36 Sirrah Street, Wainui Beach, Gisborne

Tel (06) 867 0806 or 021 250 4918
Fax (06) 868 7706

Double $80 Single $45 (Full breakfast)
Dinner $25
Visa MC Diners accepted
1 Double 2 Single (2 bdrm)
Bathrooms: 1 Guest share

Our home is half a kilometre off Highway 35 at the northern end of Wainui Beach. With beautiful sea and sunrise views, surrounded by farmland and our own young olive grove. Handy to bush and coastal walkways. We have travelled overseas and enjoy the company of others. Roger is a water colour artist with examples of his overseas and local works available for viewing or purchase. Horse trekking, fishing trips, country excursions by arrangements. We have 1 friendly small dog not allowed indoors.

Gisborne *2 km NE of Gisborne*

Herons Mead Lodge *B&B Homestay*
Avril & Brian Jackson
5 Island Road, Gisborne

Tel (06) 868 1224 Fax (06) 868 1224
heronsmead@xtra.co.nz
www.roan.co.nz/heronsmead

Double $80-$90 Single $55-$65 (Full breakfast)
Child $20 sharing family room
Dinner $25pp by prior arrangement
Family room full occupancy $100-$110
2 Double 1 Single (2 bdrm)
Bathrooms: 2 Ensuite 1 Private

Herons Mead Lodge is situated on the outer boundary of Gisborne City, in a semi-rural setting. Avril and Brian offer comfortable, home from home, accommodation, where guests are welcomed as part of the family. Gisborne is New Zealand's best kept secret, with miles of clean golden beaches, and beautiful scenery. Enjoy our restaurants and cafes, where good food and a wide choice is the norm. Soak up the sunshine, the atmosphere, the history of the region, and visit local wineries and other places of interest in the area.

Gisborne *6 km N of Gisborne*

Cameron Cottage *B&B Cottage with Kitchen*
Bev & Warwick Willson
21 Cameron Road, RD 1, Gisborne

Tel (06) 863 1430 or 027 417 9876
Fax (06) 863 1432
cameroncottage@xtra.co.nz

Double $125 Single $110 (Continental)
1 Queen (1 bdrm)
Bathrooms: 1 Ensuite

Our tastefully decorated self-contained cottage is
situated on 1 hectare just 6km from Gisborne City. We
offer luxurious cotton linen and bedding, also robes
for your use. Toiletries, hairdryer, iron, heated towel rail and a complimentry bottle of wine for you to
enjoy. Fishing and helicopter tours can be arranged. Our cottage with deck gets full all day sun. We have
room for boat parking. Tasty continental breakfast in our cottage. Come and enjoy a restful visit in our
georgous cottage. Inspection welcome.

Gisborne

Cooks Quarters *B&B Homestay*
Lynn & David Nunn plus friendly foxie Zap
66 Wainui Road, Gisborne

Tel (06) 863 3708 or 025 868 408
Fax (06) 863 3708
Cooks-Quarters@hotmail.com

Double $95-$120 Single $95-$120 (Full breakfast)
Dinner by arrangement
1 Queen 1 Twin (2 bdrm)
Bathrooms: 1 Ensuite 1 Private

You will experiance friendly hospitality and relax in
the unpretentious comfort of Cooks Quarters. Enjoy
a complementary historical tour including elevated views of the city and bays. Cooks Quarters is a
centery old character home centraly located close to Captain Cooks' landing site. You can walk to the
inner harbour, wharf cafes and bars or stroll along the river walkways to the art gallery, museum and city
centre. Please ask us if you require help with planning wine or garden tours, regions attractions, fishing
trips etc.

Gisborne

Gisborne *60 km SW of Gisborne*

Rongoio Farm Stay *Farmstay Separate Suite Cottage with Kitchen*
Philippa & Willie Purvis
1055 Ruakaka Road, Tiniroto, Gisborne

Tel (06) 867 4065 Fax (06) 863 7018
rongoio@paradise.net.nz

Double $100 Single $80 (Full breakfast)
Child $20
Children welcome
1 Queen 1 Twin 1 Single (3 bdrm)
Bathrooms: 1 Guest share

Join us on our 440 hectare hill country sheep and cattle farm and enjoy all
that rural NZ life offers. Close to the homestead but secluded by established
trees is a 3 bedroom totally self-contained cottage. From this cosy home feel the remote peace and
tranquillity along with the views of the trout filled Hangaroa River and waterfall. We encourage guests to
participate in rural activities including fishing, wild game shooting, horse and motorbike riding. We have
2 beautiful daughters, 2 cats, 3 labradors and horses.

Waitara *15 km N of New Plymouth*
Trenowth Gardens *B&B Homestay Cottage with Kitchen*
Sherril George
2 Armstrong Avenue, Waitara, Taranaki

Tel (06) 754 7674 Fax (06) 754 8884
sherril@trenowth.co.nz www.trenowth.com

Double $100 Single $80 (Full breakfast)
Child $15 Dinner $25pp
Visa MC accepted
Children and pets welcome
2 Double 1 Single (2 bdrm)
Bathrooms: 1 Ensuite 1 Private

Garden Homestay plus self-contained B&B cottage situated right on the main north-south Auckland/New Plymouth/Wellington highway at historic Waitara. Large family house with guest homestay (ensuite) plus additional B&B cottage with separate bedroom, lounge/dining/kitchen area with separate bathroom/laundry/toilet. Fully equipped with TV/music/library; all set in 18 acres of landscaped gardens, private lake and orchards. Close to 4 golf courses, local fishing, bush and mountain walks. 10 minutes from New Plymouth restaurants, 20 minutes from the mountain.

New Plymouth - Omata *5 km S of New Plymouth*
Rangitui *B&B*
Therese & Tony Waghorn
58 Waireka Road, RD 4, New Plymouth

Tel (06) 751 2979 Fax (06) 751 2985
twags@xtra.co.nz
www.accommodationtaranaki.co.nz

Double $75-$95 Single $65-$85 (Full breakfast)
Child Portacot available Dinner $40
Visa MC accepted Pets welcome
1 Queen 2 Single (2 bdrm)
Bathrooms: 1 Ensuite 1 Private

Ten minutes from New Plymouth. Private, peaceful, romantic, separate chalet with ensuite, queen bed, TV, and balcony overlooking bush and sea. Twin room with guest facilities in house. Your choice of breakfast (except kippers!) Dinner with wine, $40 per head, by arrangement. Enjoy bush or orchard walks, relax by our pool, or visit some of the nearby attractions: beautiful Mt Taranaki, some of the best surf, famous gardens, art gallery, museum, historic sites and golf courses. Bookings: please phone for reservations/directions.

New Plymouth *In New Plymouth Central*
Kirkstall House *Homestay*
Ian Hay & Lindy MacDiarmid
8 Baring Terrace, New Plymouth

Tel (06) 758 3222 or (06) 758 3224
Fax (06) 758 3224
kirkstall@xtra.co.nz

Double $95 Single $85 (Continental)
Ensuite Room $95-$110
2 Queen 1 Twin (3 bdrm)
Bathrooms: 1 Ensuite 2 Private

Kirkstall House invites you to experience its old world beauty and charm, in an atmosphere of easy hospitality and relaxed surroundings. Enjoy our superb mountain views, cosy open fire and delightful garden leading down to the Te Henui river. The ocean, walkways, restaurants and shops are all within easy walking distance. Lindy, a physiotherapist, and Ian, involved with tourism, are here to help you enjoy Taranaki to the utmost. We have 2 cats and a dog named Eva.

New Plymouth *3 km S of New Plymouth*

Oak Valley Manor *B&B Farmstay*
Pat & Paul Ekdahl
248 Junction Road, RD 1, New Plymouth

Tel (06) 758 1501 or 027 442 0325
Fax (06) 758 1052   kauri.holdings@xtra.co.nz

Double $125-$150 Single $125 (Continental)
Child $1 per year up to 15 years
Visa MC accepted
Children and pets welcome
2 Queen 1 Single (2 bdrm)
Bathrooms: 2 Ensuite

Your hosts, Pat and Paul, 2 friendly people with experience in the hospitality industry, invite you to a unique bed & breakfast in their beautifully home with views of Mt Taranaki from all rooms. These beautiful views make an everlasting impression. Guests can choose their own privacy or socialise with us. We have a variety of animals, donkey, peacocks, pigs, ducks, geese and an ex guide dog. Tours available in our Family owned brewery. Golf course 5 minute drive. Tariff reduces $150-$125 pending nights stayed.

~

New Plymouth *25 km N of New Plymouth*

Cottage by the Sea and Seacliff Villa *Cottage with Kitchen*
Nancy & Hugh Mills
66 Lower Turangi Road, RD 43, Waitara

Tel (06) 754 4548 or (06) 754 7915
cottagebythesea@clear.net.nz www.cottagebythesea.co.nz

Double $130-$160 Single $120-$150
(Breakfast by arrangement)
Child negotiable Dinner restaurant nearby
Extra adults $25 Visa MC accepted
Children and pets welcome
1 Queen 1 Double (each cottage sleeps 4)
Bathrooms: 1 Ensuite 1 per cottage

Spectacular seaviews and tranquillity, our cottages are totally self-contained and nestled in their own private gardens. The Cottage has a queen-size bed, the villa has a king-size bed. Each has a lounge with sofabed, TV, videos, verandas and access to BBQ. Descend steps through bush to a secluded beach; stroll around10 acres of avocado and fruit trees; discover the sunken garden. 20 minutes from cafes, coastal walkway, mountain, gardens. Folding bed or cot available. Discounts for longer stays. Our gentle dog may greet you

~

New Plymouth

The Grange *Homestay*
Cathy Thurston & John Smith
The Grange, 44B Victoria Road,
New Plymouth Central

Tel (06) 758 1540 or 021 410 458
027 241 0458 Fax (06) 758 1539
cathyt@clear.net.nz

Double $130 Single $100 (Full breakfast)
Visa MC Amex accepted
1 King/Twin 1 Queen 2 Single (2 bdrm)
Bathrooms: 2 Ensuite

Come and stay in our modern architecturally designed award-winning home built with the privacy and comfort of our guests in mind. With unique bush views and a house designed to take full advantage of the sun our guests can enjoy relaxing in the lounge or the extensive tiled courtyards. The Grange is centrally heated, security controlled and located adjacent to the renowned Pukekura Park and Bowl of Brooklands. The city is within a short 5 minute walk.

New Plymouth *In New Plymouth Central*

93 By the Sea *B&B*
Patricia & Bruce Robinson
93 Buller Street, New Plymouth

Tel (06) 758 6555 pat@93bythesea.co.nz
www.93bythesea.co.nz

Double $120-$100 Single $100-$80. (Special breakfast)
Child by arrangement Dinner by arrangement
Children welcome
1 King/Twin 1 Queen (2 bdrm)
Bathrooms: 1 Private

Park beside your own front door; enjoy a 2 minute wander down to sandy surf beaches; follow the mountain-fed Te Henui stream through parks and native bush; stroll the popular Coastal Walkway to many excellent city restaurants/attractions, (15-20 minutes); share a sumptious breakfast while enjoying the view over gardens, to the ever-changing Tasman sea; relax in a private B&B suite (2 bedrooms, lounge, spabath) that our guests say is warm, comfortable, spacious and well-appointed. We look forward to meeting and greeting you.

~

New Plymouth

Vineyard Holiday Flat *B&B*
Shirley & Trevor Knuckey
12 Scott Street, Moturoa, New Plymouth

Tel (06) 751 2992 or 027 310 3669
Fax (06) 751 2995
shirley12vineyard@xtra.co.nz

Double $80 Single $55 (Full breakfast)
Child $20 2 adults + 2 children $115
Visa MC accepted Children welcome
1 Double 2 Single (1 bdrm)
Bathrooms: 1 Ensuite

Situated in New Plymouth's port-view Moturoa suburb. Enter through hobby vines to the spacious upstairs open-plan studio, maximising 320 views of harbour, mountains, city; coast north and south. Near surf and shoreline pleasures. Guests may be as self-contained as wished - with lock-up garage, separate entrance, mini-kitchen. Lounge has private balcony, dining-table, Sky TV, phone. Extra bed(s) by arrangement. Ideally situated for exploring Taranaki's attractions, or the perfect R&R retreat. There is a pet cat.

~

New Plymouth *8 km N of New Plymouth*

Rockvale Homestay *B&B Homestay*
Jeannette & Neil Cowley
97 Manutahi Road, RD 2, New Plymouth

Tel (06) 755 0750 or 027 682 1236
Fax (06) 755 0750
rockvale@xtra.co.nz

Double $100 Single $70 (Full breakfast)
Child $35 Dinner $25 by arrangement
Visa MC accepted
Children welcome
1 Queen 2 Single (2 bdrm)
Bathrooms: 1 Private Spa Bath

We welcome you to our large, country-style home, surrounded by deer farm, with Mt Egmont as a backdrop. Guests' double room and lounge open onto a balcony, with rural views. Your comfort is our concern. We will book 1 guest party at a time. Relax in your private spabath. Join us for dinner, in our spacious living area or on the deck in summer. We are close to airport, city, beaches, parks and mountain. 6 18-hole golf courses are within easy drive. We look forward to welcoming you to our home . Families welcome.

New Plymouth *5 km W of New Plymouth centre*

            ♿   B&B Approved

Whaler's Rest *B&B*
Maureen & Denis Whiting
86A Barrett Road, New Plymouth

Tel (06) 751 4272
whalersrest@clear.net.nz
www.whalersrest.co.nz

Double $100 Single $80 (Full breakfast)
Child $20
Children and pets welcome
1 Double 1 Twin (2 bdrm)
Bathrooms: 1 Ensuite 1 Private

Large double bedroom with ensuite, with your own deck for drinks, plus twin room with private bathroom. Breakfast, continental or cooked. We are on the gateway to Surf Highway, 10 minutes to Oakura beach and 5 minutes to New Plymouth City Centre featuring the Wind Wand, coastal walkway, Puke Ariki Museum and Pukekura Park. Your hosts Maureen and Denis who love their tennis and garden welcome you. Children and pets by arrangement. We have a Jack Russell, Angus and 2 fat cats, Tuffy and Biscuit.

~

New Plymouth *0.5 km W of New Plymouth*

B&B Approved

Airlie House *B&B Apartment with Kitchen*
Gabrielle Masters
161 Powderham Street, New Pymouth

Tel (06) 757 8866 or 021 472 072
Fax (06) 757 8866
email@airliehouse.co.nz   www.airliehouse.co.nz

Double $135-$150 Single $100-$120 (Full breakfast)
Child negotiable   Studio $150 double
Visa MC Amex accepted
Children welcome
1 King/Twin 2 Queen 1 Double 3 Single (4 bdrm)
Bathrooms: 1 Ensuite 3 Private

Airlie House is a 110 year old character home nestled among mature trees and garden. This home has been beautifully renovated to provide 3 guest bedrooms with ensuites or private bathrooms, plus a studio apartment with its own kitchen and private bathroom. Located in central New Plymouth Airlie House is an easy 5 minute walk from shops, restaurants, the sea front, parks and many other local attractions. All rooms have many features and amenities available for your comfort, including Sky Digital TV, broadband and wireless internet access.

~

New Plymouth - Inglewood *12 km SE of New Plymouth*

B&B Approved

Araheke Cottage *B&B Cottage with Kitchen*
John Apps
Egmont Road, RD 6, Inglewood

Tel (06) 752 2722 or 025 609 1173
arahekecottage@xtra.co.nz

Double $130 Single $100 (Full provisions)
Children welcome
1 Queen 1 Double (1 bdrm)
Bathrooms: 1 Private With complimentary bubbles!

Escape to this beautifully warm, comfortable and peaceful haven, just minutes from New Plymouth. Comprehensively equipped with everything the most discerning traveller will need. Ideally situated for easy access to Egmont National Park, Mangamahoe Forest & Lake mountain bike tracks, Inglewood Athletics Complex, as well as the many attractions of New Plymouth. Nestling amidst lush pasture, mature trees, and overlooking a bubbling stream, Araheke Cottage enjoys grand views of Mount Taranaki. Inside tasteful quality furnishings create an ambience that is guaranteed to both welcome and relax.

New Plymouth *12 km NE of New Plymouth*
Villa Heights *B&B*
John & Rosemary Lucas
333 Upland Road, RD 2, New Plymouth

Tel (06) 755 2273 or 027 4164131
villaheights@xtra.co.nz   www.villaheights.co.nz

Double $110-$130 Single $70-$90 (Full breakfast)
Child $30 Dinner $25
Visa MC accepted
Children welcome
2 Queen (2 bdrm)
Bathrooms: 1 Ensuite 2

We welcome you to the peace and tranquillity of country life. Our Victorian villa is set in lovely gardens with panoramic views of Mt Taranaki to the sea. We offer warm hospitality, quality accommodation, good food, guest lounge with tea and coffee making facilities with home-made baking. We have comfortable beds. Our 3 children are married. We have 2 friendly dogs that live outside. We are just 15 minutes away from beaches, golf courses, beautiful gardens, restaurants and lovely walkways. We are only 30 minutes to Egmont National Park

New Plymouth
City Lights *B&B*
Carol & John Donaldson
4 Nadine Stanton Drive, Bell Block,
Kingsdown, New Plymouth

Tel (06) 755 0149 or 025 221 9267
Fax (06) 755 0149
carol.sharpe@clear.net.nz

Double $80-$120 Single $75 (Full breakfast)
Child $20
Children welcome
2 Queen 1 Twin (3 bdrm)
Bathrooms: 1 Ensuite 1 Guest share

Spectacular sunsets, peaceful relax country, city and sea views. Modern architecturally designed home, comfortable big bedrooms. 10 minutes to New Plymouth; 5 minutes to airport; drop-off or pick-up by arrangement. A guest lounge is available to make tea/coffee and has a microwave. Hop, skip, and jump to New Plymouth Golf course. John and I are happy and comfortable here with Barnie and Flash, our cats.

New Plymouth *2 km NE of Post Office*
Holsworthy House *Homestay*
Caroline & Peter Winstanley
22A Holsworthy Road, Brooklands, New Plymouth

Tel (06) 757 2728 or 027 475 7011
Fax (06) 757 2778
winnies@xtra.co.nz

Double $120 Single $90 (Full breakfast)
Visa MC accepted
Not suitable for children
1 King/Twin 1 Queen (2 bdrm)
Bathrooms: 2 Ensuite

Holsworthy House is down a private driveway nestled amongst native bush which extends into the world famous Pukekura Park & Bowl of Brooklands, only 5 minutes easy walk away. Relax in our private outdoor spa pool surrounded by our tranquil gardens. 15 minutes stroll to New Plymouth CBD and Coastal Walkway. Spacious bedrooms with guests own tea/coffee facilities, TV, hair dryer and internet connections.

Taranaki, Wanganui, Ruapehu, Rangitikei

New Plymouth

Issey Manor *Guest House*
Jan & Brian Mason
32 Carrington Street, New Plymouth

Tel (06) 758 2375 Fax (06) 758 2375
issey.manor@actrix.co.nz
www.isseymanor.co.nz

Double $110-$175 Single $110-$150
(Full Breakfast)
Child negotiable
Special winter rates available.
Visa MC Amex Eftpos accepted
1 King/Twin 3 Queen (4 bdrm)
Bathrooms: 4 Ensuite

A stylish blend of old architecture and modern living. Issey offers 4 contemporary suites all with designer bathrooms. Well appointed for business or pleasure with separate guest lounge and kitchen, Sky TV, and just a minutes stroll to the city centre, wonderful restaurants, cafes, parks, Pukeariki, art gallery and coastal walkway. If you enjoy comfort, stylish decor, privacy and awesome service - try Issey. Jan, Brian, Louie the Bichon and Wattie the cat welcome you.

New Plymouth

Timata Ora *Luxury B&B*
Carol & Rodney Hall
55 Gover Street, New Plymouth, Taranaki

Tel (06) 757 9917 or 0274 523 885
Fax (06) 757 9917   carolandrodneyhall@clear.net.nz
www.timataora.co.nz

Double $120-$130 Single $100-$110 (Full breakfast)
Family suite when both bedrooms used $200
Visa MC Eftpos accepted
Children welcome
1 King/Twin 3 Queen 1 Double (5 bdrm)
Bathrooms: 3 Ensuite 1 Family share Family suite has own bathroom

We warmly welcome guests to our fully refurbished (in 2003) central city home. A 1920s heritage home, Timata Ora offers 3 luxurious queen suites (1 with 4 Poster) each with own bathroom, TV, hair drier, iron/ironing board, heated towel rails, complimentary beverages and in room treats. The famiy suite has 2 bedrooms with private bathroom and amenities as other suites. Gregarious cats Splat and Murphy share Timata Ora. Breakfast in your suite, dining room, in the conservatory or on the terrace.

New Plymouth *5 km S of Waitara*
Loggers Retreat *B&B Cottage with kitchen*
John & Brenda Reumers
42 Richmond Road, RD 3, New Plymouth

Tel (06) 754 3131 or (06) 754 7668
Mobile 021 031 0375
Fax (06) 754 7668
heathenbear@xtra.co.nz

Double $100-$120 Single $80-$10 (Full provisions)
Dinner by arrangement
Not suitable for children Pets welcome by arrangement
1 Double (1 bdrm)
Bathrooms: 1 Private plus private outdoor bath

A rustic character-filled private board and battened 2 storyed cottage. Situated on 6 acres of beautiful rural land, which hosts a hand-built double storeyed log house and surrounded by native gardens. Enjoy a wine on the deck or on the bridge over the lake outside your door. This is a family with teenaged children, a cat and a dog, chooks and ducks. All under the watchful gaze of the majestic Mt Taranaki.

Directions: 12km north of New Plymouth on SH3; 5 minutes from the local airport. Well signposted on the corner of SH3 and Richmond Rd.

Stratford *1/2 km N of Stratford*

Stratford Lodge (Stallards) *B&B Homestay Farmstay*
Billieanne & Corb Stallard
3514 State Highway 3, Stratford Northern Boundary

Tel (06) 765 8324 Fax (06) 765 8324
stallardbb@infogen.net.nz   www.stratfordlodge.co.nz

Double $90-$100 Single $50-$55 (Full breakfast)
Child $20 Dinner by arrangement
Double is 2 people Visa MC Amex accepted
Children welcome
2 Double 2 Twin 2 Single (4 bdrm)
Bathrooms: 4 Ensuite 1 Guest share

Quality "Upstairs Downstairs" comfort. Cooked or
continental breakfast included. Free sel-catering kitchen, tea, coffee, biscuits. Homely or private. Own
key. Optional separate lounge. Restaurants, taverns, shops nearby. Rooms are antique, romantic with TV,
heaters, electric blankets, serviced daily. Gardens, BBQ, row boat, bush bath, river walks. 15 minutes
to Mt Egmont ski fields, climbing, tramping. Centrally located on edge of Stratford, easy distance to
New Plymouth, museums, famous gardens, tourist attractions. Interests include gemstones travel, art.
Welcome.

Egmont National Park *9 km W of Stratford*

Anderson's Alpine Lodge *Homestay Farmstay*
Berta Anderson
PO Box 303, Stratford, Taranaki

Tel (06) 765 6620 Fax (06) 765 6100
mountainhouse@xtra.co.nz www.mountainhouse.co.nz

Double $155-$195 Single $155 (Full breakfast)
Dinner a la carte
Visa MC Diners Eftpos accepted
Pets welcome
1 King/Twin 1 Queen 1 Double 2 Single (3 bdrm)
Bathrooms: 3 Ensuite

Swiss style chalet surrounded with native gardens
and bush. Offering luxury accommodation with special Alpine Ambiance. Spectacular views of Mount
Egmont/Taranaki and Egmont National Park opposite our front gate. Five kilometres to Mountain
House and its famed restaurant, further 3km to Stratford Plateau and skifields. Tramps, summit climbs,
trout stream, gardens and museums nearby. Private helicopter summit flights. Pet sheep, pig, ducks
etc. Swiss Berta Anderson has owned Mountain Lodges since 1976, winning many awards. Beautiful
paintings from Keith, her husband (Died 1 Feb 03) are on display.

Stratford *15 km NE of Stratford*

Te Popo Gardens *Country Garden Retreat*
Bruce & Lorri Ellis
Te Popo Gardens, 636 Stanley Road, RD 24, Stratford

Tel (06) 762 8775 Fax (06) 765 7182
tepopo@clear.net.nz
www.tepopo.co.nz

Double $130-$170 Single $110-$150
(Special breakfast)
Dinner $30-$40 by arrangement
Visa MC Diners Amex accepted
2 King/Twin1 King 1 Queen 2 Single (4 bdrm)
Bathrooms: 4 Ensuite

Te Popo Gardens is a garden of national significance and we love to share this special place - expansive
(34 acres) and beautiful woodland and perennial garden encircled by a deep river gorge and native forest.
Each of the 4 spacious suites opens to the garden and has private access, ensuite, woodfire, TV, sound
system, and superior bed and linen. Special breakfast is served in the sunny conservatory or beside the
fire. Fine food and wine for dinner by arrangement. Self-catering available. Wonderful dogs.

Hawera *1.5 km S of Hawera Central*

Tairoa Lodge *B&B Cottage No Kitchen*
Linda & Steve Morrison
3 Puawai Street, PO Box 117, Hawera

Tel (06) 278 8603 Fax (06) 278 8603
tairoa.lodge@xtra.co.nz   www.tairoa-lodge.co.nz

Double $140-$185 Single $120 (Full breakfast)
Dinner by arrangement
Self-contained cottage (sleeps 6) $195-$355
Visa MC Diners Amex accepted
Children welcome
2 Queen 1 Single (2 bdrm)
Bathrooms: 2 Ensuite

Originally built in 1875 our kauri villa has been renovated to its former Victorian glory and is nestled amongst established grounds. Polished kauri floors add a golden glow to the tastefully decorated guest rooms. Enjoy; private garden setting, swimming pool, sumptuous breakfasts, afternoon tea or aperitif on arrival, robes, hairdryers, toiletries and fresh flowers. For peace, privacy and retreats our self-contained Tairoa Cottage is perfect for honeymooners, families or special occasions. Sleeps 6. Linda, Steve, Hannah, & Caitlyn assure you a memorable stay.

Waitotara - Wanganui *29 km W of Wanganui*

Ashley Park *Farmstay Cottage No Kitchen*
Wendy Pearce
State Highway 3, Box 36, Waitotara, Wanganui

Tel (06) 346 5917 Fax (06) 346 5861
ashley_park@xtra.co.nz
www.ashleypark.co.nz

Double $95-$120 Single $70 (Full breakfast)
Dinner $30
Visa MC Diners Amex accepted
1 Queen 4 Single (3 bdrm)
Bathrooms: 1 Ensuite 1 Guest share

We have a 500 acre sheep and cattle farm and live in a comfortable home, set in an attractive garden with a swimming pool and tennis court. Also in the garden is an antique shop selling Devonshire teas. 100 metres from the house is a 4 acre park and lake, aviaries and a collection of hand fed pet farm animals. We welcome guests to have dinner with us. Self-contained accommodation is available in the park.

Wanganui *5 min N of Wanganui Centre*

Bradgate *B&B Homestay*
Frances
7 Somme Parade, Wanganui

Tel (06) 345 3634 Fax (06) 345 3634
vige@value.net.nz

Double $80 Single $40-$50 (Full breakfast)
Dinner $25
1 Queen 1 Twin 1 Single (3 bdrm)
Bathrooms: 1 Guest share

Welcome to Bradgate, a gracious 2 storey home. With its beautiful entrance hall and carved rimu staircase which reflects the original character and gracefulness of the house. 30 years ago my husband and I came to New Zealand. We owned a restaurant by Virginia Lake. 20 years later we retired and decided to welcome guests into our home. My Mum and I share an energetic young labrador named Crunchy. I enjoy playing golf, gardening and meeting people. Non-smoking house, dinner by arrangement.

Wanganui *2 km NW of Wanganui City centre*

Kembali *B&B Homestay*
Marylyn & Wes Palmer
26 Taranaki Street, St Johns Hill, Wanganui

Tel (06) 347 1727
wespalmer@xtra.co.nz

Double $90 Single $60 (Full breakfast)
Visa MC accepted
Not suitable for children
1 Queen 1 Twin (2 bdrm)
Bathrooms: 1 Private

Kembali is a modern, centrally heated, sunny home in a quiet street overlooking trees and wetlands. Upstairs guest bedrooms, bathroom and lounge (with TV, fridge, tea/coffee) are for 1 party/groups exclusive use. Retired, no pets, children married, we offer a restful stay. We enjoy meeting people, gardening, travel, reading and have Christian interests. Off-street parking and laundry available. 5 minutes drive to city, heritage buildings, restored paddle steamer, restaurants, museum, art gallery and walks. We look forward to welcoming you.

Wanganui *20 km NE of Wanganui*

Misty Valley Farmstay *Farmstay*
Linda & Garry Wadsworth
RD 5, 97 Parihauhau Road, Wanganui

Tel (06) 342 5767
linda.garry.wadsworth@xtra.co.nz

Double $80 Single $50 (Full breakfast)
Child $20 Dinner $30 by arrangement
Visa MC accepted
Children welcome
2 Double 2 Twin (2 bdrm)
Bathrooms: 1 Guest share

Misty Valley is a small organic farm at 3.7 hectares. We prefer to use our own produce whenever possible. There are farm animals for you to meet including our brittany, George and cats, Alice and Calico, who all live outside. Our 2 grandchildren visit us regularly and children will be made very welcome. We are non-smoking, but have pleasant deck areas for those who do. Our famous river and historical city offer plenty of activities for the whole family to enjoy.

Wanganui *2 km N of Wanganui centre*

Braemar House *B&B Guest House*
Clive Rivers & Rob Gooch
2 Plymouth Street, Wanganui

Tel (06) 347 2529 Fax (06) 347 2529
contact@braemarhouse.co.nz
www.braemarhouse.co.nz

Double $70-$90 Single $45-$55 (Continental)
Child $10 Dinner $25 by arrangement
Visa MC Eftpos accepted Children welcome
2 Queen 3 Double 3 Twin (8 bdrm)
Bathrooms: 3 Guest share

Welcome to 'Olde Worlde Charm'. This restored historic homestead circa 1895, nestled alongside the Wanganui River, has a homely ambience that makes your stay restful and enjoyable. The graceful entrance leads to centrally heated, comfortable period-designed bedrooms, guest lounge and dining room. Laundry facilities and fully equipped kitchen available. Off-street parking surrounded by lovely gardens. The homestead is close to the city and tourist attractions. We look forward to you visiting. Clive, Rob, the hens and Pippin, the resident cat, all welcome you.

Wanganui *20 km NW of Marton*

Te-Aunui Farmstay *Farmstay Cottage with Kitchen*
Mike & Marg Webster
RD 11, Wanganui

Tel (06) 327 3821 Fax (06) 3273 823 TE-AUNUI@xtra.co.nz

Double $80-$140 Single $80 (Full breakfast)
Child $25   Dinner $40 by arrangement
Picnic hamper $40   Children and pets welcome
2 King 1 Queen 1 Single (3 bdrm)
Bathrooms: 1 Private

Te-Aunui is a 300 acre sheep and beef farm. We offer a fully self-contained 3 bedroomed homestead for guests to explore the farm from or join Marg and I as we work our way through the farm year, shearing, rearing calves, lambing etc. Or enjoy the novelty golf hole and claybird shooting(extra). Te-Aunui is an ideal base to tour the Rangitikei from with one of Marg's picnic hampers. TV, phone and internet access but no cell phone coverage in the valley.
Directions: Turn up the Turakina Valley Rd at Turakina. We're 13.5kms up the valley on the left rapid no 1315. Alturnatively turn off SH1 onto Jeffersons Line(between Rata and Marton) 8.5 kms then turn right onto Tutaenui Rd for 1.7kms then left onto Makohau Rd, then right into Turakina Road, drive 2km, we are rural 1315.

Taumarunui *5 km NE of Taumarunui*

Jones' Farmstay *Farmstay*
Shirley & Allan Jones
213 Taringamotu Road, Taumarunui

Tel (07) 896 7722
costleyj@xtra.co.nz

Double $100 Single $70 (Full breakfast)
Child half price
Dinner by arrangement
Children welcome
1 King 1 Twin (2 bdrm)
Bathrooms: 1 Private

Our spacious home is situated 5km from the centre of Taumarunui surrounded by a peaceful 1 acre garden with a native bush backdrop filled with NZ native birds. The bedrooms open on to a large verandah. Laundry available. A stream runs along 1 boundary of the 80 acre property suitable for walks and summertime swimming. A golf course is located within 2km, along with guided mountain walks, canoeing, hot pools, scenic flights, skiing, trout fishing and white-water rafting are all within an hours drive.

Taumarunui *3 km N of Taumarunui*

Le Cornu Farms Bed & Breakfast *B&B Farmstay Cottage with Kitchen*
Rosemary & John Filleul
31 Simmons Road, Taumarunui

Tel (07) 896 8901
filleul.family@xtra.co.nz
www.lecornufarms.com

Double $80 Single $40 (Continental)
Child $20
Children and pets welcome
1 Queen 1 Single (1 bdrm)
Bathrooms: 1 Private

Self-contained farmstay and B&B on 700 acres of farmland only 3 minutes from town. You might like to walk or mountain-bike across our hills, do a little fishing or swimming in our river, chat with the livestock and family pets or just having a wine on the sundeck. You can also cross the road to the golf course, shoot into town for a coffee, canoe the Wanganui, or go skiing. Cooked breakfast, evening meals and packed lunches available. Child minders, pet sitters on call.

Taumarunui - Piriaka *10 km S of Taumarunui*

Awarua Lodge *B&B Separate Suite*
Raewyn & Jack Vernon
1063 State Highway 4, Piriaka, Taumarunui

Tel (07) 896 8100 Fax (07) 896 8102
info@awarualodge.co.nz
www.awarualodge.co.nz

Double $180 (Full breakfast)
Suite $350
Visa MC Eftpos accepted
1 King/Twin1 King (2 bdrm)
Bathrooms: 1 Private

Awarua Lodge, set in parkland grounds overlooking
the Whanganui River, is self-contained guest accommodation offering a suite that sleeps 4. The decor simply commands you to relax. Visit the Whanganui & Tongariro National Parks. Try your hand golfing on Taumarunui's premiere golf course, rated in the top NZ 50. Plan your adventures; tramping, fishing, canoeing, skiing, mountain biking. Watch sheep shearing and the milking of a large NZ dairy herd. Beau the retired sheep dog could be on hand to met you!

Owhango - Taumarunui *15 km S of Taumarunui*

Fernleaf *Farmstay*
Carolyn & Melvin Forlong
58 Tunanui Road, RD 1, Owhango

Tel (07) 895 4847 Fax (07) 895 4837
fernleaf.farm@xtra.co.nz

Double $100 Single $75 (Full breakfast)
Dinner $20 Cottage $75
Children welcome
2 Queen 1 Double 1 Single (3 bdrm)
Bathrooms: 2 Guest share

Relax in the tranquil Tunanui Valley just 500 metres
from SH4. Close for convenience, far enough away for
peace and quiet. We are the third generation to farm Fernleaf and our Romney flock has been recorded every year since the First World War. The views from various vantage point on the farm are awesome, taking in the mountains: Ruapehu, Ngaruahoe, Tongariro and Taranaki. Enjoy our generous country hospitality, wonderful breakfast, a beautiful dalmatian and friendly cats. Other meals by arrangement.

Raetihi *0.5 km N of Raetihi*

Log Lodge *B&B*
Jan & Bob Lamb
5 Ranfurly Terrace, Raetihi

Tel (06) 385 4135 Fax (06) 385 4835
Lamb.Log-Lodge@Xtra.co.nz

Double $115 Single $60 (Full breakfast)
Child under 14 $50 Spa $5pp
Visa MC Diners Amex accepted
2 Double 4 Single (open plan bdrm)
Bathrooms: 2 Private

A unique opportunity to stay in a modern authentic
log home sited high on 7 acres on the edge of town.
Completely private accommodation, with own bathroom. All sleeping on mezzanine, your own lounge with wood fire, snooker table, TV/video, stereo and dining area, opening onto large verandah, with swimming pool and spa available. Panoramic views of Mts Ruapehu, Ngauruhoe and Tongariro. Tongariro National Park and Turoa Skifield is half hour scenic drive.

Ohakune *6 km W of Ohakune*
Mitredale *Homestay Farmstay*
Audrey & Diane Pritt
Smiths Road, RD, Ohakune

Tel (06) 385 8016 or 027 453 1916
Fax (06) 385 8016   mitredale@ihug.co.nz

Double $100 Single $50 (Continental)
Dinner $25pp by arrangement
Visa MC accepted
Pets welcome
1 Double 2 Single (2 bdrm)
Bathrooms: 1 Family share

We farm sheep, bull beef and run a boarding kennel
in a beautiful peaceful valley with magnificent views of Mt Ruapehu. Tongariro National Park for
skiing, walking, photography. Excellent 18 hole golf course, great fishing locally. We are members of
Ducks Unlimited (a conservation group)and our local wine club. We have 2 labradors. We offer dinner
traditional farmhouse (Diane, a cook book author), or breakfast with excellent home-made jams. Take
Raetihi Road, at Hotel/BP Service Station corner. 4km to Smiths Road. Last house 2km.

≈

Taihape *1 km N of Taihape*
Korirata Homestay *B&B Homestay*
Patricia & Noel Gilbert
25 Pukeko Street, Taihape

Tel (06) 388 0315 Fax (06) 388 0315
korirata@xtra.co.nz

Double $80 Single $50 (Special breakfast)
Child half price under 10
Dinner by arrangement
Visa MC accepted
4 Single (2 bdrm)
Bathrooms: 1 Guest share

A warm welcome awaits you at the top of the hill
in Taihape, where panoramic views of the mountains, ranges and surrounding countryside, add to the
tranquil surroundings. 3 quarters of an acre has been landscaped with shrubs, hydroponics, home-grown
vegetables and chrysanthemums in season. Meals, if desired, are with hosts, using produce from the
garden where possible. Comfortable beds with electric blankets. Rafting, bungy jumping and farm visits
can be arranged. 1 hour to Ruapehu, Lake Taupo and 2 and a half hours to Wellington and Rotorua.

≈

Taihape
Grandvue *Homestay*
John & Dianne McKinnon
Wairanu Road, RD 4, Taihape

Tel (06) 388 1308 or 025 244 1309
Fax (06) 388 1308

Double $90 Single $50 (Continental)
Child under 10 years half price
Dinner by arrangement
Visa MC accepted
Children welcome
1 Queen 2 Twin (2 bdrm)
Bathrooms: 1 Guest share

We welcome you to our home situated on 90 acres of farmland, 6 minutes south of Taihape, 2 minutes
off State Highway 1, en route to Mokai Gravity Canyon. Our home boasts magnificent views of Mt
Ruapehu to the north and the Ruahine Ranges to the east. Comfortable beds with electric blankets. River
rafting, golf, farm walks, or a visit to Gravity Canyon can be arranged. 1 hour to Ruapehu, Taupo 2
hours and Wellington 3 hours. Our burmese cat also enjoys people. Dinner by arrangement.

Taihape/Rangitikei *26 km NE of Taihape*

Tarata Fishaway *Luxury B&B Homestay Farmstay Cottage No Kitchen*

Stephen & Trudi Mattock
Mokai Road, RD 3, Taihape

Tel (06) 388 0354 Fax (06) 388 0954
fishaway@xtra.co.nz
www.tarata.co.nz

Double $100-$180 Single $50-$90
(Continental provisions)
Child under 12 half price Dinner $30pp
Visa MC accepted Children and pets welcome
4 King/Twin 5 Queen 1 Double 3 Single (10 bdrm)
Bathrooms: 4 Ensuite 1 Guest share 1 Private spa bath

We are very lucky to have a piece of New Zealand's natural beauty. Tarata is nestled in bush in the remote Mokai Valley where the picturesque Rangitikei River meets the rugged Ruahine Ranges. With the wilderness and unique trout fishing right at our doorstep, it is the perfect environment to bring up our 3 children.

Stephen offers guided fishing and rafting trips for all ages. Raft through the gentle crystal clear waters of the magnificent Rangitikei River, visit Middle Earth and a secret waterfall, stunning scenery you will never forget. Our spacious home and our large garden allow guests private space to relax and unwind. Whether it is by the pool on a hot summers day with a good book, soaking in the spa pool after a day on the river or enjoying a cosy winters night in front of our open fire with a glass of wine.

Come on a farm tour meeting our many friendly farm pets, experience our nightlife on our free spotlight safari and Tarata is only 6km past the new flying fox and bungy jump. Stay in our Homestead or in Tarata's fully self-contained River Retreats where you can enjoy a spa bath with million dollar views of the river and relax on the large decking amidst native birds and trees. Peace, privacy and tranquillity at its best! We will even deliver a candle light dinner to your door. We think Tarata is truly a magic place and we would love sharing it with you. Approved pets welcome.

Directions: Tarata Fishaway is 26 scenic kilometres from Taihape. Turn off SH1, 6km south of Taihape at the Gravity Canyon Bungy and Ohotu signs. Follow the signs (14km) to the bungy bridge. We are 6 km past here on Mokai Road. Features & Attractions Trout Fishing and Scenic Rafting Visit LOTR, Anduin, Middle Earth 6 kms past Bungy & Flying Fox Mini golf (with a difference) Swimming & Spa pool Bush walks/spotlight safaris Camp outs Clay Bird shooting

173

Hunterville *10 km NE of Hunterville*
Richmond Station - Vennell's Farmstay *Farmstay*
Oriel & Phil Vennell
Mangapipi Road, Rewa, RD 10, Hunterville

Tel (06) 328 6780 or 0800 220 172
Fax (06) 328 6780
From March 2006 Tel/Fax (06) 322 8286

Double $120 Single $60 (Full breakfast)
Child negotiable
Dinner $30
1 King/Twin 1 Queen 1 Twin 4 Single (3 bdrm)
Bathrooms: 2 Private

We are fifth generation farmers on Richmond Station, a 1200 acre sheep/cattle hill country farm. Our spacious home is in a tranquil setting. You will enjoy great farm walks and beautiful views. Central to private gardens. We are midway Rotorua/Wellington. Enjoy great country fare and hospitality. Farmstay hosts since 1980. We look forward to having you stay. March 2006 we move to Richmond Hill. Our Elegant, comfortable home and surroundings is on 350 acres, near Hunterville on State Highway 1. We have 2 shy outdoor cats.

Hunterville *1/3 km NW of Hunterville*
Hunterville Hills *B&B Cottage with Kitchen*
Laddie Bush
69 Ongo Road, Hunterville

Tel (06) 322 8071 or (06) 332 8055
huntervillehills@yahoo.com
www.huntervillehills.com

Double $85 Single $65 (Continental)
Entire cottage $160
Children welcome
1 Queen 1 Double (2 bdrm)
Bathrooms: 1 Guest share

Experience true rural Kiwi lifestyle in this newly remodeled, very private, 2 bedroom home in the heart of the beautiful Rangatikei River District. Near to restaurants, river, golf, mountains but in a rural farm environment on the edge of town.

Directions: From SH1, turn NW on Bruce Street in the center of Hunterville and proceed past the sheep statues. Bruce Street changes to Ongo Road at the edge of town, continue a third of a kilometre on Ongo Road and watch for sign on left.

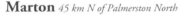

Marton *45 km N of Palmerston North*
Rea's Inn *B&B Homestay*
Keith and Lorraine Rea
12 Dunallen Avenue, Marton

Tel (06) 327 4442 Fax (06) 327 4442
keithandlorraine@xtra.co.nz

Double $85 Single $50 (Continental)
Child half price
Dinner $20
Visa MC accepted
Children welcome
1 Queen 1 Twin (2 bdrm)
Bathrooms: 1 Guest share

We have a warm comfortable home offering hospitality, peace and tranquility. Situated in quiet cul-de-sac with a private garden setting. Guests stay in separate wing of home. Close to Nga Tawa and Huntley Schools. Ideal for weekend retreat or stopover. (Only 2 hours from Wellington Ferry). Organic farm tour available by arrangement. Your comfort and pleasure are important to us. Our birman cat likes people too, and we all welcome you to come, relax and enjoy the friendly atmosphere at Rea's Inn.

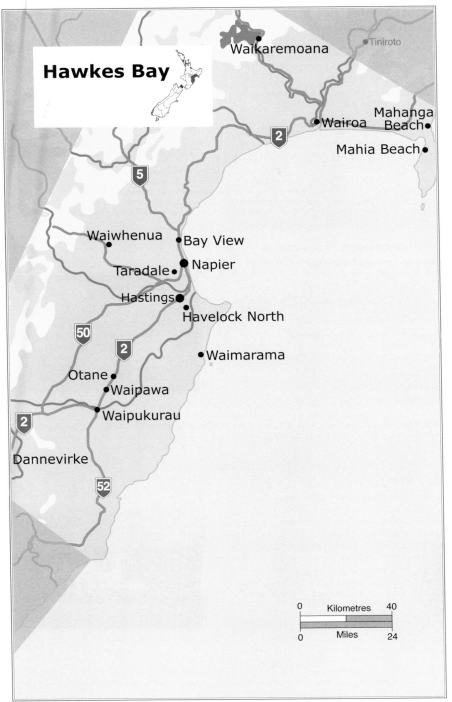

Hawkes Bay

Tiniroto

Waikaremoana

Wairoa

Mahanga Beach

Mahia Beach

Waiwhenua

Bay View

Taradale

Napier

Hastings

Havelock North

Waimarama

Otane

Waipawa

Waipukurau

Dannevirke

Kilometres

Miles

Mahia Peninsula - Mahanga Beach *50 km N of Wairoa*

Reomoana *Farmstay Cottage No Kitchen*
Louise Schick
RD 8, Nuhaka, Hawkes Bay

Tel (06) 837 5898 Fax (06) 837 5990
reomoana@paradise.net.nz

Double $120-$150 Single $60 (Continental)
Child $20 Dinner $30 Cottage $100
Visa MC accepted
Children and pets welcome
2 Queen 1 Twin 1 Single (4 bdrm)
Bathrooms: 1 Ensuite 1 Private

Reomoana - The voice of the sea. Pacific Ocean front
farm at beautiful Mahia Peninsula. The spacious, rustic home with cathedral ceilings, hand-crafted
furniture overlooks the Pacific with breathtaking views. Enjoy the miles of white sandy beaches, go
swimming, surfing or fishing. A painter's paradise. Attractions in the area include: Morere Hot Springs,
Mahia Native Bush Reserve, golf course and fishing charters by arrangement. 6km to Sunset Point
Restaurant. Also self-contained cottage in avocado orchard, ideal for families, 3 minutes walk to beach.

Waikaremoana *50 km W of Wairoa*

Waikaremoana Homestay *B&B Homestay*
Bev Macharper
Tuai Village, RD5, Wairoa

Tel (06) 837 3701 Fax (06) 837 3709
ykarestay@xtra.co.nz
www.waikaremoanahomestay.co.nz

Double $85 Single $55 (Continental)
Dinner $30 by arrangement
Visa MC accepted
Pets welcome
1 Queen 1 Twin (2 bdrm)
Bathrooms: 1 Family share

Lake Waikaremoana is a unique native forest wilderness bordering eastern Te Urewera National Park.
The homestay, set in the picturesque village of Tuai, is an ideal base for hiking, flyfishing or boating.
Tuai Village is nestled around Lake Whakamarino, 1km from Highway 38. The house, 70 years old,
is cosy and comfortable and from the verandah you may view the lake and relax. Home cooking uses
garden and local produce. Relax in outdoor spa. House pets are 3 cats and a little dog.

Bay View *12 km N of Napier*

Beachfront Homestay *B&B Homestay Separate Suite*
Christine & Jim Howard
20A Le Quesne Road, Bay View, Napier

Tel (06) 836 6530 or 021 159 0162
Fax (06) 836 6531 j-howard@clear.net.nz
www.beachfronthb.co.nz

Double $120 Single $60 (Full breakfast)
Child $25 Dinner $30 4 person apartment $200
Visa MC Diners Amex accepted Children welcome
1 Queen 1 Double 1 Single (2 bdrm)
Bathrooms: 1 Private

Jim, Christine and Sarcha (Jack Russell) will welcome
you to their beachfront home with breathtaking views of Hawkes Bay and walking distance to local
wineries. Guests are offered self-contained accommodation and own entrance on ground floor. Jim's
a local transport operator and Christine works at a local winery both enjoy meeting people and their
interests are fishing and the outdoor life. Surfcasting and Kontiki fishing available. Beachfront homestay
is just 5 minutes from the Napier Taupo turn off and 12 minutes from Napiers Marine Parade and cafes.
Personalised wine and sightseeing tours available.

Bay View - Napier *12 km N of Napier*

Kilbirnie *Homestay*
Jill & John Grant
84 Le Quesne Road, Bay View, Napier

Tel (06) 836 6929 or 027 2347363
jill.johng@xtra.co.nz
www.bnb.co.nz/kilbirnie.html

Double $80-$90 (Special breakfast)
Child not suitable
Dinner $30pp by arrangement
Visa MC accepted
Not suitable for children
2 Queen (2 bdrm)
Bathrooms: 1 Ensuite 1 Private

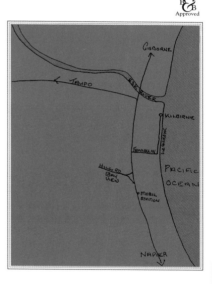

We moved with our dog in 1996 to the quiet end of an unspoiled fishing beach by the Esk River, attracted by the beauty and position away from the traffic, while only 15 minutes from the main attractions. Nearby are vineyards, gardens, walks and a full range of harbourside restaurants north of Napier. Kilbirnie is near the Taupo Road intersection with the Pacific Highway to Gisborne, with off-road parking. Upstairs, air-conditioned guest rooms have restful views of the Pacific Ocean one side or vineyards on the other, private bathrooms, excellent showers, abundant hot water, comfortable firm beds and guest lounge. Special breakfast overlooking the ocean is an experience which makes lunch seem superfluous. We are retired farmers with time to share good company, fresh imaginative food and juice, real coffee, an eclectic range of books, who invite you to enjoy our hospitality in modern surroundings. We have 15 years home hosting experience and are non-smokers. Directions: from Taupo first left after intersection Highways 2 & 5. Franklin Road to Le Quesne, proceed to far end beachfront. From Napier first right after Mobil Station. Prior contact appreciated.

The View

~

Bay View - Napier *12 km N of Napier*

The Grange Farmstay *B&B Farmstay Self-contained Lodge*
Roslyn & Don Bird
263 Hill Road, Eskdale, Hawkes Bay
PO Box 136 Bay View, Hawkes Bay

Tel (06) 836 6666 or 027 28 15738
Fax (06) 836 6456
thefarmstay@xtra.co.nz
www.thefarmstay.com

Double Farmstay $100 Single $85 (Full breakfast)
Self-contained lodge $120-$140 Single $100
$25 extra person. Optional breakfast provisions $9pp
Dinner - $45pp by arrangement
Visa MC accepted Children welcome
1 King/Twin1 King 1 Double 2 Single
(1 bdrm in farmstay, 1+ Loft in Lodge)
Bathrooms: 2 Private

home

Inside the Lodge

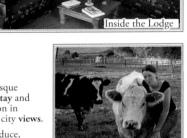

The Farm

In the heart of a thriving **wine region** overlooking the picturesque Esk Valley nestles The Grange, our delightfully modern **farmstay** and superior **self-contained lodge**. Private, spacious accommodation in relaxing peaceful surrounds with spectacular rural, coastal and city **views**.

Feel the comforts of home as we tempt you with our farm produce, baking, and preserves. We're an outgoing family who really enjoy the company of guests. Hospitality is guaranteed! Experience our **farm** life with Roslyn, Zac (our weimaraner farm dog), and Sparkie(our resident cat). Feed the sheep(Lisa, Charlotte and Rose etc), cows (especially Snowy), pigs (Bubble and Squeek), chickens and dairy goats (try milking Betsy) or bottle-feeding a lamb (seasonal).

Don a third generation **winemaker** with more than 29 years experience is passionate about the wine industry and is happy to share his knowledge over dinner or to help you plan your **Hawkes Bay Wine Adventure.**

Explore the world's **art deco** capital **Napier** 12 minutes drive away and Hawke's Bay's many regional attractions within 30 minutes. Discover part of Cultural New Zealand along the nearby rivers with Te Awa Maiden, our very talented local fishing guide. We are always happy to advise on any tours or special requests as our knowledge, information and contacts throughout Hawkes Bay are invaluable.

Unwind on the Deck to the soothing chorus of native birds in the surrounding gardens and trees and at day's end spend time romancing over our wonderful night sky. Email access available. We also offer our Taupo (Kinloch) holiday home to those wishing to stay in that area. Share our home or retreat in the Lodge. "Our Place Is Your Place." 1km off SH5 at Eskdale or 3km off SH2 at Bay View.

Bay View - Napier *10 km N of Napier*
Bev's on the Bay *B&B*
Beverley White
32 Ferguson Street North, Bay View, Napier

Tel (06) 836 7637 bevann@paradise.net.nz
www.bnb.co.nz/hosts/bevs.html

Double $110-$140 Single $90 (Full breakfast)
Visa MC Amex accepted Pets welcome
1 King 1 Queen (2 bdrm)
Bathrooms: 1 Ensuite 1 Private

The rooms at Bev's on the Bay are large, modern, have quality beds & linen, own bathrooms, TVs, tea & coffee facilities, sitting areas, and private entrances. The king room has a balcony and panoramic sea views, the queen room opens to a courtyard. Paths through a fascinating cacti and succulent garden lead to the beach. Undercover parking provided. Close to the airport, restaurants and Napier's art deco, there is a winery in walking distance. Host Beverley White is a former businesswoman.

Napier *1 km N of Napier*
Spence Homestay *B&B Homestay*
Kay & Stewart Spence
17 Cobden Road, Napier

Tel (06) 835 9454 or 025 235 9828
0800 117 890
Fax (06) 835 9454
ksspence@actrix.gen.nz

Double $135 Single $90-$95 (Full breakfast)
Visa MC accepted
1 Queen 1 Single (1 bdrm)
Bathrooms: 1 Ensuite

Welcome to our comfortable near new home. Quiet area 10-15 minutes walk from art deco city centre. Guest suite opens outside to patio, petanque court and colourful garden. Lounge includes double bed settee, TV, kitchenette with tea making facilities, fridge and microwave. Bedroom has queen and single beds, ensuite bathroom. We have hosted for over 10 years and enjoy overseas travel. Able to meet public transport. Directions: port end Marine Parade, Coote Road, right into Thompson Road, left into Cobden Road opposite water tower.

Napier *1.5 km N of Post Office*
A Room with a View *B&B Homestay*
Robert McGregor
9 Milton Terrace, Napier

Tel (06) 835 7434 Fax (06) 835 1912
roomwithview@xtra.co.nz

Double $100 Single $70 (Continental)
Visa MC accepted
1 Queen (1 bdrm)
Bathrooms: 1 Private

Having hosted for 10 years with my late wife, I'm continuing to enjoy companionship, conversation and laughter with guests. Spacious room with sea view. Fourth generation property with large 100 year old garden and sunny hill location. Only a 15 minute walk to restaurants at historic Port Ahuriri or our world famous art deco city centre. Private bathroom with bath and shower. Laundry facilities available. Free pick-up service if required. Off-street parking. No smoking inside please. I'm interested in travel, gardening, the arts, and especially local history, as I'm Executive Director of the Art Deco Trust.

Napier *1.2 km N of Napier Central*

Hillcrest *B&B Homestay*
Nancy & Noel Lyons
4 George Street, Hospital Hill, Napier

Tel (06) 835 1812
lyons@inhb.co.nz
www.hillcrestnapier.co.nz

Double $100 Single $65 (Continental)
Visa MC accepted
Not suitable for children
1 Double 2 Single (2 bdrm)
Bathrooms: 1 Guest share

If you require quiet accommodation just minutes from the city centre, our comfortable home provides peace in restful surroundings. Relax on wide decks overlooking our garden, or enjoy the spectacular sea views. Explore nearby historic places and the botanical gardens. Your own lounge with tea/coffee making; laundry and off-street parking available. We have travelled extensively and welcome the opportunity of meeting visitors. Our interests are travel, music, bowls and embroidery. We will happily meet you at the travel depots. Holiday home at Mahia Beach available.

Napier *5 km S of Napier*

Snug Harbour *Homestay*
Ruth & Don McLeod
147 Harold Holt Avenue, Napier

Tel (06) 843 2521 Fax (06) 843 2520
donmcld@clear.net.nz

Double $85-$95 Single $60 (Full breakfast)
Dinner $30 by arrangement
Visa MC accepted
1 Queen 1 Twin (2 bdrm)
Bathrooms: 1 Ensuite 1 Family share

Ruth & Don welcome you to their comfortable home with its rural outlook and sunny attractive patio. The garden studio with ensuite and tea making facilities has its own entrance. We are situated on the outskirts of Napier City, the art deco city of the World, and in close proximity to wineries and many other tourist attractions. We both have a background in teaching, with interests in travel, gardening and photography.

Napier

Blue Water Lodge Ltd *B&B*
Blue Water Lodge Ltd
471 Marine Parade, Napier

Tel (06) 835 8929 Fax (06) 835 8929
bobbrown2@xtra.co.nz

Double $80-$90 Single $40 (Continental)
Child under 14 $10
Visa MC Diners Amex Eftpos accepted
6 Double 9 Single (9 bdrm)
Bathrooms: 1 Ensuite 2 Guest share

Blue Water Lodge is on the beach front opposite the aquarium on Napier's popular Marine Parade. Close to all local tourist attractions and within walking distance to the city centre, information centre, family restaurants, RSA and Cosmopolitan Club. Owner operated.

Napier *1 km N of Napier*
The Coach House *Cottage with Kitchen*
Jan Chalmers
9 Gladstone Road, Napier

Tel (06) 835 6126 or 021 251 5847
janchalmers@paradise.co.nz
www.thecoachhouse.co.nz

Double $100 **Single** $80 (Full breakfast)
Child $25-babies free
Children and pets welcome
1 Queen 2 Single (2 bdrm)
Bathrooms: 1 Private

On the hill over-looking a gorgeous Mediterranean garden and sea views, the historic Coach-house is tastefully renovated and totally self-contained. It contains 2 bedrooms, open plan kitchen, dining, living rooms, bathroom and separate toilet. The fridge will be full of a variety of breakfast supplies. TV and radio included and fresh flowers in all rooms. The sunny deck has a table and chairs and gas barbecue. Off-street parking and easy access plus peace and privacy complete the picture.

Napier - Taradale *10 km W of Napier*
Otatara Heights *B&B Apartment with Kitchen*
Sandra & Roy Holderness
57 Churchill Drive, Taradale, Napier

Tel (06) 844 8855 Fax (06) 844 8855
sandroy@xtra.co.nz

Double $90 **Single** $65 (Continental)
Extra guest $30
1 Queen 1 Double (1 bdrm)
Bathrooms: 1 Private

Comfortable, quiet apartment in the heart of our foremost wine producing area. Superb day and night views over Napier and local rural scenes. 10 minutes drive to the art deco capital of the world. 2km to Taradale Village. Safe off-street parking. Top quality restaurants and wineries nearby. We are a friendly couple who have enjoyed B&B overseas and like meeting people. Our interests are travel, theatre, good food and wine. Bella, our cat, keeps to herself. Handy to EIT and golf course.

Napier - Taradale *7.5 km SW of Napier*
279 Church Road *B&B Homestay*
Sandy Edginton
279 Church Road, Taradale, Napier

Tel (06) 844 7814 or 021 447 814
Fax (06) 844 7814sandy.279 @homestaynapier.co.nz
www.homestaynapier.co.nz

Double $120 **Single** $90 (Full breakfast)
Dinner by arrangement
Smoking area available
Visa MC accepted
1 Queen 1 Double 1 Single (2 bdrm)
Bathrooms: 1 Guest share

279, An elegant and spacious home set amongst mature trees and gardens, offers excellent hospitality in a relaxed, friendly atmosphere to domestic and international visitors. Located adjacent to Mission Estate and Church Road Wineries, restaurants and craft galleries, 279 is within a short drive of Art Deco Napier, Hastings, golf courses, and tourist activities. I welcome you to 279 and will help make your visit the highlight of your travels.

Hawkes Bay

Napier *0.5 km N of Post Office*

Cameron Close *Homestay*
Joy & Graeme Thomas
33 Cameron Road, Napier

Tel (06) 835 5180 Fax (06) 835 4115
besco@xtra.co.nz

Double $100 Single $80 (Continental)
Not suitable for children
1 Queen 1 Double 1 Single (3 bdrm)
Bathrooms: 1 Guest share

Come and share our beautifully restored 1920s home, complete with pool and garden. We are situated above and within a 5 minute stroll to the centre of the marvellous art deco city of Napier. Continental breakfast, yes! But fresh and upmarket. Laundry facilities and parking available. Shiraz, our cat shares this home too. Some of our interests include food, wine, classic cars, art deco and good company. Our knowledge of NZ is willingly shared. Smoke free and regret not suitable for children.

Napier - Marine Parade *In Napier*

Mon Logis *B&B*
Gerard Averous
415 Marine parade, PO Box 871, Napier

Tel (06) 835 2125 or 027 472 5332
Fax (06) 835 8811
monlogis@xtra.co.nz
www.babs.co.nz/monlogis

Double $120-$200 Single $120-$145 (Full breakfast)
Visa MC Diners Amex accepted
Not suitable for children
2 King/Twin 2 Queen (4 bdrm)
Bathrooms: 3 Ensuite 1 Private

A little piece of France nestled in the heart of the beautiful wine-growing region of Hawkes Bay. Built as private hotel in 1915, this grand colonial building is a few minutes walk from the city. Now lovingly renovated Mon Logis will cater to a maximum of 8 guests. Downstairs, an informal guest lounge invites relaxation, television viewing or a quiet time reading. Guests can help themselves to coffee/tea and home-made biscuits at any time. French and Spanish spoken. Casual elegance at a price you can afford.

Napier *1 km N of Napier*

Cobden Garden Homestay *B&B Homestay*
Rayma and Phillip Jenkins
1 Cobden Crescent, Bluff Hill, Napier

Tel (06) 834 2090 or 0800 426 233
025 540062 Fax (06) 834 1977
info@cobden.co.nz
www.cobden.co.nz

Double $140-$170 Single $120-$150 (Full breakfast)
Child negotiable
Visa MC Diners Amex Eftpos accepted
2 King/Twin1 King 1 Single (3 bdrm)
Bathrooms: 3 Ensuite

We invite you to stay in our quiet and sunny colonial villa on Bluff Hill. Enjoy the spacious bedrooms with lounge furniture, TV, tea and coffee facilities, electric blankets and hairdryers. Take a stroll in our beautiful garden. Each evening join us for complimentary tastings of local wine and hors d'oeuvres. Choose your gourmet breakfast from the menu of local foods and homemade delights. We make sure your stay will be extra special and memorable. We have 2 unobtrusive cats in residence.

Napier *0.5 km N of Town Centre*
The Green House On The Hill *B&B*
Ruth Buss & Jeremy Hutt
18B Milton Oaks, Milton Road, Napier

Tel (06) 835 4475 or 021 187 3827
Fax (06) 835 4475 ruth@the-green-house.co.nz
www.the-green-house.co.nz

Double $100-$120 Single $70-$80 (Special breakfast)
Child negotiable
Visa MC Eftpos accepted
Pet free home Children welcome
2 Queen 1 Twin (3 bdrm)
Bathrooms: 1 Ensuite 1 Guest share

The Green House on the Hill is a Vegetarian owned B&B, only 5 minutes walk from the heart of art deco Napier, yet set in quiet woodland, with plenty of native birds and sea views! We offer a friendly, smoke-free environment to our guests. Home-made bread and preserves for breakfast. Our hillside home is built on several levels and unsuitable for wheelchairs or toddlers, although babies and older children are very welcome. We have ample parking or can pick up from airport, buses etc. Email access available.

Napier Hill *1 km N of Napier*
Maison Béarnaise *B&B*
Christine Grouden & Graham Storer
25 France Road, Bluff Hill, Napier 4001

Tel (06) 835 4693 or 0800 624 766
Fax (06) 835 4694
chrisgraham@xtra.co.nz
www.hawkesbaynz.com/pages/maisonbearnaise

Double $140 Single $95 (Full breakfast)
Visa MC accepted
2 Queen (2 bdrm)
Bathrooms: 2 Ensuite

Christine, Graham & Brewster (shy cat), welcome you to our attractive, peaceful oasis. Walk to city centre, restaurants, Bluff Hill lookout. Off-street parking, internet, laundry services available. Each bedroom has TV, electric blankets, heating, and ensuite for complete privacy. Relax with tea or coffee in your room or guest lounge where magazines, books, games are at your disposal. Delicious breakfasts served in dining room or colourful courtyard. Warm and friendly atmosphere. Christine, Napier born, is happy to assist with helpful local, national sightseeing suggestions.

Napier - Taradale *west km N of Napier*
Dudley's Bed & Breakfast/Homestay *B&B Homestay*
Marie & Colin Dudley
12 Weathers Place, Taradale, Napier

Tel (06) 844 6580 or 027 280 6610
Fax (06) 844 6580 c.dudley@clear.net.nz

Double $105-$115 Single $75-$80 (Full breakfast)
Dinner $30 by arrangement
Visa MC accepted
Not suitable for children
1 King (1 bdrm)
Bathrooms: 1 Private

Peaceful retreat to recharge your batteries. Located in a quiet cul-de-sac with attractive private gardens, in ground pool, barbecue area. Bright sunny bedroom with super king bed which can separate into twin beds. Tea/coffee making facilities. Private bathroom with luxury spa bath, shower. Separate guests toilet. Guests lounge, TV, or join us for coffee and chat or watch Sky Digital TV. Laundry facilities available. Continental/full breakfast provided. Off-street parking. Handy to shops, restaurants. 2 famous wineries and a top New Zealand golf course are nearby. Tours to numerous wineries can be arranged.

Napier *In 5 min walk to Napier City centre*
Inglenook *B&B*
Mieko S. & Chieko O.
3 Cameron Terrace, Napier Hill, Napier

Tel (06) 834 2922 Fax (06) 835 9538
napierin@hotmail.com

Double $110 Single $80 (Full breakfast)
1 Queen 1 Twin (2 bdrm)
Bathrooms: 2 Ensuite

Inglenook is situated on the hill in a peaceful
garden setting overlooking city and sea, and only 5
minutes stroll to get there. Inglenook offers privacy
(own separate entrances & keys) and a quiet restful
atmosphere. It is immaculately presented and serviced. Guests are asked to remove their shoes inside the
house. Cooked breakfast is delivered to guest rooms. TV, telephone line, hair-dryer, refrigerator and
tea/coffee making facilities are available in each suite. Laundry service is provided if necessary. No pets or
children please.

～

Napier *1 km N of Napier*
East Towers *Homestay*
Dale & Alan East
121 Thompson Road, Napier

Tel (06) 834 0821 or 027 661 2806
Fax (06) 834 0824
alandales.easttowers@xtra.co.nz

Double $120 Single $70-$90 (Full breakfast)
Pet free home
1 Queen 2 Single (2 bdrm)
Bathrooms: 1 Private

Dale & Alan welcome you to East Towers. Quality
accommodation for a couple or group of up to 4 people.
2 bedrooms with queen, double or 2 king singles. Own lounge, tea making facilities, TV. Quiet area,
stunning views, native birds, rambling gardens. Off-street parking. 15 minutes walk to Napier City. 10
minutes walk to Bluff Hill lookout. Arrive as guests, leave as friends.

～

Napier *In Napier Central*
Seaview Lodge *B&B Homestay*
Catherine & Evert Van Florenstein
5 Seaview Terrace, Napier

Tel (06) 835 0202 or 021 180 2101
Fax (06) 835 0202
cvulodge@xtra.co.nz
www.aseaviewlodge.co.nz

Double $140 Single $90 (Continental)
Visa MC accepted
1 King/Twin 1 King 1 Single (3 bdrm)
Bathrooms: 1 Ensuite 2 Private

Seaview Lodge offers spectacular sea and city views. A
lovingly renovated late Victorian home situated above Napieris Marine Parade and a three minute stroll
to the inner city. Enjoy your continental breakfast of fresh croissants and seasonal fruit salad on the lower
verandah while watching the sun rise and the waves break on the shore. At the end of the day relax in the
comfortable guest lounge or on the large upstairs balcony and enjoy a glass of local wine. All rooms are
stylishly furnished and show attention to detail.

Napier - Westshore *3 km NW of Napier*
A Bed at the Beach *Separate Suite*
Averil & Bayne Smart
88 Charles Street, Westshore, Napier

Tel (06) 833 6566 or 027 2759759
Fax (06) 833 6569
abedatthebeach@xtra.co.nz
www.bed-at-the-beach.co.nz

Double $110-$125 Single $95 (Continental)
Visa MC accepted
Not suitable for children
1 Queen (1 bdrm)
Bathrooms: 1 Private

J ust 100m from the beach, Averil, Bayne and Chelsea our Sheltie, welcome you to stay in our charming self catering studio suite situated upstairs with private entrance and off street parking. A continental breakfast tray will be delivered to you each morning to enjoy at your leisure. We are central to Hawkes Bay wineries, art deco and tourist attractions well known to the Bay as well as being walking distance to cafe's, and restaurants. We are Smokefree and regret not suitable for children.

Napier *1 km N of Napier*
17 on Roslyn Bed & Breakfast *B&B Homestay*
Lyn & John Andrews
17 Roslyn Road, Napier Hill, Napier

Tel (06) 833 7566 or 025 693 2174
lj.andrews@paradise.net.nz

Double $140-$150 Single $90 (Full breakfast)
Visa MC accepted Children welcome
1 King/Twin 1 Queen (2 bdrm)
Bathrooms: 1 Ensuite 1 Private

17 On Roslyn is set in tranquil gardens where guests enjoy the peaceful surroundings and panoramic views of the ocean. A great start to the day begins with a full delicious breakfast on the balcony, where you dine and take in the lovely views of the sea. 17 on Roslyn is situated on the Napier Hill just 15 minutes from the famous art deco city, short drives to the wineries/ restaurants, and in close proximity to the gannet colony at Cape Kidnappers.

Napier *1 km N of Napier Central*
Villa Vista B&B & Apartment *B&B Apartment with Kitchen*
Susana Lustig
22A France Road, Bluff Hill, Napier

Tel (06) 835 8770 or 027 435 7179
Fax (06) 835 8770 accommodation@villavista.net
www.villavista.net

Double $160 Single $125 (Full breakfast)
Self-contained $185
Visa MC Amex accepted
Children welcome
4 Queen 3 Single (5 bdrm)
Bathrooms: 4 Ensuite

A grand Edwardian villa with fantastic views over the sea to Cape kidnappers from every large and private bedroom offering ensuite, air-conditioning, television, tea/coffee making facilities and other amenities. Selection of continental and cooked breakfasts are served in the spacious dining room. Also offering a fully self-contained 2 bedroom apartment ($185, breakfast not included). Off-street parking and close to city. 10% discount for more than 2 nights. Special discounts for more than 5 nights. Welcome to Napier.

Napier - Hastings *7 km S of Napier*

B&B Approved

Lawndale Lodges & Gardens *Cottage with Kitchen*
Tony & Heather Orsborn
527 Lawn Road, East Clive, Hawkes Bay

Tel (06) 870 0302 Fax (06) 870 0346
info@lawndalelodges.com
www.lawndalelodges.com

Double $180-$250 Single $120-$150 (Continental provisions)
Child $10-$30 Dinner by arrangement Additional persons $35 per night
Visa MC Diners Amex Eftpos accepted Pet free home Children welcome
3 Queen 3 Double 3 Twin (6 bdrm)
Bathrooms: 3 Ensuite

The only accommodation of its kind in Clive, Lawndale Lodges & Gardens offer you a restful, rural setting conveniently located between the cities of Napier and Hastings and only 10 minutes drive from the smaller village of Havelock North.

Flax, Magnolia and Hydrangea Lodges are private and spacious with decks that overlook the landscaped lake and Award winning Gardens. All 3 lodges provide total self-containment with plenty of space within for up to 6 people. Each has 2 bedrooms, 1 with a queen bed, the other with 2 single beds plus a double pull-out couch in each lounge.

The lodges have been designed for your comfort and convenience and every detail has been attended to. Quality linens, comfortable beds, toiletries and entertainment systems are just some of the luxuries provided. You can cater for yourself in the fully-equipped kitchen and a continental breakfast is supplied daily. Each lodge has its own outdoor entertainment space and a gas BBQ is available for those who like to cook outdoors during the long summer evenings.

Lawndale Lodges are centered in Hawkes Bay's prestigious Wine Country. Many of the surrounding wineries offer outstanding dining in their beautiful vineyard settings, along with the chance to sample some of New Zealand's award winning wines. Hawkes Bay is not only well known for its outstanding food and wine but also offers a fantastic, warm, dry climate and friendly, relaxed people.

While you are here you can explore many other wonderful attractions such as award winning golf courses, fly fishing, sea fishing and hunting. Enjoy arts and crafts trails, hot salt water pools, art deco architecture and the famous Earthquake Museum. Wonder at the natural beauty of our National Aquarium, seahorse farm and spectacular gannet colony. Indulge yourself with gourmet delights and the very freshest produce from the farmers/growers markets, Silky Oak Chocolate Factory, Arataki Honey Hive and the Squirrel's Pantry.

Whatever you decide to do while you are here, we can always assure you of a warm welcome and a very luxurious stay. We look forward to meeting you soon.

Napier - Hastings *In btw Napier/ Hastings*
Copperfields *B&B Apartment with Kitchen Cottage with Kitchen*
Pam & Richard Marshall
Pakowhai Road, Napier

Tel (06) 876 9710 or 021 212 9631
Fax (06) 876 9710 rich.pam@clear.net.nz
www.copperfields.co.nz

Double $100-$130 Single $80-$100
(Breakfast by arrangement) Child under 12 $15
Dinner $35pp by arrangement
Separate self-contained flat, weekly rates negotiable
Visa MC accepted Children and pets welcome
1 King/Twin 1 Double 3 Single (3 bdrm)
Bathrooms: 2 Private

Welcome to Copperfields lifestyle orchard within 10 minutes of Napier, Hastings, Havelock North and Taradale - central for all tourist attractions. Guests stay in Glen Cottage, spacious self-contained cottage attached to our house with private entrance. Large lounge with log fire, fully equipped kitchen/dining Also Chapel Flat-unique self-contained accommodation in an "historic church and a fibre, craft and antiques gallery. Family rates negotiable. Dogs welcome (conditions apply)

Napier - Cape Kidnappers *12 km E of Hastings & Napier*
Merriwee Homestay *Homestay Separate Suite*
Jeanne Richards
29 Gordon Road, Te Awanga, Hawkes Bay

Tel (06) 875 0111 or 021 214 5023
Fax (06) 875 0111
merriwee@xtra.co.nz
www.merriwee.co.nz

Double $150-$240 Single $100-$180 (Full breakfast)
Dinner by arrangement Extra person $50
Visa MC accepted
1 King 3 Queen 1 Twin (5 bdrm)
Bathrooms: 2 Ensuite 1 Private

The 10 acre property lies secluded, on the coastal strip between Napier and Hastings, just a stroll from Te Awanga beach, and close to Cape Kidnappers Golf Course, gannet colony, and wineries. Merriwee homestead, built 1908, is spacious, with sea views, quality furnishings, open fires and french doors to gardens. The large grounds include swimming pool and petanque. A self-contained suite, has kitchen/sittingroom, and private entrance. Terrier Mags, and cat Poppy reside. We are approximately 15 minutes from Napier, Hastings and Havelock North.,

Hastings City *In Hastings Central*
McConchie Homestay *Homestay*
Barbara & Keila McConchie
115A Frederick Street, Hastings

Tel (06) 878 4576 or 021 0785328
barbaramcconchie@xtra.co.nz
www.bnb.co.nz

Double $90 Single $55 (Full breakfast)
Child $25 Dinner $25 by arrangement
Visa MC accepted Children welcome
1 Queen 2 Single (2 bdrm)
Bathrooms: 1 Guest share

Enjoy our peaceful garden back section, no traffic noises, yet central to Hastings City. My siamese cat says 'Hi'. Nearby are parks, golf courses, wineries, orchards and the best icecream ever. Short trips take you to spectacular views, Cape Kidnapper's gannet colony, or Napier's art deco, hot pools, or just relaxing and enjoying great hospitality. Directions: from Wellington, arriving Hastings City, turn left into Eastbourne Street, right into Nelson Street, right into Frederick Street, cross Caroline Road. Driveway on right. 115A first house off driveway.

Hastings *14 km NW of Hastings*
Grandvue Country Stay *B&B Homestay*
Dianne & Keith Taylor
Grandvue, 2596 State Highway 50, RD 5 Hastings

home

Tel (06) 879 6141 or 025 668 0252
homestays@xtra.co.nz

Double $95-$120 Single $65 (Full breakfast)
Child negotiable Dinner $25
Visa MC accepted Children welcome
1 King/Twin 1 Queen (2 bdrm)
Bathrooms: 1 Ensuite 1 Family share

Recently retired and moved from our farm but still the same genuine and caring hospitality. Enjoy with us in a relaxed atmosphere in our extensive private garden the wonderful views over vineyards and to Havelock North hills in the distance.

Comfortable beds with firm mattresses make for a good nights sleep (electric blankets for winter warmth) Sit and chat when time allows over a generous breakfast cooked or continental with homemade preserves and goodies - inside or alfresco. Dinner available on request.

Our interests include tramping, bushwalks, gardening, travel and genealogy. Having travelled extensively we do enjoy meeting local and overseas visitors. Let us advise you on all the wonderful things to see and do while in our lovely Hawkes Bay. There are many wineries close by with restaurants, Safari trips to the gannets, Orchard tours, Trout fishing, Golf courses, Panoramic views from Te Mata Peak, Havelock North with boutique shops and cafes and Napier the Art Deco City of the world are just a few. We can arrange tours for you too, and also advise you on your travel through NZ.

After nearly 18 years of hosting we have an ever increasing circle of friends with many returning. Please read our guests comments on our B & B Book website. Guests are welcome to use the swimming pool in summer and the tennis court. Dianne is one of a few in NZ who has a certificate in Homestay Management. We look forward to meeting you and our aim is to make your stay memorable arrive as a guest and leave as our friends. Easy access and plenty of parking.

Hastings *2.5 km N of Hastings*
Woodbine Cottage *B&B Homestay*

Ngaire & Jim Shand
Woodbine Cottage, 1279 Louie Street, Hastings

Tel (06) 876 9388 or 029 876 9388
025 529 522 Fax (06) 876 9666
nshand@xtra.co.nz

Double $100 Single $70 (Continental)
Dinner $25pp by arrangement
Visa MC accepted
1 Queen 1 Twin (2 bdrm)
Bathrooms: 1 Guest share

Our home is set in half an acre of cottage garden on the
Hastings boundary close to Havelock North. A tennis court for the energetic, and a spa bath to relax in at night. Hastings City centre is 5 minutes by car and Havelock North 2 minutes. Splash Planet, with its many water features and hot pools is only 2 minutes away. We look forward to your company and can assure you of a comfortable and relaxing stay. Not suitable for small children or pets.   @ Home New Zealand 930

Hastings *3 km S of Hastings*
Raureka *B&B Separate Suite*

Rosemary & Tim Ormond
26 Wellwood Road, RD 5, Hastings

Tel (06) 878 9715 or 021 104 5124
Fax (06) 878 9728
r.t.ormond@xtra.co.nz

Double $100 Single $80 (Continental)
Visa MC Amex accepted
Not suitable for children
1 Queen (1 bdrm)
Bathrooms: 1 Ensuite

Quietness and privacy are the main ingredients
of staying at Raureka. The accommodation is situated separately from the house but close enough for visitors to feel welcome and cared for. Hosts Rosemary and Tim will provide help and advice for planning a successful day around this beautiful region. Fresh flowers, home-baking and complimentary wine are among the many treats ensuring your stay here is a home away from home. Relax by our pool or enjoy a walk amongst our unique 100 year old oak trees.

Hastings *12 km W of Hastings, 12km S of Taradale*
Stitch-Hill Farm *B&B Homestay Farmstay*

Charles Trask
170 Taihape Road, RD 9, Hastings

Tel (06) 879 9456 Fax (06) 879 9806
cjtrask@xtra.co.nz

Double $120 Single $65 (Continental)
Dinner $30 by arrangement
Payments cash
2 King/Twin2 King (2 bdrm)
Bathrooms: 2 Ensuite

Welcome to Hawkes Bay, the premier food and wine
region of New Zealand. Stitch-Hill invites you to relax in the quiet countryside surrounded with panoramic views. Our prime location is just minutes from the city centres, wineries, attractions, fishing and tramping. In our comfortable smoke-free home we offer the very best hospitality. Your requirements our challenge. Your choice of 2 rooms, twin or super king in each, with ensuite. Stroll in our gardens or around our acres. Unsuitable for children and pets.

Hawkes Bay

Hawkes Bay

Hastings *3 km S of Hastings*
Primefruit Orchard *B&B Cottage No Kitchen Cottage with Kitchen*
Elly & Dick Spiekerman
74 Longlands Road East, Hastings

Tel (06) 876 4163 or 021 429 491
Fax (06) 876 4163
info@holidaynewzealand.co.nz
www.holidaynewzealand.co.nz

Double $90-$120 Single $70-$100 (Continental)
Child $20 Extra adult $30
Visa MC accepted
Children and pets welcome
2 Queen 1 Double 2 Single (4 bdrm)
Bathrooms: 3 Private

We would like to be your host on our orchard you can take part in a guided tour through the orchard. We offer a double bedroom with private bathroom in the house, continental breakfast included; or should you prefer privacy and tranquility, we have 2 self-contained cottages. Choose from a 1 or 2 bedroom cottage, each with its own deck and BBQ. For the guests we also have available: spa, swimming pool, tennis court, table tennis, petanque and lawn croquet.

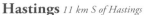

Hastings *11 km S of Hastings*
Imperial Orchards *B&B Homestay*
Vivian & Robert Dickson
68 Montana Road, Bridge Pa, Hastings

Tel (06) 879 4533 or 021 034 7424
Fax (06) 879 4337
homestay_bb@yahoo.co.nz

Double $95-$120 Single up to $75 (Special breakfast)
Visa MC accepted
Pets welcome
1 King/Twin 1 Double 1 Single (3 bdrm)
Bathrooms: 1 Guest share

Welcome to a haven set in the heart of the Hawkes Bay wine district, We offer superking/twin and double rooms, a guest living room with TV, fridge and tea and coffee facilities. Enjoy a special breakfast including home-made preserves and fresh baking. Relax with a glass of wine around the pool or on the terrace and enjoy the garden and rural views. We back onto Hawkes Bay Golf Course with the Equestrian Centre, Hawkes Bay Car Club and aerodrome nearby.

Havelock North - Hastings *16 km S of Havelock North*
Wharehau *Homestay Farmstay*
Ros Phillips
1604 Middle Road, Havelock North, RD 11, Hastings

Tel (06) 877 4111 or 027 444 6132
Fax (06) 877 4111
ros.phillips@xtra.co.nz.

Double $120-$100 Single $60 (Full breakfast)
Child half price Dinner $25
Beach bach available
Visa MC accepted Children welcome
2 Queen 2 Twin 1 Single (4 bdrm)
Bathrooms: 1 Family share 1 Guest share

Wharehau is in the beautiful Tuki Tuki valley -a great base for Hawkes Bay experience. Quarter of an hour travel from Hastings or Havelock North in the midst of Wine Country. Close to golf courses, Splash Planet, gannets and art deco. Or enjoy the peace and space on the farm. Weather permitting a farm 4WD tour is available. Walks available locally. Trout fishing (local guide can be hired) in the Tuki Tuki River. Comfortable beach bach at Kairakau Beach is available for rent

Hastings - Waiwhenua *50 km W of Napier/Hastings*
Waiwhenua Homestead & Farmstay *B&B Homestay Farmstay Annie's Cottage*
Kirsty Hill, Gary Holden & family
808 River Road, RD 9, Hastings

Tel (06) 874 2435 Fax (06) 874 2465
info@waiwhenua.co.nz
www.waiwhenua.co.nz

Double $120-$150 Single $60-$100 (Continental)
Child $50-$60 Dinner $20
The Annie Cottage $120-$200 double
Visa MC accepted
Children and pets welcome
1 Queen 1 Double 3 Single (2 bdrm)
Bathrooms: 1 Family share 1 Private Claw foot bath

Waiwhenua - The perfect place to experience a genuine
farmstay and friendly rural hospitality at our 120 year
old historic homestead or cottage. Come and join us on
our extensive 440 hectare sheep, beef and deer farm in
heartland Hawkes Bay. Enjoy informative guided farm
tours and join in farm activities on the day. Try trout
fishing in our Tutaekuri River (in the season October-
April - rental equipment avaiable). Relax with a book
on our cool verandahs, beside our swimming pool or
in the garden. Watch and listen to the many native
birds visiting our garden. Our home and family offer
guests a friendly environment catering for individuals
or families interested in the outdoor life (2 night stay
recommended). Enjoy specialty farm cooked meals of
home-grown beef, lamb or venison complemented with
fresh garden vegetables and fruit.

Annie's Cottage - For those seeking total privacy and a
longer stay at Waiwhenua. Our recently renovated, fully self-contained, cozy, 3 bedroom, historic rural
retreat awaits families and visitors wanting a holiday away from the hassle and bustles of every day life.
Relax and unwind at Annie's Cottage and enjoy the extensive views over farm land and to the cliffs of
the river beyond. Self-catering continental breakfast available. All guests welcome to join us for dinner at
the homestead. Sleeps up to 6 people at $120-$200 per night. Extended stay options available. Napier
art deco home also available. Enrich your stay by including other outdoor activities at our backdoor;
hunting, fishing, bush and farm walks, garden tours, jet boating and extensive mountain hikes plus many
attractions in the greater sunny Hawkes Bay area. To avoid disappointment please book ahead

Directions: Turn off SH 50 between Napier and Hastings into Taihape Rd at Omahu/Fernhill. Travel
35km to River Road on right. Travel along River Rd for 8kms. Waiwhenua #808. Main drive, 100m
from mail box on right. Cottage #746 on right.

Hawkes Bay

Havelock North *1 km N of Havelock North*

Weldon Boutique Bed & Breakfast *B&B Homestay Boutique*
Pracilla Hay
98 Te Mata Road, Havelock North, Hawkes Bay

Tel (06) 877 7551 Fax (06) 877 7051
pracilla@weldon.co.nz
www.weldon.co.nz

Double $130-$150 **Single** $100-$120
(Special breakfast) Dinner $45
Twin $130 Queen $130-$150
Visa MC Amex accepted Children welcome
1 Queen 2 Double 1 Twin 1 Single (5 bdrm)
Bathrooms: 1 Guest share 2 Private

Nearly 100 years old, Weldon offers quality, comfort and peace with a romantic olde worlde charm and a French Provincial ambience. Accommodation is in spacious, elegantly appointed bedrooms, furnished with period and antique furniture. TV & tea/coffee are provided in each room. Fresh flowers, fine linen and fluffy towels reflect the luxury of fine accommodation. Breakfast of fresh local fruits & gourmet cooked options is served alfresco in summer or in the dining room during winter. 2 toy poodles (James and Thomas) will greet you enthusiastically!

Havelock North *5 km N of Havelock North*

Totara Stables *B&B Homestay*
Sharon A. Bellaart & John W. Hayes
324 Te Mata - Mangateretere Road,
Havelock North, RD 2, Hastings

Tel (06) 877 8882 or 025 863 910
Fax (06) 877 8891
totarastables@xtra.co.nz
www.geocities.com/totarastables

Double $120-$140 **Single** $100 (Continental)
Visa MC accepted
1 King/Twin 1 Queen 1 Twin (3 bdrm)
Bathrooms: 1 Ensuite 1 Private

Offering a unique Bed & Breakfast experience in a lovingly restored 1910 villa. Take a peek into the museum of early pioneer farming displayed in the century old stables or marvel at the simplicity of early stationary motors. Feed the hand reared deer or arrange a ride in a classic 1951 Sunbeam Talbot motor car. We are located in the heart of the Te Mata wine region only minutes from the pictureque village of Havelock North. Non-smoking and not suitable for children under 12 years.

Havelock North *4 km E of Havelock North*

Borak B&B *B&B Homestay*
Doris & Mike Curkovic
433 Te Matamangateretere Road,
RD 12, Havelock North

Tel (06) 877 6699 or 027 408 2575
Fax (06) 877 6615
dcurkovic@clear.net.nz
www.borakbed-breakfast.co.nz

Double $120 **Single** $100 (Full breakfast)
Visa MC accepted
2 Queen 1 Single (2 bdrm)
Bathrooms: 1 Guest share

Experience relaxing hospitality on a producing apple orchard. We are located in the heart of Te Mata wine region nestled amongst 7 wineries with Craggy Range along the road. 5 minutes to the Havelock North Village centre, 7 minutes to Hastings and 15 minutes to Napier. Waimarama, Ocean Beach and Te Awanga within easy reach. For the trout-fisher there is paradise at the back of our orchard. Play petanque, relax. We speak English, German and Croatian. Not suitable for children under 12. Pet cat.

Waimarama Beach *34 km SE of Hastings*
Waimarama Bed & Breakfast *B&B Homestay*
Rita & Murray Webb
68 Harper Road, Waimarama, Hawkes Bay

Tel (06) 874 6795 Fax (06) 8746 795
rwebb@xtra.co.nz

Double $100 Single $55 (Full breakfast)
Dinner $25pp
Visa MC accepted
2 Double (2 bdrm)
Bathrooms: 1 Guest share

Lovely beach for surfing, swimming, diving, boating, fishing etc. Bushwalks and golf course nearby. Situated only 5 minutes walk from beach with lovely views of sea, local park and farmland. Nearest town is Havelock North - 20 minutes drive, with Napier 40 minutes. We have 2 double rooms available and separate toilet and bathroom for guests. Cooked breakfast is offered and dinner is available if required. Please phone for reservations phone (06) 874 6795. No smoking inside please. Pets: 1 cat, 1 dog.

Otane *8 km N of Waipawa*
Ludlow Farmstay *B&B Farmstay Cottage with Kitchen*
Gwen and Neil White
53 Drumpeel Road, RD 1, Otane

Tel (06) 856 8348 or 027 441 8354
Fax (06) 856 8348
ludlow.white@xtra.co.nz
www. ludlowfarmstay.co.nz

Double $150 Single $90 (Full provisions)
Child $20-$30 Dinner $25 by arrangement
Children welcome
1 King/Twin 1 Queen 1 Double (3 bdrm)
Bathrooms: 1 Private

Ludlow is a 480 hectare extensive cropping farm, including squash, sweetcorn and peas with lamb and beef finishing, and an 8 hectare apple orchard. Our recently renovated shearers' cottage is situated in private surroundings, 50 metres from main homestead, with full kitchen facilities, BBQ, laundry, open fire and views over the Drumpeel Valley Farmland, with stock grazing alongside the cottage. Swimming pool and Astrograss tennis court available for guests' use. Farm tour available on request. Expect a warm welcome from Hogan & Zinga, the Jack Russells.

Waipawa *2 km E of Waipawa*
Haowhenua *Farmstay*
Caroline & David Jefferd
77 Pourerere Road, RD 1, Waipawa 4170

Tel (06) 857 8241 or 027 268 4854
Fax (06) 857 826
1d.jefferd@xtra.co.nz

Double $120 Single $90 (Full breakfast)
Child half price Dinner $30pp
Visa MC accepted
Children welcome
1 Queen (1 bdrm)
Bathrooms: 1 Ensuite

Come and enjoy an evening or 2 at Haowhenua, with a farming family in a spacious and comfortable old country home, set in park like surrounds with lovely gardens and swimming pool, and share your adventures with us. We have a cat, a labrador and numerous other farm animals and are only 2km off State Highway 2 and in close proximity to all of Hawkes Bay's attractions. Please phone for directions.

Waipawa *40 km S of Hastings*

Abbotsford Oaks *Luxury B&B*

Nicolette Brasell & Chris Davis

85 Abbotsford Road, Waipawa, Central Hawke's Bay

Tel (06) 857 8960 or 025 296 1160
Fax (06) 857 8961
nicolette@abbotsfordoaks.co.nz
www.abbotsfordoaks.co.nz

Double $140-$240 **Single** $100-$200 (Full breakfast)
Dinner by arrangement
Visa MC accepted
1 King 3 Queen (4 bdrm)
Bathrooms: 1 Ensuite 3 Private

Nicolette and Chris warmly welcome you to Abbotsford Oaks. Nestled in picturesque Central Hawkes Bay and surrounded by 3.5 acres of gardens and orchards, Abbotsford Oaks offers a special venue for those wanting a break from their busy lifestyle. Ideal for that restful getaway (as our 2 cats have found), corporate retreat, or as a base to explore the many attractions Hawkes Bay has to offer. Beaches, wineries and art deco/Spanish mission architecture are only 30 minutes away. Golf courses and trout fishing are close by.

Our property was purpose built as a childrens home in the 1920s and has been extensively renovated to provide quality boutique bed & breakfast accommodation. It has spacious rooms most with their own sitting/sun room and private bathroom, with wonderful views of the grounds and countryside. There is also a substantial and elegantly furnished guest lounge with open fire where you can watch TV or just relax. The large dining room also has a comfortable lounge area in which to relax, listen to music or read a book.

Breakfast either cooked or continental can be served in the dining room, the garden or your private lounge. Complimentary coffee, tea and biscuits are available throughout the day. Dinner is available by arrangement. Visit our website www.abbotsfordoaks.co.nz for more details.

Waipawa *1 km NE of Waipawa*
Abbot Heights *B&B*
Jacqui & Charlie Hutchison
6 Parkland Drive, Waipawa

Tel (06) 857 8585 Fax (06) 857 8580
chipper@paradise.net.nz

Double $130-$150 Single $80-$10 (Continental)
2 Queen (2 bdrm)
Bathrooms: 1 Ensuite 1 Private

Welcome to Parkland Drive! Your relaxed, easy going hosts (and their cat Myrtle) enjoy meeting all new guests at their stunning modern manor set in 12 acres of private gardens. Facilities include a splendid private lounge, luxury goose down duvets, plush bathrobes, top quality linen, spa bath and electric blankets. New gym, indoor heated pool, golf, vineyard, hot-air ballooning, art gallery, theatre, museum, cafes and antique shops are only 5 minutes away. Golden sandy beaches, tramping, hunting and fishing are within 30 minutes. .

Waipukurau *20 km S of Waipukurau*
Hinerangi Station *Farmstay Cottage with Kitchen*
Caroline & Dan von Dadelszen
615 Hinerangi Road, RD 1, Waipukurau

Tel (06) 855 8273 Fax (06) 855 8273
caroline@hinerangi.co.nz
www.hinerangi.co.nz

Double $130 Single $90 (Full breakfast)
Child $30 Dinner $35pp
Self-contained cottage $120 double
Extra guests $40pp
Children and pets welcome
1 King/Twin 2 Queen 3 Single (4 bdrm)
Bathrooms: 2 Private

Hinerangi Station is an 1800 acre sheep, cattle and deer farm set in the rolling hills of Central Hawkes Bay. Our spacious 1920 homestead was designed by Louis Hay of Napier Art Deco fame. It has a full size billiard table and there is a tennis court and swimming pool in the garden. Guests have their own private entrance. "The Cookhouse", a recently renovated 100 yr old cottage offers self contained accommodation for couples and families. We have one terrier and a cat.

Waipukurau *9 km W of Waipukurau*
Mynthurst *Farmstay*
Annabelle & David Hamilton
912 Lindsay Road, RD 3, Waipukurau

Tel (06) 857 8093 or 027 232 2458
Fax (06) 857 8093
mynthurst@xtra.co.nz

Double $175 Single $95 (Full breakfast)
Child $35 Dinner $35pp
Extra space available for families
1 King/Twin 1 Double 1 Twin 1 Single (4 bdrm)
Bathrooms: 1 Ensuite 1 Private

Mynthurst, genuine working sheep and cattle farm 560 hectares. Guests from NZ and overseas welcomed for 20 years. The homestead is large, warm and comfortable. Observe farm activities, enjoy swimming, trout fishing, golf, tennis, wineries. Dinner available on request, using finest local produce. Whether travelling north or south, visiting beautiful Hawkes Bay, you'll find Mynthurst the perfect retreat. 1/2 hour from Hastings SH2. Booking avoids disappointment. Phone for directions. No smoking. Children welcome. 2 cats. Expect excellence. Farm tour included. Superb environment.

Hawkes Bay

Waipukurau *7 km E of Waipukurau*

Mangatarata Country Estate *Farmstay*
Judy & Donald Macdonald
415 Mangatarata Road, RD 5, Waipukurau

Tel (06) 858 8275 Fax (06) 858 8270
mangatarata@xtra.co.nz
www.hawkesbaynz.com/pages/mangataratacountryestate

Double $150-$170 **Single** $85 (Full breakfast)
Dinner $35pp
2 Queen 1 Double 3 Single (4 bdrm)
Bathrooms: 1 Guest share 1 Private

Retreat to a beautiful historic homestead nestled in the
heart of Hawkes Bay, Wine Country. Unwind with
uninterrupted farm views from the gracious Victorian verandah. Experience beef and sheep farming first
hand or wander through the extensive gardens with swimming pool, pathways and a pond where birdlife
prevails. Enjoy a generous breakfast and good coffee. Other sumptuous meals may be arranged by
request. Gourmet lamb is Judy's speciality, complimented with fresh produce from the kitchen garden or
grown locally.

Waipukurau *4.5 km S of Waipukurau*

Pukeora Vineyard Cottage *Cottage with Kitchen*
Kate Norman
Pukeora Estate, 208 Pukeora Scenic Road, RD 1
(off SH2 south of Waipukurau), Waipukurau

Tel (06) 858 9339 or 021 701 606
Fax (06) 858 6070
cottage@pukeora.com
www.pukeora.com

Double $110 **Single** $80 (Continental)
Child $25 Extra guest $35pp Children welcome
1 Queen 1 Double 2 Twin 1 Single (3 bdrm)
Bathrooms: 1 Private

Exclusive hire of our charming, hilltop country cottage which boasts stunning views over the vineyard,
river, plains and beyond. The spacious cottage built circa 1920, with character wooden floors, sunny
verandah, and open plan lounge/kitchen with log fire, is a private annex to our house. Pukeora Estate, set
on 86 acres, is a working 5 hectare vineyard, boutique winery and a conventions venue. Your hosts Kate
and Max, with daughters Jessica (age 3) and Marika (age 2), and 3 cats, welcome you. Wine tasting and
sales available.

If you need any information ask your hosts,
they are your own personal travel agent and guide.

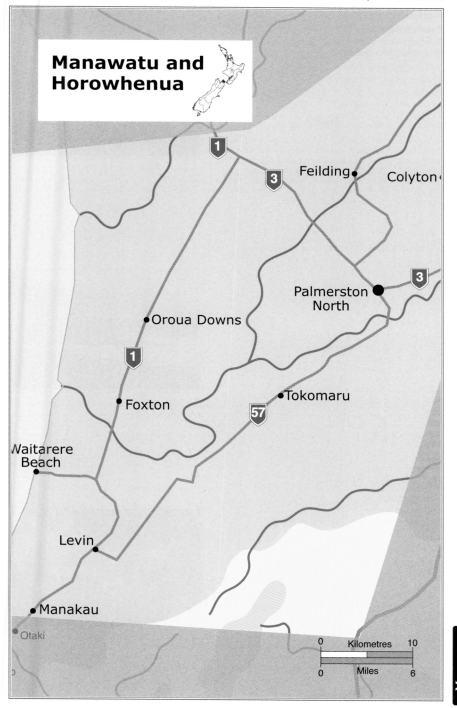

Manawatu and Horowhenua

Feilding

Colyton

Palmerston North

Oroua Downs

Foxton

Tokomaru

Waitarere Beach

Levin

Manakau

Otaki

| 0 | Kilometres | 10 |
| 0 | Miles | 6 |

Feilding *In Feilding Central*

Avoca Homestay *Homestay*
Margaret Hickmott
12 Freyberg Street, Feilding

Tel (06) 323 4699
margh-avoca@inspire.net.nz

Double $90 Single $55-$70 (Full breakfast)
Dinner $25 by arrangement
1 Queen 2 Twin (2 bdrm)
Bathrooms: 1 Ensuite 1 Family share

Enjoy a break in friendly Feilding, 12 times winner of New Zealand's Most Beautiful Town Award. You are assured of a warm welcome and an enjoyable stay in a comfortable smoke-free home set in an attractive garden with mature trees and a spectacular shrubbery. Off-street parking is provided for your vehicle. The main bedroom has a queen-size bed, ensuite and an outside entrance for your convenience. We are within easy walking distance of the town centre and well situated for the Manfield Park complex.

Palmerston North *3 km W of Palmerston North*

Andellen *Farmstay Separate Suite*
Kay and Warren Nitschke
RD 8, Palmerston North

Tel (06) 355 4155 or 021 900 226
027 244 1393 Fax (06) 355 4155
kw@inspire.net.nz

Double $90 Single $45 (Continental)
Child $30 Dinner $25pp by arrangement
Visa MC accepted
Children and pets welcome
1 King 1 Queen 4 Single (4 bdrm)
Bathrooms: 1 Ensuite 1 Private spa bath

Kay, Warren and Libby (9 years) welcome you to Andellen, a lovely spacioius modern homestead set on 65 acres with extensive lawn and garden. We offer guests the opportunity to relax in a lovely tranquil and private country setting. Own lounge and spa bath and seasonal farm activities available. Children very welcome. City 3km away. We have a pet cat and dog. Dinner by arrangement.

Palmerston North *5.5 km E of City Centre*

Clairemont *B&B*
Joy & Dick Archer
10 James Line, RD 10, Palmerston North

Tel (06) 357 5508 Fax (06) 357 5501
clairemont@inspire.net.nz

Double $80 Single $50 (Full breakfast)
1 Double 1 Twin (2 bdrm)
Bathrooms: 1 Guest share

Welcome to Clairemont. We are a rural spot within the city boundary, plenty of trees and a quite extensive garden. On our 1 1/4 acres we keep a few sheep, silky bantams, and our little dog Toby. We are handy to river walks, golf course, and shops are a few minutes away. We have a cosy, spacious family home we would like to share with you. Our interests are walking, gardening, model engineering and barbershop singing. Good off-street parking. Home-baked suppers provided.

Palmerston North *In Palmerston North*

Panorama B&B *B&B*
Claire & Bill Sawers
105 Dittmer Drive, Riverdale,
Palmerston North Central

Tel (06) 354 8816
panorama.bb@paradise.net.nz

Double $90 Single $70 (Full breakfast)
Child $20
Visa MC accepted
Children welcome
1 Double 1 Twin (2 bdrm)
Bathrooms: 1 Private

A warm welcome awaits you at our home in Palmerston North. With our 1 party at a time policy guests enjoy a private sitting/dining room with fridge and TV. Refreshments always available. 2 large bedrooms, bath and separate shower. Own entrance via the sunny patio. River walkways across from our home lead to the Esplanade Cafe, rose gardens, bird aviary and childrens play area. The Lido Swimming Complex is close by. Walk or bus to Massey University, restaurants and town centre. Off-street parking.

Palmerston North *13 km E of Palmerston North*

Country Lane Homestay *B&B Homestay*
Fay & Allan Hutchinson
52 Orrs Road, RD 1 Aokautere, Palmerston North

Tel (06) 326 8529 or 027 448 5833
Fax (06) 326 9216
countrylane@xtra.co.nz

Double $90-$12 Single $50-$75 (Full breakfast)
Dinner $25-$30
1 King/Twin1 King 1 Queen 1 Double 1 Single
(3 bdrm)
Bathrooms: 1 Ensuite 1 Family share 2 Private

Luxury country living, short distance from Palmerston North, near Manawatu Gorge, below wind farm. 10km from Pacific College and 2km from Equestrian Centre. Excellent stop over en route to/from Wellington or East Coast. Our home is newly decorated, with antiques in a country traditional style surrounded by our garden. Sawmill on the property, coloured sheep, horses and calves. Manawatu River borders our property. It is our pleasure to provide home-cooked meals with some local produce. Directions: please phone. A brochure with map is available.

Palmerston North *5 km SW of Central Palmerston North*

Udys on Anders *B&B Apartment with Kitchen*
Glenda & Tim Udy
52 Anders Road, Palmerston North

Tel (06) 354 1722 or 027 440 9299
Fax (06) 354 1711
kiwitim@clear.net.nz   www.udysonanders.co.nz

Double $120 Single $90 (Full breakfast)
Child $20 Dinner negotiable
Visa MC accepted
Children welcome
1 Queen 1 Double (1 bdrm)
Bathrooms: 1 Ensuite

We offer superior accommodation. An elegantly furnished self-contained apartment, own lounge and full kitchen. Quiet country location, huge lawn, edge of town, 7 minutes to CBD. Plexipave tennis court, beautiful mediterranean courtyard and large games room for our guests to make use of. Cleanliness, attention to detail and great hospitality are our priorities. We are well travelled and love meeting people. Enjoy your own space or get to know us. So... come, relax, enjoy. Tariff includes full breakfast. Apartment is smoke-free. Dinner by arrangement.

Palmerston North *5 km E of Palmerston North*

Weltevreden B&B *B&B*
Diann & Harry Vyver
11 The Bush Track, RD 1, Aokautere,
Palmerston North

Tel (06) 357 6346 or (025) 411 803
d.vyver@xtra.co.nz

Double $90 Single $60 (Full breakfast)
Family $120, separate lounge
Children welcome
1 Queen 1 Twin (2 bdrm)
Bathrooms: 1 Guest share

Shadowed beneath the undulating landscape of the
Tararua Ranges and only 5 minutes (5km) drive from Palmerston North's city centre. Weltevreden offers
guests a warm welcome and comfortable stay. Nestled amongst 20 acres of native NZ bush with 2.5 acres
of spacious landscaped gardens. The bush is frequently visited by native bird life, namely the tui, fantail
and wood pigeon. Guests share separate bathroom and lounge with TV, log fire, tea and coffee facilities.

Tokomaru *19 km S of Palmerston North*

Hi-Da-Way Lodge *Cottage with Kitchen*
Sue & Trevor Palmer
21 Albert Road, RD 4, Palmerston North

Tel (06) 329 8731 Fax (06) 329 8732
hi-da-way-lodge@xtra.co.nz
www.hidawaylodge.co.nz

Double Cottage $95-$195 (Continental breakfast)
Dinner by arrangement
1 Double 2 Single (2 bdrm)
Bathrooms: 1 Private

Looking for something unique - then Hi-Da-Way
lodge extends a warm welcome. The fully self-contained
rustic cabin is set in a peaceful garden setting surrounded by trees and has its own spa, TV, video and
fridge/freezer. Guests may enjoy volley ball, shared swimming pool, BBQ or just meander around our
6.5 hectare property. Situated just 10 minutes from Massey University and 1.5 hours from Wellington
off State Highway 57. We have 2 boys still at home and 2 pet dogs who enjoy meeting people. Treat
yourself.

Waitarere Beach *14 km NW of Levin*

Dunes *Homestay*
Robyn & Grant Powell
10 Ngati Huia Place, Waitarere Beach 5500

Tel (06) 368 6246 or 027 285 3643
sand.dunes@xtra.co.nz

Double $115 Single $75 (Continental)
Dinner $30
Visa MC accepted
2 Queen (2 bdrm)
Bathrooms: 2 Ensuite

Robyn & Grant Powell welcome you to our new
absolute beachfront retreat. Enjoy beach walks and
magnificent views of Kapiti and Mounts Taranaki and Ruapehu. We offer 2 queen-size bedrooms with
own private entrance and deck areas, ensuites, own living areas with TV, tea/coffee making facilities
- continental breakfast provided. Situated 14km north west of Levin, approximately 1 and a half hours
from Wellington and 35 minutes from Palmerston North. Laundry facilities, off-street parking, non-
smoking. Dinner by arrangement.

Levin *5min km N of Levin*

Fantails *B&B Cottage with Kitchen Self-contained cottages*
Heather Watson
40 MacArthur Street, Levin

Tel (06) 368 9011 Fax (06) 368 9279
fantails@xtra.co.nz
www.fantails.co.nz

Double $100-$150 Single $80-$100 (Special breakfast)
Child negotiable Dinner by arrangement
Self-contained cottages $110-$150
Visa MC accepted
Children and pets welcome
1 King 2 Queen 1 Twin 4 Single (4 bdrm)
Bathrooms: 3 Ensuite 1 Private

Welcome to Fantails, a hidden oasis of native bush, mature trees, native birds and other species, all set in 2 acres of park-like gardens only minutes from the town centre by car. Experience our garden where you can pick fruit of the season from our trees, view our raised vegetable garden made of ponga logs. Learn about worm farming and companion planting plus a little humour tossed in.

Our breakfasts are quite a treat with a lovely view of fantails, native pigeons and other bird life. Different diets are catered for and all our meals are Certified Organic.

If you require timeout for a few days take one of out 2 cottages; they sleep 2-4 people. They are very private and have everything you require. In the evening why not try our sauna and whirlpool spa and then rest in our quiet and secure environment and very comfortable beds Bikes for hire.

We are also only 1 hour away from the Wellington Ferry Terminal and are smoke-free.

Levin *3.4 km E of Levin*
Lynn Beau Ley *Farmstay*
Beverley & Peter Lynn
Queen Street East, RD 1, Levin

Tel (06) 368 0310 Fax (06) 368 0310
lynnbeauley@paradise.net.nz

Double $90-$100 Single $70 (Full breakfast)
Dinner $25 by arrangement
Visa MC accepted
1 Double 2 Single (2 bdrm)
Bathrooms: 1 Ensuite 1 Private

A superb rural outlook - 10 acre farmlet 4 minutes
from town centre. We invite you to our comfortable
spacious home, attractive guest rooms with ensuite or master bathroom, delightful dinners served with
wine and delicious home-made breakfasts. Relax on patio or wander through our large garden and lawn
areas with lovely farm views of sheep and cattle. Maybe catch a glimpse of free-range hens, Beau the cat
and Bailey our Wheaton Terrier. East off SH1 into Queen Street East, 3.4km on left, sign at gate.

Levin *1 km N of Levin*
Greenacres *Farmstay*
Derek & Dorothy Burt
88 Avenue North, Levin,

Tel (06) 368 7062 Fax (06) 368 7062
info@levinbb.com
www.levinbb.com

Double $100 Single $70 (Full breakfast)
Child negotiable Dinner $25
Children welcome
2 Queen 1 Single (2 bdrm)
Bathrooms: 2 Ensuite

Quality accommodation in peaceful, relaxing rural
surrounds, warm hospitality and every comfort considered. Spacious bedrooms with ensuite, TV, coffee
& tea in room. Laundry, computer, fax/phone. Derek & Dorothy Burt your hosts, Somerset & Edward
their cats. New house on 10 acres 1km north of Levin. Hand feeding cattle. Dinner available on request,
full English or continental breakfast. 100m off SH1 on Avenue North. Horses and floats accommodated.
Camper vans.Room to land a helicopter, park a balloon or keep your horses & alpacas.

Levin *5 km S of Levin*
Ardo Highland Haven *B&B Farmstay*
Malcolm & Rachel Phillips
170 McLeavey Road, RD 20, Levin

Tel (06) 368 7080 or 021 506 990
Fax (06) 368 7080
info@ardohighlandhaven.co.nz
www.ardohighlandhaven.co.nz

Double $90 Single $60 (Full breakfast)
Dinner by arrangement
Visa MC accepted
1 Queen 1 Twin 1 Single (3 bdrm)
Bathrooms: 1 Private

Country home on 10 acres - highland cattle and coloured sheep to pamper. A private, peaceful haven
for a good night's sleep. Situated 5 minutes south of Levin - the perfect stopover on your way to or from
Wellington. Airport/ferry transfers readily arranged. Refreshments on arrival. Dinner by arrangement.
Laundry facilities available. After dairy farming for 25 years we are enjoying our change of lifestyle and
look forward to meeting you. Family have left home, just Mandy, our Australian terrier, and Lola, our
grey tabby ,to greet you.

Levin *6 km W of Levin*

Dragonfly Countrystay *Cottage with Kitchen*
Jim & Elizabeth Eade
257 Hokio Sand Road, Levin

Tel (06) 367 9165 Fax (06) 367 9165
dragonflylevin@actrix.co.nz
www.dragonflylevin.co.nz

Double $190 Single $160 (Full breakfast)
Child $30 Dinner by arrangement
Extra person $50
Visa MC accepted
Children welcome
2 Double 1 Single (3 bdrm)
Bathrooms: 1 Private

Private rural hideaway near town. 1 party in the self-contained cottage with wood fire. Connected to the main house by a covered solar-heated pool. Outdoor hot spa, decks with tables, gardens, paths, trees, lawns in 4 acres of park-like grounds. Small pet dog in hosts house. Horse to ride. Portacot, highchair, car seat available. Levin town 5 minutes away and Wellington 75 minutes away.

Levin *In Levin*

Serendipity Bed & Breakfast *B&B Homestay*
Chris Lloyd & Barbara Lucas
86 MacArthur Street, Levin

Tel (06) 368 6766 or 027 413 1504
Fax (06) 368 6764
relax@serendipitynz.co.nz www.serendipitynz.co.nz

Double $90-$120 Single $90-$120 (Continental)
Child $25 Extra adult $25
Visa MC accepted
Children and pets welcome
1 King 1 Queen 1 Single (2 bdrm)
Bathrooms: 1 Ensuite 1 Private

Experience Kiwi heartland hospitality on the Nature Coast. Stop, relax and take your time. Chris & Barbara invite you to unwind at Serendipity - in a quiet corner of town. A pleasant 30 minute walk or 5 minute drive from the centre - close to the theatre and restaurants. Explore the lower North Island. 1and a half hours to Wellington, 40 minutes to Palmerston North, 3 hours to the Hawkes Bay or Taranaki. Enjoy fine foods, museums, bird life, unspoiled beaches, outdoor pursuits, golf and the work of craftspeople.

Please let us know
how you enjoyed your B&B experience.
Ask your host for a comment form
or leave a comment on www.bnb.co.nz

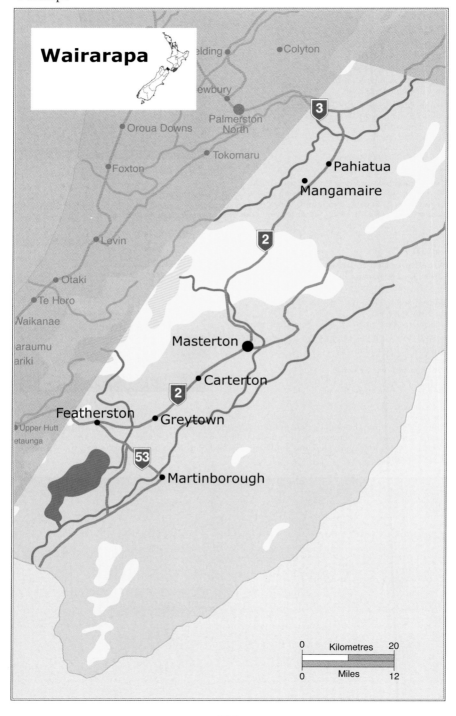

Pahiatua - Mangamaire *8 km S of Pahiatua*

Lizzie's Country Bed & Breakfast *B&B Separate Suite Apartment with Kitchen Countrystay* B&B Approved

Lizzie & Craig Udy

86 Mangamaire Road, Mangamaire, Pahiatua

Tel (06) 376 7367 or 027 204 2648
Fax (06) 376 7367 craigandlizudy@inspire.net.nz
www.bnb.co.nz/hosts/lizzies.html

Double $100 Single $70 (Full provisions)
Child negotiable Extra adult $30
Visa MC Diners Amex accepted
Children welcome
1 King 1 Twin (2 bdrm)
Bathrooms: 1 Private

Lizzie and Craig welcome you to our friendly home and mini-farm. Your tastefully decorated, self-contained, private accommodation is the entire lower storey of our spacious home and includes a private lounge and dining with log fire. Relax and watch a movie in our luxurious home cinema or soak under the stars in our outdoor hot water bath in an intimate bush setting. You can dine out at our award-winning local restaurant or relax and have the cuisine delivered to your dining table

~

Pahiatua *19 km E of Palmerson North*

Borderlands B&B *B&B Cottage with Kitchen* B&B Approved

Tania & Mark McBride

933 Makomako Road, RD 3, Pahiatua

Tel (06) 376 6064
borderlands@xtra.co.nz

Double $100 Single $70 (Full provisions)
Child negotiable
Visa MC accepted
Children welcome
1 Queen (1 bdrm)
Bathrooms: 1 Private

Come on in, unwind, sip a mug of hot chocolate while stretching out on a comfy couch in front of a
glowing logfire. Soak away any cares in an antique clawfoot bath. Wake refreshed to songs from the tui, bellbird or magpie. Let your eyes wander over the beautiful hills and farmland of the Tararua's, as you enjoy an ample breakfast. Lose yourself in our large well known garden (we suggest taking a picnic). Fly fishing? Sheep shearing? Shopping? And so close to Palmerston North, Pahiatua or Woodville.

~

Masterton *3 km W of Masterton*

Harefield *B&B Farmstay Cottage with Kitchen* B&B Approved

Marion Ahearn

147 Upper Plain Road, Masterton

Tel (06) 377 4070 Fax (06) 377 4070

Double $80 Single $45 (Full breakfast)
Child half price Dinner $20 by arrangement
Self-contained flat for 2 $55
Children welcome
1 Double 1 Single (1 bdrm)
Bathrooms: 1 Private

A warm welcome awaits you at Harefield, a small
farmlet on the edge of town. A quiet country garden
surrounds the cedar house and self-contained flat. The flat has 1 bedroom with double and single beds. 2 divan beds in living area. Self-cater or have breakfast in our warm dining room. Convenient for restaurants, showgrounds, vineyards, schools, tramping. 1.5 hour drive to Picton Ferry. We enjoy meeting people, aviation, travel, reading, art, farming and tramping. Baby facilities available. Smoke-free.

Masterton *10 km W of Masterton*

Tidsfordriv *B&B Homestay*
Glenys Hansen
4 Cootes Road, Matahiwi RD 8, Masterton

Tel (06) 378 9967 Fax (06) 378 9957
ghansen@contact.net.nz

Double $85-$90 Single $55 (Full breakfast)
Child half price Dinner $20 by arrangement
Visa MC accepted
Children welcome
1 Queen 2 Single (2 bdrm)
Bathrooms: 1 Private

A warm welcome awaits you at Tidsfordriv - a 64 acre
farmlet - seven kilometres off the main bypass route. You can enjoy the comforts for a modern home set
in parklike surroundings with large gardens & lakes. You can bird watch with ease and enjoy the peaceful
serenity of this 'Rural Retreat'. Glenys invites you to join her for dinner and enjoy good conversation
about gardening, conservation and travel. A Labrador dog is the family pet. You'll enjoy visits to
National Wildlife Centre, vineyards & Tararua Forest Park.

Masterton *1 km E of Masterton*

Mas des Saules *Homestay*
Mary & Steve Blakemore
9A Pokohiwi Road, Homebush, Masterton

Tel (06) 377 2577 or (027) 620 8728
Fax (06) 377 2578 mas-des-saules@wise.net.nz

Double $110 Single $75 (Full breakfast)
Child $40 Dinner $35
Visa MC accepted
Children and pets welcome
2 Queen (2 bdrm)
Bathrooms: 1 Guest share

Hidden down a tranquil country lane, discover our
authentic French Provencal farmhouse with its landscaped garden, stream, and courtyard. Swimming
and trout fishing in nearby river. Our children have departed, leaving us with a cat, small dog, and cattle
on our small farm. Guest lounge and bathroom with bath and shower. Open fire and central heating.
Enjoy farmhouse cooking with fresh vegetables from our large country garden, barbecues and picnic
lunches. We are a well-travelled couple who enjoy helping guests discover the unspoilt Wairarapa.

Masterton *In Central Masterton*

Victoria House *B&B*
Marion & Sara Monks & Mike Parker
15 Victoria Street, Masterton

Tel (06) 377 0186 Fax (06) 377 0186
parker.monks@xtra.co.nz

Double $80 Single $50 (Continental)
Twin $80
Visa MC accepted
3 Double 1 Twin 2 Single (6 bdrm)
Bathrooms: 2 Guest share

Victoria House is a 2 storey house built pre-1886,
renovated to retain the character of the period. The
peaceful nature of the furnishings and outdoor area create a quiet, relaxing atmosphere, great for a
"get away from it" weekend. We are also only a 3 minute walk from the town centre and Masterton's
excellent restaurants. Being wine-friendly hosts, we enjoy discussing wines and freely offer advice on the
Wairararapa's growing wine industry.

Masterton *3 km N of Masterton*

Llandaff *B&B Farmstay*
Elizabeth & Robin Dunlop
155 Upper Plain Road Masterton

Tel (06) 378 6628 or 021 359 562
Fax (06) 378 6628 llandaff@xtra.co.nz
www.wairarapa.co.nz/llandaff

Double $100-$120 Single $60-$70 (Full breakfast)
Child $25 Dinner $30
Children welcome
1 King 2 Queen 1 Double 1 Twin (5 bdrm)
Bathrooms: 1 Ensuite 1 Guest share

Elegantly restored, the homestead boasts beautiful
native NZ timbers throughout, wood panelled rooms, polished floors, old pull-handle toilets, a 'coffin' bath, open fireplaces and cosy woodburning kitchen stove. Explore the historic hayloft and stables, washhouse, longdrop, produce shed, gardener's shed, pavilion and dove cote. Relax in the majestic garden beneath 120 year old trees, or wander the farm and feed the animals. Bike riding, croquet and petanque are available to guests. Enjoy a cooked breakfast with Dinner available on request.

Masterton *2 km E of Masterton*

Apple Source Orchard Stay *Farmstay*
Mary & Roger Smith
Te Ore Ore, RD 6, Masterton

Tel (06) 377 0820 or 025 238 0228
Fax (06) 370 9401
rapukesmith@xtra.co.nz

Double $100 Single $75 (Full breakfast)
Visa MC accepted
2 Queen 2 Single (2 bdrm)
Bathrooms: 2 Ensuite

Try an experience that's a little different! Our colonial
style homestead is set in an operating apple orchard and
has a separate guest wing with lounge and 2 bedrooms with ensuites. You are welcome to share dinner (special diets catered for) with us and enjoy the ambience of Stanley range cooking along with relaxing by the open fire, or on the deck. There are orchard walks and a garden haven. Watch the daily orcahrd activities and pick some fruit in season.

Carterton *1 km N of Carterton*

Homecroft *B&B*
Christine & Neil Stewart
Somerset Road, RD 2, Carterton

Tel (06) 379 5959 homecroft@xtra.co.nz

Double $85-$95 Single $60 (Full breakfast)
Dinner $30pp by arrangement
1 Queen 1 Double 1 Twin (3 bdrm)
Bathrooms: 1 Ensuite 1 Private

Homecroft is surrounded by our country garden and
farmland yet handy to the vineyards, crafts, antiques,
and golf courses of the Wairarapa. Wellington
and the inter-island ferry 90 minutes away. Guests
accommodation, with own entrance, in a separate wing of the house with small lounge, the sunny bedrooms open onto a deck. The double room with ensuite, The Croft, is separate from the house. All bedrooms overlook the garden. A leisurely breakfast at Homecroft is an enjoyable experience. We look forward to making your stay with us happy and relaxing.

Greytown *80 km N of Wellington*
The Ambers *B&B Separate Suite*

Approved

Marilla Rankin
58A McMaster Street, Greytown

Tel (06) 304 8588 or 027 499 4394
Fax (06) 304 8590 ambershomestay@xtra.co.nz
www.ambershomestay.co.nz

Double $100-$130 Single $75-$100 (Continental)
Child $25 Self-contained cottage available
Visa MC accepted
Children welcome
1 King 1 Queen 2 Double 1 Single (4 bdrm)
Bathrooms: 3 Ensuite 1 Family share 1 Guest share

The Ambers is now in a 1920s 2 storey home originally from Lowry Bay in Wellington, moved over the Rimutaka Ranges and set on a lovely private section with mature trees. We offer spacious accommodation in this new home.

The Cherub Room has a large ensuite bathroom, queen bed, TV and coffee making facilities, french doors opening onto deck.

The Vintage Suite provides a large ensuite bathroom, king bed, private lounge with TV and coffee making facilities, a single bed for extra guests or children in the same group.

The Oak-Aged Room has a shared bathroom, double bed. This room is ideal for any overflow or big groups wishing to stay together.

The Ambers now offers a **serviced apartment** Petit Maison, with french doors to own outdoor area (see Photo). Great for romantic weekends. Facilities include a mini kitchen with microwave and fridge, lounge area with TV and sofa bed for the kids, a double bed and bathroom, woodburner.

If you desire the ultimate privacy or a romantic getaway we offer a blissful cottage set in its own private garden featuring lovely old trees. **Ambrosia Cottage** has 2 double bedrooms, with own amenities including fire and bath. For tariff please contact Marilla Rankin at above numbers.

Greytown *In Greytown Central*

Serenity Homestay *B&B Homestay Cottage with Kitchen*
Ursula Curtis & Bob Walker
37 Jellicoe Street, Greytown

Tel (06) 304 8666
serenity.homestay@ihug.co.nz

Double $100-$120 Single $80 (Full breakfast)
2 Queen 1 Single (3 bdrm)
Bathrooms: 1 Ensuite

Set in an acre of grounds, we offer a private or romantic getaway in 'The Cottage'; a fully self-contained 1 bedroom home with its own facilities for cooking, washing and relaxing. Or you can stay in our home. Either way you will enjoy the 'serenity' and beauty of our landscaped gardens and can relax in the separate spa pool. Non-smokers preferred. We are situated within easy walking distance of the Greytown shops and restaurants. The wine fields of Martinborough and NZ's Stonehenge are just 15 minutes away by car.

~

Greytown *2 km N of Greytown*

Totara Manoir *Homestay*
Lyn & Peter Besseling
RD 1 Woodside Road, Greytown

Tel (06) 304 7972 or 027 457 9130
Fax (06) 304 7960
p.besseling@xtra.co.nz

Double $110 Single $60 (Continental)
1 Queen 1 Double (2 bdrm)
Bathrooms: 2 Ensuite

Totara Manor, is a rural homestay situated 2km from the heart of Greytown. Enjoy expansive rural views while meandering on the wrap arround verandahs. Relax in the internal courtyard, read a book or two. Wander around the property or explore the small totara forest. Play petanque, feed the alpacas and gotland sheep. A pleasant 30 minute walk sees you in the heart of Greytown with its many shops and restaurants.

~

Featherston

Woodland Holt Bed & Breakfast *B&B*
Judi Adams
47 Watt Street, Featherston

Tel (06) 308 9927
woodland-holt@xtra.co.nz

Double $115-$115 Single $65 (Continental)
Dinner $35
Children welcome
1 Queen 1 Twin 1 Single (3 bdrm)
Bathrooms: 1 Guest share

Providing friendly hospitality. Interests include travelling, gardening, books, music, cross-stitch and collecting. Secluded gardens contain native, exotic and rare plants. Warm, luxury accommodation with off-street parking. Breakfast includes home-made treats and preserves. Explore beautiful Wairarapa or relax in comfort. View Meakin-at-Woodland, an extensive private collection of china by Alfred Meakin and J&G Meakin. Dine at a local restaurant or arrange to join me for an evening meal. Picnic hampers are available (additional charge). We look forward to your company and making your stay enjoyable.

Martinborough *0.5 km NW of Martinborough*

Oak House *B&B Homestay*
Polly & Chris Buring
45 Kitchener Street, Martinborough

Tel (06) 306 9198 Fax (06) 306 8198
chrispolly.oakhouse@xtra.co.nz
burings.co.nz

Double $100-$120 **Single** $55 (Special breakfast)
Child by arrangement Dinner by arrangement
Visa MC accepted
Children welcome
2 Queen 2 Single (3 bdrm)
Bathrooms: 1 Ensuite 1 Guest share

Our characterful 80 year old Californian bungalow offers gracious accommodation. Our spacious lounge provides a relaxed setting for sampling winemaker Chris's wonderful products. Our guest wing has its own entrance, bathroom (large bath and shower) and separate toilet. Our new bedroom has ensuite facilities. Bedrooms enjoy afternoon sun and garden views. Breakfast features fresh croissants, home-preserved local fruits and conserves. Creative cook Polly matches delicious dishes (often local game) with Chris's great wines. Tour our onsite winery with Chris. Meet our multi-talented cats.

Take time to enjoy your journey and the company of your hosts.

Martinborough *1 km SW of Martinborough*

Ross Glyn *Homestay*
Kenneth & Odette Trigg
1 Grey Street, Martinborough

Tel (06) 306 9967 Fax (06) 306 8267
rossglyn1@hotmail.com

Double $95 **Single** $65 (Full breakfast)
Dinner from $25 by arrangement
Children welcome
1 Double 2 Single (2 bdrm)
Bathrooms: 1 Guest share 1 Private

Our home nestles in over 2 acres of landscaped gardens which includes a rose garden, orchard, Japanese garden and we are surrounded by vineyards. Both our guestrooms have french doors opening onto a sunny deck with private access. Guests are welcome to relax with us and our small spoilt dog and cat in our large cosy (woodburner heated) lounge. Breakfast includes fresh croissants, home-made jams, jellies and preserved fruit. Cooked breakfast on request and dinner by arrangement.

Martinborough *In Martinborough Central*
Beatson's of Martinborough *B&B Guest House*
Karin Beatson & John Cooper
9A Cologne Street, Martinborough, Wairarapa

Tel (06) 306 8242 or 027 449 9827
Fax (06) 306 8243
beatsons@wise.net.nz
www.beatsons.co.nz

Double $150 Single $120 (Full breakfast)
Dinner by arrangement
Visa MC accepted
4 King/Twin 5 Queen (9 bdrm)
Bathrooms: 9 Ensuite

Beatsons offer a friendly and relaxed stay. Harrington and Cologne are restored villas operated as hosted guest houses for your year round comfort. Individually decorated spacious bedrooms with ensuites feature. In the living rooms, french doors open onto verandahs overlooking the gardens. Full country breakfasts use local produce, home-made breads and preserves. Dinner and functions by arrangement. Beatson's are just 5 minutes walk from Martinborough Square with its cafes and restaurants. Close to great wineries.

Martinborough *1 km W of Martinborough*
The Old Manse *B&B Homestay*
Sandra & John Hargrave
Corner Grey & Roberts Streets, Martinborough

Tel (06) 306 8599 or 0800 399 229
Fax (06) 306 8540 info@oldmanse.co.nz
www.oldmanse.co.nz

Double $150-$170 (Full breakfast)
Visa MC Diners Amex Eftpos accepted
Not suitable for children
5 Queen 1 Twin (6 bdrm)
Bathrooms: 6 Ensuite

In the heart of the wine district, a beautifully restored Presbyterian Manse, built 1876, has been transformed into a boutique homestay. Spacious, relaxed accommodation in a quiet, peaceful setting. 1 twin, 5 queen-size bedrooms all with their own ensuites. All day sun. Off-street parking, open fireplace. Amenities include spa pool, petanque, billiards. Enjoy breakfast or wine overlooking vineyard. Walking distance to Martinborough Square with selection of excellent restaurants. Close to vineyards, antique and craft shops, adventure quad bikes and golf courses. Qualmark 4+

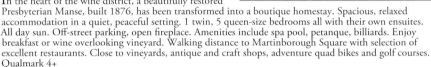

Please let us know
how you enjoyed your B&B experience.
Ask your host for a comment form
or leave a comment on www.bnb.co.nz

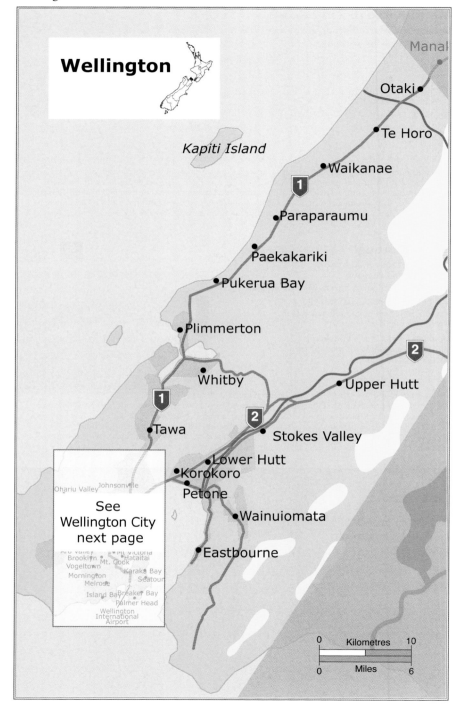

Wellington

Kapiti Island

Otaki

Te Horo

Waikanae

1

Paraparaumu

Paekakariki

Pukerua Bay

Plimmerton

2

Whitby

Upper Hutt

1

2

Tawa

Stokes Valley

Lower Hutt

Korokoro

Oharu Valley   Johnsonville

Petone

See
Wellington City
next page

Wainuiomata

Aro Valley   Mt. Victoria
Brooklyn   Hataitai
Vogeltown   Mt. Cook
Melrose   Karaka Bay
Mornington   Seatoun
Island Bay   Breaker Bay
Palmer Head
Wellington
International
Airport

Eastbourne

Manal

0   Kilometres   10

0   Miles   6

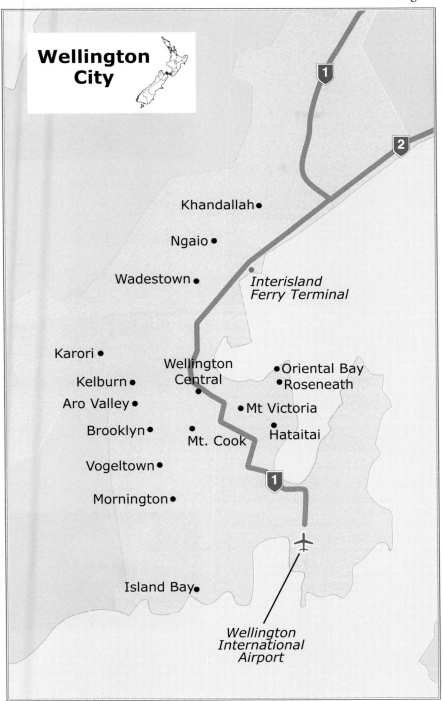

Wellington

Wellington City

Khandallah•

Ngaio•

Wadestown•

Interisland Ferry Terminal

Karori•

Wellington Central

•Oriental Bay
•Roseneath

Kelburn•

Aro Valley•

•Mt Victoria

Brooklyn•

Mt. Cook

Hataitai

Vogeltown•

Mornington•

Island Bay•

Wellington International Airport

Te Horo *7 km N of Waikanae*

Pateke Lagoons Wetlands *B&B Homestay Farmstay*
Peter & Adrienne Dale
152 Te Hapua Road, Te Horo, RD 1, Kapiti Coast

Tel (06) 364 2222 or 021 439661
Fax (06) 364 2214
peter@pateke-lagoons.co.nz
www.pateke-lagoons.co.nz

Double $195 Single $175 (Special breakfast)
Dinner $65 including wine
Visa MC accepted
2 Queen 1 Single (2 bdrm)
Bathrooms: 2 Ensuite 1 Private

Pateke Lagoons overlooks a private 50 acre wetland and waterfowl refuge. It offers peace and quiet in tranquil rural surroundings. 2 guest rooms, each with ensuite and private courtyard. Large lounge with wildfowl and wetland ecology library. Beautiful views of farmland, sea and wetland. Easy 30 minute walking tracks through native bush and wetland, with golf cart available. Fresh seafood is our specialty with garden fresh vegetables. Special breakfast using local products. Feed the horses and pet the cats. Open wetlands are unsuitable for children.

Waikanae *59 km N of Wellington*

Shepreth Homestay *B&B Homestay*
Lorraine & Warren Birch
12 Major Durie Place, Waikanae Beach 6010

Tel (04) 905 2130 or 027 444 1088
Fax (04) 905 2139
shepreth@paradise.net.nz

Double $100-$120 Single $70-$80 (Full breakfast)
Visa MC accepted
Not suitable for children
1 Queen 2 Twin (2 bdrm)
Bathrooms: 1 Private

You will find it easy to relax and enjoy your surroundings in our comfortable modern home overlooking Kapiti Island and the beach. The spacious guest rooms have their own lounge and kitchenette. Breakfasts are delicious! We only take 1 party of guests at a time, and enjoy spending time with both New Zealand and overseas guests. We're 50 minutes from Wellington, easy to find, with several cafes and restaurants close by. Our cat lives here too. You are assured of a warm welcome.

Waikanae Beach *5 km W of Waikanae*

Konini Cottage & Homestead *Cottage with Kitchen & Separate Suite*
Maggie & Bob Smith
26 Konini Crescent, Waikanae Beach, Kapiti Coast

Tel (04) 904 6610 Fax (04) 904 6610
konini@paradise.net.nz   www.konini.co.nz

Double $130 Single $85-$115 (Full breakfast)
Child $25 Extra person $45   Dinner $40
Less $15 per head if self-catering
Visa MC accepted
Children welcome
2 Queen 2 Single
(Cottage 2 bdrm Homestead 1 bdrm)
Bathrooms: 2 Private

Set in an acre of tranquil grounds, both the Lockwood Cottage and Homestead offer a restful haven 300 metres from the beach and bordering the golf links. For the independent traveller the Cottage is your choice with full self-catering facilities. Deduct $15 per head if breakfast not required. The Homestead suite (bedroom with adjoining sitting room} offers a traditional B&B. Directions: turn off SH1 at traffic lights to beach, 4km to old service station, take right fork, then first right, 1km to Konini Crescent.

Waikanae *1 km E of Waikanae*

Country Patch *Apartment with Kitchen*

Sue & Brian Wilson

18 Kea Street, Waikanae

Tel (04) 293 5165 Fax (04) 293 5164
stay@countrypatch.co.nz
www.countrypatch.co.nz

Double $110-$185 Single $85-$13 (Continental)
Child $25 Dinner by arrangement
Visa MC accepted
Children welcome
2 King/Twin 1 Queen 2 Single (3 bdrm)
Bathrooms: 3 Ensuite

2 Delightful self-contained accommodation sites. Country patch studio with its own entrance and deck has a queen bed with ensuite and twin beds on the mezzanine floor of the kitchen lounge. Country patch villa has an open fire and a large verandah with magic views. It is wheelchair accessible and the 2 bedrooms (each with ensuite) have king beds that unzip to twin. We warmly invite you to share our patch of the country with Kate (16), Simon (14) and Holly our labrador.

~

Waikanae *6 km E of Waikanae*

RiverStone *B&B Cottage with Kitchen*

Paul & Eppie Murton

111 Ngatiawa Road, Waikanae

Tel (04) 293 1936 Fax (04) 293 1936
riverstone@paradise.net.nz
www.riverstone.co.nz

Double $100-$120 Single $70 (Full breakfast)
Child $45
Visa MC accepted
1 Queen 1 Twin (2 bdrm)
Bathrooms: 1 Private

Birdsong, the sound of the river and complete privacy. Peace and quiet with a scrumptious breakfast and comfortable accommodation. Riverstone has 5 hectares of paddocks and garden with river walks and local pottery and cafe. Waikanae, Raumati and Paraparaumu have a variety of cafes, shops, boutiques, Lindale Farm Park, the Southward Car Museum, Nga Manu Bird Sanctuary, golf courses and beautiful beaches. Pick up from train or bus. Laundry facilities. Smoke-free. No pets.

~

Waikanae *In Waikanae*

Camellia Cottage @ Sudbury Estate *B&B Cottage with Kitchen*

Glenys & Brian Daw

39 Manu Grove, Waikanae 6010, Kapiti Coast

Tel (04) 902 8530 or 021 129 6970
Fax (04) 902 8531
1stay@sudbury.co.nz   www.sudbury.co.nz

Double $150-$195 Single $120-$195
(Special breakfast) Dinner by arrangement
Visa MC accepted
Not suitable for children
2 Queen (2 bdrm)
Bathrooms: 1 Guest share 1 Private Spa bath in house

"The Place to Stay in Kapiti", only 50 minutes from Wellington ferries. Recently described as a jewel in Kapiti's crown. Experience sincere Kiwi hospitality in a superb location. Lovely self-contained cottage with own courtyard, tastefully furnished - nestled in a beautiful 2 1/2 acre garden. Traditional B&B also offered. Break your journey or stay longer in this idyllic setting. 4 golf courses - Bush and beach walks nearby - Excellent local restaurants - Off-street parking - TV/DVD/Hi-Fi. Guest email/fax/phone - dinner by prior arrangement.

Wellington

Waikanae Beach

Helen's Waikanae Beach B&B *B&B Homestay*

Helen Anderson

115 Tutere Street, Waikanae Beach, Kapiti Coast

Tel (04) 902 5829 or 021 259 3396
Fax (04) 902 5840
waikanaebeachbandb@paradise.net.nz
www.waikanaebeachbandb.net

Double $110-$130 Single $90-$110 (Full breakfast)
Child negotiable   Dinner by arrangement
Visa MC accepted
2 Queen 1 King/Single (2 bdrm)
Bathrooms: 1 Ensuite 1 Private

Need to relax and unwind? Then come and experience Helen's warm, friendly hospitality in her home by the sea. Count stars (not sheep) and fall asleep to the soothing sound of the ocean. Direct access to a sandy safe swimming beach where you can enjoy long leisurely walks, beautiful sunsets, spectacular views of Kapiti Island, and the Tararua Ranges. Crisp cotton bed linen. Tea-making facilities. Generous breakfasts. Dinner by prior arrangement. Guest laundry. Good restaurants nearby. Helen looks forward to making your acquaintance soon.

∽

Waikanae Beach

Gekkenhuis B&B *B&B Separate Suite*

Katrina & Franck van Dooren

26 Freyberg Crescent, Waikanae Beach 6010

Tel (04) 293 7768 Fax (04) 293 7762
enquiries@gekkenhuis.co.nz   www.gekkenhuis.co.nz

Double $120-$180 Single $90-$120
(Continental provisions)
Child $20-$40 Dinner by arrangement
Visa MC accepted
Children and pets welcome
1 King/Twin 1 Queen (2 bdrm)
Bathrooms: 2 Private

Welcome to the Gekkenhuis - the place to unwind and rediscover the simple pleasures in life. Explore the many and varied Kapiti Coast tourist attractions and beaches. You'll share our home with son Lucas, dog Molly and cat Zwarty, so children and pets are most welcome. Babysitting service available. Spacious rooms feature all the home comforts including TV/DVD, CD player, fridge and tea and coffee making facilities. Cooked breakfast and other meals available on request. Dutch/German/French speaking. We'll make sure your stay with us is memorable.

∽

Raumati

The Boathouse Bed & Breakfast *B&B Cottage with Kitchen Self-contained house*

Liz Kirkland

39 Matatua Road, Raumati Beach

Tel (04) 293 1483 or 027 554 5175
Fax (04) 293 1583
stay@theboathouse.co.nz   www.theboathouse.co.nz

Double $150-$225 (Full provisions)
Child $15 Dinner by arrangement Extra adult $30
Visa MC accepted
Children and pets welcome
1 Queen 2 Single (2 bdrm)
Bathrooms: 1 Private outside bath in garden

Raumati Beach and cafes just moments away. A large deck overlooks the eastern hills with outdoor furniture and barbeque, see the sunrise. Quality furnishings and refreshments provided. Stylish kitchen with all mod cons, even a dishwasher. Bathroom and full laundry. You'll even find a 28 foot whale chaser boat right next to the house. Take a walk up the garden path to the hammock in the trees and an outdoor bath with hot and cold running water. Great for the whole family or your honeymoon.

Paraparaumu *55kms km N of Wellington*
Avion Homestay *Homestay*
Jude & Vic Young
3 Avion Terrace, Paraparaumu

Tel (04) 902 0199 or 021 177 6195
Fax (04) 902 0199
judeandvicyoung@paradise.net.nz

Double $90 Single $50-$60 (Full breakfast)
Child half price Dinner $25 by arrangement
Children welcome
1 Double 1 Single (2 bdrm)
Bathrooms: 1 Guest share Bath & shower

Our quiet, Mediterranean style house is situated
one block back from Marine Parade. Shops, golf course, airport, cafes and excellent restaurants are a
1.5km walk away. Off-street parking is provided and we will meet bus or train. Special diets catered
for. We enjoy walking, food, music, and Citroens. We have a cat. Directions: from south, turn at Nyco
Chocolate & Prenzel Shop into Raumati Road, then follow road north from Raumati Beach shops for
1.5km, turning sharp right into Avion Terrace just before S bend to Marine Parade.

Paraparaumu Beach *5. km NW of Paraparaumu*
Beachstay *Homestay*
Ernie & Rhoda Stevenson
17 Takahe Drive, Kotuku Park, Paraparaumu Beach

Tel (04) 902 6466 or 025 232 5106
Fax (04) 902 6466
ernandrho@paradise.net.nz

Double $80 Single $55 (Continental)
Dinner $25 by arrangement
Visa MC accepted
1 Double 2 Single (2 bdrm)
Bathrooms: 1 Private

Enjoy warm friendly hospitality in the relaxing
atmosphere of our modern new home. Peaceful surroundings next to river estuary and beach. Wonderful
views of sea, lake and hills. Lovely coastal and river walks. Close to Paraparaumu Beach world ranking
golf course and Southwards Car Museum. Trips to Kapiti Island Bird Sanctuary can be arranged with
prior notice. South Island Ferry Terminal 45 minutes away. We enjoy meeting people and sharing our
love of NZ scenery and bush walking. Ernie paints landscapes. Enquiries welcome.

Paraparaumu *43 km N of Wellington*
Rosetta House Bed & Breakfast Plus Garden Suite *B&B Homestay Separate Suite*
Lorraine & Michael Sherlock
349 Rosetta Road, Raumati, Paraparaumu

Tel (04) 905 9055 or 021 122 0939
Free Phone 0800 299 955 Fax (04) 905 9055
rosettahouse@paradise.net.nz www.rosetta.co.nz

Double $125-$165 Single $75-$125 (Full breakfast)
Visa MC accepted
1 King/Twin 2 Queen 1 Double (4 bdrm)
Bathrooms: 2 Ensuite 1 Private

Travelling on unfamiliar roads? Going to or from the Picton Ferry? Business
or pleasure, it's time to relax... a warm welcome awaits you. Our charming
and elegant homestead has 3 lounges with bedrooms opening out to the glass-
covered pergola and gardens. Beach, restaurants are 1-2 minutes easy walk
away. Spend a few days exploring the many attractions of our coastal paradise
here on the Kapiti Coast. Generous cooked/gourmet breakfast with home-made bread and jams, fresh
fruit, etc. Laundry/internet. 35 minutes from Wellington and Picton Ferry.

Wellington

Paekakariki *40 km N of Wellington*

Killara Homestay *B&B*
Carole & Don Boddie
70 Ames Street, Paekakariki

Tel (04) 905 5544 or 027 4 944 551
Fax (04) 905 5533
killara@paradise.net.nz
www.killarahomestay.co.nz

Double $120-$140 Single $110-$120 (Continental)
Visa MC accepted
Pet free home Not suitable for children
1 Queen 1 Twin (2 bdrm)
Bathrooms: 1 Private

Relax, enjoy the sound of the sea, fabulous views and beach access from our absolute beachfront home. Spacious apartment-like accommodation upstairs includes a guest lounge. All rooms have outstanding views from Kapiti Island to the South Island. Internet and laundry facilities available. We host 1 party at a time. Have a relaxing spa bath, enjoy beach activities (surf-casting gear available), walk to village cafes/restaurants, or explore the Kapiti Coast. Within 15 minutes of 5 golf courses; 30 minutes drive to Wellington City. Close to shops/transport.

∾

Paekakariki *5 km S of Paraparaumu*

Seaside Getaway *Apartment with Kitchen*
Marion & Eddie Clark
27/8 Beach Road, Paekakariki

Tel 027 442 1111 or 027 284 1002
Business (04) 232 4178 or Home (04) 232 8528
Fax (04) 232 4171
marion.clark@harcourts.co.nz
www.seasidewellington.co.nz

Double $160-$190 Single $160
(Breakfast by arrangement) Weekly rates available
2 Queen (2 bdrm)
Bathrooms: 1 Private

Unwind and get away to this slice of paradise - watch the sea roll in, revel in the glorious sunsets and the panoramic views of Kapiti and the South Island from this superbly refurbished self-contained seaside retreat. New kitchen, bathroom. Garage, plus extra car parking. Private decking for outdoor relaxation, barbeques. Enjoy the quaint village with 3 great restaurants. Easy access to Wellington City (30 minutes). Swim, fish or walk the sandy beach. Golf courses and scenic QE2 park (walking/biking), are nearby. Kayaks available.

∾

Pukerua Bay *30 km N of Wellington*

Sheena's Homestay *Homestay*
Sheena Taylor
2 Gray Street, Pukerua Bay 6010, Kapiti Coast

Tel (04) 239 9947 Fax (04) 239 9942
homestay@sheenas.co.nz

Double $90 Single $50 (Full breakfast)
Child $25 Dinner by arrangement
Visa MC Amex Eftpos accepted
Children and pets welcome
1 Double 1 Twin 1 Single (2 bdrm)
Bathrooms: 1 Family share

Come share our warm, sunny refurbished smoke-free home. Relax in the conservatory and enjoy the views. We have 2 friendly cats - Tabitha & Sienna. Pukerua Bay, home of creative people, has an interesting beach about 15 minutes walk away. Railway station closeby. Sheena is a keen spinner - spinning wheel/fibre available to use. Restaurants and cafes 5-15 minutes drive. Most special diets catered for, lunches arranged. Smokers seating undercover; off-street parking; laundry facilities; garaging for bikes; powerpoint small campervans; cot & highchair. Personal care for people with disabilities.

Plimmerton *6 km N of Porirua*

Aquavilla *B&B Cottage No Kitchen Cottage with Kitchen*
Graham & Carolyn Wallace
16 Steyne Avenue, Plimmerton

Tel (04) 233 1146 or 027 231 0141
aquavilla@paradise.net.nz
www.aquavilla.co.nz

Double $150 **Single** $140 (Special breakfast)
Child negotiable
Dinner $50 Extra adults $50
Visa MC accepted
Children welcome
1 Queen 1 Single (1 bdrm)
Bathrooms: 1 Private

Aquavilla ia an upmarket self-contained Bed & Breakfast situated in one of Wellington's finest areas, with beach at you back door, beautiful walks,garden setting.All this with just a 20min drive or train ride to Wellington CBD or 1 min. walk to local restaurants and all amenities. You will have parking at the door,fun hosts who would love to have a wine down on the beach with you.

Plimmerton *20min km N of Wellington*

Southridge Farm *Farmstay Cottage with Kitchen*
Katrina & Andrew Smith
Southridge, 96 The Track, Plimmerton, Wellington

Tel (04) 233 1104
aksmith@paradise.net.nz

Double $95-$110 **Single** $75-$90 (Continental)
Child free
Children and pets welcome
1 Queen 1 Single (1 bdrm)
Bathrooms: 1 Ensuite

Looking for something special away from the city noise? Southridge Farm has it. Rural in a residential area. We have a lovely modern self-contained cottage with full kitchen including washing machine if self-catering is preferred. Couch has a sofabed. Cot and foldaway bed also available. Beach, trains and restaurants 1km away. Major shopping centre 7km. Our pets: ponies, sheep and goats are waiting to greet you. Andrew & Katrina, children Lachlan & Ella, farm dog Penny warmly invite you to share in our relaxing rural experience.

Whitby *10 km NE of Porirua*

Oldfields *Homestay*
Elaine & John Oldfield
22 Musket Lane, Whitby, Wellington

Tel (04) 234 1002
oldfields@ihug.co.nz
www.oldfieldshomestay.co.nz

Double $115 **Single** $95 (Full breakfast)
Dinner $25 by arrangement
Visa MC accepted
2 Queen (2 bdrm)
Bathrooms: 1 Guest share

Would you enjoy a stay in a tranquil home with bush views and overlooking a mature and well-tended garden? Oldfields is situated in a quiet cul-de-sac in the suburb of Whitby, 10 minutes by car from Paremata Station and 25 minutes from central Wellington. Having travelled and lived overseas we are always interested in meeting people, whether they are from just up the road in New Zealand or further a field. We welcome you to stay with us and our cats Tinker & Roxy.

Wellington

Whitby *30 km N of Wellington*

Scoresby Manor *B&B Homestay*
Virginia and Paul Green
13 Scoresby Grove, Whitby, Wellington

Tel (04) 234 7795 or 021 620 320
Fax (04) 234 7703
info@scoresbymanor.co.nz   www.scoresbymanor.co.nz

Double $160 Single $160 (Special breakfast)
Dinner $40
Visa MC accepted
Children and pets welcome
1 King 1 Queen 2 Single (3 bdrm)
Bathrooms: 2 Private

Scoresby Manor is situated on the outskirts of Whitby and Pauatahanui; 20 minutes north of Wellington. Surrounded by native bush reserve we offer you a relaxing and tranquil environment. Virginia and Paul provide warm hospitality and superb accommodation and food for the discerning traveller. If you are looking for something special then look no further! We take pride in ensuring our guests' stay is both memorable and comfortable. Virginia and Paul and their 3 miniature schnauzers welcome you to the country's most vibrant city; Wellington.

Tawa *15 km N of Wellington*

Tawa Homestay *Homestay*
Jeannette & Alf Levick
17 Mascot Street, Tawa, Wellington

Tel (04) 232 5989 Fax (04) 232 5987
milsom.family@xtra.co.nz

Double $90 Single $50 (Full breakfast)
Dinner 3 course candle-lit $20pp
Visa MC accepted
1 Queen 1 Single (2 bdrm)
Bathrooms: 1 Family share

Our comfortable family home is in a quiet street in Tawa. We have a separate toilet, shower and spa bath. Freshly ground coffee a speciality, with breakfast of your choice. Jeannette's interests are: Japanese language, porcelain painting, knitting, dressmaking, playing tennis, learning to play golf and the piano and gardening. Alf's interests are: Amateur radio, woodwork, Toastmasters International - and being allowed to help in the garden. We are both members of Lions International.

Tawa *15 km N of Wellington*

Chaplin Homestay *Homestay*
Joy & Bill Chaplin
3 Kiwi Place, Tawa, Wellington

Tel (04) 232 5547 or 021 146 5717
021 298 4569 Fax (04) 232 5547
chapta@xtra.co.nz

Double $90 Single $50 (Continental)
Dinner by arrangement
Pet free home
Not suitable for children
1 King 1 Double 1 Single (3 bdrm)
Bathrooms: 1 Guest share

You will find No 3 in a quiet cul-de-sac with safe off-street parking 7 minutes by car and rail to Porirua City and 15 minutes to Wellington and the InterIsland Ferry Terminal. Relax in comfort and enjoy good restaurants, close proximity to beaches, tenpin bowling, swimming pool and fine walks. Phone for directions and notification for dinner if required. Laundry facilities available.

Tawa *15 km NW of Wellington CBD*
Perry Homestay *B&B Homestay*
Jocelyn & David Perry
5 Fyvie Avenue, Tawa, Wellington 6006

Tel (04) 232 7664
djperry@actrix.co.nz

Double $90 Single $50 (Continental)
Child $20
Dinner By arrangement
Children welcome
1 Double 1 Twin 1 Single (3 bdrm)
Bathrooms: 1 Family share 1 Guest share

We are a retired couple. Together we welcome you to stay with us. There is a 5 minute walk to the suburban railway station with a half hourly service into the city (15 minutes) and north to the Kapiti Coast. Alternatively you can drive north to the coast, enjoying sea and rural views before sampling tourist attractions in this area. We are happy to provide transport to and from the Interislander ferry. Laundry facilities available.

Upper Hutt - Te Marua *7.4 km N of Upper Hutt*
Te Marua Homestay *Homestay*
Sheryl & Lloyd Homer
108A Plateau Road, Te Marua, Upper Hutt

Tel (04) 526 7851 or 0800 110 851
027 450 1679 Fax (04) 526 7866
sheryl.lloyd@clear.net.nz

Double $90 Single $60 (Continental)
Dinner $25pp by arrangement
Visa MC Diners Amex accepted
Children welcome
1 Queen 1 Double (2 bdrm)
Bathrooms: 1 Private

Our home is situated in a secluded bush setting. Guests may relax on 1 of our private decks or read books from our extensive library. For the more energetic there are bush walks, bike trails, trout fishing, swimming and a golf course within walking distance. The guest wing has a kitchenette and television. Lloyd is a landscape photographer with over 30 years experience photographing New Zealand. Sheryl is a teacher. Travel, tramping, skiing, photography, music and meeting people are interests we enjoy.

Upper Hutt *30 min km N of Wellington*
Tranquility Homestay *B&B Homestay*
Elaine & Alan
136 Akatarawa Road, Birchville, Upper Hutt

Tel (04) 526 6948 Fax (04) 526 6968
tranquility@xtra.co.nz

Double $100 Single $50-$90 (Continental)
Child negotiable
Dinner $20 by prior arrangement
Airport pick up
Children and pets welcome
1 Queen 1 Twin 1 Single (3 bdrm)
Bathrooms: 1 Ensuite 2 Family share

Tranquility Homestay. The name says it all. Escape from the stress of city life approx 30 minutes from Wellington off SH2. Close to Upper Hutt - restaurants, cinema, golf, racecourse, leisure centre (swimming), bush walks. We are near the confluence of the Hutt and Akatarawa Rivers which is noted for its fishing. 13km to Staglands. Country setting, relax, listen to NZ tuis, watch the fantails or wood pigeons, or simply relax and read. Comfortable, warm and friendly hospitality. Close by locations used for The Lord of the Rings.

Lower Hutt

Judy & Bob's Place *Homestay*
Judy & Bob Vine
11 Ngaio Crescent, Lower Hutt

Tel (04) 971 1192 Fax (04) 971 6192
bob.vine@paradise.net.nz

Double $100 **Single** $50 (Full breakfast)
Dinner $30
Visa MC Diners Amex accepted
Pet free home
1 Queen 2 Single (2 bdrm)
Bathrooms: 1 Private

Located in Woburn, a picturesque and quiet central
city suburb of Lower Hutt, known for its generous sized houses and beautiful gardens. Within walking distance of the Lower Hutt downtown, 15 minutes drive from central Wellington, its railway station and ferry terminals; airport 25 minutes; 3 minutes walk to Woburn Rail Station. Private lounge and TV. Love to entertain and share hearty Kiwi style cooking with good New Zealand wine. Laundry facilities. Transfer transport available. High speed and dial up internet connections.

Lower Hutt *12 km N of Hutt City*

Casa Bianca *B&B Separate Suite Apartment with Kitchen*
Jo & Dave Comparini
10 Damian Grove, Lower Hutt,

Tel (04) 569 7859 Fax (04) 569 7859
dcompo@xtra.co.nz

Double $95 **Single** $75 (Continental provisions)
Pet free home Children welcome
1 King 1 Single (1 bdrm)
Bathrooms: 1 Private

Our comfortable house is situated in the peaceful Eastern hills of Hutt City. We are within easy reach of the city centre, the Open Polytech and Waterloo Railway Station. Wellington is 20 minutes by train or car. We have a self-contained apartment with bedroom (double), bathroom, large lounge, fully equipped kitchen, extra single bed in lounge. Breakfast provisions provided in apartment. We specialise in long or short term stays. Come and enjoy our special hospitality. Computer (broadband) line if required. Off-street parking. No smoking please.

Lower Hutt *2 km SE of Lower Hutt*

Dungarvin *B&B Homestay*
Beryl & Trevor Cudby
25 Hinau Street, Woburn, Lower Hutt

Tel (04) 569 2125 Fax (04) 569 2126
t.b.cudby@clear.net.nz

Double $100-$115 **Single** $80-$100 (Full breakfast)
Dinner $30 by arrangement
Visa MC accepted
Pet free home Not suitable for children
1 Queen (1 bdrm)
Bathrooms: 1 Private

Our 75 year old cottage has been fully refurbished while retaining its original charm. It is 15 minutes from the ferry terminal and the stadium, and 20 minutes from Te Papa - The Museum of New Zealand. Our home is centrally heated and the sunny guest bedroom looks over our secluded garden. The bed has an electric blanket and wool duvet. Vegetarians are catered for, laundry facilities are available and we have ample off-street parking. Our main interests are travel, music, gardening, shows and NZ wines.

Lower Hutt *0.5 km SE of Lower Hutt Central*
Rose Cottage *B&B Homestay*
Maureen & Gordon Gellen
70A Hautana Street, Lower Hutt, Wellington

Tel (04) 566 7755 or 021 481732
Fax (04) 566 0777
gellen@xtra.co.nz

Double $110-$120 **Single** $80-$90 (Full breakfast)
Dinner $30 by arrangement
Visa MC accepted
Not suitable for children
1 King/Twin 1 Queen (2 bdrm)
Bathrooms: 1 Ensuite 1 Family share

Relax in the comfort of our cosy home which is just a 5 minute walk to the Hutt City Centre. Originally built in 1910 the house has been fully renovated. We have travelled extensively overseas and in NZ. Interests include travel, gardening, sports and live theatre. As well as TV in guest room there's coffee and tea-making facilities. Breakfast will be served in our dining room at your convenience. Unsuitable for children. We look forward to welcoming you into our smoke-free home which we share with Scuffin our cat.

Lower Hutt *3 km N of Hutt City Centre*
Park Avenue B&B *Homestay*
Pam & Ray Ward
788 High Street, Lower Hutt

Tel (04) 567 4788
pam.ray.ward@xtra.co.nz

Double $90-$130 **Single** $60-$90 (Continental)
Dinner by arrangement
Visa MC Diners accepted
Children welcome
1 Queen 1 Double 1 Twin (3 bdrm)
Bathrooms: 1 Ensuite 2 Private

A warm, friendly welcome awaits guests in this gracious home. Conveniently situated 1500 metres off SH2 (Avalon exit). 15km to ferry terminal and Westpac Stadium. Short walk to trains or Airport Flyer bus stop. All essential services and facilities available at nearby Park Avenue shops. 1km to hospitals and golf courses, short stroll to Avalon Park and Hutt Riverbank Walkway. Indoor Pool (heated, spring-autumn). Centrally heated home with secluded garden and off-street parking. Capital, realistically priced, accommodation for Capital visitors.

Lower Hutt *2 km E of Lower Hutt*
Tyndall House *Homestay*
Paulene & Nigel Lyne
6/2 Tyndall Street, Lower Hutt, Wellington 6009

Tel (04) 569 1958 Fax (04) 569 1952
tyndallhouse@xtra.co.nz

Double $110-$115 **Single** $80-$95 (Full breakfast)
Dinner $30
Visa MC accepted
2 Queen (2 bdrm)
Bathrooms: 2 Ensuite

Nigel and Paulene warmly invite you to share their home which is situated beneath a bush reserve in a tranquil haven. We offer a high standard of accomodation, secure parking, sunny elegant bedrooms with garden views, Sky TV and tea/coffee making facilities,electric blankets and a heat pump. We are 15 minutes from the ferry terminal and 20 minutes from Te Papa ń the museum of New Zealand. Come and relax in our peaceful surroundings. We look forward to welcoming you into our home.

Lower Hutt - Stokes Valley *8 km NE of Lower Hutt*

Kowhai B&B *B&B Homestay*
Glenys & Peter Lockett
88A Manuka Street, Stokes Valley, Lower Hutt

Tel (04) 563 6671 or 027 443 3341
p_g.lockett@xtra.co.nz

Double $95-$110 Single $70-$80 (Full breakfast)
Visa MC accepted
Pet free home
1 Queen 1 Double (2 bdrm)
Bathrooms: 1 Private

Awake to birdsong in our spacious, tasteful bedrooms with bath robes and hairdriers provided. Relax in the lovely guest lounge with deck, Sky TV, CD player and tea & coffee facilities. We offer off-road parking at the door and delicious breakfast with seasonal fresh fruits. Sports, theatre and travel are our interests and we have a wide knowledge of the greater Wellington area.

Petone *3 km S of Lower Hutt*

Homestay
Anne & Reg Cotter
1 Bolton Street, Petone, Wellington

Tel (04) 568 6960 Fax (04) 568 6956

Double $80 Single $40 (Full breakfast)
Child over 10 half price
Dinner $15
Visa MC accepted
Children welcome
1 Double 2 Single (2 bdrm)
Bathrooms: 1 Guest share

We have a 100 year old home by the beach. We are two minutes from a Museum on beach, shop and bus route to the city. A restaurant is nearby. We are ten minutes from Picton Ferries. Off street parking available. Children are very welcome. Reg is a keen amateur ornithologist and goes to the Chatham Islands with an expedition trying to find the nestling place of the Taiko - a rare sea bird, on endangered list. Other interests are genealogy and conservation. Laundry facilities are available.

Petone - Korokoro *2 km W of Petone*

Korokoro Homestay *Homestay*
Bridget & Jim Austin
100 Korokoro Road, Korokoro, Petone

Tel (04) 589 1678 or Freephone 0800 116 575
Fax (04) 589 2678
jaustin@clear.net.nz
www.bnb.co.nz/korokorohomestay.html

Double $100-$120 Single $70-$80 (Continental)
Dinner by arrangement
Visa MC accepted Not suitable for children
1 King/Twin 1 Double (2 bdrm)
Bathrooms: 1 Ensuite 1 Guest share ensuite has bath and large shower etc.

Our 1 acre property is secluded and quiet but only 12 minutes to ferries and central Wellington. Easy to find. We came from England to New Zealand in 1957 and enjoy travel. Jim is a desultory woodworker with a machinery background. Bridget was a teacher and is an artist/weaver/feltmaker. We enjoy visual arts, theatre, cinema, music, books, gardening, and the outdoors. Your food will be mainly organic as we prefer an environmentally friendly lifestyle. The new house reflects our interests and skills.

~

Lower Hutt - Korokoro *12 km N of Wellington*
Devenport Estate *B&B Hobby Vineyard*
Alasdair & Christopher
1 Korokoro Road, Korokoro, Petone, Wellington 6008

Approved

Tel (04) 586 6868 Fax (04) 586 6869
devenport_estate@hotmail.com
homepages.paradise.net.nz/devenpor

Double $115-$145 Single $100-$115 (Continental)
Visa MC Diners accepted
Children welcome
3 Queen 2 Single (3 bdrm)
Bathrooms: 2 Ensuite 1 Private
Ensuites with showers, Private with shower over bath

Stay at the closest hobby vineyard to the capital. Only
15 minutes to ferry, city & stadium yet with the
privacy and quietness of a country retreat. Devenport
Estate is an Edwardian-styled homestead overlooking
Wellington Harbour, built at the turn of the century
(2000!) based upon the MacDonald family home in
Scotland.

Nestled amongst native bush we have carved out a
colourful garden around the homestead and planted
over 400 Pinot Gris/Pinot Noir grapevines in our
hobby vineyard. Devenport was built for views, comfort
and peacefulness

Guests enjoy stunning sea, bush and garden views.
Bedrooms contain queen-sized bed, writing desk, chairs, TV, tea-making services, hair dryer, electric
blanket with either an ensuite or private bathroom. Relax in the guest living room or outside in the sun
on the titanic deck chairs. Play petanque or deck quoits, admire the vines and water features or watch the
yachts sail past on the harbour.

Avoid city stress and leave your car here, we are only a 15 minute train ride to central Wellington. We
offer free arrival/departure transfers from Petone Station. Devenport provides; free internet, free laundry
service for stays of 2 or more nights. Some limits apply. We have plenty of off street parking. Breakfast
in the formal dining room or alfresco, overlooking Somes Island. At night, enjoy the vast variety of
restaurants of Petone's Jackson Street - only a 5 minute drive from Devenport. Alasdair, Chris and our 2
cocker spaniels, welcome you to a comfortable stay in Wellington on our vineyard estate.

Petone - Korokoro *2 km W of Petone*

Matairangi *B&B*
Kate & Barry Malcolm
29 Singers Road, Korokoro, Petone

Tel (04) 566 6010
barrym@actrix.co.nz
www.bnb.co.nz/matairangi.html

Double $90 Single $60 (Full breakfast)
Child $30
1 Twin (1 bdrm)
Bathrooms: 1 Private

Welcome to our hectare of peaceful natural bush and native birds, a hilltop perch with amazing views over Wellington Harbour and links to an extensive network of popular walking tracks. Such a special spot needs to be shared. Your private ground floor space includes a sitting room with tea/coffee facilities, TV, books and information about Petone restaurants. Upstairs, breakfast may include new-laid eggs, our own honey, fresh-baked bread and muesli. The ferry terminal is 15 minutes drive away. Also email, laundry, parking.

Wainuiomata *6 km E of Lower Hutt*

Kaponga House *B&B Homestay Cottage No Kitchen*
Hilary & Neville
22 Kaponga Street, Wainuiomata

Tel (04) 564 3495 Fax (04) 564 3495
hilwha@xtra.co.nz

Double $100 Single $80 (Continental)
Pet free home
Not suitable for children
1 Queen (1 bdrm)
Bathrooms: 1 Private

Hilary & Neville offer you top quality accommodation in a quiet bush setting just 20 minutes drive from Wellington City. Our ground floor apartment includes 1 double bedroom, private bathroom with heated towel rail, laundry, spacious lounge/living room with gas heating, TV, tea/coffee making facilities and fridge. Nearby attractions include the Rimutaka Forest Park, seal colony and 18 hole golf course. We enjoy gardening, golf, tennis, travel and meeting new people. We look forward to welcoming you to our home. Genuine Kiwi hospitality guaranteed.

Eastbourne *3 km N of Eastbourne*

Bush House *Homestay*
Belinda Cattermole
12 Waitohu Road, York Bay, Eastbourne

Tel (04) 568 5250 or 027 408 9648
Fax (04) 568 5250
belindacat@paradise.net.nz

Double $100 Single $75 (Full breakfast)
Dinner by arrangement
1 Double 1 Single (2 bdrm)
Bathrooms: 1 Family share 1 Private

Come and enjoy the peace and tranquility of the Eastern Bays. You will be hosted in a restored 1920's settler cottage nestled amongst native bush and looking towards the Kaikoura mountains of the South Island. My love of cordon-bleu cooking and the pleasures of the table are satisfied through the use of my country kitchen and dining room. Other attractions: A Devon Rex cat. Eastbourne is a small seaside village across the harbour from Wellington City with a range of attractions.

Eastbourne *12 km E of Wellington*

Treetops Hideaway *B&B Apartment with Kitchen sofabeds in lounge*
Robyn & Roger Cooper
7 Huia Road, Days Bay, Eastbourne

Tel (04) 562 7692 or 027 616 9826
Fax (04) 562 7690
bnb@treetops.net.nz   www.treetops.net.nz

Double $145-$165 Single $115-$135
(Continental provisions)
Child $30 Extra adults $40
Visa MC accepted Children welcome
1 Queen (1 bdrm)
Bathrooms: 1 Private

Ride our private cable car through native bush to Treetops, a secluded romantic retreat overlooking Wellington Harbour. Sparkling sea views from bedroom and lounge; fully-equipped kitchenette, bath/shower, phone, computer port, separate entrance. Wake to bellbird song; breakfast on your garden patio; relax with books, games, TV. Portacot, highchair available. Beach, cafes, galleries, ferry to Central Wellington 200 metres (20 minute ride, berths near Te Papa and The Stadium). Inter-island ferry 20 minutes. From the guest book: 'This place is Dreamland - a Kiwi Shangri-la.'

~

Eastbourne *17 km N of Wellington*

Lowry Bay Homestay *B&B Homestay*
Pam & Forde Clarke
35 Cheviot Road, Lowry Bay, Eastbourne, Wellington

Tel (04) 568 4407 or 0508 266 546
Fax (04) 568 4408
homestay@lowrybay.co.nz   www.lowrybay.co.nz

Double $100-$130 Single $80-$110 (Full breakfast)
Child negotiable
Visa MC Diners Amex accepted
Pet free home Children welcome
1 King/Twin 1 Queen 1 Single (2 bdrm)
Bathrooms: 1 Private

Enjoy our hospitality. Warm, restful, peaceful, yet close to Wellington and Hutt Cities, transport, local restaurants and art galleries. Play tennis on our court, stroll to the beach, walk in the bush, sail on our 28 foot yacht, or relax under a sun umbrella on the deck. Native birds abound. Our sunny, elegant bedrooms have garden views, TV, tea/coffee and central heating. We share with our 2 grown up daughters, Isabella and Kirsty, interests in sailing, skiing, tennis, ballet and theatre. Laundry. From SH2 follow Petone signs then Eastbourne.

~

Eastbourne *17 km E of Wellington*

Frinton by the Sea *B&B Homestay boutique bed and breakfast*
Wendy & Doug Stephenson
55 Rona Street, Eastbourne, Wellington

Tel (04) 562 7540 or 0274 417365 Fax (04) 562 7860
frinton@xtra.co.nz   www.frintonbythesea.co.nz

Double $125-$145 Single $100-$130
(Special breakfast) Child not suitable
Dinner by arrangement   Discounts for extended stays
Visa MC accepted Not suitable for children
2 Queen (2 bdrm)
Bathrooms: 1 Ensuite 1 Private
Private bathroom with double 3 cornered bath

You are invited to share in the peace and tranquillity of our bush clad home overlooking Wellington Harbour. We offer cosy well appointed bedrooms with doors opening out onto a balcony. Enjoy the unique village atmosphere of Eastbourne with its restaurants, galleries, gift shops and beach, or take the harbour ferry to Wellington. Our interests are the arts, theatre and music. Wendy, Doug, our golden lab Max, JR Missy and 2 cuddly cats look forward to greeting you. Be assured of a warm welcome in our smoke-free haven.

Wellington

Eastbourne *20 km E of Wellington*

The Anchorage *B&B Homestay*
Bet & Wal Louden
107 Marine Parade, Eastbourne, Wellington

Tel (04) 562 8310 or 021 329 993
betandwal@paradise.net.nz

Double $130 Single $100 (Continental)
Extra guests $50
Visa MC accepted
Children welcome
1 Queen 1 Single (2 bdrm)
Bathrooms: 1 Private

Welcome to our waterfront property, wonderful
views of Wellington Harbour and city. One minute walk to Eastbourne Village and wharf, supermarket, cafes, restaurants, pub, antique shops and art gallery. We offer for the more adventurous a choice of guided bush walks from an easy 2 hours to a demanding 7 hours (bookings essential; Mon-Friday only), panoramic views of Wellington Harbour, outstanding beech, northern rata and podocarp forests. Coastal walks (mountain bike rides) to Pencarrow Lighthouse. Kayak trips also available. Labrador, Splash on property.

Wellington - Khandallah *7 km N of Wellington*

Clothier Homestay *Homestay*
Sue & Ted Clothier
22 Lohia Street, Khandallah, Wellington

Tel (04) 479 1180 or 025 246 6158
Fax (04) 479 2717
sclothier@xtra.co.nz

Double $100 Single $70 (Full breakfast)
Not suitable for children
1 Twin (1 bdrm)
Bathrooms: 1 Ensuite

This is a lovely, sunny and warm open plan home with
glorious harbour and city views. A quiet easily accessible
street just 10 minutes from the city and 5 minutes from the ferry. Close to Khandallah Village where you can make use of the excellent local restaurant, cafe or English country pub. We are a non-smoking household. Another family member is an aristocratic white cat called Dali. We enjoy sharing our home with our guests.

Wellington - Khandallah *6 km N of Wellington*

The Loft in Wellington *B&B Separate Suite*
Phillippa & Simon Plimmer
6 Delhi Crescent, Khandallah, Wellington

Tel (04) 938 5015 or 021 448 491
plimmers@paradise.net.nz

Double $120 Single $90 (Full breakfast)
Visa MC accepted
Pet free home
Not suitable for children
1 Queen (1 bdrm)
Bathrooms: 1 Ensuite

The Loft in Wellington offers the discerning traveller comfort and style in a beautifully appointed self-contained studio (no cooking facilities). Enjoy complete privacy with your own entrance and new ensuite bathroom. Sky TV, off-street parking, laundry, email/phone/internet access available. 10 minutes from downtown Wellington. 300 metres to local train and bus. 15 minutes train ride direct to Westpac Stadium. 500 metres from Khandallah Village and local restaurants. Studio not suitable for pets. We have 2 young boys, Ben and Sam.

Wellington - Ngaio *7 km NW of Wellington*

Ngaio Homestay *B&B Homestay Apartments with Kitchen*
Jennifer & Christopher Timmings
56 Fox Street, Ngaio, Wellington

Tel (04) 479 5325 Fax (04) 479 4325
jennifer.timmings@clear.net.nz

Double $130-$140 Single $100-$140 (Continental)
Child negotiable Dinner $35pp by arrangement
Self-contained $130 double, extra person $45
Visa MC accepted
1 Queen 1 Double 1 Twin 3 Single (4 bdrm)
Bathrooms: 3 Ensuite 1 Private

Welcome to Wonderful Wellington! Share your visit with
us and enjoy helpful personal hospitality! Our unusual multi-
level open plan character home [built1960] is in the suburb
of Ngaio. Guests may leave their car here and take the train to
CBD [10 minutes]

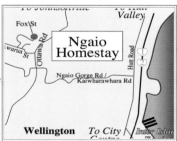

Our double room has tea/coffee facilities, quality bedding,
tiled ensuite and french doors opening onto a deck and private
jungle garden. Breakfast is continental. Evening meals an
optional extra.

2 self-contained apartments, 1 queen, 1 twin, adjacent to our
property, are comfortable, convenient, tastefully furnished and
recently re-decorated. Each apartment also has a couch with a
fold-out bed in lounge, fully equipped kitchen, shower, bath,
laundry facilities, cable TV, phone and internet [small fee]
There is a large garden with trees, birds and views. Perfect for
business, holiday or relocating.

Jennifer plays harp at home and live piano music daily in
NZ's top department store. Our adult son Christopher lives
at home and is a computer whiz. Compliment from guest:
"This is a home where there is beautiful music, art and love."
Do come and share! Please phone before 11am or after 3pm
or fax or email. Bookings essential.

Wellington - Karori *5 km W of Wellington*

Campbell Homestay *Homestay*

Murray & Elaine Campbell

83 Campbell Street, Karori, Wellington

Tel (04) 476 6110 or 027 44766110
Fax (04) 476 6593   ctool@ihug.co.nz

Double $100 Single $65 (Continental)
Child half price Dinner $30
Visa MC accepted Children and pets welcome
1 Queen 2 Twin 4 Single (3 bdrm)
Bathrooms: 1 Guest share

Welcome to our quiet and spacious home in the suburb of Karori, 5 minutes from the central city. We are happy to pick you up from ferry, train, bus or airport terminals and of course make sure you do not miss your onward connection. We are situated just off the main road near our Karori Village, close to the Karori Wildlife Sanctuary, botanic gardens and Otari-Wilton's bush, Cable Car, historic Thorndon's boutique shopping centre, Katherine Masefield's birthplace and Westpac Stadium.

Dine with us, or eat out at the local taverns, restaurants or cafes. Or enjoy our local village shops. We are on 3 bus routes, so guests, if they wish, can leave their car off the street and take the bus into the city. Wonderful Wellington is a dynamic ever changing compact city where it is easy to walk from one sight to next and with

simply the most friendly helpful people. Take advantage of Wellington's cultural events: orchestra, ballet, opera, galleries and theatres. Visit our fabulous modern museum, Te Papa or take a shuttle ferry across the harbour.

We have 3 guest bedrooms: 1 large queen, 1 large twin, 1 smaller twin/single room. Guests have the sole use of a shower room, separate toilet and a full-sized bathroom. Relax and make yourself at home - use our laundry, large garden, spacious lounge, email/internet facilities. Meet Charlie, our border collie dog. Children of all ages welcome. Our large home is perfect for business travellers or families relocating. Weekly rates on application Evening meals are an optional extra, $30 per person. From the motorway, when coming into Wellington from the north, take the Hawkestone Street/Karori exit off the motorway and follow the signs up past the botanic gardens, through the tunnel, up the hill into the Karori Village

Wellington - Karori *4 km W of Wellington CBD*

Bristow Place *B&B Apartment with Kitchen*
Helen & Tony Thomson
8 Bristow Place, Karori, Wellington

Tel (04) 476 6291 or 021 656 825
Fax (04) 476 6293
h.t.thomson@xtra.co.nz

Double $160-$200 **Single** $120-$160 (Full breakfast)
Dinner by arrangement
Long stay or self-catered by arrangement
Visa MC accepted Children welcome
1 Queen 2 Double (2 bdrm)
Bathrooms: 2 Private

We offer a private apartment, able to sleep up to 4, that can be enjoyed either as a regular B&B facility or on a self-catered, self-serviced basis. In addition we have another guestroom with double bed and private bathroom. Enjoy Sky TV, electric blankets, bathrobes, heated towel rails, etc. Share coffee and conversation with us. We enjoy music, theatre, travel, sports and bridge. German spoken. Inner suburb location with ample parking, good transport and local shops and restaurants. Internet, fax and laundry service at small charges.

Wellington - Karori *5 km W of Wellington*

Karori Cottage *Cottage with Kitchen*
Kaye & Peter Eady
11 Shirley Street, Karori, Wellington

Tel (04) 977 5104
eady1@paradise.net.nz

Double $120-$140 (Continental)
Child $20
Children welcome
1 Queen 1 Twin (2 bdrm)
Bathrooms: 1 Private

A cosy self-contained cottage at the rear of our section with drive on access. Queen and twin bedrooms and bathroom upstairs, lounge/dining area with open fire and kitchen downstairs opening onto a sunny courtyard. Children can play on the large front lawn, climb trees and share the trampoline with our 3 children (9, 12 and 14 years). Laundry facilities. Close to bus route and great local deli/cafe.

Wellington - Karori *6 km W of Wellington*

Norlan Homestay *Homestay*
Dale Mansill
15 Cathie Place, Karori, Wellington

Tel (04) 476 4469 Fax (04) 476 4472
dale.mansill@xtra.co.nz

Double $95 **Single** $60 (Continental)
Dinner by arrangement Twin $90
Children welcome
1 Queen 1 Twin 1 Single (2 bdrm)
Bathrooms: 1 Ensuite 1 Family share

Enjoy comfort and good company at Norlan Homestay in the suburb of Karori 15 minutes from the city centre. Close to transport, local shops, restaurants, and cable car. Relax in front of the log burner with Sox the cat or take advantage of Wellington's many sights and cultural activities. Continental breakfast provided. Laundry facilities, internet, Sky TV available. Plenty of parking. Happy to pick up from airport or ferry terminals. Choice of queen with ensuite and single or twin share bathroom. Dinner by arrangement.

Wellington - Wadestown *2.5 km NW of Wellington*
The Nikau Palms Bed & Breakfast *B&B*
Diane & Bill Boyd
95 Sar Street, Wadestown, Wellington

Tel (04) 499 4513 Fax (04) 499 4517
thenikaupalms@xtra.co.nz
www.thenikaupalms.co.nz

Double $120-$160 Single $100-$115 (Full breakfast)
Visa MC accepted
2 Queen 1 Single (2 bdrm)
Bathrooms: 2 Ensuite

You are invited to share our spectacular views of Wellington Harbour overlooking the city, ferry and Westpac Stadium, all within walking distance. Our home is a few minutes drive from Wellington's attractions, Historic Thorndon's restaurants, shops and Heritage Trail and Katherine Mansfield's birthplace. The bedrooms include ensuites, one with private sitting room. Full cooked or continental breakfast provided. The guests' dining room includes tea and coffee making facilities and refrigerator. Off street parking provided

Wellington - Wadestown *2 km N of Wellington*
Harbour Lodge Wellington *B&B*
Lou & Chris Bradshaw
200 Barnard Street, Wadestown, Wellington

Tel (04) 976 5677 or 021 032 6497
lou@harbourlodgewellington.com
www.harbourlodgewellington.com

Double $180-$260 (Continental)
Child negotiable
Visa MC Amex accepted
Children welcome
4 King (4 bdrm)
Bathrooms: 4 Ensuite

Let your stresses be gently lulled away in the luxurious comfort of this beautiful new lodge. Admire the fabulous views of Wellington Harbour from the large sunny deck. Swim in the 11 metre indoor heated pool or take a spa. Laze in the comfort of a large guest lounge with an open fire and stunning harbour views. All this is only a few minutes drive from central Wellington, ferry terminal or Wellington Stadium. Children of all ages welcome, no pets please.

Wellington - Wadestown *2.3 km N of Central Wellington*
Annaday Homestay *B&B*
Anne & David Denton
39 Wadestown Road, Wellington

Tel (04) 499 1827 Fax (04) 499 9561
annaday@tavis.co.nz
www.tavis.co.nz/annaday

Double $120-$160 Single $90-$130 (Full breakfast)
Child $20
Dinner $15-$35
Cot, Spa, Sauna $5 each Pet free home
Children and pets welcome
 2 King/Twin1 King 2 Queen 1 Double 2 Twin
(5 bdrm)
Bathrooms: 1 Ensuite 2 Family share 1 Guest share

For a comfortable, convenient and interesting stay in the capital city, try this lovely restored character home. There's music, books, art and technology inside, and glorious views outside. Hosts who take trouble to meet your needs. Guest lounge with kitchenette. Many extra services including transport available. Pets accommodated - none resident. Children welcome - one resident.

Wellington - Kelburn *1 km W of Wellington Central*

Rawhiti *B&B*
Annabel Leask
40 Rawhiti Terrace, Kelburn, Wellington

Tel (04) 934 4859 Fax (04) 972 4859
rawhiti@paradise.net.nz   www.rawhiti.co.nz

Double $190-$264 Single $165-$185
(Special breakfast)
Longer stay rates available
Visa MC accepted Children welcome
1 King/Twin1 King (2 bdrm)
Bathrooms: 2 Ensuite
1 with bath and shower; 1 with shower

Rawhiti is located in the prime suburb of Kelburn and within walking distance of the city centre. Magnificent views of harbour and city are seen from all rooms including the small private garden at the rear. A charming 1903 2 storeyed Victorian home is furnished to create an elegant and tranquil ambience. It's historical features, wonderful outlook and quality chattels combine to offer guests a special stay in Wellington. A 2 minute walk to the cable car, botanic gardens and Victoria University.

Wellington - Kelburn *2 km W of Wellington*

Rangiora B&B *B&B Homestay*
Lesley & Malcolm Shaw
177 Glenmore Street, Kelburn, Wellington 6005

Tel (04) 475 9888
rangiora.bnb@xtra.co.nz
www.rangiorabnb.co.nz

Double $120 Single $90 (Continental)
Child negotiable
Visa MC accepted
Children welcome
1 Queen 1 Double (2 bdrm)
Bathrooms: 1 Guest share

Location, location, location!!! Our modern hillside home is very easy to find. From north, take the Hawkestone Street motorway exit, follow brown signs for 1km to botanic gardens. We are another 1km on the left past the gardens entrance. 5 minutes drive from central city, stadium, ferry/bus/train terminals. Walking distance from 8 restaurants, cable car, Victoria University & Karori Sanctuary. Tea/coffee/TV in rooms. Free email access. On-street parking. Courtesy car from/to ferry/bus/train. On city bus route. We have a small dog named Patsy.

Wellington - Aro Valley *2 km SW of Information Centre*

Millie's Bed & Breakfast *B&B Homestay*
Miriam Busby
33 Holloway Road, Aro Valley, Wellington

Tel (04) 381 2968 or 021 254 7308
Fax (04) 381 2969
miriam.busby@paradise.net.nz
www.milliesbb.co.nz

Double $120 Single $80 (Full breakfast)
Child $40 Dinner $14.00
1 Double 1 Single (2 bdrm)
Bathrooms: 1 Family share

Named after Millie, the pet cat, at Millie's you awake to the sound of native birdsong. The house is nestled in a bushy valley near the Karori Sanctuary, and is situated on a heritage trail. Millie's is close to a bus-stop, Aro Street cafes, restaurants and shops. 20 minutes walk to city. Free off-street parking available. Complimentary breakfast. 1 extra divan bed in kitchen. Deck with BBQ. Dinner, scenic drives, walks & therapeutic, art sessions are extra services available.

Wellington - Oriental Bay *0.75 km N of Wellington*

No 11 *B&B*
Virginia Barton-Chapple
11 Hay Street, Oriental Bay, Wellington

Tel (04) 801 9290 Fax (04) 801 9295
v.barton-chapple@xtra.co.nz

Double $130-$150 **Single** $110-$125 (Full breakfast)
Visa MC accepted
1 King/Twin (1 bdrm)
Bathrooms: 1 Family share

Step up to a bed & breakfast with stunning views of Wellington Harbour and the inner city. No 11 is an easy stroll to Te Papa: the museum of New Zealand, the City Art Gallery, all the major theatres and cinemas, great restaurants and cafes. Virginia has extensive knowledge of what's going on, and where to go. The comfortable room has an adjacent bathroom, electric blankets, and tea & coffee facilities. Breakfast will be an occasion. Cat in residence.

Wellington - Mt Cook *In Wellington*

Apartment One *B&B Homestay*
Jim & Colleen Bargh
2 King Street, Mt Cook, Wellington

Tel (04) 385 1112 or 027 247 8145
027 275 0913
apartmentone@yahoo.co.nz

Double $130-$140 **Single** $90-$100 (Full breakfast)
Visa MC accepted
Not suitable for children
2 Queen (2 bdrm)
Bathrooms: 2 Ensuite

Experience apartment living in the city. We moved off the farm into our converted warehouse to try city life. We love its ever-changing beauty and the people are simply the best. Come try it for yourself. Buses depart every few minutes. 2 minutes walk to the Basin Reserve and 10-15 minutes walk to Courtenay Place (Wellington's restaurant, cafe and theatre district). Less than 10 minutes drive to the ferry terminal and airport. We serve a deluxe breakfast to get you through your eventful day.

Wellington - Mt Victoria *1 km E of Central Wellington*

Scarborough House *B&B Homestay*
Sue Hiles & Miles Davidson
36 Scarborough Terrace, Mt Victoria, Wellington

Tel (04) 801 8534 or 027 450 1346
Fax (04) 801 8536
info@scarborough-house.co.nz
www.scarborough-house.co.nz

Double $145-$160 **Single** $120 (Full breakfast)
Visa MC accepted
1 King/Twin 1 Queen (2 bdrm)
Bathrooms: 2 Private

Enjoy a hassle-free visit to Wellington. Share our modern centrally-heated home in sunny Mt Victoria. Walk to city centre, Te Papa Museum, Courtenay Place with its restaurants and nightlife, Oriental Bay beach and the waterfront. 10 minutes drive from airport and ferry terminal. Option of king, queen or twin accommodation. Private guest bathrooms. Breakfast of your choice with fresh seasonal fruits. Tea/coffee facilities, hairdryer, bathrobes, Sky Digital TV, laundry and garaging available. Our interests include promoting Wellington, travel, skiing, golf. Children over 12 welcome.

Wellington - Mt Victoria *0.5 km E of Central Wellington*

Villa Vittorio *B&B Homestay*

Annette & Logan Russell

6 Hawker Street, Mt Victoria, Wellington

Tel (04) 801 5761 or 027 432 1267
Fax (04) 801 5762
villa@villavittorio.co.nz
www.villavittorio.co.nz

Double $180-$220 Single $125-$135 (Full breakfast)
Dinner from $50
Visa MC Diners Amex accepted
1 Double (1 bdrm)
Bathrooms: 1 Private

Welcome to Villa Vittrio. Centrally located close by Courtenay Place. Short walk to restaurants, theatres, shopping, conference centres, Te Papa Museum, Parliament & Stadium. Guest bedroom with TV, tea & coffee facilities. Adjoining sitting room with balcony overlooking city. Bathroom with shower and bath.

Breakfast served in Italian styled dining room or outside in courtyard. We enjoy having guests, having travelled extensively ourselves. Transport and gourmet dinner by arrangement. Garaging and laundry at small charge. No children or pets.

Directions: phone, fax, email or write.

Wellington

Wellington - Mt Victoria *In Wellington City*

Austinvilla *B&B Apartment with Kitchen*
Averil & Ian
11 Austin Street, Mt Victoria, Wellington

Tel (04) 385 8334 or 027 273 7760
Fax (04) 385 8336
info@austinvilla.co.nz   www.austinvilla.co.nz

Double $120-$160 Single $100-$120 (Continental)
Visa MC accepted
Children welcome
2 Queen (2 bdrm)
Bathrooms: 2 Ensuite

Top location: a warm welcome to one of Mt Victoria's most elegant turn of the century villas. Set amongst beautiful gardens, and only a few minutes walk to theatres, restaurants, Oriental Bay and Te Papa. Close to public transport and short drive to airport, ferries, and Westpac Stadium. 2 spacious, elegant apartments offer sun, privacy, and include kitchen, queen bed, ensuite with bath and shower, lounge, cable TV, and phone. Apartments have french doors to private courtyard and own entrance way. Laundry facilities and garaging available. Continental breakfast provided. Children welcome. Smoke-free.

Wellington - Roseneath *3 km E of Wellington*

Harbourview Homestay and B&B *B&B Homestay*
Hilda & Geoff Stedman
125 Te Anau Road, Roseneath, Wellington

Tel (04) 386 1043 or 021 0386 351
hildastedman@clear.net.nz
nzhomestay.co.nz/harbourview_homestay

Double $120-$170 Single $95-$110 (Full breakfast)
Dinner from $35
Visa MC accepted
Children welcome
1 Double 2 Single (2 bdrm)
Bathrooms: 2 Private

Five minutes drive from Wellington city, 10 minutes drive from the airport and on the No. 14 bus route. The house offers comfortable hospitality and elegance. Each bedroom opens to a wide deck, offering expansive views of Wellington harbour. Pleasantly decorated rooms quality beds and linen, separate guest's bathroom with shower and spa bath. Harbourview is situated in a peaceful setting close to the city, catering for Businesspeople, Tourists and Honeymooners. A surcharge will be added if paying by credit card.

Wellington - Hataitai *3 km E of Wellington CBD*

Top O' T'ill *B&B Homestay Apartment with Kitchen*
Cathryn & Dennis Riley
2 Waitoa Road, Hataitai, Wellington 6003

Tel (04) 976 2718 or 025 716 482
Fax (04) 976 2719
top.o.hill@xtra.co.nz   www.topotill-homestay.co.nz

Double $110-$130 Single $70-$110 (Full breakfast)
Self-contained $110-$130
Visa MC accepted   Not suitable for children
2 Queen 1 Twin 1 Single (4 bdrm)
Bathrooms: 2 Ensuite 1 Guest share 1
Private Studio has ensuite

Hataitai - 'breath of the ocean', is a popular eastern suburb midway between the airport and central Wellington. City attractions are 5-10 minutes by bus or car. Our comfortable family home of 60 years is a welcome retreat for guests. The quality studio/apartment is fully equipped - long and short term rates on application. We share a range of cultural interests, have travelled widely, and will help you make the most of your visit to Wellington. Unsuitable for young children. @home NZ approved. Directions: included in web site.

236

Wellington - Brooklyn (city end) *3 km SW of Wellington City Centre*

Karepa *Homestay*
Ann & Tom Hodgson
56 Karepa Street, Brooklyn, Wellington

Tel (04) 384 4193 Fax (04) 384 4180
golf@xtra.co.nz
www.holidayletting.co.nz/karepa

Double $130-$165 Single $95-$120 (Full breakfast)
Child by arrangement Dinner $35 by arrangement
Extra guest $35pp
Visa MC accepted
Children welcome
2 King 1 Double 1 Single (3 bdrm)
Bathrooms: 1 Ensuite 1 Guest share

Stay at Karepa, our sunny, spacious home overlooking city, harbour and mountains. The secluded rear garden adjoins native bush. Private guest rooms have TV and tea/coffee facilities. City 5 minutes, ferry 10 and airport 15. Residents of 23 years, ex-UK, we have travelled widely, play golf and tennis, and enjoy Wellington's many attractions. Ann gardens and Tom watches from his deckchair. On-site parking. Bus at door. Laundry facilities. Sorry, no smokers or pets. Please phone/fax for directions.

Wellington - Vogeltown *3 km S of Wellington CBD*

Finnimore House *B&B Homestay*
Willie & Kathleen Ryan
2 Dransfield Street, Vogeltown, Wellington

Tel (04) 389 9894 Fax (04) 389 9894
w.f.ryan@xtra.co.nz
www.finnimorehouse.co.nz

Double $95-$120 Single $75-$90 (Full breakfast)
Child $20
Visa MC accepted Children welcome
2 Queen 2 Single (2 bdrm)
Bathrooms: 1 Guest share

Welcome to our Victorian manor 5 minutes drive from downtown Wellington. Your hosts, Willie and Kathleen Ryan, offer a warm welcome, good conversation, large comfortable rooms and a hearty breakfast. We guarantee hospitality, from a traditional B&B experience, to a welcoming family homestay with a genuine Irish flavour. Our great location is close to: airport, ferries, local cafes, Basin Reserve, hospital, Massey University, Hurricanes rugby training ground, National School of Dance and Drama. Secure parking, convenient public transport. Wellington is yours at Finnimore House.

A homestay is a B&B
where you share the family's living area.

All our B&Bs are non-smoking
unless stated otherwise in the text.

Wellington - Mornington

Ngahere House *Homestay*
Hilary & David Capper
147 The Ridgeway, Mornington, Wellington

Tel (04) 389 4501 or 025 686 7003
h.capper@xtra.co.nz

Double $120 - Please note that agents fees are extra
(Full breakfast)
2 Queen (2 bdrm)
Bathrooms: 1 Family share 1 Private

Relax in our private, sunny and contemporary home. Enjoy the panoramic views of the city, harbour and mountains from our sunroom and deck or sit by our cosy fire. We are 5 minutes drive from downtown Wellington and close to the airport and ferries. Guest facilities - spacious double room, roomy cupboard, coffee table, 2 lounge chairs, televsion, desk and private balcony. The bathrooms are well appointed. We enjoy meeting people, travel, reading, films, walking and the arts, and welcome time spent talking to guests over breakfast.

Wellington - Island Bay/Melrose *4 km S of Courtenay Place*

Buckley Homestay *B&B Separate Suite Also a self-contained fully furnished 2 level townhouse*
Mrs Wilhelmina Muller
51 Buckley Road, Melrose, Island Bay, Wellington

Tel (04) 934 7151 or 025 607 1853 Fax (04) 934 7152
kandwmuller@paradise.net.nz
www.buckleyhomestay.co.nz

Double $95-$130 (Continental)
Child negotiable Dinner by arrangement
Visa MC accepted Children and pets welcome
1 King/Twin 1 Queen 1 Double 3 Single (3 bdrm)
Bathrooms: 1 Family share 1 Private

Large 2 storey sunny home with spectacular scenery and beautiful views over Wellington. New tastefully decorated, private entrance, 1 bedroom, self-contained, double flat with private balcony, TV, conservatory, fridge & microwave. Close to hospitals. We are interested in food, wine, travel, relaxing and meeting people. Willy is a nurse, enjoys cooking, gardening and speaks Dutch. No pets or children at home. Off-street parking is provided. Complimentary tea, coffee & biscuits available, Dinner by arrangement. On bus route. Inspection invited. Also double bedroom with super king-size bed available.

Wellington - Island Bay *6 km S of Welington City Central*
The Lighthouse & The Keep *Self-contained*
Bruce Stokell
326 The Esplanade & 116 The Esplanade, Island Bay, Wellington

Tel (04) 472 4177 or 027 442 5555
Fax (04) 472 4177
bruce@thelighthouse.net.nz
www.thelighthouse.net.nz

Double $180-$200 (Full provisions)
Visa MC accepted
Not suitable for children
1 Double (1 bdrm)
Bathrooms: 1 Private

Island Bay - 10 minutes city centre, 10 minutes airport, 20 minutes ferry terminal.

The Lighthouse is on the south coast and has views of the island, fishing boats in the bay, the beach and rocks, the far coastline, the open sea, the shipping and, on a clear day, the South Island. There are local shops and restaurants.

The Lighthouse has a kitchen and bathroom on the first floor, the bedroom/sitting room on the middle floor and the lookout/bedroom on the top. Romantic.

The Keep is a stone tower just 2 minutes from The Lighthouse. It has a lounge/kitchen on 1 level and a bed with ensuite on the next level. Also a spa bath in the bedroom. It is very cosy and has excellent views of the sea, especially in a storm. Stairs from the bedroom lead to a hatch which opens on to the roof.

Wellington - Island Bay *3 km S of Courtenay Place*
Ma Maison *B&B Boutique B&B*
Margo Frost
9 Tamar Street, Island Bay, Wellington

Tel (04) 383 4018 or 025 2429 827
Fax (04) 383 4018
bedandbreakfast@paradise.net.nz
www.nzwellingtonhomestay.co.nz

Double $120 Single $100 (Full breakfast)
2 Queen (2 bdrm)
Bathrooms: 1 Ensuite 1 Private

Luxury in a warm, comfortable home at a realistic price, our 1920s home is decorated with a French flavour. Drive to door, lovely garden.

The brown guest room has it's own entrance and ensuite, the blue room has private bathroom. Both rooms have queen posturrepedic beds and are equipped with everything to make your stay as comfortable as possible.

Island Bay is a popular seaside suburb with excellent local restaurants. We are 8 minutes by car to the city and very handy to great bus service.

A full delicious breakfast is served at a time to suit you. Resident family cat.

240

Wellington - Island Bay *7 km S of Wellington City Central*

Nature's Touch Guest House *B&B*

B&B Approved

Maarten & Natsuko Groeneveld
25A Happy Valley Rd, Owhiro Bay, Wellington

Tel (04) 383 6977 or 021 490 966
Fax (04) 383 6977
happyvalley@paradise.net.nz
naturestouchguesthouse.com

Double $90-$120 Single $70-$90 (Full breakfast)
Child $45 Dinner $40
Visa MC accepted
Children welcome
1 King 1 Double 1 Single (1 bdrm)
Bathrooms: 1 Family share

Ìt was restful mentally and physically for us having had a
long trip to have warm & homely hospitality while we enjoy
seeing ferry boats in the Cook Strait.î Mr & Mrs Ito and
Mrs Tamakoshi from Japan

We are glad to have been here! We will never forget you.
Clemens & Ans from the Netherlands.

A warm welcome from us and our friendly dog, Lucky!

We are just a short stroll to the beach and the reserve. Only
10 minutes drive to the city, 15 minutes to the ferry terminal and
the airport.

Whole of upstairs is yours to enjoy elevated views as well as privacy.
Natureís Touch Guest House offers a free 45 minute Wild Seals
Tour within an agreed time to the reserve to share the beauty of
nature.

For more info, feel free to contact us anytime.

Island Bay - Wellington *In Wellington*

Island Bay Homestay *Homestay*
Theresa & Jack Stokes
52 High Street, Island Bay, Wellington 6002

Tel (04) 970 3353 or 0800 335 383
Fax (04) 970 3353
tandjstokes@paradise.net.nz
www.wellingtonhomestay.com

Double $80 Single $50 (Full breakfast)
2 Double (2 bdrm)
Bathrooms: 2 Private

We live in a Lockwood house, at the end of High Street in a very private section. Our land goes three quarters of the way up the hill and above that is Town Belt. Wonderful views, overlooking the Cook Strait with its ferries, cargo and fishing boats on the move day and night. We see planes landing or taking off (depending on wind direction) but the airport is round a corner and we get no noise from it.

We only let two of our rooms and each has its own private bathroom, just outside the bedroom door. TV in rooms. A warm, comfortable smoke-free home with warm clean comfortable beds and 2 warm owners who enjoy meeting people. We do our best to provide good, old fashioned Homestay, without charging the earth! We have 2 lovely Moggies.

Directions:
From State Highway 1 or 2 take the Aotea Quay turn-off. (From the ferry take the city exit). Follow the main road which bears slightly to the left until you come to a T junction (Oriental Parade). Turn right in to Kent Terrace and get in the right hand lane before going round the Basin Reserve (cricket ground) and in to Adelaide Road. Keep going straight, up the hill and the road becomes The Parade. Keep going until you reach the sea and then turn **SHARP** right (new guests can easily miss this turn-off) into Beach Street. Left and left again in to High Street and up the private road at the end.

From Wellington Airport: take the rear exit (past the cargo warehouses) and turn right. Follow the coast road for 10 minutes and Beach Street is on the right.
For the Navigator we live at - Lat. S.41.20.54 Long E.174.45.54.

Full breakfast 7:30am onwards. Regrets we cannot accept bookings from guests arriving from Australia on the midnight arrivals or guests leaving on the 6am departures.
Not suitable for children under 14.

"We've put a number of friends onto this place as it is so reasonable for such an amazing setting."

"We stayed at Island Bay Homestay with Theresa& Jack Stokes in April. There are no nicer people in this world. We give them a 10."

"With grateful Thanks to Jack who welcomed us at 2.00 in the morning after we had attended a Wedding in Wellington. And special thanks to both Theresa and Jack for the beautiful breakfast and comfy beds and wonderful views."cvv

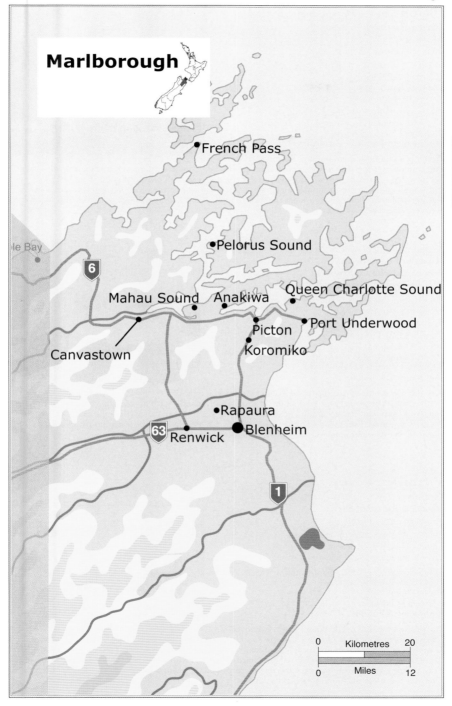

Marlborough

French Pass

Pelorus Sound

6

Mahau Sound   Anakiwa   Queen Charlotte Sound

Canvastown

Picton   Port Underwood

Koromiko

Rapaura

63 Renwick   Blenheim

1

0   Kilometres   20

0   Miles   12

243

Marlborough

Picton *1 km E of Picton Central*

Retreat Inn *B&B Homestay*
Alison & Geoff
20 Lincoln Street, Picton

Tel (03) 573 8160 or 021 143 2224
Fax (03) 573 7799
elliott.orchard@xtra.co.nz
www.retreat-inn.co.nz

Room-rate $100-$130 (Special breakfast)
Visa MC accepted Not suitable for children
2 Queen 2 Single (3 bdrm)
Bathrooms: 1 Ensuite 1 Guest share 1 Private

Set in peaceful bush surroundings, Retreat Inn offers you comfort and rest with a yummy breakfast! 1 guest bedroom downstairs - ensuite queen with outside access to fern/seating area. And 2 rooms upstairs - queen, twin with private or guest share bathroom. Great for a group of 4. Not suitable for children. A 2 night stay is recommended as this diverse and unforgettable Marlborough region has so much to offer. Flat off-street parking. Local pick-up available. A happy 2 person/2 cat household!

Picton *0.25 km SE of Picton*

Rivenhall *B&B Homestay*
Nan & Malcolm Laurenson
118 Wellington Street, Picton

Tel (03) 573 7692 Fax (03) 573 7692
rivenhall.picton@xtra.co.nz

Double $110 Single $80 (Full breakfast)
Dinner $35pp by arrangement
Visa MC accepted
Pet free home Children welcome
1 Queen 1 Double (2 bdrm)
Bathrooms: 2 Private

Up the rise, on the left, at the top of Wellington Street, is Rivenhall. A gracious home with all the warmth, comfort and charm of days gone by, overlooking the town of Picton with its background of surrounding hills. Yet it is an easy walk to the centre of town or the ferry's beyond. Evening meal on request, courtesy car pick up from the ferry, bus or train. Laundry facilities. The Marlborough Sounds start at the bottom of our street.

Picton *In Picton Central*

Grandvue *B&B Apartment with Kitchen*
Rosalie & Russell Mathews
19 Otago Street, Picton

Tel (03) 573 8553 Fax (03) 573 8556
grandvue-mathews@clear.net.nz
www.nzhomestay.co.nz/mathews.htm

Double $100 Single $70 (Continental)
Child $30 Visa MC accepted
Pet free home
1 Queen (1 bdrm)
Bathrooms: 1 Ensuite

Situated on the hills overlooking Picton, Grandvue offers panoramic views of Queen Charlotte Sound and surrounding areas. At the end of a cul-de-sac Grandvue is a quiet haven in a secluded garden, 5 minutes walk to town and its assortment of restaurants. Accommodation is a quality, warm, self-contained apartment with TV, video and access to a barbecue. Feast on scenic views from our upstairs conservatory, while enjoying a delicious and satisfying breakfast. Courtesy transport and laundry facilities available.

Picton *800m km N of Picton*
Echo Lodge *B&B Homestay*
Lyn & Eddie Thoroughgood
5 Rutland Street, Picton

Tel (03) 573 6367 Fax (03) 573 6387
echolodge@xtra.co.nz

Double $90 Single $60 (Full breakfast)
1 Double 1 Twin 1 Single (2 bdrm)
Bathrooms: 2 Ensuite

Lyn, Eddie and our little dog Osca welcome you to home-style comfort at Echo Lodge. Starting your day with a smorgasbord breakfast of home-grown produce and freshly baked bread. A 5 minute stroll into Picton takes you to great restaurants. From our front gate there are lovely bush walks to Bob's Bay, The Snout or Marina. Tea and coffee in your room, ensuite or private facilities, a sunny patio and log fire for chilly nights ensures your comfort. Courtesy car and off-street parking

Picton - Kenepuru Sounds *80 km NE of Havelock*
The Nikaus *B&B Farmstay*
Alison & Robin Bowron
86 Manaroa Road, Waitaria Bay, RD 2, Picton

Tel (03) 573 4432 or 027 454 4712
Fax (03) 573 4432
info@thenikaus.co.nz
www.thenikaus.co.nz

Double $100 Single $50 (Full breakfast)
Dinner $30 Visa MC accepted
1 Queen 2 Single (2 bdrm)
Bathrooms: 1 Guest share

The Nikaus sheep & cattle farm is situated in Waitaria Bay, Kenepuru Sound, 2 hours drive from Blenheim or Picton. We offer friendly personal service in our comfortable spacious home. Large gardens contain rhododendrons, roses, Camellia, lilies and perennials, big sloping lawns and views out to sea. We have Minny (Jack Russel-cross), Other animals include the farm dogs, donkeys, pet wild pigs, turkeys, hens and peacocks. Good hearty country meals, home-grown produce. Operators available for fishing trips, launch charters, golf and various walks.

Picton *In Picton Central*
The White House *Homestay*
Gwen Stevenson
114 High Street, Picton

Tel (03) 573 6767 Fax (03) 573 8871
thewhitehousepicton@xtra.co.nz

Double $65 Single $45 (Continental)
Twin $65
2 Double 3 Single (4 bdrm)
Bathrooms: 2 Guest share

The White House, in Picton's main street, offers affordable luxury - just ask any previous guest - a minute's walk to Picton's fabulous cafes and restaurants for your evening meal. Bedrooms and lounge are upstairs and guests are welcome to make tea/coffee in the kitchen. Laundry available at small charge. Non-smoking. Not suitable for children.

Marlborough

Picton - Ngakuta Bay *11 km W of Picton*

Bayswater *B&B Homestay Apartment with Kitchen*
Paul & Judy Mann
25 Manuka Drive, Ngakuta Bay,
Queen Charlotte Drive, RD 1, Picton

Tel (03) 573 5966 Fax (03) 573 5966

Double $85-$100 Single $65 (Continental)
2 people in self-contained unit $100
4 people in self-contained unit $150
1 Queen 1 Twin (2 bdrm)
Bathrooms: 1 Ensuite 1 Private

Welcome to Bayswater B&B in Ngakuta Bay, situated 11km from Picton and 24km from Havelock on Queen Charlotte Drive in the beautiful Marlborough Sounds. Your accommodation consists of a self-contained apartment with 2 double bedrooms, 2 bathrooms, kitchen, dining and lounge. Spectacular views over Ngakuta Bay and the surrounding bush. The Bay has a picnic area and safe swimming; the Queen Charlotte Track is close by. Remember to bring food if self-catering. Suitable for longer stays. Come and relax in paradise. Complimentary transport available.

Picton - Queen Charlotte Sounds *16 km W of Picton*

Tanglewood *B&B Homestay Separate Suite*
Linda & Stephen Hearn
1744 Queen Charlotte Drive, The Grove, RD 1, Picton

Tel (03) 574 2080 or 027 481 4388
Fax (03) 574 2044
tanglewood.hearn@xtra.co.nz

Double $125 Single $90 (Full breakfast)
Dinner $35 Self-contained $170
Visa MC accepted
2 King/Twin (2 bdrm)
Bathrooms: 2 Ensuite

Nestled amongst the native ferns overlooking Queen Charlotte Sounds. Our private guest wing includes spacious rooms with ensuites, lounge, kitchenette and barbeque area. Relax in our spa surrounded by our beautiful native garden, listen to the birds or take a walk with us to view the glow-worms. Enjoy a delicious generous breakfast before your day's pursuits, swimming, fishing, kayaking, walking the Queen Charlotte Track or exploring Marlborough Wineries. Kiwi hospitality at its best,we look forward to making you welcome.

Pelorus - Mahau Sound *33 km W of Picton*

Ramona *B&B Homestay*
Phyl & Ken Illes
460 Moetapu Bay Road, Mahau Sound, Marlborough

Tel (03) 574 2215 or 025 247 6668
Fax (03) 574 2915
illes@clear.net.nz

Double $110 Single $75 (Continental)
Dinner & lunch by arrangement
Visa MC accepted
Children welcome
2 Double 2 Twin (2 bdrm)
Bathrooms: 1 Private

Our beachfront home on the beautiful Mahau Sound has been designed for you to share. Our guest floor has its own conservatory, here you can view the passing water traffic. Awake to the call of bellbirds and tuis, and after breakfast stroll around our rhododendron garden, or fossick on the beach. In the evening, see our glowworms. Phyl, a quilter and keen gardener, and Ken, a retired builder, will arrange visits to local art and craft studios, at your request. We host only 1 party at a time.

246

Picton - Whatamango Bay *10 km E of Picton*
Whatamango Lodge *B&B Homestay Apartment with Kitchen*
Ralph and Wendy Cass
17 McCormicks Road, Whatamango Bay, Picton

Tel (03) 573 5110 Fax (03) 573 5110
whatamango.lodge@paradise.net.nz
www.picton.co.nz/whatamango

B&B
Approved

Double $120-$150 **Single** $90 (Full breakfast)
Dinner $35
Not suitable for children
2 Queen (2 bdrm)
Bathrooms: 2 Ensuite

Welcome to Whatamango Lodge, situated at the
head of Whatamango Bay, looking out towards Queen
Charlotte Sound. We invite you to share our modern,
waterfront home and enjoy total peace and tranquillity.

Relax on your own private balcony and watch the magnificent birdlife. Take a stroll around the beach or
swim in the crystal clear water. There are also numerous bush walks. You may like to use our dinghy or
fish off the rocks. Kayaks are available to paddle round the bay.

We are situated 10 mins on a sealed road from Picton. Follow the Port Underwood Road from Waikawa
to Whatamango Bay, turn left into McCormicks Road, waterfront location, number 17. A courtesy car is
also available for transport to or from the ferry.

Guest accommodation comprises 1. A self-contained unit (sleeps 4), Queen-sized bedroom, lounge (sofa
bed), full kitchen facilities, large deck. 2. Queen-sized bedroom with ensuite. Use of spacious lounge and
balcony. Laundry facilities available. Sky TV in unit.

Dinner is available by arrangement and features traditional New Zealand cuisine, served with
complimentary wine. For breakfast choose either a full country style cooked breakfast, or a light
continental breakfast, or if you prefer a delectable combination of both. We are a non-smoking
household. Not suitable for children. We have a small dog, Sam

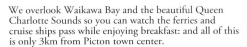

Picton *3 km NE of Picton*
Michiru *B&B*
Rosemary & Paul Royer
247B Waikawa Road, Waikawa, Picton

Tel (03) 573 6793 Fax (03) 573 6793
royer@xtra.co.nz
www.picton.co.nz/for/michiru

Double $110-$130 Single $75 (Special breakfast)
Dinner $35 by arrangement Visa MC accepted
Children welcome
1 King 1 Queen 2 Single (3 bdrm)
Bathrooms: 1 Ensuite 2 Private

B&B
Approved

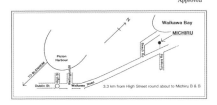

We only have one aim - to give you the finest and most memorable experience that we are able to provide.

We overlook Waikawa Bay and the beautiful Queen Charlotte Sounds so you can watch the ferries and cruise ships pass while enjoying breakfast: and all of this is only 3km from Picton town center.

The bright and sunny rooms are all located on the ground floor with a lovely private guest lounge and garden patio. Guests have the use of laundry facilities, bikes and kayaks around the bay. We invite you to join us for Rosemary's delightful 3 course dinners with a glass of wine (by arrangement). We will of course meet or drop you at the ferry terminal, especially if you are walking the Queen Charlotte Track and don't have your own transport. There is a waterside restaurant and a café/bar within 5 minutes walk of the house. You'll love this location!

Walk the Queen Charlotte Track - Kayak or sail the Queen Charlotte Sounds - Take half or whole day winery tours - Daily dolphin watch tours -Re-live "The Edwin Fox" experience - she's the world's ninth oldest ship - Visit the fascinating "Seahorse World" - Our favourite place - Karaka Point historical site Superb accommodation for the discerning guests!

Picton - Anakiwa *22 km W of Picton*

Tirimoana House *Homestay Apartment with Kitchen*
Jan & Brian Watts
257 Anakiwa Road, RD 1, Picton

Tel (03) 574 2627 Fax (03) 574 2647
jan.w@xtra.co.nz
www.tirimoanahouse.com

Double $110-$150 Single $95 (Full breakfast)
Dinner $35
Self-contained flat (sleeps 5) $110 double
Extra person $20
Visa MC Eftpos accepted
1 King/Twin 3 Queen 1 Double 1 Single (4 bdrm)
Bathrooms: 3 Ensuite 1 Private

Every room in our long-established homestay commands spectacular views down Queen Charlotte Sound. Our considerable reputation has been built on creating a warm and friendly environment for our guests.

Dinners are available using local cuisine and wines. All bedrooms and our stunning Sunrise Suite have own ensuites and self-contained flat has own private deck.

After kayaking, walking, mountain biking or visiting local wineries, relax in our swimming or hot spa pools.

Jan, Brian and Pepsi the poodle would love to meet you. Arrive as guests, leave as friends.

Picton - Queen Charlotte Sound *11 km W of Picton*
Waterfront Bed & Breakfast *B&B Homestay*
Vicki & David Bendell
Queen Charlotte Drive, 2383 Little Ngakuta Bay,
RD 1, Picton

Tel (03) 573 8584 or 021 216 5955
bendell@xtra.co.nz
www.picton.co.nz/for/kotare

Double $145-$165 Single $135 (Full breakfast)
Child $40 Dinner by arrangement
Diners accepted Children welcome
1 Queen 1 Double 2 Single (2 bdrm)
Bathrooms: 1 Ensuite 1 Family share 1 Private

Our waterfront accommodation is as close to the waters edge as you can get. The aptly named Boatshed with ensuite and Pacific Room with private bathroom are seperate from the cottage. A 180 metre jetty is right out front - ideal for fishing or evening stroll to see the water fluoresce. Kayak, fishing rods, sun loungers, petanque, sportscruiser available or row the clinker dinghy with picnic hamper. Handy to Queen Charlotte Track our young family and dog welcome you for a break from the ordinary.

Picton - Koromiko *5 km S of Picton*
Koromiko Valley Homestead *B&B*
Caryll & Vic Hewson
30 Freeths Road, Koromiko, Picton

Tel (03) 573 5674 or 027 240 8632
Fax (03) 573 7682
hewson@clear.net.nz
www.koromikohomestead.co.nz

Double $120 (Full breakfast)
Dinner with prior notice
Visa MC accepted
Not suitable for children
2 Queen (2 bdrm)
Bathrooms: 2 Private

Approved

Koromiko Valley Homestead is situated 5km south of Picton just off State Highway 1. We offer quality accommodation, evening meal, rural setting, ferry & airport transfers with prior request. The home is situated on 10 acres with various animals. Stroll in the large gardens, go for a game of golf on the nearby course. Relax in the spa or enjoy a glass of wine by the fire or on the deck. Sky TV and internet available. Not suitable for children or pets. Friendly resident dog.

Picton *0.5 km W of Picton*
Glengary *B&B*
Glenys & Gary Riggs
5 Seaview Cresent Picton

Tel (03) 573 8317 or 027 498 6388
inquires@glengary.co.nz

Double $100-$120 Single $55 (Continental)
2 King/Twin 2 Queen (3 bdrm)
Bathrooms: 1 Ensuite 1 Guest share

Located a short drive from Picton Ferry Terminal and a few minutes walk to the town centre. Inner harbour across the road. Whether you are interested in visiting wineries, fishing, bush walking, cruising, sea kayaking or simply relaxing in idyllic surroundings Glengary Bed & Breakfast is ideally located to explore the Marlborough area. Your friendly hosts will provide you with the best service to ensure your stay in the beautiful Marlborough Sounds is relaxing and enjoyable. They will pick you up from ferry and provide you with advice on local trips. Family cat in residence.

Picton *In Picton Central*

Palm Haven *B&B Homestay*
Eleanor & Kevin Sexton
15A Otago Street, Picton

Tel (03) 573 5644 Fax (03) 573 5648
palmhaven@xtra.co.nz

Double $120 Single $85 (Continental)
Visa MC accepted
1 King/Twin 3 Queen 2 Twin (4 bdrm)
Bathrooms: 3 Ensuite 1 Private

Couples, families and singles are welcome at Palm Haven, a modern purpose-built home designed for your comfort and convenience with a lovely outlook from the balcony over Picton and Mt Freeth. It's just a few minutes walk to the town centre to cafes, restaurants and all leisure activities. Guest rooms, 3 with queen beds and ensuites, 1 room with twin beds and private bathroom have tea making facilities and TVs. Cot and highchair available. We provide courtesy pick up from the ferry terminal and public transport.

Blenheim *3 km S of Blenheim*

Hillsview *Homestay*
Adrienne & Rex Handley
Please phone for address

Tel (03) 578 9562 Fax (03) 578 9562
aidrex@xtra.co.nz

Double $80-$90 Single $60 (Full breakfast)
Less 10% if pre booked by the night before
1 King/Twin 1 Double 2 Twin (3 bdrm)
Bathrooms: 2 Private

Welcome to our warm, spacious, non-smoking home in a quiet suburb with outdoor pool, off-street parking, and no pets. All beds have quality mattresses, electric blankets and wool underlays. Interests: Rex's (retired airline pilot) - are aviation oriented - models, microlights, homebuilts and gliding. Builds miniature steam locomotives, has 1930 Model A soft-top tourer vintage car and enjoys barbershop singing. Adrienne's - cooking, spinning, woolcraft. Let us share these hobbies, plus our caring personal attention, complimentary beverages and all the comforts of home with you.

Blenheim - Rapaura *12 km NW of Blenheim*

Thainstone *Homestay Cottage with Kitchen*
Vivienne & Jim Murray
120 Giffords Road, RD 3, Rapaura

Tel (03) 572 8823 Fax (03) 572 8623
thainstone@xtra.co.nz
www.thainstone.co.nz

Double $120 Single $70 (Full breakfast)
Self-contained house (sleeps 2-4) $120-$180
Breakfast not provided in self-contained Dinner $35
Visa MC Amex accepted Not suitable for children
1 King 2 Queen 1 Double 1 Twin 1 Single (5 bdrm)
Bathrooms: 1 Ensuite 1 Guest share 1 Private

Our large home is surrounded by vineyards and within walking distance of the Wairau River and several wineries. In our home there are 3 upstairs bedrooms and a guest lounge which opens onto an enclosed, solar heated swimming pool. The self-catering house has 2 bedrooms and is fully equipped for longer stays. We are widely travelled and some interests are bird watching, trout fishing, woodworking and cards. Evening meals, by prior arrangement, are served with Marlborough wines. Unsuitable for children.

Marlborough

Blenheim *500 m W of Blenheim Central*

Beaver B&B *Homestay Cottage with Kitchen*
Jen & Russell Hopkins
60 Beaver Road, Blenheim

Tel (03) 578 8401 or 021 626 151
Fax (03) 578 8401
rdhopkins@xtra.co.nz
marlborough.co.nz/beaver/

Double $90 Single $60 (Continental)
Visa MC accepted
1 Queen (1 bdrm)
Bathrooms: 1 Ensuite

Our self-contained unit can accommodate 1 couple
or a single. Features include your own entrance, queen-size bed, mini kitchen, bathroom with large bath, shower and separate toilet. Use of our laundry can be made upon request. 2 cats and a bird live with us. We have off-street parking and are within 10 minutes walk from central Blenheim. Please phone before 8am or after 4.30pm during the working week. If no response, Jennie can be contacted via her cell-phone. Fax us anytime.

Blenheim *2 km N of Blenheim*

Philmar *B&B Homestay*
Wynnis & Lex Phillips
63 Colemans Road, Blenheim

Tel (03) 577 7788 Fax (03) 577 7788

Double $80 Single $60 (Continental)
Dinner $20pp
2 Queen 1 Twin (3 bdrm)
Bathrooms: 1 Guest share

Welcome to our home 2km from the town centre.
Guests can join us in our spacious sunny living
areas. We both enjoy all TV sports and our other
interests include wood turning, handcrafts and the Lions organisation. Blenheim is an ideal place to visit Picton, Nelson and the many wineries, whale watch, parks and craft shops in the area . Smoking is not encouraged. Just phone to be picked up at airport, train or bus. Dinner on request.

Blenheim

Baxter Homestay *Homestay*
Kathy & Brian Baxter
28 Elisha Drive, Blenheim

Tel (03) 578 3753 or 021 129 2062
Fax (03) 578 3796 baxterart@clear.net.nz
www.baxterhomestay.com

Double $110-$150 (Continental)
Children welcome
1 King/Twin 1 Queen 1 Double (3 bdrm)
Bathrooms: 2 Ensuite 1 Guest share
Bath & shower in king/twin ensuite

Brian, a renowned New Zealand artist, and Kathy, a
keen gardener, welcome you to their spacious, sunny, modern home and art gallery. Original artwork throughout house. TV in all bedrooms (smoke-free). Guests can enjoy magnificent panoramic views over Blenheim and nearby vineyards, or explore terraced gardens of roses, rhododendrons, camellias, perennials, deciduous trees etc. We can arrange tours to wineries, gardens, ski-field, golf courses etc. Laundry facilities. Our interests include gardening, music, travel, fishing, skiing, art, video production, and meeting people from all over the world.

Blenheim *2 km N of Blenheim*

The Willows *B&B Homestay*
Millie Amos
6 The Willows, Springlands, Blenheim

Tel (03) 577 7853 Fax (03) 577 7853

Double $85 Single $60 (Continental)
1 Queen 2 Twin (2 bdrm)
Bathrooms: 1 Private

Only 2km from the centre of town. The Willows is a spacious and modern home in close proximity to shops, restaurants and wineries.
Peaceful location surrounded by lovely gardens. I welcome you to my home, so please phone first.

Blenheim *In Blenheim Central*

Maxwell House *Homestay*
John and Barbara Ryan
82 Maxwell Road, Blenheim

Tel (03) 577 7545 Fax (03) 577 7545
mt.olympus@xtra.co.nz

Double $125 Single $100 (Full breakfast)
Visa MC accepted
Children welcome
1 Queen 1 Twin (2 bdrm)
Bathrooms: 2 Ensuite

Welcome to Marlborough. We invite you to stay at Maxwell House, a grand old Victorian residence. Built in 1880 our home has been elegantly restored and is classified with the Historic Places Trust. Our large guest rooms are individually appointed with ensuite, lounge area, television and tea & coffee making facilities. Breakfast will be a memorable experience, served around the original 1880's kauri table. Set on a large established property Maxwell House is an easy ten minute walk to the town centre. Non-smoking.

Marlborough

Blenheim *0.1 km W of Blenheim*
Henry Maxwell's Central B&B *B&B*
Rae Woodman
28 Henry Street, Blenheim

Tel (03) 578 8086 Fax (03) 578 8086
stay@henrymaxwells.co.nz
www.henrymaxwells.co.nz

Double $100-$140 Single $70 (Full breakfast)
3 Queen 4 Twin 3 Single (4 bdrm)
Bathrooms: 2 Ensuite 1 Private

Welcome to Henrys, a gracious 75 year old home.
Guests have spacious quiet rooms, 2 with ensuites,
2 share bathroom. TV, tea, coffee, cookies and
complimentary port. Queen size beds and large comfortable arm chairs. All overlook gardens. Breakfast
in the unique dining room (maps and charts) is something to remember. 3 minutes stroll to town, many
excellent restaurants, shops, theatre, movies, etc. Find Henrys, corner of Henry and Munro Streets
between High Street and Maxwell Road. Off-street parking. Relax and enjoy the garden and sun.

Blenheim *7 km N of Blenheim*
Blue Ridge Estate *B&B Homestay*
Lesley & Brian Avery
50 O'Dwyers Road, RD 3, Blenheim

Tel (03) 570 2198 Fax (03) 570 2199
stay@blueridge.co.nz
www.blueridge.co.nz

Double $175-$195 Single $150-$175 (Full breakfast)
Dinner by arrangement
Visa MC accepted
2 Queen 2 Twin (3 bdrm)
Bathrooms: 1 Ensuite 2 Private

Set on a 20 acre purpose-designed homestay property,
Blue Ridge Estate, 2002 Marlborough Master Builders' "House of the Year", enjoys a rural setting with
stunning views across vineyards to the Richmond Range and is close to many of Marlborough's fine
wineries, restaurants and gardens. Our home has proven most popular with both international and New
Zealand visitors. Come share our home with Bella our friendly young labrador, where comfort and
privacy will ensure your Marlborough visit is indeed a memorable one.

Blenheim *9 km NW of Blenheim*
Stonehaven Vineyard Homestay *B&B Homestay*
Paulette & John Hansen
414 Rapaura Road, RD 3, Blenheim

Tel (03) 572 9730 or 027 682 1120
Fax (03) 572 9730 stay@stonehavenhomestay.co.nz
www.stonehavenhomestay.co.nz

Double $195-$220 Single $99-$130 (Full breakfast)
Child suitable 10 years and over
Dinner $50pp wine available Visa MC accepted
1 King 1 Queen 1 Twin (3 bdrm)
Bathrooms: 2 Ensuite 1 Private

Stonehaven is surrounded by beautiful gardens
and 17 acres of Sauvignon Blanc vines in the premium grape growing area of Marlborough. Spacious
and comfortable, our home commands exquisite views over the vineyards to the Richmond Ranges.
Close by are some of NZ's most outstanding wineries. Our delicious breakfasts are often served in the
summerhouse overlooking the pool. Dinner available by arrangement We have a cat and a labrador. We
look forward to making your stay with us as relaxing or as active as you choose. Book on-line at
www.stonehavenhomestay.co.nz

Renwick *10 km W of Blenheim*

Clovelly *Homestay*
Don & Sue Clifford
2A Nelson Place, Renwick, Marlborough 7352

Tel (03) 572 9593 or 025 986 917
Fax (03) 572 7293
clifford@actrix.co.nz
www.clovelly.co.nz

Double $130 Single $80 (Special breakfast)
Visa MC accepted
Children welcome
1 King/Twin 1 Queen (2 bdrm)
Bathrooms: 2 Private

Our colonial style home is set in lovely private grounds in the heart of vineyard country. We overlook organic orchards and out to the Richmond Range. Complimentary refreshments on arrival. Visit the quaint local English pub - dine in the village or vineyard restaurants. We are close by a number of prestigious vineyards. Comlimentary bicycles (including a 1938 vintage tandem!) are available for guests to cycle the vinyards. Don,Sue and our Scottish terriers Chloe and Phoebe and cat Sophie, will welcome you most warmly.

Renwick *10 km W of Blenheim*

Olde Mill House B&B & Bike Hire *B&B Homestay*
Diane Sutton
9 Wilson Street, Renwick, Marlborough

Tel (03) 572 8458 or 0800 653 262
0800 Old BNB Fax (03) 572 8458
info@oldemillhouse.co.nz
www.oldemillhouse.co.nz

Double up to $110 Single up to $85 (Continental)
Visa MC accepted
Children welcome
1 Queen 1 Twin (2 bdrm)
Bathrooms: 1 Ensuite 1 Guest share

Welcome to our elevated 1929 three-bedroom character bungalow. Refurbished for your comfort whilst retaining the olde world charm. We have an extensivebarbeque/spa area for guests to relax in and enjoy the views to the Richmond Ranges. We also have complimentary cycle hire for guests to cycle the local wine trail at their leisure. Robert and I both enjoy gardening - and are re-landscaping our property. He is a member of the Ulysses Club of NZ & the Moto Guzzi Association of America. We have two border collie dogs - Rosie & Vinnie.

Canvastown *10 km W of Havelock*

Woodchester *B&B Homestay*
Judy & Ted Tomlinson
84 Te Hora Pa Road, Canvastown, RD 1, Havelock

Tel (03) 574 1123
woodchesterlodge@woodchesterlodge.co.nz
www.woodchesterlodge.co.nz

Double $120 Single $80 (Full breakfast)
Child from $18 Dinner $35
Single divan in queen room Children welcome
1 Queen 1 Twin (2 bdrm)
Bathrooms: 1 Private

Woodchester Lodge, located in historic goldmining Canvastown, is on the Picton, Nelson, Abel Tasman route. Consider three nights as our location provides access to Blenheim and New Zealand's finest wines, also gateway to world famous Pelorus Sounds mailboat trips, Guided fly fishing on nearby Pelours River, bush walking and tramping tracks are prolific. Dinner at the lodge can be arranged, or enjoy renowned mussel seafood from Havelcok restaurants. Ted and I and Mr Fox, our friendly Jack Russel dog, say welcome to Woodchester Lodge and enjoy.

French Pass, Pelorus Sounds *110 km NE of Nelson*

Ngaio Bay Homestay, B&B, & Retreat *B&B Homestay*
Jude & Roger Sonneland
Ngaio Bay, French Pass Road, Pelorus Sounds

Tel (03) 576 5287   homestay@ngaiobay.co.nz
www.ngaiobay.co.nz

Double $155 Single $105 (Full breakfast)
Child $55, under 2 $30 all inclusive
Dinner $35pp, children $15
Visa MC Eftpos accepted Children welcome
2 Queen 3 Single (2 bdrm)
Bathrooms: 2 Private

Ngaio Bay, 2 hours scenic drive from Nelson or Blenheim, in remote Pelorus Sounds wilderness with private beach, near awesome waters of French Pass. The Garden Cottage and Rose & Dolphin offer comfortable private accommodation overlooking beach, garden and bush. A honeymoon favourite. Guests linger at our table enjoying scrumptious food and good conversation, open fire for cool evenings. Organic vegetable garden and orchard, colourful flower garden. Swimming, walking, boating. Private fireheated bath on beach a speciality. Children welcome. 3 loveable labradors.

French Pass *25 km NE of Rai Valley*

Rocklea at Okiwi Bay *B&B Homestay*
Vivienne & Gerhardt Hechenberger
6 Field Terrace, Okiwi Bay, RD 3
Rai Valley, Marlborough

Tel (03) 576 5575 Fax (03) 576 5575
rocklea@xtra.co.nz
www.okiwibay.co.nz

Double $140 Single $120 (Full breakfast)
Child by arrangement Dinner by arrangement
Visa MC accepted
Pet free home Children welcome
1 Queen (1 bdrm)
Bathrooms: 1 Private

Okiwi Bay, on the road to French Pass, is either an hour's drive from Nelson or the Marlborough wineries. Sip a latte on the deck and take in the view, or relax in the garden as you listen to the soft trickle of the fountain. Your spacious room has a fabulous bay view, complete with a TV and CD player. We enjoy the good things in life (fresh air, food, wine and laughter) and we would like to share our piece of paradise with you.

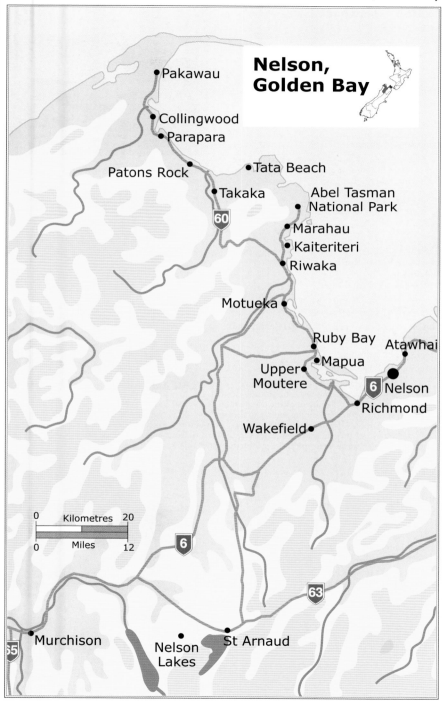

Nelson, Golden Bay

Pakawau

Collingwood

Parapara

Patons Rock

Tata Beach

Takaka

60

Abel Tasman
National Park

Marahau

Kaiteriteri

Riwaka

Motueka

Ruby Bay

Atawhai

Upper
Moutere

Mapua

6 Nelson

Richmond

Wakefield

0   Kilometres   20

0   Miles   12

6

63

Murchison

Nelson
Lakes

St Arnaud

65

Nelson - Atawhai *6 km NE of Nelson*

Mike's B&B *B&B Homestay*
Mike Cooper & Lennane Cooper-Kent
4 Seaton Street, Nelson

Tel (03) 545 1671 Fax (03) 545 1671
cooperkent@actrix.co.nz
www.bnb.co.nz/hosts/kent

Double $65-$75 Single $65-$70 (Full breakfast)
Dinner $35pp with prior notice
Visa MC Diners accepted
2 Queen (2 bdrm)
Bathrooms: 2 Ensuite

5 Minutes from Nelson City we welcome you to
our comfortable home in a quiet neighbourhood with extensive views out over Tasman Bay to the mountains beyond. Our guests accommodation is almost self contained and includes 2 ensuite bedrooms a kitchenette with a fridge/freezer, microwave and complimentary tea and coffee making facilities, a small lounge with TV and housing some of our large collection of books. Laundry facilities are available for your use. Our interests include travel, education, sea fishing and our beautiful schnauzer dog.

Nelson *2 km SW of Nelson*

Harbour View Homestay *B&B Homestay*
Judy Black
11 Fifeshire Crescent, Nelson

Tel (03) 548 8567 Fax (03) 548 8667
harbourview-homestay@xtra.co.nz

Double $125-$145 Single $90-$120 (Continental)
Full breakfast extra $10pp
Visa MC accepted
2 Queen 2 Single (3 bdrm)
Bathrooms: 2 Ensuite 1 Private

Our home is above the harbour entrance. Huge
windows capture spectacular views of beautiful Tasman
Bay, Haulashore Island, Tahunanui Beach, across the sea to Abel Tasman National Park and mountains. Observe from the bedrooms, dining room and decks, ships and pleasure craft cruising by as they enter and leave the harbour. If you can tear yourself away from our magnificent view, within walking distance along the waterfront there are excellent cafes and restaurants. Your hosts, Judy and David and Possum the cat, offer you a warm welcome and a memorable stay.

Nelson *5 km SW of Nelson*

Arapiki *B&B Self-contained Homestay Units*
Kay & Geoff Gudsell
21 Arapiki Road, Stoke, Nelson

Tel (03) 547 3741 Fax (03) 547 3742
bnb@nelsonparadise.co.nz
www.nelsonparadise.co.nz

Double $75-$110 Single $70-$90
Continental breakfast optional $7.50pp
Visa MC accepted
1 Queen 1 Double 1 Single (2 bdrm)
Bathrooms: 2 Ensuite

Enjoy a relaxing holiday in the midst of your trip. The
2 quality smoke-free units in our large home offer comfort, privacy and offstreet parking in a central location. The larger Unit 1 is in a private garden setting. A ranchslider opens on to a deck with outdoor furniture. It has an electric stove, microwave, TV, auto washing machine & phone. Unit 2 has a balcony with seating to enjoy sea and mountain views. It has a microwave, hotplate, TV & phone. We have a tonkinese cat.

Nelson *2 km W of Nelson Central*

Jubilee House *Homestay*

BC&B
Approved

Patsy & Sheridan Parris
107 Quebec Road, Nelson

Tel (03) 548 8511 or 027 448 7767
0800 118 891 Fax (03) 548 8511
info@jubileehouse.co.nz
www.jubileehouse.co.nz

Double $100-$110 Single $70-$80
(Special breakfast)
Not suitable for children
2 Double 2 Single (4 bdrm)
Bathrooms: 1 Guest share

Please Note: We no longer except
credit-cards. www.jubileehouse.co.nz
Many of our guests have told us we
have some of the finest views of any
bed & breakfast in New Zealand.
High on a ridge overlooking the
whole of Nelson City, beautiful
Tasman Bay, mountains and harbour
entrance. Drive downtown in 3
minutes, or try the walkway from the top of Quebec Road to the valley below.

Breakfast is special, our own Muesli made with beech honey and cinnamon, home-made yoghurt, breads, muffins or scones. Taste Sheridan's special blend of coffee. Waffles are our specialities, topped with seasonal fruit and real Canadian maple syrup. You might like to go savoury with salami, tasty bacon and fruit. We can serve something traditional or different, or cater for your special diet, with adequate notice.

As Nelson leads the rest of the country in sunshine hours stay a while in this beautiful region. You may even get to see one of our spectacular sunsets. We are happy to help or advise you on places of interest, or on the many great restaurants and cafe's we have in our city. Use our freephone to book or advise us of your arrival. Book-in time after 4pm preferred. We provide a smoke-free environment, off-street parking.Courtesy pick up from bus depot. KJ our Devon Rex cat may grace you with his presence, he is non-allergenic.

Nelson *3 km E of Nelson*

Brooklands *B&B Homestay*
Lorraine & Barry Signal
106 Brooklands Road, Atawhai, Nelson

Tel (03) 545 1423 Fax (03) 545 1423
barry.lori@xtra.co.nz

Double $100-$140 Single $75 (Full breakfast)
Child by arrangement Dinner $35
Visa MC accepted
Pet free home Children welcome
1 King 1 Queen 1 Double 1 Twin (3 bdrm)
Bathrooms: 1 Ensuite 1 Guest share spa bath

Spacious, luxurious 4 level home with superb sea views.
Spacious well furnished king room on top level. Next level has 2 bedrooms sharing large bathroom with spa bath for 2. 1 bedroom has a private balcony. Spacious indoor/outdoor living areas. We enjoy sports, travel and outdoors. Lorraine and Barry make dolls and bears and enjoys crafts, gardening and cooking. We are close to Nelson's attractions - beaches, crafts, wine trails, national parks, lakes and mountains. We enjoy making new friends. Smoke-free. Courtesy transport available.

Nelson *2.5 km S of Nelson*

Sunset Waterfront B&B *B&B Separate Suite*
Bernie Kirk & Louis Balshaw
455 Rock Road, Nelson

Tel (03) 548 3431 or 027 436 3500
Fax (03) 548 3743
waterfrontnelson@xtra.co.nz

Double $140-$150 Single $110-$120 (Full breakfast)
Self-catering cottage $135
Visa MC accepted
2 Queen 1 Twin 1 Single (2 bdrm)
Bathrooms: 2 Ensuite

Sunset Waterfront B&B provides wonderful
panoramic sea and mountain views of Tasman Bay. Ideally situated to walk to quality seafood restaurants. Stroll along the promenade to enjoy the sunset or take an evening walk along the beach. 10 minutes drive from the airport and bus station. Quiet and secluded location. Freshly brewed coffee and local fresh produce provided. Home-made fruitbread, scones and muffins. Also freshly picked raspberries and strawberries when in season. No children under 12. Bono is our golden retriever. Come enjoy our paradise! Cottage available next door.

Nelson *800m km E of Trafalgar/Hardy intersection*

The Baywick Inn *B&B*
Tim Bayley & Janet Southwick
51 Domett Street, Nelson

Tel (03) 545 6514 Fax (03) 545 6517
baywicks@xtra.co.nz
www.baywicks.com

Double $140-$165 Single $110-$130
(Special breakfast) Dinner $45-$50pp
Visa MC accepted
3 Queen 1 Single (3 bdrm)
Bathrooms: 2 Ensuite 1 Private

Overlooking the Maitai River, Brook Stream and
Centre of New Zealand, this elegantly restored 1885 Victorian offers spacious and luxuriously appointed rooms. Each has its own character and charm with antique furnishings, comfortable beds and modern amenities. Enjoy afternoon tea or cappuccino in the cozy guest lounge, sunroom or garden and chat with Tim about his classic MG's. Janet, a cook by profession, makes breakfast to order, healthy or indulgent, cooked or continental. This Canadian/New Zealand ambiance is enhanced by their lively fox terrier.

Nelson Central *0.8 km E of Nelson*
Sunflower Cottage *B&B*
Marion & Chris Burton
70 Tasman Street, Nelson

Tel (03) 548 1588 Fax (03) 548 1588
marion@sunfloweraccommodation.co.nz
www.sunfloweraccommodation.co.nz

Double $110 Single $75 (Continental)
2 King/Twin 2 Twin 2 Single (2 bdrm)
Bathrooms: 2 Ensuite

Welcome to our home on the banks of the Maitai River. Our large bedrooms, with ensuite bathrooms, are serviced daily with fresh flowers, complimentary basket of fruit and contain TV, microwave, fridge, tea/coffee making facilities, and toaster. Breakfast is self-service. We are very close to Queen's Gardens, Suter Art Gallery and the Botanical Hill, where after an easy walk to the centre of New Zealand, you experience wonderful views over Tasman Bay and Nelson City. Courtesy car to airport or bus depot.

Nelson *2 km S of Nelson*
Beach Front B&B *B&B*
Oriel & Peter Phillips
581 Rocks Road, Nelson

Tel (03) 548 5299 or 021 063 9529
Fax (03) 548 5299 peterp@tasman.net
www.bnb.co.nz

Double $100-$125 Single $100 (Full breakfast)
Visa MC accepted
Not suitable for children
1 Queen 1 Double (2 bdrm)
Bathrooms: 1 Ensuite 1 Private

As recommended by The Rough Guide. Our home is situated overlooking Tahunanui Beach, Haulashore Island and Nelson waterfront with amazing daytime mountain views and magnificent sunsets. Enjoy a wine out on the deck with your hosts. Excellent restaurants and cafes within walking distance, stroll to beach or 5 minute drive to city. Golf course, tennis courts and airport nearby. 1 hour drive to Abel Tasman. Both rooms have ensuite/private bathrooms, quality beds, electric blankets, fridge, TV, tea & coffee making facilities, heaters, iron and hairdryers. Kiwi Host.

Nelson *In Nelson Central*
Peppertree B&B *B&B*
Richard Savill & Carolyn Sygrove
31 Seymour Avenue, Nelson

Tel (03) 546 9881 Fax (03) 546 9881
c.sygrove@clear.net.nz

Double $100 (Continental)
Child $15 Dinner $25-$35 by arrangement
Extra adult $30
Visa MC accepted
Children welcome
1 Queen 1 Double 1 Single (1 bdrm)
Bathrooms: 1 Ensuite

Enjoy space and privacy in our heritage villa, only 10 minutes riverside walk from Nelson's city centre. The master bedroom has an ensuite bathroom and walk-in wardrobe. Your private adjoining rooms include a large lounge with double innersprung sofabed, single bed, heat pump, Sky TV, fridge, microwave, kettle etc. Also sunroom with cane setting and private entrance. Email/internet/fax facilities and off-street parking available. Children are welcome. We have 2 daughters aged 11 and 9, and a friendly cat called Chocolate.

Nelson *0.5 km N of Nelson*

Grampian Villa *B&B*

John & Jo Fitzwater
209 Collingwood Street, Nelson

Tel (03) 545 8209 or 021 459 736 (Jo)
021 969 071 (John) Fax (03) 548 7888
Jo@GrampianVilla.co.nz
GrampianVilla.co.nz

Double $115-$350 Single $115-$350
(Special breakfast)
Child POA Dinner POA
Visa MC Eftpos accepted
Pet free home Not suitable for children
1 King/Twin2 King 5 Queen (8 bdrm)
Bathrooms: 7 Ensuite 1 Private

Located in the tree-lined streets below The
Grampians overlooking Nelson City, historic
Grampian Villa & Cottage are a pleasant 5 minute
walk to Nelson's City Centre.

Grampian Villa offers 4 spacious ensuites (3
SuperKing, 1 Queen w/clawfoot bath and shower)
each have french doors opening onto the spacious
verandahs with views of Nelson City and the sea.
Grampian Cottage offers 4 great value-for-money
Queen ensuites. Grampian Villa

Facilities: spacious tiled showers with heated floors
and large heated towel rails. Wireless DSL internet
access, Writing desk in all rooms., TV, DVD,
in-house movies etc. available in all bedrooms. Complimentary tea/coffee, port, local chocolates, cookies.
Enjoy a Latte/Expresso from our professional coffee machine. Gourmet/Special breakfast changes every
day. TV, VCR, CD, DVD, Stereo & SKY available in Lounge Central heating for your comfort.

We regret that we cannot accommodate children under the age of 12 years or pets.

Nelson *In Central*
Mikonui *B&B*
Elizabeth Osborne
7 Grove Street, Nelson

Tel (03) 548 3623
bess.osborne@xtra.co.nz

Double $100 Single $70 (Full breakfast)
1 Queen 1 Double 1 Twin (3 bdrm)
Bathrooms: 3 Ensuite

One hundred metres from the Visitor Information Centre in the heart of Nelson City is the Mikonui. This delightful house built in the 1920s, has been the Blair Family home for more than 50 years. The lovely rimu staircase leads to 3 tastefully appointed guest rooms all with ensuites. A delicious continental and cooked breakfast are served each morning. Just a short stroll to restaurants, cafes, the cinema and the beautiful Queens Gardens. Come and enjoy the hospitality at the Mikonui, you won't be disappointed. Off-street parking.

Nelson *4.5 km S of Nelson*
Annesbrook House *B&B*
Kath & Tony Charlton
201 Annesbrook Drive, Tahunanui, Nelson

Tel (03) 548 5868 Fax (03) 548 5802
tony.kath@paradise.net.nz
www.annesbrookhouse.co.nz

Double $95 Single $85 (Continental Breakfast)
Not suitable for children
1 Queen 1 Double (2 bdrm)
Bathrooms: 2 Ensuite

Drive up our private drive from Highway 6 to our peaceful home in a quiet sunny tree setting, with views of the sea and mountains. Each bedsit has its own separate entrance, (do your own thing, safe parking, ensuite, TV, fridge, electric blanket, hairdryer, heating, table and chairs, microwave. Telephone available. We are centrally situated near Tahuna Beach, golf, airport, clubs, restaurants. Look for the sign on the lime green letterbox.

Nelson
Lamont B&B *B&B*
Pam & Rex Lucas
167A Tahunanui Drive, Nelson, New Zealand

Tel (03) 548 5551 or 0274 351 678
Fax (03) 548 5501
rexpam@xtra.co.nz

Double $105 Single $65 (Full breakfast)
Child by arrangement
Dinner $30
Children welcome
1 Queen 1 Double (2 bdrm)
Bathrooms: 1 Private

We are in a position to offer high standard accommodation having 2 double bedrooms with own toilet and bathroom facilities. Our house is on a private property in Tahunanui Drive opposite the Nelson Surburban Club where it is possible to get an evening meal most nights. A 2 minute drive to Tahuna Beach and 5 minutes to a number of waterfront restaurants gives plenty of variety and choice. We are a few minutes from the airport. Pick-up from airport and bus. 2 cats in residence

Nelson *In Nelson central*

Haven House Bed & Breakfast *B&B*

Paula Waters
89 Haven Road, Nelson

Tel (03) 545 9321 or 0800 446 783
Fax (03) 545 9320
havengh@xtra.co.nz
www.havenguesthouse.co.nz

Double $120-$140 Single $95-$110 (Continental)
Triple $160 Visa MC Diners Amex Eftpos accepted
Children welcome
2 King 2 Queen 1 Twin (5 bdrm)
Bathrooms: 5 Ensuite

Recent extensive renovations to Haven House, one of Nelson's oldest homes, now provides 5 elegant bedrooms all with ensuite, Sky TV and phone. Originally built circa 1860 for the first collector of customs, it is situated opposite the Trafalgar Center, just a 5 minute walk to town and a 5 minute drive to the beach. A delicious continental breakfast is served in the dining room and tea/coffee making facilities are provided in your room. My 2 delightful daughters, a very friendly burmese cat and I look forward to welcoming you.

Nelson - Atawhai *5 km N of Nelson on SH6*

Strathaven Lodge *B&B Homestay*

Julie & Hugh Briggs
42 Strathaven Place, Atawhai, Nelson

Tel (03) 545 1195 or 027 243 5301
Fax (03) 545 1195 strathavenlodge@xtra.co.nz
www.strathavenlodge.com

Double $125-$175 Single $100-$125 (Full breakfast)
Child $50 Dinner $35pp
Visa MC Diners accepted
Pet free home Children welcome
1 King 1 Queen 1 Single (3 (2 suites) bdrm)
Bathrooms: 2 Private

Imagine relaxing in the terrace spa, appreciating the beautiful sea and mountain views, the spectacular sunsets, listening to the melodious songs of the tuis and bellbirds. Sleep deeply in your comfortable suites, with their own private bathrooms, robes, TV's and hairdryers. Savour Hugh's generous breakfasts! "Bring your runnning shoes to burn off those breakfasts" said one guest. Enjoy this slice of paradise with Hugh and Julie. Share your travel experiences with your well travelled hosts, over a glass of local wine. "It is luxury with a smile".

Nelson - Atawhai *6 km N of Nelson*

Five Smooth Stones *B&B Homestay*

Liz & Chris Chinnery-Jack & Bowyer
784A Atawhai Drive on State Highway 6,
(Off SH 6, second house on right up the drive), Nelson

Tel (03) 545 1230
fivesmoothstones@clear.net.nz

Double $85-$100 (Special breakfast)
Dinner by arrangement
Off season discount available
Pet free home
2 Double (2 bdrm)
Bathrooms: 2 Ensuite

New Zealanders Liz & Chris welcome you to Five Smooth Stones. Not glitzy, up-market or intimidating just wonderful water and mountain Nelson views and warm, welcoming Kiwi hospitality with comfortable indoor/outdoor guest areas. Off-street parking. With prior notice we will cook you a real Kiwi dinner using home grown and local produce. Guests comments include: "lovely stay, great food and conversation." "Beautiful view, super comfy bed and great breakfast." "Lovely to get to know the Kiwis on a more personal basis."

Nelson - Atawhai *7 km N of Nelson*
A Culinary Experience *Luxury B & B Homestay*
Kay & Joe Waller
71 Tresillian Avenue, Atawhai, Nelson

Tel (03) 545 1886 or 0800-89-1886
Fax (03) 545 1869 kpastorius@xtra.co.nz
www.a-culinary-experience.com

Double $120-$175 Single $105-$160
(Special breakfast) Dinner $45-$60
Cooking Classes $85 Visa MC accepted Pets welcome
2 King/Twin2 King (2 bdrm)
Bathrooms: 2 Ensuite heated tile floors

Welcome to our lovely home filled with art, laughter,
great food and our adorable Yorkshire Terrier. We lead gourmet European tours and enjoy cruising our
boat in North America. Kay, author and former cooking school owner, can provide delightful dinners or
cooking classes. Joe, with a degree in naturopathic medicine, offers therapeutic massage. Our boutique
accommodation, near Nelson, is nestled in the hills: beautifully appointed bedrooms, ensuites, spa, sun-
drenched patios, sensational sunsets overlooking bay and mountains. Pets and children by arrangement.
Complementry glass of wine.

Nelson *1 km E of Nelson Central*
Te Maunga - Historic House *B&B Apartment with Kitchen*
Anne Kolless
82 Cleveland Terrace, Nelson

Tel (03) 548 8605
temaungahouse@xtra.co.nz
nelsoncityaccommodation.co.nz

Double $90-$130 Single $75-$90 (Continental)
Child $20 Self-catered $140
Visa MC accepted
Pet free home
1 Queen 2 Double 1 Single (3 bdrm)
Bathrooms: 1 Family share 1 Private

Anne welcomes you to her family's 1930's character, registered Historic
House, a stunning native timbers example. Still mainly as original with modern facilities, Te Maunga sits
on a knoll, within a rambling garden, giving commanding views over Nelson City, sea and Maitai Valley,
and only 5 minutes to downtown. Enjoy your continental style breakfast including local fruits, yoghurts,
cheeses and home-made breads, muffins etc. or maybe your aperitif, while taking in the amazing views.
Self-catered unit is next door!

Nelson - Atawhai *2 km N of Post Office*
Havenview Homestay B&B *B&B Homestay*
Bruce & Shirley Lauchlan
10 Davies Drive, Walters Bluff, Nelson

Tel 03 546 6045 or 027 420 0737
0800 546 604
havenview@paradise.net.nz
www.havenview.co.nz

Double $120-$145 Single $90 (Full breakfast)
Dinner $30pp by arrangement
Visa MC accepted
Not suitable for children
2 Queen 1 Single (3 bdrm)
Bathrooms: 1 Ensuite 1 Private

Welcome to our modern home just a few minutes from the city centre. Relax on our deck with a
complimentary local wine and admire the view across the sea to the Able Tasman Park. Our large ensuite
has a bay window, also with delightful sea views. Share a meal with us as we help you plan your activities
for the next day. Together with our friendly ginger cat we look forward to welcoming you to our home.
Don't miss Nelson's Saturday market..always fun with a great selection of local art and crafts.

Nelson *0.5 km E of Nelson Central*
Sussex House Bed & Breakfast *B&B Historic B&B*
Victoria & David Los
238 Bridge Street, Nelson

Tel (03) 548 9972 Fax (03) 548 9975
reservations@sussex.co.nz
www.sussex.co.nz

Double $130-$160 **Single** $110-$140 (Full breakfast)
Visa MC accepted
5 Queen 3 Twin 3 Single (5 bdrm)
Bathrooms: 4 Ensuite 1 Private

Experience the peace and charm of the past in our fully restored circa 1880s B&B, one of Nelson's original family homes. Situated beside the beautiful Maitai River, Sussex House has retained all the original character and romantic ambience of the era. It is only minutes' walk from central Nelson's award-winning restaurants and cafes, the Queens Gardens, Suter Art Gallery and Botanical Hill (The Centre of NZ) and many good river and bushwalks.

The 5 sunny bedrooms all have TVs and are spacious and charmingly furnished. All rooms have access to the verandahs and complimentary tea and coffee facilities are provided. Breakfast includes a variety of fresh and preserved fruits, muffins baked fresh every morning, hot croissants and pastries, home-made yoghurts, cheeses and a large variety of cereals, rolls, breads and crumpets. Cooked breakfasts are available.

Other facilities include: wheelchair suite; free email/internet station; fax; courtesy phone; laundry facilities; separate lounge for guest entertaining; complimentary port; tea & coffee facilities; very sociable cat (Riley). We have lived overseas and have travelled extensively. We speak French fluently.

Nelson *2 km S of Nelson*

Francois Heights B&B *B&B Separate Suite*
Ellie and Bob
4 Francois Way, Enner Glynn, Nelson

Tel (03) 547 7390 Fax (03) 547 7390
e.rudd@xtra.co.nz
www.francoisheights.co.nz

Double $180-$220 Single $150 (Full breakfast)
Child welcome Visa MC accepted
Children and pets welcome
1 King/Twin 1 Queen 2 Twin (3 bdrm)
Bathrooms: 1 Ensuite 1 Guest share

We offer quality accommodation. The suite has king bed, ensuite and your own comfortable sitting area, with TV and DVD, looking out onto a private patio and over Tasman Bay to the ranges. A barbque is available. The kitchenette has fridge, microwave, toaster and electric jug. We have 2 gorgeous friendly burmese cats. We live on a lifestyle block and have sheep, cattle and free range hens. Our other rooms share a large bathroom and seperate toilet. All rooms have cotton linen,d own duvets, bathrobes & fresh flowers. We are conveniently halfway between the airport and town.

Richmond *0.5 km E of Richmond*

Hunterville *Homestay*
Cecile & Alan Strang
30 Hunter Avenue, Richmond, Nelson

Tel (03) 544 5852 Fax (03) 544 5852
strangsa@clear.net.nz.

Double $100 Single $60 (Full breakfast)
Child half price
Dinner $30 by arrangement
Children and pets welcome
1 King 1 Twin 1 Single (3 bdrm)
Bathrooms: 1 Family share 1 Private

Experience a family welcome in a real Kiwi home with drinks poolside in summer, or a cuppa and home-made biscuits. Our home is up a short driveway where we enjoy birdsong from surrounding trees. We are enroute to Golden Bay and Able Tasman park but just 15 minutes from Nelson City. We travel frequently so appreciate travellers needs;comfortable beds, laundry, generous breakfasts, dinner with local food and wine. Our interests: music, reading, bridge, our friendly dogs (Waldo & Coco) and the company of guests.

Richmond *1 km E of Richmond*

Antiquarian Guest House *B&B*
Robert & Joanne Souch
12A Surrey Road, Richmond, Nelson

Tel (03) 544 0253 or (03) 544 0723
021 417 413 Fax (03) 544 0253
souchebys@clear.net.nz

Double $95 Single $75 (Full breakfast)
Child $10 Visa MC accepted
Children and pets welcome
1 King 1 Queen 1 Twin (3 bdrm)
Bathrooms: 1 Ensuite 1 Guest share

Bob & Joanne Souch welcome you to their peaceful home only 2 minutes from Richmond (15 minutes drive south of Nelson) - excellent base for exploring National Parks, beaches, arts/crafts, ski fields etc. Relax in the garden, beside the swimming pool or in our large TV/guest lounge. Tea/coffee facilities, home-baking and memorable breakfasts. Our family pet is Gemma (friendly border collie). As local antique shop owners we know the area well.

Nelson, Golden Bay

Richmond *12 km SW of Nelson*

Idesia *B&B Homestay*
Jenny & Barry McKee
14 Idesia Grove, Richmond, Nelson

Tel (03) 544 0409 or 0800 361 845
Fax (03) 544 0402
idesian@xtra.co.nz
www.idesia.co.nz

Double $95-$110 Single $80-$85 (Full breakfast)
Dinner $35 by arrangement
Visa MC accepted Pet free home
1 King/Twin 1 Queen (2 bdrm)
Bathrooms: 1 Ensuite 1 Private

A warm welcome to our home centrally located to explore the Nelson/Tasman region. 2km from Highway 6, in a quiet grove. Our modern house is elevated to catch the sun and views. Your choice of full or continental breakfast will include local and home-made produce. Join us for dinner, by prior arrangement, however Richmond's restaurants are within 2km. Pet-free. Smoke-free. Internet access. Off-road parking. With our local experience our aim is to enable you to enjoy our regions attractions for a truly memorable stay.

Wakefield *27 km S of Nelson*

Lansfield Bed & Breakfast Homestay *B&B Homestay*
Dianne & Malcolm Tillier
133, Eighty-Eight Valley Road, Wakefield, Nelson

Tel (03) 541 9789 or 021 131 3415
Fax (03) 541 9780
mdtillier@xtra.co.nz

Double $110-$130 (Full breakfast)
Dinner $25
1 King/Twin 2 Queen (3 bdrm)
Bathrooms: 3 Ensuite

We welcome you to our comfortable new home set in a tranquil valley with rural views. Well situated if travelling via the West Coast and Nelson Lakes and close to Nelson and Tasman Bay. Our interests include gardening and classic cars and we have a Burmese cat, Pheobe. Tea, coffee and home-baking provided, laundry facilities available and dinner is offered, by prior arrangement. A great golf course and cafe are close by. We are located on the outskirts of Wakefield Village, and look forward to meeting you.

Mapua *10 km N of Richmond*

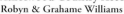

Atholwood Country Accommodation *B&B Self-contained Country Accomodation*
Robyn & Grahame Williams
Bronte Road East, off Coastal Highway 60, near Mapua

Tel (03) 540 2925 or 025 310309
Fax (03) 540 3258 atholwood@xtra.co.nz
www.atholwood.co.nz

Double $180-$200 Single $150
(Special breakfast)
Dinner $45pp by arrangement
Self-contained $200 Visa MC accepted
Children welcome by arrangement
1 King/Twin 2 Queen 3 Single (3 bdrm)
Bathrooms: 3 Ensuite

Beauty, seclusion and tranquillity. We welcome you to share our home situated on the shores of the Waimea Inlet with 2 acres of garden and bush. The Gatehouse is self-contained with full amenities, opening out to a terrace. The guest wing is upstairs within the house and has 2 rooms, each with ensuites and a guest lounge (B&B basis). Start your day with a special breakfast and to finish - award-winning Restaurants are closeby in Mapua. Our beautiful cat Carlos completes the family.

⁓

Mapua *4 km S of Mapua*

Kimeret Place Boutique B&B *Luxury B&B Suites or Apartments*
Clare & Peter Jones
Bronte Road East (off SH60), near Mapua, Nelson

Tel (03) 540 2727 Fax (03) 540 2726
stay@kimeretplace.co.nz
www.kimeretplace.co.nz

Double $185-$340 Single $135-$275
(Special breakfast)
2 bedroom cottage $240-$320
Visa MC Diners accepted
4 King/Twin (4 bdrm)
Bathrooms: 4 Ensuite

A tranquil coastal setting in the heart of the wine & craft region with stunning views, heated swimming pool and spa. Just 4km to award-winning restaurants and 30 minutes from the Abel Tasman National Park. A range of accommodation all with ensuite facilities, (2 with spa-baths), TV, Hi-fi, tea/coffee, fridge, sitting area and views from either balcony or deck. The 2 bedroom cottage also has a kitchenette and dining area. Light meals, local wines, laundry and internet are also available. Dog-lovers may wish to meet our 2 friendly labradors.

⁓

Mapua Village *30 km W of Nelson*

Mapua Seaview B&B *B&B Homestay*
Murray & Diana Brown
40 Langford Drive, Mapua Village, Nelson

Tel (03) 540 2006 seaview@mapua.co.nz
www.mapua.co.nz

Double $125-$115 (Full breakfast)
Visa MC accepted
2 Queen (2 bdrm)
Bathrooms: 2 Ensuite

Seaview B&B commands stunning views of both Waimea Estuary and Richmond Mountains. Local waterfront restaurants are within just a few minutes stroll, enjoying our direct estuary pathway . Easy 25 minute drive to Nelson or Abel Tasman Park, which has become very popular with guests for the variety of day walks. Our modern home is nestled on elevated sunny garden setting being off-street,and very peaceful. Enjoy our estuary vista while breakfasting on the deck. Queen-size beds, private bathrooms, TV etc,in the Estuary View or Garden guest rooms.

Mapua *30 km W of Nelson*

Hartridge *B&B*
Sue & Dennis Brillard
103 Aranui Road, Mapua, Nelson

Tel (03) 540 2079 or 021 189 7622
Fax (03) 540 2079 stay@hartridge.co.nz
www.hartridge.co.nz

Double $130-$185 Single $95-$150 (Continental)
Dinner $45pp Visa MC accepted
Not suitable for children
1 King/Twin 1 Queen 1 Double (3 bdrm)
Bathrooms: 2 Ensuite 1 Private

Delightful 1915 home set in mature gardens in
coastal village of Mapua between Nelson and Abel Tasman National Park. Listed with NZ Historic
Places Trust, Hartridge has period furnishings, inherited fine arts, whilst new upstairs accommodation is
private, sunny and comfortable. Every effort made for that vital good night's sleep. Sue's well presented,
memorable, continental breakfasts include daily baking, fresh local fruit, choice of teas, great coffee.
Den's 1939 Morgan available for a spin. Stroll to cafes, beach, wharf. Off-road parking. Dinner by
arrangement.

~

Upper Moutere *1 km N of Upper Moutere*

Summer Forever *B&B Farmstay Cottage with Kitchen*
Kaye & Owen Pope
28 Kelling Road, Upper Moutere, Nelson

Tel (03) 543 2843 ext 902 or 021 543 780
Fax (03) 543 2847 anathoth@xtra.co.nz
www.summerforever.co.nz

Double $120-$160 Single $120-$150
(Breakfast by arrangement)
Barbecue available Visa MC accepted
Pet free home Not suitable for children
1 Queen (1 bdrm)
Bathrooms: 1 Ensuite

Owen and Kaye Pope founders of Anathoth Jams and Pickles are now offering their Summer Forever
accommodation on their Upper Moutere Raspberry orchard and Roxburgh Apricot orchard in Central
Otago. With all children left home and no resident pets they can offer at Upper Moutere a 1 bedroom
(Queen) self catering flat with ensuite also use of the heated swimming pool and spa to relax and a
barbecue. Roxburgh Apricot orchard has a spacious two bedroom (1 queen, 1 twin) self catering flat.

~

Upper Moutere *18 km S of Motueka*

Neudorfs Gingerbread House *Country B&B & Self-contained Cottage*
Peter Bullock & Doris Lindegger
Neudorf Road, Upper Moutere, Nelson

Tel (03) 543 2472 dandp@gingerbreadhousenz.com
www.gingerbreadhouseNZ.com

Double $85-$150 Single $70-$100 (Continental)
Child under 12 half price Dinner by arrangement
Organic cuisine Pet free home Children welcome
1 King/Twin 2 Queen 1 Double
(2 bdrm in B&B, 1 in Cottage)
Bathrooms: 1 Ensuite in Self-contained Cottage
1 Guest share 1 Private

You need some time and space just to yourself. Relax on the sunny veranda of your self-contained
cottage. Let magic colours and scents, the song of birds and thousands of stars, take you into a world
where you forget daily life's rush and stress. Or join your Swiss/Kiwi hosts and their two lovely
children in their homely country kitchen, sharing stories, local wine and good laughter by the smell of
garden fresh food. Either or, what you'll need for sure, is our central location, a gateway to the regions
attractions.

Ruby Bay *20 km W of Nelson*
Broadsea B&B *B&B*
Rae & John Robinson
42 Broadsea Avenue, Ruby Bay, Nelson

Tel (03) 540 3511 Fax (03) 540 3511

B&B
Approved

Double $120 Single $100 (Full breakfast)
Not suitable children
1 Queen (1 bdrm)
Bathrooms: 1 Ensuite 1 Private

Beach front accommodation, with lovely walks on beach and reserve; cafes and tavern close by, as are wineries and restaurants. We are 15 minutes from Richmond and Motueka, 30 minutes from Nelson and the airport. Abel Tasman and Kaiteriteri are within 40 minutes drive. We want our guests to feel at home and have their privacy in a peaceful and private setting. Coffee, tea and old fashioned home-made biscuits available. Our birman cat Bogart will greet you when you arrive.

Ruby Bay *32 km W of Nelson*
Sandstone House *B&B*
John and Jenny Marchbanks
30 Korepo Road, Ruby Bay, Nelson

Tel (03) 540 3251 Fax (03) 540 3251
sandstone@rubybay.net.nz
www.rubybay.net.nz

B&B
Approved

Double $220 Single $200 (Full breakfast)
Visa MC accepted Not suitable for children
2 Queen (2 bdrm)
Bathrooms: 2 Ensuite

Welcome to Sandstone House - the ideal place to relax - stay a few days and explore this delightful region. We enjoy a maritime and semi-rural situation, ideally situated midway between Nelson and Motueka. We are handy to all the fine attractions that this region has to offer - National Parks, wineries, award winning restaurants, beaches, arts and crafts, the famous Mapua Wharf and lots lots more. We have 35 years local knowledge and are happy to assist you to make the most of your holiday.

Tasman - Upper Moutere *10mins km N of Mouteka*
Maple Grove *B&B Separate Suite*
Judy Stratford & George Page
72 Flaxmore Road, RD 2, Upper Moutere, Nelson

Tel (03) 543 2267 Fax (03) 543 2267
george1judy@xtra.co.nz
www.maplegrove.co.nz

B&B
Approved

Double $130-$160 (Full breakfast)
Child negotiable
Children welcome
1 Queen 1 Double 2 Twin (2 bdrm)
Bathrooms: 1 Private

The perfect private hideaway on 4 acres in the heart of the wine country and at the gateway to Able Tasman National Park. Enjoy ambience and charm of bygone days. Magnificent views of the grand avenue of mature trees, private pond and the mighty Mount Arthur Range. This 2 bedroom boutique cottage with modern conveniences is designed with your comfort in mind. Indulge in home-baked goodies from the breakfast hamper. Close to vineyards, cafes and award-winning restaurants.

Motueka Valley *25 km S of Motueka*

The Kahurangi Brown Trout *B&B Homestay Farmstay Apartment with Kitchen*
David Davies & Heather Lindsay
2292 Westbank Road, Pokororo, RD 1, Motueka

Tel (03) 526 8736 enquiries@kbtrout.co.nz
www.kbtrout.co.nz

Double $130 Single $115 (Full breakfast)
Child $25 share room Dinner $35
Visa MC accepted Children and pets welcome
2 King 1 Single (2 bdrm)
Bathrooms: 2 Ensuite
We also have an outdoor wood fired bath

Enjoy the sound of the beautiful Motueka River
which runs past our house. Step across the road for
trout fishing, or a refreshing swim. Come "home" for
a delicious meal made with our home grown organic
fruit and veges. Enjoy the garden with its pizza oven fish
pond, ducks and the wood fired bush bath.

Comments from last years visitors book say it all: "We
ended up in utopia - (the brown troutB&B). We
enjoyed everything, from the breakfast, room, the
garden and the excellent dinner. One thing we well
never forget is how welcome you made us feel. What a
remarkable environment. The hospitality - absolutely
splendiferous. We shall return. The food gorgeous,
especially the fresh raspberries, bread, hazel nut cake
and David's scones. The beds were so comfortable we all
slept like logs. Your home is warm and welcoming and
we had the best nights sleep in perfect peace. Truly a
home from home. Warming to the soul! Fantastic place,
food, people - why would anyone go anywhere else?
Berries were out of this world. We have had a brilliant
time. It's hard to leave but we leave feeling refreshed."

Come and share this piece of paradise with us and
our dog, cat, ducks, goldfish and cows. Occasionally
our adult children return to join us as well. Pets and
children are welcome.

Motueka Valley *18 km S of Motueka*
Mountain View Cottage/Dexter Farmstay *Farmstay Cottage with Kitchen*
A & V Hall
Waiwhero Road, RD 1, Motueka

Tel (03) 526 8857 Fax (03) 526 8857
ajandvhall@xtra.co.nz

Double $95 Single $60 (Special breakfast)
Dinner $25 Cottage $95
Visa MC accepted
1 King/Twin 1 Queen (2 bdrm)
Bathrooms: 1 Ensuite 1 Private

Your hosts Alan & Veronica offer B&B, farmstay and separate cottage accommodation on our 35 acre organic property complete with unique dexter cows and native bush covenanted area. Perfectly situated for anglers, close to 3 National Parks and art/craft/garden trails. Mountain View Cottage is completely self-contained while our homestead offers spacious bedroom with own ensuite, tea/coffee & TV facilities. Meals are cooked on our wood-fired range and breakfast comprises choice of home-made muesli, bread, yoghurt, and organic eggs. A very warm welcome completes the picture.

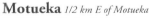

Motueka *1.4 km E of Motueka*
Williams B&B *B&B Homestay*
Rebecca & Ian Williams
186 Thorp Street, Motueka

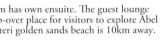

Tel (03) 528 9385 Fax (03) 528 9385
B&B@motueka-homestay.co.nz
www.motueka-homestay.co.nz

Double $100-$110 Single $60 (Full breakfast)
Child $20
Dinner by arrangement
1 Queen 1 Double 1 Single (2 bdrm)
Bathrooms: 2 Ensuite

We only look expensive. We are 1.4km to Motueka shopping centre and 1.2km to 18 hole golf course. Each bedroom has own ensuite. The guest lounge has tea & coffee making facilities and fridge. Motueka is the stop-over place for visitors to explore Abel Tasman and Kahurangi National Parks. Golden Bay and Kaiteriteri golden sands beach is 10km away. We have a Jack Russell dog. Visa and Mastercard accepted.

Motueka *1/2 km E of Motueka*
Golf View Chalet *B&B and Apartment with Kitchen*
Kathleen & Neil Holder
20A Teece Drive, Motueka

Tel (03) 528 8353 info@GolfViewChalet.co.nz
www.GolfViewChalet.co.nz

Double $95-$120 Single $75 (Special breakfast)
Child $20, in apartment $10
Self-contained apartment $100 double Extra adult $15
Visa MC accepted
Children welcome
3 Queen 1 Double 4 Single (4 bdrm)
Bathrooms: 1 Ensuite 2 Private

Welcome to our sunny home with mountain views, adjoining 18 hole golf course, beside the sea. Enjoy our lovely garden setting. Sleep well in comfortable beds. Close to restaurants, National Parks and golden beaches. Central in the Nelson region for day trips. Breakfast option available for self-cater apartment (extra). Carport with apartment. Complimentary laundry, tea/coffee making facilities, guest fridge, BBQ. Directions: from High Street (main street), State Highway 60, turn into Tudor Street, left Thorp Street, right Krammer Street, left into Teece Drive.

273

Motueka *2 km S of Motueka*

Grey Heron - The Italian Organic Homestay *B&B Homestay*
Sandro Lionello & Laura Totis
110 Trewavas Street, Motueka 7161

Tel (03) 528 0472 Fax (03) 528 0472
sandro@greyheron.co.nz
www.greyheron.co.nz

Double $90-$110 Single $50-$80 (Continental)
Dinner $35pp Children welcome
3 Queen 1 Single (4 bdrm)
Bathrooms: 1 Ensuite 1 Guest share

We are a couple from Northern Italy, much travelled and keen on tramping, mountaineering and motorbiking.

Our garden faces the Moutere River Estuary, birdwatchers' paradise with colonies of migrant and permanent native birds: you will have the chance to see the spectacular Royal Spoonbills and White Heron feeding in the estuary.

You can enjoy our breakfast (Continental-plus with Italian specialities, organic home-made bread and jams), overlooking a superb tidal view of the estuary and of the Kahurangi National Park mountain range.
Profit by Sandro's experience in Geology, Outdoor Activities and Italian Language Teaching and book with us: * 1-day botanical/geological/birdwatching guided walks. *Special half-day option in the beautiful Kahurangi National Park. * Rock-climbing lessons by special arrangements. * Italian Language lessons for beginners and advanced.

The Guest Accommodation includes both ensuite and shared-facilities with toilet room and bathroom each separate. The ensuite bedroom is small and cosy with private driveway and ground-floor entrance.

Enjoy our Organic Italian Dinner (available on booking) and Sandro's huge collection of jazz records. Tea/coffee facilities. Secure off-street parking. Water Taxi ticketing service available. Regrettably we don't accept Visitor Information Centres Vouchers. "Benvenuti tutti gli amici italiani!".

Directions: From Nelson: at the southern roundabout in High Street, turn right towards Port Motueka then turn left into Trewavas Street. From the West Coast: at the intersection with High Street go straight, drive up to the end of Old Wharf Rd. and turn right into Trewavas Street. Look for our signs.

Motueka *10 km S of Motueka*

River Hills Bed & Breakfast *B&B*
Anthea Garmey & Andrew Claringbold
398 Westbank Road, RD 1, Okaihau, Motueka

Tel (03) 528 8979 or 027 208 3106
Fax (03) 528 8979
ant.andy@paradise.net.nz
www.riverhills.co.nz

Double $100-$140 Single $100 (Full breakfast)
Children welcome
1 King/Twin (1 bdrm)
Bathrooms: 1 Ensuite

River Hills is nestled on the foothills of the Kahurangi
National Park above the Motueka River. We have stunning views over rural Motueka, Tasman Bay
and out to D'Urville Island. Listen to the Morepork while you relax and unwind in the steaming hot
outdoor bath. Awake to a gorgeous sunrise and the chorus of native birds. Enjoy a continental or cooked
breakfast. We love the outdoors and enjoy boating. Andrew is a keen fly fisherman. We share our home
with our daughter Hannah and Basil, the cat.

Motueka Valley *15 km S of Motueka*

Lakeside Lodge *Luxury Farmstay Separate Suite Cottage No Kitchen*
Robert & Gaynor Brooks
Ngatimoti, Motueka, RD 1

Tel (03) 526 8844 or 021 205 0602
Fax (03) 526 8844
enquiries@lakeside-lodge.co.nz
www.lakeside-lodge.co.nz

Double $150-$220 Single $120-$150 (Full breakfast)
Child $50 Dinner $40
Visa MC accepted
Children welcome
4 Queen 2 Twin (6 bdrm)
Bathrooms: 3 Ensuite Showers

The accommodation consists of the east wing of a large log house. The rooms are all timber panel
ceilings and walls. Ensuite and seperate entrance to rooms from the rest of the house. Stunning views of
mountains and river. For 2006 we will have seperate log cottages available next to lake. Excellent trout
fishing.Kyaking on the lake. We have one boy aged 8. All meals can be provided. Swimming pool.

Motueka - Marahau *20 km N of Motueka*

The Point *B&B*
Kerstin & Urs Uhlmann
37 Tokongawa Drive,
Split Apple Rock, RD 2 Motueka

Tel (03) 527 8572
uhlmann@hotmail.com

Double $150-$250 Single $120-$220 (Continental)
Dinner $35pp
Visa MC accepted
Pet free home Not suitable for children
2 King (2 bdrm)
Bathrooms: 2 Ensuite

Welcome to The Point @ Toko Ngawa - the perfect base for all
outdoor activities and relaxation. Unwind and relax on the terrace
of our unique eco- and environmental friendly earthblock home, stroll to the golden beaches nearby and
explore the magnificent Abel Tasman National Park. Enjoy delicious breakfasts on your own private deck
ñ all in an informal and relaxed atmosphere spiced with spectacular views and set within lush native bush.
We are looking forward to welcoming you soon. English, German, Swiss, French spoken.

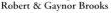

Nelson, Golden Bay

Riwaka *2 km N of Motueka*

Bridge House B&B *B&B*
Michelle & Malcolm Greenwood
274 Main Road, Riwaka, RD 3, Motueka

Tel (03) 528 9117 Fax (03) 528 9117
bridgehouse@ihug.co.nz
homepages.ihug.co.nz/~malandmichelle

Double $150-$150 (Full breakfast)
Dinner $33.50 by arrangement
Visa MC Eftpos accepted
Not suitable for children
3 Queen (3 bdrm)
Bathrooms: 3 Ensuite

Relax in the queen-size suites with big baths. Our guest lounge has Sky TV, video, complimentary beverages, books, games etc. Home-cooked evening meals by arrangement. Internet, fax and laundry facilities available. Enjoy your generous full cooked breakfast before you take in the local scenery or experience the many varied activities the Tasman region has to offer. Malcolm & Michelle look forward to meeting you with Tui and Tiki our very cuddly birman kittens. Regret no pets.

Kaiteriteri *12 km N of Motueka*

Bayview *B&B*
Aileen & Tim Rich
Kaiteriteri Heights, RD 2, Motueka

Tel (03) 527 8090 Fax (03) 527 8090
book@kaiteriteribandb.co.nz
www.kaiteriteribandb.co.nz

Double $165-$195 (Full breakfast)
Visa MC accepted
1 King/Twin1 King 1 Twin (2 bdrm)
Bathrooms: 2 Ensuite

Welcome to our piece of paradise. Our modern house has huge windows with outstanding seaviews overlooking Kaiteriteri Beach out to Abel Tasman National Park. Large, beautifully furnished guest rooms have every convenience you could want. Enjoy delicious home-cooked breakfast with your hosts or on your private terrace. Laundry, email and booking facilities for boat trips, walking and kayaking are available. We are happy to share our home, and general lifestyle with you. Recommended 2 nights minimum stay to explore this unique area.

Kaiteriteri *10 km N of Motueka*

Bracken Hill B&B *B&B*
Grace & Tom Turner
265 Kaiteriteri Road, RD 2, Motueka

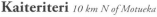

Tel (03) 528 9629 Fax (03) 528 9629
gracet@ihug.co.nz

Double $120-$130 Single $100 (Continental)
Visa MC accepted
Pet free home Not suitable for children
2 Queen 1 Twin (3 bdrm)
Bathrooms: 3 Private

Coastal Luxury. Welcome you to our tasteful, spacious modern home. Cosy rooms all have wonderful sea views over Tasman Bay. Enjoy mountains, native bush, magical sunrises, sunsets & stars! A large viewing sundeck leads to a unique natural rock garden. Guests TV lounge, tea/coffee, fridge, pool table, laundry facility. Experience (5-15 minutes) to golden Kaiteriteri Beach, Marahau, Kahurangi/Abel Tasman National Parks; (1 hour) to Golden Bay. Kayaking, walks, & water taxis. Restaurants close by. Interests: travel & guests will delight in a refreshing breakfast at our peaceful haven. Friendly hosts, Grace & Tom

Kaiteriteri *13 km N of Motueka*
Everton B&B *B&B*

Martin & Diane Everton
Kotare Place, Little Kaiteriteri, RD 2 Motueka

Tel (03) 527 8301 or 021 527 830
Fax (03) 527 8301
everton@xtra.co.nz
www.evertonbandb.co.nz

Double $120 Single $100 (Continental)
Visa MC accepted
1 King/Twin 1 Queen (2 bdrm)
Bathrooms: 1 Guest share

We live 2 minutes from the golden sands of Little Kaiteriteri Beach with wonderful sea views. Breakfast includes fresh home-baked bread or muffins. Our interests include golf, music, travel, walking, conversation and reading. The Abel Tasman National Park is right here where you can kayak, walk and take boat trips. Nearby are excellent restaurants and wineries. We are licensed to take you on a personalised trip in our boat if you choose. Email is offered and even a piano to play! We have no pets and are non-smokers.

Kaiteriteri *15 km N of Motueka*
Bellbird Lodge *Luxury B&B*

Anthea & Brian Harvey
Sandy Bay Road, Kaiteriteri, RD2, Motueka

Tel (03) 527 8555 or 021 057 1470
Fax (03) 527 8556 stay@bellbirdlodge.com
www.bellbirdlodge.com

Double $165-$250 Single $120-$180
(Special breakfast) Dinner by arrangement (May-Sept)
Visa MC accepted
Pet free home Not suitable for children under 10
1 King/Twin 1 Queen 1 Twin (3 bdrm)
Bathrooms: 1 Ensuite 1 Private

Welcome to our home where warm friendly hospitality, superb food and fine accommodation await you. Nestled on a quiet hillside with panoramic sea views, Bellbird Lodge is close to Kaiteriteri Beach and the Abel Tasman National Park. Enjoy gourmet breakfasts featuring a speciality hot course of the day served in the dining room, or alfresco on the terrace accompanied by songs of bellbirds and tuis. Laundry, phone, fax, email available. Bookings for local activities arranged. We look forward to welcoming you soon.

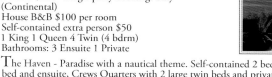

Kaiteriteri *13 km N of Motueka*
The Haven *B&B Cottage with Kitchen*

Tom & Alison Rowling
Rowling Heights, RD 2, Kaiteriteri, Motueka

Tel (03) 527 8085 Fax (03) 527 8065
thehaven@internet.co.nz
www.thehaven.co.nz

Double $200 Single party bookings only
(Continental)
House B&B $100 per room
Self-contained extra person $50
1 King 1 Queen 4 Twin (4 bdrm)
Bathrooms: 3 Ensuite 1 Private

The Haven - Paradise with a nautical theme. Self-contained 2 bedrooms, Captains Cabin with king-size bed and ensuite, Crews Quarters with 2 large twin beds and private bathroom. Galley kitchen with generous breakfast provisions. 2 decks providing outdoor living. B&B available in our home offering queen or twin rooms with ensuites. Enjoy relaxed family atmosphere, spectacular views, swimming pool, private bush track to beach. Minimum stay 2 nights, not suitable for small children.

Nelson, Golden Bay

Kaiteriteri *15 km N of Motueka*

Ngaiomi *Separate Suite*
Julie & Allan Hunter
Kaiteriteri / Sandy Bay, Motueka RD 2, Nelson

Tel (03) 527 8274 or 027 454 3009
Fax (03) 527 8309
homes@goldensands.co.nz
www.goldensands.co.nz

Double $85-$130 (Continental)
1 Queen (1 bdrm)
Bathrooms: 1 Ensuite

Welcome to Ngaiomi. Your private villa set in our garden has ensuite facilities, kitchenette and TV. You will wake to the song of the bellbird and tui. Partake of breakfast on your deck while enjoying the sea views. We are just minutes away from the golden sands of Kaiteriteri Beach and start of the Abel Tasman National Park. This area offers kayaking, bush walks and marvellous boat trips. Top rated wineries, restaurants and craft shopping beckon. Hosts Julie and Allan and friendly cat Ben.

Kaiteriteri *13 km N of Motueka*

Robyn's Nest B&B *Separate Suite Apartment with Kitchen*
Robyn & Mike O'Donnell
1 Rowling Road, Kaiteriteri

Tel (03) 527 8466 or 021 431 735
Fax (03) 527 8466
robynod@ihug.co.nz
www.accommodationkaiteriteri.co.nz

Double $120-$150 Single $100-$120 (Continental)
Child negotiable
Visa MC accepted Children welcome
2 Queen 1 Single (2 bdrm)
Bathrooms: 2 Ensuite

Take the track through our garden and walk 100 metres to the beautiful Kaiteriteri Beach with golden sand, clear water and safe swimming. Kaiteriteri is also the departure point for Launches, Water-Taxis and Kayaking into the Abel Tasman National Park. Private entry via your own terrace, television, hairdryer, refrigerator and tea, coffee & toast making facilities. We have off-street parking, guests BBQ area, petanque court and JJ, the mischievous cat. Continental breakfast includes home-made muesli and preserves.

Kaiteriteri - Tapu Bay *12 km N of Motueka*

Maison Luc *B&B Cottage with Kitchen*
Angie & Martin Lucas
Tapu Bay, Kaiteriteri Road, RD 2, Motueka

Tel (03) 527 8247 or 0800 468 815
027 221 6090 Fax (03) 527 8347
maison_luc@xtra.co.nz www.maisonluc.co.nz

Double $90 Single $85 (Continental)
Cottage Double $130 Single $110 Extra guest $15
(Some breakfast provided)
Visa MC accepted Children welcome
2 Queen 1 Double 1 Twin (4 bdrm)
Bathrooms: 1 Guest share 1 Private

Angie, Martin and Lu (dog) welcome you to Maison Luc. 2 minute walk to Tapu and Stephens Bays, 1km to Kaiteriteri beaches. Gateway to Abel Tasman. Self-contained separate unit in peaceful orchard garden. Sleeps 4 (2 on sofa), children welcome. B&B: 2 double bedrooms upstairs. Guests share bathroom. Continental breakfast served in dining room or on terrace with views across the bay. Swimming pool. Good restaurants nearby. Hunting/tramping guiding available. We look forward to meeting you and introducing you to the magic of this special area.

Kaiteriteri *12 km N of Motueka*
Wall Street Accommodation *B&B Separate Suite*
Dr Hans Brutscher & Fiona Thornton
Wall Street, C/O Postal Centre, Kaiteriteri, Nelson

Tel (03) 527 8338 or 021 544 335
025 283 1890 Fax (03) 527 8338
HansFiona@xtra.co.nz

Double $105-$120 Single $95-$100 (Continental)
Visa MC accepted
Not suitable for children
1 Queen (1 bdrm)
Bathrooms: 1 Ensuite

Situated in a peaceful setting close to nearby beaches and centrally located to explore the Abel Tasman National Park and Golden Bay. We offer a modern studio room with queen bed, kitchenette with fridge and microwave plus tea & coffee making facilities, ensuite and TV. Separate entry with outdoor courtyard and bordering a native bush reserve. Only minutes from Tapu Bay, Stephens Bay and golden-sanded Kaiteriteri beach and just a short drive to nearby restaurants. Accommodation only also offered. German & French spoken.

Abel Tasman National Park - Marahau *18 km NW of Motueka*
Abel Tasman Bed & Breakfast *B&B Homestay Motels*
George Bloomfield
Abel Tasman National Park, Marahau

Tel (03) 527 8181 Fax (03) 527 8181
abel.tasman.stables.accom@xtra.co.nz
www.abeltasmanstables.co.nz

Double $100-$125 Single $70-$90 (Special breakfast)
Cottage $140 (sleeps 4)
Visa MC accepted
3 Queen 2 Double 4 Single (6 bdrm)
Bathrooms: 5 Ensuite 1 Family share 1 Private

Great views, hospitality, peaceful garden setting are yours at Abel Tasman Stables accommodation. Closest ensuite facility to Abel Tasman National park. Guests comments include: 'I know now that hospitality is not just a word', TH, Germany. 'Wonderful place, friendly hospitality. The best things for really special holidays. We leave a piece of our hearts', P&M, Italy. 'The creme-de-la-creme of our holiday. What a view', MN & JW, England. Homestay bed & breakfast or self-contained options. Cafe close by.

Abel Tasman National Park *17 km NW of Motueka*
Split Apple Rock Homestay *B&B Homestay*
Thelma & Rodger Boys
Tokongawa Drive, Split Apple Rock, RD 2, Motueka

Tel (03) 527 8182
splitapplerock@hotmail.com
www.splitapplerock.com

Double $130-$140 Single $115-$120 (Full breakfast)
Dinner $30 by arrangement
Children welcome
1 Queen 1 Twin (2 bdrm)
Bathrooms: 2 Ensuite

Enjoy 180 degree panoramic sea views of Tasman Bay and Abel Tasman National Park. Our Eco-log home rooms have private entrances and decking. We are within walking distance of 2 golden beaches, 5 minutes drive to Marahau and the start of Abel Tasman National Park where walking, kayaking, boating, swimming and more are available. 2 cats in residence. Directions: on the Marahau/Kaiteriteri Road take the Tokongawa Drive turn-off, 1.2km up Tokongawa Drive the "Split Apple Rock Homestay" sign is on your right.

Patons Rock Beach - Takaka *10 km W of Takaka*

Patondale *Farmstay Cottage with Kitchen*
Vicki & David James
Patons Rock, RD 2, Takaka

Tel (03) 525 8262 or 0800 306 697 (NZ only)
025 936 891 Fax (03) 525 8262
patondale@xtra.co.nz
www.patonsrockbeachvillas.co.nz

Double $125 Single $125 (Provisions first night)
Child $20
Visa MC accepted
Children welcome
4 King 8 Single (8 bdrm)
Bathrooms: 4 Private

Golden Bay's newest villas. 4 sunny, spacious, deluxe self-contained units, own attached carports. 2 bedrooms. Peaceful rural setting at the seaward end of our dairy farm yet only a few minutes walk to beautiful Patons Rock Beach. Central location. Simply the Best. Your Kiwi hosts, David & Vicki invite you to be our guests.

Takaka - Tata Beach *15 km NE of Takaka*

The Devonshires *B&B Homestay*
Brian & Susan Devonshire
32 Tata Heights Drive, Tata Beach, RD 1, Takaka

Tel (03) 525 7987 Fax (03) 525 7987
devs.1@xtra.co.nz

Double $95 Single $65 (Full breakfast)
Not suitable children
Dinner $25-$30 by arrangement
Visa MC accepted
1 Queen (1 bdrm)
Bathrooms: 1 Ensuite

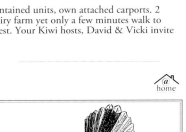

The Devonshires live at Tata Beach and invite you to enjoy their new home and stroll to the nearby beautiful golden beach. A tranquil base for exploring the truly scenic Golden Bay, the Abel Tasman Walkway, Kahurangi National Park, Farewell Spit, amazing coastal scenery, fishing the rivers or visiting interesting craftspeople. Brian, an educator, wine and American Football buff is a keen fisherman. Susan enjoys crafts, painting, gardening and practising her culinary skills. Charlie Brown and Hermione are the resident cats. Longer visits welcomed.

Takaka *5 km S of Takaka*

Rose Cottage *B&B Cottage with Kitchen*
Margaret & Phil Baker
Hamama Road, RD 1, Takaka

Tel (03) 525 9048 Fax (03) 525 9043

Double $77-$87 Single $60-$67 (Continental)
Self-contained units $97-$127
Visa MC accepted
1 Queen 2 Single (2 bdrm)
Bathrooms: 1 Guest share 1 Private

Rose cottage, much loved home of Phil & Margaret, is situated in the beautiful Takaka valley, in 2.5 acres of garden amongst 300 year old Totara trees, ideally situated to explore Golden Bay's many attractions. Our 3 self-contained units have full kitchens, private sun decks and quality furniture made by Phil in his craft workshop. The 12 metre indoor solar-heated swimming pool is available to our guests. Our interests are travel, photography, gardening, arts and crafts. Ask about our seniors specials

Takaka *2 km S of Takaka*

Croxfords Homestay *Homestay*
Pam & John Croxford
Dodson Road, RD 1, Takaka, Golden Bay

Tel (03) 525 7177 or 0800 276 156
Fax (03) 525 7177
croxfords@xtra.co.nz
www.kahurangiwalks.co.nz

Double $100 Single $70 (Full breakfast)
Child $10 Dinner $30 Visa MC accepted
Pet free home Children welcome
1 Queen 1 Double 1 Single (2 bdrm)
Bathrooms: 2 Ensuite

You are welcome to our spacious home in a peaceful rural setting close to Takaka. Views of Kahurangi National Park are spectacular. Pam loves cooking evening meals, including special diets, using home grown produce. Breakfasts include home-made bread, muesli, yoghurt and preserves. We enjoy assisting visitors make the most of their visit. We are near beaches and national parks. We have many New Zealand books. No children at home, or pets. Non-smokers preferred. We offer guided walks in the Abel Tasman and Kahurangi National Parks.

Takaka *5 km W of Takaka*

BenGar-Pohara *B&B*
Joan & John Garner
91 Selwyn St, Pohara, Golden Bay, Takaka,RD

Tel 03 525 9088 jjgarner@xtra.co.nz

Double $100-$100 (Full breakfast)
Dinner by arrangement
Eftpos accepted
Not suitable for children
2 Queen (2 bdrm)
Bathrooms: 1 Guest share seperate toilet room

Joan & John have built a new house by Pohara's beach & golf course. The house is just across the road from the beach. A challenging 9 Hole Golf course is a minute's walk from the house. The rooms have their own private deck & look out towards the mountains that surround Golden Bay. All guests will be welcomed by Jed the Jack Russell, who is ever ready to give a guided tour of his "beach". Tess, our Birman cat will make the occasional appearance.

Parapara *20 km NW of Takaka*

Hakea Hill House *B&B*
Vic & Liza Eastman
PO Box 35, Collingwood 7171

Tel (03) 524 8487 Fax (03) 524 8487
vic.eastman@clear.net.nz

Double $120 Single $80 (Full breakfast)
Child $40 Dinner by arrangement
Visa MC accepted
Children welcome
2 Double 6 Single (3 bdrm)
Bathrooms: 1 Guest share

Hakea Hill House at Parapara has views from its hilltop of all Golden Bay. The 2 story house is modern and spacious. 2 guest rooms have large balconies, the third for children has 4 bunk beds and a cot. American and New Zealand electric outlets are installed. Television, tea or coffee, and telephone lines are available in rooms. Vic is a practising physician with an interest in astronomy. Liza is a quilter and cares for 2 outdoor dogs. Please contact us personally for reservations and directions.

Pakawau Beach - Collingwood *12 km N of Collingwood*

Pakawau Homestay *Homestay Cottage with Kitchen*
Val & Graham Williams
Pakawau Beach, RD, Collingwood

Tel (03) 524 8168 Fax (03) 524 8168

B&B
Approved

Double $100-$120 Single $80-$90 (Continental)
Dinner $25 Self-contained $100
3 Queen 1 Single (2 bdrm)
Bathrooms: 2 Ensuite

We are one of the most northern homestays in the South Island, just 10km from Farewell Spit.

The Puponga Farm Park and Wharariki Beach provide many walking options. Nearby Kaihoka Lakes, Westhaven Inlet, Mangarakau Swamp and beyond offer a remote an rugged landscape worth exploring. The Farewell Spit tour will pick you from our gate.

Walk through our garden to a safe swimming beach. We have kayaks available for our guests.

Our main guest room has a fridge, tea/coffee making facilities, own private deck with access to the beach. We have self-contained cottages available which sleep 2-6 people from $100 per night.

Local seafoods available, e.g. whitebait, scallops, or you can walk across the road to a licensed cafe. We are non-smokers, have 2 cats, and look forward to sharing our lifestyle with you.

Collingwood *25 km N of Takaka*

Skara Brae Garden Motels & Bed and Breakfast *B&B Cottage with Kitchen*
Joanne & Pax Northover
Elizabeth Street, Collingwood

Tel (03) 524 8464 Fax (03) 524 8474
skarabrae@xtra.co.nz
www.accommodationcollingwood.co.nz

Double $130 Single $100 (Continental)
2 self-contained units $95
Visa MC accepted
2 Queen 1 Double 1 Twin 2 Single (4 bdrm)
Bathrooms: 1 Ensuite 3 Private

Skara Brae, the original police residence in
Collingwood built in 1908, has been tastefully renovated over the years. Our historic home is in a quiet,
peaceful garden setting. Join us in the house for bed & breakfast, or our 2 self-contained motel units.
Either way you will experience a warm welcoming atmosphere and individual attention. We are a minute
away from the excellent Courthouse Cafe and local tavern bistro bar and it is a short stroll to the beach.
Farewell Spit trips depart close by.

Nelson Lakes - St Arnaud *85 km S of Nelson*

Nelson Lakes Homestay *Homestay*
Gay & Merv Patch
RD 2, State Highway 63, Nelson

Tel (03) 521 1191 Fax (03) 521 1191
Home@Tasman.net
www.nelsonlakesaccommodation.co.nz

Double $125 Single $90 (Full breakfast)
Dinner $35pp by arrangement
Visa MC accepted
2 King/Twin 1 Queen (2 bdrm)
Bathrooms: 2 Ensuite

Nestled on the sunny slopes of the St Arnaud
Mountain Range, Nelson Lakes National Park, our spacious modern home is designed for the comfort
and convenience of our guests. Spacious ensuite rooms, with doors opening on to our garden, large
comfortable lounge and terrace to relax on at the end of the day and admire the magnificent mountain
views. Laundry facilities are available and 3 course meals by prior arrangement. We have a house cat.
Directions: State Highway 63, 4km east of St Arnaud.

Murchison *0.5 km N of Murchison*

Murchison Lodge *B&B*
Shirley & Merve Bigden
15 Grey Street, Murchison,

Tel (03) 523 9196 or 021 266 7016
Fax (03) 523 9196
info@murchisonlodge.co.nz
www.murchisonlodge.co.nz

Double $145-$175 Single $115-$160 (Full breakfast)
Dinner by arrangement
Visa MC accepted
Not suitable for children
1 King/Twin 2 Queen 1 Single (4 bdrm)
Bathrooms: 3 Ensuite 1 Private

Enjoy our warm and relaxed hospitality, comfortable beds and hearty BBQ breakfasts. Our unique
timber lodge is set on three acres surrounded by rivers and mountains. Here you will feel miles from
anywhere, yet be within an easy walk to town. Murchison makes a great base to unpack your bags.
Explore three national parks in this stunning area, fly fish, raft or play golf then come home to a cold
beer on the veranda or a wine in front of the log fire.

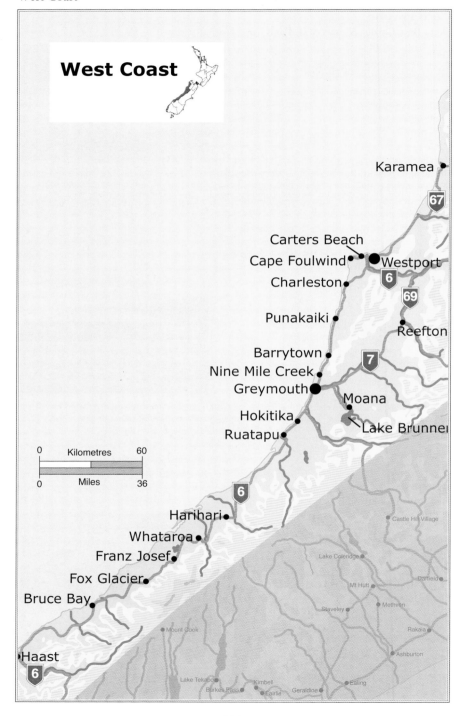

West Coast

Karamea

67

Carters Beach
Cape Foulwind
Charleston
Westport
6
69
Punakaiki
Reefton
Barrytown
Nine Mile Creek
7
Greymouth
Moana
Hokitika
Lake Brunner
Ruatapu

0 Kilometres 60
0 Miles 36

6

Harihari
Castle Hill Village
Whataroa
Franz Josef
Lake Coleridge
Fox Glacier
Darfield
Bruce Bay
Mt Hutt
Methven
Mount Cook
Staveley
Rakaia
Haast
Ashburton
6
Lake Tekapo
Kimbell
Burkes Pass
Geraldine
Ealing
Fairlie

Karamea *84 km N of Westport*

Beachfront Farmstay B&B *B&B Farmstay*
Dianne & Russell Anderson
Karamea, SH 67, Karamea

Tel (03) 782 6762 or 021 782676
Fax (03) 782 6762
farmstay@xtra.co.nz
www.WestCoastBeachAccommodation.co.nz

Double $130-$150 Single $100 (Special breakfast)
Child $35 Dinner $40
Visa MC accepted Children welcome
1 King 1 Queen 1 Twin (3 bdrm)
Bathrooms: 2 Ensuite 1 Family share

Our home is 2 minutes walk to an unspoiled sandy beach with wonderful sunsets, ideal for walking, jogging or just beachcombing. We are a working farm milking 420 cows. Enjoy a special whitebait breakfast with fresh baked bread. Join us for delicious evening meals with organic vegetables, home-made desserts and NZ wine. Ensuite rooms are tastefully decorated with every convenience. Our area offers day walks, guided tours in limestone caves, unique limestone arches, golf, bird watching, trout fishing. Come and relax in our spacious home and garden.

Karamea *0.5 km N of Karamea*

Bridge Farm *Farmstay Apartment with Kitchen*
Rosalie & Peter Sampson
Bridge Street, Karamea, RD 1, Westport

Tel (03) 782 6955 Fax (03) 782 6748
Enquires@karameamotels.co.nz

Double $95-$130 (Continental)
Child $10 Extra adult $20
Visa MC accepted
Children welcome
6 Queen 8 Single (10 bdrm)
Bathrooms: 8 Private

Since relinquishing their dairy farm to daughter Caroline and son-in-law Bevan, Rosalie and Peter have purpose-built on the property accommodation that neatly bridges the gap between motel and farm stay. Both are happy to share their extensive knowledge of their district, its people and environment and introduce guests to the many short walks that Karamea offers. Each quality suite is self contained and has a private lounge that overlooks the farm to Kahurangi National Park beyond. A small mob of tame deer and alpaca graze nearby.

Westport - Cape Foulwind *11 km SW of Westport*

Steeples Cottage & B&B Homestay *B&B Homestay Cottage with Kitchen*
Pauline & Bruce Cargill
48 Lighthouse Road, Cape Foulwind, Westport

Tel (03) 789 7876 or 0800 670 708
021 663 687 steepleshomestay@xtra.co.nz
www.baches.co.nz/bhh/listing/0/1005

Double $100 Single $60 (Full breakfast)
Child $15
Self-contained cottage $110 (Continental breakfast)
1 Queen 2 Single (2 bdrm)
Bathrooms: 1 Ensuite 1 Private

Enjoy our peaceful rural home or cottage with gardens, magnificent views of the Tasman Sea, rugged coastline, beautiful beaches & tranquil sunsets. Great swimming, surfing, fishing. Walk the very popular seal colony walkway, dine at The Bay House Restaurant or the friendly Star Tavern. Local attractions include full golf course, Coaltown Museum, jet-ski & jet boating, horse riding, underworld & white water rafting, bush walks & Punakaiki National Park. We have a Jack Russell dog and a cat. Laundry available and off-street parking. Cottage includes continental breakfast. Whitebait meals by arrangment.

Westport *In Westport Central*
Havenlee Homestay *B&B Homestay*

Jan & Ian Stevenson
76 Queen Street, Westport

Tel (03) 789 8543 or 0800 673 619
Fax (03) 789 8502
info@havenlee.co.nz
www.havenlee.co.nz

Double $100-$150 **Single** $75 (Continental)
Child negotiable
Visa MC accepted Children welcome
2 Queen 1 Double 1 Twin (3 bdrm)
Bathrooms: 1 Guest share suite 1 Private

Peace in Paradise - this is Havenlee: a welcoming, relaxed, spacious, quality homestay where you will feel at home right away. Centrally located, an idyllic base from which to explore the environmental wonderland, share local knowledge or just to tke time out. Checkout the adventure experiences and local attractions. Soak up the nature, rest and restore body and soul in the peace and quiet of a garden oasis. Fantastic continental-plus breakfast. Laundry facilities available. Treat yourself - stay awhile and feel exhilerated.

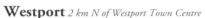

Westport *2 km N of Westport Town Centre*
Chrystal Lodge *Apartment with Kitchen*

Ann & Bill Blythe
Corner of Craddock Drive & Derby Street, Westport

Tel (03) 789 8617 or 0800 259 953
Fax (03) 789 8617
blythea@xtra.co.nz

Double $85 **Single** $65 (Breakfast by arrangement)
Continental breakfast optional $10pp
Visa MC accepted
Children welcome
2 Queen 1 Single (2 bdrm)
Bathrooms: 2 Ensuite

Ann and Bill would like to welcome you to Chrystal Lodge. We are established on 20 acres beside a beach ideal for walking, surfing and fishing. Our separate self-contained units have a fully equipped kitchen/lounge with ensuite bedrooms. The garden setting has ample off-street parking. Free guest laundry. Pony available for children. We have 1 shy cat. Seasonal rates. Directions: turn right at the post office, continue down Brougham Street, turn left at Derby Street until at the beach.

Westport - Cape Foulwind *10 km W of Westport*
Lighthouse Homestay *B&B Homestay*

Helen Jenkins
32 Lighthouse Road, Cape Foulwind, Westport

Tel (03) 789 5352 or 021 432 472
0800 555 569
hj.jenkins@xtra.co.nz

Double $90-$150 **Single** $80 (Continental)
Visa MC accepted
Children welcome
2 Queen 1 Double 1 Single (3 bdrm)
Bathrooms: 1 Ensuite 1 Family share 1 Guest share

Enjoy the soothing tranquillity of amazing sea views from your bedroom/patio. Walk the impressive Cape Foulwind Walkway with its seals and captivating coastline, ending at the award winning Bay House Restaurant overlooking Tauranga Bay. Numerous outdoor activities and attractions nearby. Let Poppy my fox terrier take you beachwalking below the cliffs. Helen can take you on short or half day walks in native rainforest, or organise golf and other outdoor activities. Short walk to friendly country pub.

Westport - Carters Beach *3 km S of Westport*

Bellaville *B&B*

Marlene & Ross Burrow
10 State Highway 67, Carters Beach
Po Box 157, Westport

Tel (03) 789 8457 or 0800 789 845
bellaville@xtra.co.nz

Double $90 Single $60 (Full breakfast)
Child $15 Children welcome
1 Queen 1 Twin (1 bdrm)
Bathrooms: 1 Private

Come stay with us at Carters Beach. Wake to the
sound of the waves pounding on our safe walking
and swimming beach. Plenty of off-street parking. Ouiet sunny extra large, spacious studio room with
private entrance, own patio, private bathroom with spa bath, shower and separate toilet. Sleeps 4 people
in comfort. Ideal for a family. Laundry available, Electric blankets,TV, tea & coffee and home-baking.
Close to all activities, coastal walks, seal colony. Short walk to friendly licensed country cafe/bar, golf
course, beach and airport.

Westport - Carters Beach *4 km S of Westport*

Carters Beach B&B *B&B*

Sue & John Bennett
Main Road Carters Beach,
On State Highway 67A, Westport

Tel (03) 789 8056 or 0800 783 566
cartersbeachaccom@xtra.co.nz
www.bnb.co.nz/cartersbeachbb.html

Double $100 Single $70-$80 (Continental)
Pet free home Children welcome
2 Queen 1 Twin (3 bdrm)
Bathrooms: 1 Ensuite 1 Private

Carters Beach B&B, a lovely relaxed atmosphere,
Situated only 4km south of Westport. A 3 minute walk will take you to our beach, with fully licenced
resturant/cafe and bar. golf links, world famous seal colony and Bay House Cafe within a few minutes
drive. Our rooms are very spacious with TV and tea/coffee making facilities. Own private entrance ways
with sun decks. Laundry facillities available by arrangement. Ideal accommodation for couples travelling
togeather. We look forward to meeting and sharing our local knowledge with you. Cheers, Sue and John
Bennett.

Westport *14 km S of Westport*

Okari Lake Hideaway *Cottage with Kitchen*

Marie Dickson
Virgin Flat Road, Westport

Tel (03) 789 6841 Fax (03) 789 6841
marie.greg@xtra.co.nz
www.nz.hideaway.com

Double $150-$200 (Full breakfast)
Children welcome
1 Queen (1 bdrm)
Bathrooms: 1 Private

If you are looking for peace and tranquillity, this
private exclusive cottage, which is built over a private
lake, is the perfect place for you. There is a boat moored on the cottage jetty for your use. The location of
the lake allows for all-weather trout fishing. This is a bird watches paradise - there are many varieties of
native birds and water foul. A book on native birds and binoculars are to help identify them. We are only
35 minutes from Punakaiki and 30 minutes from the Bay House.

West Coast

Westport *4 km SW of Westport Central*
Lakeside Terrace B&B *B&B*
Anne & Wynne Goldie
12 Lakeside Terrace, RD 2, Westport

Tel (03) 789 7438 or 021 458 508
Fax (03) 789 6269
wa.goldie@xtra.co.nz

Double $90-$110 Single $80-$90 (Continental)
1 Queen 1 Double 1 Single (3 bdrm)
Bathrooms: 1 Private

We offer quality accommodation for 1 party of guests at a time in our new and modern sunny home, set in a peaceful rural area, surrounded by native trees and shrubs and the native ducks on nearby lakes. Experience the amazing outdoor activities and attractions our district has to offer, or just relax and enjoy the tranquillity of your back to nature surrounds with magical panoramic views. Hospitality is our heritage. You can be assured of a warm welcome and a memorable stay.

Westport - Cape Foulwind *11 km S of Westport*
Cape House *B&B Homestay*
Dave Low
Tauranga Bay Road, Cape Foulwind, Westport

Tel (03) 789 6358 or 027 481 8672
stay@capehouse.co.nz
www.capehouse.co.nz

Double $100-$120 Single $65-$75 (Continental)
Child $20
Dinner from $25 by arrangement
Extra guest $20
2 Queen 2 Single (2 bdrm)
Bathrooms: 1 Ensuite 1 Private

Cape House is a large and warm open style house in a secluded environment with a funky and friendly atmosphere. Your hosts are Dave the surfer and fisherman and Mark the technical guy. Chill out or enjoy the outdoors. Very near by are the Cape Foulwind walkway, seal colony, beaches, surfing and fishing. Options for eating out are a stroll to the local tavern, or the award winning Bayhouse Cafe. Free internet access is available. We have an inside cat.

Please let us know
how you enjoyed your B&B experience.
Ask your host for a comment form
or leave a comment on www.bnb.co.nz

Our B&Bs range from homely to luxurious,
but you can always be assured of superior hospitality.

Westport - Carters Beach *3 km S of Westport*

home

Beach Haven *B&B*
Leslie & Gary Broderick
35 Marine Parade, Carters Beach, Westport

Tel (03) 789 8207 or 0800 111 585
027 622 8044 Fax (03) 789 8207
leslie.gary@xtra.co.nz
www.bnb.co.nz/beachhaven.html

Double $110-$130 Single $110 (Continental)
Visa MC accepted
2 Queen 1 Double 1 Twin (3 bdrm)
Bathrooms: 1 Ensuite 1 Guest share 1 Private

Welcome to Beach Haven situated on the shoreline of Carters Beach. Take a stroll on the beach, enjoy a glass of wine whilst watching the sun go down and be lulled to sleep by the sound of surf. Gary a born Coaster can impart his knowledge of local history and places of interest to visit. We have beautiful walks,underwater rafting, horse treking and more. Be as busy or as relaxed as you choose. Stay a day or two, you,ll be glad that you did.

Westport *In Westport*

B&B
Approved

Riverlea Cottage *B&B Cottage with Kitchen*
Margaret Broderick
89 Snodgrass Road, RD 2 Ext, Westport

Tel (03) 789 8655 or 025 245 7258
0800 45 7258 Fax (03) 789 8655
marg.b@xtra.co.nz

Double $100-$150 Single $100-$150 (Continental)
Child negotiable
Dinner negotiable
Children welcome
2 Queen 2 Twin (3 bdrm)
Bathrooms: 1 Family share 2 Private

Riverlea Cottage, situated on Orowaiti River, in one of Westport's most peaceful and tranquil areas. Marg offers a warm welcome, with friendly relaxed accommodation in a self-contained unit, or her riverside room with shared facilities. Fancy a wine on the deck watching fantastic sunsets or the moon on the river, Take a short walk along the river edge or maybe do some spear fishing. Continental breakfast is generous and delicious. This is a feel at home friendly place welcoming you to come, stay and enjoy.

Charleston *17 km S of Westport*
Birds Ferry Lodge *Luxury B&B*
Alison & Andre Gygax
Birds Ferry Road, 8KM North Charleston, SHW 6, Westport

Tel 0800 212 207 or 021 337 217
info@birdsferrylodge.co.nz
www.birdsferrylodge.co.nz

Double $110-$175 Single $90-$140 (Special breakfast)
Child by arrangement Dinner our speciality - by arrangement
Check availability now via our web site Visa MC accepted
Children and pets welcome
2 Queen 1 Twin (3 bdrm)
Bathrooms: 3 Ensuite Purpose Built wheelchair use, ensuite
shower room

Allow yourselves to relax and unwind at Birds Ferry Lodge.
Along with the native birdlife, you will enjoy an exceptionally
tranquil spot with panoramic views of Paparoa Mountains,
Tasman Sea and native forest.
Step onto the deck from your room and enjoy the ocean
sunset from the heated spa. Or take a break in the luxuriously
appointed guest lounge in front of the log fire.
Privately accessed guest accommodation is ensuite with
bath, shower and lashings of hot water. Room tariff includes
refreshments, laundry service, internet and full cooked breakfast served at a time to suite you. Purpose
built disabled/wheelchair access. We share our lodge with 2 Norfolk/Norwich Terriers.
Alison has 15 years experience in hospitality business and her home cooking is her speciality. Dinner is
available by arrangement. Our own home produced vegetables and free-range eggs are used wherever
possible. Alison and Andre are keen gardeners. House bar, with New Zealand Wines.
The historic Buller has a multitude of activities, accessible areas of dense, luxuriant forest, rich birdlife
and a wild coastline; there is something for everyone. Andre, a New Zealand tour guide with 15 years
experience can accompany you on a personal tailor made local tour which includes a picnic lunch. He
will help you find those places seldom visited by others. If your stay is for more that one night this service
is complimentary. On arrival, many of our guests ask to extend their visit to more than 1 night. "Why?",
you might ask. On arrival you will discover the answer to this.
Close by there are numerous coastal and forest walks. 5 Minutes away, visit an exhibition gold mine. 10
minutes away take the Charleston Nile River Forest Train. 30 minutes away is Punakaiki . A day trip
distance north of us you can visit Heaphy Track, Karamea, Oparara Arches and historic Denniston.
To check availability or make a secure reservataion go to the 'contact us' page on our website.

Reefton *In Reefton Central*

Reef Cottage B&B and Cafe *B&B Cottage with Kitchen*
Susan & Ronnie Standfield
51-55 Broadway, Reefton

Tel (03) 732 8440 or 0800 770 440
Fax (03) 732 8440 reefton@clear.net.nz
www.reefcottage.co.nz

Double $90-$140 Single $80-$120 (Full breakfast)
Child half price Dinner $10-$35
Visa MC Diners Amex Eftpos accepted
1 King/Twin 1 Queen 2 Double (4 bdrm)
Bathrooms: 2 Ensuite 2 Private

Built in 1887 from native timbers for a local barrister. This historical Edwardian home has been carefully renovated to add light and space without losing its olde world charm. Elegantly decorated the house features charming character rooms serviced daily. Centrally heated. Reefton is nestled in historic gold and coal mining country, between native beech forests and the Inangahua River. Reef Cottage is unrivalled as the finest accommodation in Reefton. Reef Cafe next door offers casual dining, specialist coffees and decadent desserts. Trout fishing, hiking, and 4WD.

Reefton *In Reefton Central*

Quartz Lodge *B&B*
Toni & Ian Walker
78 Sheil Street, Reefton, West Coast

Tel (03) 732 8383 or 0800 302 725
Fax (03) 732 8083
quartzlodge@xtra.co.nz
www.quartzlodge.co.nz

Double $100-$130 Single $75-$95 (Full breakfast)
Child $35 Dinner $30
Visa MC accepted
Pet free home Children welcome
1 King 1 Queen 1 Twin 1 Single (3 bdrm)
Bathrooms: 1 Ensuite 1 Guest share 1 Private

You will be sure of a friendly welcome when you arrive at Quartz Lodge, in the heart of Reefton. Guests only entrance will take you upstairs to huge picture windows in every room. Luxurious beds, robes and so much more. We are surprised how often our guests compliment us on our comfortable beds. Laundry service available. Complimentary coffee and a selection of teas are available in your private lounge/dining area. We pride ourselves on making you feel at home. Quality and comfort says it all.

Punakaiki *45 km N of Greymouth*

The Rocks Homestay *B&B Homestay*
Peg & Kevin Piper
No. 33 Hartmount Place, PO Box 16, Punakaiki 7850

Tel (03) 731 1141 Fax (03) 731 1142
therocks@minidata.co.nz
www.therockshomestay.com

Double $130-$190 Single $110-$160
(Special breakfast) Dinner $40-$55 by arrangement
Self-contained house $140-$180 Visa MC accepted
2 Queen 2 Twin (3 bdrm)
Bathrooms: 3 Ensuite

At Punakaiki, in view of the Pancake Rocks and Blowholes, adjacent Truman Track and beach, The Rocks Homestay sits above the forest - comfortable, modern, well-appointed, warm, friendly - unique in its wilderness location. Huge windows provide astounding panoramic views - coast, sea, crags, rainforest, National Park. Healthy breakfasts with home-baking. Home-cooked evening meals (by arrangement). Take time to experience unspoiled New Zealand. Walk a track, stroll on a beach, photograph limestone gorges, enjoy the reference library. Midway Greymouth and Westport, turn 200 metres north of Truman Track.

West Coast

Punakaiki - Barrytown *27 km N of Greymouth*

Golden Sands Homestay *Homestay*
Sue & Tom Costelloe
4 Golden Sands Road, Barrytown, Runanga

Tel (03) 731 1115 Fax (03) 731 1116
goldensands@paradise.net.nz

Double $95-$100 Single $55 (Continental)
Child by arrangement
Dinner by arrangement
Visa MC accepted
Children welcome
2 Queen 1 Twin (3 bdrm)
Bathrooms: 1 Ensuite 2 Private

Nestled between the Paparoa Range and the Tasman Sea on the Greymouth to Westport Scenic Highway, Golden Sands Homestay offers a friendly atmosphere and comfortable rooms. It is handy to Punakaiki, the Pancake Rocks and the Paparoa National Park to the north, with Greymouth a 25 minute drive to the south. As well as stunning views and wonderful sunsets, Golden Sands Homestay has Sky television, internet facilities, a cosy fire in winter and a contented cat. Access and facilities for disabled people. Nearby restaurants.

Punakaiki - Barrytown *20 km N of Greymouth*

Kallyhouse *B&B Homestay Apartment with Kitchen*
Kathleen & Alister Schroeder
13 Cargill Road, Barrytown, RD 1, Westland

Tel (03) 731 1006 Fax (03) 731 1106
kallyhouse@xtra.co.nz
www.bnb.co.nz/schroeder.html

Double $100-$120 Single $75 (Continental)
Visa MC accepted
Pet free home
3 Queen 1 Twin (4 bdrm)
Bathrooms: 1 Ensuite 1 Guest share 1 Spa Bath

We have a new spacious home on a quiet rear section, a garden setting, with native bush backdrop and sea views. We offer a self-contained flat downstairs, with queen room and twin beds in spacious living area. Full kitchen, bathroom, washing machine, parking and separate entrance. We also have 2 queen rooms upstairs. Breakfast with host. Punakaiki Pancake Rocks and adventure activities in Paparoa National Park, 10 minutes north. Greymouth is 20 minutes south. Turn at Barrytown Hotel corner, past 3 houses on left, up the lane, house on left.

Nine Mile Creek *14 km N of Greymouth*

The Breakers *Homestay*
Jan Macdonald
PO Box 188, Greymouth, Westland

Tel (03) 762 7743 Fax (03) 762 7733
stay@breakers.co.nz
www.breakers.co.nz

Double $150-$235 (Full breakfast)
Visa MC accepted
Not suitable for children
2 King 2 Queen 2 Twin (4 bdrm)
Bathrooms: 4 Ensuite

One of the West Coast's most spectacularly located B&Bs, with stunning views over the ocean. Private beach access allows you to fossick for jade and beautiful stones. All rooms are ensuite with TV and hot beverage making facilities. Fall asleep to the sound of the waves on the beach below. The Breakers is a wonderful base to visit the Pancake Rocks, the Paparoa National Park and the best stretch of coastline in NZ. Sorry, unsuitable for children

Greymouth *In Greymouth Central*
Ardwyn House *Homestay*
Mary Owen
48 Chapel Street, Greymouth

Tel (03) 768 6107 Fax (03) 768 5177
ardwynhouse@hotmail.com

Double $85-$90 Single $55 (Full breakfast)
Child half price
Visa MC accepted
Children welcome
2 Queen 3 Single (3 bdrm)
Bathrooms: 1 Guest share

Ardwyn House is 3 minutes walk from the town centre in a quiet garden setting offering sea, river and town views. The house was built in the 1920s and is a fine example of an imposing residence with fine woodwork and leadlight windows, whilst being a comfortable and friendly home. Greymouth's ideally situated for travellers touring the West Coast being central with good choice of restaurants. We offer a courtesy car service to and from local travel centres and also provide off-street parking.

Greymouth *4 km S of Greymouth*
Piners Homestay *Homestay*
Bev & Graham Piner
75 Main South Road, Karoro, Greymouth

Tel (03) 768 5397 Fax (03) 768 5396
tpiner@paradise.net.nz

Double $85-$95 Single $60-$65 (Full breakfast)
Child negotiable
Dinner $30
Visa MC accepted
Children welcome
1 Double 1 Twin (2 bdrm)
Bathrooms: 1 Guest share 2 toilets

We have been welcoming guests to our home for many years. Our elevated home is near the beach and you will see amazing sunsets. There is off-road parking. Your hostess enjoys creating delicious food using home-grown and local produce. Dinner $30pp. We take a maximum of 4 guests. There is a second toilet adjacent to the bedrooms. We have 2 spoilt cats. Courtesy pick up from TranzAlpine or bus; also rental cars can be arranged at competative rates. See you soon.

West Coast

Greymouth *6 km S of Greymouth*

Paroa Homestay (formerly Pam's Homestay) *Homestay*
Pam Sutherland
345 Main South Road, Greymouth

Tel (03) 762 6769 or 027 323 3118
Fax (03) 762 6765 paroahomestay@xtra.co.nz
www.paroahomestay.co.nz

Double $110-$130 **Single** $79-$99 (Special breakfast)
Child negotiable Visa MC accepted
Children over 5 welcome
1 King/Twin1 King 1 Double (3 bdrm)
Bathrooms: 1 Ensuite 1 Guest share 1 Private

Relax on terraces overlooking the sea and watch incredible sunsets. 3 minutes walk to the beach. Towering trees, native bush surrounds spacious classic home with luxurious guest lounge. Excellent restaurants within 3-6 minutes drive. Experience superb continental breakfast as baking and cooking is Pam's forte (previously owning Greymouth's busiest cafe/bar). Pam has NZQA Food Hygiene qualifications. West Coast born, Pam's local knowledge is invaluable. Pam enjoys hospitality, antiques, china, organic gardening and bush walking. Courtesy transport from train/bus (including complimentary drive to Shantytown).

Greymouth *3 km S of Greymouth*

Maryglen Homestay *Homestay*
Allison & Glen Palmer
20 Weenink Road, Karoro, Greymouth

Tel 0800 627 945 or (03) 768 0706
Fax (03) 768 0599 mary@bandb.co.nz
www.bandb.co.nz

Double $110-$140 **Single** $85-$10 (Continental)
Child negotiable Dinner $30pp
Visa MC accepted
Children welcome
2 King/Twin 1 Queen 1 Single (3 bdrm)
Bathrooms: 3 Ensuite

Native ferns and bush surround our hillside home overlooking the sea. Our guests comment- amazing location. The sound of the surf will lull you to sleep. Off the main road, quiet location, 2 rooms have own deck entrance. Amazing sunsets, family spa pool. Complimentary transport available from bus/train. Let us share our wonderful coast with you as we help you plan your days-scenic tours, bush walks, Argo Bike tours, Trans-scenic train (a must), Shantytown History Village, Punakaiki Pancake Rocks. We look forward to hearing from you.

Greymouth *6 km S of Greymouth*

Sunsetview *B&B Homestay Apartment with Kitchen*
Russell & Jill Fairhall
335 Main South Road, Greymouth 7801, South Island

Tel (03) 762 6616 Fax (03) 762 6616
sunsetview@xtra.co.nz

Double $100-$140 **Single** $90-$120 (Full breakfast)
Child by arrangement
Dinner by arrangement
Visa MC accepted
Children and pets welcome
2 King/Twin1 King 1 Queen (4 bdrm)
Bathrooms: 2 Ensuite 1 Private

Jill & Russell welcome you to our sunny modern home with amazing sea and mountain views. We offer well-appointed superior bedrooms. Sky TV in rooms. Home-cooked meals available on request. Outdoor areas, pool and barbecue. Short walk to beach, shop. Courtesy car available to local resturants, travel centres. Off-street parking. Downstairs apartment has two bedrooms (either can be king double or single beds) bathroom with wardrobe /dressing room. Kitchen with dining/lounge area. Own entrance with undercover parking.

Greymouth *12 km N of Greymouth*
Westway *B&B Homestay Campavan site*
John Best & Wayne Margison
58 Herd Street, Dunollie, Greymouth

Tel (03) 762 7077 or 027 495 2844
Fax (03) 762 7377 westway@xtra.co.nz
www.westway.co.nz

Double $100-$120 Single $85-$95 (Continental)
Child negotiable Dinner $25-$40
Cooked breakfasts avalable
Campavan from $15 Children welcome
1 King 2 Queen 1 Twin (3 bdrm)
Bathrooms: 1 Ensuite 1 Guest share 1 Private

Just minutes from Greymouth, Westway is situated in a native forest clad valley, including an historic tunnel and glowworms. Only 5 minutes drive from a sandy beach. There are private places in the garden where you can experience nature and the tranquility of Westway. We have a friendly and relaxing lifestyle; take pleasure in sharing our local knowledge and in creating an environment that visitors enjoy. There's space for your leisure equipment. Evening meals available. Complimentary transport. Come and let us spoil you.

Greymouth *15 km S of Greymouth*
Chapel Hill *B&B Homestay Farmstay*
Gay Sweeney
783 Rutherglen Road, Paroa, Greymouth

Tel (03) 762 6662 or 025 816 736
Fax (03) 762 6664
gay@chapelhill.co.nz

Double $90-$110 Single $75 (Full breakfast)
Dinner $25 Visa MC accepted
Children and pets welcome
2 Queen 1 Twin 1 Single (3 bdrm)
Bathrooms: 1 Ensuite 1 Guest share 1 Private

Touch the ferns out your window! Spectacular architect-designed country stay in a rainforest setting, 15 minutes south of Greymouth on the Christchurch-Glaciers Highway. Huge log fire, free email, and big comfy beds with electric blankets. Hearty country breakfasts included. Home-grown food. Dinner, wine, beer available. 40 minutes to Pancake Rocks & Hokitika Gorge, 60 minutes to Arthurs Pass. Non-smoking inside. Pets, farm and wildlife on the property. Unusual multi-level design is unsuitable for toddlers or disabled.

Greymouth *3 km N of Greymouth*
Oak Lodge *B&B Homestay*
Colette & Brian MacKenzie
286 State Highway 6, Coal Creek, Greymouth

Tel (03) 768 6832 or 0800 625 563
Fax (03) 768 4362
relax@oaklodge.co.nz
www.oaklodge.co.nz

Double $130-$290 Single $110 (Full breakfast)
Children welcome
2 King/Twin 2 Queen 1 Twin (5 bdrm)
Bathrooms: 4 Ensuite 1 Private

This 100 year old farmhouse is full of character, and only 3 minutes from Greymouth. It is surrounded by extensive gardens, has a spa/jacuzzi, swimming pool, sauna, tennis court, billiard room, guest lounge and laundry facilities. This 20 acre hobby farm has an unusual collection of black sheep, hens, and a very friendly donkey called Finias. Colette and Brian, who have travelled themselves, extend a very warm welcome to you. A generous farmhouse breakfast is served. "We came as guests and leave as friends."

Moana - Lake Brunner *35 km E of Greymouth*

Lancewood *B&B Homestay*

Jan & Simon Wilkins
2177 Arnold Valley Road, Moana, Lake Brunner

Tel (03) 738 0844 or 027 436 9706
lancewood.upon.moana@paradise.net.nz
www.lancewood.co.nz

Double $215 Single $195 (Full breakfast)
Child by arrangement
Bunk-room for older children
Visa MC Diners accepted Children welcome
1 Queen (1 bdrm)
Bathrooms: 1 Ensuite

A warm welcome awaits you at Lancewood?. Relax with us enjoying captivating views of Lake Brunner, amidst a scenic backdrop of the Southern Alps. Spend time enjoying bush walks, gold panning, trout fishing or a launch trip. Your choice of accommodation has a double queen bed with ensuite, complimentary tea and coffee facilities plus TV and fridge. A continental breakfast is served at a time suitable to you. A bunk room is available for older children. For further information please refer our website

Moana - Lake Brunner *35 km E of Greymouth*

Lake View B&B *Cottage with Kitchen*

Brent & Madeline Beadle
18 Johns Road, Moana, Westland

Tel (03) 738 0886 or 0274 318022
Fax (03) 738 0887
browntrout@minidata.co.nz
www.fishnhunt.co.nz/guides/brunner/index.htm

Double $100-$120 Single $90-$100
(Continental provisions)
Child $20 Extra adult $20
Visa MC accepted Children welcome
1 King 2 Single (2 bdrm)
Bathrooms: 1 Private

Lake View B&B offers guests fantastic views of Lake Brunner from the lounge, the decking or while lying in bed. Accommodation is a very private self-contained cottage adjacent to our house only five minutes walk to the village centre, cafe or hotel. The lake is famous for its trout fishing 365 days and Brent is a fishing guide. Lake tours, canoe hire, bush walks and a pottery are all close by. The Tranz Alpine stops at Moana. Christchurch is three hours away by road.

Moana - Lake Brunner *34 km E of Greymouth*

Lake Brunner B&B & Golf Course *B&B*

Pete & Deb Connor
2046 Arnold Valley Road, Moana, Lake Brunner

Tel (03) 738 0646 Fax (03) 738 0647
brunnerb&b&golf@xtra.co.nz
www.brunnerb&b&golf@xtra.co.nz

Double $150-$200 Single $130-$180 (Full breakfast)
Visa MC Diners Amex Eftpos accepted
Not suitable for children
6 King (6 bdrm)
Bathrooms: 6 Ensuite

Lake Brunner B&B and Golf Course

A warm welcome awaits you at our new purposely built B&B. Nestled along side beautiful native bush only minutes away from the lake front. All our rooms have king-sized beds, fridge, TV and ensuite facilities. Complimentary tea and coffee are available in both your room and the guests lounge. Your room opens to a peaceful deck to enjoy the scenery and golf course. The attractions in the area are countless from fishing, bush walks, gold panning and not forgetting the best little golf course in the area.

Hokitika *2 km N of Hokitika*

Hokitika Heritage Lodge *Luxury B&B Homestay*
Dianne & Chris Ward
46 Alpine View, Hokitika

Tel (03) 755 7357 or 0800 261 949
027 437 1254 Fax (03) 755 8760
hokitikaheritage@xtra.co.nz
www.hokitikaheritagelodge.co.nz

Double $165-$195 Single $165 (Full breakfast)
Dinner by arrangement
Visa MC accepted
Not suitable for children
1 King 2 Queen 1 Single (3 bdrm)
Bathrooms: 3 Ensuite

B&B Approved

West Coast

Dianne (Literacy Teacher) and Chris (Property Consultant and Rotarian) have planned and built a purpose-built lodge, based on their experience over a number of years hosting B&B guests.

Heritage is the theme for our lodge, the bricks are from a hotel built in Christchurch in the 1800s; our guest rooms are "Gold", "Jade", and "Heritage" to reflect the West Coast history.
The colours are stunning, making modern stylish accommodation, with old world charms.
The rooms are quiet; all have ensuites; wonderful views of the sea, mountains or bush; tea/coffee making; Sky TV; broadband and wireless internet are available.

You are warmly welcomed with a drink and home-made baking in our comfortable and gracious lounge, where you can enjoy magnificent views from the Tasman Sea to the mountains, including Mounts Cook and Tasman. The sunsets are magical.

We love to chat with our guests over a complimentary pre-dinner drink about your travels and we can help with planning and bookings for the next stage of your holiday, as we have a wide knowledge of what New Zealand has to offer..

Guests comments have included: "night to remember, a home not to forget!", "Delightful warm and friendly atmosphere. We felt so welcome, and were treated like friends.", "What a beautiful place", "We love your decor - would like to stay longer!", "The best!! Warm & gracious hospitality.", "Tell your friends"

We can offer dining in our beautiful dining room where views once again can be enjoyed along with a 4-course dinner. A bush-setting spa pool will be operating for your use, and our large garden is really beginning to take shape.

Find us by following 'Lodge' signs from the main road to the airport, along Tudor Street, turning left into Airport Drive. Turn right at the top of the hill into Alpine View. Travel to the end of the street, turning left into our drive. Follow the road around the house to the parking area and main entrance.

Hokitika *3 km S of Hokitika*

Meadowbank *B&B Rural Homestay*
Alison & Tom Muir
Takutai Road, RD 3, Hokitika

Tel (03) 755 6723 Fax (03) 755 6723

Double $90 Single $60 (Full breakfast)
Child half price Dinner by arrangement
Children welcome
1 Double 2 Single (2 bdrm)
Bathrooms: 1 Guest share

Tom and Alison welcome you to their lifestyle
property, situated just minutes south of Hokitika. Our
large home, which we share with 2 cats, is modern,
sunny and warm, and has a large garden.
Nearby we have the beach, excellent golf-links, Lake Mahinapua, paddleboat, river, and of course
Hokitika, with all its attractions. Directions: travel south 2km from south end of Hokitika Bridge on
SH6, turn right - 200 metres on right. North-bound traffic - look for sign 1km north of Golf-links and
Paddleboat.

Hokitika *1 km N of Hokitika*

Montezuma *Homestay*
Russell & Alison Alldridge
261 Revell Street, Hokitika, Westland

Tel (03) 755 7025 montezuma@actrix.co.nz

Double $95 Single $65 (Continental)
Pet free home Not suitable for children
1 Queen 1 Double (2 bdrm)
Bathrooms: 1 Ensuite 1 Family share 1 Guest share

Welcome to Montezuma by the sea. So named
after a ship that was wrecked here in 1865. Alison a
Queenslander, Russell a genuine West Coaster. Enjoy a
leisurely walk along the beach, watch the breathtaking
sunset, visit the nearby glowworm dell and take time out to enjoy our West Coast hospitality. Directions:
when travelling to Hokitika from north take first turn to your right (Richards Drive). Our house is the
last on the street. When travelling from south turn left at the last street out of town.

Hokitika *0.9 km E of Hokitika*

Larry's Rest *B&B Homestay Apartment with Kitchen Cottage with Kitchen*
Linda & Paul Hewson
188 Rolleston Street, Hokitika

Tel (03) 755 7636 or 021 220 3295
info@larrysrest.co.nz
www.larrysrest.co.nz

Double $125-$150 Single $115-$125 (Continental)
Apartment/cottage (sleeps 4) from $150
Visa MC Amex accepted Children and pets welcome
3 Queen 2 Twin (5 bdrm)
Bathrooms: 1 Ensuite 2 Private

Receive a warm welcome at Larry's Rest where
outdoor enthusiasts Linda & Paul will willingly share their extensive knowledge of South Island walks,
activities and attractions, enabling you to make the most of your holiday. We offer a range of quality
accommodation: queen studio unit with ensuite; secluded self-contained modern apartment (pictured)
with wheelchair friendly bathroom; and our restored colonial cottage (both with queen and twin rooms).
Both have all modern conveniences including laundry. Families welcome. Signposted from the main
highway opposite the 4 Square store.

Hokitika - Lake Kaniere *15min km E of Hokitika*

Serenity *Apartment with Kitchen*
Kay & Dave Clausen
6 Stuart Street, Hans Bay, Lake Kaniere,
Postal: PO Box 133, Hokitika

Tel (03) 755 5038 or 027 437 2666
dmkeclausen@xtra.co.nz

Double $80 Single $60 (Continental)
Child under 15 years $20
Extra adult over double $40
Children welcome
1 Queen 2 Single (1 bdrm)
Bathrooms: 1 Private

Lake Kaniere is set amongst beautiful New Zealand native bush. The scenery is breathtaking. There are many bush-walks around the lake, and Dorothy Falls is just a short drive from Serenity. Our studio apartment is self-catering and has full kitchen and bathroom facilities. All linen is provided. Restaurants and cafe-bars are just a shortdrive away, at Hokitika, or it's great to just relax and enjoy the surroundings at Lake Kaniere - a very unspoilt place! Serenity is 2 minutes walk from the lake. Separate access, studio apartment.

Hokitika - Upper Kokatahi *28 km E of Hokitika*

Sheridan Farmstay *Farmstay Cottage with Kitchen*
Trish & Terry Sheridan
Middle Branch Road, Upper Kokatahi RD 1, Hokitika

Tel (03) 755 7967
tpsheridan@xtra.co.nz

Double $100 Single $60 (Full breakfast)
Child negotiable
Dinner $30 by arrangement
Self-contained cottage from $75
Children and pets welcome
1 Queen 2 Double 3 Twin (6 bdrm)
Bathrooms: 1 Ensuite 1 Family share 2 Guest share

Welcome to our 1000 acre dairy farm at the top of Kokatahi Valley 28km east of Hokitika. Numerous day walks, 3 rivers with trout fishing and kayaking and Lake Kaniere are all minutes away. Share our home or stay in our fully serviced self-contained unit. We enjoy meeting people and love travelling. Terry enjoys current affairs and all sports while Trish is happy in the kitchen or garden. Enjoy dining with us in peaceful surroundings.

Hokitika *7 km E of Hokitika*

Riverside Villa *B&B Homestay*
Margaret & Alan Stevens
185 Woodstock-Rimu Road, RD 3, Hokitika

Tel (03) 755 6466 or 027 437 1515
amstevens@actrix.co.nz

Double $90-$110 Single $70 (Full breakfast)
Child negotiable
Dinner $30 by arrangement
Pet free home Children welcome
1 Queen 1 Twin (2 bdrm)
Bathrooms: 1 Guest share

Set in extensive grounds with tranquil river and mountain views, Riverside Villa is a haven for relaxation a short drive away from Hokitika. We combine the elegance of a 100 year old villa with the warmth of large open plan lounge and sunny verandahs. An ideal place for peaceful stopover. With the Hokitika river on the boundary, it is a fisherman's paradise with our own glowworm grotto. We are keen travellers, have an extensive knowledge of NZ outdoors and enjoy meeting people. Warm hospitality assured.

West Coast

Hokitika *2 km E of Hokitika*

Woodland Glen Lodge *Luxury B&B*
Janette & Laurie Anderson
Hau Hau Road, Blue Spur, Hokitika

Tel (03) 755 5063 or 0800 361 361 (NZ Only)
027 201 6126 Fax (03) 755 5063
l.anderson@xtra.co.nz
www.hokitika.net

Double $140-$280 Single $130-$180 (Full breakfast)
Visa MC Diners Amex Eftpos accepted
Children welcome
5 Queen 2 Twin (5 bdrm)
Bathrooms: 3 Ensuite 1 Guest share

Our 6500 square foot lodge is located on 21 acres and is surrounded in native kahikatea trees providing complete quiet and privacy. A great place for a retreat or just time out. Most guests base themselves in Hokitika for visits to the glaciers and Punakaiki, allow 2 nights. Laurie & Janette welcome you to Woodland Glen Lodge, both are widely travelled and have many experiences to share with you. Laurie is a retired police officer and commercial pilot, Janette is a health professional with a keen interest in quilting.

Hokitika *1 km N of Hokitika*

Top View Homestay/B&B *B&B Homestay*
Lin & Colin Jackson
24 Whitcombe Terrace Hokitika
PO Box 295 Hokitika

Tel (03) 755 7060 Fax (03) 755 7060
topview24@xtra.co.nz

Double $100-$110 Single $70 (Full breakfast)
Child price depending age
Reduced rates for longer stays
Pet free home Children welcome
2 Queen 2 Twin (3 bdrm)
Bathrooms: 1 Ensuite 1 Guest share

We offer you a place to relax with a superb view of mountains, sea and sunsets. Colin and Lin are retired farmers with many interests including Lions and Diabetes Societies. For those with Alergies, this is a pet free home. We look forward to your company over a cup of tea or coffee. From the main road north, turn at the Airport sign on Tudor Street, take the next left into Bonar Drive to the top of the hill on to Whitcombe Terrace, turn left.

Ruatapu *12 km S of Hokitika*

Berwick's Hill *B&B Country Stay*
Eileen & Roger Berwick
Ruatapu, Ruatapu-Ross Road,
State Highway 6, RD 3, Hokitika

Tel (03) 755 7876 or 025 673 7387
Fax (03) 755 7870
berwicks@xtra.co.nz
www.berwicks.co.nz

Double $100-$120 Single $70 (Full breakfast)
Dinner $40 by arrangement
Visa MC accepted
2 King/Twin 1 Queen (2 bdrm)
Bathrooms: 1 Ensuite 1 Private 1 bath in ensuite

Welcome to Berwick's Hill. We offer you a warm and relaxed stay in our comfortable home. Magnificent views of the Tasman Sea and the Southern Alps are seen from the main living areas. Experience the sunsets and sunrises. We are close to Lake Mahinapua, bush walks, the beach and golf course. We run sheep and cattle and grow pine trees on our hobby farm. We have one farm dog and we share our home with our cat and our house dog.

~

Harihari *0.5 km S of Hari Hari*
Wapiti Park Homestead *Luxury Farmstay*
Bev & Grant Muir
RD 1, Hari Hari 7953, South Westland

Tel (03) 753 3074 Fax (03) 753 3024
wapitipark@xtra.co.nz
www.wapitipark.co.nz

Double $165-$375 Single $125-$300 (Special breakfast)
Dinner $75pp Visa MC Eftpos accepted
Not suitable for children
3 King/Twin 2 King 4 Single (5 bdrm)
Bathrooms: 4 Ensuite 1 Private

"Superb in evey way and our best trout fishing day in NZ!" (S&M UK) "Surpassed expectations - wonderful hospitality, superb meals, 5 star accommodations and a magical experience with the elk. A truly memorable stay." (M&C USA) "Near perfect and our most enjoyable stay to date." (A&B NZ)

Hosts Grant and Beverleigh invite you to join them and discover the unique experience of staying at Wapiti Park Homestead. Enjoy a special combination of elegance, informal sophistication, and warm hospitality. Relax in complete comfort and affordable luxury.

Nestled beneath the forest-clad foothills of the Southern Alps and set in tranquil surroundings amid extensive gardens, our modern colonial style luxury lodge is built on the site of the original Hari Hari accommodation house, coaching stop, and post office. The homestead overlooks its own small farm which specialises in the breeding of Wapiti (Rocky Mountain Elk). Join Grant on the farm tour to handfeed the Wapiti, meet the farm pet Vicki, and learn about Elk Antler Velvet and it's potential health benefits.

Enjoy spacious indoor/outdoor areas; large bedrooms with superior comfort beds and ensuites or private facilities; 2 lounges and a trophy games room; a well stocked bar fridge and extensive selection of NZ wines; and our renowned "all you can eat" country-style 5 course dinners. Special diets catered for by prior arrangement.

Our location on State Highway 6 makes us the ideal stopover between the Nelson/Christchurch-Wanaka/Queenstown areas. However to explore this scenic wonderland of rainforests, glaciers, lakes and National Parks; to pursue the challenges of our renowned brown trout fishery; to hunt; or to simply catch your breath and relax, a minimum 2 night stay is recommended. Log on to our website www.wapitipark.co.nz for our suggested activities programs and more information. Unsuitable for children under 12. Advance booking recommended. Spoil yourself!

West Coast

Whataroa *35 km N of Franz Josef*

Matai Lodge *Farmstay*
Glenice & Jim Purcell
Whataroa, South Westland

Tel (03) 753 4156 or 021 395 068
021 395 068, 0800 787 235
Fax (03) 753 4156
jpurcell@xtra.co.nz

Double $150-$180 Single $120 (Full breakfast)
Dinner $40pp
1 King/Twin1 King 2 Single (3 bdrm)
Bathrooms: 1 Ensuite 1 Private

When your coming to the Glaciers, walk in the world
heritage park or visit the White Heron Bird Sanctuary we warmly welcome you to share our spacious home, this tranquil rural valley retreat. 20 minutes from Franz Josef Glacier. Upstairs is a suite of 2 bedrooms, conservatory and private bathroom. Downstairs a king-size ensuite. You're welcome to join us for a home-cooked dinner with NZ wines. Our motto is: A stranger is a friend we have yet to meet. Glenice speaks Japanese.

Whataroa *13 km (10 mins) N of Whataroa*

Mt Adam Lodge *B&B Farmstay*
Elsa & Mac MacRae
State Highway 6, Whataroa, South Westland

Tel (03) 753 4030 Fax (03) 753 4264
mtadamlodge@paradise.net.nz
www.mountadamlodge.co.nz

Double $90-$120 Single $75-$90 (Continental)
Fold-away bed $15 extra
Visa MC accepted
2 Queen 1 Double 4 Twin (7 bdrm)
Bathrooms: 5 Ensuite 2 Guest share

If you're wanting to escape the crowds in the busy
tourist centres then we are an ideal place for you to stay. Just a short 35 minute drive north of Franz Josef Glacier. We are situated on our farm at the foot of Mt Adam surrounded by farmlands and beautiful native bush. Our lodge is just newly established and offers comfortable accommodation and a fully licensed restaurant. You can stroll along the river bank and the farm tracks meeting our variety of animals along the way.

Whataroa *30 km N of Franz Josef Glacier*

Heritage Gateway B&B *B&B*
Clare & Rob Shaw
State Highway 6, Whataroa, South Westland

Tel (03) 753 4158 Fax (03) 753 4159
heritage.gateway@xtra.co.nz
www.heritage-gateway.co.nz

Double $100-$130 Single $70-$10 (Continental)
Visa MC Eftpos accepted
Children welcome
2 Queen 2 Single (3 bdrm)
Bathrooms: 2 Ensuite

We welcome you to our home in Whataroa, gateway
to South Westland's World Heritage Area, a scenic 25 minute drive north of Franz Josef Glacier. We offer a friendly, quiet retreat from the busy glacier towns in our comfortable, spacious 1930s home. Clare is a fourth generation member of a pioneering family who first settled on the West Coast in 1871. Rob originally from Auckland has been gold mining in this area for the past 30 years. Pet cat on property. Please view our web page.

Whataroa *3.6 km NW of Whataroa*
Whataroa Country Home Stay *B&B Homestay*
Stellamaris & Bruce Graham
360 Whataroa Flat Road, RD 1, Whataroa

Tel (03) 753 4130
bruceandstell@xtra.co.nz

Double $110 Single $80 (Continental)
Pet free home
Children welcome
1 Queen 2 Twin (3 bdrm)
Bathrooms: 1 Family share 1 Guest share

Stay with us on our 85 Hectare, 200 cow dairy farm, with a recently renovated homestead. Take a visit to the local native white heron colony, or travel 30 minutes south to Franz Josef and view its magnificent glacier. Skiplane or helicopter up to a landing on the snow, or take one of the many walks. The farm has a 450 metre gravel airstrip so why not fly in, though phone first. We have 2 cats, would not mind children over 12, but no pets please.

Franz Josef *5 km N of Franz Josef Glacier*
Ribbonwood Retreat *B&B Cottage No Kitchen*
Julie Wolbers & Jo Crofton
26 Greens Road, Franz Josef Glacier

Tel (03) 752 0072 Fax (03) 752 0272
ribbon.wood@xtra.co.nz
www.ribbonwood.net.nz

Double $160-$220 Single $150 (Continental)
Visa MC accepted Children welcome
1 King 2 Queen 1 Single
(2 doubles, king plus single bdrm)
Bathrooms: 1 Ensuite 1 Family share 1 Private Power showers, private bathroom has bath and shower.

Ribbonwood Retreat offers breathtaking views of forests, mountains and glaciers from your bedroom window. Keen travellers themselves hosts Julie & Jo welcome you to their modern home and new self-contained cottage only 5 minutes drive from bustling Franz Josef. Refresh yourself in luxury bathrooms and sleep soundly in comfortable beds. An ideal base for guided glacier walks, scenic flights, kayaking, bird watching or simply walking forest trails and secluded beaches. See you soon! Longhaired cat on premises. Children welcome. Tranquil rural location

Franz Josef *3 km S of Franz Josef Glacier*
Knightswood Bed and Breakfast *B&B*
Gerry Findlay
State Highway 6, Franz Josef Glacier

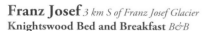

Tel (03) 752 0059 or 0800 752 0059
027 433 0312 Fax (03) 752 0061
knightswood@xtra.co.nz
www.knightswood.co.nz

Double $160-$210 Single $130-$170 (Continental)
Child price dependent on age
Dinner by arrangement
Visa MC accepted Children welcome
2 King/Twin 1 Queen 1 Single (3 bdrm)
Bathrooms: 2 Ensuite 1 Family share

Enjoy my modern home on 24 acres, with spectacular alpine views. 3km from Franz Josef Town, I assure you peace and tranquility. Ensuite rooms have private entrances and outdoor area. I am a former local helicopter pilot and wildlife ranger, and am well travelled and enjoy convivial conversations and sharing experiences. Enjoy an interpretive guided walk through my own native bush, view the prolific bird life or venture further for a scenic glacial flight or hike.

Fox Glacier *0.5 km W of Fox Glacier*

The Homestead *B&B Farmstay*
Noeleen & Kevin Williams
PO Box 25, Cook Flat Road, Fox Glacier

Tel (03) 751 0835 Fax (03) 751 0805
foxhmstd@xtra.co.nz

Double $135-$168 (Full breakfast)
Cooked breakfast $7pp
Not suitable for children
1 King/Twin1 King (3 bdrm)
Bathrooms: 2 Ensuite 1 Private

Kevin and Noeleen, welcome you to our 2200 acre beef cattle and sheep farm. Beautiful native bush-clad mountains surround on 3 sides, and we enjoy a view of Mt Cook.

Our spacious 105 year old character home, built for Kevin's grandparents, has fine stained glass windows. The breakfast room overlooks peaceful pastures to the hills, and you are served home-made yoghurt, jams, marmalade, scones etc, with a cooked breakfast if desired.

The guest lounge, with its beautiful wooden panelled ceiling, has an open plan fire for cool autumn nights.

A rural retreat within walking distance of village facilities, with Matheson (Mirror Lake) and glacier nearby. It is our pleasure to help you with helihikes, helicopter scenic flights and glacier walks.

Unsuitable for small children. Bookings recommended. Smoke-free.

Directions: On Cook Flat Road, fifth house on right, 400 metres back off road before church.

Fox Glacier *In Fox Glacier*

Roaring Billy Lodge *Homestay*
Kathy & Billy
PO Box 16, 21 State Highway 6, Fox Glacier

Tel (03) 751 0815 Fax (03) 751 0815
kathynz@xtra.co.nz

Double $85-$100 Single $70-$90 (Special breakfast)
Visa MC accepted
Not suitable for children
1 King/Twin 1 Double 1 Twin (2 bdrm)
Bathrooms: 1 Guest share 1 Private

Welcome to the comfort, warmth and hospitality of
our 2 storey home. Our livingroom, kitchen, diningroom and veranda are upstairs and lined with local
timbers, with 360-degree views of glacier valley, mountains, farms and the township. We're the closest
homestay to the glacier and 2 minutes walk to all eating and tourist facilities. We are happy to book your
local activities. The bus goes past our home. We offer a special cooked vegetarian breakfast. We have 1
cat, Koko and 1 dog, Angel.

Fox Glacier

Fox Glacier Homestay *Homestay*
Eunice & Michael Sullivan
64 Cook Flat Road, Fox Glacier

Tel (03) 751 0817 Fax (03) 751 0817
euni@xtra.co.nz

Double $90-$120 Single $80-$90 (Continental)
Children and pets welcome
1 Queen 1 Double 1 Twin 1 Single (3 bdrm)
Bathrooms: 1 Family share

Eunice and Michael are third generation farming
and tourism family. We have 3 grown children, 1 dog
(Ruff) and 3 cats (Bushy Tail, Sabrina & Tig). Our
grandparents were founders of the Fox Glacier Hotel. We are a couple who enjoy meeting people and
would like to share the joys of living in our little paradise (rain and all). Our home is surrounded by a
large garden and has views of the mountains and Mt Cook. A 5 minute walk from township.

Please let us know
how you enjoyed your B&B experience.
Ask your host for a comment form
or leave a comment on www.bnb.co.nz

Fox Glacier *2 km W of Fox Glacier*

Fox Glacier Mountain View B&B *B&B Homestay Cottage with Kitchen*

Karen Simpson
Williams Drive, Fox Glacier

Tel (03) 751 0770 Fax (03) 751 0774
info@foxglaciermountainview.co.nz
www.foxglaciermountainview.co.nz

Double $155-$170 Single $145 (Full breakfast)
Visa MC Eftpos accepted
Children welcome
3 King (3 bdrm)
Bathrooms: 3 Ensuite 1 Family share

Welcome to my peaceful hideaway set on 8 acres of pure nature at its best. This 6 year old country home has it all. With wide-open landscape, breathtaking views of Mt Cook and Mt Tasman, and surrounded by bush-clad hills with magnificent reflection on my own special pond.

I have a cosy self-contained cottage with basic kitchenette facility and ensuite. Inside my home, are ensuited super king/twin bedrooms, and super king/twin bedrooms with shared bathroom, which include a shower unit and a spa bath. (Pure heaven after a day out on the glacier!). 3 bedrooms have private access.

The area is ecologically diverse, from the West Coast's sub-temperate rain forest, to one of the lowest flowing Glaciers in the Southern Hemisphere at Fox Glacier.

Situated near one of the most photographed mirror lakes in New Zealand (Lake Matheson), and just a short distance further, is access to the wild West Coast (Gillespie's Beach) with long tracks of rugged coastline, which is home to many New Zealand fur seal colonies. From walking adventures to adrenaline activities. I can happily assist enhancing your Glacier experience to the full.

It's truly "a piece of paradise" - I'd like to share the comfort and individual uniqueness with you.

I have travelled extensively in New Zealand as part of my career, gaining a wealth of tourism knowledge, and can help in your travel plans (where to go or what to do) around the rest of our beautiful country

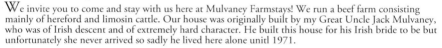

Bruce Bay *50 km S of Fox Glacier*
Mulvaney Farmstay *Farmstay*
Peter & Malai Millar
PO Box 117, Bruce Bay, South Westland

Approved

Tel (03) 751 0865 Fax (03) 751 0865
mulvaney@xtra.co.nz

Double $95-$95 Single $70 (Continental)
Dinner $30 Not suitable for children
1 Queen 1 Double 1 Twin (3 bdrm)
Bathrooms: 1 Family share 1 Guest share

West Coast

We invite you to come and stay with us here at Mulvaney Farmstays! We run a beef farm consisting mainly of hereford and limosin cattle. Our house was originally built by my Great Uncle Jack Mulvaney, who was of Irish descent and of extremely hard character. He built this house for his Irish bride to be but unfortunately she never arrived so sadly he lived here alone unitl 1971.

We have lived here for over 20 years with our children who have since grown and are now living away from home. Enjoy a pleasant and peaceful stay at our home by relaxing in our serene rural environment.

Unwind by taking a leisurely walk around our farm and surrounding areas (we are a short drive to numerous rivers and the beach) and absorb the tranquility and beaty of the deep South Westland landscape. Our local rivers are ideal for trout and salmon fishing. If you are too tired and weary for a walk then a long soak in a hot bath in the garden may be more appealing. Enjoy a bath the old fashioned country way outside in the garden looking toward the mountains - by prior arrangment preferably as it takes a while to get the fire hot enough to heat the bath water!

Malai, orignially from Thailand, offers a dinner option of authentic delicious cuisine or a home style European meal if preferred. Dinner is by prior arrangment only. We are situated 50km south of Fox Glacier (40 minutes) and 60km north of Haast (50 minutes). We are well sign posted from the main highway.

Haast *16 km S of Haast*

Okuru Beach *B&B Homestay Cottage with Kitchen*

Marian & Derek Beynon
Okuru, Haast, South Westland

Tel (03) 750 0719 Fax (03) 750 0722
okurubeach@xtra.co.nz
www.okurubeach.co.nz

Double $85-$95 Single $55 (Continental)
Child $20 Dinner $25 by arrangement
Self-contained $85-$95
Visa MC accepted
4 Double 6 Single (7 bdrm)
Bathrooms: 1 Ensuite 1 Guest share 2 Private

Okuru Beach gives you the opportunity to stay in a unique part of our country, in a friendly relaxing environment. Enjoy coastal beaches with driftwood, shells and penguins in season. Walk in the rainforest and view the native birds. We and our friendly labrador dogs enjoy sharing our comfortable home and local knowledge. Dinner served with prior notice. Our interests are our handcraft shop, coin collecting, fishing and tramping. Also available - Seaview Cottage, self-contained sleeps 8 persons. Directions: turn into Jacksons Bay Road, drive 14km turn into Okuru.

All our B&Bs are non-smoking
unless stated otherwise in the text.

The difference between a B&B and a hotel
is that you don't hug the hotel staff when you leave.

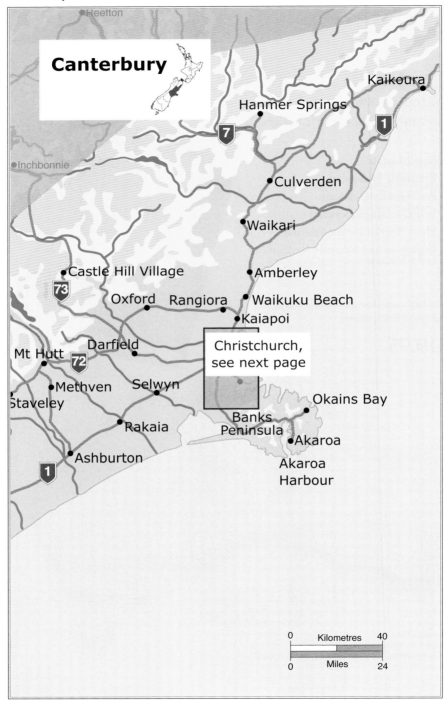

Canterbury

Reefton

Inchbonnie

Kaikoura

Hanmer Springs

Culverden

Waikari

Castle Hill Village

Amberley

Oxford

Rangiora

Waikuku Beach

Kaiapoi

Christchurch,
see next page

Okains Bay

Mt Hutt

Darfield

Selwyn

Staveley

Methven

Banks
Peninsula

Akaroa

Rakaia

Akaroa
Harbour

Ashburton

0   Kilometres   40

0   Miles   24

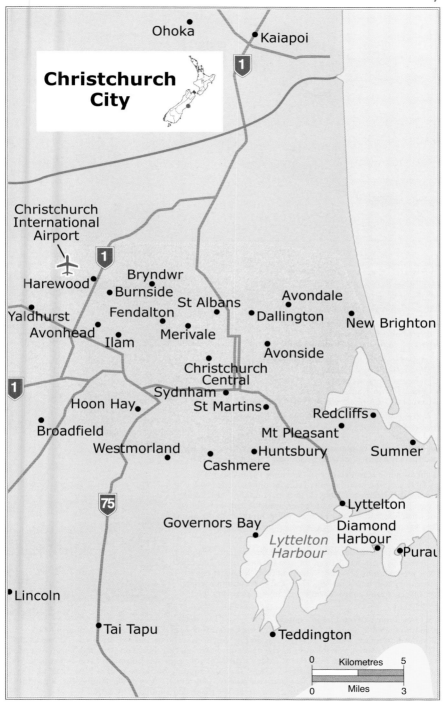

Ohoka

Kaiapoi

Christchurch City

1

Christchurch International Airport

1

Harewood

Bryndwr

Burnside

Fendalton

St Albans

Avondale

Dallington

New Brighton

Yaldhurst

Avonhead

Ilam

Merivale

Avonside

Christchurch Central

1

Sydnham

St Martins

Hoon Hay

Redcliffs

Broadfield

Mt Pleasant

Sumner

Westmorland

Huntsbury

Cashmere

75

Lyttelton

Governors Bay

Diamond Harbour

Lyttelton Harbour

Purau

Lincoln

Tai Tapu

Teddington

0 Kilometres 5

0 Miles 3

Kaikoura *130 km S of Blenheim*

Bay-View *Homestay*
Margaret Woodill
296 Scarborough Street, Kaikoura

Tel (03) 319 5480 Fax (03) 319 7480
bayviewhomestay@xtra.co.nz
www.bnb.co.nz/bayviewkaikoura.html

Double $85-$95 Single $55 (Full breakfast)
Child under 14 $15 Dinner $30
Children and pets welcome
1 Queen 1 Twin 1 Single (3 bdrm)
Bathrooms: 1 Ensuite 1 Guest share 1 Private

B&B
Approved

Our spacious family home on Kaikoura Peninsula has splendid mountain and sea views and is exceptionally quiet. Only 5 minutes from the Kaikoura township, off the main highway south. The house nestles in an acre of colourful garden and there is plenty of off-street parking.

A guest lounge is available or you are more than welcome to socialise with the host. Laundry facilities and tea/coffee with home-made baking available. Traditional breakfast with home-baked bread, muesli, home preserves, available early as required for whale/dolphin watching guests. Enjoy breakfast in the dining area or out on the sunny deck whilst taking in the magnificent mountain view.

We book local activities and happily meet bus or train. Margaret, your friendly host, has lived in the area for most of her life. She has a grown family of 4 and 7 grandchildren. Margaret enjoys gardening, golf, bowls, sewing, choir and her amusing burmese cat. She especially enjoys warmly welcoming guests into her home.

"Let Our Home be Your Home". Guests comments: "This B&B is an unforgettable memory for me in NZ 5 weeks travel" (Japan). "Beautiful place, beautiful food, fabulous hospitality, Margaret. Thank you for opening up your home and welcoming us. Be back again" (Wellington). "Thank you for meeting the train and showing us the area. You were highly recommended and we absolutely endorse this" (UK). "Many thanks for your generous hospitality. You and your lovely home are a credit to B&B Homestays" (UK). "The most amazing breakfast in all of New Zealand. The views are amazing too and so is Margaret's hospitality" (Australia). "We felt like family! Thank you for such a lovely visit and wonderful, delicious meals. We thank you a million!" (USA).

Kaikoura *5 km N of Kaikoura*

Ardara Lodge *B&B Cottage with Kitchen*

Alison & Ian Boyd

233 Schoolhouse Road, RD 1, Kaikoura

Tel (03) 319 5736 or 0800 226 164   Fax (03) 319 5732
aemboyd@xtra.co.nz
www.ardaralodge.com

Double $110-$150 Single $100-$120 (Continental)
Child by arrangement   Cottage $140-$250
Visa MC accepted
Children welcome
7 Queen 3 Twin 4 Single (7 bdrm)
Bathrooms: 5 Ensuite 1 Private

You will enjoy a relaxed and peaceful stay in a beautiful rural setting near the magnificent Kaikoura mountains. Relax on our deck and enjoy Alison's colourful garden which completes the panoramic view. Enjoy our outdoor hot tub (spa), view the Kaikoura mountains by day and the stars by night or read a book in our new guest lounge.

Ian's Great, Great, Uncle Jim, left Ardara, Ireland in 1876. He bought our land here in Kaikoura in 1883 and milked cows. He established an orchard and planted macrocarpa trees for shelter. One macrocarpa tree was milled and used to build the cottage which was designed and built by Ian in 1998. The cottage has an upstairs bedroom with a queen and two single beds. Downstairs there is a bedroom with a queen bed, a bathroom with a shower, and a lounge, kitchen, dining room. The deck is private with a great view of the mountains. It has been very popular with groups, families and honeymoon couples.

The house has ensuite bathrooms with queen beds,plus a two bedroom unit all with TV, fridge, settee and coffee/tea facilities. You have your own private entrance and you can come and go as you please. We offer laundry facilities, off-street parking, courtesy car from bus/train.

Bookings for local tourist attractions, restaurants and farm tours can be arranged. Ian's brother Murray, has Donegal House, an Irish Garden Bar and Restaurant, which is within walking distance. Ian is a retired teacher and Alison a librarian. Our hobbies are tennis, golf, designing and building houses, gardening, handcrafts, spinning and we like to travel. No smoking indoors please. We look forward to your company. Directions: Driving north, 4km from Kaikoura on SH1, turn left, 1.5km along Schoolhouse Road

Kaikoura *130 km S of Blenheim*

Churchill Park Lodge *B&B*

Moira & Stan Paul

34 Churchill Street, Kaikoura, Marlborough

Tel (03) 319 5526 or 0800 363 690
Fax (03) 319 5526
cplodge@ihug.co.nz
www.churchillparklodge.co.nz

Double $100-$120 Single $100-$120 (Continental)
Child $20
Visa MC accepted
Children welcome
1 Queen 1 Double 1 Single (2 bdrm)
Bathrooms: 2 Ensuite

We proudly offer you the choice of 2 separate upstairs suites with ensuite bathrooms, TV, fridge, lounge settee, dining suite, and tea/coffee making facilities including coffee percolator, heater and electric blankets. We have designed your room to guarantee your stay with us is comfortable and enjoyable. Our rooms are smoke-free.

We believe the sea and mountain views we offer from your room and balcony is unbeatable in Kaikoura. Take time to relax and enjoy your continental breakfast while watching the sunrise out of the sea, or your complimentary wine & nibbles enjoying the sea and mountain views. We offer laundry facilities and off-street parking.

Our home is only 5 minutes walk through Churchill Park to the town centre where you will find a restaurant that will suit your taste buds, souvenir shops, Visitor Information Centre and a walk along the beach. We are in close walking distance to Whalewatch and Dolphin Encounter Tour departure stations and are happy to book local tours and offer a courtesy pick up from train or bus stations.

We are a Christian couple and like Muffy, our cat, are friendly and welcoming and look forward to making your stay a time to remember.

Kaikoura - Oaro *22 km S of Kaikoura*

Waitane Homestay *B&B Homestay Cottage with Kitchen*

Kathleen King
Oaro, RD 2, Kaikoura

Tel (03) 319 5494 Fax (03) 319 5524
waitane@xtra.co.nz

Double $75-$85 Single $50 (Full breakfast)
Child $20
Dinner $20 by arrangement
Visa MC accepted
1 Double 4 Single (1 in B@B, 2 in cottage bdrm)
Bathrooms: 2 Private

Waitane is 48 acres, close to the sea and looking north
to the Kaikoura Peninsula. Enjoy coastal walks to the Haumuri Bluff with bird watching, fossil hunting etc, or drive to Kaikoura along our beautiful rocky coast. This is a mild climate and we grow citrus and sub-tropical fruits, mainly feijoas. Guest room in house has 2 single beds. Self-contained unit has 2 bedrooms, sleeps 4. 1 friendly cat lives here. Join me for dinner - fresh vegies, home preserves and home-made ice cream.

Kaikoura *3 km N of Kaikoura*

Carrickfin Lodge *B&B*

Roger Boyd
Mill Road, Kaikoura

Tel (03) 319 5165 or 025 315 076
Fax (03) 319 5162
rogerboyd@xtra.co.nz
www.carrickfinlodge.co.nz

Double $100-$120 Single $100-$120 (Full breakfast)
Child not suitable
Carreickfin Cottage, self-contained sleeps 6 $100-$120
5 Queen 2 Single (6 bdrm)
Bathrooms: 6 Ensuite

Carrickfin has been home of the Boyds since 1867. The lodge is on 100 acres on town boundary making it quiet and peaceful. Most rooms have stunning views of Kaikoura Mountains. 2 large lounges with open fire, guest bar (BYO) and 24 hour coffee/tea making facilities making it most welcome. The main feature of the Lodge is the Big Irish Breakfast!! which is legendary. We are 3km from Whale Watch, Dolphin Encounter. Directions: Mill Road is 3 km north of Kaikoura Township on State Highway 1

Kaikoura *180 km N of Christchurch*

Austin Heights *Luxury B&B Separate Suite Luxurious outdoor spa tub available from 1st Oct*

Lynley & John McGinn
19 Austin Street, Kaikoura--Canterbury, New Zealand

Tel (03) 319 5836 or 0800 080 324
Fax (03) 319 6836
austinheights@xtra.co.nz
www.austinheights.co.nz

Double $150-$240 Single $150-$180 (Continental)
Child negotiable Dinner by arrangement only
Visa MC accepted
Children welcome
1 King 1 Queen 1 Single (2 bdrm)
Bathrooms: 2 Ensuite

Austin Heights is close to Kaikoura's unique attractions, with whale watching and the towns centre only a minutes away. We have 2 luxury, spacious and warm ensuite units with large sliding doors opening directly out onto a balcony where you can sit with a glass of local wine and enjoy the stunning view. Both suites have quality furnishings, kitchenette,dining suite, microwave, TV, DVD player, stereo, CD & hairdryer.

Kaikoura *In Central Kaikoura*

Bendamere House *B&B Homestay*
Ellen & Peter Smith
37 Adelphi Terrace, Kaikoura

Tel (03) 319 5830 or 0800 107 770
Fax (03) 319 7337
bendamerehouse@xtra.co.nz
www.bendamere.co.nz

Double $110-$180 Single $70-$90 (Full breakfast)
Child negotiable
2 King 4 Queen 1 Twin 4 Single (7 bdrm)
Bathrooms: 6 Ensuite 1 Private

We are retired dairy farmers and fourth generation Kaikourians with extensive knowledge of the area.

Our 1930s restored home and large garden are just 5 minutes from the township, beach, Whale Watch, a great selection of restaurants, cafes and tourist other attractions. Incredible views of the Pacific Ocean and Seaward Kaikoura Mountains.

All rooms have electric blankets, heaters, hairdryers, bathrobes, television and tea making facilities. Fax and laundry facilities available. We have major additions for this season with 4 new luxury rooms, 2 at ground level and 2 elevated, all facing out to our superb views with private balconies.

We enjoy meeting people and assisting guests with their visits to our wonderful activities and attractions Kaikoura has to offer. We offer true country breakfasts and other home-made treats. Courtesy car available to meet buses and trains.

Kaikoura *4 km N of Kaikoura Central*
The Point *B&B*
Peter & Gwenda Smith
Fyffe Quay, Kaikoura

Tel (03) 319 5422 Fax (03) 319 7422
pointsmith@xtra.co.nz
www.pointbnb.co.nz

Double $90-$10 Single $80-$90 (Continental)
1 Queen 1 Double (2 bdrm)
Bathrooms: 2 Ensuite

We offer you a warm and friendly welcome to our
family home, which we share with our 2 daughters.
Enjoy the quietness and unique location of this
beautiful 125 year old farmhouse. On the waterfront and surrounded by 90 acres of farmland (part of
Kaikoura Peninsula). Spectacular views of the sea and mountains. Ideally situated for walks around the
Kaikoura peninsula and seal colony. 5 minutes walk to one of Kaikoura's top restaurants. We run daily
sheep shearing shows, have farm dogs and a cat.

Kaikoura
Nikau Lodge *B&B*
John & Lilla Fitzwater
53 Deal Street, Kaikoura (central), Kaikoura

Tel (03) 319 6973 or 021 682 076
Fax (03) 319 6973
stay@NikauLodge.com
www.NikauLodge.com

Double $135-$225 Single $135-$225 (Full breakfast)
Visa MC Eftpos accepted
Pet free home Not suitable for children
1 King/Twin 4 Queen 1 Double (6 bdrm)
Bathrooms: 5 Ensuite 1 Private

Conveniently located in the heart of Kaikoura on SH1 with magnificent hilltop views of sea and
mountains, Nikau offers high quality affordable B&B accommodation. 5 minutes walk takes you to
Kaikoura's main street where you can enjoy local rock lobster. Relax in the hot-tub or garden with a glass
of wine and gaze at the stars and snow-capped mountains. Internet access, Sky TV, complimentary tea/
coffee, laundry, in-room TV/movies etc. Friendly hosts John & Lilla Fitzwater welcome the opportunity
to make your stay enjoyable and memorable.

Kaikoura *In Kaikoura Central*
Driftwood Villa *Deluxe B&B*
Suzy James & Chris Valkhoff
166A Beach Road, Kaikoura

Tel (03) 319 7116 or 027 476 7000
Fax (03) 319 7116
chrisandsuzy@xtra.co.nz
www.driftwoodvilla.co.nz

Double $130-$180 Single $105-$125 (Full breakfast)
Child $20
Visa MC accepted
Children welcome
1 King 3 Queen 1 Twin 4 Single (4 bdrm)
Bathrooms: 4 Ensuite

Quality beachfront accommodation with great young hosts who know what is important to guests.
We offer 4 delightful ensuite bedrooms decorated with warmth and style. Comfortable beds - powerful
showers - full cooked and continental breakfast - private beach bench - spa pool and bath robes - homely
guest lounge and kitchen - electric blankets - TV - Dutch and German also spoken - and much more....
Chris, Suzy & the cat look forward to your stay with us.

Canterbury

Kaikoura *In Central Kaikoura*

Admiral Creighton B&B *Luxury B&B*
Yvonne & Tony Steadman
191 Beach Road, Kaikoura

Tel 0800 742 622 or (03) 319 7111 Fax (03) 319 7111
admiral.creighton.b2b@ihug.co.nz
www.admiral-creighton.com

Double $100-$200 **Single** $95 (Full breakfast)
Dinner $30
Visa MC Amex accepted
Not suitable for children
4 Queen 1 Twin (5 bdrm)
Bathrooms: 3 Ensuite 2 Private

You will love staying at this lovely B&B which has been designed for your every comfort. Enjoy a complimentary wine or beer as you soak up the magnificent vista of the Seaward Kaikoura Mountains. Choose your breakfast dining time, select from the menu your favorite cooked or continental breakfast. Feed the trout, eels and ducks in our stream boundry. Ideal small conference venue with spacious living and BBQ area. Dinners by prior arrangement. A courtesy car is available and off-street parking. Our well behaved cockatoo Creighton will welcome you warmly. On line booking at www.admiral-creighton.com

~

Hanmer Springs *5 km SW of Hanmer Springs*

Mira Monte *B&B Countryhomestay*
Anna & Theo van de Wiel
324 Woodbank Road, Hanmer Springs

Tel (03) 315 7604 Fax (03) 315 7604
relax@miramonte.co.nz
www.miramonte.co.nz

Double $120-$140 **Single** $95-$11 (Special breakfast)
Child negotiable Dinner by arrangement
Visa MC accepted Children welcome
2 King 1 Single (2 bdrm)
Bathrooms: 2 Ensuite

Close to the thrills of Hanmer Springs, at the foot of the mountains, lies our peaceful home. Our guest rooms have been tastefully decorated to make your stay special. Relax in your own sitting room or join us. We make a great espresso! Years in the hospitality trade have taught us how to pamper you. There is a grand piano and our large garden has a swimming pool. We speak Dutch and German. Mindy, our Jack Russell is part of the family. Come as a Stranger! Leave as a Friend!

~

Hanmer Springs *In Hanmer village*

Cheltenham House *B&B Cottage No Kitchen*
Maree & Len Earl
13 Cheltenham Street, Hanmer Springs

Tel (03) 315 7545 Fax (03) 315 7645
enquiries@cheltenham.co.nz
www.cheltenham.co.nz

Double $170-$210 **Single** $140-$180
(Special breakfast)
Child by arrangement Extra person $30
Visa MC Diners Eftpos accepted
Children and pets welcome
2 King/Twin 5 Queen 1 Single (6 bdrm)
Bathrooms: 5 Ensuite 1 Private

Located on a quiet street, 200 metres from the Thermal Pools, restaurants and forest walks, this gracious 1930s home was renovated with the guests comfort paramount. The 4 spacious, sunny suites in the house and 2 cottage suites in the park-like garden, are all centrally heated. Enjoy breakfast of your choice served in the privacy of your suite and complimentary local wine in the original rimu panelled billiard room in the evening. Together with our sociable siamese, we look forward to meeting you.

Hanmer Springs *130 km N of Christchurch*

Albergo Hanmer Lodge & Alpine Villa
B&B & Self-contained Villas   **Bascha & Beat Blattner**
88 Rippingale Road, Hanmer Springs

Tollfree 0800 342 313 Ph/fax 03 315 7428 albergo@paradise.net.nz
www.albergohanmer.com   **Check web for packages!**

Double $150-$230 Single $100 Villa $260-$525
(Special breakfast) Dinner by prior arrangement
Visa MC Diners Amex accepted
3 Superking/Twin, 1 King (4 ensuite)

BREAKFAST - WELLNESS - CUISINE

Arrive at Albergo Hanmer to blitz your senses in the fresh n' fun eclectic interiors with whimsical touches. **Dramatic Alpine Views** stream in from all windows. **Stretch out on super king beds**, with TV/fridge/tea & coffee and spacious ensuites (great water pressure) - choose the spa one for that bubble bath delight! Relax in cosy corners in the ambient guest lounges or the Feng Shui courtyard, with soothing waterfall & fragrant lavenders galore. **Privacy & all day sun:** 2 minutes from Hot Pools, shops & cafes. **Ask about hunting & fishing tours, pamper package delights.**

Your dedicated hosts have spent 6 years refining the Albergo accommodation experience by creating the Alpine Villa, for privacy plus. The living area features kitchen and lounge, double doors lead to the opulent American king bedroom with awesome in-room cinema and DVD library. The marbled ensuite boasts 'wow' views from the high panorama window, while you shower! Slip on a fluffy bathrobe, wander out to the split level courtyard with **private jacuzzi** and soak up Hanmer's starry night skies.

We are passionate about breakfasts! Served at a time to suit you, **Albergo's renowned breakfast** offers over 10 choices: Start with a creative fruit platter or Swiss Birchermuesli, followed by the wafting smell of **Home-made swiss bread & fine Italian coffee.** Help yourself to tempting cereals, while the hosts prepare your mains: Salmon Eggs Benedict, French fluffy omelets, wafer-thin crepes, 'Albergo Egg Nests' with crispy bacon. Candlelight fine dining by prior arrangment.

'*There are few places in the world with an energy quite like this, altruistic cuisine, interiors and a sense of calm*' Sarah and Roger, London, UK. '*Albergo is the most warmest, adorable and fun place I have ever visited. Your kindness and spirit shine through in everything*' Marcia & Paul, Colorado, USA

Directions: At junction before main village, 300 metres past Shell Garage, take **Argelins Rd** (Centre branch), take 2nd road left **Rippingdale Rd**. Albergo Hanmer is 700 metres down on the left hand side (Sign at drive entrance).

Canterbury

Hanmer Springs *In Hanmer Springs*

Hanmer View *B&B*
Will & Helen Lawson
8 Oregon Heights, Hanmer Springs, 8273

Tel (03) 315 7947 Fax (03) 315 7958
hanmerview@xtra.co.nz   www.hanmerview.co.nz

Double $160-$185 Single $130-$150 (Full breakfast)
Child N/A
Visa MC Eftpos accepted
Not suitable for children
1 King/Twin 2 Queen (3 bdrm)
Bathrooms: 3 Ensuite

Hanmer View, surrounded by beautiful forest and
adjoining Conical Hill track. Stunning panoramic alpine views. Purpose built to ensure guests enjoy
quiet, relaxing stay in warm, spacious quality ensuite rooms. Individually decorated with TV, wool
duvets and hand made patchwork quilts. Tea, coffee and cake always available and your hosts, Will and
Helen delight in serving you a generous scrumptious cooked & continental breakfast. No-one goes away
hungry. Short stroll to village, thermal pools and tourist attractions. See letterbox sign, on right, end
Oregon Heights.

~

Hanmer Springs *1.5hrs km N of Christchurch*

Cheshire House *Luxury B&B*
Jan & Chris Ottley
164C Hanmer Springs Road, Highway 7A,
Hanmer Springs

Tel (03) 315 5100 or 0800 337 332
janandchris@xtra.co.nz

Double $130-$150 Single $100-$120 (Full breakfast)
Child over 10 years
Pet free home Children welcome
2 Queen 1 Twin (3 bdrm)
Bathrooms: 3 Ensuite

Cheshire House is conveniently situated 1 minutes
drive from Hanmer township. Come and be spoilt with our English hospitality and relax in one of our 3
beautifully furnished ensuite bedrooms with private guest entrance and stunning mountain views. Jan &
Chris will ensure that you have a memorable stay and breakfast in Hanmer Springs where many activities
can also be enjoyed if you wish. Experience Hanmer's delightful thermal pools and relax by indulging
into health, body and mind.

~

Hanmer Springs *140 km N of Christchurch*

Alpine B&B Hanmer *B&B*
Cobie & Gavin Bickerton
21A Leamington Street, Hanmer Springs, North
Canterbury 8273

Tel (03) 315 5051 Fax (03) 315 5051
gavinandco@callplus.net.nz

Double $120-$145 Single $100-$120 (Full breakfast)
Visa MC Diners Amex accepted
Pet free home   Not suitable for children
1 King/Twin 1 Queen (2 bdrm)
Bathrooms: 2 Ensuite

We invite you to come and stay at our purpose
designed brand new B&B home which opened in February 2005. We are in a very tranquil residential
street with views across the Hanmer Valley to the mountains and a short level walk to the famed hot
springs, forest walks, restaurants, and shops. Each of our 2 guest rooms has their own ensuite, entrance,
tea & coffee making facilities, and deck. Breakfast will be served in your room. Your hosts (NZ and
Dutch) believe they can offer you complete unobtrusive hospitality.

Culverden *3 km S of Culverden*
Ballindalloch *Farmstay*
Diane & Dougal Norrie
Culverden, North Canterbury

Tel (03) 315 8220 Fax (03) 315 8220
dianedougal@xtra.co.nz

Double $110 Single $60 (Full breakfast)
Child $30
Dinner $30 by arrangement
Children welcome
1 Queen 2 Single (2 bdrm)
Bathrooms: 1 Guest share

Welcome to Ballindalloch, 2090 acre irrigated farm
3km south of Culverden. We milk 1400 cows (2 herds) through a new 70 bail rotary dairy and a floating dairy. We have 1000 corriedale sheep stud. We are just over 1 hour north of Christchurch, half hour to Hanmer Springs, Kaikoura whales 1.5 hour drive. Having travelled extensively overseas we appreciate relaxing in a homely atmosphere - this we extend to our guests. I am involved in the nutrition field and enjoy discussing health care. Our cat is Thomas. We look forward to welcoming you.

Waikari *28 km NW of Amberley*
Tullach Glas Motel B&B *B&B Homestay Separate Suite*
Patsy & Ivor McMillan
38 Princes Street, Waikari, North Canterbury

Tel (03) 314 4931 Fax (03) 314 4936
info@countrystay.co.nz
www.countrystay.co.nz

Double $80-$90 Single $50 (Continental)
Child $15
Dinner $20pp by arrangement
Visa MC accepted
3 Queen 1 Twin (4 bdrm)
Bathrooms: 2 Ensuite 1 Guest share 2 Private

Welcome to our country home. We are 50 minutes from Christchurch International Airport and an ideal stop off point to major tourist attractions nearby. We have our own small farm, Biddy the sheep dog and BC our very aloof black cat. Rest awhile with us, lunch at local wineries, fish in our lakes and river, walk, horse trek, play golf or just admire the view.

Amberley *1 km S of Amberley*
Bredon Downs Homestay *Homestay Farmstay*
Bob & Veronica Lucy
Bredon Downs, Amberley, RD 1, North Canterbury

Tel (03) 314 9356 or (03) 314 8018
Fax (03) 314 8994
lucy.lucy@xtra.co.nz
www.bredondownshomestay.co.nz

Double $110-$130 Single $75 (Full breakfast)
Dinner $40 (including wine)
Visa MC accepted
1 Queen 1 Twin 1 Single (3 bdrm)
Bathrooms: 1 Ensuite 1 Private

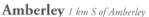

Our drive goes off SH1 and so we are conveniently en route to and from the Interisland Ferry, just 48km north of Christchurch and 100km south of the Kaikoura whales, and easy to find. The house is surrounded by an English style garden with swimming pool, and close to the Waipara wineries, beach and attractive golf course. We breed ostriches which we are pleased to show visitors, have travelled extensively and lived abroad, and now share our lives with a newfoundland and a labrador, 2 geriatric donkeys and Hugo the cat!

Canterbury

Amberley *1 km W of Amberley*

Kokiri B&B *B&B Apartment with Kitchen*
Pat & Graham Shaw
65 Douglas Road, Amberley, North Canterbury

Tel (03) 314 9699 or 021 033 3173
Fax (03) 314 9699
grahampat@actrix.co.nz

Double $120-$100 (Continental)
Child $15
Extra guest in apartment $15
Children and pets welcome
1 King 1 Queen 1 Single (2 bdrm)
Bathrooms: 1 Ensuite 1 Private

Kokiri is set in the countryside opposite Amberley Domain with views of Mount Gray. Our colonial home awaits you with the doves, fish and labrador. Centrally heated throughout. Relax and enjoy strolling around our large gardens or play croquet! Good restaurants within walking distance. 5 minutes from many wineries, 1 hour to Hanmer Springs and Mount Lyford Skiing. 40 minutes to Christchurch, marine interests at Kaikoura 100km north.

Waikuku Beach *30 km N of Christchurch*

Emmanuel House *B&B*
Graham & Mary Dacombe
20 Allin Drive, Waikuku Beach,
North Canterbury 8254

Tel (03) 312 7782 Fax (03) 312 7783
emmanuel.house@xtra.co.nz

Double $95 Single $55 (Continental)
Child under 5 free, under 12 half price
Dinner $20 by arrangement
Children welcome
1 Double 1 Twin 1 Single (3 bdrm)
Bathrooms: 1 Guest share

You are special to us, and we warmly invite you to our new 1 level purpose-built home in its park-like setting with wheelchair access throughout. Emmanuel House is 2km from the main highway, within walking distance of the beach and 30km north of Christchurch. Close by is the thriving rural township of Rangiora. Amateur radio ZL3NZ and ZL3MD, music, correspondence, and people are our interests. Complimentary tea/coffee/home-baking always available.

Rangiora *30 km N of Christchurch*

Willow Glen *B&B*
Glenda & Malcolm Ross
419 High Street, Rangiora,

Tel (03) 313 9940 or 027 498 4893
Fax (03) 313 9946
rosshighway@xtra.co.nz
www.willowglenrangiora.co.nz

Double $110 Single $75 (Continental)
Cooked breakfasts $7.50
Visa MC accepted Not suitable for children
1 Queen 1 Double (2 bdrm)
Bathrooms: 1 Ensuite 1 Private

Nestled on the northern side of Rangiora township on Highway 72, towards Oxford 30 minutes from Christchurch, 90 minutes to Mt Hutt. Walking distance to cafes, restaurants. We invite you to share our enchanting English style home for Kiwi hospitality. Off-street parking available. Comfortable beds, electric blankets, quality linen, continental breakfast or a hearty cooked breakfast ($7.50 pp). Bedrooms overlook garden and surrounding countryside. Relax in the spa with a glass of wine. Meet Lucy our foxy and our 2 spoilt cats. Email available.

Rangiora *25 km N of Christchurch*
Silverlea B&B *B&B Homestay*
Geoff & Shirley Cant
12 Janelle Place, Rangiora, North Canterbury

Tel (03) 313 0001 or 021 141 7660
021 299 1705 Fax (03) 313 0304
silverlea@paradise.net.nz
homepages.paradise.net.nz/thecantz

Double $95-$120 Single $75-$85 (Full breakfast)
Child $35 Dinner $25
Visa MC accepted Children welcome
2 Queen 1 Single (2 bdrm)
Bathrooms: 1 Guest share 1 Private

Our place is located a short distance north of Christchurch. Our home is a modern house, comfortable with all mod cons. Children welcome. Breakfast includes home-made bread, jams and preserves. Your hosts are semi-retired with a hospitality background. We are 2.5 hours from Kaikoura for whale watching and central to Marlborough and North Canterbury wine areas. Hanmer Springs is 1.25 hours away for year round hot baths and winter skiing. Plentiful off-steet secure parking. Airport transfers arranged.

Rangiora *14 km NW of Rangiora*
Sarolych Farm Homestay *B&B Homestay*
Lin & Chris Leppard
387 Stonyflat Road, North Loburn, RD 2 Rangiora

Tel (03) 312 8910 or 021 160 5087 leplin@hotmail.com

Double $110 Single $75 (Full breakfast)
Child by arrangement Dinner $25 by arrangement
Visa MC accepted Children welcome
1 Double 1 Twin (2 bdrm)
Bathrooms: 1 Ensuite 1 Family share

We welcome you to join us on our small alpaca farm. Our home is warm and comfortable with wonderful mountain views where you can relax in the quiet countryside. Watch the fantails and listen to the bellbirds in the native section of our large garden. Breakfast includes home-made jams from locally grown fruit and dinners are by prior arrangement using seasonal vegetables from our organic vegetable plot. We are 40 minutes from Christchurch and the airport and centrally located for many North Canterbury attractions, such as Hanmer Springs hotpools, the Canterbury wine growing regions, skifields and Kaikoura's whale watching. Come and join us and our 2 lazy cats, where we will guarantee to make your stay a happy and relaxing experience.

Rangiora *N of Rangiora*
Jotori Homestay *Homestay*
Lyn Kean
90 Carrs Road, Loburn, Rangiora

Tel (03) 312 8784 or 021 251 8867
Fax 03 3128784
jotori@xtra.co.nz

Double $100 Single $75 (Continental)
Child 1 or 2
Dinner by arrangement - gluten free meals available
Children welcome
1 Queen 1 Double 1 Single (3 bdrm)
Bathrooms: 1 Guest share

Large home and grounds set on elevated 10 acre farmlet. Goat, hens and cat. Quiet and private with panoramic views over Canterbury Plains and the mountains. Spa available. 30 minutes from Christchurch Airport.

Canterbury

Oxford *60 km W of Christchurch*

Country Life *B&B Self-contained Homestay*
Helen Dunn
137 High Street, Oxford, North Canterbury

Tel (03) 312 4167

Double $60-$75 Single $35-$40 (Full breakfast)
Dinner $20 by arrangement
Children and pets welcome
3 Double (3 bdrm)
Bathrooms: 1 Ensuite 1 Family share

Country life has been operating since 1987, the house is 80 years old and has a spacious garden, warm and sunny. Helen enjoys meeting people from far and wide - whether overseas visitors or those wanting a peaceful break away from Christchurch - all are welcomed at Country Life. High Street is left off the Main Road. Sign outside the gate.

Oxford *40mins km W of Christchurch Airport*

Hielan' House *B&B Homestay*
Shirley & John Farrell
74 Bush Road, Oxford, North Canterbury

Tel (03) 312 4382 or 0800 279 382 (freephone)
Fax (03) 312 4382
hielanhouse@ihug.co.nz   www.hielanhouse.co.nz

Double $120-$130 Single $100-$110
(Special breakfast)
Child price on application   Dinner by arrangement
Visa MC accepted Children and pets welcome
1 King/Twin 1 Queen 1 Twin (2 bdrm)
Bathrooms: 2 Ensuite

Nestled on 6 acres in peaceful rural surroundings with Oxford foothills as a backdrop, we have 2 quality upstairs guest rooms with their own relaxing areas, ensuites, separate entrance. TV, tea/coffee facilities. Inground swimming pool, laundry, fax/internet facilities. Christchurch 40 minutes away. Delicious menu breakfasts, dinners, organic meat and home-grown vegetables in season. Your warm welcome includes home-baking and cup of coffee/tea. Friendly farm animals. From Inland Scenic Route 72 (Oxford's main street) turn into Bay Road and then left into Bush Road.

Oxford *1/4 km E of Oxford*

The Country Garden *B&B Homestay*
Yolanda & Fred Lewis
3103 Oxford Road, Oxford 8253, North Canterbury

Tel (03) 312 3486
yolandaandfred@xtra.co.nz

Double $85-$85 Single $50-$50 (Full breakfast)
Child up to 15 years - 1 only
Dinner by arrangement
Children welcome
1 Twin (1 bdrm)
Bathrooms: 1 Private

The Country Garden B&B has a tranquil 4 acre garden setting with views of the foothills, on Scenic Route 72. Friendly, country hospitality. Dinner by arrangement possibly with vegies. fresh from Fred's garden and a glass of wine. The pool room is available for those who enjoy a game. We have a house cat and a retired horse on the property. Relax & unwind, dine with us or at Oxford's smart new restaurant. Go golfing, fishing, maybe just enjoy the garden. The TranzAlpine is nearby for a scenic trip to the West Coast.

Kaiapoi *15 km N of Christchurch*
Morichele *B&B*
Helen & Richard Moore
25 Hilton Street, Kaiapoi,

Tel (03) 327 5247 Fax (03) 327 5243
morichele@xtra.co.nz

Double $90 Single $60 (Full breakfast)
Child negotiable Dinner by arrangement
1 Double 1 Twin (2 bdrm)
Bathrooms: 1 Guest share

Your hosts Helen & Richard provide comfortable accommodation in a beautiful garden setting, close to rivers and beaches for fishing, golf course and walks. With off-street parking, your own entrance, sitting/dining area with fridge, tea and coffee making facilities, TV and video. Cafes and restaurants within walking distance alternatively, if you prefer,you are welcome to bring back takeaways or barbeque in the garden. A 2 hour drive will take you to ski fields, Hanmer Springs themal reserve, Akaroa (home of the Hector's Dolphin) and Kaikoura (whale watching). Extra bed, email, fax and laundry available.

Kaiapoi *20 km N of Christchurch*
Fairway View Kaiapoi B&B Motel *B&B Cottage No Kitchen*
Christine and Michael Cole
465 Williams Street (formally Main North Road),
RD1 Kaiapoi, Christchurch

Tel (03) 327 5688 Fax (03) 327 5629
stay@fairwayviewkaiapoi.co.nz
www.fairwayviewkaiapoi.co.nz

Double $95-$120 Single $95-$110 (Continental)
New motel $135 double
3 King/Twin 1 Queen 1 Single (4 bdrm)
Bathrooms: 1 Ensuite 1 Private

Travellers Retreat/Golfers Delight. 20 mins north of Christchurch and international airport. Turn off SH1 at Kaiapoi River Town exit, drive along Williams St past golf course, look for blue B&B sign, Fairway View is at end of drive (house cannot be seen from road). Set in 1 acre of quiet, tranquil gardens overlooking golf course, separate guest entrance, lovely guest lounge with CD, DVD, TV, fridge and dining area where we serve breakfast. New two bedroom (twin /king beds) Motel. Golf packages. Spa pool. Friendly warm welcome assured. Three minutes drive to several restaurants.

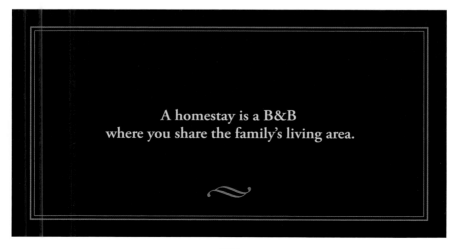

Christchurch - West Melton *15 km W of Christchurch*

Hillcrest *B&B Homestay*
Averil Dyke
Manna Place, West Melton, RD 1, Christchurch

Tel (03) 318 1948 Fax (03) 318 1948
Averil.A.Dyke@xtra.co.nz

Double $100 Single $60 (Full breakfast)
Dinner $30
1 King (1 bdrm)
Bathrooms: 1 Ensuite

Averil & David offer a warm welcome to our rural 2
acre property, conveniently situated 15 minutes from
the airport and 30 minutes from Christchurch City
centre. Lovely guest room having super king bed with ensuite, tea/coffee making facilities and television.
Full English breakfast provided and evening meals by prior arrangement. If you wish, relax in our
separate guest lounge and watch a movie on the home theatre system or catch up with your emails.

Christchurch - Harewood *7.5 km N of Christchurch Centre*

St James B&B *B&B*
Margaret & David Frankish
125 Waimakariri Road, Harewood, Christchurch 8005

Tel (03) 359 6259 or 0800 WELCOME or
0800 935 266 or 025 2244982 or 0274 320996
Fax (03) 359 6299 dj.frankish@xtra.co.nz
www.stjamesbnb.com

Double $100-$140 Single $75-$90 (Continental)
Child $40 Dinner $30
Visa MC accepted Children welcome
1 King/Twin 1 Queen (2 bdrm)
Bathrooms: 1 Private

Located 5 minutes from Christchurch Airport, 10 minutes from city. Begin or end your South Island
trip in our warm, modern home with its tranquil garden setting, and the horses who live on the 3 acre
property. Our lovely guest rooms include private lounges with a spa bath/ bathroom upstairs. Rooms
have tea/coffee facilities and TV. Internet access is available. We have 2 teenage children and a spaniel.
Close by are golf courses, excellent restaurants, shopping, Wildlife Reserve, McLeans Island Recreation
Area and Antarctic Centre.

Christchurch - Harewood *7.5 km N of Christchurch City Centre*

Evansleigh *B&B Homestay*
Faye Forsyth
344 Gardiners Road, Harewood, Christchurch

Tel (03) 359 8872 Fax (03) 359 6683
bookings@Evansleigh.com
www.Evansleigh.com

Double $110-$130 Single $80-$90 (Full breakfast)
Child negotiable
Visa MC accepted
Children and pets welcome
2 Queen 1 Twin (3 bdrm)
Bathrooms: 1 Ensuite 1 Guest share 1 Private 2

Evansleigh offers gracious accommodation in a private rural setting. It is a Victorian villa set in a
large English garden on a 12 acre lifestyle block. Situated just minutes from the airport, city centre,
International Golf Resort, wildlife reserves, award-winning restaurants and shops. Private entrance, guest
sitting room and spacious well appointed bedrooms and bathrooms. A full cooked breakfast is served in
the dining room or alfresco on the veranda. I share my property with dog, cat, and horses. Well travelled
host, warm reception.

Christchurch - Yaldhurst *8 km W of Christchurch Central*

Gladsome Lodge *B&B Homestay*
Stuart & Sue Barr
314 Yaldhurst Road, Russley, Christchurch 8004

Tel (03) 342 7414 or 0800 222 617
Fax (03) 342 3414
sue@gladsomelodge.com   www.gladsomelodge.com

Double $90-$120 Single $75 (Continental)
Child 0-5 free, 5-12 $20 Dinner $25
Cooked breakfast available
Visa MC Diners Amex accepted Children welcome
3 Queen 1 Double 2 Twin 2 Single (5 bdrm)
Bathrooms: 2 Ensuite 3 Guest share

Located close to airport with easy access to key attractions. Be assured of professional, attentive hosting in a friendly environment. Enjoy our property which has a tennis court, swimming pool,spa and sauna available. We are able to accommodate couples travelling together. Have knowledge of Maori history and culture. Our house is centrally heated. On bus route to city. On route to ski fields and West Coast Highway. Hosts Sue and Stuart, New Zealanders who have travelled and have a wide variety of interests.

Christchurch - Yaldhurst *10 km W of Christchurch*

GP's Place *Homestay*
Gwenda & Peter Bickley
164 Old West Coast Road, RD 6, Christchurch

Tel (03) 342 9196 or 021 158 6208
Fax (03) 342 4196
gpsplace_@hotmail.com

Double $100 Single $60 (Full breakfast)
Pet free home
1 Queen 2 Twin (2 bdrm)
Bathrooms: 1 Private

We invite you to come and enjoy the ambience of our warm and spacious home set in a large garden with magnificent views of the Southern Alps. Our home is situated on 7.5 acres where we farm ostriches and various other farm animals. We are ideally located just 7 minutes from the airport and 10 minutes from the city. Also closely situated to ski fields, beautiful lakes, fine wineries and golf courses. A full sized tennis court is available for guests use.

Christchurch - Avonhead *10 min km W of Christchurch central*

Ash Croft *Luxury Cottage with Kitchen*
Sky & Raewyn Williams
6 Fovant Street, Avonhead, Christchurch

Tel (03) 342 3416 or 0275 663724
Fax (03) 342 3415
bookings@ashcroftgroup.co.nz
www.ashcroftgroup.co.nz

Double $115-$125 (Provisions first night)
Child under 5 free extra persons $15 per night
Visa MC accepted
Pet free home Children welcome
2 Queen 2 Twin (3 bdrm)
Bathrooms: 1 Private spa bath

Quality accommodation for the visitor to Christchurch, offering privacy and comfort, off-street parking and a child-friendly environment. Modern facilities, full kitchen, dining area, lounge with comfortable furnishings, TV, VCR, CD/radio/tape player, collection of video tapes, book library and childrens games/toys. Bathroom includes full bath and separate shower. Laundry with washing machine and dryer. Easy access to airport, city centre, local shopping centres and tourist attractions.

Canterbury

Christchurch - Avonhead *10 km W of Christchurch Central*

Russley 302 *B&B Homestay Farmstay*
Helen & Ron Duckworth
302 Russley Road, Avonhead, Christchurch 8004

Tel (03) 358 6510 or 021 662 016
Fax (03) 358 6470
haduck@ducksonrussley.co.nz
www.ducksonrussley.co.nz

Double $120-$130 Single $75-$12 (Full breakfast)
Dinner by arrangement
Visa MC accepted
1 King 1 Twin 1 Single (3 bdrm)
Bathrooms: 1 Ensuite 1 Family share 1 Private

Located on the main north/south highway near Christchurch airport and main west highway Russley 302 is well placed for guests arriving and departing Christchurch. A 10 acre farmlet, with sheep and chickens (providing freshest breakfast eggs) each ensuite guest rooms has refreshment facilities, refrigerator, television electric blankets. Laundry options, email, fax available. Alfresco dining on warm summer evenings and a log fire in winter create a relaxing atmosphere. Stay awhile, Christchurch is an ideal base for excursions to Canterbury's hinterland.

Christchurch - Burnside *8 km NW of Christchurch*

Burnside Bed & Breakfast *B&B*
Elaine & Neil Roberts
31 O'Connor Place, Burnside 8005, Christchurch

Tel (03) 358 7671 Fax (03) 358 7761
elaine.neil.roberts@xtra.co.nz

Double $90-$110 Single $65 (Continental)
Children welcome
1 Queen 1 Twin (2 bdrm)
Bathrooms: 1 Guest share

Welcome to our comfortable, modern home in quiet street, 5 minutes from the airport and 15 minutes to the city centre. Relax in the garden with tea or coffee and freshly baked muffins. Enjoy a generous continental breakfast with home-baking and preserves. Free broadband internet, laundry facilities and off-street parking available. Private bathroom facilities arranged with prior booking at $110.00. Our interests include sport, gardening, reading,travel and local history. We enjoy sharing our home with guests and look forward to meeting you.

Christchurch - Burnside

Stableford *B&B*
Margaret & Tony Spowart
2 Stableford Green, Burnside, Christchurch 8005

Tel (03) 358 3264
stableford@xtra.co.nz
www.stableford.co.nz

Double $130 Single $120 (Continental)
Visa MC accepted
2 Queen 1 Twin (3 bdrm)
Bathrooms: 2 Ensuite 1 Private

Welcome to Stableford, the closest B&B to the Christchurch Airport, making it ideal for arriving or departing visitors. City bus-stop at door. We are situated adjacent to the prestigious Russley Golf Club. Stableford is new, clean and comfortable with a separate guest lounge available. Airport transfers are available. Good restaurants are close by. Snacks by request. Our interests are travel, music, antiques. Let us know if you require a tee booking at the Russley Golf Course.

Christchurch - Burnside *8 km NW of City Centre*

Watson Homestay *B&B Homestay*

Lorna Watson
29 O'Connor Place, Burnside, Christchurch 8005

Tel (03) 358 2635 Fax (03) 358 2665
blossomtree@xtra.co.nz

Double $100-$120 Single $60-$80 (Continental)
Child $20
Children welcome
1 Queen 2 Double (3 bdrm)
Bathrooms: 1 Guest share 2 Private

Located 5 minutes from Christchurch Airport, 15
minutes from City Centre. Good bus services closeby.
Russley Golf Course and a variety of excellent restaurants and cafes nearby. Modern 6 year old home,
along with it's owners, Lorna & Lyndsay and lovely cat Emma, welcomes bed & breakfast guests. Enjoy
lovely surroundings and a generous continental breakfast. Off-street parking and laundry facilities
available. We look forward to welcoming you.

Christchurch - Ilam *7.5 km NW of Christchurch*

Anne & Tony Fogarty Homestay *Homestay*

Anne & Tony Fogarty
7 Westmont Street, Ilam, Christchurch 8004

Tel (03) 358 2762 Fax (03) 358 2767
tony.fogarty@xtra.co.nz

Double $90 Single $50 (Continental)
Dinner $30 by arrangement
Visa MC accepted
4 Single (2 bdrm)
Bathrooms: 1 Family share 1 Guest share

Our home is in the beautiful suburb of Ilam, only
minutes from Canterbury University and The
Christchurch College of Education. Close to Christchurch Airport (7 minutes by car) and the railway
station (10 minutes). A bus stop to the central city, with its many attractions is 50 metres from our home.
Willing to arrange transport from airport or train. Guests are welcome to use our laundry. We have a
wide range of interests. Complimentary tea and coffee at any time. Stay with us and get value for money.

Christchurch - Bryndwr *In Christchurch*

Bryndwr B&B *B&B Homestay*
Kathy & Brian Moore
108 Aorangi Road, Christchurch

Tel (03) 351 6299
eroom.b@clear.net.nz

Double $95 Single $75 (Special breakfast)
1 Double 1 Single (2 bdrm)
Bathrooms: 1 Guest share

Welcome, share our comfortable home with
relaxing outdoor garden. Located northwest corner of
Christchurch, 5km from airport off Wairakei Road
or via Memorial Avenue, left onto Ilam Road, past
Aqualand, on to Aorangi Road. Walking distances to local shops and restaurants. Welcome to bring
home takeaways. Complimentary tea and coffee. Laundry, ironing facilities available. 3 minute walk
to bus route, 10 minutes ride to city centre, passing botanical gardens, museum, art centre. Inspection
welcomed. Ring if you have questions, we may be able to help.

Christchurch - Fendalton *5 min km NW of Central Christchurch*

Ambience on Avon *B&B*
Lawson & Helen Little
9 Kotare Street, Fendalton, Christchurch

Tel 0800 226 628 or (03) 348 4537
Fax (03) 348 4837
lawsonh@xtra.co.nz www.ambience-on-avon.co.nz

Double up to $190 Single up to $180
(Special breakfast) Visa MC Amex accepted
Pet free home Not suitable for children
1 Queen 1 Double (2 bdrm)
Bathrooms: 1 Ensuite 1 Private spa bath

Ambience on Avon in a private, picturesque garden on the Avon. Helen & Lawson, your gracious hosts enjoy welcoming guests into their home with its elegant comfortable understated furnishings, guest lounge with a large open fire, TV. Enjoy home-baking, complimentary wine & refreshments antipasto under the large elm tree or in the river garden, or relax in leather therapeutic chairs in family room opening into garden. Art, comfortable beds, fine linen, electric blankets, room heaters and all modern conveniences for a relaxing, friendly, hosted stay. Courtesy pick up. Off-street parking, no pets, no children.

Christchurch - Fendalton *4 min km NW of Central Christchurch*

Anselm House *B&B*
Jan & Leigh Webber
34 Kahu Road, Fendalton, Christchurch

Tel (03) 343 4260 or 0800 267 356
Fax (03) 343 426
1anselm@paradise.net.nz www.anselmhouse.co.nz

Double $130-$170 Single $100-$120 (Full breakfast)
Dinner $45pp
Visa MC accepted
Not suitable for children
2 Queen (2 bdrm)
Bathrooms: 2 Ensuite

Anselm House is beside the Avon River; a landmark building constructed of pink Hanmer marble and designed by the famous architect Heathcote-Helmore. Special attractions include: 4 minute walk to Riccarton for restaurants, banks and shopping mall; private, courtesy airport and TranzAlpine pick up and drop off; safe off-street parking; within easy walking distance of Hagley Park, art galleries, city centre; adjacent to historic Riccarton House; close to university; on city centre bus route; friendly, family atmosphere. Not suitable for pets or children under 12.

Christchurch - Dallington *4 km NE of Christchurch*

Killarney *B&B Separate Suite*
Lynne & Russell Haigh
27 Dallington Terrace, Dallington, Christchurch

Tel (03) 381 7449 or 027 305 0603
Fax (03) 381 7449
haigh.killarney@xtra.co.nz

Double $95 Single $75 (Full breakfast)
Child negotiable
2 Double (2 bdrm)
Bathrooms: 1 Ensuite 1 Private

Peace, tranquillity and a cottage garden on the banks of the river Avon. Detached double (ensuite) accommodation is warm and cosy with fridge, microwave, TV, extra single couch-bed available, and private garden. Double accommodation, lounge and private bathroom available inside. Tea/coffee, home-baking and laundry service always available. Scenic river walks or borrow our dinghy and row! 6 minutes drive to city centre. Buses stop nearby. Ensuite room-only rate available if you provide own breakfast. Both of us and our cat look forward to meeting you.

Christchurch - Merivale *2 km N of Christchurch*

Leinster Homestay B&B *B&B Homestay*
Kay and Brian Smith
34B Leinster Road, Merivale, Christchurch

Tel (03) 355 6176 or 027 4330 771
Fax (03) 355 6176
brian.kay@xtra.co.nz

Double $130-$135 Single $120 (Special breakfast)
Child negotiable
Visa MC accepted Children welcome
1 Queen 1 Double 1 Single (2 bdrm)
Bathrooms: 1 Ensuite 1 Private

At Leinster Bed & Breakfast we pride ourselves
on creating a relaxed friendly atmosphere in our modern sunny home. Only 5 minutes to city centre (art gallery, museum, botanical gardens, Cathedral Square, casino, town hall etc), 10 minutes from the airport. For evening dining convenience there are excellent restaurants just a leisurely stroll away at Merivale Village. Laundry, email, fax and off-street parking facilities makes us your home away from home. Bedrooms have TV, electric blankets, heaters, tea/coffee. Well behaved puss & pooch in residence.

Christchurch - Merivale *3min km N of Christchurch*

Melrose *B&B*
Elaine & David Baxter
39 Holly Road, Merivale, Christchurch

Tel (03) 355 1929 or 027 647 5564
Fax (03) 355 1927
BaxterMelrose@xtra.co.nz
www.melrose-bb.co.nz

Double $120 Single $75 (Full breakfast)
Child $30
Visa MC accepted Children welcome
3 Queen (3 bdrm)
Bathrooms: 1 Ensuite 2 Guest share 1 Private

A warm welcome awaits you at Melrose, a charming character home (1910) located in a small quiet street, just off Papanui Road only minutes away from the city and all the shops, restaurants and cafes of Merivale. Our house is spacious, we offer large rooms with tea & coffee making facilities and a private dining room/lounge. We have many interests and having travelled extensively, are keen to accommodate your needs. Our family comprises of 2 daughters and a boxer, Milly. Off-street parking. Children are welcome.

Christchurch - Merivale *1.5 km N of Cathedral Square*

Chestnuts on Holly *Luxury B&B*
John & Edell Pereira
27 Holly Road, Merivale, Christchurch

Tel (03) 355 7977 or 021 046 9684
Fax (03) 355 7977
enquiries@chestnutsonholly.co.nz
www.chestnutsonholly.co.nz

Double $140-$175 Single $90-$10 (Special breakfast)
Visa MC Amex Eftpos accepted
Children welcome
1 Queen 1 Double 1 Single (3 bdrm)
Bathrooms: 3 Ensuite

Chestnuts on Holly was built in circa 1901 from native kauri timber and has been restored to reflect the charm and elegance of a bygone era. The 3 tastefully furnished ensuite bedrooms are cosy in winter and lovely and cool during the summer. Guests have their own private lounge and dining room where they can relax. Special gourmet breakfasts are served in the dining room or in summer, on the verandah. Cathedral Square is an easy stroll away with buses and restaurants within a few minutes walk.

Christchurch - Avondale *8 km NE of Christchurch Central*

Hulverstone Lodge *B&B*
Diane & Ian Ross
18 Hulverstone Drive, Avondale, Christchurch

Tel (03) 388 6505 or 0800 388 650 (NZ only)
Fax (03) 388 6025
hulverstone@caverock.net.nz
www.hulverstonelodge.co.nz

B&B
Approved

Double $110-$140 Single $80-$11 (Full breakfast)
Visa MC accepted
3 King/Twin 1 Single (4 bdrm)
Bathrooms: 1 Ensuite 1 Guest share 1 Private

Gracing the bank of the Avon River in a quiet suburb, yet only 10 minutes from the city centre, stands picturesque Hulverstone Lodge. From our charming guest rooms watch the sun rise over the river, catch glimpses of the Southern Alps or enjoy views of the Port Hills. Delightful riverside walks pass the door. A pleasant stroll along the riverbank leads to New Brighton with its sandy Pacific Ocean beach and pier. Numerous golf courses and the QEII Leisure Complex are close at hand.

Located just off Christchurch's Ring Road system, Hulverstone Lodge offers easy access to all major tourist attractions, while frequent buses provide convenient transport to the city. An ideal base for holidays year-round, Hulverstone Lodge is only a couple of hours from quaint Akaroa, Hanmer Hot Springs thermal attraction, Kaikoura's Whale Watch, and several ski fields.

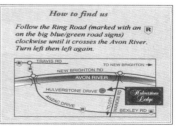

You are guaranteed warm hospitality and quality accommodation at Hulverstone Lodge. All our rooms are decorated with fresh flowers from our garden. We regret our facilities are not suited to young children.

We offer: complimentary pick up; fax and email facilities; king or twin beds; advice on onward travel planning; French and German languages spoken; a delicious breakfast.

Come and experience the ambience of Hulverstone Lodge.

Christchurch - New Brighton *8 km E of Christchurch*

Tudor House *B&B*

Rosa Rijk & Alex Isherwood

17 Hood Street, New Brighton, Christchurch

Tel (03) 382 1077 Fax (03) 382 1177
alexish@xtra.co.nz
www.bnb.co.nz/tudorhousebb.html

Double $100 Single $80 (Full breakfast)
Visa MC accepted
3 Queen 2 Double (5 bdrm)
Bathrooms: 2 Guest share

Welcome to Tudor House, our beautiful and comfortable residence which offers a homely atmosphere created by Alex and Rosa. You are promised clean quality accommodation with heated rooms and all beds have electric blankets.

We guarantee fresh baked home-made breakfasts. Tudor House offers a spectacular visual seascape with wonderful sunrises and sunsets, as well as a myriad of opportunities to become involved in a wide range of beach activities. Enjoy safe bathing and a picnic lunch on sparkling sands which stretch forever, and offering fantastic shortline walks where native birds can be sighted.

Our village, which is within walking distance, is full of interesting cafes and bars with a distinctive local flavour, or if you want an evening at the theatre, we are only 10 minutes from the city centre. An excellent bus service is available from our door.

For golf enthusiasts there are a number of courses within easy access to Tudor House, and we are only to pleased to assist you to organize any day trips you wish to make to our many tourist attractions. There is a swimming pool on the property for guests who wish to spend a day at home with a glass of wine and a good book.

Tea and coffee facilities are also on tap. Since neither of us smoke we prefer our guests who wish to do so, to use our pleasant outside area.

We look forward to sharing our home with you.

Canterbury

Christchurch - St Albans *3 km N of Christchurch City*
Severn Street B&B *B&B*

Tina & Peter Reynolds
15 Severn Street, St Albans, Christchurch 8001

Tel (03) 960 3185 or 027 332 5219
Fax (03) 960 3186
tina.reynolds@paradise.net.nz

Double $105 Single $75 (Full breakfast)
Child $20
Visa MC accepted
Children welcome
2 King/Twin 2 Queen (3 bdrm)
Bathrooms: 1 Ensuite 2 Private

Severn Street B&B is a warm character home in a tree lined street, 5 minutes drive from town, and close to the bus route. Facilities include; large warm bedrooms, guest kitchen, cot, highchair, fax/email, off-street parking, hot spa, tea and coffee, courtesy pick up, Deutsche Sprache. Peter and I and are well travelled New Zealanders. Peter is an English language teacher, and I am a retired Occupational Therapist and now have time for painting and potting.

Christchurch - Avonside *4 km E of Christchurch*
Treeview *B&B Homestay*

Kathy & Laurence Carr
6 Lomond Place, Woolston, Christchurch 6

Tel (03) 384 2352

Double $90 Single $50 (Continental)
Child $20 Dinner $20
1 Double 2 Single (2 bdrm)
Bathrooms: 1 Guest share

Welcome. Kiwi hospitality. Smoke-free sunny home in quiet cul-de-sac. Garden with seating. Guests carport. Comfortable beds, electric blankets, hair drier. 10 minutes by car to city and beaches. Close to Jade Stadium, Eastgate Mall and bus. Courtesy transport from railway station. Airport shuttle service. From Cathedral Square take Gloucester Street to traffic lights at Linwood Avenue. Turn right. Pass Eastgate Mall to traffic lights end of avenue of trees. Right into Hargood Street. First left into Clydesdale, first left Lomond Place.

Christchurch - Avonside *4 km E of Christchurch*
Avon Park Lodge *B&B & Cottage No Kitchen*

Murray & Richeena Bullard
144A Kerrs Road, Avonside, Christchurch

Tel (03) 389 1904 or 0276419692
Fax (03) 389 1904
avonparklodge@clear.net.nz
home.clear.net.nz/pages/avonparklodge/

Double $95-$110 Single $70-$95 (Full breakfast)
Child by arrangement
Garden studio $95-$110
Visa MC accepted
2 Queen 2 Twin (3 bdrm)
Bathrooms: 1 Ensuite 1 Guest share

Enjoy quiet surroundings in our beautiful garden and 2 storey home close to the Avon river, Porritt Park rowing and hockey and QE2 leisure centre. The 2 upstairs guest bedrooms are comfortably furnished with tea & coffee making facilities, etc. Our garden studio has ensuite, fridge and microwave. Close to frequent public transport (including bus to the railway station). 5 minutes drive to the city. Your hosts and their lovable boxer dog Gus assure you of a warm, friendly welcome. Complimentary pick up

Christchurch City *Christchurch Central*

Windsor B&B Hotel *B&B Hotel*

Carol Healey & Don Evans
52 Armagh Street, Christchurch 1

Tel (03) 366 1503 or 0800 366 1503
Fax (03) 366 9796
reservations@windsorhotel.co.nz
www.windsorhotel.co.nz

Double $120 Single $85 (Full breakfast)
Triple $150, Quad/Family $164
Visa MC Diners Amex Eftpos accepted
(40 bdrm)
Bathrooms: 24 Guest share

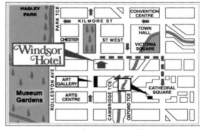

Canterbury

Looking for Bed & Breakfast in Christchurch, then try The Windsor. Built at the turn of the century this inner city residence is located on the Tourist Tram Route and is within 5-10 minutes walk of the city centre, restaurants, convention centre, casino, galleries, museum and botanical gardens.

Guests are greeted on arrival by our pet dachshund, Miss Winnie and shown around our charming colonial style home. Often described as traditional, this family operated bed & breakfast hotel prides itself on the standard of accommodation that it offers. The warm and comfortable bedrooms are all decorated with a small posy of flowers and a watercolour by local artist Denise McCulloch.

The shared bathroom facilities have been conveniently appointed with bathrobes provided, giving warmth and comfort in the bed & breakfast tradition. Such things as "hotties" and "brollies" add charm to the style of accommodation offered, as does our 1928 Studebaker sedan.

Our generous morning breakfast (included in the tariff) offers fruit juice, fresh fruits, yogurt and cereals followed by bacon and eggs, sausages, tomatoes, toast and marmalade, and is served in the dining room each morning between 6.30 and 9.00. The 24 hour complimentary tea & coffee making facilities allow guests to use them at their own convenience. "Supper" (tea, coffee and biscuits) is served each evening in the lounge at 9.00.

As part of our service the hotel offers email/internet facilities, laundry, off-street parking for the motorist and bicycle and baggage storage. *QUOTE THIS BOOK FOR 10% DISCOUNT*

Christchurch City *In Christchurch Central*

Riverview Lodge *B&B Cottage No Kitchen Apartment with Kitchen*

Ernst and Sabine Wipperfuerth

361 Cambridge Terrace, Christchurch 1

Tel (03) 365 2860 Fax (03) 365 2845
riverview.lodge@xtra.co.nz
www.riverview.net.nz

Double $170-$195 Single $100-$150 (Full breakfast)
Self-contained suites/holiday house $225
Visa MC accepted
Children welcome
3 Queen 1 Double 1 Twin 1 Single (5 bdrm)
Bathrooms: 4 Ensuite 1 Private

If you like quality accommodation in a relaxed and quiet atmosphere, still just minutes walking away from the centre of an exciting city: this is the place to stay.

Riverview Lodge is a restored Edwardian residence that reflects the grace and style of the period with some fine kauri carvings. Guest rooms are elegant combining modern facilities with colonial furnishings. Balconies provide wonderfull river views.

The Edwardian townhouse next door has 2 very spacious (80m2) apartments (1 or 2 bedrooms) for a private stay. Guests find antiques and quality furniture, a fully equipped kitchen, lounge, bathroom, TV and private telephone.

For full breakfast we invite guests into the lodge or if requested supply a continental breakfast in the suite. For information on our inner city holiday cottages please look up www.moacottages.co.nz. As ex-tour operators we'll be happy to help you with planning and bookings. Kayaks, bicycles and golf clubs are for guests to use. We are multilingual.

Christchurch City

Croydon House *B&B Hotel Guest House Fully furnished apartments*
Nita Herbst
63 Armagh Street, Christchurch

Tel (03) 366 5111 Fax (03) 377 6110
welcome@croydon.co.nz
www.croydon.co.nz

Double $140-$180 Single $110-$140
(Full breakfast)
Child under 12 $30
Self-contained apartment $220-$300
Visa MC Eftpos accepted
Children welcome
1 King 4 Queen 2 Double 4 Twin 3 Single
(12 bdrm)
Bathrooms: 10 Ensuite 2 Guest share

Croydon House is a charming hotel offering
fine accommodation in the Heart of New
Zealand's Garden City. All bedrooms are tastefully
refurbished with share or ensuite bathroom.

Start your day with our scrumptious buffet and
indulge yourself in a deliciously cooked breakfast
prepared especially for you.

Historic tram, art gallery, casino, art centre.
Explore the city's major attractions, great
restaurants, conference venues and the famous
botanical gardens are within easy walking distance.

We provide internet access. For more information
visit our home-page on the internet with on-line
booking form.

***Croydon House has received the Community
Pride Garden Award for the last 4 consecutive years.***

Canterbury

Christchurch City *In Christchurch Central*
Home Lea B&B *B&B Homestay*
Pauline & Gerald Oliver
195 Bealey Avenue, Christchurch

Tel (03) 379 9977 or 0800 355321
Fax (03) 379 4099
homelea@xtra.co.nz www.homelea.co.nz

Double $100-$140 Single $70-$115 (Special breakfast)
Child negotiable Dinner by arrangement
Extra adult $30
Visa MC Amex accepted
Children welcome
1 King 3 Queen 3 Single (5 bdrm)
Bathrooms: 2 Ensuite 1 Guest share 1 Private

Home Lea offers the traveller a comfortable and enjoyable stay. Built in the early 1900s, Home Lea has the charm and character of a large New Zealand home of that era: rimu panelling, leadlight windows, and a large lounge with a log fire. Tea, coffee, biscuits and fruit are available at all times. Off-street parking, and email/fax facilities available for guests. Pauline and Gerald are happy to share their knowledge of local attractions and their special interests are travel, sailing and music.

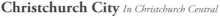

Christchurch City *In Christchurch Central*
Orari B&B *B&B*
Ashton Owen
42 Gloucester Street, Christchurch 1

Tel (03) 365 6569 Fax (03) 365 2525
orari.bb@xtra.co.nz
www.orari.net.nz

Double $160-$198 Single $130-$160
(Special breakfast)
Visa MC Amex accepted
2 King/Twin 8 Queen 5 Single (10 bdrm)
Bathrooms: 8 Ensuite 2 Private

Orari was built in 1893. Of kauri construction with beautifully proportioned rooms, Orari is located in the heart of the city directly opposite the new Christchurch Art Gallery. Orari is within easy walking distance of the art centre, the botanic gardens, museum, Hagley Park, town hall, casino, convention centre and Cathedral Square. Featuring 10 bedrooms with private bathrooms, off-street parking and wheel chair access, it provides comfortable, friendly accommodation for travellers, business people and small group conferences. Enjoy the convenience of the inner city in an elegant heritage home

Christchurch City *In Christchurch Central*
Apartment 37 B&B *Homestay*
Lynne & David
Apartment 37, PO Box 177, Old Government Buildings, Cathedral Square, Christchurch

Tel (03) 377 7473 or 027 622 0849
Fax (03) 377 7863 apartment37@xtra.co.nz

Double $155-$155 Single $145-$155
(Breakfast by arrangement)
Visa MC accepted
Pet free home Not suitable for children
1 King/Twin 1 Queen (2 bdrm)
Bathrooms: 2 Ensuite

In the heart of Christchurch (Cathedral Square), Apartment 37 (homestay) is unique offering warm friendly hospitality and elegant accommodation in a grand historic building with central city convenience. In addition enjoy many extras including Sky TV, tea/coffee making facilities, and access to in-building facilities (lap pool, gymnasium, spa, sauna, restaurant). Walk to Christchurch's vibrant attractions - arts centre, museum, botanic gardens, Hagley Park, shops, cafes, conference centre, and entertainment; or use transport right on door step. Perfect for holidays, conferences or business.

Christchurch City *In Christchurch Central*
Eliza's Manor on Bealey *B&B*
Ann Zwimpfer & Harold Williams
82 Bealey Avenue, City Central, Christchurch

Tel (03) 366 8584 or 0800 366 859
Fax (03) 366 4946
info@themanor.co.nz www.themanor.co.nz

Double $175-$265 Single $155-$245
(Special breakfast)
Visa MC Diners Amex Eftpos accepted
Not suitable for children
5 King/Twin 3 Queen 1 Single (8 bdrm)
Bathrooms: 8 Ensuite

Eliza's Manor on Bealey is a beautifully restored Victorian mansion, built in 1861. The original architecture includes a magnificent entrance foyer, lead light windows and wood panelling. The tariff includes a full continental and cooked breakfast. We are a short drive from the airport and a 15 minutes level walk to the art centre, botanical gardens, art galleries, museums, city centre, golf course and restaurants. Free parking and internet access is available to guests. We are a day trip to Hanmer Springs, Akaroa, and Kaikoura.

Christchurch City *In Christchurch Central*
The Devon B&B *B&B*
Sandra & Benjamin Humphrey
69 Armagh Street, Christchurch

Tel (03) 366 0398 Fax (03) 366 0392
bandbdevonhotel@xtra.co.nz
www.devonbandbhotel.co.nz

Double $115-$150 Single $80-$110 (Full breakfast)
Child under 15 years $20
Extra adults $35
Visa MC Diners Amex accepted
6 Queen 3 Twin 2 Single (11 bdrm)
Bathrooms: 6 Ensuite 4 Guest share 1 Private

The Devon is a personal guest house located in the heart of beautiful Christchurch City, which offers elegance and comfort in the style of an olde worlde English manor. Just 5 minutes walk to Christchurch Cathedral, Town Hall, and Convention Centre, casino, museum, art gallery, hospital and botanical gardens in Hagley Park. TV lounge, tea & coffee making facilities. Off-street parking.

Christchurch City
Holly House *B&B*
Erica & Allister Stewart
1/337 Cambridge Terrace, Inner City, Christchurch

Tel (03) 371 7337
a.e.stewart@xtra.co.nz

Double $130 Single $120 (Special breakfast)
1 King/Twin (1 bdrm)
Bathrooms: 1 Private

We would be pleased to welcome you to our home which is within walking distance to anywhere in the inner city. We have 1 lovely bedroom which can be arranged as twin beds or 1 king-size bed. The guests' bathroom is adjacent to the bedroom. The sitting room overlooks the beautiful tree-lined Avon River. A comment from our visitors' book: "Holly House is an absolute gem." Erica is an artist working with mixed media, and clay sculpture. Allister is a retired school teacher.

Christchurch City - East *1.5 km E of Christchurch*

Lanslow Lodge *B&B Homestay Cottage No Kitchen*
Lance Ching & Dennis Munslow
564 Cashel Street, City East, Christchurch

Tel (03) 389 1009 or 027 262 4377
027 637 3795 Fax (03) 389 1009
lanslowlodge@xtra.co.nz
https://www.seekom.com/catalogue/op_srch.
php?op=lanslowlodge

Double $80-$15 Single $50-$80 (Continental)
Dinner $20 Video/Spa $5
Visa MC accepted Not suitable for children
6 Queen 1 Double 1 Twin 2 Single (6 bdrm)
Bathrooms: 1 Ensuite 1 Family share 1 Private

Lanslow Lodge (House) character 1930's villa home-away-from-home, atmosphere, where you can relax, read or just stroll around garden with Amy & Chelsea, our friendly westhighland terriers. Join us for a chat over pre-dinner drinks by the fire. 10 minutes to city center. Bus at gate. 5 minutes walk to Eastgate Mall. We do our best to suit everyone and if we don't offer a service please ask and we will endeavor to provide it. Not suitable for children. The house is smoke-free. New Spa pool area at a little extra cost.

~

Christchurch City *3 km N of Square*

Summers House B&B *B&B Homestay Apartment with Kitchen*
Jackie & Kieran
274 Papanui Road, Merivale, Christchurch 8005

Tel (03) 355 1145 or (03) 355 2500
Fax (03) 355 2501
stay@summers.net.nz
www.summers.net.nz

Double $120-$150 Single $90 (Full breakfast)
Visa MC accepted
Children welcome
1 King/Twin1 King 1 Queen (2 bdrm)
Bathrooms: 1 Family share 1 Guest share 1 Private

Summers B&B at Knowles Court, a Christchurch listed Heritage Home of grand and regal proportions set on nearly half an acre surrounded by a high brick wall and mature trees in prestigious Merivale. Handy to the city centre, transport and airport. Easy walking distance to quality restaurants and shopping. Variety of accommodation available including self catering flat - from $120 double, $90 single including tax and breakfast. "Affordable, spacious, gracious and tranquil - A home away from home."

~

Christchurch City *0.5 km N of Cathedral Square*

Martina Bed & Breakfast *B&B*
Sunny Morley
302 Gloucester Street, Central City, Christchurch

Tel (03) 377 7150 Fax (03) 377 7476
martinabedandbreakfast@ihug.co.nz

Double $85-$110 Single $75-$90 (Continental)
1 Queen (1 bdrm)
Bathrooms: 1 Family share ensuite from July

Martina is a charming, Victorian house with a peaceful garden, 4 blocks from Cathedral Square. A short walk takes you to all the city has to offer - restaurants, shopping, museum, arts centre, art galleries, botanical gardens, movies and theatre. Your downstairs room has a queen bed, bay window, TV, video and telephone. Bathroom upstairs. Downstairs toilet. Ensuite from July. We have off-street parking and a bus stop at the gate. Host and teenage children are well travelled, lived overseas and speak Spanish. Small pet cat.

Christchurch City *1 km E of Centre*
The Chester *B&B*
Jennifer & Jan van den Berg
Suite 3, 173 Chester Street East, Christchurch City

Tel (03) 366 5777 or 021 365 495
Fax (03) 365 6314
thechester@clear.net.nz
www.thechester.com

Double $95-$120 **Single** $65-$75 (Continental)
Visa MC accepted
Pet free home   Not suitable for children
1 King/Twin 1 Single (2 bdrm)
Bathrooms: 2 Ensuite

The Chester B&B Apt 3,situated in the historic Old Wards Brewery Building, dates back to the 1850's. Now converted into elegant apartments, this unique suite offers all modern comforts and amenities in close walking distance of the city centre, restaurants, banks, town hall, arts centre, casino & convention centre. Perfect for holiday or business. Your hosts Jan & Jennifer van den Berg will ensure your stay is comfortable and memorable. Airport transfers, theatre & concert bookings can be arranged on request.

Christchurch City *1 km NW of Info centre*
Turret House *B&B*
Pam & Michael Hamilton
435 Durham Street North, Christchurch,

Tel (03) 365 3900 Fax (03) 365 5601
turretb.bchch@xtra.co.nz www.turrethouse.co.nz

Double $95-$15 **Single** $75-$85 (Continental)
Visa MC Eftpos accepted
Children welcome
3 King/Twin1 King 2 Queen 1 Twin 1 Single (8 bdrm)
Bathrooms: 8 Ensuite some with baths some without

Cead Mile Failte' (1 hundred thousand welcomes)
Turret House is a gracious superior Bed & Breakfast accommodation located in downtown Christchurch. It is within easy walking distance of Cathedral Square, the Botanical Gardens, Museum, Art Gallery, the Arts Centre and Hagley Park 18 hole golf course. Also Casino, new Convention Centre, Town Hall. Built around 1900 this historic residence is one of only 3 in the area protected by the New Zealand Historic Places Trust. It has been restored to capture the original character and charm..

Christchurch *5 km NW of Christchurch*
Condell Bed & Breakfast *B&B*
Barbara & Roger Arnold
83 Condell Avenue, Papanui, Christchurch 5

Tel (03) 352 4535 Fax (03) 352 7656
condell@ihug.co.nz

Double $120-$140 **Single** $120 (Full breakfast)
Child by arrangement
Visa MC accepted
Pet free home
2 Queen 1 Single (3 bdrm)
Bathrooms: 1 Guest share

We invite you to the friendly atmosphere of our home in its beautiful, secluded garden. Make yourself tea, coffee or juice. Enjoy delicious breakfasts, home-baking and freshly brewed coffee, relax in attractive guest lounge. Laundry facilities. With a bus stop on our doorstep you can reach Christchurch City in 10 minutes with its art gallery, botanical gardens, museum, arts centre and restaurants. Airport 10 minutes, beach 25 minutes, mountains 2 hours for year-round enjoyment. We take pleasure in making your stay special.

Christchurch - Sydenham *2 km S of Christchurch City Square*

The Designer Cottage *B&B Homestay*

Chet Wah

53 Hastings Street West, Sydenham, Christchurch City

Tel 0800 161 619 or (03) 377 8088
021 210 5282 Fax (03) 377 8099
stay@designercottage.co.nz
www.designercottage.co.nz

Double $80-$250 Single $45-$60 (Continental)
Whole house (sleeps 6) $120-$250
Visa MC accepted
Pet free home
4 Queen 1 Double 1 Twin 1 Single (7 bdrm)
Bathrooms: 1 Ensuite 5 Guest share 1 Private

The Designer cottage B&B Homestay is a charming place to stay. Just off Colombo Street situated in peaceful surroundings, and within 20 minutes walk to the city centre or 1 minute walk to amenities. There is off-street parking and free pick up from city centre on arrival (by arrangement only). Once settled in you will be welcomed with a 'mean' cup of coffee or tea by the friendly host.

~

Christchurch - St Martins *3 km S of Christchurch City Centre*

Kleynbos B&B *B&B Separate Suite Apartment with Kitchen*

Gerda De Kleyne & Hans van den Bos

59 Ngaio Street, Christchurch

Tel (03) 332 2896
KLEYNBOS@xtra.co.nz or kleynbos@paradise.net.nz

Double $80-$90 Single $75 (Continental)
Apartment $ 100-$130
Visa MC accepted
Children welcome
2 Queen 2 Double 2 Single (4 bdrm)
Bathrooms: 2 Ensuite 1 Guest share 1 Private

Quality accommodation with a personal touch, sins 1991. 3km to city centre, in an easy to find, friendly, tree-lined street. Your large ensuite rooms are $90 with microwave, fridge and juge. A computer is available to keep in contact with friends and family. A self-catering option is available in the apartment, sleeps 5 for $100-$130. The children are 15 and 12 years old. DIRECTIONS; SH74 Barbadoes Street, Waltham Road, Wilsons Road, right into Gamblins Road, first left is Ngaio Street.

~

Christchurch - St Martins *In Christchurch Central*

Locarno Gardens *Luxury Apartment with Kitchenette*

Aileen & David Davies

25 Locarno Street, St Martins, Christchurch 8002

Tel (03) 332 9987 or 027 439 9747
Fax (03) 332 9687 locarno@xtra.co.nz
www.cottagestays.co.nz/begonia/cottage.htm

Double $130-$150 (Continental)
Self-catering double/single $85-$115 Extra person $30
1 King 1 Queen 1 Twin 1 Single (3 bdrm)
Bathrooms: 2 Ensuite 1 Private

Aileen and David invite you to their fine 80 year old character villa, with stained glass windows, surrounded by mature trees and established gardens. Choose between the King bed studio within villa with private verandah entrance, and if required, adjoining twin bedroom (extra person $30) or the Stand-alone architecturally designed Garden Apartment (Begonia Cottage). Relax in the picturesque garden courtyard by the goldfish pond. River walks and a tennis court close by. Public transport 3 minutes walk away, plus the Orbiter bus which circles Christchurch city. Amenities closeby. Laundry facilities and off-street parking. As listed in The Lonely Planet. Aileen's knowledge of restaurants is extensive and David enjoys diving, deer hunting and outdoor activities."

Christchurch - Mt Pleasant *7 km E of Central Christchurch*

A Nest on Mount Pleasant *B&B Apartment with Kitchen*
Kathryn & Kai Tovgaard
15 Toledo Place, Mount Pleasant, Christchurch 8

Tel (03) 3849 485 Fax (03) 3848 385
thenestonMP@xtra.co.nz www.anestbnb.co.nz

Double $85-$1105 Single $75-$105 (Full breakfast)
Child discounted Dinner by arrangement
Visa MC Diners Amex accepted
Pet free home Children welcome
2 Queen 2 Twin (3 bdrm)
Bathrooms: 1 Ensuite 1 Private

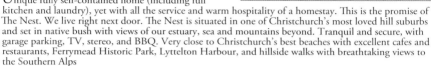

Unique fully self-contained home (including full kitchen and laundry), yet with all the service and warm hospitality of a homestay. This is the promise of The Nest. We live right next door. The Nest is situated in one of Christchurch's most loved hill suburbs and set in native bush with views of our estuary, sea and mountains beyond. Tranquil and secure, with garage parking, TV, stereo, and BBQ. Very close to Christchurch's best beaches with excellent cafes and restaurants, Ferrymead Historic Park, Lyttelton Harbour, and hillside walks with breathtaking views to the Southern Alps

Christchurch - Mt Pleasant *8 km E of Christchurch*

Mt Pleasant Bed & Breakfast *B&B Separate Suite*
Nicola & Paul Kristiansen
14 Hobday Lane, Mt Pleasant, Christchurch

Tel (03) 384 9220 Fax (03) 384 9235
Kristiansen@xtra.co.nz
mtpleasantbandb.co.nz

Double $110 Single $80 (Continental)
Child $20
Visa MC accepted
Pet free home Children welcome
1 Queen (1 bdrm)
Bathrooms: 1 Ensuite

This unique home offers a friendly and relaxed stay in your private suite. Enjoy your spacious and comfortable queen bedroom, ensuite bathroom with king-size vintage cast-iron bath (such bliss our guests tell us!) Sitting room with private entrance leading to deck and sauna (takes 6). Own kitchen facilities. Explore the huge rambling garden facinating with waterwheel, plentiful trees and abundant bird life. Conveniently situated 15 minutes from city, 10 minutes to popular Sumner Beach, 5 minutes to paragliding, windsurfing, gondola, walking and mountain-bike tracks. You'll love it!

Christchurch - Redcliffs *8 km E of Christchurch*

Redcliffs on Sea *B&B Homestay*
Cynthia & Lyndsey Ebert
125 Main Road, Redcliffs, Christchurch 8

Tel (03) 384 9792 Fax (03) 384 9703
redcliffsonsea@xtra.co.nz
www.redcliffsonsea.co.nz

Double $120 Single $75 (Continental)
Visa MC accepted
Pet free home Children welcome
1 Queen 1 Single (1 bdrm)
Bathrooms: 1 Ensuite

Relax and enjoy our comfortable home by the sea, situated approximately 15 minutes from the city, our home is "absolute water front ", on the Avon-Heathcote Estuary with magnificent views of the sea, birds and boating. We are non-smoking, and our sunny guest room contains a queen and single bed with its own ensuite and TV. Local restaurants offer a choice of cuisine, continental breakfast is included in the tariff, laundry facilities and off-street parking. What more could you wish for?

Christchurch - Redcliffs *8 km E of Christchurch centre*
Pegasus Bay View *B&B Separate Suite*
Denise & Bernie Lock
121A Moncks Spur Road, Redcliffs, Christchurch

Tel (03) 384 2923 or 021 254 2888
pegasusbay@slingshot.co.nz
www.pegasusbayview.co.nz

Double $120-$130 Single $115 (Continental)
Extra person $25
Visa MC accepted
1 Queen 1 Double
(1 bedroom plus sofa bed in loung)
Bathrooms: 1 Private

Enjoy spectacular views over the South Pacific and across the city to the Southern Alps from our modern home. The private guest suite, with its own entrance, is tastefully furnished, with queen-size bedroom, TV lounge and private bathroom. The lounge can be converted to a second double bedroom for additional friends/family. Relax over a delicious breakfast, served outside or in our dining room, while enjoying the stunning panorama. Close to beach and restaurants and 15 minutes from Christchurch City centre. We have a friendly cat.

Christchurch - Sumner *10 km E of Christchurch*
Villa Alexandra *B&B Homestay Apartment with Kitchen*
Wendy & Bob Perry
1 Kinsey Terrace, Christchurch 8

Tel (03) 326 6291 Fax (03) 326 6096
villa_alexandra@xtra.co.nz
www.villaalexandra.co.nz

Double $100-$125 Single $80 (Full breakfast)
Child under 12 $10
Children and pets welcome
1 Queen 1 Double 1 Twin 1 Single (3 bdrm)
Bathrooms: 2 Ensuite 2 Private

Enjoy the warmest hospitality in our spacious turn of the century villa overlooking Sumner Bay. Our home retains the graciousness of a bygone era while offering all modern comforts. In winter enjoy open fires, cosy farmhouse kitchen and on sunny days the verandah and turret. Spectacular sea views from Sumner to the Kaikouras. We enjoy food, wine, music, gardening, tramping, travel. The children have flown, but we still have 3 hens. 5 minutes walk to beach; off-street parking; laundry. Also self-contained beach front apartment, 2 double bedrooms, $150 per night, minimum 3 nights.

Christchurch - Sumner Beach *8 km E of Christchurch*
Cave Rock Bed & Breakfast *B&B*
Gayle & Norm Eade
16 Esplanade, Sumner, Christchurch

Tel (03) 326 6844 or 027 436 0212
Fax (03) 326 5600 eade@chch.planet.org.nz
www.caverockguesthouse.co.nz

Double $130-$140 Single $105-$115
(Continental provisions)
Child $20
Visa MC Eftpos accepted
4 Queen (4 bdrm)
Bathrooms: 4 Ensuite

The Cave Rock B&B - Christchurch's ultimate seafront accommodation opposite Sumner's famous Cave Rock. Hosts Gayle & Norm Eade have been in the industry for 19 years and enjoy meeting people from overseas and within NZ. Large double rooms all with sea views, colour TV, heating and ensuite bathrooms, can sleep up to 4. Kitchen facilities available. Sumner - the ideal location, 15 minutes from Christchurch City, excellent bus service - cafe/bars, shops, cinema, within walking distance. We have a friendly dalmatian dog.

Christchurch - Sumner *15 km E of Central Christchurch*
Abbott House Sumner Bed & Breakfast *B&B Apartment with Kitchen*
Janet & Chris Abbott
104 Nayland Street, Sumner, Christchurch

Tel (03) 326 6111 or 0800 020 654
Mobile 021 654 344   Fax (03) 326 7034
info@abbotthouse.co.nz   www.abbotthouse.co.nz

Double $105-$125 **Single** $90-$100 (Continental breakfast)
Cheaper rates apply to one-room Studio, dearer ones to four-room Suite.
Child $10   Extra Adult $20   Discounts for weekly stays (15%-40%)
Visa MC accepted   Children welcome
3 King/Twin 1 Single (2 bdrm)
Bathrooms: 1 Ensuite 1 Private

Your hosts, Chris and Janet Abbott welcome you to our historic restored
1870s villa in Christchurch's unique seaside village. Our home is 1 block from the beach, and an easy
10 minute walk along the beach to Sumner's many cafÈs, restaurants, boutique shops and cinema. Both
suite and studio have king-sized beds, own kitchen areas, TV and DVD, internet access. Off-street
parking. Laundry facilities. We also have nearby 2 holiday houses each sleeping 6-8 people. See our
website for full details.

Christchurch - Sumner *12 km E of Christchurch*
Scarborough-Heights *B&B*
Barbara and Brian Hanlon
21 Godley Drive, Scarborough, Christchurch 8008

Tel (03) 326 7060 or 027 229 7312
Fax (03) 326 7060
stay@scarborough-heights.co.nz
www.scarborough-heights.co.nz

Double $150 **Single** $100 (Full breakfast)
Child $50 Dinner $45 by arrangement
Visa MC accepted   Children welcome
1 King 1 Queen 3 Single (2 bdrm)
Bathrooms: 1 Ensuite 1 Private

Scarborough-Heights is a striking, modern architecturally designed home set in an award winning
garden, high on Scarborough Hill and offering luxurious bed & breakfast accommodation. All rooms
offer spectacular views of the Southern Alps, Christchurch City and South Pacific Ocean. We provide
friendly hospitality in peaceful, quiet surroundings yet are only 20 minutes from the city centre and 5
minutes from the seaside village of Sumner with its many cafes, speciality shops and cinema. We have no
children living at home, only 2 cats.

Christchurch - Sumner *8 km E of Christchurch*
Tiromoana *B&B Guests' kitchen facilities*
Helen Mackay & Brian Lamb
89 Richmond Hill Road, Sumner, Christchurch

Tel (03) 326 6209 Fax (03) 326 6208
relax@tiromoana.co.nz
www.tiromoana.co.nz

Double $120-$140 **Single** $90-$120 (Continental)
Child $25
Visa MC accepted Children welcome
1 King/Twin 1 Queen 1 Double (3 bdrm)
Bathrooms: 1 Ensuite 1 Private
Plus bath under the stars!

Sumner, only 15 minutes from the city, within easy walking of village cafes, movie theatres, specialty
shops and the beach. Tiromoana was built in 1904 in a spectacular position overlooking the beach. A
perfect spot to relax, wander the garden, have a bath outside under the stars and sleep to the sound of
the sea. The atmosphere is friendly, relaxed and informal, providing guests' lounge and kitchen facilities,
with a fresh and generous breakfast provided. Laundry facilities are available. We look forward to
welcoming you.

Canterbury

Christchurch - Hoon Hay *5 km SE of Christchurch*

Sparks Road *B&B Apartment with Kitchen*
Micky & Alistair Watson
330 Sparks Road, Hoon Hay, Christchurch

Tel (03) 339 0138 or 021 145 9597
Fax (03) 339 0139
alandmic@xtra.co.nz
www.sparksroad.co.nz

Double $120-$130 Single $90 (Continental)
Self-contained (sleeps 4) $190
Visa MC accepted
Pet free home   Children welcome
2 Queen 1 Twin (3 bdrm)
Bathrooms: 2 Private 2 baths, 2 showers

Welcome to a touch of country, 10 minutes from the city. Kick off your shoes, make a cup of tea, sink into a comfy sofa, and enjoy the views. Your comfort is our priority and we offer you a spacious lounge, tea/coffee making facilities, laundry, shower & bath with handmade soaps,a stack of towels and "the best bed yet" (guests' comment). The main highway to Akaroa is close, plus several wineries and golf courses. We can assist with forward bookings and plans. Internet available. Courtesy pick up.

~

Christchurch - Cashmere *5 km S of Christchurch Centre*

Milne B&B *B&B*
Janet Milne
12A Hackthorne Road, Cashmere, Christchurch

Tel (03) 337 1423

Double $100 Single $50 (Continental)
1 Queen 1 Single (1 bdrm)
Bathrooms: 1 Ensuite 1 Family share

Two storeyed home in quiet back section on Cashmere Hills. Lower storey is an independent suite comprising 2 hand basins, shower, lavatory, king-size bed with electric blanket, 2 single bunks, television, telephone, heaters, and table and chairs. Tea/coffee making facilities. Non-smokers only. I am a registered general nurse; obstetrics nurse; a university student studying for a degree in linguistics; and an English language teacher. The piano loves attention. Spanish and English are my favourite languages. 'Explorer' of foreign countries.

~

Christchurch - Cashmere *6 km S of City Centre*

Edgehill *Separate Suite private bathroom*
Malcolm & Judie Douglass
51A Bowenvale Avenue,, Cashmere, Christchurch

Tel (03) 332 5504 Fax (03) 332 5506
douglass.edgehill@clear.net.nz

Double $140 (Continental provisions)
2 Double (2 Doubles bdrm)
Bathrooms: 1 Private

Edgehill is a comfortable home in a quiet leafy location on the edge of the Port Hills, only 10 minutes from the city centre and 25 minutes from the airport. Separate suite with private bathroom, a double bedroom and also a sitting room with a pull out double bed. Relax in this private rear section with sunny verandah, courtyard, terraced garden and trees. Cafe/restaurants , attractive parks, riverside and hillside walks are close by. Share your experiences with Malcolm (civil engineer and town planner) and Judie (professional actress).

Christchurch - Westmorland *7 km SW of Christchurch*

Slippers *B&B Homestay*
Georgie & Ron McKie
66 Penruddock Rise, Westmorland 8002, Christchurch

Tel (03) 339 6170 or 021 1142189
Fax (03) 339 6170
mckiepic@paradise.net.nz

Double $190 Single $120 (Full breakfast)
Dinner $50 including wine
Visa MC accepted
Not suitable for children
1 King/Twin 1 Single (2 bdrm)
Bathrooms: 1 Private

Pure New Zealand wool slippers are ready for your use the moment you arrive at Slippers. Relax in a beautiful Port Hills home and enjoy the stunning views of the Alps, the Caterbury Plains and Christchurch City.

You will be our only guests and your suite of rooms includes 2 bedrooms, lounge, private bathroom & private entrances in a smoke free environment. Central heating, down duvets, electric blankets, bathrobes, hairdryers, hand-made toiletries, Sky TV & an extensive library combine to make your stay comfortable and memorable.

A fruit bowl, home-baking, wonderful PNG plunger coffee and Twinings teas are always available at you finger tips. Dinner is available on 24 hours notice and features fine wine. Special diets can be catered for.

Enjoy a superb collection of museum quality primitive Papua New Guinea artefacts, intriguing antique maps and fine images from leading NZ photographers.

Complimentary email and internet are available. Parking is off-street and a city centre bus frquently stops at the gate.

Our photographic guests may access a fine chemical darkroom, or digital facilities and tutoring can be arranged on request. Allow us to assist with your touring plans, advise on photographic opportunities and introduce you to local photographic clubs and like minded people. Cat lovers will be enchanted by Mangi and Liklik. Georgie and Ron look forward to meeting you.

Christchurch - Tai Tapu *20 km SE of Christchurch*

Fantail Lodge on Greenpark *Country B&B*
Pamela & Doug Hueston
164 River Road, Tai Tapu, Christchurch RD 2

Tel (03) 325 7572 or 027 433 7706
Fax (03) 325 7572
riversidegpk@xtra.co.nz

Double $100-$130 Single $90 (Full breakfast)
Visa MC accepted
1 King 1 Double (2 bdrm)
Bathrooms: 1 Ensuite 2 Family share

Located on River Road meandering along the Halswell
River. Artist Pamela and Photographer Doug share the
comfort of their elegant and spacious home, with guests separate lounge (with piano) for privacy. Ensuite,
TV, electric blankets. Set in extensive landscaped grounds, in tranquil country surroundings, views of
the Alps, sunsets, nestled in our 10 acre farmlet, farming cattle and sheep. Native birds: Fantails and
Pukeko's often frequent our garden. Pick-up from Airport, (25km.) buses or train by arrangement. Local
award winning winery, restaurants within 12 km

Lyttelton *9 km E of Christchurch*

Shonagh O'Hagan's Guest House *B&B*
Shonagh O'Hagan
Dalcroy House, 16 Godley Quay, Lyttelton

Tel (03) 328 8577
shonagh.ohagan@xtra.co.nz

Double $115 Single $90 (Full breakfast)
Child $25 Dinner $35
Visa MC accepted
Children welcome
1 King/Twin 2 Queen 1 Double (4 bdrm)
Bathrooms: 2 Family share 1 Guest share

Dalcory House built 1859, has been a boarding school,
private residents, rental property, and hostel for naval ratings in WW2. Shonagh your hostess is a cook,
nurse, educator, health manager and mother. Have a comfortable nights sleep in pleasant surroundings
with a clear view of Lyttelton Port and Harbour, 5 minutes walk from the centre of Lyttelton and 15
minutes drive to the centre of Christchurch. Shonagh and her son will ensure your stay is comfortable
and memorable.

Governors Bay *13 km SE of Christchurch*

Governors Bay Bed & Breakfast *B&B Apartment Style No kitchen*
Karen & Kevin McGrath
14 Hays Rise, Governors Bay, Lyttelton RD 1

Tel (03) 329 9930 or 021 622 657
karen@gbbedandbreakfast.co.nz
www.gbbedandbreakfast.co.nz

Double $120 Single $100 (Continental)
Visa MC accepted
Pets welcome
1 Queen (2 bdrm)
Bathrooms: 1 Private

Unique timber home designed to accommodate our B&B private guest wing. Separate entrance with sunny morning deck. Enjoy brekky (self-contained) at your leisure. King room, panoramic views of Lyttelton Harbour. TV, fridge, CD player. Private guest lounge, convert to double room (sofa bed). Rural walking tracks start at rear of property. 20 minute drive to Christchurch, 15 minutes to Lyttelton, 2 minutes to local hotel and cafe. Karen operates Earth Healer Aromatherapy, offers complimentary aromatherapy baths. Full treatments and Reiki by appointment. We and our lab X, Bella-Brae look forward to welcoming you.

Teddington - Lyttelton Harbour *20 km S of Christchurch*

Bergli Hill Farmstay *Farmstay*
Rowena & Max Dorfliger
265 Charteris Bay Road, Teddington, RD 1 Lyttelton

Tel (03) 329 9118 or 027 482 9410
Fax (03) 329 9118
bergli@ihug.co.nz   www.vmacgill.net/bergli

Double $105-$125 Single $70-$90 (Full breakfast)
Dinner from $25 by arrangement
Visa MC accepted
Children welcome
1 King/Twin 1 Queen 1 Double 2 Twin 3 Single
(3 bdrm)
Bathrooms: 2 Ensuite 1 Family share

Lyttelton Harbour and the Port Hills create a dynamic panorama you can enjoy from our custom-built log chalet. Rowena speaks Japanese (but is a Kiwi) and Max speaks German. We are both self-employed (woodworker and shadow puppeteer) and enjoy sharing a sail on Max's yacht. Our pet cat, alpacas and sheep, welcome guests enthusiastically. Whether relaxing on the veranda at Max's hand-crafted table or sipping wine in the spa bath, we are sure you will make good memories.

Diamond Harbour - Church Bay *35 km S of Christchurch*

Kai-o-ruru Bed & Breakfast *B&B Cottage No Kitchen*
Robin & Philip Manger
32 James Drive, Church Bay, Lyttelton, RD 1

Tel (03) 329 4788 Fax (03) 329 4788
manger@xtra.co.nz

Double $95 Single $60 (Full breakfast)
Dinner $25
2 Single (1 bdrm)
Bathrooms: 1 Ensuite

Explore Banks Peninsula from Church Bay. Our cosy, ensuite unit overlooks Quail Island and our coastal garden. The room has a tea/coffee tray, home-made biscuits, books, TV, fridge. We are a non-smoking household with an unobtrusive cat. Philip and I are travelled, retired teachers who enjoy welcoming travellers to our wonderful area. Languages: German, Dutch (some French, Italian, Spanish).

Lyttelton Harbour - Purau *35 km SE of Christchurch*

Mt Evans B&B *B&B Cottage No Kitchen*
Pauline Croft & Barry Kendall
53 Purau - Port Levy Road, Purau, Lyttelton Harbour

Tel (03) 329 4414 Fax (03) 329 4414
kendallcroft@hyper.net.nz

Double $75-$100 Single $70-$95 (Continental)
Child $15 Dinner by arrangement
2 separate cottages
2 Queen 2 Single (3 bdrm)
Bathrooms: 2 Private

Our home is situated on 1.5 hectares, amongst mature trees on the gentle slopes of Mt Evans. Just 500 metres from the beach, we offer tranquil rural accommodation in two separate and sunny modern cottages. A perfect base for exploring Banks Peninsula and Christchurch (ferry 7 minutes to Lyttelton) or to relax and unwind. Local attractions include swimming, boating etc, wildlife cruises in the harbour. Mountain biking, tramping (we are experienced outdoor people happy to share our knowledge) abundant bird life and wonderful views.

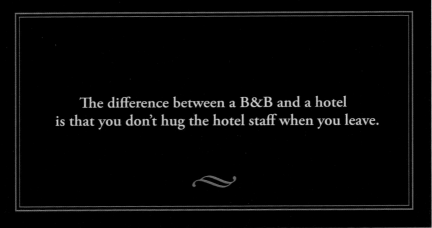

The difference between a B&B and a hotel
is that you don't hug the hotel staff when you leave.

Selwyn - Dunsandel *30 km SW of Christchurch*

Selwyn Bed & Breakfast *B&B*
Susan Askew & John Baker
Camden Street, Selwyn Village,
Near Dunsandel, Canterbury

Tel (03) 325 4184 Fax (03) 325 4195
selwyn@baskcontrol.co.nz

Double $110 Single $80 (Continental)
Child negotiable
Children welcome
2 Queen 1 Single (2 bdrm)
Bathrooms: 2 Ensuite

Our modern home with half acre garden is just off SH1 near Dunsandel. Surrounded by farmland, we are also close to vineyards, skiing and salmon fishing. Comfortable upstairs guest rooms, each with large ensuite, TV and radio/alarm, open onto a guest lounge, or feel at home in our family lounge with 2 quiet children and friendly cats. Continental or cooked breakfast and other meals available at adjacent restaurant - The Famous Whitehouse Cafe. Email, facsimile and laundry facilities.

Banks Peninsula - Okains Bay *20 km N of Akaroa*

Kawatea *Farmstay*
Judy & Kerry Thacker
Okains Bay, Banks Peninsula

Tel (03) 304 8621 Fax (03) 304 8621   kawatea@xtra.co.nz

Double $110-$135 Single $70-$90 (Full breakfast)
Child by arrangement Dinner $30
Visa MC accepted
3 Queen 2 Single (3 bdrm)
Bathrooms: 1 Ensuite 1 Guest share 1 Private

Experience the grace and charm of yesteryear, while enjoying the fine food and wine of NZ today. Revel in the peace of country life, but still be close to sights and activities. Escape to Kawatea, an historic Edwardian homestead set in spacious gardens, and surrounded by land farmed by our Irish ancestors since the 1850s. Built in 1900 from native timbers, it features stained glass windows and handcrafted furniture, and has been carefully renovated to add light and space without losing its old world charm.

Linger over your choice of breakfast in the sunny conservatory. Join us for barbeques on the expansive verandahs, savouring seafood from the Bay, and creative country fare from our garden and farm. Gather around the dining table by the fire, sharing experiences with fellow travellers.

Participate in farm activities such as moving stock, feeding pet sheep, lambing, calving or shearing. Wander our 1400 acre hillside farm, climbing to enjoy a panoramic view of Banks Peninsula. Relax or swim at Okains Bay, observe the birdlife on the estuary, or walk along the scenic coastline to secluded beaches and a seal colony with excellent photographic opportunities. Learn about Maori culture and the life of early settlers at the acclaimed Okains Bay Museum. Explore Akaroa with its strong French influence, visit art galleries and craft

shops. Play golf, go horse riding, sample local wines and watch traditional cheeses being made. Take a harbour cruise or swim with the rare Hector's dolphin.

We have been providing farmstays since 1988, and pride ourselves on thoughtful personal service. Romantic weekends and special occasion dinners are also catered for. We hope you come as a visitor but leave as a friend. Directions: Take Highway 75 from Christchurch through Duvauchelle. Turn left at signpost marked Okains Bay. Drive to the top of the Bay - we are 6km downhill on the right

Canterbury

351

Akaroa - Barry's Bay *12 km W of Akaroa*

Rosslyn Estate *B&B Homestay Farmstay*

Ross, Lynette, Kirsty (13) & Matt (11) Curry
Barry's Bay, RD 2, Akaroa

Tel (03) 304 5804 Fax (03) 304 5804
Rosslyn@xtra.co.nz

Double $120-$140 Single $100 (Full breakfast)
Child negotiable   Dinner $35pp
1 night stay $140, 2 or more nights $120 per night
Visa MC accepted
2 Queen (2 bdrm)
Bathrooms: 2 Ensuite

Rosslyn is a large historic homestead built in the 1860s, overlooking the serene Akaroa Harbour. It has been our family home and dairy farm for 4 generations. 2 large ground floor rooms have been refurbished to accommodate you in comfort. A spa room, pool and laundry are also available, at no charge. We have enjoyed sharing our life style with guests for the past 17 years and look forward to welcoming you too. Directions: SH75, "Rosslyn Estate" sign behind picket fence on left travelling to Akaroa.

Akaroa - Paua Bay *12 km E of Akaroa*

Paua Bay Farmstay *B&B Farmstay*

Murray & Sue Johns
Postal: C/- 113 Beach Road, Akaroa, Banks Peninsula

Tel (03) 304 8511 or 021 133 8194
Fax (03) 304 8511
info@pauabay.com
www.pauabay.com

Double $120-$140 (Full breakfast)
Child negotiable Dinner $30
1 Queen 1 Twin (2 bdrm)
Bathrooms: 1 Ensuite 1 Guest share

Set in a private bay, our 900 acre sheep, deer and cattle farm is surrounded by coast-line, native bush and streams. You are spoilt for choice - walk to the beach, enjoy seals and extensive bird life, join in seasonal farming activities or horse riding. Swim in the pool, laze in the hammock and don't miss the secluded moonlit bath under the stars overlooking the pacific ... In the evening share a meal of fresh farm produce with relaxed conversation gathered around the large kitchen table.

Akaroa *5 km N of Akaroa*

LeLievre Farmstay *Farmstay*

Hanne & Paul LeLievre
Box 4, Akaroa, Banks Peninsula

Tel (03) 304 7255 Fax (03) 304 7255
Double.L@Xtra.co.nz
www.sealsafari.com

Double $95 Single $50 (Full breakfast)
Dinner $25
Children welcome
1 Double 1 Single (1 bdrm)
Bathrooms: 1 Ensuite

Our home is situated 1.5km up the Takamatua Valley and 5km from Akaroa. We farm sheep, cattle and deer and usually have a menagerie of orphaned pets etc around. Our interests include golf and bridge and we invite you to enjoy some good old fashioned country hospitality. A trip to the Akaroa Seal Colony Safari, which was recently featured on the TV programmes A Flying Visit, Totally Wild and The Great Outdoors, should be considered a must. The safari includes a scenic drive, to and through, a working farm, with the farmer.

Akaroa *5 km S of Akaroa*
Onuku Heights - Historic Farmstay *B&B Farmstay*
Eckhard Keppler
Onuku Heights, Akaroa,

Tel (03) 304 7112 Fax (03) 304 7116
onuku.heights@paradise.net.nz
www.onuku-heights.co.nz

Double $190-$240 (Full breakfast)
Dinner $40-$60 by prior arrangement
Visa MC accepted
3 King (3 bdrm)
Bathrooms: 3 Ensuite

Onuku Heights is a charming, carefully restored 1860s homestead overlooking the Akaroa Harbour. Nestled in orchard and tranquil gardens with an abundance of bird life, it is surrounded by native bush reserves, streams and waterfalls on a 309 hectare working sheep farm.

Enjoy spacious rooms furnished with antiques, comfortable firm king-size beds and exquisite ensuite bathrooms. The 2 guest rooms in the homestead have majestic sea views, the sunny cottage room is looking to the rose garden. There is a separate well-appointed guest lounge with an open fire and verandah. Explore the beautiful scenery on well maintained walking tracks, going up to 700 metre altitude with breathtaking panoramic views of the Akaroa Harbour, the ocean and the Alps.

Our property is part of the Banks Peninsula Track. Join us in the farm activities, recline in a sun-lounger, or just dream the day away under an apple tree. Indulge yourself at the heated pool; soak up the sun, listening to the trickling fountain and basking in the stunning views.

In the morning we prepare you a delicious breakfast with freshly baked bread, home-made jam, cereals, fruits from the orchard; bacon and eggs if you like. In the evening you may choose one of Akaroa's fine restaurants, a mere 15 minute drive away or we may provide supper / dinner by prior arrangement. Then relax on the veranda with a glass of wine, enjoy the sunset and beautiful birdsong.

Canterbury

Akaroa *80 km SE of Christchurch*
The Maples *B&B*
Lesley & Peter Keppel
158 Rue Jolie, Akaroa

Tel (03) 304 8767 Fax (03) 304 8767
maplesakaroa@xtra.co.nz
www.themaplesakaroa.co.nz

Double $120 **Single** $90 (Full breakfast)
Visa MC accepted
3 Queen 1 Single (3 bdrm)
Bathrooms: 3 Ensuite

The Maples is a charming historic 2 storey home built
in 1877. It is situated in a delightful garden setting, 3
minutes walk from the cafes and waterfront. We offer 2 queen bedrooms with ensuites upstairs and a
separate garden room with a queen and single bed also ensuited. You can relax in the separate guests
lounge where tea and coffee is available. Our delicious continental and cooked breakfasts usually include
freshly baked brioche and croissants.

Akaroa *80 km SE of Christchurch*
Wilderness House *Luxury B&B*
Jim & Liz Coubrough
42 Rue Grehan, Akaroa,

Tel (03) 304 7517 or 021 669 381   Fax (03) 304 7518
info@wildernesshouse.co.nz
www.wildernesshouse.co.nz

Double $220-$240 **Single** $180-$200 (Full breakfast)
Dinner by arrangement
Visa MC accepted
1 King/Twin 3 Queen (4 bdrm)
Bathrooms: 3 Ensuite 1 Private

Gracious accommodation in one of Akaroa's finest
historic homes set in a large traditional garden containing protected trees, old roses and a petite vineyard.
Charming bedrooms, with their own character, feature fine linen, fresh flowers, tea/coffee and home-
baking. Elegant lounge opens to verandah and garden. Enjoy our scrumptious country-cooked breakfasts.
We take particular care to make you feel comfortable, relaxed and welcome in our home. Join us for a
glass of wine in the evening. Short stroll to harbour, restaurants and shops. Resident cats, Beethoven and
Harry.

Akaroa Harbour - French Farm *70 km SE of Christchurch*
Bantry Lodge *B&B Cottage with Kitchen*
Dolina & David Barker
French Farm, RD 2, Akaroa

Tel (03) 304 5161 or 025 284 8260 Fax (03) 304 5162
barker.d@xtra.co.nz   www.bantrylodge.co.nz

Double $120-$140 (Full breakfast)
Dinner $40 by arrangement
Self-contained cottage sleeps 4
Visa MC Diners Amex accepted
Children and pets welcome
2 Queen 2 Double (3 bdrm)
Bathrooms: 1 Guest share 2 Private

Our historic home has views across Akaroa Harbour 50 metres away. Groundfloor queen room has
french doors to verandah and sea views, private bath. Upstairs queen room with balcony overlooks
harbour , private bath. Coffee, tea facilities provided with home-baking. Our comfortable sitting room
is for relaxing or joining us for a drink. Full breakfast is served in our elegant dining room. We offer
comfort, tranquillity, space. A self-contained cottage sleeps 4, linen, breakfast supplies available. 1 shy cat.

Akaroa *3 km N of Akaroa*
Akaroa Country House *B&B*
David & Sue Thurston
19 Bells Road, Takamatua, Akaroa

Tel (03) 304 7499 Fax (03) 304 7499
takamatua@xtra.co.nz
www.akaroacountryhouse.com

Double $160-$185 **Single** $150 (Continental)
Visa MC accepted
Children welcome
3 Queen (3 bdrm)
Bathrooms: 3 Ensuite

A peaceful rural retreat set amongst bush, birds and
creeks. Enjoy the private swimming pool, croquet or petantque. All rooms are private and ensuite, the
provencial style French hut set in the bush beside the creek with an outside bath. David, a cabinetmaker,
built the house which has many examples of his work including 2 sleigh beds in the guest rooms, he is
happy to welcome visitors to his workshop. Sumptuous breakfast includes fresh fruit from the orchard,
croissants, home-made preserves and freshly ground coffee.

Akaroa *80 km SE of Christchurch*
La Belle Villa *B&B*
Alice & Paul Hewitson
113 Rue Jolie, Akaroa

Tel (03) 304 7084 Fax (03) 304 7084
bookings@labellevilla.co.nz
www.labellevilla.co.nz

Double $125-$130 **Single** $105-$110
(Special breakfast)
Visa MC accepted
Children welcome
1 King 2 Queen 1 Twin (4 bdrm)
Bathrooms: 4 Ensuite

A warm welcome awaits you. Relax in the comfort of a bygone era, and appreciate the antiques in our
picturesque historic villa with separate guest lounge. Built in the 1870s as the first doctor's surgery in
Akaroa it is now established on beautiful, mature grounds. Enjoy the indoor/outdoor living, and gently
trickling stream. We offer to make your stay with us special. Breakfast alfresco with real coffee. Being
centrally situated, restaurants, cafes, wine bars and beach are all in walking distance.

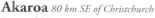

Akaroa *80 km SE of Christchurch*
Lavaud House *B&B Homestay*
Alison & Gavin Porteous
83 Rue Lavaud, Akaroa

Tel (03) 304 7121 Fax (03) 304 7121
lavaudhouse@xtra.co.nz
www.lavaudhouse-akaroa.co.nz

Double $160-$210 (Continental)
Visa MC Eftpos accepted
Not suitable for children
1 King 2 Queen (3 bdrm)
Bathrooms: 2 Ensuite 1 Private

Lavaud House is a gracious, historic home which
overlooks the beach and harbour. Being centrally located, you are only 5 minutes walking distance from
restaurants, galleries and shops. Relax in the comfort of elegant furnishings, or wander in our peaceful
garden with its magnificent harbour views and enchanting native birds. Lavaud House has been home to
Alison, Gavin, daughter Lucy and Maddie the golden retriever since July 2004.

Canterbury

Akaroa *80 km SE of Christchurch*

Chez Fleurs *B&B*
Jan & Paul Wallace
15 Smith Street, Akaroa 8161

Tel (03) 304 8674 Fax (03) 304 8974
chezfleurs@xtra.co.nz
www.chezfleurs.co.nz

Double $150 **Single** $130 (Continental)
Visa MC accepted
Not suitable for children
2 Queen 1 Twin (3 bdrm)
Bathrooms: 2 Ensuite 1 Private

Bonjour! Chez Fleurs is ideally situated 150 metres
up from the beach and 3 minutes walk to cafes, galleries, restaurants, shops and Information Centre.
Enjoy our stunning waterfront views, beautiful garden and native birdlife, while relaxing on your own
private balcony. We offer superior accommodation with private tea/coffee making facilities, fridge, TV,
hairdryers and fresh flowers in suites. Complimentary guest laundry and BBQ. Secure off-street parking.
Your delicious breakfast, using fresh home-grown produce is served alfresco, on your own balcony. 'A
Bientot'. See you soon!

Akaroa *80 km SE of Christchurch*

Mullberry House *B&B Homestay*
Anne Craig & Jack Clark
9 William Street, Akaroa 8161

Tel (03) 304 7778 or (03) 304 7793
Fax (03) 304 7778
anneandjacknz@yahoo.com
www..house.co.nz

Double $100-$150 **Single** $90 (Special breakfast)
1 night stay $10 surcharge
1 King 1 Queen 1 Twin 1 Single (3 bdrm)
Bathrooms: 2 Ensuite 1 Private

Experience the best in homestyle accommodation and
delight in the setting of Mulberry House, a 100 year old historic home furnished with antiques, only two
minutes' walk from the village and restaurants. There is a choice of double rooms with private bathroom
or ensuite or a twin room. All rooms are beautifully decorated and feature quality beds and fine linen.
The romantic poolside summerhouse has its own kitchen, ensuite and garden to provide total privacy
if desired. Breakfasts are a speciality and feature a choice of American, European, English and New
Zealand styles. Well travelled and semi-retired, Anne and Jack offer unparalleled hospitality.

Akaroa *1 km NE of Akaroa*

Mill Cottage *Luxury B&B Cottage with Kitchen Suite of rooms in Homestead*
Louisa Hobson & Cliff Corry
81 Rue Grahan, Akaroa 8161

Tel (03) 304 8007
millcottage@xtra.co.nz
www.akaroa.gen

Double $195-$295 **Single** $175-$275 (Full breakfast)
Child under 12 $50
Visa MC Diners Amex Eftpos accepted
Pet free home
1 Queen 2 Single (3 bdrm)
Bathrooms: 1 Private

Enjoy the unique experience of staying in a fully restored, listed historic cottage, in a tranquil garden
setting. Wake to the dawn chorus, the sound of the nearby stream and a generous breakfast hamper.
The privacy and peace provide an ideal atmosphere for those seeking a romantic setting for a special
break. The character and charm of the original cottage have been largely retained, while providing all
essential amenities for guest comfort. The cottage is exclusively yours during your stay. Smoke-free. No
pets.

Akaroa *75 km SE of Christchurch*
The Olive Grove *Luxury B&B*
Andy & Alison Beck
36 Sawmill Road, Robinsons Bay, Akaroa

Tel (03) 304 5190 or 021 153 1713
Fax (03) 304 5190
the_olive_grove@clear.net.nz www.theolivegrove.net.nz

Double $165-$215 **Single** $120-$165 (Full breakfast)
Dinner available on request
Visa MC Eftpos accepted
Children welcome
2 King 1 Queen 1 Twin (4 bdrm)
Bathrooms: 2 Ensuite 1 Guest share

Nestled in a sheltered valley near Akaroa, The Olive Grove is the perfect tranquil getaway. High quality renovation combines modern day comforts with original character in this 1915 home. Breathtaking view of the bay from bed, balcony, bath or outdoor spa under the stars. Open fire in cosy guest lounge. 4 stunning rooms with gorgeous linen, bathrobes, flowers, candles, TV and central heating. Taste olive oil grown on the property. Join us for a complimentary glass of wine in the evening. Resident soft dog, Clive.

Akaroa *80 km SE of Christchurch*
Maison de la Mer *Luxury*
Carol & Bruce Hyland
1 Rue Benoit, Akaroa, Banks Peninsula

Tel (03) 304 8907 or 021 986 221
Fax (03) 304 8917
maisondelamer@xtra.co.nz
www.maisondelamer.co.nz

Double $250-$295 (Special breakfast)
Child over 12
Visa MC Amex Eftpos accepted
3 Queen 1 Single (3 bdrm)
Bathrooms: 3 Ensuite

Life is too short not to not treat yourself to something special when you visit such a magic place as Akaroa, Indulge yourself, with that pampered feeling of luxury, romance and fine food. Enjoy panoramic waterfront vistas from every room. Feel extra special in luxurious private surroundings with antiques, fine art, and wondrous comfort. TV/DVD movies in all rooms. Guest computer. Delicious gourmet breakfasts served overlooking the harbour. Steps from all restaurants and attractions. As experienced hosts, we offer personal attention and many complimentary surprises .

Canterbury

Highcountry Canterbury - Castle Hill *33 km W of Springfield*
The Burn Alpine B&B *B&B Homestay*
Bob Edge & Phil Stephenson
11 Torlesse Place, Castle Hill Village, Canterbury

Tel (03) 318 7559 Fax (03) 318 7558
theburn@xtra.co.nz www.theburn.co.nz

Double $120 **Single** $70 (Continental)
Child under 13 half price Dinner $30
Dinner, Bed & Breakfast $100
Visa MC accepted Children welcome
3 Queen 1 Twin (4 bdrm)
Bathrooms: 2 Guest share Two bathrooms with
showering facilites and seperate toilets

1 Hour west of Christchurch, a carefree atmosphere prevails at The Burn. Nestled in the heart of the Southern Alps, it's arguably New Zealand's highest B&B. We designed and built our alpine lodge to maximise mountain vistas. Centered in the mystic Castlehill Basin, surrounded by native forest, this is a fantastic place to return after a days activity or just kick back and relax on the sunny deck. A host of outdoor sports include ski/snowboarding, hiking, mountain biking, and flyfishing. Professional flyfishing guiding available in house.

Canterbury

Darfield *4 km W of Darfield*

The Oaks Historic Homestead *B&B Homestay*
Madeleine de Jong
State Highway 73, Corner of Clintons Road, Darfield

Tel (03) 318 7232 or 027 241 3999
Fax (03) 318 7236
theoaks@quicksilver.net.nz
www.theoakshomestead.co.nz

Double $150-$275 Single $140 (Continental)
Dinner $38pp on request
Visa MC Eftpos accepted   Children and pets welcome
3 Queen 1 Single (4 bdrm)
Bathrooms: 1 Ensuite 2 Private

One of Canterbury's oldest homesteads, restored to its former glory. Located amidst stunning scenery of the Southern Alps to the Westcoast, with ski fields, golf courses and tourist attractions on its doorstep. The Oaks features: guest rooms with ensuite/private bathrooms, a guest dining and living room featuring stunning open fires, a traditional large homestead kitchen, beautiful verandas for outdoor entertaining. Children welcome. Pets on request. Your Host Madeleine speaks 5 languages and is a keen cook. Wherever possible I try to use fresh organic produce.

Mt Hutt - Methven *6 km E of Methven*

Pagey's Farmstay *B&B Farmstay*
Shirley & Gene Pagey
Chertsey Road, Methven Mt-Hutt Village, 12 RD Rakaia

Tel (03) 302 1713 Fax (03) 302 1714
pageysfarmstay@wave.co.nz

Double $110 Single $90 (Special breakfast)
Child under 12 half price   Dinner $30pp   spa pool
Pet free home Children welcome
1 King 1 Queen 4 Single (3 bdrm)
Bathrooms: 2 Private

Enjoy hospitality and freedom in our lovely expansive home, set amidst aged oak trees and large rose garden. Watch our 47" TV and its many channels. Enjoy pre-dinner drinks, wine, crystal clear mountain water and home-grown cuisine. Star gaze in our luxurious massaging spa. Surrounding activities include breathtaking bush walks, 2 superior golf courses, ballooning and skiing. Short notice is our peciality. Directions from Methven town centre, turn down Methven Chertsey Road, signposted 6km on the left.

Mt Hutt - Methven *7 km N of Methven*

Alaska Park Tranquill House *Executive self-contained cottage & farmstay*
Patrick & Pat Mason
Alaska Park, 703 Pudding Hill Road, Methven, RD 12
Rakaia Canterbury

Tel (03) 302 9335 Fax (03) 302 9335
ppjm@xtra.co.nz
www.tranquilhouse.co.nz

Double $120-$160 Single $90-$13 (Full breakfast)
Child under 12 half price   Dinner by arrangerment
Children welcome
2 Double 1 Twin 1 Single
(4 in cottage)
Bathrooms: 1 Private

Set in 350 acres of picturesque farm land offering Summer/Winter retreat for couples or families. Tranquil house provides executive s/c accommodtion, barbecue area, private garden, b/b, farm tour with stay, dinner by arrangement. Tranquil House is a warm, modern family home, tastefully furnished with modern facilities, just 7km from Methven, 5km to ski field, 5 mins from golf course, club hire available Transport to/from Christchurch Airport, 1 hour away by arrangement.

~

Mt Hutt - Methven *4 km NW of Methven - Mt Hutt Village*

Green Gables Deer Farm *B&B Farmstay*
Roger & Colleen Mehrtens
185 Waimarama Road No 12 R.D. Rakaia,

Tel 0064 3 3028 308 Fax 0064 3 3028 309
greengables@xtra.co.nz
www.nzfarmstay.com

Double $140-$180 **Single** $110-$140 (Special breakfast)
Child $55Dinner $50pp
Visa MC accepted
Children welcome
2 King 2 Twin (3 bdrm)
Bathrooms: 2 Ensuite 1 Private

Green Gables 4 star qualmarked "Supreme Award Winners Ashburton District Tourism Awards 2004" Bed and Breakfast........1 hour Christchurch International Airport, 3 hrs Kaikoura for Whale Watching or swimming with Dolphins. 3.5 hrs Mt Cook and 5.5 hrs Queenstown approx. Relax with a welcome cup of tea on arrival with your hosts, meet pet deer and our semi retired portly Labrador.

Tranquil surroundings, private entrances. superking beds, electric blankets, clock radios, ensuites, heaters, hair dryers, curling wands, toiletries, bathrobes, tea and coffee facilities.Fridges, Irons-ironing boards. Laundry available free with two nights or more accommodation.

Sumptuous breakfasts. Dinner by arrangement. Complimentry pre dinner drinks when dining in. Superb restaurants..... 4kms to Methven-Mt Hutt village.

ACTIVITIES:- International Golf courses Methven & Terrace Downs....club & cart hire available. Hot air ballooning, Bush, Mountain & Rhododendron Walks, Visit nearby "Edoras" the "Lord of the Rings" film site at Mt Sunday......4WD scenic tours available by arrangement. Fishing, Jet Boating, Scenic Flights, Ecotours, Bird Watching, Horse Trekking, Heliski,Snow boarding, Skiing-Mt Hutt. Seven club-fields - all activities nearby.

LOCATION:- Situated on S/H77 4kms N/W Methven. From Inland Scenic-Route 72 turn into S/H77 travel 5kms Green Gables Deer Farm on right.

Mt Hutt - Methven *11 km W of Methven*

Glenview Farmstay *B&B Farmstay Cottage No Kitchen*
Helen & Mike Johnstone
142 Hart Road, Methven,

Tel (03) 302 8620 Fax (03) 302 8620
helenmikejohnstone@yahoo.com

Double $100 **Single** $60 (Full breakfast)
Child $25 Dinner $25
Children welcome
2 Queen 1 Double 2 Twin 1 Single (5 bdrm)
Bathrooms: 1 Ensuite 1 Guest share Ensuite in unit

Glenview farmstay is situated at the base of Mt Hutt
Ski Field, with the house designed to look at the
mountains and down the Canterbury Plains to the Port
Hills.

Our 1200 acre farm consists of mainly cattle with a few
sheep. We have a golden labrador and a cat.

There is a peaceful unit in the garden which is suitable
for a couple or a family which has 1 queen and 2 single
beds, ensuite, TV, tea & coffee making facilities and
wonderful views. The rooms in the house have seperate
access, good heating and are non-smoking. Dinner by
arrangement. Free farm tours on request.

Methven is only 10 minutes away and we are very close
to good fishing, golf, ballooning, bush walks and jet
boating. Free transfers to local walkways.

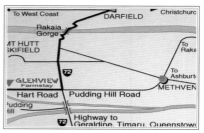

360

Staveley - Mt Somers *20 km SW of Methven*

Korobahn Lodge *B&B Homestay*
Caroline & John Lartice
Burgess Road, Staveley

Tel (03) 303 0828
carolinel@xtra.co.nz
www.korobahnlodge.co.nz

Double $120-$160 **Single** $90-$12 (Full breakfast)
Dinner $45 Children welcome
2 Queen 1 Twin (3 bdrm)
Bathrooms: 3 Ensuite

Welcome to our unique North American barn style
homestead. Korobahn is tucked into the foot of Mt
Somers and stands in several acres of gardens, surrounded by farmland. The property has recently been
totally refurbished, and offers very high quality accommodation and comfort. Korobahn Lodge is on
Inland Scenic Highway 72, approximatly 110 kilometres (75 minutes drive) southwest of Christchurch
Airport and on the way to Mt Cook and Queenstown. Local activites include bush walking, horse treks,
jet boating, fishing, in season skating and skiing. (Close to Mt Hutt ski field.)

Rakaia *50 km S of Christchurch*

St Ita's Guesthouse *B&B Homestay*
Miriam & Ken Cutforth
11 Barrhill/Methven Road,
Rakaia Township, Canterbury

Tel (03) 302 7546 Fax (03) 302 7546
stitas@xtra.co.nz www.stitas.co.nz

Double $110-$120 **Single** $70 (Full breakfast)
Child $30   Dinner $30pp
Visa MC accepted
Children welcome
1 Queen 1 Double 4 Single (3 bdrm)
Bathrooms: 3 Ensuite

Relax in our elegant and comfortable historic former convent, 600 metres from SH1 in small town New
Zealand. Excellent base for exploring Ashburton District. Excellent first and last stop from Christchurch
International Airport. All bedrooms have ensuites and garden views. Walking distance to local shops,
hotels, crafts and winery. Close to golf and salmon fishing, 30 minutes to skiing, jet boating and more.
Dinner based on local produce served with wine. Full breakfasts. Share the open fire with our cat and
golden retriever.

Ashburton

Weir Homestay *Homestay*
Pat & Dave Weir
35 Leeston Street, Ashburton Central

Tel (03) 308 3534 d&sweir@xtra.co.nz

Double $80 **Single** $45 (Full breakfast)
Dinner $20
Visa MC accepted
1 Double 3 Single (2 bdrm)
Bathrooms: 1 Ensuite 1 Family share 1 Guest share

Our comfortable home is situated in a quiet street
with the added pleasure of looking onto a rural
scene. We are 10-15 minutes walk from town or 1-2
minutes to riding for the disabled grounds or river walkway. Guest rooms have comfortable beds with
electric blankets. We welcome the opportunity to meet and greet visitors and wish to make your stay a
happy one. Your hosts are retired but active, hobbies general/varied from meeting people to walking etc.
Request visitors no smoking inside home. Laundry facilities available. Off-street parking.

Ashburton *8 km W of Ashburton*

Carradale Farm *B&B Farmstay*
Karen & Jim McIntyre
Ferriman's Road (Rapid no. 200), RD 8, Ashburton

Tel (03) 308 6577 Fax (03) 308 6548
jkmcintyre@xtra.co.nz
www.ashburton.co.nz/carradale

Double $100-$120 Single $70 (Full breakfast)
Child under 12 half price Dinner $30 by arrangement
Caravan powerpoint $25
Visa MC accepted
1 Double 2 King/Twin (3 bdrm)
Bathrooms: 1 Ensuite 2 Private

Our homestead, which captures the sun in all rooms, is cosy and inviting. It is situated in a sheltered garden where you can enjoy peace, tranquillity and fresh country air or indulge in a game of tennis.

All guest rooms have comfortable beds, electric blankets, reading lamps and tea/coffee making facilities. Laundry and ironing facilities available.

Dinner is by arrangement and features traditional New Zealand cuisine including home grown meat and vegetables. Breakfast is served with delicious home-made jams and preserves.

We have a 220 acre irrigated sheep and cattle farm. You may like to be taken on a farm tour or enjoy a walk on the farm. As we have both travelled extensively in New Zealand, Australia, United Kingdom, Europe, North America and Zimbabwe. We would like to offer hospitality to fellow travellers. Our hobbies include meeting people, travel, reading, photography, gardening, sewing, cake decorating, rugby, cricket, Jim belongs to the Masonic Lodge and Karen is involved in Community Affairs.

For the weary traveller a spa pool is available. For young children we have a cot and high chair. There is a power point for camper vans. We are one hour from Christchurch International Airport.

CARRADALE FARM "WHERE PEOPLE COME AS STRANGERS AND LEAVE AS FRIENDS."

Ashburton *1 km S of Ashburton Centre*

A Welcome Inn *B&B Homestay*
Betty & Bruce Arnst
13 Thomson Street, Tinwald, Ashburton

Tel (03) 308 7297 Fax (03) 308 7297
bb_arnst@xtra.co.nz
www.awelcomeinn.co.nz

Double $100-$120 Single $60-$70 (Full breakfast)
Child negotiable by age Dinner $30pp
Visa MC accepted
Children welcome
1 Double 1 Twin 1 Single (3 bdrm)
Bathrooms: 1 Guest share

We are a retired couple who have travelled overseas and in New Zealand and love sharing experiences. We provide a friendly stay in our warm comfortable modern home with an opportunity for travellers to meet New Zealanders. Our 2 elderly pets live outdoors. Join us for a chat in our large lounge or in our pleasant garden. 5 minutes from Lake Hood. 1 hour south of Christchurch International Airport. Near all sports venues and Lake Hood. 30 minutes to Mt Hutt Village/Methven.

Ashburton *In Ashburton*

Falcutt House *B&B*
Nola & Stuart Lovett
23 Falcon Drive, Ashburton

Tel (03) 308 9253 or 025 685 4312

Double $90 Single $50 (Full breakfast)
Child under 12 $30
Dinner $30 by arrangement
2 Twin (2 bdrm)
Bathrooms: 1 Private

A new house situated in a quiet cul-de-sac surrounded by pleasant garden, with private areas. 2 comfortable twin bedrooms. Guests' private bathroom with separate toilet. Visit farm upon request. Close to town and restaurants. Off-street parking available.

Ashburton *1 km N of central Ashburton*

Ferriman House *B&B Homestay*
Gail Cooper & Neville Gutsell
10 Ferriman Street, Ashburton

Tel (03) 307 2600 or 027 2416371
gailcook@xtra.co.nz

Double $100-$120 Single $85-$95 (Full breakfast)
Dinner $30 by arrangment
1 King/Twin1 King (2 bdrm)
Bathrooms: 1 Ensuite 1 Private

A warm welcome to our new sunny home built in 2004. We are situated on a quiet street just off the main road and close to motels and town centre. Retired moteliers of 21 years we enjoy golf, fishing, boating and travelling. We have 2 comfortable rooms; 1 is purpose built with ensuite and access to a private lounge or join us in our large dining room. Both bathrooms have heated towel rails, underfloor heating. TV in rooms. Directions from Christchurch: second left turn off East Street to King Street, then first right.

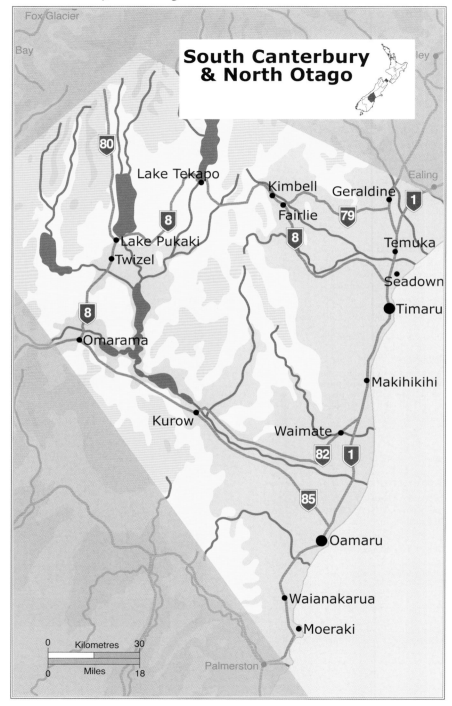

South Canterbury & North Otago

Geraldine *3 km N of Geraldine*

The Crossing Boutique B&B Guest Lodge and Licensed Restaurant

Boutique B&B Guest Lodge & Licenced Restaurant

Dale & Patti Epp (Hosts)
Dick & Barbara Sahlie (Owners)
124 Woodbury Road, RD 21, Geraldine

Tel (03) 693 9689 Fax (03) 693 9789
srelax@xtra.co.nz
www.thecrossingbnb.co.nz

Double $160-$190 Single $140-$170 (Full breakfast)
Extra person $30 Children over 12 welcome
In-house restaurant - 3 course a la carte dinner
Visa MC accepted Pet free home
2 Queen 1 Double 2 Single (3 bdrm)
Bathrooms: 2 full tub ensuites, 1 shower ensuite

Experience New Zealand history on 37 tranquil acres near the base of the Four Peaks Range.

The Crossing is a beautifully restored and furnished English style manor house built in 1908. Our spacious lounges have open fires and comfortable seating. A shaded verandah overlooks the lovely gardens, where you can relax and read or enjoy a leisurely game of croquet or petanque. Enjoy dinner and your choice of beverages in our fully licensed restaurant. Dinners by prior arrangement.

The Crossing is your perfect base for exploring the central South Island. Local attractions include fishing for salmon and trout, white water rafting, nature treks in Peel Forest, and ski fields are nearby. Golfers, spend a week and play 14 uncrowded courses each within 1 hours drive. All have low green fees and welcome visitors. We are located on the main route between Christchurch and Queenstown or Mount Cook. Directions: signposted on SH 72/79 approx 3km north of Geraldine, turn into Woodbury Road, then 1km on right hand side. Children over 12 welcome.

Geraldine *0.5 km S of Geraldine*

Victoria Villa *B&B Cottage with Kitchen*
Leigh & Jerry Basinger
55 Cox Street, Geraldine 8751

Tel (03) 693 8605 or 0800 537 533
, 027 482 1842 Fax (03) 693 8605
jbasinger@xtra.co.nz

Double $80-$120 Single $80-$100 (Full breakfast)
Child $10-$15 Dinner by arrangement
Detached studio unit Visa MC Amex accepted
3 Queen 2 Double 2 Single (4 bdrm)
Bathrooms: 3 Ensuite 1 Private

Welcome to our historical villa, completely refurbished - spacious bedrooms with ensuites or private bathroom. Off-street parking, private entrance and lounge. Molded ceilings, native woods. Also, separate studio with ensuite and light cooking area; ideal for family up to 5 people. On Highway 79 to Mt Cook and Queenstown. 7 minutes walk to Geraldine Village which has boutique movie theatre, fine restaurants, sports pub, antiques, world class glass blower, boutique shops, 2 golf courses. Adjacent to domain. Personality pet dog and cat. Your hosts will assist to make your stay enjoyable.

Geraldine *0.2 km S of Geraldine*

Lilymay *B&B*
Lois & Les Gillum
29 Cox Street, Geraldine,

Tel (03) 693 8838 or 0800 545 9629
elgillum@chc.quik.co.nz

Double $85-$95 Single $60-$65 (Full breakfast)
Child $20-$25
Visa MC accepted
2 Queen 1 Double 3 Twin 3 Single (3 bdrm)
Bathrooms: 2 Guest share

A charming character home set in a large garden where Sammy the cat plays. A friendly, warm welcome is assured with tea/coffee and Lois' home-baked cookies. Ample off-street parking and separate guest entrance. Teas, coffee, etc. available at all times in the guestlounge with cosy open fire. The village, shops, cafes, restaurants, crafts a short stroll away. We are on the main highway to the Southern Lakes and mountains and the ideal stopover from Christchurch (137km).

Geraldine *0.5 km S of Geraldine*

Forest View *B&B*
Joyce & John Leverno
128 Talbot Street, Geraldine

Tel (03) 693 9928 or 0800 572 740
021 440 349 Fax (03) 693 9928
forest.view@xtra.co.nz

Double $80-$110 Single $55-$75 (Full breakfast)
Child negotiable Dinner $30 by arrangement
Sleep-out $45 Children welcome
Visa MC Amex accepted
1 King 1 Queen 1 Double 1 Twin 1 Single (4 bdrm)
Bathrooms: 1 Ensuite 1 Guest share 1 Private

We have a charming 2 storey, character home set in a cottage garden where our dogs, Oscar & Emmy love to play. You will be warmly welcomed on arrival and a refreshing cup of tea or coffee is available in the guest lounge at all times. We are a short stroll to the cafes and restaurants in the charming village of Geraldine which is the ideal first stop from Christchurch (137km) as you travel towards the Southern Lakes and mountains.

Geraldine *3 km N of Geraldine*

Rivendell *B&B Homestay Apartment with Kitchen*
Erica & Andrew Tedham
Woodbury Road, RD 21, Geraldine

Tel (03) 693 8559 or 021 264 1520
rivendellnz@xtra.co.nz

Double $100-$110 Single $85 (Full breakfast)
Self-contained apartment with kitchen $100
1 Queen 1 Single (2 bdrm)
Bathrooms: 1 Ensuite 1 Family share

Set in over 3 acres, Rivendell is a traditional New Zealand villa and has beautiful secluded gardens that can be enjoyed relaxing on the large verandah or in the spa pool. Our home provides all modern facilities including internet and laundry. The delightful village of Geraldine with its numerous cafes, restaurants, shops and cinema is only 5 minutes drive. We offer you a truly warm welcome together with our dogs, Lady Lou (collie) & Sophie Pippin (New Zealand huntaway) horse Bracken and peacocks Aragorn & Arwen.

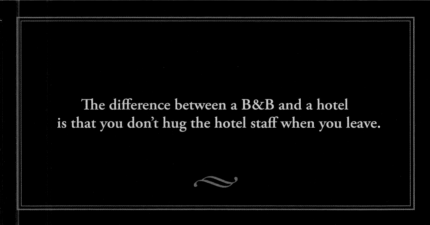

The difference between a B&B and a hotel
is that you don't hug the hotel staff when you leave.

Geraldine *1.5 km W of town centre*

The Downs B&B *B&B*
Alycen & Myron Cournane
5 Ribbonwood Road, The Downs, RD 21, Geraldine

Tel (03) 693 7388 or 021 675 249
Fax (03) 693 7388
cournane.m.a@xtra.co.nz
www.thedowns.co.nz

Double $150-$250 Single up to$150 (Full breakfast)
Visa MC Diners Amex accepted
Children welcome
3 Queen 1 Twin (4 bdrm)
Bathrooms: 3 Ensuite 1 Private

Alycen, Myron & Max (the cat) opened this new business early in 2005. The house dates from the 70s but since then has undergone some major alterations. The upper level is now totally for guest use. There are 3 high quality ensuite guest rooms (1 with extra bedroom if required). Free guest laundry. Guestlounge/breakfast room with open bar, tea, coffee etc. Step from the lounge onto the balcony and down to the large lawn and gardens. Enjoy the peace and quiet!

Temuka *16 km N of Timaru*

Ashfield House B&B *B&B Homestay*
Ray & Wendy Pearson
71 Cass Street, Temuka

Tel (03) 615 6157 Fax (03) 615 9062
ashfield@paradise.net.nz
www.ashfield.co.nz

Double $100-$150 Single $65-$85 (Full breakfast)
Visa MC accepted
Not suitable for children Pets welcome
1 King 2 Queen 1 Double (4 bdrm)
Bathrooms: 1 Ensuite 1 Guest share

Ashfield House, a Victorian villa built in 1883 is set
in 4 acres of woodlands complete with stream, ducks and trout. The house features the original marble
fireplaces, gilt mirrors, and a full size snooker table. Only 15 minutes walk from shops and restaurants,
Ashfield House is close to skifields, salmon and trout fishing. 2 of our upstairs bedrooms open out to a
balcony with a lovely view of the garden. Join us with our cats and newfoundland dogs for a wonderful
stay in a lovely setting. Guests welcome to use laundry.

Temuka *16 km N of Timaru*

Temuka Grange *B&B Cottage with Kitchen*
Chris Pullin & Andrew Lush
4 Grange Settlement Road, Temuka, South Canterbury

Tel (03) 615 8385 or 027 661 5888
thegrange@ihug.co.nz

Double $95 Single $65 (Full breakfast)
Cottage (studio unit) $95 per night
Visa MC accepted
Pet free home Children welcome
1 Queen 1 Twin (2 bdrm in B&B, 1 in Cottage)
Bathrooms: 1 Ensuite 1 Private

Temuka Grange is set in 1 acre of tranquil established
gardens with pathways meandering through an abundance of rhododendrons, azaleas and roses. All
bordered by a private stream, home to the property's family of ducks. Fruit trees, berry bushes and home-
grown vegetables complete the picture. Temuka is a thriving, busy and bustling village, home to the
famous pottery and the pioneer aviator Richard Pearse. With easy access to some of the best salmon and
trout fishing in the world, golf courses, scenic tours and ski fields.

Timaru Central

Jones Homestay *Homestay*
Margaret & Nevis Jones
16 Selwyn Street, Timaru

Tel (03) 688 1400 Fax (03) 688 1400

Double $100 Single $60 (Full breakfast)
Child half price Dinner $25 by arrangement
Visa MC accepted
2 Double 1 Twin (3 bdrm)
Bathrooms: 2 Ensuite 1 Guest share

Welcome to our spacious character brick home built
in the 1920s and situated in a beautiful garden with a
grass tennis court. A secluded property with off-street
parking and views of the surrounding sea and mountains. Centrally situated, only 5 minutes from the
beach and town with an excellent choice of cafes and restaurants. On arrival tea is served on our sunny
verandah. Hosts have lived and worked extensively overseas, namely South Africa, UK and the Middle
East, and enjoy music, theatre, tennis and golf. Dinner by arrangement.

Timaru - Seadown *4.8 km N of Timaru*
Country Homestay *Homestay*
Margaret & Ross Paterson
491 Seadown Road, Seadown, RD 3, Timaru

Tel (03) 688 2468 or 021 213 7434
Fax (03) 688 2468

Double $80 Single $50 (Full breakfast)
Child half price Dinner $25
Visa MC Diners Amex accepted
1 Double 2 Single (3 bdrm)
Bathrooms: 1 Guest share

Our homestay is approximately 10 minutes north of
Timaru, situated 4.8km on Seadown Road off State
Highway 1 at Washdyke - second house on left past Pharlap Statue. We have hosted on our farm for
11 years - now retired and have a country farmlet with some farm animals, with views of farmland and
mountains. Day trips to Mt Cook, Hydro Lakes and ski fields, fishing, golf course few minutes away.
Electric blankets on all beds - laundry facilities available. Interests are farming, gardening, spinning,
embroidery and overseas travel.

Timaru *In Timaru Central*
Bidwill House *Homestay*
Dorothy & Ron White
15 Bidwill Street, Timaru

Tel (03) 688 5856 or 027 238 8122
Fax (03) 688 5870
bidwillhouse@xtra.co.nz

Double $110 Single $80 (Full breakfast)
Child half price
Dinner $20-$30 by arrangement
Visa MC accepted
1 King/Twin 2 Single (2 bdrm)
Bathrooms: 1 Ensuite bath & shower

Bidwill House offers superior personalised homestay in a classic 2 storeyed centrally heated home with a
delightful garden in a quiet street in central Timaru - 5 minutes walk to the town centre, restaurants and
Caroline Bay. The guest bedroom has a super king/twin with a smaller bedroom with 2 single beds. The
2 rooms are only available to the 1 booking. Laundry facilities available. We look forward to welcoming
guests to our home, and offer our hospitality to those who prefer a homestay.

Timaru *3 km S of Timaru*
Mountain View B&B *B&B Homestay Farmstay*
Marlene & Norman McIntosh
23 Talbot Road, RD 1 Kingsdown, Timaru

Tel (03) 688 1070 or 021 113 8517
Fax (03) 688 1069
mvhomestay@xtra.co.nz
www.bnb.co.nz/mtview.html

Double $90 Single $60 (Full breakfast)
Dinner $25 by arrangement
Visa MC accepted   Children welcome $20 under 13
1 Queen 1 Double 1 Twin (3 bdrm)
Bathrooms: 2 Private 1 bath

Mountain View is a farmlet on Talbot Road, 200 metres from State Highway 1. Blue and white Bed &
Breakfast signs on highway, 3km from Timaru. Semi-retired farmers with pet deer and sheep. Home is
situated in tranquil garden overlooking farmland with views of mountains. Private bathrooms - laundry
facilities available. Tea & coffee. Nearby fishing, golf courses, swimming and walk to sea coast. Day trips
comfortably taken to Mt Cook, hydro lakes and ski fields. We enjoy meeting people and look forward to
offering our hospitality.

Timaru *In Timaru Central*

Etheridge Gardens *B&B*
Nan & Wynne Raymond
10 Sealy Street, Timaru

Tel (03) 684 4910 or 027 436 5365
Fax (03) 684 4918
wynne.raymond@timaru.com

Double $140 **Single** $90 (Full breakfast)
Child $40
Visa MC accepted
Children and pets welcome
1 Queen 1 Twin 1 Single (3 bdrm)
Bathrooms: 1 Private

Etheridge Gardens is a beautiful character home built in 1911, set in romantic English style gardens. We offer the very best in hospitality. Guests are encouraged to relax in our spacious sitting room which leads on to the terrace and garden with heated swimming pool. TV in main bedroom. Tea, coffee, chocolates and fresh flowers and robes in the bedrooms. Afternoon tea and complimentary wine, aperitifs on arrival. Excellent restaurants nearby. Children, pets welcome. Wynne is former mayor of Timaru, Nan is a renowned NZ gardener.

Timaru *8 km W of Timaru*

Berrillo *B&B Homestay*
Owen & Liz Berrill
32 Gladstone Road, RD 4, Timaru

Tel (03) 686 1688 or 021 295 2451
Fax 03 686 1678
oberrill@xtra.co.nz

Double $110-$120 **Single** $90 (Full breakfast)
Child $45 Dinner $40
Visa MC accepted
1 Queen 2 Twin (3 bdrm)
Bathrooms: 2 Ensuite 1 Guest share

A Touch of Tuscany in Timaru. A warm welcome awaits you and we offer a complimentary glass of wine on the terrace overlooking stunning views of Mt Cook. Our award winning Home of the Year 2000 is nestled in an olive grove. We have a purpose-built guest wing with separate antique furnished lounge, Sky TV, tea/coffee making facilities. Sit and chat with us or just relax and enjoy the peace. We enjoy golf, art and music. Golf courses nearby, skifields 1 hour away. Resident labrador.

Timaru Central *.5 km W of Information Centre*

Sefton Homestay *B&B Homestay*
Trish & John Blunden
32 Sefton Street, Seaview, Timaru

Tel (03) 688 0017 Fax (03) 688 0042
trish@seftonhomestay.co.nz
www.seftonhomestay.co.nz

Double $95-$110 **Single** $70-$80 (Full breakfast)
Visa MC accepted
Children welcome half price
1 King/Twin 1 Queen 1 Single (3 bdrm)
Bathrooms: 1 Ensuite 1 Guest share 1 Private

Relax in our superbly appointed and spacious 2 storey character brick home with sweeping views from the mountains to the sea. Refurbished with the feel of yesteryear, but with ambience and style you will love.
All our children have left home with the exception of our labrador Ollie who enjoys meeting people as we do.

Makikihi - Waimate *10 km N of Waimate*

Alford Farm *Farmstay*
June & Ken McAuley
Lower Hook Road, RD 8, Waimate

Tel (03) 689 5778 or 027 319 8391
Fax (03) 689 5779
alfordfarmstays@paradise.net.nz
www.bnb.co.nz/alfordfarm.html

Double $90 Single $60 (Continental)
Dinner $25 Visa MC accepted
1 Double 2 Single (2 bdrm)
Bathrooms: 1 Family share

Halfway between Dunedin and Christchurch; stop over to enjoy the peaceful surroundings on our deer and cattle farm. Hosting since 1985 we enjoy sharing our home, farm, attractive garden and native birds with visitors. Attractions in our area include: trout and salmon fishing, penguin colony, 2 golf courses, bush walks and day trips to Mount Cook and the lake district. Directions: 4km south of Makikihi, turn inland into Lower Hook Road. Second on the right (2km). Rapid No. 202.

Fairlie *3 km W of Fairlie*

Fontmell *B&B Homestay Farmstay*
Anne & Norman McConnell
Nixons Road 169, RD 17, Fairlie

Tel (03) 685 8379 Fax (03) 685 8379

Double $90-$110 Single $65 (Full breakfast)
Child $35 Dinner $25
2 King/Twin 1 Queen 1 Double
2 Twin 1 Single (4 bdrm)
Bathrooms: 1 Guest share 1 Private

Our farm consists of 400 acres producing fat lambs, cattle and deer, with numerous other animals and bird life. The house is situated in a large English style garden with many mature trees in a tranquil setting. In the area are 2 ski fields, golf courses, walkways and scenic drives. Informative farm tours available. Our interests include golf, gardening and music. Directions: travel 1 km from town centre, along Tekapo highway, then turn left into Nixon's Road when 2 more kilometres will bring you to the Fontmell entrance.

Fairlie *1.5 km NW of Fairlie*

Ashgrove *B&B*
Maria & Stewart Evans
Mt Cook Road, Fairlie,

Tel (03) 685 8797 or 027 289 5323
Fax (03) 685 8795
maria@ashgrove.co.nz
www.ashgrove.co.nz

Double $125 Single $80 (Continental)
Child negotiable Visa MC accepted
Pet free home Children welcome
1 King/Twin 1 Double (2 bdrm)
Bathrooms: 1 Ensuite 1 Private

Enjoy a restful stopover on your South Island journey at our 3 acre farmlet. Our house is set amongst established trees and gardens. Guest facilities include a private sunny sitting room, microwave, fridge, TV, tea & coffee are available. There is a cot available. We also offer refreshments for sale. Only 10 minutes walk to award winning restaurants. We have no pets inside. We are happy to share our knowledge of the South Island, especially to trampers and those keen to fish the clear lakes & rivers of the region.

South Canterbury
North Otago

Kimbell *8 km W of Fairlie*

Rivendell Lodge *B&B Countrystay*
Joan Gill
15 Stanton Road, Kimbell, RD 17, Fairlie

Tel (03) 685 8833 or 027 4819 189
Fax (03) 685 8825
Rivendell.lodge@xtra.co.nz
www.fairlie.co.nz/rivendell

Double $110-$130 **Single** $65-$75 (Full breakfast)
Child negotiable Dinner $40
Visa MC accepted
2 Queen 2 Double 3 Single (4 bdrm)
Bathrooms: 2 Ensuite 2 Guest share

Quality country comfort and hospitality offered in a peaceful historic village. Joan writes and shares her passion for travelling, mountains, literature and good conversation with Richard, a retired Argentine engineer, exploring local history. We enjoy cooking and gardening and delight in sharing our home grown produce. Take time out for fishing, skiing, walking, golf or water sports. Relax in the garden, complete with stream and cat, or come with us to some of our favourite places. Complimentary refreshments on arrival. Laundry facilities and internet available

Lake Tekapo *40 km W of Fairlie*

Freda Du Faur House *B&B Homestay*
Dawn & Barry Clark
1 Esther Hope Street, Lake Tekapo

Tel (03) 680 6513 dawntek@xtra.co.nz
www.fredadufaur.co.nz

Double $110-$120 **Single** $70 (Continental)
Child negotiable Visa MC accepted
1 Queen 1 Double 2 Single (3 bdrm)
Bathrooms: 1 Guest share

Experience tranquillity and a touch of mountain magic. A warm and friendly welcome. Comfortable home, mountain and lake views. Rimu panelling, heart timber furniture, attractive decor, blending with the McKenzie Country. Bedrooms in private wing overlooking garden, two opening onto balcony. Refreshments on patio surrounded by roses or view ever changing panorama from lounge. Walkways nearby. Mt Cook one hour away. Views of skifield. Five minutes to shops and restaurants. Call for Directions.

Lake Tekapo *43km*

Creel House *B&B*
Grant & Rosemary
36 Murray Place, Lake Tekapo

Tel (03) 680 6516 Fax (03) 680 6659
creelhouse.l.tek@xtra.co.nz
www.bnb.co.nz/hosts/creelhouse.html

Double $140-$150 **Single** $75 (Special breakfast)
Off-season tariff $110 double/twin
Visa MC accepted
Children welcome
2 Queen 1 Twin (3 bdrm)
Bathrooms: 1 Ensuite 2 Private

Built by Grant, our three storied home with expansive balconies offers panoramic views of the Southern Alps, Mt John, Lake Tekapo and surrounding mountains. All rooms are spacious and comfortable, with guest lounge and separate guest entrance. A NZ native garden adds an attractive feature. Restaurants in township. Our two daughters are 15 & 17 years, we live on the ground floor with two cats thus separate from our guest accommodation. Grant is a professional flyfishing guide (NZPFGA) and offers guided tours.

Lake Tekapo *43 km W of Fairlie*

Alpine Vista *Luxury B&B*
Gillian & Peter Maxwell
12 Hamilton Drive, Lake Tekapo

Tel (03) 680 6702 or 021 415 544
0800 390 637 Fax (03) 680 6707
info@alpinevista.co.nz
www.alpinevista.co.nz

Double $170-$225 **Single** $120-$185 (Full breakfast)
Visa MC Diners Amex Eftpos accepted
Children welcome
2 King 1 Twin (3 bdrm)
Bathrooms: 3 Ensuite

Welcome to Alpine Vista, our recently renovated home offering amazing views of the Southern Alps, beautiful Lake Tekapo and a Panorama of Mt John. Our warm modern home offers 3 fully ensuited guests rooms, tea & coffee making facilities, email facilities, laundry and large lounge where we encourage you to meet with us and fellow guests. Having lived in the Mackenzie Country for 30 years we would enjoy sharing our knowledge of what this area has to offer. We assure you of a warm and comfortable stay.

Lake Pukaki - Mt Cook *7 km N of Twizel*

Rhoborough Downs, Pukaki *Homestay*
Roberta Preston
State Highway 8 Tekapo/Twizel

Tel (03) 435 0509 Fax (03) 435 0509
ra.preston@xtra.co.nz

Double $120 **Single** $70 (Continental)
Child $50 **Dinner** $40
1 Double 1 Twin 1 Single (3 bdrm)
Bathrooms: 1 Guest share

A quiet place to stop, halfway between Christchurch and Queenstown or Christchurch and Dunedin via Waitaki Valley. 40 minutes to Mt Cook. The 18,000 acre property has been in the family 85 years. Merino sheep graze to 6000 feet, hereford cattle. Views of the southern sky. The homestead is set in tranquil gardens. Afternoon tea/drinks served on the veranda. We have a black lab. Twizel has a bank, doctor, restaurants, shops. Dinner by arrangement. Please phone for bookings and directions. Cot available.

Lake Pukaki *27 km N of Lake Tekapo*

Tasman Downs Station *Farmstay*
Linda, Bruce & Ian Hayman
Lake Pukaki, Lake Tekapo

Tel (03) 680 6841 Fax (03) 680 6851
samjane@xtra.co.nz

Double $110-$130 **Single** $85 (Full breakfast)
Dinner $40pp by arrangement
1 Queen 1 Twin (2 bdrm)
Bathrooms: 1 Guest share 1 Private

"A place of unsurpassed beauty" located on the shores of Lake Pukaki, magnificent views of the lake, Mount Cook and Southern Alps. Our local stone home blends in with the natural peaceful surroundings. This high country station has been in our family since 1914 and runs mainly angus cattle. Bruce an ex-RAF pilot and Linda enjoy sharing their knowledge of farming with guests. An opportunity to experience true farm life with friendly hosts, dinner by arrangement. Met our good natured corgi.

South Canterbury
North Otago

Twizel - Mt Cook *2 km W of Twizel Info Centre*

Artemis B&B *B&B*
Jan & Bob Wilson
33 North West Arch, Twizel

Tel (03) 435 0388 Fax (03) 435 0377
artemistwizel@paradise.net.nz

Double $125 **Single** $95 (Special breakfast)
2 Queen 1 Single (2 bdrm)
Bathrooms: 1 Ensuite 1 Private

Welcome to the magnificent Mackenzie basin. Our modern home has stunning mountain views along with peace and tranquility. We are only 45 minutes from Mount Cook and 3 minutes drive to nearby restaurants. A guest sitting room with balcony - tea, coffee and complimentary snack and television. Our special continental breakfast includes a choice of juices, fruits, cereals, cheeses and home-made croissants, toast and jams. A selection of teas and coffees. We look forward to sharing our home with you.

Twizel *1 km W of Twizel*

Heartland Lodge *Homestay Apartment with Kitchen*
Kerry & Steve Carey
19 North West Arch, Twizel, South Canterbury

Tel (03) 435 0008 or 021 230 7502
Fax (03) 435 0387
heartlandlodge@xtra.co.nz
www.heartland-lodge.co.nz

Double $200-$220 **Single** $150 (Full breakfast)
Child negotiable
Extra adult from $120
Visa MC accepted Children welcome
2 King/Twin 1 King 1 Queen (4 bdrm)
Bathrooms: 4 Ensuite 3 spabaths, 1 sauna

Welcome to our friendly, comfortable homestay lodge, only 45 minutes from Mt Cook. Luxuriously appointed guest rooms feature ensuites with spa baths or sauna. Relax in our garden or sunny lounge before dining at one of several nearby restaurants. Complimentary laundry, refreshments and email services are available . The Loft is a large self-service apartment above our garage, ideal for families sleeping 2-6 people with kitchen and bathroom facilities. $120 double and $15 for each extra person.

Twizel

Aoraki Lodge *B&B*
Oksana & Vlad Fomin
32 Mackenzie Drive, Twizel / Mt Cook 8773

Tel (03) 435 0300 Fax (03) 435 0305
aorakilodge@xtra.co.nz
www.aorakiadventure.co.nz

Double $145-$150 **Single** $100 (Continental)
Child $30 Visa MC accepted
Children welcome
2 Queen 1 Double 1 Twin 4 Single (5 bdrm)
Bathrooms: 4 Ensuite 1 Family share 1 Private

Haere Mai ki Aoraki (Welcome to Aoraki Lodge). If you prefer a casual informal atmosphere with friendly hosts then Aoraki Lodge is the place for you. Relax in our comfortable lodge and sunny private garden. Vlad a well known guide can offer helpful advice on all local attractions We look forward to welcoming you.

Twizel - Lake Ruataniwha *4 km SW of Twizel*

Lake Ruataniwha Homestay *Homestay*

Robin & Lester Baikie

146 Max Smith Drive, Twizel, P O Box 9 Twizel

Tel (03) 435 0532 or 027 432 1532
027 437 3294 Fax (03) 435 0522
robinandlester@xtra.co.nz

Double $120-$150 Single $75-$100 (Full breakfast)
Child negotiable Dinner $35pp
Visa MC accepted
Children welcome
2 Queen 2 Twin (3 bdrm)
Bathrooms: 1 Ensuite 1 Guest share

Welcome to our new home, built on 4 hectares overlooking Lake Ruataniwha with 360 degree views of the lake and mountains. We have travelled overseas and enjoy meeting people. All bedrooms open onto a patio. We have a variety of farm animals close to our house. Lester and his horses were extras on Lord of the Rings and he enjoys talking about his experiences. Our interests are farming, horse trekking, sport and WI. Email and fax facilities available. An ideal stopover between Christchurch and Queenstown.

Twizel - Mt Cook

Hunters House and Hunters Cottage *B&B Homestay Cottage with Kitchen*

Anne & Matt Hunter

58 Tekapo Drive, Twizel

Tel (03) 435 0038 Fax (03) 435 0038
annehunter@xtra.co.nz

Double $145 Single $95 (Full breakfast)
Visa MC accepted
Not suitable for children
2 King/Twin (2 bdrm)
Bathrooms: 2 Ensuite

Hunters House was built in 2003. It is architecturally designed for guests and features every comfort and a warm welcoming environment. It overlooks the native tussocks and trees of the Green Belt on the township boundry with the mountains as a backdrop. All rooms are tastefully decorated with all facilities and french doors opening to the peaceful outdoors sited for the sun and views. We also have a self contained cottage fully equiped with all home comforts and same views as Hunter's House. Situated on its own private setting. Available short or long term. "Cead Mile Failte"

Omarama *1 km S of Omarama*

Omarama Station *Farmstay*

Beth & Dick Wardell

Omarama, North Otago

Tel (03) 438 9821 Fax (03) 438 9822
wardell@paradise.net.nz
www.omaramastation.co.nz

Double $110 Single $60 (Full breakfast)
Child $20-$50 Dinner $35
2 Queen 2 Single (3 bdrm)
Bathrooms: 1 Ensuite 1 Private

Omarama Station is a merino sheep and cattle property adjacent to the Omarama township. The 100 year old homestead is nestled in a small valley in a tranquil park-like setting of willows, poplars and a fast flowing stream (good fly fishing), pleasant walking environs, and interesting historical perspective to the high country as this was the original station in the area. Swimming pool and a pleasant garden. An opportunity to experience day to day farming activities. Dinner by arrangement.

Kurow *60 km W of Oamaru*

Glenmac Farmstay *Farmstay Cottage No Kitchen Cottage with Kitchen Campervan facilities*

Kaye & Keith Dennison
RD 7K, Oamaru

Tel (03) 436 0200 Fax (03) 436 0202
glenmac@farmstaynewzealand.co.nz
www.farmstaynewzealand.co.nz

Double $80-$100 Single $40-$50 (Full breakfast)
Dinner $25 Self-contained price on application
Children and pets welcome Child under 13 half price
Visa MC accepted
1 Queen 2 Double 2 Twin (4 bdrm)
Bathrooms: 1 Ensuite 1 Family share 1 Guest share

A peaceful situation, away from traffic noises, enjoy home-cooked meals, a comfortable bed, relax and be treated as one of the family. Explore our 4000 acre high country farm. See merino sheep and beef cattle. On farm enjoy horse riding, take a 4 wheel drive farm tour, walk some of our many tracks. Nearby fly and spinner fishing (guide available), mountain biking, golf or explore the Fossil Trail. Directions: Situated at end of Gards Road which is 10km east of Kurow on right or 13km west of Duntroon on left.

Kurow *2.7 km E of Kurow*

Western House *B&B Cottage No Kitchen*

Bernadette & Michael Parish
Highway 83, Kurow, North Oago

Tel (03) 436 0876 Fax (03) 436 0872
mbparish@xtra.co.nz
www.westernhouse.co.nz

Double $100-$120 Single $90-$120 (Full breakfast)
Dinner $40
Visa MC accepted
2 Queen 1 Double 1 Twin (4 bdrm)
Bathrooms: 1 Ensuite 1 Guest share 1 Private

Western House, built in 1871 as an accomodation house, is surrounded by extensive garden and orchard with mountain views. Enjoy wood fires, fresh flowers, hearty breakfasts and wholesome dinners. A warm welcome awaits guests for an enjoyable stay with us and our cat Simba. Attractions: Trout and salmon fishing (guide available), golf (clubs on-site), tennis, squash, walks, mountain biking, 4WD, swimming pool, beehive tours, and historic water wheel built 1899.

Oamaru

Wallfield *Homestay*

Pat & Bill Bews
126 Reservoir Road, Oamaru

Tel (03) 437 0368 or 025 282 7303
bpbews@xtra.co.nz

Double $85 Single $50 (Continental)
Pet free home
1 Queen 2 Single (2 bdrm)
Bathrooms: 1 Guest share

Our modern home is situated high above the north end of Oamaru with superb views to the east. We have 4 children, all happily married. We have been home hosting for the last 14 years and although now retired from farming, still enjoy the buzz of meeting new friends. Our interests include gardening and tramping.

Oamaru - Waianakarua *27 km S of Oamaru*

Glen Dendron *B&B Farmstay*
Anne & John Mackay
284 Breakneck Road, Waianakarua, 9 ORD, Oamaru

Tel (03) 439 5288 Fax (03) 439 5288
anne.john.mackay@xtra.co.nz
www.glenhomestays.co.nz

Double $120-$145 **Single** $80-$100 (Full breakfast)
Child $45 **Dinner** $35 with wine Visa MC accepted
2 King/Twin 2 Queen (4 bdrm)
Bathrooms: 2 Ensuite 1 Guest share Spa bath

Whitestone Waitaki Tourism Award Winner 2003.
Enjoy tranquility and beauty when you stay in our
stylish modern home, spectacularly sited on a hilltop
overlooking the picturesque Waianakarua River and
surrounded by 5 acres of landscaped garden.

After a sumptuous farm-cooked breakfast, feed the
sheep and alpacas. Then take a stroll through the forest,
native bush complete with waterfalls and birds or beside
the river. Play a round on our private golf course. Later,
watch the seals and penguins on a beach nearby. Then,
complete a perfect day with our gourmet 3 course
dinner with fine NZ wine before snuggling down for a
peaceful sleep in the fresh country air.

After a lifetime spent in farming and forestry we relish
the opportunity to share our home and semi-retired
lifestyle with guests. Our adult family lives overseas so we travel frequently and have a great interest in
other countries and cultures. We are very keen gardeners, read widely and enjoy antiques. Anne is a floral
artist and John is involved with the Lions organization.

An overnight stay is not enough to do justice to this lovely area - with so much to see, why not stay
awhile! We can plan customised itineraries of the area's many attractions. Oamaru's historic architecture.
Garden, heritage and fossil trails. Beaches, fishing, seals and penguins. Famous Moeraki Boulders and
other interesting geological features. Use us as a base for day visits to Oamaru, Dunedin, Waitaki Valley
and Mt Cook. Christchurch International Airport - 3.5 hours. We don't mind short notice!

South Canterbury
North Otago

Oamaru *8 km SW of Oamaru*

Tara *Homestay*
Marianne & Baxter Smith
Springhill Road, 3 ORD, Oamaru

Tel (03) 434 8187 Fax (03) 434 8187
smith.tara@xtra.co.nz
www.tarahomestay.com

Double $100 **Single** $60 (Full breakfast)
Dinner $30 by arrangement
2 Single (1 bdrm)
Bathrooms: 1 Private

Want to be pampered? Tara is the place for you. Enjoy the comfort and luxuries of our character Oamaru stone home. Tara boasts all day sun and the privacy to soak up the country atmosphere. Nestled amongst 11 acres of roses, mature trees and rural farmland Tara is the perfect place to unwind. Our livestock include alpacas, coloured sheep, donkeys and an aviary. We also have a burmese cat and a Lassie collie. My husband Baxter and I will ensure your visit is an enjoyable experience. Please phone for directions.

Oamaru *3 km S of Oamaru, just off SH1*

Springbank *B&B Cottage with Kitchen*
Joan & Stan Taylor
60 Weston Road, Oamaru,

Tel (03) 434 6602 or 027 403 5410
Fax (03) 434 6602

Double $85 **Single** $50 (Continental)
Child $10 Visa MC accepted
1 Double 1 Twin (1 bdrm)
Bathrooms: 1 Private

We look forward to sharing our retirement haven with visitors from overseas and New Zealand. Our modern home and separate guest flat are set in a peaceful and private large garden. Feed the goldfish and pamper Oscar our cat. Our guest flat is sunny, warm, spacious and comfortable. We enjoy helping visitors discover our district's best kept secrets! Penguins, gardens, Moeraki Boulders, beaches, pool, fishing and golf. Our interests: travel, gardening, grandchildren. Stan, Lions and follows sports. Joan all handcrafts, patchwork, floral design.

Oamaru *1.3 km N of Oamaru Centre*

Highway House Boutique B&B *B&B Homestay*
Stephanie & Norman Slater
43 Lynn Street, (Corner of Thames Highway & Lynn Street), Orana Park, Oamaru

Tel (03) 437 1066 or 0800 003 319
, 025 200 2976 Fax (03) 437 1066
cns@ihug.co.nz

Double $100-$120 **Single** $80-$100 (Full breakfast)
Child negotiable Dinner by arrangement
Pet free home Children welcome Visa MC Amex accepted
2 King 1 Twin (3 bdrm)
Bathrooms: 1 Family share 1 Guest share

Our character residence on Thames Highway, the main north road (1.3km from town centre), has been entirely refurbished to the highest standard. We provide a full cooked breakfast and other refreshments as required. We can assist with tours of historic Oamaru or visits to the nature sites. Our courtesy car can collect or take you to nearby dining establishments. If you appreciate a quality ambiance and particular assistance from Stephanie and Norman who have travelled widely overseas, Highway House will be ideal for you. French spoken.

Oamaru *10 km S of Oamaru*
Sunnyside B&B *B&B*
Andrina & Tony Butcher
3 Kakanui Road, 5 ORD, Oamaru 8921

Tel (03) 439 5442 Fax (03) 439 5442
tonyandrina@xtra.co.nz

Double $80 Single $50 (Continental)
1 Queen (1 bdrm)
Bathrooms: 1 Ensuite

Kakanui is a pretty coastal village on the Vanished
World Fossil Trail. You can walk swim, surf, fish,
kayak on the river, fossick for interesting stones or just
relax. We are close to the village store and 2 restaurants.
We are centrally located for many attractions in Otago including historic Oamaru, Moeraki Boulders,
Maniototo plane, Waitaki Lakes, yellow eyed & little blue penguins. Andrina and Tony are retired from
arboriculture and forestry. You will receive a warm welcome from us and our 2 cats.

Oamaru *2 km N of Oamaru Central*
Coral Sea Cottage & Ocean View *B&B Cottage with Kitchen*
Nicola & Peter Mountain
34 Harlech Street, Oamaru

Tel (03) 437 1422 or 021 659 757
021 042 6997 Fax (03) 437 1427
nmountain@xtra.co.nz

Double $85-$135 Single $38-$80 (Special breakfast)
Child 5-16 $20-$25 Visa MC accepted
Children and pets welcome
4 King/Twin 1 Double 2 Single (5 bdrm)
Bathrooms: 1 Ensuite 2 Private Ensuite is shower room
Private has bath and shower

Come and relax on a peaceful hillside in our cosy cottage with secluded grounds or in bright self-
contained accommodation in our home, Ocean View. Both newly equipped, including Sky TV and cot.
Enjoy wonderful views, pet farm animals and our son's art gallery. Resident dogs, cats and teenager! Near
local shops and restaurants. 2km to historic town centre, art galleries and blue penguin colony. We look
forward to welcoming you and offering help with planning your visit to our area. "Best stay we had."
(European Guest)

Oamaru *0.5 km W of Oamaru centre*
Homestay Oamaru *B&B Homestay*
Doug Bell
14 Warren Street, Oamaru

Tel (03) 434 1454 or 027 408 2860
Fax (03) 434 1454
homestayoamaru@paradise.net.nz
www.bellview.co.nz

Double $75-$95 Single $45-$60 (Full breakfast)
Dinner $25 Not suitable for children
2 Queen 1 Double (3 bdrm)
Bathrooms: 2 Ensuite 1 Family share

Sweeping views over the town and harbour. Warm, spacious and comfortable accommodation for the
travelling enthusiast, with books, maps, atlases and guides for you perusal. Quiet, private site, close
to town centre. (see map on website). Off-street parking. Southern scenic walkway access at property
boundary. Some of the area's attractions include sea and river fishing, historic architecture, unique
geological features and eco-tourism. Host has detailed local knowledge. Site unsuitable for young
children or pets.

Oamaru - Airedale *8 km NW of Oamaru*

Seadowns Farmstay *Farmstay*
Lynne & Colin Gibson
1D RD Oamaru, North Otago, Rapid No 217
Rosebery Road, Airedale, Oamaru

Tel (03) 434 9479 or 021 188 9865
Fax (03) 434 9499
lynne.col.seadowns@xtra.co.nz

Double $110 **Single** $70 (Full breakfast)
Child $40
Children and pets welcome
2 Double 1 Twin (3 bdrm)
Bathrooms: 1 Family share 1 Guest share

Seadowns is an intensive breeding property of 1100 acres of rolling hill country, with hereford, romney and dorset downs studs. The homestead built in 1939 is a relaxing home set in a lovely country garden with coastal views. We have a fox terrier and cat. View or participate in seasonal farm activities. Historic sites on the property include: Oamaru stone quarrying site, limestone cliffs, lobster catching, guided farm walks. Experience penguin colonies, historic Oamaru precinct, with important 19th century architecture, Moeraki Boulders and salmon fishing.

~

Moeraki - Oamaru *38 km S of Oamaru*

Moeraki Boulder Downs Farmstay & B&B *B&B Farmstay*
Jan & Ken Wheeler
State Highway 1, Moeraki, RD 2,
Palmerston, North Otago

Tel (03) 439 4855 or 025 989 362
Fax (03) 439 4355
farmstay@moerakiboulders.co.nz
www.moerakiboulders.co.nz

Double $90-$120 **Single** $70 (Full breakfast)
Child $40 Dinner by arrangement
Visa MC accepted
2 Queen 2 Single (2 bdrm)
Bathrooms: 1 Guest share

Indulge yourself and enjoy warm hospitality at our charming country homestead by the sea. Breakfast with the bellbirds - then stroll along the beautiful beach to Moeraki Boulders and quaint fishing village. Sheep farm tours available. Stay 2 nights and experience the Moeraki penguins, seals, historic Oamaru, golf courses and antique shops nearby. We are en route to Christchurch, Dunedin, Queenstown and Mt Cook.

Just as we have a variety of B&Bs
you will also be offered a variety of breakfasts,
and they will always be generous.

~

380

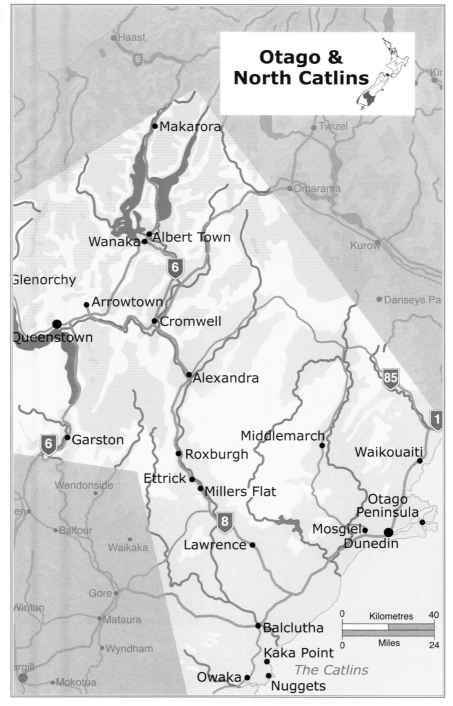

Otago & North Catlins

Makarora *65 km N of Wanaka*

Larrivee Homestay *Homestay*
Andrea & Paul
Makarora, via Wanaka

Tel (03) 443 9177 andipaul@xtra.co.nz
www.larriveehomestay.co.nz

Double $120-$150 Single $80
(Breakfast by arrangement)
Child under 12 half price
Dinner $35 BYO
Visa MC accepted Children welcome
2 Double 2 Single (3 bdrm)
Bathrooms: 1 Ensuite 1 Guest share 1 Private

Nestled in native bush bordering Mt Aspiring National Park, our unique home and cottage are secluded, quiet and comfortable. Originally from the USA, we have lived in Makarora for over 25 years and like sharing our mountain retreat and enjoying good food and conversation. Many activities are available locally, including fishing, bird watching, jet boating, scenic flights and bush walks - including the wonderful 'Siberia Experience', fly/walk/boat trip. We are happy to help make arrangements for activities.

Makarora *65 km N of Wanaka*

Makarora Homestead *Separate Suite Cottage with Kitchen*
Kenna Fraser
53 Rata Road, Makarora

Tel (03) 443 1532 Fax (03) 443 1525
bnb@makarora.com
www.makarora.com

Double $105-$115 Single $95 (Continental provisions)
Children welcome
7 Queen 1 Double 7 Twin (8 bdrm)
Bathrooms: 2 Ensuite 3 Guest share

Makarora Homestead offers a secluded retreat in the midst of the Southern Alps and is perfect for travellers looking for the warmth and ambience of a home. A self-contained comfortable house with a private sunny deck leads into the open plan kitchen/dining/living area. 2 new detached bedrooms have queen beds, ensuite bathrooms and verandah. With tame farm animals to feed Makarora Homestead provides a fun rural experience for any age.

Wanaka *In Wanaka Central*

Lake Wanaka Homestay *B&B Homestay*
Gailie & Peter Cooke
85 Warren Street, Wanaka

Tel (03) 443 7995 Fax (03) 443 7945
wanakahomestay@xtra.co.nz
www.lakewanakahomestay.co.nz

Double $110-$120 Single $75-$80 (Full breakfast)
Visa MC accepted
Not suitable for children
2 Double (2 bdrm)
Bathrooms: 1 Guest share

Welcome to our home. Relax with us enjoy breathtaking views of lake and mountains, just 5 minutes walk to shops, restaurants and lake. Peter, a keen fly fisherman, is happy to show guests where to find the big ones. Complimentary tea, coffee and home-made cookies during your stay. Warm home, cooked breakfast, comfortable beds and electric blankets. We have shared our home with guests for many years, making wonderful friendships. We both enjoy meeting and helping people, fishing, golf, skiing, walking, gardening. Kate, our labrador dog everyones friend. Freephone 0800 443 799.

Lake Wanaka *In Wanaka*

Beacon Point *B&B Homestay Apartment with Kitchen*
Diana & Dan Pinckney
302 Beacon Point Road, PO Box 6, Lake Wanaka

Tel (03) 443 1253 or 025 246 0222
027 435 4847 Fax (03) 443 1254
dan.di@lakewanaka.co.nz
www.beaconpoint.co.nz

Double upto$120 **Single** up to $90 (Continental)
Child $30 **Dinner** $40 Rolla Beds
Pet free home Children welcome
1 Queen 1 Twin (2 bdrm)
Bathrooms: 1 Ensuite

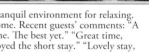

Beacon Point B&B is surrounded by an acre of lawn and garden for your enjoyment. Leads to a walking track to the village around the edge of the lake. Private spacious studio with ensuite, queen and single beds (2 rooms), kitchen, TV, sundeck and BBQ. Studio equipped with every need for perfect stay. We enjoy planning your days with you. Our intrests include farming, forestry, fly fishing, real estate, boating, gardening and grandchildren. Turn right at lake - Lakeside Road - then to Beacon Point Road 302.

Wanaka *In Wanaka*

Harpers *B&B Homestay*
Jo & Ian Harper
95 McDougall Street, Wanaka

Tel (03) 443 8894 Fax (03) 443 8834
harpers@xtra.co.nz
www.harpers.co.nz

Double $130 **Single** $90 (Continental)
Visa MC accepted
1 King/Twin 2 Single (2 bdrm)
Bathrooms: 1 Ensuite 1 Private Bath and Shower

We take pride in offering a friendly, comfortable home. Share breakfast and awesome lake and mountain views with us. Also explore our extensive garden, which provides a tranquil environment for relaxing. We offer a drink and muffins on your arrival. This is a smoke-free home. Recent guests' comments: "A wonderful stay - hot bath, hot pancakes, hot view and such a welcome. The best yet." "Great time, great views, great atmosphere, great flowers and great pancakes. Enjoyed the short stay." "Lovely stay, wonderful views, pancakes delicious."

Wanaka *4 km S of Wanaka*

Stonehaven *Homestay*
Deirdre & Dennis
Halliday Lane, RD 2, Wanaka

Tel (03) 443 9516 Fax (03) 443 9513
moghul@xtra.co.nz
www.stonehaven.co.nz

Double $115 **Single** $85 (Full breakfast)
Portacots and highchairs available
Visa MC accepted
Children welcome
2 Queen 2 Single (2 bdrm)
Bathrooms: 1 Ensuite 1 Private

Our home is set in two acres about five minutes drive from Wanaka. All beds have electric blankets. Tea and coffee is freely available. We have extensive views of surrounding mountains. Children are welcome and child care by arrangement. Our nearby tree collection has an accent on autumn colour. Local walks a speciality. Organic fruit both in season and preserved. We have twin sixteen year old girls, a small dog and a cat. No smoking inside please. Please phone for directions.

Wanaka *10 km N of Wanaka*

The Stone Cottage *B&B Apartment with Kitchen*

Belinda Wilson

Wanaka, RD 2, Central Otago

Tel (03) 443 1878 Fax (03) 443 1276
stonecottage@xtra.co.nz
www.stonecottage.co.nz

Double $240-$270 Single $220 (Full breakfast)
Child under 12 half price
Dinner $65
Visa MC accepted
1 King 1 Queen 1 Double 2 Single (2 bdrm)
Bathrooms: 1 Ensuite 1 Private

50 years ago, a spectacular garden was created at Dublin Bay on the tranquil shores of Lake Wanaka. Its beauty still blooms today against a backdrop of the majestic Southern Alps. Accommodation is private, comfortable and elegantly decorated.

The Stone Cottage offers 2 self-contained loft apartments with breathtaking views over lake Wanaka to snow clad alps beyond. Featuring your own bathroom, bedroom, kitchen, living room and balcony. Television, VCR/DVD, fax and email available. Private entrance.

Enjoy breakfast at leisure, made from fresh ingredients from your well stocked fully equipped kitchen, Pre-dinner drinks, delicious 3 course dinner and NZ wines or a gourmet picnic hamper is available by arrangement.

Walk along the beach just 4 minutes from The Stone Cottage or wander in the enchanting garden. Guests can experience trout fishing, nature walks, golf, boating, horse riding, wine tasting and ski fields nearby. Only 10 minutes from Wanaka, this is the perfect retreat for those who value privacy and the unique beauty of this area. Relax in the magic atmosphere at The Stone Cottage and awake to the dawn bird chorus of native bellbirds and fantails.

Wanaka *2min km N of Wanaka*
Hunt's Homestay *Homestay*
Bill & Ruth Hunt
56 Manuka Crescent, Wanaka 9192, Central Otago

Tel (03) 443 1053 Fax (03) 443 1355
relax@huntshomestay.co.nz
www.huntshomestay.co.nz

Double $110-$120 Single $70-$80 (Continental)
Child by arrangement Full breakfast $12
Visa MC accepted
1 Queen 2 Single (2 bdrm)
Bathrooms: 1 Ensuite 1 Private 1

Welcome to our modern home in Wanaka where we
will greet you with tea or coffee in our smoke-free house and settle you in your spacious ground-floor
accommodation. After farming near Wanaka, we built this house over looking the mountains and lake,
and so have a good knowledge of the area. Through our membership of Lake Wanaka Tourism we are
kept informed of all tourist activities in the area. Our interests are golf, gardening, travel and meeting
people. We have no resident children or pets.

Wanaka *2 km NW of Wanaka Central*
Lake Wanaka Home Hosting *B&B Homestay*
Joyce & Lex Turnbull
19 Bill's Way, Wanaka

Tel (03) 443 9060 Fax (03) 443 1626
lex.joy@xtra.co.nz
www.lakewanakahomehosting.co.nz

Double $100-$140 Single $70 (Full breakfast)
Child under 10 years $25 Dinner $40
Children welcome
1 King/Twin 1 Double 1 Twin (3 bdrm)
Bathrooms: 2 Private

We welcome visitors to Wanaka, enjoy sharing our
natural surroundings with others. We have a large peaceful home where our guests can experience not
only the austerity of the lake and mountains around them, but also experience the ambience of Wanaka
itself. Guest room with super king bed has adjoining TV lounge with TV, tea & coffee facilities, private
bathroom. Good laundry facilities. We wish your stay in Wanaka will be a very happy one. Directions:
please ring for directions. We enjoy your company.

Wanaka *2.5 km E of Wanaka*
Riverside *B&B Homestay*
Lesley & Norman West
11 Riverbank Road, RD 2, Wanaka

Tel (03) 443 1522 or 027 464 0333
Fax (03) 443 1522
n.l.west@paradise.net.nz
www.riversidewanaka.co.nz

Double $120-$150 Single $75-$90 (Full breakfast)
Visa MC accepted
1 King 1 Queen 2 Twin (3 bdrm)
Bathrooms: 1 Ensuite 1 Guest share 1 Private

We welcome guests to the quiet location of our quality
home with extensive grounds. Overlooking the Cardrona River with sweeping mountain and rural
views,we are 100 metres off SH84, 5 minutes drive from the Lake and Wanaka's excellent restaurants.
Individually decorated and well appointed rooms offer a high level of comfort. Enjoy the open fire and
central heating in winter, or shady terraces in summer. Delicious continental or home-cooked breakfasts
and friendly hosts ensures your stay will be enjoyable. We have 2 cats and a small friendly dog (outdoors).

Wanaka *In Wanaka Central*

Te Wanaka Lodge *B&B*

Graeme & Andy Oxley
23 Brownston Street, Wanaka

Tel (03) 443 9224 **Fax** (03) 443 9246
tewanakalodge@xtra.co.nz
www.tewanaka.co.nz

Double $155-$205 Single $145-$195 (Full breakfast)
Garden cottage $205
Visa MC Amex accepted
9 Queen 4 Twin (13 bdrm)
Bathrooms: 13 Ensuite

Nestled in the heart of Wanaka, Te Wanaka Lodge is a 2 minute walk to the lake, restaurants, shops and golf course. Tastefully decorated with fishing and skiing memorabilia, Te Wanaka Lodge has a distinctive Alpine ambience.

On a hot summers day laze under our walnut tree with a cool drink from the house bar, or in winter relax by the warmth of our log fire after enjoying a soak in our secluded garden hot tub.

*All bedrooms with ensuite and private balcony
*Full cooked breakfast included
*House bar specialising in local beers and wines
* Sky TV, video, CD and book library
*Off-street parking

Wanaka - Albert Town *6 km N of Wanaka*
Riversong *B&B Homestay*
Ann & Ian Horrax
5 Wicklow Terrace, Albert Town, RD 2, Wanaka

Tel (03) 443 8567 or 021 113 6397
Fax (03) 443 8564 info@happyhomestay.co.nz
www.happyhomestay.co.nz

Double $120-$150 **Single** $90-$95 (Full breakfast)
Child $25 Dinner $35pp by arrangement
Visa MC accepted Children welcome
1 King/Twin 1 Queen 1 Single (3 bdrm)
Bathrooms: 1 Ensuite 1 Private

Riversong is 5 minutes from Wanaka Township, at
historic Albert Town, on the banks of the majestic Clutha River. At our secluded haven all rooms have
river and mountain views, with immediate access to the river. Ann's background is healthcare and Ian's
law. We invite you to share all the comforts of our home and garden and Ian's knowledge of the region's
fishing and guidance service. We aim to provide a peaceful and comfortable atmosphere (books galore!)
where you can simply relax. We have 2 outside lab dogs.

Lake Wanaka *2.3 km NW of Wanaka Centre*
Peak-Sportchalet *B&B Apartment with Kitchen*
Alex & Christine Schafer
36 Hunter Crescent, Wanaka

Tel (03) 443 6990 Fax (03) 443 4969
stay@peak-sportchalet.co.nz
www.Peak-Sportchalet.co.nz

Double $105-$135 **Single** $70 (Special breakfast)
2 bedroom chalet $140-$160
Visa MC accepted
Pet free home Children welcome
1 King/Twin 1 Queen 1 Twin (3 bdrm)
Bathrooms: 2 Ensuite 1 Private

Welcome at Peak-Sportchalet - your Qualmark 4 star accommodation in Wanaka. Feel like at home
in our guest suites including our self-contained chalet; all are individually designed and appointed with
fine furniture and ensuite bathrooms. Sliding doors open onto private verandahs. Awake refreshed after
a relaxing nights sleep on our prime quality mattresses and in luxury duvets. Start your day healthy with
our memorable breakfast buffet. Experience our hospitality and ambience.

Wanaka *1.5 km N of Wanaka central*
Temasek House *B&B Homestay*
Vivien Reid & Mandy Madin
7 Heuchan Lane, Wanaka 9192

Tel (03) 443 1655 Fax (03) 443 1655
temasek.house@xtra.co.nz

Double $95-$11 **Single** $65 (Full breakfast)
Twin $95 Children welcome
1 Queen 1 Twin 1 Single (3 bdrm)
Bathrooms: 1 Ensuite

Only 1.5km from the town centre, Temasek House
offers guests a friendly, homely atmosphere. Our home
is ideally situated for the local ski fields and Mount
Aspiring National Park. A large comfortable lounge opens on to a balcony with mountain views. A gentle
stroll to local restaurants and lakeside. Tea & coffee complimentary with home-made treats. Internet/
email and laundry facilities available for small extra charge. 1 small dog on property.

Otago, North Catlins

Wanaka *2 km E of Wanaka*

Oregon Hollow *B&B Apartment with Kitchen*
Robyn & Gene Clements
426 Aubrey Road, RD 2, Wanaka, Otago

Tel (03) 443 4086 or 021 418 878
Fax (03) 443 4086
gene@oregonhollow.co.nz
www.oregonhollow.co.nz

Double $165-$185 Single $140 (Full provisions)
Visa MC accepted
Children welcome
1 Queen (1 bdrm)
Bathrooms: 1 Private

Oregon Hollow is a luxury one bedroom apartment (renovated 2003) attached to our house. Set in a peaceful location yet less than 2km to Wanaka's restaurants and amenities. The apartment has a separate entrance, private bathroom, and large living area with a kitchenette and log burner, TV, DVD and stereo. Quality bed linen, furnishings are fitted throughout. A private patio is set in our acre of country garden. A speciality breakfast hamper is provided. We have a son, Oliver and 2 Jack Russell terriers. Bookings Essential.

Wanaka *2.4 km E of Wanaka*

The Cedars *B&B Homestay*
Mary & Graham Dowdall
7 Riverbank Road, RD 2, Wanaka 9192

Tel (03) 443 1544 Fax (03) 443 1580
thecedarswanaka@xtra.co.nz

Double $130-$170 Single $90-$12 (Full breakfast)
Dinner by arrangement
Visa MC accepted
Children welcome
2 Queen 1 Single (2 bdrm)
Bathrooms: 1 Guest share Bathroom with Spa Bath

Cead Mile Failte - One hundred thousand welcomes.
A warm Irish/Kiwi welcome awaits at The Cedars, by Mary, Graham, pet English Collie and cat Cara. Our stone home set on 11 acres includes panoramic views, expansive gardens, guest lounge with large open fire. Nearby attractions include The Maze, Warbirds Museum (both internationally acclaimed), golf, ski fields, walking tracks, paragliding, lakes and rivers for water pursuits: shops and restaurants. Full breakfast is served with fresh and home-made produce. We offer evening meals or BBQ by prior arrangement.

Wanaka *In In*

Criffel Peak View *B&B*
Caroline Holland
98 Hedditch Street, Wanaka

Tel (03) 443 5511 Fax (03) 443 5521
stay@criffelpeakview.co.nz
www.criffelpeakview.co.nz

Double $110-$140 Single $80-$10 (Full breakfast)
2 King/Twin1 King 1 Queen (2 bdrm)
Bathrooms: 1 Ensuite 1 Private

A cosy modern cottage situated in a quiet cul-de-sac, just a short walk from the lake and town. Great mountain views, large sunny deck, friendly young hosts and a crazy cat called Splodge. We are only minutes from the stunning Wanaka Golf Club and local icon the Cinema Paradiso. Our 2 guest rooms look out towards the Criffel Range and are equipped with super king and queen sized beds, TVs and tea/coffee facilities.

Wanaka *In Wanaka Central*

Wanaka Springs Boutique Lodge *Luxury*
Lyn & Murray Finn
21 Warren Street, Wanaka, Central Otago

Tel (03) 443 8421 or 027 241 4113
Fax (03) 443 8429
relax@wanakasprings.com
www.wanakasprings.com

Double $295-$330 (Full breakfast)
Visa MC Diners Amex Eftpos accepted
Not suitable for children
2 King/Twin 5 Queen 1 Twin (8 bdrm)
Bathrooms: 8 Ensuite

Welcome to Wanaka's in-town retreat, a purpose built, boutique lodge set in the tranquility of natural springs and native gardens. It is within a 5 minute stroll to the lakefront, golf course and Wanaka's shops, cafes, bars and restaurants. 8 spacious guestrooms, each with private ensuite, have superior king, queen or twin beds. The guest lounge has a welcoming log fire, quality furnishings, book collection and entertainment systems. Full breakfast, afternoon tea, pre-dinner drinks and nightcaps are included in the tariff.

Wanaka *2 km W of Wanaka*

Sequora Lodge *B&B Homestay*
Lew Crawford
137 Anderson Road, RD 2, Wanaka

Tel (03) 443 1961 Fax (03) 443 1964
stay@sequoralodge.co.nz
www.sequoralodge.co.nz

Double $120-$160 Single $90-$10 (Continental)
Child negotiable
Visa MC accepted
3 Queen (3 bdrm)
Bathrooms: 3 Ensuite

Sequora Lodge is a quality purpose built B&B in a large new home set on 2 acres, 2 minutes drive to town, with spectacular lake and mountain views. Quiet and spacious guest rooms. The guest lounge has a piano, open fire, TV, VCR and DVD player. Facilities include guest verandah, ski drying room, central heating, library, email access, laundry facilities, and complimentary classic/vintage car tour of Wanaka. Mountain bikes and fishing rods available. 2 children at home, pet on property. A warm welcome assured.

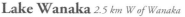

Lake Wanaka *2.5 km W of Wanaka*

Wanaka Jewel *B&B Homestay Separate Suite*
Pam & Bruce Mayo
7 Foxglove Heights, Far Horizon Park, Lake Wanaka

Tel (03) 443 5636 or 025 285 6234
Fax (03) 443 5637 Wanakajewel@xtra.co.nz
www.bnb.co.nz/wanakajewel.html

Double $120-$150 Single $80-$90 (Full breakfast)
Visa MC accepted
2 Queen (2 bdrm)
Bathrooms: 1 Ensuite 1 Private

Welcome to Wanaka Jewel - a stay in paradise. 3 minutes from township. Wanaka Jewel is a brand new modern home with purpose built bed & breakfast suite, set on 1 acre surrounded by magestic mountains and superb lake views, close to town. Own private entrance and parking. This suite is beautifully appointed with quality linen. Complimentary pool (summer months only), spa, tennis courts, gymnasium, BBQ, pitch and putting green available to guests. Complimentary tea, coffee and home-made treats, sumptious breakfast. You can be assured of a warm welcome and a memorable stay. Friendly outside dog.

Wanaka *In Wanaka Central*

Wanaka Homestead Lodge & Cottages *B&B Cottage with Kitchen*
Shonagh & Roger North
1 Homestead Close, Wanaka

Tel (03) 443 5022 Fax (03) 443 5023
stay@wanakahomestead.co.nz
www.wanakahomestead.co.nz

Double $195-$299 **Single** $195-$245 (Full breakfast)
Cottages $310-420 all facilities included
Visa MC Diners Amex Eftpos accepted
Children welcome
4 King/Twin 1 Twin (5 bdrm)
Bathrooms: 5 Ensuite Baths in cottages

Welcome to our friendly new luxury lodge and cottages just 200 metres from the shores of Lake Wanaka. Peacefully located overlooking parkland, the accommodation is within walking distance of Wanaka's vibrant township and is also well positioned for lakefront walking tracks, ski field, and National Park access. Wanaka Homestead opened in 2003 and has since won awards for its environmentally friendly buildings, offering affordable luxury and a choice of accommodation types to couples and families alike.

Luxury Lodge. The homestead lodge is a boutique bed & breakfast, which, during winter, has a "ski lodge" feel. The 5 ensuited bedrooms have extremely comfortable twin, super-king or huge California king beds. Gourmet breakfast and the sociable evening wine and nibbles? are optional, served by the log fire, exposed beams and sumptuous sofas in the guest lounge.

Alternatively, our charming new cottages are family friendly and offer self-contained and serviced home from home? style accommodation with real warmth and character. Each cottage is serviced daily, has a well appointed kitchen, a lounge with french doors opening onto a grassy courtyard, a dining area, 2 bathrooms, underfloor heating, CD/DVD and comfortable new king or twin beds. The 2 bedroom stone cottage? and 3 bedroom timber barn comfortably accommodate 4 and 7 people respectively, and are sometimes also available as a 1 bedroom option.

All guests enjoy complementary facilities, such as under-the-stars hot tub, broadband internet, hot spot internet, mountain bikes and laundry. Our website is well worth a visit too.

Wanaka

Shep's Place *B&B*
Heather & Murray Sheppard
21 Hedditch Street, Wanaka

Tel (03) 443 5663 or 021 058 7742
the.sheppards@xtra.co.nz

Double $110-$140 **Single** $75-$10 (Continental)
Child negotiable
Children welcome
1 Queen 2 Twin (2 bdrm)
Bathrooms: 1 Guest share

Shep's Place offers guests an opportunity to relax and enjoy magnificent views of Lake Wanaka and surrounding mountains. The guest sitting room with television, fridge, tea, coffee and home-made biscuits opens onto a sunny balcony. Guests only on first floor - single party bookings. Family cat in residence. Less than 5 minute walk to restaurants. Laundry available. We look forward to meeting you.

Wanaka

Beaconfield *B&B Homestay*
Carla & Michael Rackley
251 Beacon Point Road, Wanaka

Tel 021 056 2996
rackleymike@hotmail.com

Double $140-$195 **Single** $120-$175 (Full breakfast)
2 Queen (2 bdrm)
Bathrooms: 2 Ensuite

Welcome to our lovely brand new home set on 1 acre with breath-taking lake and mountain views. We invite you to share our Kiwi hospitality and local knowledge. Your guest room with ensuite has french doors opening to a verandah with stunning views. You will never tire of the beauty and tranquility. Share our interests of food, wine, music, local art, antiques, travel. Gourmet breakfast and refreshments included. Carla is an RN and Michael was a lawyer and hospital manager.

Wanaka *5 km N of Wanaka*

Ferryman's Cottage *B&B Homestay*
Marie Lewis & Bryan Lloyd
4 Arklow Street, Albert Town, RD 2, Wanaka

Tel (03) 443 4147 or 021 144 7513
ferrymanscottage@xtra.co.nz
www.ferrymanscottage.co.nz

Double $125-$140 **Single** $85-$95 (Full breakfast)
Dinner $35 by arrangement
Visa MC accepted
2 Queen (2 bdrm)
Bathrooms: 1 Ensuite 1 Private

Ferryman's is our lovingly restored historic cottage, located 5 minutes from Wanaka, on the banks of the beautiful Clutha River (famous for fishing). The warmth, peace, and tranquility of our home, has been created for you to enjoy. A unique garden fresh breakfast experience from Marie's kitchen awaits you. Laze in our cottage garden. Stroll, 1 minute to fish, or walk riverside tracks to Lake Wanaka. Bryan, lawyer by day, laidback host by night, Marie, (foodie and teacher), and our cat, Indy, invite you to relax in our corner of Paradise.

Cromwell

Stuart's Homestay *Homestay*
Elaine & Ian Stuart
5 Mansor Court, Cromwell

Tel (03) 445 3636 Fax (03) 445 3617
ian.elaine@xtra.co.nz

Double $100-$120 Single $70-$80 (Full breakfast)
Dinner $20-$30 by arrangement
Visa MC accepted
Pet free home
2 Queen 2 Single (3 bdrm)
Bathrooms: 1 Ensuite 1 Guest share

Welcome to our home which is situated within
walking distance to most of Cromwell's amenities. We are semi-retired Southland farmers who have
been home hosting for over 15 years. Now enjoying living in ths stone fruit and wine region. Cromwell
is a quiet and relaxed town with historic gold diggings, vineyards, orchards, trout fishing, boating, walks,
close to ski fields. 45 minutes to Wanaka or Queenstown. Share dinner with us or just bed & breakfast.
Tea and coffee, home-made cookies available. We enjoy sharing our home and garden with visitors and a
friendly stay is assured.

Cromwell *1 km N of Cromwell*

Cottage Gardens *B&B Homestay, Detached twin studio*
Jill & Colin McColl
3 Alpha Street, corner State Highway 8B,
Cromwell, Central Otago

Tel (03) 445 0628 Fax (03) 445 0628
cottage.gardens@ihug.co.nz   www.fiordland.gen.nz/jill.htm

Double $80-$95 Single $45-$65 (Continental)
Dinner $25 Visa MC accepted
2 Twin 1 Single (3 bdrm)
Bathrooms: 2 Ensuite 1 Host share

Hospitality is our specialty. For 11 years we have offered
travellers good food and company. Our spacious guest room and detached twin studio have ensuites,
TV, tea making facilities and private entrances. Guest room has veranda overlooking garden and lake.
Cromwell is surrounded by orchards & vineyards with ever-changing scenery. Excellent sporting facilities.
Accompany labrador Jessica May on lakeside walks. Fritta is a retired pre-school cat. Members of Lions
International, retired orchardists and pre-school teacher. Queenstown and Wanaka 45 minutes, Te Anau
two & half hours, Free laundry.

Cromwell - Northburn *4 km N of Cromwell*

Quartz Reef Creek Bed & Breakfast *B&B Apartment with Kitchen*
June Boulton
Quartz Reef Creek, RD 3, Northburn,
State Highway 8, Cromwell

Tel (03) 445 0404 Fax (03) 445 0404
june-boulton@xtra.co.nz
www.quartzreefcreek.co.nz

Double $110-$120 Single $70-$90 (Continental)
Visa MC accepted
1 Queen 1 Twin 1 Single (3 bdrm)
Bathrooms: 1 Ensuite 1 Private

You are invited to stay at my peaceful and modern
lakeside home located in Central Otago, a rapidly expanding wine growing region. Panoramic views
from your sunny room include Lake Dunstan and surrounding mountains. Both rooms have total
privacy with their own entrances. 1 has its own deck, tea making facilities, fridge, microwave and TV.
Another room has twin beds, TV and sitting room with another single bed. I enjoy making pottery in my
studio and supply local galleries. I have 2 friendly pets, a dog Guinness and cat, Tom.

Cromwell *5 km N of Cromwell*
Lake Dunstan Lodge *Homestay*
Judy & Bill Thornbury
Northburn, RD 3, Cromwell

Tel (03) 445 1107 or 027 431 1415
Fax (03) 445 3062
william.t@xtra.co.nz
www.lakedunstanlodge.co.nz

Double $110-$130 Single $80 (Full breakfast)
Child negotiable Dinner $25pp by arrangement
Visa MC accepted Children welcome
2 Queen 3 Single (3 bdrm)
Bathrooms: 1 Ensuite 1 Guest share

Friendly hospitality awaits you at our home privately situated beside Lake Dunstan. We are ex-Southland farmers and have a cat Ollie. Our interests include Lions, fishing, boating, gardening and crafts. Bedrooms have attached balconies, fridge, tea and coffee facilities. Guests share our living areas, spa pool and laundry. Local attractions: orchards, vineyards, gold diggings, fishing, boating, walks, 4 ski fields nearby. Enjoy dinner with us or just relax in the peaceful surroundings. No smoking indoors please. Directions: 5km north of Cromwell Bridge on SH8.

Cromwell - Bannockburn *6 km N of Cromwell*
Aurum *B&B Separate Suite Cottage with Kitchen Self-contained*
Janette & Maurice Middleditch
RD 2, Bannockburn, Lawrence Street - Short Street

Tel (03) 445 4024 or 025 693 8248
Fax (03) 445 4028
aurumgallery@xtra.co.nz
www.nzsouth.co.nz/aurumhomestay

Double $110-$130 Single $90 (Continental)
Child negotiable Dinner by arrangement
Visa MC accepted
1 Queen 1 Double (2 bdrm)
Bathrooms: 1 Ensuite 1 Private big bathroom

Welcome to our garden retreat at aurum, situated in Bannockburn and surrounded by local wineries and historic gold mining sites. Our location is 5 minutes drive from Cromwell, tourist centres at Lake Wanaka and Queenstown are 40 and 50 minutes drive away respectively. Aurum provides warm and sunny guest living in a private and self-contained unit. For your own privacy, we accommodate only 1 group of guest at any time. Maurice is a scenic artist who has exhibitions throughout New Zealand and Janet loves sharing the garden and meeting people.

Cromwell *5 km W of Cromwell*
Serendipity Vineyard *B&B Farmstay Cottage with Kitchen*
Joanna Lewis
229 Ripponvale Road, RD 2, Cromwell

Tel (03) 445 1864 or 027 454 7351
Fax (03) 445 1864
serendipityvineyard@xtra.co.nz

Double $110 Single $80 (Continental)
Family self-contained $100 per night
Family self-contained with breakfast $130
Children welcome
1 Queen 2 Double 6 Single (2 bdrm)
Bathrooms: 1 Ensuite 2 Private

Situated 5 minutes from Cromwell on our family vineyard. Self-contained queen bedsit unit with luxurious ensuite bathroom and private courtyard. Separate self-contained family accommodation with private garden, 2 modern toilets and showers, full cooking and laundry facilities, telephone and internet.

Arrowtown *18 km NE of Queenstown*

Bains Homestay *Homestay Cottage with Kitchen*
Ann & Barry Bain
R32 Butel Road, Arrowtown 9196, Otago

Tel (03) 442 1270 F ax (03) 442 1271
bainshomestay@ihug.co.nz
www.dotco.co.nz/bainshomestay

Double $120 (Full breakfast)
Child negotiable Bunkroom $70 double
Visa MC accepted
Children and pets welcome
1 Queen 2 Single (2 bdrm)
Bathrooms: 2 Ensuite

We are a retired business couple who have travelled extensively. We welcome our guests to a peaceful, spacious, sunny self-contained upstairs suite complete with kitchen, and a balcony with panoramic views of surrounding mountains and the famous Millbrook Golf Resort. Meet our friendly cocker spaniel. Extra continental breakfast with freshly baked bread, jams etc is provided in your suite; or join us for a cooked starter. Complimentary laundry, road bikes, gold mining gear, BBQ etc. Our courtesy car is an Archbishop's 1924 Austin drophead coupe.

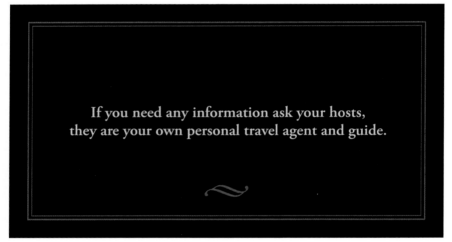

If you need any information ask your hosts, they are your own personal travel agent and guide.

Arrowtown *In Arrowtown Central*

Miller's *Separate Suite*
Pam Miller
23 Berkshire Street, Arrowtown

Tel (03) 442 1126

Double $110 Single $90 (Full breakfast)
Visa MC accepted
1 Queen (1 bdrm)
Bathrooms: 1 Private

You will be made very welcome at my home which is centrally located on the main road, entering Arrowtown from Queenstown. I am 3 blocks from the Arrowtown Village centre. My accommodation for guests has a private entrance, double bedroom, small sitting room with TV and tea/coffee making facilities. Also a private bathroom with laundry facilities. Delicious continental or full breakfast is served in the dining room upstairs. Off-street parking. Only 20 minutes drive to Queenstown.

Willowbrook is within easy reach of four ski fields and three very picturesque golf courses

Arrowtown - Queenstown *4 km W of Arrowtown*

Willowbrook *B&B Apartment with Kitchen*
Cottage with Kitchen
Tamaki & Roy Llewellyn
Malaghan Road, RD 1, Queenstown

Tel (03) 442 1773 or (027) 451 6739
Fax (03) 442 1780
info@willowbrook.net.nz
www.willowbrook.net.nz

Double $140-$165 **Single** $115-$135 (Continental)
Cottage (sleeps 4) $295 BBQ $10
Visa MC Diners Amex accepted
2 King 2 Queen 3 Twin (7 bdrm)
Bathrooms: 5 Ensuite 1 Private

Willowbrook is a 1914 homestead at the foot of Coronet Peak in the beautiful Wakatipu Basin. The setting is rural, historical and distinctly peaceful, and with the attractions of Queenstown and Arrowtown only 15 and 5 minutes away respectively, Willowbrook can truly claim to offer the best of both worlds. 4 acres of mature garden contain a tennis court, luxurious spa pool and several outhouses. The former shearers quarters have been rebuilt and a hay barn renovated allowing Willowbrook to offer varied styles of accommodation:

Bed & Breakfast in the Main House - centrally heated double rooms, ensuite bathrooms, guest lounge with open fires and Sky TV.

The Barn offers warm, spacious ensuite accommodation with kitchenette, separate from the Main House. Super king bed, bunks for children, TV and covered deck. Annex available for extra members of same party.

The Cottage is a delightfully cosy 2 bedroom cottage with full kitchen and laundry facilities. Ensuite bathrooms, underfloor heating throughout, spacious sundecks and private lawn.

Willowbrook is within easy reach of 4 ski fields and 3 very picturesque golf courses. Kate and Allan are your hosts. Expect a warm welcome, friendly advice and traditional South Island hospitality.

**Otago
North Catlins**

Arrowtown - Queenstown *14 km N of Arrowtown*

Crown View *B&B Farmstay*
Caroll & Reg Fraser
457 Littles Road, Dalefield, Queenstown 9197

Tel (03) 442 9411 Fax (03) 442 9411
info@crownview.co.nz
www.crownview.co.nz

Double $150-$170 (Full breakfast)
Visa MC accepted
Children welcome
2 King (2 bdrm)
Bathrooms: 1 Ensuite 1 Private

Peaceful and quite rural setting with views of
Remarkables and Crown Range. 15 minutes from either Queenstown and Arrowtown. 2 double bedrooms both with super king-size beds, that can be made into single beds if required. Both rooms have tea & coffee facilities, TV & radios. Breakfast can be had on upstairs balcony or outside on our secluded terrace both with views of the mountains. Relax and enjoy our rural lifestyle, along with our 2 white highland westies (Dougal & Archie) sheep and chickens. Come as a guest leave as a friend.

Queenstown *1.5 km NE of Queenstown Central*

Birchall House *B&B*
Joan & John Blomfield
118 Panorama Terrace, Larchwood Heights,
Queenstown

Tel (03) 442 9985 Fax (03) 442 9980
birchall.house@xtra.co.nz
www.zqn.co.nz/birchall

Double $135-$150 Single $110-$120 (Full breakfast)
Child $50 Visa MC accepted
Children welcome
1 Queen 2 Twin (2 bdrm)
Bathrooms: 1 Ensuite 1 Private

Welcome to our home in Queenstown, purpose built to accommodate guests in a beautiful setting. At Birchall House, enjoy a magnificent 200 degree view of lake and mountains within walking distance of town centre. Guest accommodation is spacious, private, separate entrance, centrally heated, electric blankets, smoke-free. Continental or cooked breakfast available. From Frankton Road, turn up Hensman Road, left into Sunset Lane. Or, Frankton Road, turn up Suburb Street, right into Panorama Terrace. Access via Sunset Lane. Off-street parking. Visit our website: www.zqn.co.nz/birchall.

Queenstown *1/2 km N of Queenstown*

Adelaide Street Guest House *B&B*
Dave, Mandy & family Wright
PO Box 998, 27 Adelaide Street, Queenstown

Tel (03) 442 6207 Fax (03) 442 6202
adelaidehouse@xtra.co.nz
www.adelaidehouse.co.nz

Double $70-$110 Single $47-$70 (Continental)
Visa MC accepted
Children welcome
2 King 2 Double 2 Twin 4 Single (6 bdrm)
Bathrooms: 1 Ensuite 1 Family share 2 Guest share

Adelaide Street Guest House is perfectly situated just
35 metres from the shores of the beautiful Lake Wakatipu in the heart of Queenstown, just a short scenic walk to the centre of town. The sundecks, spacious lounge and most or our rooms enjoy breathtaking views of the lake and golf course enveloped by stunning mountain ranges. All rooms are heated and have electric blankets and duvets. Tea and coffee available anytime. Colourful sunsets in summer. Skiing in Winter. Book with us for tours and sightseeing. Off season rates.

Queenstown .3 km S of Queenstown Central
The Stable *B&B Homestay*
Isobel & Gordon McIntyre
17 Brisbane Street, Queenstown 9197

Tel (03) 442 9251 Fax (03) 442 8293
gimac@queenstown.co.nz
www.thestablebb.com

Double $160-$180 Single $120 (Full breakfast)
Visa MC accepted
Not suitable for children
1 King/Twin 1 Double 2 Single (2 bdrm)
Bathrooms: 1 Ensuite 1 Private

A 135 year old stone stable, converted for guest accommodation, and listed by the New Zealand Historic Places Trust, shares a private courtyard with our home.

The Garden Room is in the house, providing convenience and comfort with lake and mountain views. Our home is in a quiet cul-de-sac and set in a garden abundant with rhododendrons and native birds. It is less than 100 metres from the beach where a small boat and canoe are available for guests' use.

The famous Kelvin Heights Golf Course is close and tennis courts, bowling greens and ice skating rink are in the adjacent park. All tourist facilities, shops and restaurants are within easy walking distance, less than 5 minutes stroll on well lit footpaths. Both rooms are well heated with views of garden, lake or mountains. Tea and coffee making facilities are available at all times.

Guests share our spacious living areas and make free use of our library and laundry. A courtesy car is available to and from the bus depots. We can advise about and are booking agents for all sightseeing tours. Do allow an extra day or two for all the activities in the Queenstown region.

Your hosts, with a farming background, have bred Welsh ponies and now enjoy weaving, cooking, gardening, sailing and the outdoors.

We have an interest in a successful vineyard and enjoy drinking and talking about wine. We enjoy meeting people and have travelled extensively overseas.

Directions: Follow State Highway 6A (Frankton Road) to where it veers right at the Millenium Hotel. Continue straight ahead. Brisbane Street (no exit) is second on left. Phone if necessary.

Otago
North Catlins

Queenstown
Bed & Breakfast
NUMBER 12
.... a quiet convenient location

Queenstown *In Queenstown Central*
Number Twelve *B&B Homestay Separate Suite*
Barbara & Murray Hercus
12 Brisbane Street, Queenstown

Tel (03) 442 9511 Fax (03) 442 9755
hercusbb@queenstown.co.nz
www.number12bb.co.nz

Double $140-$150 Single $100-$110 (Full breakfast)
Visa MC Amex accepted
Children welcome
2 King 2 Twin (2 bdrm)
Bathrooms: 1 Ensuite 1 Private

B&B Approved

We would like you to come and share our conveniently situated house in a quiet no exit street. You only have a 5 minute stroll to the town centre. We have mountain and lake views.

Our home is warm and sunny, windows double glazed and we have central heating for the winter months. Our bedrooms have TVs, coffee/tea making facilities, hair dryers and instant heaters. Our down stairs studio apartment has a separate entrance with a view of our rose garden. Email & laundry is available.

We have a solar heated swimming pool (Dec/March) the sun deck and BBQ are for your use. Our sun room is available for your comfort. Guests have the choice of either a full or continental breakfast in our dining room with its panoramic views.

Once settled in you will seldom need to use your car again. There are several easy walking routes into the town centre, restaurants, shops and tourist centres. We are very close to the lake and our botanical gardens.

Whilst you are with us we will be happy to advise on tourist activities and sightseeing and make any arrangements you would wish.

Barbara has a nursing/social work background and Murray is a retired chartered accountant. We have travelled extensively within our country and overseas. We have an interest in classical/choral music.

Queenstown Central *200m km N of Queenstown*

Queenstown House *Luxury B&B*
Louise Kiely, Family & Friends
69 Hallenstein Street, Queenstown

Tel (03) 442 9043 Fax (03) 442 8755
queenstown.house@xtra.co.nz
www.queenstownhouse.co.nz

Double $250-$595 Single $225-$250
(Special breakfast)
Dinner by arrangement
Visa MC Diners Amex accepted
Children welcome
10 King/Twin 4 Queen (14 bdrm)
Bathrooms: 14 Ensuite

Queenstown house is a unique and charming B&B hotel, overlooking Queenstown Bay with majestic lake and mountain views. 300 metres walk to the town centre. Deluxe breakfast and pre-dinner hospitality included. Fireside sitting rooms and rose scented patios. Room choices include 5 luxurious villa suites and studio rooms with private lake-view decks Hospitality and ambience specialists. 'Your memories make us famous'.

～

Queenstown *800m km N of Queenstown*

Monaghans *B&B*
Elsie & Pat Monaghan
4 Panorama Terrace, Queenstown

Tel (03) 442 8690 Fax (03) 442 8620
patmonaghan@xtra.co.nz
www.bandbclub.com/pages/monaghan

Double $100 Single $90 (Continental)
1 Queen (1 bdrm)
Bathrooms: 1 Ensuite

Welcome to our home in a quiet location, walking distance to town. Enjoy this panoramic view while you breakfast. 1 couple - personal attention. Spacious comfortable room with separate entrance and garden patio. Queen bed, own bathroom, TV, fridge and tea/coffee biscuits. Interests - music, gardening, sport, travel. We will enjoy your company but respect your privacy. Off-street parking. Directions: turn right up Suburb Street off Frankton Road which is the main road into Queenstown then first right into Panorama Terrace.

～

Queenstown *In Queenstown Central*

Anna's Cottage & Rose Suite *Cottage with Kitchen*
Myrna & Ken Sangster
67 Thompson Street, Queenstown

Tel (03) 442 8994 or 025 693 3025
Fax (03) 441 8994
carl.linda@xtra.co.nz

Double $120-$145 Single $90
Extra person $10
Visa MC accepted
1 King/Twin 2 Queen (2 bdrm)
Bathrooms: 2 Private

A warm welcome to Anna's Cottage. Myrna a keen gardener and golfer, Ken with a love of fishing. Enjoy the peaceful garden setting and mountain views. Full kitchen facilities and living room combined. Washing machine. Tastefully decorated throughout, the bedroom is furnished with Sheridan linen. Only a few minutes from the centre of Queenstown. Private drive and parking at cottage. Attached to the end of our home is The Rose Suite, self-contained, 1 queen bed with ensuite, small kitchen, washing machine, furnished with Sheridan linen.

~

Queenstown *0.8 km NW of Central Queenstown*
Coronet View Apartments & B&B *B&B Cottage with Kitchen*
Karen & Neil
30 Huff Street, Queenstown

Tel (03) 442 6766 or 0800 89 6766
027 432 089 Fax (03) 442 6767
stay@coronetview.com
www.coronetview.com

Double $120-$240
Child negotiable
Dinner $25-$70
Apartments from $130-$600
Visa MC accepted
Children welcome
8 King/Twin 1 Queen 1 Twin (10 bdrm)
Bathrooms: 9 Ensuite 1 Private

We welcome you to our beautifully appointed rooms that offer every comfort in either hosted accommodation or private apartments. Superb views of Coronet Peak, The Remarkables and out to Lake Wakatipu.

Guest areas include elevated and spacious dining and living areas, outdoor decks, a sunny conservatory, outdoor BBQ, pool and jacuzzi area and computers with internet access.

Apartments feature fully equipped kitchens and laundries and generous living areas.

Full booking and/or tour guide service. Friendly persian cats on property.

Queenstown *1.5 km NE of Queenstown*
Campbells B&B *B&B and Cottage with Kitchen*
Ruth Campbell
10 Wakatipu Heights, Queenstown

Tel (03) 442 9190 Fax (03) 442 4404
roosterretreat@xtra.co.nz

Double $150 Single $100 (Continental)
Self-contained Unit $280
Visa MC accepted
1 King/Twin 1 Queen 1 Double 1 Single (3 bdrm)
Bathrooms: 2 Private

Our tranquil home has off-street parking, relaxing
garden, outstanding views over Lake Wakatipu and the
Remarkables. Option 1: super king/twin room with private bathroom, down duvets etc. Complimentary
tea, coffee, laundry facilities. Option 2: fully self-contained 2 bedroom unit, sleeps 4/5. Unit faces sun
and has own garden. Fully equipped kitchen, laundry, books, hair dryer etc. No stairs, all guest facilities
on ground level. Enjoy a generous continental breakfast with fresh-baked bread and real coffee, at your
leisure.

Queenstown *400m km N of Queenstown Central*
The Historic Stone House Inn *B&B*
Jo & Steve Weir
47 Hallenstein Street, Queenstown

Tel (03) 442 9812 Fax (03) 441 8293
stone.house@xtra.co.nz
www.stonehouse.co.nz

Double $250-$300 (Special breakfast)
Visa MC accepted
Not suitable for children
4 King (4 bdrm)
Bathrooms: 3 Ensuite 1 Private featuring an extra-large
claw foot tub as well as shower.

The Stone House, built in 1874 of local stone and lovingly restored, is a heritage-listed inn 500 metres
from central Queenstown. Steve and Jo's warm hospitality includes advice on sightseeing and dining
options as well as complimentary wine and cheese by the fire each evening. Fresh flowers welcome guests
to rooms whose amenities include telephones, radio alarms, bathrobes and hair dryers. Laundry service,
free broadband internet and a garden spa are also provided and cats Baz & Lump help make guests feel at
home.

Queenstown *300m km NW of Central Queenstown*
Browns Boutique Hotel *B&B*
Bridget & Nigel Brown
26 Isle Street, Queenstown

Tel (03) 441 2050 F ax (03) 441 2060
stay@brownshotel.co.nz
www.brownshotel.co.nz

Double $240-$260 Single $220-$240 (Continental)
Visa MC Diners Amex accepted
10 King/Twin (10 bdrm)
Bathrooms: 10 Ensuite

Located only 2 blocks walk from downtown
Queenstown with views over Queenstown Bay to the
Remarkables. Every guest room is well appointed, spacious and boasts a super king-size bed along with
french doors opening onto balconies over the courtyard. All rooms have their own generous sized ensuite
including showers and baths. The guest lounge and dining room feature leather couches, open fireplace
and mahogany dining tables and chairs. Nigel and Bridget believe they are offering a unique product in
Queenstown with a quality built and furnished hotel with superior service.

Queenstown

Delfshaven *Homestay*
Irene Mertz
11 Salmond Place (off Kent Street), Queenstown

Tel (03) 441 1447 Fax (03) 441 1383
irenemertz@xtra.co.nz

Double $175 **Single** $150 (Special breakfast)
Visa MC accepted Pet free home
1 Queen (1 bdrm)
Bathrooms: 1 Private

Nestled at the base of Queenstown is my sunny, warm,
modern home, offering magnificent unobstructed
180 degree views over town, lake and mountains. The
comfortable guest room, with its own TV and tea-making facilities, opens out to the garden and those
beautiful views. It is only a 5 minute downhill walk to the town. I am a retired teacher, widely travelled,
enjoy good food and wine, love art, music and enjoy meeting people. A piano is waiting to be played.
Welcome to Salmond Place.

Queenstown *14 km N of Queenstown*

Kahu Rise *B&B Homestay*
Angela & Bill Dolan
455 Littles Road, RD 1, Queenstown

Tel (03) 441 2077 or 0800 436 111
021 104 0009 Fax (03) 441 2078
info@kahurise.co.nz www.kahurise.co.nz

Double $190-$220 **Single** $140-$170
(Special breakfast) Dinner by arrangement
Additional person $50
Visa MC accepted Children welcome
1 Queen 2 Single (2 bdrm)
Bathrooms: 1 Private

In the country, yet close to Queenstown, local attractions and ski fields we offer tranquility and
convenience. Catering exclusively for single party bookings (1-4), our guest wing has a private bathroom,
underfloor heating, tea & coffee facilities, refrigerator, TV, hairdryer etc. Rooms enjoy mountain views
and open directly onto the lawn. Laundry facilities available. We prepare you a delicious home-cooked
breakfast each morning and are happy to offer dinner with complimentary wine, by arrangement. Angela,
Bill and Tess, our friendly dog, warmly welcome you.

Queenstown *1.3 km N of Queenstown*

Matterhorn Chalet Lodge *Luxury B&B Homestay*
Maria & Joe Arnold
20 Wakatipu Heights, Queenstown
PO Box 1427, Queenstown

Tel (03) 441 3935 Fax (03) 441 3935
info@matterhornchalet.com
www.matterhornchalet.com

Double $190-$210 **Single** $180-$195 (Full breakfast)
Visa MC accepted
3 King 1 Queen 2 Single (4 bdrm)
Bathrooms: 1 Ensuite 1 Guest share 1 Private

Imagine a European alpine lodge magically moved
to the shores of Lake Wakatipu. Matterhorn Chalet is a luxury B&B with views as breath-taking as
any in Europe (all rooms have lake views). Only 15 minutes walk to the bustling heart of downtown
Queenstown. For peace and tranquility stay; this is the place for you. Great breakfasts. Maria and Joe
speak English, Swiss, German and Dutch. For the most panoramic views over Remarkables and Lake
Wakatipu. We provide a courtesy shuttle to Queenstown Airport.

Queenstown *500mtr km N of Queenstown*

B&B
Approved

Chalet Queenstown *B&B*
Dianalyn Kaahu & Murray Colson
1 Dublin Street, Queenstown

Tel (03) 442 7117 Fax (03) 442 7508
chalet.queenstown@xtra.co.nz
www.chalet.co.nz

Double $145-$185 **Single** $130-$170 (Continental)
4 King/Twin 1 Queen (5 bdrm)
Bathrooms: 5 Ensuite

You will love the location of Chalet Queenstown, a sunny site, 500 metres from the central post office, and botannical gardens, an easy stroll will take you to the lakeside walking track and the millenium walk, Queenstown Hill is on our doorstep.

Murray & Dianalyn have been involved in the tourism industry for many years and have a great knowledge of Queenstown and all its activities. We enjoy meetng people, very keen outdoor enthusiasts, especially tramping, fishing, sightseeing. Dianalyn is also a qualified therapeutic masseuse, cranial sacral therapist, reiki instructor, we also have onsite our own healing room (appointments essential).

Our well appointed rooms all have views of lake or mountains, ensuite facilities (shower),TV, refrigerator, tea/coffee, hair dryer, oil heating, electric blankets, lovely linen and super comfortable beds, where a good night's sleep is assured.

We endeavour to provide guests with wholesome, organic, preservative-free food and beverages. You will enjoy the hearty continental breakfast consisting of lots of fresh fruit, organic and flavoured yoghurts, your choice of milk, home-made muesli, seeds, nuts and dried fruits, 100% juices. Fresh-baked croissants, cereals, toast, tea, good quality coffee and herbal teas. Other features of our home: - complimentary mountain bike use - off street parking - laundry facilities - filtered water - relaxed and friendly atmosphere We are more than happy to assist with all your reservations for Queenstown's activities and onward bookings through the NZ B&B Book.

Queenstown *10 km E of Queenstown*

Milestone *Luxury B&B Cottage No Kitchen Cottage with Kitchen*
Betty & John Turnbull
Ladies Mile, RD 1, SH6, Queenstown

Tel (03) 441 4460 or 027 541 4460
Fax (03) 441 4438
jcturnbull@xtra.co.nz
www.themilestone.co.nz

Double $165-$225 Single $125-$165 (Full breakfast)
Dinner by arrangement
Visa MC Amex accepted Children welcome
1 King 3 Queen 1 Single (4 bdrm)
Bathrooms: 2 Ensuite 1 Private

Milestone, has 3 acres of gardens and water features, located on the main highway into Queenstown. Close to ski fields and golf courses, the airport, supermarket, shops and lakes. The rose-covered stone schist cottage with its romantic bedroom is a favourite with honeymooners. In the main house are the Coronet Queen Suite and the Remarkables King Suite which can include the Crown Range Room to accommodate a family. Betty is a marriage celebrant and many couples have been married in their home and garden. Welcome to Milestone

~

Queenstown

Campbells on Earnslaw *B&B*
Aderianne & Bevan Campbell
9 Earnslaw Terrace, Queenstown

Tel (03) 442 7783 Fax (03) 442 7784
stay@campbells.net.nz
www.campbells.net.nz

Double $175 Single $135 (Full breakfast)
Extra person $50 Children welcome
1 Queen 2 Single (2 bdrm)
Bathrooms: 1 Private

We look forward to welcoming you to our home, which has 180 degree spectacular panoramic views of lake, mountains and golf course. Guests own private living room with balcony, TV, fridge, toast, tea & coffee making facilities. Ideal for 2 couples or family, only 1 party at a time. Experienced hosts we can advise and arrange your sightseeing and activities. From Frankton Road turn up Suburb Street, right into Panorama Terrace, right into Earnslaw Terrace. We are only a 10 minute stroll (1.2km) into town centre.

~

Queenstown - Glenorchy *45 mins N of Queenstown*

Lake Haven *B&B Homestay*
Ronda
Benmore Place, Glenorchy

Tel (03) 441 1327
lakehaven@xtra.co.nz

Double $120 Single $80 (Full breakfast)
Child by arrangement
Dinner by arrangement
Visa MC accepted
Children welcome
2 King/Twin (2 bdrm)
Bathrooms: 2 Ensuite

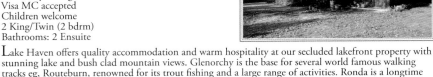

Lake Haven offers quality accommodation and warm hospitality at our secluded lakefront property with stunning lake and bush clad mountain views. Glenorchy is the base for several world famous walking tracks eg, Routeburn, renowned for its trout fishing and a large range of activities. Ronda is a longtime local and is happy to assist you in exploring and enjoying our unique and beautiful area. Children welcome. Laundry facilities. Fishing guide available. Glenorchy - gateway to paradise.

Garston *50 km S of Queenstown*

Menlove Homestay *B&B Homestay Cottage No Kitchen*

Bev & Matt Menlove

17 Blackmore Road, Private Bag, Garston 9660

Tel (03) 248 8516
mattmenlove@xtra.co.nz

Double $80 Single $50 (Continental)
Dinner $25 by arrangement
1 Double 1 Single (1 bdrm)
Bathrooms: 1 Ensuite

We are organic gardeners and our other interests
include lawn bowls, sailing, gliding and alternative
energy. Garston is New Zealand's most inland village
with the Mataura River (famous for its fly fishing) flowing through the valley, surrounded by the Hector
Range and the Eyre Mountains. A fishing guide is available with advance notice. For day trips, Garston is
central to Queenstown, Te Anau, Milford Sound or Invercargill. We look forward to meeting you.

Alexandra - Earnscleugh *6 km W of Alexandra*

Iversen *Orchardstay*

Robyn & Roger Marshall

47 Blackman Road, RD 1 Alexandra, Central Otago

Tel (03) 449 2520 Fax (03) 449 2519
r.r.marshall@xtra.co.nz
www.otagocentral.com

Double $150 Single $100 (Continental)
Child by arrangement
Dinner $25 by arrangement
Visa MC accepted
Children welcome
2 Queen (2 bdrm)
Bathrooms: 2 Ensuite

Our seperate guest accommodation offers you privacy and comfort. Combined with a warm welcome
into our home, you can share with us, the peaceful and relaxing setting our our cherry orchard. While at
Iversen you can experience the grandeur and contrasts of the Central Otago landscape, walk the thyme
covered hills, visit local wineries or just relax. Directions: from Alexandra or Clyde, travel on Earnscleugh
Road, turn into Blackman Road and look for our sign on the left. Advanced bookings preferred.

Alexandra *3.5 km N of Alexandra*

Duart *B&B Homestay*

Mary & Keith McLean

Bruce's Hill Lane, Rapid No. 356,
Highway 85, RD 3, Alexandra

Tel (03) 448 9190 or 027 316 3569
Fax (03) 448 9190 duart.homestay@xtra.co.nz
www.duarthomestay.co.nz

Double $100 Single $80 (Continental)
Child negotiable Dinner $25 by arrangement
Visa MC accepted Children and pets welcome
1 Double 1 Twin 1 Single (3 bdrm)
Bathrooms: 1 Ensuite 1 Guest share

Your accredited Kiwi Hosts, Mary and Keith, welcome you to our secluded home, 5 minutes from
Alexandra. Your privacy is assured, but we enjoy company and conversation if that is your wish. Relish
the spectacular views from our extensive stone terraced garden, or relax on the verandahs, sitting room or
library. Revel in the myriad activities and experiences Alexandra offers; e.g. the climate, Rail Trail, award
winning vineyards, art tours, mountain biking, kyaking etc. Laundry, Sky TV, complimentary tea, coffee,
biscuits, fruit anytime, pre-dinner drink and nibbles.

**Otago
North Catlins**

Roxburgh - Ettrick *15 km SW of Ettrick*
Wilden Station Homestead *B&B Homestay Farmstay*
Sarah & Peter Adam
Wilden School Road, near Dunrobin, West Otago

Tel (03) 204 8115 Fax (03) 204 8116
wildenstation@xtra.co.nz

Double $140 Single $100 (Special breakfast)
Child $15 Dinner $30
Visa MC accepted
Children welcome
2 Queen 2 Single (3 bdrm)
Bathrooms: 1 Ensuite 1 Private

Experience high-country farm life with us, our two
boys and two cats. Watch our dogs work the sheep. Stroll through trees to a small lake, explore our
historic farm buildings, fish the Pomahaka River, tour the property by vehicle or on horseback, or simply
relax in our gracious homestead. Enjoy superb meals prepared by your internationally experienced chef/
hostess (all by prior arrangement). Unwind in our tranquil surroundings about 2 hours from Dunedin,
Queenstown, Wanaka. Families most welcome. Please telephone for directions.

Lawrence *45 mins N of Balclutha*
The Ark *B&B*
Frieda Betman
8 Harrington Place (Main Road)

Tel (03) 485 9328
the.ark@xtra.co.nz
www.theark.co.nz

Double $90 Single $50 (Full breakfast)
Child $15
2 Double 1 Twin 1 Single (4 bdrm)
Bathrooms: 1 Family share

My home is situated on the main road near the picnic
ground with its avenue of poplars. My garden is special
to me, the home is 100 years old, has character, charm and a lived in feeling. It's home to Ambrose &
Pumpkin, my cats and Holly, a miniature Foxie. Guestrooms are restful with fresh flowers, fruit, and
breakfast includes hot bread, croissants, home-made jams. Free-range eggs. There is a lovely peaceful
atmosphere in our early gold mining town. Approx. 45 minutes to Dunedin airport, just over an hour to
Dunedin.

Middlemarch *4 km SW of Middlemarch*
The Farm *Homestay Farmstay*
Lynley & Glynne Smith
Farm Road, RD 2, Middlemarch

Tel (03) 464 3610 Fax (03) 464 3612
glynley@xtra.co.nz

Double $95 Single $70 (Full breakfast)
Dinner $30pp
Children and pets welcome
1 King 1 Twin (2 bdrm)
Bathrooms: 1 Guest share

Our charming old stone house and gardens are set
amoungst mature oaks, with the spectacular Rock
and Pillar Range as a backdrop. Lynley & Glynne welcome you to their peaceful relaxed haven which
includes a 200 acre farm, sheep, cattle, horses, 2 family cats & a Jack Russell dog. From high country
farming background, interested in horses, hunting and a tranquil lifestyle. On the Central Otago Rail
Trail, 1 hour from Dunedin, this is a convenient and hospitable stop for exploring this picturesque area.

Waikouaiti *5 km N of Waikouaiti*
Boutique Bed & Breakfast *B&B Farmstay Separate Suite*
Barbara & John Morgan
107 Jefferis Road, Waikouaiti RD 2

Tel (03) 465 7239 or 027 224 8212
Fax (03) 465 7239
info@boutiquebedandbreakfast.co.nz
www.boutiquebedandbreakfast.co.nz

Double $150-$180 Single $150 (Full breakfast)
3 Queen (3 bdrm)
Bathrooms: 3 Ensuite

Wake up to the birds singing. In a setting of
mature of trees and garden, relax in your own luxury
accommodation, separate and private from adjacent homestead. 3 new units purpose built for your
comfort and pleasure. Each unit opens on to a verandah or courtyard and includes TV, refrigerator,
microwave oven, toaster, tea/coffee facilities and iron/ironing board. Tariff includes delicious home-made
cooked breakfast, home-baking, fruit bowl, use of tennis court, has barbeque and John's deer farm tour.

Dunedin *2 km W of Dunedin*
Magnolia House *B&B*
Joan & George Sutherland
18 Grendon Street, Maori Hill, Dunedin 9001

Tel (03) 467 5999 Fax (03) 467 5999
mrsuth@paradise.net.nz

Double $100 Single $80 (Special breakfast)
Not suitable for children
1 Queen 1 Double 2 Single (3 bdrm)
Bathrooms: 2 Private

Our quiet turn-of-the-century villa sits in broad,
flower-bordered lawns backed by native bush with
beautiful, tuneful birds. All rooms have electric heating,
comfortable beds with electric blanket, and antiques, while the queen room has an adjoining balcony.
Close by is Moana Pool, the glorious Edwardian house Olveston, and Otago Golf Course. Our special
breakfast will set you up for the day. We have a courtesy car, a burmese and a siamese cat. It is not
suitable for children or smokers.

Dunedin *7 km NE of Dunedin*
Harbourside B&B *B&B Homestay*
Shirley & Don Parsons
6 Kiwi Street, St Leonards, Dunedin

Tel (03) 471 0690 Fax (03) 471 0063
harboursidebb@xtra.co.nz

Double $80-$95 Single $60-$95 (Full breakfast)
Child $20 Dinner $25
Visa MC Diners accepted
Children welcome
1 King/Twin 2 Queen 3 Single (3 bdrm)
Bathrooms: 1 Ensuite 1 Guest share

We are situated in a quiet suburb overlooking Otago
Harbour and surrounding hills. Within easy reach of all local attractions. Lovely garden or harbour
views from all rooms. Children very welcome. Directions: drive into city on one-way system watch for
Highway 88 sign follow Anzac Avenue onto Ravensbourne Road. Continue approx 5km to St Leonards
turn left at Playcentre opposite Boatshed into Pukeko Street then left into Kaka Road, straight ahead to
Kiwi Street turn left into Number 6.

Dunedin *In Dunedin Central*

Deacons Court *B&B*

Keith Heggie & Gail Marmont

342 High Street, Dunedin

Tel (03) 477 9053 or 0800 268 252
Fax (03) 477 9058
Deacons@es.co.nz
www.deaconscourt.co.nz

Double $100-$150 Single $60-$90 (Full breakfast)
Child $20-$30 Visa MC accepted
Children welcome
1 King 2 Queen 3 Single (3 bdrm)
Bathrooms: 2 Ensuite 1 Private

Deacons Court is a charming superior spacious Victorian villa 1km walking distance from the city centre and on a bus route. We offer you friendly but unobtrusive hospitality in a quiet secure haven. Guests can relax in our delightful sheltered rose garden and conservatory. All our bedrooms are large, have ensuite or private bathrooms, heaters, TV and electric blankets. Complimentary 24 hour tea or coffee, free parking and laundry service available. We cater for non-smokers and have a quiet cat. Family groups welcome.

Dunedin - Otago Peninsula *8 km N of Dunedin City*

Captains Cottage *B&B Tours*

Christine & Robert Brown

422 Portobello Road, RD 2, Dunedin

Tel (03) 476 1431 or 027 435 2734
Fax (03) 476 1431 wildfilm@actrix.co.nz
www.wildfilm.co.nz

Double $155 Single $110 (Special breakfast)
Tours by arrangment
Visa MC accepted Not suitable for children
1 King/Twin 1 Queen (3 bdrm)
Bathrooms: 1 Ensuite 1 Guest share 1 Private

Enjoy the spectacular views from our waterfront home, in a bush setting beside Glenfalloch Gardens, on the ruggedly beautiful Otago Peninsula. Enroute to albatross, penguin and seal colonies. Christine & Robert are wildlife film makers, having filmed for BBC, National Geographic and Discovery. Wildlife/photography day trips, by arrangement,to our special locations include a picnic lunch and an opportunity to share Robert's experience and knowledge of wildlife and filming. Great food, hospitality, barbeques, or relax by the fire in our comfortable, character filled home.

Dunedin *4.5 km SE of Dunedin Central*

Alloway *Luxury B&B Homestay*

Lorraine & Stewart Harvey

65 Every Street, Andersons Bay, Dunedin

Tel (03) 454 5384 or 0800 387 245
Fax (03) 454 5364 alloway@xtra.co.nz
www.alloway.co.nz

Double $120-$200 Single $110-$175 (Continental)
Visa MC accepted Not suitable for young children
2 Queen 2 Single (2 bdrm)
Bathrooms: 1 Guest share 1 Private
We only have 1 guest bathroom, but prices vary depending whether guests are willing to share

We are at the gateway to the Otago Peninsula, which features wildlife, walking tracks, Taiaroa Head Albatross Colony, disappearing gun, seal colonies, yellow eyed penguins, Glenfalloch Gardens and much more. We are 7 minutes to town centre. Our home is set in 1 acre of gardens and lawns, with indoor/outdoor living. Awaken to the sound of abundant bird life in a quiet and secure neighbourhood. We serve delicious healthy breakfasts. All rooms have tea making facilities, TV, heaters, electric blankets. Separate facilities with modern guest bathroom.

Dunedin *3 km N of Dunedin Central*
Dalmore Lodge *B&B Homestay*
Loraine Allpress
9 Falkirk Street, Dalmore, Dunedin

Tel (03) 473 6513 or 027 287 1517
Fax (03) 473 6512
bookings@dalmorelodge.co.nz
www.dalmorelodge.co.nz

Double $110-$150 Single $85-$110 (Special breakfast)
Child negotiable Visa MC accepted Children welcome
2 Queen 1 Twin 2 Single (4 bdrm)
Bathrooms: 1 Guest share 1 Private

In its peaceful setting, 2 minutes off the Northern
Motorway you'll find Dalmore Lodge, offering views of the harbour, Pacific Ocean and Otago Peninsula.
The balcony leads out onto a sheltered garden, relax, enjoy watching and listening to native birds along
with our cat, Teagan. Public transport at gate. Off-street parking. A 3 minute drive takes you into the
city centre. We look forward to meeting you and sharing delights of Dunedin and its local attractions.
Dunedin City Council Building Code Compliant, allowing accommodation for up to 8 guests.

Dunedin *2 km N of central*
Arden Street B&B Dunedin Central *B&B Homestay*
Joyce Lepperd
36 Arden Street, North East Valley, Dunedin Central

Tel (03) 473 8860 Fax (03) 473 8861
joyce-l@clear.net.nz
www.ardenstreethouse.co.nz

Double $75-$120 Single $45-$90 (Continental)
Child $10-15 Dinner $10-$25
Visa MC Eftpos accepted Children welcome
2 Queen 1 Double 2 Twin 3 Single (5 bdrm)
Bathrooms: 1 Ensuite 1 Private

Comfortable, quiet 1930s character homestay, built
by a sea captan with stained glass themes. Guests describe it as having a warmth far beyond temperature!
Good parking. Close to botanical gardens, university, Knox College, city & hospice. Arty, quirky, sunny,
great views, birdsong, garden. Modern bathrooms, ensuite. Social dinners using organic produce from
Joyce's garden - meet 'the locals'. Good guests piano. Children welcome. We practice recycling! Cat
called QT! From the north turn left towards North East Valley (North Road, first right (Glendining
Avenue up to 36 Arden Street.)

Dunedin *1 km W of Dunedin Central*
Highbrae Guesthouse *B&B Homestay*
Fienie & Stephen Clark
376 High Street, City Rise, Dunedin

Tel (03) 479 2070 or 025 328 470
Fax (03) 479 2100
highbrae@xtra.co.nz
www.highbrae.co.nz

Double $90-$120 Single $70-$85 (Continental)
Child $20 Full breakfast extra
Visa MC Amex accepted
Children welcome
1 King 1 Queen 1 Twin (3 bdrm)
Bathrooms: 1 Family share 1 Guest share

Experience a taste of early Dunedin. This heritage home in the heart of the city was built on the High
Street Cable Car route in 1908 to provide first class accommodation to its residents. Today it is still an
impressive home with spectacular views of the city and harbour. The 3 upstairs guest rooms are carefully
restored to preserve their character for visitors, who delight in the many features in the home. A courtesy
van can meet you at the bus or train if required.

Dunedin *In Dunedin Central*

Albatross Inn *B&B*
Glynis Rees
770 George Street, Dunedin

Tel (03) 477 2727 or 0800 441 441
Fax (03) 477 2108
albatross.inn@xtra.co.nz

Double $100-$140 Single $85-$95 (Continental)
Child $15
Children welcome
1 King 4 Queen 3 Double 5 Single (9 bdrm)
Bathrooms: 8 Ensuite 1 Private

Welcome to Dunedin and Albatross Inn! Our beautiful late Victorian house is ideally located on the main street close to the university, gardens, museum, shops and restaurants.

Our attractive rooms have ensuite/private bathrooms, telephone, TV, radio, tea/coffee, warm duvets and electric blankets on modern beds. Firm beds upon request. Quiet rooms at rear of house. Several rooms have kitchenette and fridge.

Enjoy your breakfast in front of the open fire in our lounge. We serve freshly baked bread and muffins, fresh fruit salad, yoghurt, juices, cereals, teas, freshly brewed coffee. We are happy to recommend and book tours for you. All wildlife tours pick up and drop off here. We can recommend many great places to eat, most just a short walk down George Street. Nearby laundry, non-smoking, cot and highchair.

Some comments from our visitors Book! The right balance of everything location, breakfast and lovely room. Delightfully different. Absolutely fantastic as always. Home away from Home. A touch of Class, lovely home beautifully presented. Perfecto! Homepage:

www.albatross.inn.co.nz. Winter special $75 Double - special conditions apply. Complimentary e-mail and internet.

Dunedin *In Dunedin Central*
Grandview *B&B Homestay*
Steve Scott
360 High Street, Dunedin 9001

Tel (03) 474 9472 Freephone 0800 749472
Fax (03) 474 9473
nzgrandview@msn.com
www.grandview.co.nz

Double $90-$1705Single $70-$125 (Continental)
Child $15   Children welcome
1 King 3 Queen 1 Double 1 Twin 3 Single (6 bdrm)
Bathrooms: 2 Ensuite 1 Family share 1 Guest share
2 Private

Grandview is centrally located! The casino, restaurants, shops, cafes and bars are only a short stroll away! Relax in luxury in this charming 1901 heritage listed Edwardian mansion. Featuring magnificent panoramic views from our viewing platforms and spa area. Also 154cm BIG TV, satellite TV, videos, free internet, laundry facilities and scrumptious continental breakfasts are all a complimentary part of the Grandview experience. Rooms to suit all budgets! From basic rooms to our luxury trendy spa suites for your pleasure!

Dunedin - St Clair *4 km S of Dunedin*
Aberdeen B&B *B&B Homestay*
Robert O'Shea
43A Aberdeen Road, St Clair, Dunedin

Tel (03) 479 7617 or (03) 487 8217
43AAR@bigfoot.com
thor.prohosting.com/43aar/brochure.htm

Double $130-$160 Single $95-$130 (Continental)
Child $35 Visa MC Diners accepted
Children welcome
2 Queen 1 Single (2 bdrm)
Bathrooms: 2 Ensuite

Aberdeen B&B is a large, warm house, set in a quiet, sunny enclave on St Clair headland with spectacular views of beach and peninsula. It's 2 minutes drive from St Clair Beach and about 8 minutes' drive from the Visitor Centre. There are 2 large ensuite rooms, 1 with a large spa bath. My son Joel and I enjoy meeting people; we've travelled in USA, Canada, Europe, and Australia. We offer peace and privacy with the comforts of home.

Otago Peninsula - Portobello *20 km NE of Dunedin*
Captain Eady's Lookout *B&B Homestay*
Richard & Ana Good
2 Moss Street, Portobello, Dunedin

Tel (03) 478 0537 or 021 478 785
capteady@earthlight.co.nz
capteady.co.nz

Double $130-$155 Single $120-$145
(Special breakfast)
Child negotiable Dinner $25 Twin room $100
Visa MC accepted Children welcome
2 Queen 1 Twin (3 bdrm)
Bathrooms: 2 Ensuite 1 Family share

Captain Eady's Lookout is a delightful bed and breakfast situated on the water's edge. This character house, built early last century by Captain Eady, a ferry master, is set on a small bluff overlooking Otago Harbour. 1 bedroom opens onto a secluded garden, 1 overlooks the harbour. You may have a special breakfast in our conservatory whilst taking in the splendid harbour views. The house has many antiques and on the walls are paintings by local artists. You may sample the very large jazz collection. Cats in residence.

Otago Peninsula - Broad Bay *16 km E of Dunedin*

B&B Approved

Chy-an-Dowr *B&B*
Susan & Herman van Velthoven
687 Portobello Road, Broad Bay, Dunedin

Tel (03) 478 0306 or 021 036 5190
021 156 0715
hermanvv@xtra.co.nz
www.chy-an-dowr.co.nz

Double $150-$195 (Special breakfast)
Visa MC accepted
1 King/Twin1 King 1 Queen (3 bdrm)
Bathrooms: 1 Ensuite 1 Private

Chy-an-Dowr (House by the Water), a quality B&B located midway on scenic Otago Peninsula. Our character 1920's home with its harbourside location has panoramic views, is situated opposite a small beach and enroute to the albatross and penguin colonies. The upstairs guest area is spacious and private with comfortable rooms, bathrobes, tea/coffee, TV, fridge, ensuite/private facilities and sunroom. Enjoy a delicious breakfast at your leisure. Originally from Holland, we enjoy welcoming people and sharing our wonderful location with them.

Otago Peninsula - Macandrew Bay *11 km E of Dunedin*

B&B Approved

Mac Bay Retreat *B&B Cottage with Kitchen*
Jeff & Helen Hall
38 Bayne Terrace, Macandrew Bay, Dunedin 9003

Tel (03) 476 1475 Fax (03) 476 1975
jhall9@ihug.co.nz
www.otago-peninsula.co.nz/macbayretreat.html

Double $105 Single $85 (Continental)
Extra guest $25pp
Visa MC accepted
1 King 1 Double (2 bdrm)
Bathrooms: 1 Ensuite

Mac Bay Retreat - Otago Peninsula. Welcome to your private self-contained smoke-free retreat, 15 minutes from Dunedin centre on the Otago Peninsula. Relax with the spectacular view overlooking the harbour from Dunedin City to Port Chalmers. Your cosy retreat is separate from the host's house and gives you a choice of either a super king or double bed plus an ensuite, modern kitchen and TV. Suitable for 1 couple, possibly 2 couples, travelling together. Only minutes from Dunedin's most popular attractions, Larnach Castle, albatross and penguin colonies, etc.

Otago Peninsula - Broad Bay *16 km E of Dunedin*

B&B Approved

Broad Bay White House *B&B Homestay*
Chris & Margaret Marshall
11 Clearwater Street, Broad Bay, Dunedin

Tel (03) 478 1160 Fax (03) 478 1159
broadbaywhitehouse@paradise.net.nz
www.broadbaywhitehouse.co.nz

Double $140-$165 (Full breakfast)
Dinner $30 by arrangement
Visa MC Diners Amex accepted
2 Queen 1 Double 1 Single (3 bdrm)
Bathrooms: 2 Ensuite 1 Private

Looking for peace and quiet, privacy, panoramic views over the harbour, superb meals with silver service? Look no further. We are a tranquil semi-rural hideaway located on the Otago Peninsula. Handy to albatross, penguin and seal colonies. All bedrooms enjoy spacious decks and panoramic views over the harbour. House is centrally heated throughout. Relax and wander through gardens and enjoy the abundant bird life. Have fun with a game of petanque (no experience required).

Otago Peninsula - Portobello *20 km NE of Dunedin*

Peninsula B&B & Treetop Lodge *B&B*

Toni & Stephen Swabey
4 Allans Beach Road, Portobello, Dunedin

Tel 0800 478 090 or (03) 478 0909   027 634 3661
Fax (03) 478 0909
toni@peninsula.co.nz   toni@treetop.co.nz
www.peninsula.co.nz   www.treetop.co.nz

Double $105-$165 **Single** $85-$125 (Full breakfast)
Child POA Dinner by arrangement Apr-Oct
Free wireless broadband internet
Visa MC accepted Children welcome
1 King 2 Queen 1 Twin (4 bdrm)
Bathrooms: 2 Ensuite 1 Guest share

Treetop Lodge - Double $95-$125 Single $85-$105
(Continental breakfast)
Cottage $105-$145 (sleeps 4)
Visa MC accepted Children welcome
3 queen 1 double 1 twin (5 bedrooms)
2 ensuite 1 private 1 guest share

Would you prefer to relax in the elegant and romantic Victorian ambience of Peninsula B&B in our beautiful 1880s villa - or enjoy the tranquility of Treetop Lodge, a more rustic B&B with a separate self-catering cottage, nestled in a manuka forest? Peninsula B&B is situated in peaceful gardens, with views of the harbour from your room. When you arrive you will be warmly welcomed by Charlie, our friendly cat.

In summer evenings you may wish to visit the wildlife or perhaps just unwind in the lounge or on the verandah. In winter the fire will be roaring. After a day enjoying the sights, make yourself a hot drink and snuggle down in your comfortable king or queen size bed. Relish your delicious cooked breakfast in the morning, with fresh scones and home-made jam. In winter we offer evening meals. Alternatively, enjoy the tranquility of Treetop Lodge, perched above the village of Portobello in a secluded garden. Relax in the quaint wood-and-stained-glass rooms and take in the fabulous views of the Otago harbour from your comfortable room.

Start your day with a delicious continental breakfast with home-baked bread, home-made jam and pastries. If you are traveling in a group, choose the cosy self-catering cottage, which sleeps 4. Take breakfast on the deck while the many species of native birds and our chickens entertain you in the garden. It ís just a short walk from either B&B to the delights of Portobello's 2 restaurants.
The village of Portobello is at the heart of the Otago Peninsula and ideally situated for penguins, albatrosses and seals and for exploring the stunning scenery. We will help you find the best places to see Peninsula wildlife.

Si vous ne parlez pas anglais bien, Stephen parle francais. Both B&Bs have internet access (wireless broadband at Peninsula B&B) and offer complimentary laundry facilities. We can burn digital camera images to CD for a small charge.

413

Otago Peninsula - Harington Point *30 km NE of Dunedin*

Harington Point Accommodation *B&B Cottage with Kitchen*

Dave & Marie Rodger
932 Harington Point Road, RD 2, Dunedin

Tel (03) 478 0287 Fax (03) 478 0089
mdrodger@ihug.co.nz
www.wildlifetours.co.nz

Double $95-$120 (Continental)
Self-contained cottages/motels from $85
Visa MC Eftpos accepted
3 Queen 1 Double 2 Twin 2 Single (5 bdrm)
Bathrooms: 5 Ensuite

Enjoy very comfortable self-contained individual
cottages or B&B units, looking out to Otago Harbour. Closest accommodation to albatross, penguin and
seal colonies. The area has many historic features including The Disappearing Gun and Larnach Castle.
Wake up to bellbirds and bleating of our pet sheep. 2 minutes walk to the beach for a leisurely stroll and
spectacular sunsets. Golf course, restaurants and cafes close by. The Otago Peninsula offers many scenic
walks and drives. Let our local knowledge enhance your stay on the peninsula.

∼

Mosgiel *14 km S of Dunedin*

The Old Vicarage *Homestay*

Lois & Lance Woodfield
14 Mure Street, Mosgiel, Otago

Tel (03) 489 8236
l.l.woodfield@clear.net.nz

Double $75-$95 (Continental)
Visa MC accepted
Children welcome
1 Queen 2 Single (2 bdrm)
Bathrooms: 1 Guest share 1 Private

Welcome to our English-style cottage home. Built
in 1913 and used as the Vicarage for 46 years, before
passing to private owners who made sympathetic restorations. The outstanding feature is the exquisitely
balanced garden, laid out in 'rooms'. 2 upstairs guest rooms and bathroom enjoy a commanding view of
the garden. Warm Oregan panelling and leadlight windows enhance the atmosphere. Situated in Mosgiel,
close to the airport, just 15 minutes from Dunedin. We are a retired Christian couple who enjoy
gardening, architecture, tramping and history.

∼

Mosgiel *2 km SW of Mosgiel*

The Trees *B&B*

Jenny Blackgrove & Rex Moore
70 Main South Road, East Taieri, Mosgiel

Tel (03) 489 4837 Fax (03) 477 1479
rex.moore@clear.net.nz

Double $90-$110 Single $65 (Full breakfast)
Dinner $35 by prior arrangement
Not suitable for children
1 King 1 Twin (2 bdrm)
Bathrooms: 1 Guest share

We are 15km SW of Dunedin, half-way between
Dunedin and the airport. There are 3 golf courses in
close proximity. The house is set in a large garden and we have 2 cats and a border collie dog named
Dougal. Rex enjoys flying light aircraft and sailing, and Jenny's interests include gardening, cooking and
reading. We both have travelled extensively.

Balclutha *26 km W of Balclutha*
Argyll Farmstay *B&B Farmstay*
Trish & Alan May
246 Clutha River Road, Clydevale, RD 4, Balclutha

Tel (03) 415 9268 or 027 431 8241
Fax (03) 415 9268 argyllfm@ihug.co.nz
www.argyllfarmstay.co.nz

Double $120-$150 Single $60-$100 (Full breakfast)
Child negotiable
Dinner $30 by arrangement
Visa MC accepted Children welcome
1 Queen 1 Twin 1 Single (3 bdrm)
Bathrooms: 1 Ensuite 1 Private

From the moment you step onto Argyll Farm you will experience the warmth, tranquillity and hospitality extended to you by Alan and Trish; third generation sheep, deer and cattle farmers. We will make your stay a memorable one, pampering you with exquisite accommodation and cuisine. You can enjoy our day to day farm activities or enjoy quiet times. Go for walks, fish in the Clutha River bordering our property or explore. Our home is yours. Experience us for a magical stay. Directions: please telephone.

Balclutha *4 km N of Balclutha/Catlins*
Lesmahagow *B&B Boutique*
Noel & Kate O'Malley
Main Road, Benhar, RD 2, Balclutha

Tel (03) 418 2507 or 0800 301 224 (NZ only)
027 457 8465
lesmahagow@xtra.co.nz
www.lesmahagow.co.nz

Double $100-$150 (Special breakfast)
Dinner $35 Lunches on request
Visa MC Eftpos accepted Children welcome
2 Queen 2 Double 1 Single (4 bdrm)
Bathrooms: 2 Guest share 2 Private

Lesmahagow offers excellent accommodation in an historic homestead and garden setting. Centrally situated, discerning travellers can make Lesmahagow their base to explore the Catlins region, Dunedin and the Otago Penninsula or the historic goldfields of Lawrence. Centrally heated, with delightful bedrooms and gorgeous bathrooms, you can be sure of wonderful hospitality and a truly memorable stay. Evening dining is always available and our special breakfasts will satisfy all taste buds! Teas, coffees, fruit and home-baking there for the taking. Come as strangers, leave as friends.

Balclutha - North Catlins *8 km E of Balclutha*
Balmoral *Homestay*
Yana & Barry Eaton
147 Chicory Road, Inchclutha RD 1, Kaitangata

Tel (03) 418 1444
barrye2000@xtra.co.nz

Double $100-$125 (Full breakfast)
Child $15
Dinner $40 byo
Children welcome
2 Queen 2 Twin (3 bdrm)
Bathrooms: 1 Guest share

Enjoy an unforgettable holiday at historic (1862) Balmoral. Discover this hidden storybook garden sanctuary of flowers, herbs, native birds and pet lambs. View arts and crafts; savor organic home-cooking and garden-view rooms. Easy drive to fishing, Catlins Lighthouse, (free) sea lion and penguin sites. Host Barry is wilderness guide and microlight pilot; Yana is author and artist. Balmoral is the perfect stop when on route to Dunedin or TeAnau; locatated 8km from Balclutha 'on the island.' We warmly welcome you as guests!

Otago
North Catlins

415

Nuggets - The Catlins *24 km NE of Owaka / Balclutha*

Nugget Lodge *Apartment with Kitchen*
Kath & Noel Widdowson
Nugget Road 367, RD 1, Balclutha, South Otago

Tel (03) 412 8783 Fax (03) 412 8784
lighthouse@nuggetlodge.co.nz
www.nuggetlodge.co.nz

Double upto$150 (Continental)
Extra guests $25pp Breakfast $15pp
Visa MC accepted
Not suitable for children
1 King/Twin 1 Queen 1 Single (2 bdrm)
Bathrooms: 2 Ensuite

2 Superior modern, private, fully self-contained units. Centrally heated. Absolutely on the ocean above the incoming tide, bordering the historic Nugget Lighthouse and wildlife reserve. Your own exclusive view of our secluded beaches. Sleep to the roar of the waves, and wake to our fabulous sunrises. Host experienced DOC honorary wildlife ranger and photographer. Kath spends part of her time protecting the wildlife and educating the public. Renowned for the excellent care we give our guests. Make this your base to explore the Catlins.

Kaka Point - The Catlins *21 km S of Balclutha*

Rata Cottage *B&B Cottage with Kitchen*
Jean Schreuder
31 Rata Street, Kaka Point, South Otago

Tel (03) 412 8779

Double $70 Single $65 (Continental)
Extra person $15
1 Twin (1 bdrm)
Bathrooms: 1 Ensuite

A fully self-contained sunny bed & breakfast unit in a tranquil bush garden setting, with sea view, bell birds and tuis. Bedroom with twin beds, plus double divan in lounge. Wheelchair facilities. 5 minutes from a beautiful sandy beach for swimming or long walks. next door to scenic reserve and bush walks. You can have breakfast in the garden with the birds if you wish. Non-smoking. Laundry facilities available. Cooking facilities.

Kaka Point - The Catlins *20kms km S of Balclutha & 20 kms N of Owaka*

Cardno's Accommodation *B&B Apartment with Kitchen Self-contained & Studio Unit*
Lyn & Selwyn Cardno
8 Marine Terrace, Kaka Point - The Catlins,
RD 1, Balclutha

Tel (03) 412 8181 Fax (03) 412 8101
cardnos@xtra.co.nz www.cardnosaccommodation.co.nz

Double $80-$150 Single $80-$150 (Continental)
Extra person $25 Visa MC accepted
Not suitable for children
2 Queen 1 Double 1 Single (3 bdrm)
Bathrooms: 3 Ensuite

Forty five minutes drive from Dunedin Airport, following the Southern Scenic Route. Kaka Point, the gateway to the Catlins is a seaside destination with patrolled beaches in summer and is ideal to base yourself while exploring Nugget Point Lighthouse, yellow eyed penguins, seals, sea lions, petrified forest, waterfalls, native birds and much more. With great views of the sea beach and Lighthouse, your new modern contempory furnished accommodation has off street parking, own entrance, ensuite, quality linen, bedding, filtered water, complimentry tea/coffee/chocolates.1 minute walk to restaurant/bar/shop and beach.

Kaka Point - The Catlins *20 km SE of Balclutha*

Molyneux House *B&B*

Joan & John
2 Rimu Street, Kaka Point, RD 1 Balclutha

Tel (03) 412 8002 or 021 150 4086
kaka_point@yahoo.co.nz
www.molyneuxhouse.co.nz

Double $125-$155 Single $95-$12 (Continental)
Visa MC accepted
Pet free home Not suitable for children
1 Queen 1 Double (One bdrm)
Bathrooms: 1 Ensuite

Unique waterfront seaside property. Joan & John invite you to join them at their spacious, comfortable home overlooking Molyneux Bay at the seaside village of Kaka Point, Catlins. Our accommodation features quality furnishings, ensuite and lounge area with stunning ocean views. We are within easy reach of the Catlins Coast featuring natural wildlife and unspoilt spectacular scenery. We both enjoy meeting people and would love to extend to you our hospitality. Only 5 minutes walk to The Point, restaurant and bar.

Owaka - The Catlins *15 km S of Owaka*

Greenwood Farmstay *B&B Farmstay Separate Suite Self-contained Beach Cottage*

Helen-May & Alan Burgess
739 Purakaunui Falls Road, Owaka, South Otago

Tel (03) 415 8259 or 027 438 4538
Fax (03) 415 8259 greenwoodfarm@xtra.co.nz

Double $120 Single $85 (Full breakfast)
Child $50 Dinner $40 per person (3 course)
Self-contained cottage $75 double Extra person $10
Children welcome
2 Queen 1 Twin (3 bdrm)
Bathrooms: 1 Ensuite 1 Family share 1 Guest share
1 Private

Welcome ... Situated within walking distance to beautiful Purakaunui Falls. Alan enjoys taking people around our 1900 acre sheep, cattle and deer farm. We host on dinner, bed & breakfast basis and enjoy dining with our guests. Our home offers warm, comfortable accommodation. 1 guest bedroom with ensuite and day-room opens to our large garden. A private bathroom services other guest rooms. Email or phone for directions. Ask about our self-contained beach cottage at Papatowai.

Owaka *6 km N of Owaka*

Hillview *B&B Farmstay Cottage with Kitchen*

Kate & Bruce McLachlan
Rapid 161 Hunt Road, Katea, RD 2,
Owaka, South Otago

Tel (03) 415 8457 Fax (03) 415 8650
hillviewcatlins@xtra.co.nz

Double $95-$100 Single $60 (Breakfast by arrangement)
Child $40 Dinner from $25 Visa MC accepted
Children and pets welcome
2 Queen 4 Single (4 bdrm)
Bathrooms: 2 Guest share

Our 450 acre sheep and cattle grazing property is situated 15 minutes from Nugget Point, 10 minutes from Cannibal Bay. Relax in our cosy private cottage set in a large developing garden, or enjoy the relaxed atmosphere of our home. Our pets usually live outside. Bruce enjoys working with horses and training sheepdogs and often works on another local farm. Kate is a school librarian who enjoys reading, gardening, and handcrafts. We both enjoy our grandchildren and meeting people. Breakfast with us or in private. Evening meals available, bookings essential. Phone evenings.

Otago North Catlins

Owaka - The Catlins *1/2 km N of Owaka*
J T's Catlins B&B *B&B Homestay*
John & Thelma Turnbull
Main Road, Owaka

Tel (03) 415 8127 Fax (03) 415 8129
jtowaka@ihug.co.nz
www.jtscatlinsbnb.co.nz

Double $90-$10 Single $70 (Full breakfast)
Child half price Dinner by arrangement
Children welcome
1 Queen 1 Twin (2 bdrm)
Bathrooms: 1 Guest share
Toilet, shower & bathroom, 3 seperate rooms

Welcome to our warm and comfortable home, which is situated on a 25 acre farmlet, surrounded by colourful, peaceful gardens with splendid unspoilt views. Located in the heart of the Catlins, renowned for its wildlife and spectacular scenery, we are within walking distance of Owaka Township with its restaurants, museum and other amenities. Our guests are encouraged to dine with us for the evening meal when we enjoy quality local food and wine. We look forward to meeting you. Travel safely.

Owaka - The Catlins *6 km E of Owaka*
Kepplestone by the Sea *B&B Homestay*
Esther & Jack Johnson
9 Surat Bay Road, Newhaven,
The Catlins, Owaka 9251

Tel (03) 415 8134 Fax (03) 415 8137
kepplestone@xtra.co.nz

Double $100-$110 Single $85 (Full breakfast)
Dinner by arrangement Children welcome
1 King/Twin 1 Queen 2 Twin (3 bdrm)
Bathrooms: 2 Ensuite

There are no strangers here, only friends we haven't met. Situated metres from Surat Bay, with Hooker sealions basking. Close to Catlins scenery, waterfalls, royal spoonbills, golf. Private yelloweyed penguin viewing with Catlins Natural Wonders. Delicious home-made breakfasts. Fabulous meals served with organically grown vegetables from garden. Allergy diets catered for, every care taken. Directions: Owaka, (Royal Terrace) Follow signs towards Pounawea, at golf course go across bridge, right to Newhaven, go 3km on metal road, at Suratbay Road, right first house on left.

Owaka - The Catlins *10 km W of Owaka*
Catlins Country Cottage Retreat *B&B Cottage with Kitchen*
Margaret Anderson
981 Owaka Valley Road, RD 2, Owaka

Tel (03) 415 8776 Fax (03) 415 8776
anders@ihug.co.nz

Double $100 (Continental provisions)
Child $10 Bed-sit $75
Visa MC Eftpos accepted
Children and pets welcome
2 Queen 2 Single (3 bdrm)
Bathrooms: 1 Private

We have a private, modern house available with farm and hill views. The house is suitable for families or just if you want a private getaway. The nearest town is 10 minutes away and the nearest beach is 15 minutes away. We are 1.5 hours away from both Invercargill and Dunedin. Catlins Country Cottage Retreat is situated on our 1000 acre dairy farm and offers complete seclusion in peaceful surroundings. Your hosts, Rodger and Margaret have a grown family who live away from home and 550 brown eyed beauties who will never leave home.

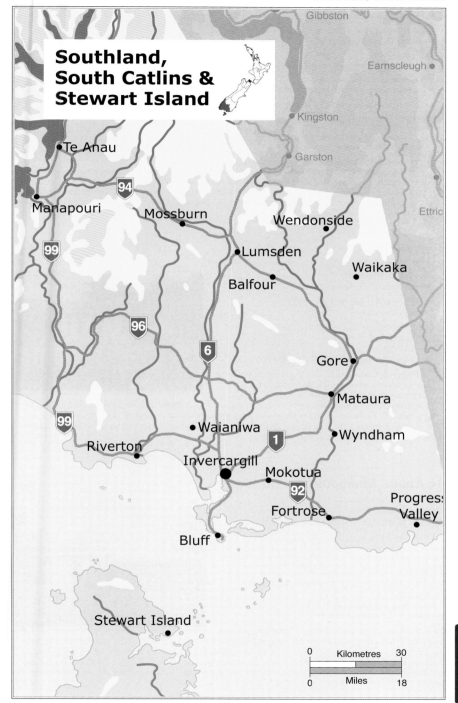

Southland, South Catlins & Stewart Island

Gibbston

Earnscleugh

Kingston

Garston

Ettric

Te Anau

94

Manapouri

Mossburn

99

Wendonside

Lumsden

Waikaka

Balfour

96

6

Gore

Mataura

99

Waianiwa

Wyndham

Riverton

1

Invercargill

Mokotua

Progress Valley

92

Fortrose

Bluff

Stewart Island

| 0 | Kilometres | 30 |
| 0 | Miles | 18 |

Southland, South Catlins

Te Anau *20 km E of Te Anau*

Tapua *Farmstay*
Dorothy & Donald Cromb
RD 2, Te Anau

Tel (03) 249 5805 Fax (03) 249 5805
Tapua.Cromb@xtra.co.nz
www.fiordland.org.nz/html/tapua.html

Double $110-$120 Single $110 (Full breakfast)
Dinner $35pp
Visa MC accepted
1 King 1 Twin (2 bdrm)
Bathrooms: 1 Guest share

You are surrounded by million dollar views while enjoying the comfort of our large modern family home. Electric blankets, heaters in rooms. Traditional farm-style meals. Excellent base for day trips to Milford or Doubtful Sound. A 2 night stay is recommended. Farm tour prior to dinner of our 348 hectare farm which has 3700 sheep and some cattle. Excellent fishing rivers within a few minutes drive as are great walking tracks, golf course etc. Smoke-free home. Directions: Please phone.

Te Anau

Rob & Nancy's Place *Homestay Cottage No Kitchen*
Rob & Nancy Marshall
13 Fergus Square, Te Anau

Tel (03) 249 8241 Fax (03) 249 7397
rob.nancy@xtra.co.nz

Double $125 Single $125 (Full breakfast)
Visa MC accepted
2 King (2 bdrm)
Bathrooms: 1 Ensuite 1 Guest share 1 Private

Rob, Nancy & Chardonnay, our Burmese cat welcome you to our quiet and tranquil home facing a park, 5 minutes walk to the lake and town centre. We are a couple retired from farming and enjoy meeting people. Our modern home includes a courtyard barbecue and gardens. Te Anau is a special place to visit with the magnificent scenery of the Fiordland National Park including spectacular Milford and Doubtful Sounds. All tours are picked up and delivered to the door. Off-street parking and storage available.

Te Anau - Manapouri *20 mins E of Manapouri*

Crown Lea *Farmstay*
Florence & John Pine
Gillespie Road, RD 1, Te Anau

Tel (03) 249 8598 or 025 22 783 66
Fax (03) 249 8598
crownlea@xtra.co.nz
www.crown-lea.com

Double $140-$160 Single $140 (Full breakfast)
Dinner $35
1 King/Twin 1 Queen 1 Twin (3 bdrm)
Bathrooms: 1 Ensuite 2 Private

Our 900 acre sheep, cattle and deer farm offers a farm tour after 6pm, and views of Lake Manapouri, Fiordland mountains, and the Te Anau Basin. Day trips to Doubtful and Milford Sounds, visits to Te Anau, glowworm caves, or hikes on the many walking tracks in Fiordland are all within easy reach. Having travelled in the UK, Europe, Canada, Hong Kong and Singapore, we enjoy meeting guests from all over the world. We and Harriet the cat look forward to welcoming you to our home.

Te Anau - Manapouri *20 km S of Te Anau*

The Cottage *B&B Homestay*
Don & Joy MacDuff
Waiau Street, Te Anau - Manapouri

Tel (03) 249 6838 or 021 138 6110
Fax (03) 249 6839
don.joymacduff@xtra.co.nz
www.thecottagefiordland.co.nz

Double $115-$130 (Special breakfast)
Not suitable for children
2 Queen 1 Single (2 bdrm)
Bathrooms: 2 Ensuite

Gateway to the scenic wonders of Doubtful and Milford Sounds. Cozy homestay B&B combining Old World charm with Kiwi ingenuity. Located in tranquil bush setting,with some mountain and water views. Warm ensuite rooms, cottage decor. Access to cottage gardens. Tea & coffee, TV and videos in room. Shared lounge, fridge, microwave. Excellent breakfasts (full breakfast and laundry extra charge). Credit card by arrangement. Walk 2minutes to where the boat departs for Doubtful Sound. We, with Rosie our skye terrier, extend a warm Kiwi welcome.

Te Anau - Manapouri *10 km N of Manapouri*

Christies Cottage *B&B Farmstay Cottage with Kitchen*
Murray Christie
Hillside/Manapouri Road, Te Anau

Tel (03) 249 6695
mchristie@xtra.co.nz
www.christiescottage.co.nz

Double $115 (Continental)
Child negotiable Extra adult $15
Visa MC accepted
Children welcome
1 Double 1 Single (2 bdrm)
Bathrooms: 1 Private

Exclusively yours, in a tranquil setting, is a delightful sunlit self-contained cottage with courtyard garden, beautiful mountain backdrop overlooking the (famous trout fishing) Mararoa River. Murray with 2 teenage children live on a sheep/cattle farm close to both Te Anau and Manapouri, Murray enjoys sharing his extensive knowledge of fishing and the region. I love gardening and helping with your travel plans if you wish. Bookings can be made for local tourist excursions. Looking forward to meeting you; travel safely - Murray.

Te Anau *5 km S of Te Anau*

Kepler Cottage *B&B Homestay Farmstay*
Jan & Jeff Ludemann
William Stephen Road, Te Anau

Tel (03) 249 7185 or 027 431 4076
Fax (03) 249 7186
kepler@teanau.co.nz
www.fiordlandaccommodation.co.nz

Double $150-$200 Single $100-$120 (Full breakfast)
Visa MC Diners accepted
1 Queen 3 Single (2 bdrm)
Bathrooms: 1 Ensuite 1 Private

Jeff, an aircraft engineer and Jan, who works from home as a marketing consultant, welcome you to their small farmlet on the edge of Fiordland, just 5 minutes drive from Te Anau. Relax outdoors in the garden and enjoy the peace and comfort of our rural location between visiting Milford or Doubtful Sounds, or walking one of the many nearby tracks. Our family includes a cairn terrier, and 2 cats. We can advise tours and sightseeing and make bookings where needed.

Southland
South Catlins

Southland, South Catlins

Te Anau *1 km N of Te Anau Centre*

Shakespeare House *B&B Separate Suite*
Margaret & Jeff Henderson
10 Dusky Street, PO Box 32, Te Anau

Tel (03) 249 7349 or 0800 249 349
Fax (03) 249 7629
marg.shakespeare.house@xtra.co.nz
www.shakespearehouse.co.nz

Double $105-$120 Single $90-$95 (Full breakfast)
Child $5-$15
Self-contained, 2 bedrooms - sleeps 5
Visa MC Eftpos accepted Pet free home
4 King 3 Queen 4 Single (8 bdrm)
Bathrooms: 8 Ensuite

Shakespeare House is a well established Bed & Breakfast, where we keep a home atmosphere with personal service. We are situated in a quiet residential area yet are within walking distance of shops, lake and restaurants. Our rooms are ground floor and have the choice of king, queen or twin beds. Each room has private facilities, TV, tea/coffee making. Tariff includes continental or delicious cooked breakfast. Guest laundry available, internet and payphone facilities on site. Winter rates May to September.

~

Te Anau *8 km S of Te Anau*

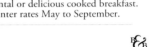

Lynwood Park *B&B Homestay Farmstay*
Trina & Daniella Baker
State Highway 94, Te Anau

Tel (03) 249 7990 Fax (03) 249 7990
lynwood.park@xtra.co.nz

Double $80-$130 Single $50-$80 (Full breakfast)
Child $40 Winter rates May-October
Visa MC accepted
Children welcome
2 Queen 1 Double 3 Single (3 bdrm)
Bathrooms: 2 Ensuite 1 Private

Lynwood Park is set amidst our families 450 acre sheep, cattle and deer farm in a lovely quiet rural oasis. Each guest room has a private entrance, TV and tea/coffee. Cooked or continental breakfast available. We offer the use of laundry facility and childrens play area which Daniella my 7 year old looks forward to sharing with you. We have 3 pet sheep, and a cat on the property. I am able to advise or arrange most activities to make your holiday a memorable experience.

~

Te Anau *2 km E of Te Anau*

Rose 'n' Reel *B&B Farmstay Cottage with Kitchen*
Lyn & Lex Lawrence
Ben Loch Lane, RD 2, Te Anau

Tel (03) 249 7582 or 025 545 723
Fax (03) 249 7582
rosenreel@xtra.co.nz
www.rosenreel.co.nz

Double $90-$100 Single $60-$70 (Continental)
Visa MC accepted
1 Queen 1 Double 1 Single (3 bdrm)
Bathrooms: 1 Guest share 1 Private

Genuine Kiwi hospitality in a magic setting 5 minutes from Te Anau. Hand feed tame fallow deer, meet our 2 friendly cats and dog. Sit on the veranda of our fully self-contained cabin and enjoy watching deer with a lake and mountain view. The 2 room cabin has cooking facilities, fridge, microwave, TV, 1 queen, 1 double plus bathroom. Our modern 2 storey smoke-free home is set in an extensive garden. 2 downstairs guest bedrooms. Lex is a fishing guide and average golfer, while I love to garden. Directions: please phone.

Te Anau *In Te Anau Central*
Cosy Kiwi *B&B*
Eleanor & Derek Cook
186 Milford Road, Te Anau 9681

Tel (03) 249 7475 or 0800 249 700
Fax (03) 249 8471
info@cosykiwi.com
www.cosykiwi.com

Double $140-$160 Single up to $120 Triple $160-$175
(Special breakfast) Child negotiable
Visa MC Eftpos accepted Children welcome
4 King/Twin 3 Queen 9 Single (7 bdrm)
Bathrooms: 7 Ensuite

Eleanor & Derek and our 2 adult children welcome you to our new Bed & Breakfast (30 years experience in hospitality industry). Privacy with comfort, quiet spacious, ensuited bedrooms, quality beds, individual heating, television and tea/coffee. Gourmet breakfast buffet of home-made breads, jams, fresh fruits, dessert fruits, yoghurt, brewed coffee, special teas, mouthwatering pancakes with maple syrup and more. Centrally located, bookings arranged for all tours, pick-up at gate. Guest lounge with internet access, laundry, off-street parking and luggage storage.

Te Anau *1.5 km N of Te Anau*
The Croft *B&B Cottage with Kitchen*
Jane & Ross McEwan
Te Anau Milford Sound Road, RD 1, Te Anau

Tel (03) 249 7393 or 027 682 0061
Fax (03) 249 7393
jane@thecroft.co.nz
www.thecroft.co.nz

Double $130-$150 (Continental)
Visa MC accepted
2 Queen 1 Single (2 bdrm)
Bathrooms: 2 Ensuite

Warm hospitality and quality accommodation are guaranteed at The Croft, a small lifestyle farm only minutes from Te Anau. Our 2 recently built self-contained cottages are set in private gardens and enjoy magnificent lake and mountain views. Timber ceilings, large ensuite bathrooms, window seats and elegant furnishings are some of the highlights. Microwaves, fridges, sinks, TVs and CD mini systems. Enjoy breakfast with Jane & Ross or have it served in your cottage. Pets include Dolly the sheep, Mac the Jack Russell, and Kitty. Lake and river access from our farm.

Te Anau *5 km E of Te Anau*
Stonewall B&B *B&B Apartment with Kitchen*
Nicky Harrison & Jim Huntington
36 Kakapo Road, RD 2, Te Anau

Tel (03) 249 8686 Fax (03) 249 8686
stonewall@hprojects.co.nz
www.hprojects.co.nz/stonewall

Double $140 Single $100 (Continental provisions)
Child negotiable Children welcome
1 Queen (1 bdrm)
Bathrooms: 1 Ensuite

Come up the driveway passed the pond and dry stonewalls to our self-contained guest studio. It is sited at our home amidst our deer farm in Kakapo Road, only 5 minutes out of Te Anau. You have your own private accomodation, including ensuite bathroom and kitchen. Your courtyard over looks our organic vegetable garden to the mountains of Fiordland. It is peaceful and quiet, we hope you will enjoy the environment as we do. Breakfasts include home produce and seasonal fruit. Great kids play area as well.

Te Anau - Manapouri *19 km S of Te Anau*
Rose Cottage B&B *B&B Cottage with Kitchen*
Mary & Rennie McRae
1809 Te Anau, Manapouri Highway, RD1 Te Anau

Tel (03) 249 6691 or 027 472 1742
Fax (03) 249 6690
renniemac@xtra.co.nz

Double $135 Single $105 (Continental)
Child $15 $25 Visa MC accepted
Children and pets welcome
1 Queen 2 Twin (2 bdrm)
Bathrooms: 1 Private

Rose Cottage is a fully self-contained 2 bedroom house with washing/cooking facilities that sleeps up to 6 people. The cottage has 1 queen, 2 singles and a fold out double sofa in the lounge. We are located on a deer/sheep farm overlooking Fiordland National Park and the beautiful Lake Manapouri. We offer a place for people to enjoy while exploring the surrounding area. We enjoy meeting people and sharing with them our local knowledge of the Fiordland area. Private parking is available and there's always a warm welcome from Biddy the Jack Russell.

Te Anau *1 km N of Town Te Anau*
Te Anau Lodge *Luxury B&B*
Nikola Trevor
52 Howden Street, Te Anau

Tel (03) 249 7477 or 021 064 9354
Fax (03) 249 7487 info@teanaulodge.co.nz
www.teanaulodge.com

Double $180-$250 Single $150-$220 (Full breakfast)
Visa MC Eftpos accepted Children welcome3 King/Twin3 King 5 Queen 3 Twin 8 Single
(8 bdrm)
Bathrooms: 7 Ensuite 1 Private , 2 with spa baths

Experience genuine warmth of traditional Kiwi hospitality in a relaxed, peaceful environment, which simply feels like home! A 1936 Convent, set on 2.7 hectares with breathtaking views. Te Anau Lodge is lovingly restored, maintaining it's original charm whilst incorporating modern facilities, along with complimentary laundry, luggage storage and wireless internet. Enjoy our famous leisurely breakfasts in the Chapel. Relax in the library or courtyard with complimentary drinks. If you desire the best in accommodation and service, we invite you to come and stay with us!

Te Anau *In Te Anau Centre*
Antler Lodge *B&B Cottage with Kitchen*
Helen & Chris Whyte
44 Matai Street, Te Anau

Tel (03) 249 8188 Fax (03) 249 8188
antler.lodge@xtra.co.nz
www.antlerlodgeteanau.co.nz

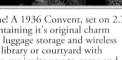

Double $120-$155 (Continental)
Visa MC accepted
1 King 2 Queen (3 bdrm)
Bathrooms: 3 Ensuite

Helen, Chris & daughter Hayley invite you to enjoy their comfortable bed & breakfast accommodation. Situated in a quiet residential area close to shops, restaurants and within walking distance of the lake. We have 2 friendly Jack Russell dogs. We offer 3 spacious smoke-free guest rooms, each with a private ensuite. The 2 cottages each have full kitchen facilities, electric heating and comfortable furnishings. Our third room is an upstairs suite with private entrance and sunroom dining area. This suite has beautiful mountain views.

Te Anau *1 km S of Central Te Anau*
Cat's Whiskers *B&B*
Anne Marie & Lindsay Bernstone
2 Lakefront Drive, Te Anau

Tel (03) 249 8112 Fax (03) 249 8112
bookings@catswhiskers.co.nz
www.catswhiskers.co.nz

Double $155-$170 Single $115 (Full breakfast)
Child $20 Visa MC accepted
Children welcome
2 King 2 Queen 4 Single (4 bdrm)
Bathrooms: 4 Ensuite

On the lakefront opposite Fiordland National Park Visitor Centre. A short walk to the town centre. Guest rooms offer comfortable king, queen and twin beds. All rooms have ensuites, TV, fridges, tea and coffee making facilities. Internet access available. A cooked or continental breakfast is served in our dining room. Booking service for local trips. Off-street parking available. Guest laundry and short term luggage storage is also available. Our cat, Lucy and a small maltese dog, Elle live with us.

∼

Te Anau *5 km N of Te Anau*
Lochvista B&B *B&B Homestay*
Viv Nicholson
454 State Highway 94, Te Anau

Tel (03) 249 7273 Fax (03) 249 7278
lochvista@xtra.co.nz

Double $140-$150 Single $130-$140 (Continental)
Full breakfast by arrangement $15pp
1 King 1 Queen 1 Twin (2 bdrm)
Bathrooms: 2 Ensuite

Welcome to Fiordland. Lochvista is situated on Te Anau Milford Highway 5km from the town centre, overlooking Lake Te Anau and Murchison mountains.
2 rooms each with queen beds and ensuite, tea/coffee making facilities, fridge, TV & hairdryer. French doors onto the patio where you can sit and take in spectacular views. Fiordland has a great deal to offer and I am more than happy to help guests with any booking to make their stay more relaxing. A cat called Mischief.

∼

Te Anau *.2 km W of central Te Anau*
House of Wood *B&B Homestay*
Merle & Cliff Buchanan
44 Moana Crescent, Te Anau

Tel (03) 249 8404 or (021)250 0802
Fax (03) 249 7676
houseofwood@xtra.co.nz
houseofwood.co.nz

Double $100-$130 Single $90-$110 (Full breakfast)
Visa MC accepted
2 King/Twin 3 Queen (4 bdrm)
Bathrooms: 3 Ensuite 1 Private

A warm welcome is assurred when you arrive at our home, the House of Wood. We really enjoy meeting guests from overseas (and locals). Our house is a unique architecturally designed home of native and exotic timber. Sit at the outdoor tables and enjoy the beautiful views from our balconies. Our interests are boating, fishing, golf and gardening. We can help you plan your activities and book trips, with pick up at the door. We are 2 minutes walk from town centre and 5 minutes to the lake. Dinner by arrangement.

Te Anau - Manapouri *8 km S of Manapouri*

Connemara *B&B Farmstay Cottage with Kitchen*
Bev & Murray Hagen
415 Weir Road, Manapouri, Te Anau

Tel (03) 249 9399 or 027 292 3651
Fax (03) 249 9399
hagen@southnet.co.nz

Double $120-$150 (Full provisions)
Child by arrangement
1 Queen 1 Double (1 bdrm)
Bathrooms: 1 Ensuite

Exclusively yours is a cosy self-contained cottage in
a tranquil garden setting with magnificent mountain
views. The bedroom has a queen bed while the lounge has a very comfortable double foldout sofa bed.
Enjoy breakfast with us or have it in the privacy of your cottage. Full breakfast, laundry extra charge.
Manapouri - The Gateway to DoubtfulSound - is 5 minutes from our 750 acre deer farm, which is close
to 2 great fishing rivers. Murray's interests include microlights, while Bev enjoys gardening bowls crafts
etc. We and Angel (cat) welcome you. Credit Cards by arrangement.

Te Anau *21 km N of Te Anau*

Waitahanui *B&B Farmstay Cottage with Kitchen*
Claire & Hunter Shaw
313 Hillside Manapouri Road, RD 1, Te Anau

Tel (03) 249 6661 Fax (03) 249 7585
theshawfamily@xtra.co.nz

Double $170 (Continental)
Child over 5 $40
1 Queen (1 bdrm)
Bathrooms: 1 Ensuite

Ti Kouka a private cottage set in serene surroundings
with magnificent mountain views. The cottage is on
a 60 acre deer farm 3km from Manapouri, the start
of your Doubtful Sound experience. Fully self-contained the cottage sleeps 4. Furnishings and colours
depict the surrounding native fauna. Full cooking facilities. Children under 12 welcome. Floors and
ceilings feature native silver beech milled from sea washed logs from Doubtful Sound. Hunter your host
is a massage therapist, relax even more during your stay, book in for a massage.

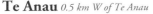

Te Anau *0.5 km W of Te Anau*

Blue Ridge *Luxury B&B Luxury Self-Contained Studio*
Julia & Phillip Robertson
13-15 Melland Place, Te Anau

Tel (03) 249 7740 or 027 258 9877
Fax (03) 249 7340
info@blueridge.net.nz
www.blueridge.net.nz

Double $145-$225 Single $135-$215 (Full breakfast)
Child negotiable Extra adult $25
Visa MC accepted Not suitable for children
2 King/Twin 2 Queen 2 Twin 1 Single (4 bdrm)
Bathrooms: 3 Ensuite 1 Private 4

Three luxury self-contained units in tranquil garden setting overlooking mountains. Units have
kitchenette, ensuites have heated towel rail, heater & under-floor heating. Delicious breakfast included
as a continental hamper delivered to your room, or join us in our dining room for a full breakfast. Meet
Latte our beautiful birman cat. Phillip is a police officer, a keen tramper and fisherman. Julia is interested
in gardening, walking, cooking, wines and is learning to paint. We are happy to assist with bookings for
local and Milford attractions.

Te Anau *1 km N of Te Anau*
Dunluce *B&B Private Guest Wing*
Wendy & Roger McQuillan
Aparima Drive, Te Anau

Tel (03) 249 7715 or 025 629 9685
Fax 03 249 7703
info@dunluce-fiordland.co.nz
www.dunluce-fiordland.co.nz

Double $185-$195 Single $155-$165 (Full breakfast)
Visa MC accepted
Not suitable for children
4 King/Twin (4 bdrm)
Bathrooms: 4 Ensuite

We are proud to have lived in Te Anau for over 30 years and welcome you to stay in our new purpose built bed & breakfast. Our guest wing includes 4 luxury ensuite rooms and a dining room where breakfast is served and coffee/tea are always available. All rooms have panoramic lake and mountain views. We have laundry facilities, parking, storage, fax, phone and internet. We are situated on the outskirts of Te Anau just a short walk to shops and restaurants. We have an unobtrusive cat.

Te Anau
Moptop Place Bed & Breakfast *B&B*
Yvonne & Ian Dickson
39 Luxmore Drive, Te Anau 9681

Tel (0)3 249 7206 or 027 222 1113
0800 249 720 Fax (03) 249 7206
info@moptopteanau.com
www.moptopteanau.com

Double $85-$100 Single $70-$90 (Continental)
Child negotiable
1 Queen 1 Double (2 bdrm)
Bathrooms: 1 Ensuite 1 Family share

Yvonne & Ian, burmese cats Mactavish & Phoebe and labrador Zara offer a warm welcome. We are ideally situated on Luxmore Drive the main road into the town centre. Our home has mountain views and is 4 minutes walk from the town centre restaurants and beautiful Lake Te Anau. A generous continental breakfast is provided. The 2 quality bedrooms have private entrances and include tea/coffee making facilities, TV and comfortable chairs. Fish guiding can be arranged.

Manapouri *In Manapouri*
About Time *B&B*
Liz and Steve Futter
2 Whitestone Court, PO Box 18, Manapouri

Tel (03) 249 6962 or 021 678 472
Fax (03) 249 6954
stay@abouttimemanapouri.co.nz
www.abouttimemanapouri.co.nz

Double $210 Single $210 (Full breakfast)
Dinner $30pp Visa MC accepted
Not suitable for children
 1 King/Twin1 King (2 bdrm)
Bathrooms: 2 Ensuite Separate showers & baths

Come and stay with us on a rise overlooking picturesque Lake Manapouri and the surrounding mountains. Our home is new and affords stunning veiws enhanced by indoor - outdoor living We offer a warm welcome and are extremely interested in meeting visitors and exchanging ideas and local knowledge. We offer for guests to join us for our evening meal. Manapouri is situated on the edge of Fiordland and is the gateway to Doubtful Sound. Our interests are boating, fishing, diving and enjoying the outdoor life style with our Scottish terrier Angus.

Southland
South Catlins

Mossburn *25 km S of Mossburn*

Turner Farmstay *Farmstay*
Joyce & Murray Turner
RD 1, Otautau, Southland

Tel (03) 225 7602 Fax (03) 225 7602
murray.joyce@xtra.co.nz
www.innz.co.nz/host/e/etalcreek.html

Double $90 Single $50 (Full breakfast)
Child under 12 $20
Dinner $30
Visa MC accepted
1 Queen 4 Single (3 bdrm)
Bathrooms: 1 Guest share 1 Private

Our modern home on 301 hectares, farming sheep & beef cattle, is situated half-way between Invercargill and Te Anau, which can be reached in 1 hour. We enjoy meeting people, will provide quality accommodation, farm-fresh food in a welcoming friendly atmosphere. You can join in farm activities, farm tour or just relax. The Aparima River is adjacent to the property. Murray is a keen fly fisherman. Guiding available. Pet Bichon Frise. Evening meal on request. Directions please phone/fax. 24 hours notice to avoid disappointment.

~

Lumsden *9 km S of Lumsden*

Josephville Gardens *Farmstay Guest House*
Annette & Bob Menlove
Rapid sign 824, State Highway 6, RD 4, Lumsden

Tel (03) 248 7114 or 021 494 149
Fax (03) 248 7114
bobannette@menlove.net
www.josephville.co.nz

Double $130-$150 (Full breakfast)
Dinner $30
Visa MC accepted
1 King/Twin 2 Double 1 Twin (4 bdrm)
Bathrooms: 1 Ensuite 1 Family share 1 Private

We have a 480 hectare farm which runs sheep, cattle and deer. Surrounding our comfortable warm home, we have a large garden with a selection of specimen trees, rhododendrons, roses, peonys and perennials. The golf course is 3km away - golf clubs are available- a good fishing river nearby. We have hiked in our mountains a lot and can give advise on where and what to see. If you wish, a 4 wheel drive trip is available.

~

Balfour *3 km N of Balfour*

Hillcrest *Farmstay*
Liz & Ritchie Clark
206 Old Balfour Road, RD 1, Balfour

Tel (03) 201 6165 Fax (03) 201 6165
clarkrl@xtra.co.nz

Double $120-$150 Single $120-$150 (Full breakfast)
Dinner $40pp
Visa MC accepted
Children welcome
2 King/Twin 1 Single (2 bdrm)
Bathrooms: 1 Family share 1 Private

Welcome to our 650 acre sheep and deer farm, 3km from State Highway 94. Relax in our garden, enjoy a farm tour with mountain views or a game of tennis. Trout fishing in the Mataura, Oreti and Waikaia Rivers. Fishing guide can be arranged with notice. Enjoy a relaxing dinner with fine food, wine and conversation. Breakfast is served with fresh baked bread, yoghurt, muesli, jams and preserves. Interests include handcrafts, tennis, photography and fishing. We have 3 children attending boarding school/tertiary education and a cat. Directions: please phone.

Wendonside *15 km N of Riversdale*

Ardlamont Farm *Farmstay*
Dale & Lindsay Wright
110 Wendonside Church Road North,
Wendonside, RD 7, Gore

Tel (03) 202 7774 Fax (03) 202 7774
ardlamont@xtra.co.nz

Double $120 Single $80 (Full breakfast)
Dinner $40
1 King/Twin 1 Double (2 bdrm)
Bathrooms: 1 Private

Experience Ardlamont, a fourth generation 1200
acre sheep and beef farm offering panoramic views of
northern Southland. Gourmet meals a specialty, served with fine New Zealand wines. Tour the farm,
then return to the renovated comforts of our 95 year old homestead. Having travelled widely we enjoy
welcoming visitors into our home. Our 3 children attend university. 2 of New Zealand's best trout
rivers only 5 minutes away. 15 minutes off SH94 (Queenstown - Gore - Dunedin route) Well worth the
detour.

~

Waikaka *30 km N of Gore*

Blackhills Farmstay *B&B Farmstay*
Dorothy & Tom Affleck
192 Robertson Road, RD 3, Gore, Southland

Tel (03) 207 2865 Fax (03) 207 2865
afflecks@ispnz.co.nz
www.bnb.co.nz/blackhillsfarmstay.html

Double $100 Single $50 (Full breakfast)
Child $25 Dinner $25 by arrangement
Visa MC accepted Children welcome
2 King/Twin 1 Queen (3 bdrm)
Bathrooms: 1 Family share 1 Guest share
1 Private Double spa

Rest between Dunedin and Te Anau gateway to Milford Sound. 15 minutes from SHW 90 means no
traffic noise. Dorothy and Tom have farmed 800 acre Blackhills for 35years. Dorothy: "We treat you as
friends we haven't met and want you to feel at home." That means as much privacy as you like, home
grown vegetables, and meat, in home cooked meals, established tree and shrub gardens. Take Tom's
farm tour, walk rolling green hills , catch trout, play golf, meet New Zealanders . Tom: "See you soon."
Ask for directions please.

~

Gore *In Gore*

Connor Homestay *Homestay*
Dawn & David Connor
29 Aotea Crescent, Gore, Southland

Tel (03) 208 3598 or 0800 372 484
027 669 1362
ddconnor@esi.co.nz
www.bnb.co.nz/connororchids.html

Double $100 Single $50 (Full breakfast)
Dinner by arrangement
Visa MC accepted
1 King/Twin 1 Queen (2 bdrm)
Bathrooms: 1 Guest share 1 Private

Dawn & David invite you to enjoy quality accommodation in their modern home, situated in a quiet
residential area overlooking the Hokonui Hills & farmland, close to golf course, driving range, bush
walks and good fishing rivers including Mataura, well known for its brown trout. Fishing guide or advise
available. We enjoy meeting people and sharing travel experiences. Laundry facilities available. Smoke-
free accommodation. Please phone for directions.

Southland, South Catlins

Gore *3 km NW of Gore*

Hokonui Homestay *B&B Homestay Rural Lifestyle*
Brian & Shona McLennan
258 Reaby Road, RD 4, Gore

Tel (03) 208 4890 or 027 568 4835
021 254 6404 Fax (03) 208 4890
bssm@sld.quik.co.nz
www.bnb.co.nz/hokonuihomestay.html

Double $100-$120 Single $60 (Full breakfast)
Child negotiable Dinner by arrangement
Visa MC accepted Children welcome
1 King 1 Queen 1 Twin (3 bdrm)
Bathrooms: 2 Ensuite 1 Private

Looking for somewhere private with a fantastic view? Only 5 minutes from Gore. We provide a spacious, modern new home on a 12 acre lifestyle block (some animals). All bedrooms are sited for views and sun. Private upstairs unit, underfloor heating and full size snooker table. Close to the Mataura River which is famous for Brown Trout Fishing, 18 hole golf course and native bush walks. A perfect base for sightseeing Southland and attending the NZ Gold Guitar Awards, Southern Waimumu Fieldays and the Hokonui Fashion Awards. Interests - golf, fishing, dog trialing, music and wine tasting. .

Mataura - Gore *12 km S of Gore*

Kowhai Place *Farmstay*
Helen & John Williams
291 Glendhu Road, RD 4, Gore

Tel (03) 203 8774 Fax (03) 203 8774
kowhaiplace@xtra.co.nz
www.southland-homestays.co.nz

Double $95-$100 Single $50 (Full breakfast)
Child half price
Dinner $25 by arrangement
Children and pets welcome
2 King/Twin 2 Queen 2 Single (4 bdrm)
Bathrooms: 1 Family share 1 Guest share 1 Private

John & Helen farm sheep and deer on our 50 acre farmlet. We live 5 minutes from one of the best brown trout fishing rivers in the world. Drive 1 hour south to Bluff, and 1.5 hours to Queenstown's ski fields. We both play golf and enjoy gardening. Fishing guide and garden tours can be arranged with prior notice. Children and outside pets welcome. Over the past years we have enjoyed sharing our spacious home and garden with lots of overseas guests. Enjoy the south.

Please let us know
how you enjoyed your B&B experience.
Ask your host for a comment form
or leave a comment on www.bnb.co.nz

Wyndham *3.65 km E of Wyndham*
Smiths Farmstay *Farmstay*
Beverly and Doug Smith
365 Wyndham - Mokoreta Road, RD 2,
Wyndham, Southland

Tel (03) 206 4840 Fax (03) 206 4847
beverly@smithsfarmstay.co.nz

Double $110-$140 Single $100 (Full breakfast)
Child negotiable Dinner $40
Visa MC accepted
Children welcome
2 King/Twin 1 Queen 1 Twin (4 bdrm)
Bathrooms: 1 Ensuite 1 Guest share 1 Private

Beverly and Doug assure you of a warm welcome to
the Modern Farm house set in 265 hectare sheep farm.
We are situated on the hills above Wyndham only 3.65
km, set in quiet and peaceful surroundings.

Farm tour included in tarif. Feeding the animals and
sheep shearing when in season. Doug will demonstrate
his sheep dogs working. Beverly a registered nurse
enjoys cooking, floral art, knitting, gardening and travel.
We enjoy meeting people and both are of a friendly
deposition, with a sense of humour.

Each bedroom has a view and is tastefully furnished to
meet your needs. Genuine home cooking. Special Diets
on request. Packed Lunches if required. You are most
welcome to join us for the evening meal, which is $40pp. Prior booking required please.

Fishermans Retreat; The Mataura, Wyndham and Mimihau Rivers are renowned for its abundance of
Brown trout. Each of these Rivers are only a short 5km away. Doug, a keen experienced fisherman is
only too happy to share his knowledge of these rivers with you. Enjoy the Mad Mataura evening Rise
a site to experience. Gateway to Catlins, Only 2 hours from Queenstown, Te Anau and Dunedin.
Laundry and fax available.

Directions: Come to Wyndham, follow signs to Mokoreta.Sign at gate, number 365.

Progress Valley - South Catlins *6 km N of Waikawa*

Catlins Farmstay B&B *B&B Farmstay*
June & Murray Stratford
174 Progress Valley Road, South Catlins, Southland

Tel (03) 246 8843 Fax (03) 246 8844
catlinsfarmstay@xtra.co.nz
www.catlinsfarmstay.co.nz

Double $180-$250 Single $110 (Full breakfast)
Child negotiable Dinner $50
Self-contained available Visa MC accepted
1 King 2 Queen 1 Twin (4 bdrm)
Bathrooms: 3 Ensuite 1 Private

Ours is a great location close to fossil forest at Curio
Bay. Superior new guest rooms plus king self-contained suite available with private entrances. Dinner available on mon, wed, thurs and fri only , featuring home-grown venison, beef or lamb, and organic vegetables, (vegetarians catered for) followed by delicious desserts - and breakfasts. We farm 1000 acres running, 2500 sheep, 500 deer, 150 cattle with 2 sheepdogs. Farm tours by arrangement. Directions: turn off at Niagara Falls into Manse Road, drive 2km. Ask about our self-contained cottage at Waikawa (www.cottagestays.co.nz/curio/cottage.htm)

~

Fortrose - The Catlins *50 km SE of Invercargill*

Greenbush *B&B Farmstay*
Ann & Donald McKenzie
298 Fortrose - Otara Road, Fortrose, RD 5, Invercargill

Tel (03) 246 9506 or 021 395 196
Fax (03) 246 9505
info@greenbush.co.nz
www.greenbush.co.nz

Double $130-$150 Single $120 (Full breakfast)
Child negotiable
Dinner $40 by arrangement
Visa MC accepted Children welcome
1 King/Twin 1 Double 1 Twin (3 bdrm)
Bathrooms: 1 Ensuite 1 Private

Greenbush Bed & Breakfast is ideally located off the Southern Scenic Route from Fortrose. Within 30 minutes drive from Greenbush you can enjoy Curio Bay, Waipapa Point and Slope Point, the southern most point in the South Island. Greenbush is nestled in 2 acres of garden. You will wake to the song of birds and magnificent views of green rolling countryside. Enjoy our private beach access, lake and farm tour. Directions at Fortrose take Coastal Route drive 4km.

~

Mokotua *20 km NE of Invercargill*

Fernlea *B&B Farmstay Cottage No Kitchen*
Anne & Brian Perkins
Mokotua, RD 1, Invercargill on Southern Scenic Route

Tel (03) 239 5432 Fax (03) 239 5432
fernlea@southnet.co.nz
www.fernlea.co.nz

Double $120 (Full breakfast)
Child $10
Dinner $30 by arrangement
2 Double (1 bdrm)
Bathrooms: 1 Private

Proof of Fernlea's success was winning both the
'Hosted Accommodation' section and the 'Supreme Tourism Award for Southland'. Anne's cottage is nestled in its own private olde world garden, is completely s/c and can sleep 4. Our dairy farm of 300 acres is home to 300 Holstein Friesian cows - farm tour included. Interests include golf, travel, tramping, fishing and people. Relax and enjoy a taste of real NZ farm life on your journey to discover the Catlins, or enroute to Stewart Island, Te Anau or Queenstown. Directions: From Invercargill on SH92, 20 mins from Invercargill turn left at Mokotua Garage.

Invercargill *5 km N of Invercargill city*
Glenroy Park Homestay *B&B Homestay*
Margaret & Alan Thomson
23 Glenroy Park Drive, Invercargill

Tel (03) 215 8464 Fax (03) 215 8464
home_hosp@actrix.co.nz

Double $100-$115 Single $65-$75 (Continental)
Child $12
Dinner $30
Children welcome
1 Queen 1 Twin 1 Single (3 bdrm)
Bathrooms: 1 Guest share 1 Private

Exclusively yours, in a quiet retreat with restaurants and parks nearby. Be our special guests and share an evening of relaxation and friendship. Our interests are golfing, meeting people, travel and cooking. We look forward to having you visit us. Invercargill is the gateway to Queenstown, Fiordland, Catlins and Stewart Island. Directions: from Queenstown turn left at first traffic lights (Bainfield Road), take first left, third house on left. From Dunedin turn right at first traffic lights (Queens Drive), travel to end, turn left, first street right, third house on left.

Invercargill *5 km W of Invercargill*
The Oak Door *B&B*
Lisa & Bill Stuart
22 Taiepa Road, Otatara, RD 9, Invercargill 9521

Tel (03) 213 0633 Fax (03) 213 0633
blstuart@xtra.co.nz

Double $100 Single $80 (Full breakfast)
Child POA
Pet free home
2 Queen 2 Twin (3 bdrm)
Bathrooms: 2 Guest share

Bill (Kiwi) & Lisa (Canadian) welcome you to their warm, self-built, unique home. Enjoy attractive gardens and native bush setting; minutes from: Invercargill CBD, Scenic route amenities, airport. Coffee/tea awaits you on arrival at The Oak Door. Guests comment on a warm comfortable visit, where beds, breakfast and hospitality are quality plus! A Warm Welcome! (Nonsmoking/no pet). Directions: Drive past the airport entrance. Take first left (Marama Avenue South). Take first right Taiepa Road second drive on right (#22).

Invercargill *3 km N of Invercargill City Centre*
Gimblett Place *B&B*
Alex & Eileen Henderson
122 Gimblett Place, Kildare, Invercargill

Tel (03) 215 6888 Fax (03) 215 6888
the_grove@xtra.co.nz
www.bnb.co.nz/hosts/thegrovedeerfarm.html

Double $95 Single $65 (Full breakfast)
Child negotiable
Dinner by arrangement
Visa MC accepted
1 Queen 2 Single (2 bdrm)
Bathrooms: 1 Guest share

Eileen & Alex are experienced hosts who are ex-farmers and offer comfortable accommodation in a quiet cul-de-sac close to city amenities, golf, parks, restaurants. We are pleased to assist with local and tourist information and can guide if required (ie Catlins). Alex is a vintage car and machinery enthusiast and can arrange good veiwing. Close to famous trout fishing rivers. Bus and airport courtesy pick up. Directions: find Queens Drive, Gimblett Street is first left north of Thomsons Bush, fourth right into Gimblett Place.

Southland South Catlins

Invercargill *10 km E of Invercargill on Southern Scenic Rte*
Long Acres Farmstay *Farmstay Self-contained*
Helen & Graeme Spain
Waimatua, RD 11, Invercargill

Tel (03) 216 4470 or 027 228 1308
Fax (03) 216 4470   longacres@xtra.co.nz
www.longacres.co.nz

Double $100-$150 **Single** $100 (Full breakfast)
Child negotiable Dinner $40
Self-contained $160-$200
Visa MC accepted Children and pets welcome
2 Queen 2 Twin (4 bdrm)
Bathrooms: 1 Guest share 1 Private

Southland hospitality. Excellent food awaits you at our friendly home. Our farm is 1000 acres carrying 4000 sheep, 80 cattle. World record shearing video available to watch. Enjoy a farm tour. Bluff is 30 minutes, you'll enjoy a day trip to Stewart Island. Guests comments: "Great hospitality." Home cooked meal always available. A peaceful relaxed place for a farm stay for the length of time you choose. Directions: from Invercargill, east on Southern Scenic Route approximately 15 minutes. Look for Long Acres Farmstay Sign.

Invercargill - Waianiwa *18 km W of Invercargill*
Annfield Flowers *B&B Homestay*
Margaret & Mike Cockeram
126 Argyle-Otahuti Road, Waianiwa,
RD 4, Invercargill

Tel (03) 235 2690 or 021 385 134
Fax (03) 235 2745
annfield@ihug.co.nz

Double $100-$110 (Full breakfast)
Dinner $30, light meal $20
Visa MC accepted
1 King/Twin (1 bdrm)
Bathrooms: 1 Ensuite

We are 1km from the Southern Scenic Route (signposted Waianiwa/Drummond) and well placed for sightseeing, fishing and golf. Dating from 1866, Annfield has been renovated to retain character and include modern facilities. Our sunny guest room opens into the garden. 2 cats and a dog have limited access inside. We are semi-retired, grow flowers for export, keep coloured sheep and alpacas. We enjoy meeting people and love to share dinner or a light meal, including our own produce. Complimentary laundry facilities.

Invercargill *4 km N of Invercargill Central*
Stoneleigh Homestay *B&B Homestay*
Joan & Neville Milne
15 Stoneleigh Lane, Invercargill

Tel (03) 215 8921 Fax (03) 215 8491
nevm@bowdens.co.nz

Double $90-$110 **Single** $65-$75 (Full breakfast)
Dinner $30
Visa MC accepted
1 Queen 3 Single (3 bdrm)
Bathrooms: 1 Guest share

We welcome guests to share our warm comfortable home, which has underfloor heating. We are situated in a quiet lane off the main North Road to Te Anau and Queenstown, and just minutes from the town centre. Neville owns a wholesale fruit and vegetable market, so fresh produce is assured. We are keen golfers and members of the Invercargill Club, the only Championship course in Southland. Our interests are golf, travel, gardening, cooking, wine and meeting people. City and airport pick up can be arranged.

Invercargill *6 km NE of Invercargill*

The Manor *B&B Homestay*
Pat & Frank Forde
9 Drysdale Road, Myross Bush, RD 2, Invercargill

Tel (03) 230 4788 Fax (03) 230 4788
the.manor@xtra.co.nz
www.manorbb.co.nz

Double $90-$130 Single $70-$85 (Full breakfast)
Child negotiable Dinner $30 by arrangement
Visa MC accepted Pet free home
2 Queen 1 Double 2 Single (3 bdrm)
Bathrooms: 1 Ensuite 1 Guest share 1 Private

Relax, enjoy our warm, comfortable home, underfloor
heating, in a sheltered garden setting on our 10 acre farmlet (sheep, lambs, horses, hens). Private guest area with television, refrigerator, tea/coffee making facilities. We are retired farmers, keen golfers, enjoy gardening, harness racing, travel, meeting people. Pleasant outdoor areas, meals of fresh home-grown produce, cooked/continental breakfasts. Courtesy pick up. A stop on your way to Stewart Island, Southern Scenic Route, Queenstown or Te Anau. We would enjoy having you stay with us. 5 minutes drive north east Invercargill along State Highway 1.

Invercargill *In Invercargill central*

Victoria Railway Hotel *B&B Hotel*
Trudy & Eian Read
3 Leven Street, off Picadilly Place, Invercargill

Tel (03) 218 1281 Fax (03) 218 1283
vrhotel@xtra.co.nz
www.vrhotel.info

Double $95-$140 Single $48-$60 (Full breakfast)
Child $15 Dinner $16-$25
Visa MC Diners Amex Eftpos accepted
5 Queen 4 Double 2 Twin 11 Single (22 bdrm)
Bathrooms: 11 Ensuite 2 Guest share

Come and enjoy old world charm and southern
hospitality in a boutique hotel in the heart of the city. Built in 1896 we are a Class 1 Historic Places heritage building and completed our architecturally designed upgrade and refurbishment in May 2004. We offer a variety of accommodation options including Executive, VIP, and 2 ground floor accessible units. Guests can relax in our bar before dining in at Gerrard's Restaurant and enjoy traditional home cooked meals and a selection of fine NZ wines.

Invercargill *0.5 km N of City Centre*

Burtonwood Bed & Breakfast *B&B Guest House Boutique Bed & Breakfast*
Peter & Amy
177 Gala Street, Avenal, Invercargill

Tel (03) 218 8884 or 021 376 399
Fax (03) 218 9148
burtonwoodbnb@woosh.co.nz www.burtonwood.co.nz

Double $125-$225 Single $100-$200 (Full breakfast)
Child negotiable Dinner by arrangment
Off Season rates available Visa MC Eftpos accepted
Not suitable for children
3 Queen 2 Twin 2 Single (4 bdrm)
Bathrooms: 2 Ensuite 1 Guest share

What a gorgeous stay awaits you at our charming Edwardian heritagehome with the distinctive "cat on the roof" Centrally situated opposite beautiful Queens Park, moments from Southland Museum & Art Gallery,Visitor Information Centre, Bus terminus and Golf course. Sunny comfortable well appointed secure guest rooms have lovely decor and views. Spacious guest lounge and dining room, beautiful garden with off street parking. Facilities include: TV, NZ Library, Wireless Internet, Fax, Laundry, hairdryers, electric blankets and Tea/coffee 24/7.

Southland, South Catlins

Bluff *25 km S of Invercargill*

The Lazy Fish *B&B Separate Suite Cottage with Kitchen*
Robyn & Roy Horwell
35 Burrows Street, Bluff

Tel (03) 212 7245 or 021 211 7424
Fax (03) 212 8868
horwell@thelazyfish.co.nz
www.thelazyfish.co.nz

Double $100-$120 (Continental)
Continental breakfast $8.50pp
Children welcome
2 Double (2 bdrm)
Bathrooms: 2 Private

Very homely fully self-contained unit attached to our home, in a peacefull garden setting. Sleeps 4, double bed in bedroom and sofa bed in lounge. Also double bedroom attached to house, tea & coffee making facilities and microwave. Sunny shelterd courtyard. Animals in residence. Gateway to Stewart Island and Southern Scenic Route. Take a break and absorb our Coastal and native bush walks, maritime museum, restaurants and supermarket all within walking distance. 5 minutes walk to Stewart Island ferry. Continental breakfast by arrangement.

Riverton *40min km W of Invercargill*

Reo Moana *B&B*
Jean & Alan Broomfield
192 Rocks Highway, Riverton, Southland

Tel (03) 234 9044 Fax (03) 234 9047
alanb@orcon.net.nz

Double $140 Single $100 (Full breakfast)
Child negotiable
2 nights or more $120 per night
Pet free home Children welcome
1 King 1 Twin (2 bdrm)
Bathrooms: 2 Ensuite

Reo Moana, meaning 'language of the sea', overlooks a beautiful secluded swimming and surfing beach with extended views to the open sea beyond, and northward to the mountains and hills of Southland. Reo Moana, recently completed, was built to take advantage of the sea views and sun. Tastefully decorated, the warm and spacious guest rooms each have ensuite bathrooms and sea views. Your hosts Jean and Alan have many years experience in the tourism industry. We welcome you to Riverton, on the Southern Scenic Route and just 45 minutes from Tuatapere and the Humbridge track.

Stewart Island *1 km of Oban*

Glendaruel Bed & Breakfast *B&B*
Raylene & Ronnie Waddell
38 Golden Bay Road, Oban, Stewart Island

Tel (03) 219 1092 Fax (03) 219 1092
r.r.waddell@xtra.co.nz
www.glendaruel.co.nz

Double $180 Single $100-$1120 (Full breakfast)
Dinner $30 by arrangement
1 King/Twin 1 Queen 1 Single (3 bdrm)
Bathrooms: 3 Ensuite

Peaceful bush setting, 10 minutes walk from village, 3 minutes from Golden Bay on beautiful Paterson Inlet. Handy for water taxis, kayak hire, sandy beaches and bush walks. Large guest lounge and three balconies with bush and sea views. Colourful garden - bird lovers' paradise. Central heating. Courtesy transfers. Advice and assistance with local activities. We have travelled widely and love welcoming guests from around the world. Our friendly cairn terrier, helps us provide traditional Scottish and Kiwi hospitality. "A Hundred Thousand Welcomes!"

Stewart Island *500m km N of Oban township*
Sails Ashore & Kowhai Lane B&B *B&B Apartment with Kitchen*
Self-catering Flat

Iris and Peter Tait
11 View Street & 6 Kowhai Lane, Stewart Island

Tel (03) 219 1151 Fax (03) 219 1151
tait@taliskercharter.co.nz
www.taliskercharter.co.nz/sailsashore.htm

Double $135-$350 (Continental)
Dinner by arrangement
Kowhai Lane $175
Self-catering Flat $135
Visa MC accepted
Pet free home
Children welcome
2 King/Twin (2 bdrm)
Bathrooms: 2 Ensuite

Enjoy with us our centrally located home with 2 new private apartments designed to maximise sun and scenery overlooking Halfmoon Bay. Stewart Island is New Zealand's newest National Park.

Peaceful beaches, undisturbed forest and wonderful wildlife make the island a haven.

We have 33 years of island life as ranger, district nurse, commercial fishers and now, hosts of a charter yacht/homestay.

We and our border terriers will delight in sharing our island and home with you.

Index

Notes

Notes

Notes

Notes

The New Zealand
Bed &Breakfast
Book

Please Help us to Keep our Standards High

To help maintain the high reputation of **The New Zealand Bed & Breakfast Book** we ask for your comments about your stay. You can simply stick a stamp on this form or save all your comment forms and return them in and= envelope.

Alternatively, leave your comment at our website
www.bnb.co.nz

Name of Host or B&B_____

Address _____
_____

Considering things such as Breakfast, meals, beds, cleanliness, hospitality and value for money, what is your overall satisfaction rating, with 1 beeing the lowest and 10 being the highest rating?

1   2   3   4   5   6   7   8   9   10

Do you have any comments?

We May display your comments on our website. The rating will be confidential and will be kept for administration purposes.
Fill in your details to go into our regular prize draws!
Your details will not be passed on to anyone else. If you do not have email we suggest you use a friend's email address.

Your name   _____

Your Town/city
and country   _____

Email   _____

Please Post this form to:
The New Zealand B&B Book,
PO Box 6843, Welington, New Zealand

Place stamp
here or send
forms in one
envelope

Moonshine Press
PO Box 6843
Wellington
New Zealand

Order Form

Extra copies of **The Bed & Breakfast Book**
may be ordered at www.bnb.co.nz
or use this form

Please mail me ☐ copies of **The Bed & Breakfast Book** - *Australia*
and ☐ copies of **The Bed & Breakfast Book** - *New Zealand* at a cost of
NZ$19.95 plus postage as applicable.

*Postage is free within New Zealand and Australia or NZ$10 per book airmail to
the rest of the world.*

Please charge my Visa/ Mastercard _____/_____/_____/_____
   Exp _____/_____
for NZ$ _____ including postage.

Signature   _____

Name   _____
Address _____
         _____
         _____

Please email, post or fax your order to;
email info@bnb.co.nz
PO Box 6843, Wellington, New Zealand
Fax +64 4 385 2694